Garfield

FAT CAT 3-PACK

VOLUME 19

Garfield
FAT CAT 3-PACK
VOLUME 19

BY
JIM DAVIS

BALLANTINE BOOKS • NEW YORK

2017 Ballantine Books Trade Paperback Edition

GARFIELD SINGS FOR HIS SUPPER copyright © 2013 by PAWS, Inc. All Rights Reserved.
GARFIELD CAUTION: WIDE LOAD copyright © 2013 by PAWS, Inc. All Rights Reserved.
GARFIELD SOUPED UP copyright © 2014 by PAWS, Inc. All Rights Reserved.
"GARFIELD" and the GARFIELD characters are trademarks of PAWS, Inc.

Published in the United States by Ballantine Books, an imprint of Random House,
a division of Penguin Random House LLC, New York.

BALLANTINE and the HOUSE colophon are registered trademarks of Penguin Random House LLC.

GARFIELD SINGS FOR HIS SUPPER and GARFIELD CAUTION: WIDE LOAD were each published separately by
Ballantine Books, an imprint of Random House, a division of Penguin Random House LLC, New York, in 2013.
GARFIELD SOUPED UP was published separately by Ballantine Books, an imprint of Random House, a division
of Penguin Random House LLC, in 2014.

ISBN 978-0-425-28561-9

Printed in China on acid-free paper

randomhousebooks.com

9 8 7 6 5 4 3 2

Garfield
SINGS FOR HIS SUPPER

BY JIM DAVIS

Ballantine Books • **New York**

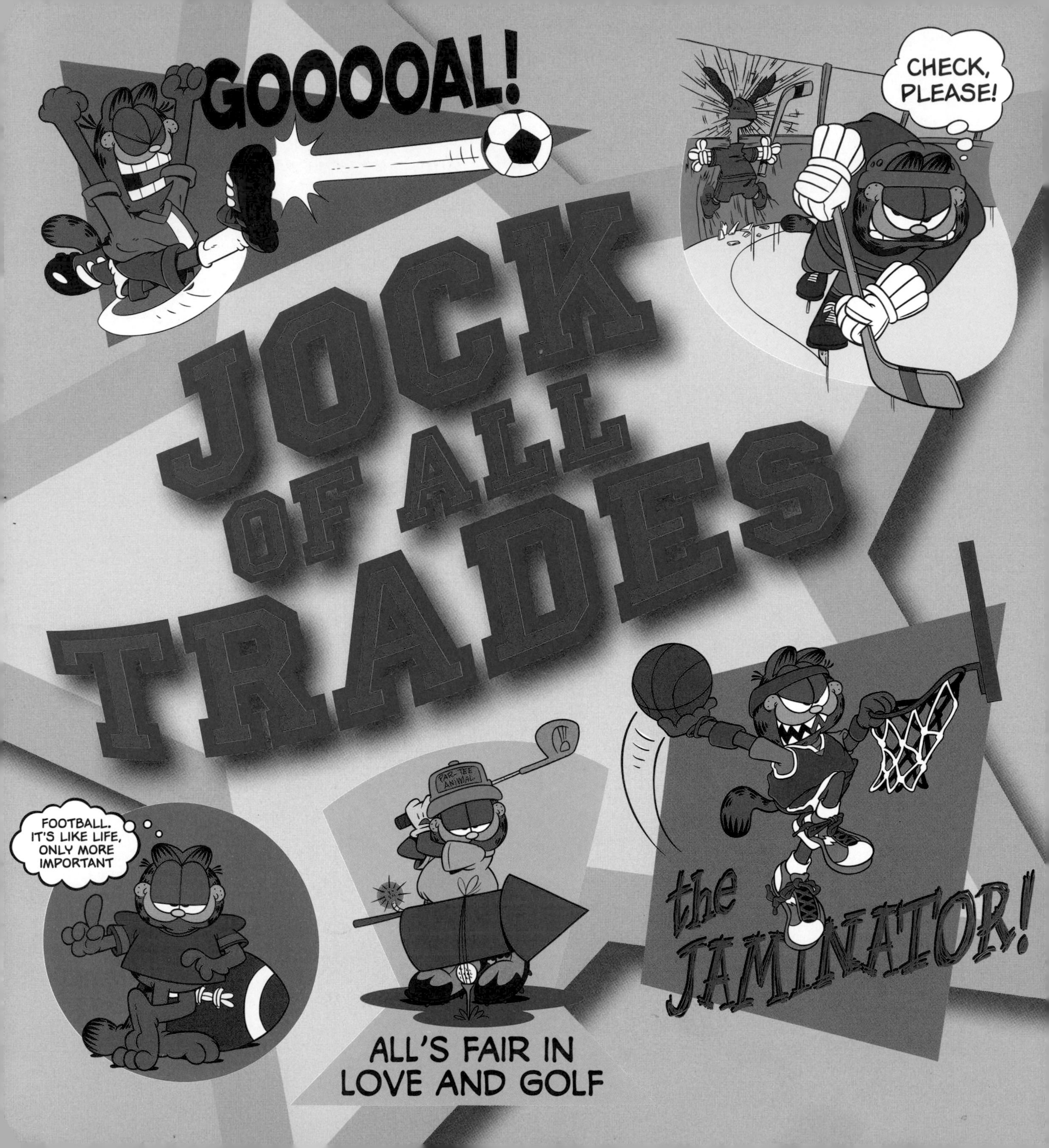
GOOOOAL!
CHECK, PLEASE!
JOCK OF ALL TRADES
FOOTBALL. IT'S LIKE LIFE, ONLY MORE IMPORTANT
PAR-TEE ANIMAL
the JAMINATOR!
ALL'S FAIR IN LOVE AND GOLF

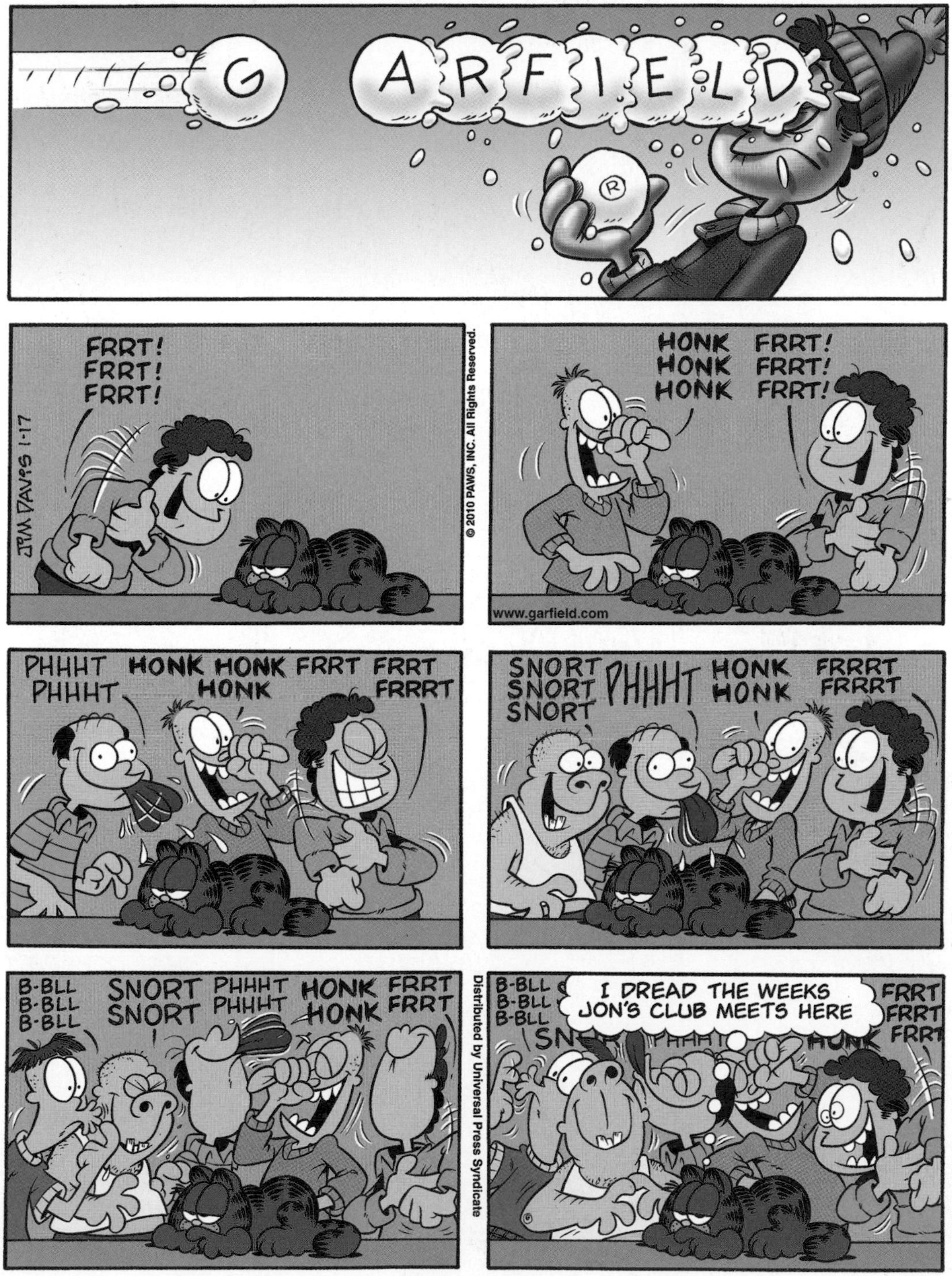
GARFIELD®
FRRT! FRRT! FRRT!
JIM DAVIS 1-17
© 2010 PAWS, INC. All Rights Reserved.
HONK HONK HONK
FRRT! FRRT! FRRT!
www.garfield.com
PHHHT PHHHT
HONK HONK HONK
FRRT FRRT FRRRT
SNORT SNORT SNORT
PHHHT
HONK HONK
FRRRT FRRRT
B-BLL B-BLL B-BLL
SNORT SNORT
PHHHT PHHHT
HONK HONK
FRRT FRRT
Distributed by Universal Press Syndicate
B-BLL B-BLL B-BLL
I DREAD THE WEEKS JON'S CLUB MEETS HERE
FRRT FRRT

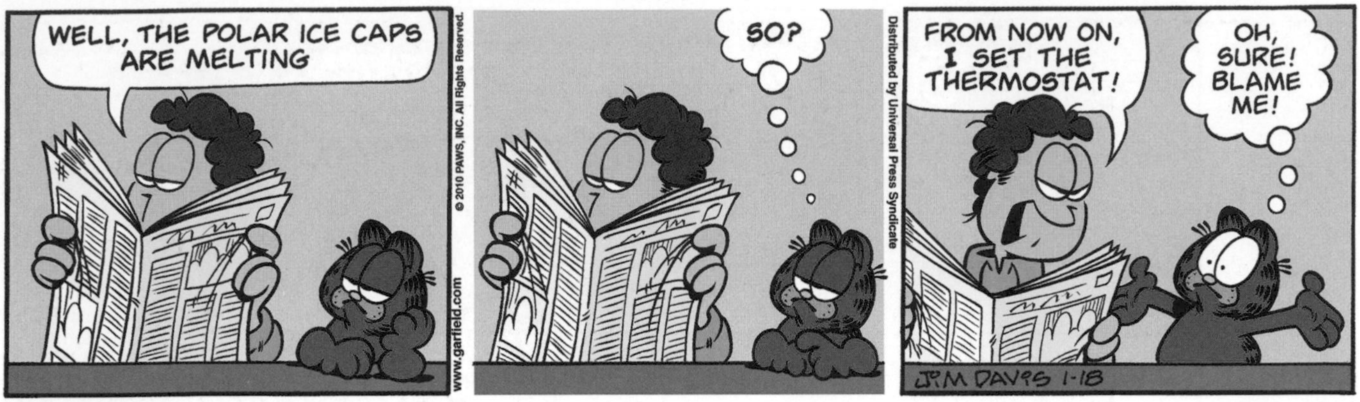
WELL, THE POLAR ICE CAPS ARE MELTING
SO?
FROM NOW ON, I SET THE THERMOSTAT!
OH, SURE! BLAME ME!
JIM DAVIS 1-18
© 2010 PAWS, INC. All Rights Reserved.
www.garfield.com
Distributed by Universal Press Syndicate

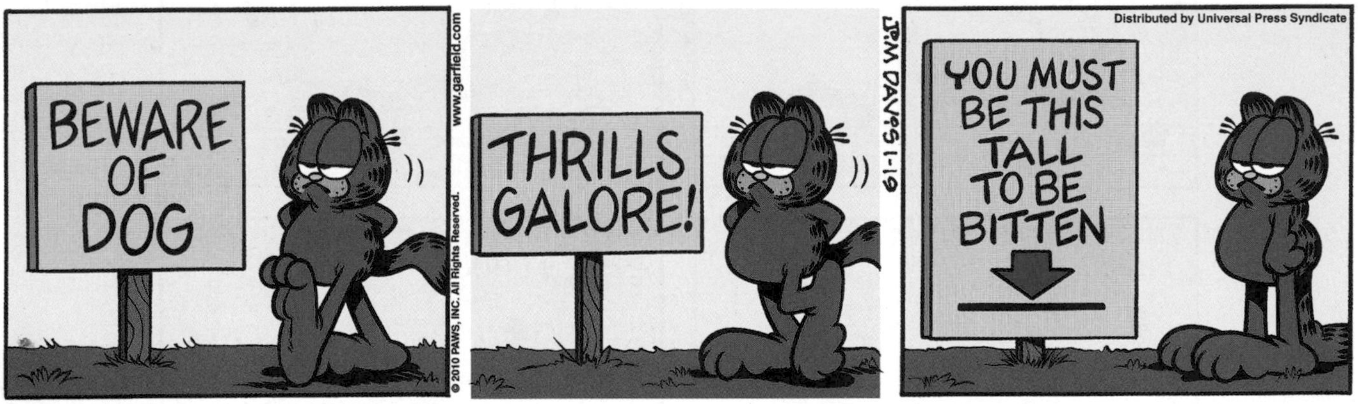
BEWARE OF DOG
THRILLS GALORE!
YOU MUST BE THIS TALL TO BE BITTEN
JIM DAVIS 1-19
© 2010 PAWS, INC. All Rights Reserved.
www.garfield.com
Distributed by Universal Press Syndicate

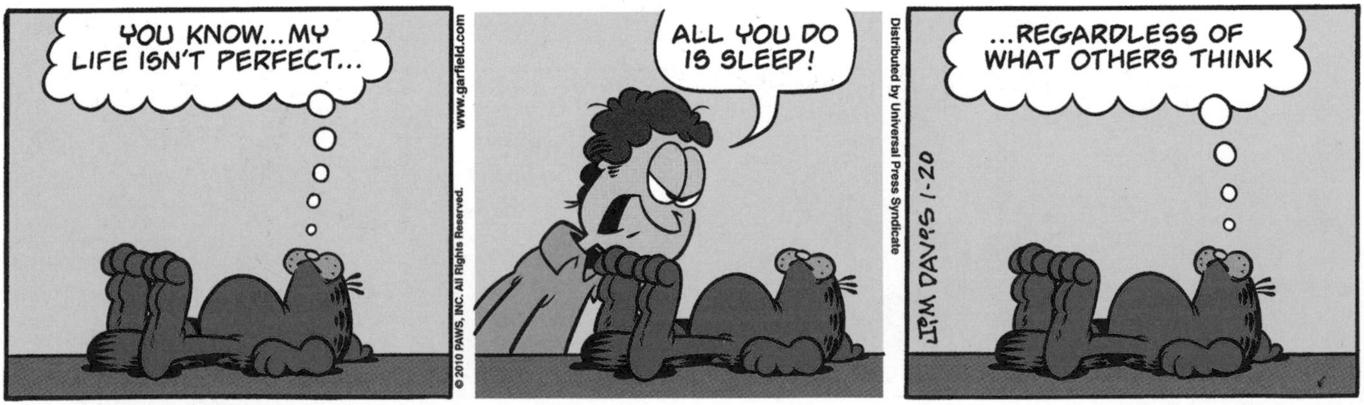
YOU KNOW...MY LIFE ISN'T PERFECT...
ALL YOU DO IS SLEEP!
...REGARDLESS OF WHAT OTHERS THINK
JIM DAVIS 1-20
© 2010 PAWS, INC. All Rights Reserved.
www.garfield.com
Distributed by Universal Press Syndicate

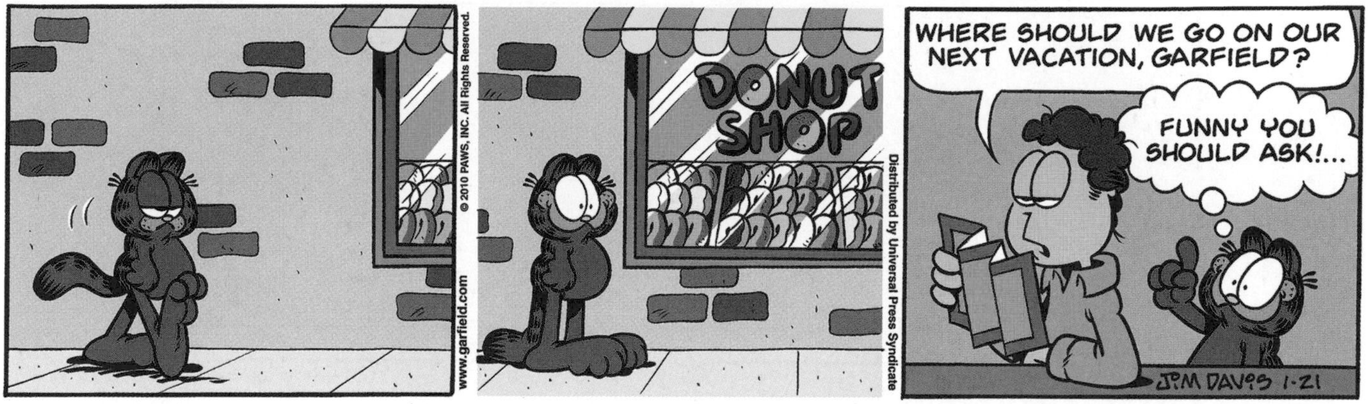
www.garfield.com
© 2010 PAWS, INC. All Rights Reserved.
DONUT SHOP
Distributed by Universal Press Syndicate
WHERE SHOULD WE GO ON OUR NEXT VACATION, GARFIELD?
FUNNY YOU SHOULD ASK!...
JIM DAVIS 1-21

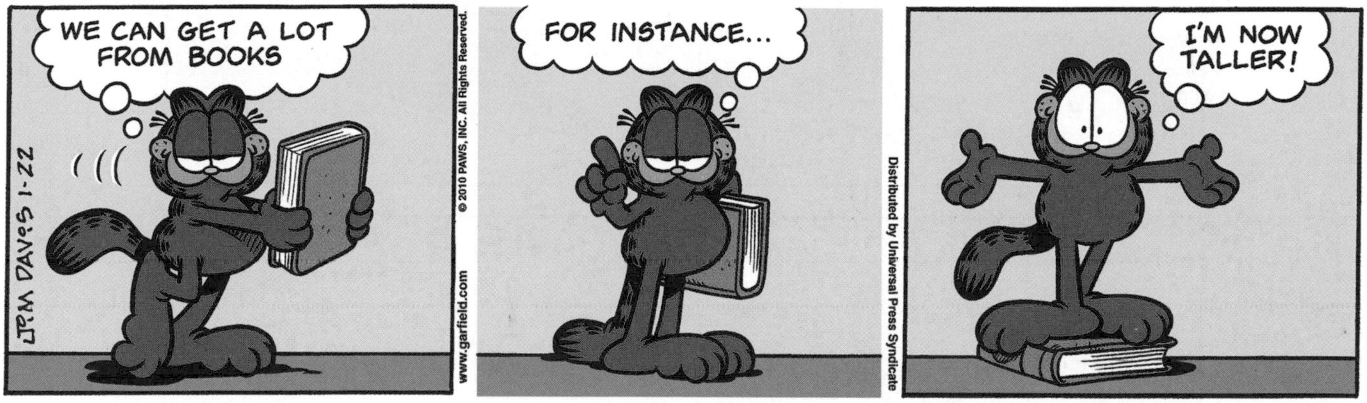
WE CAN GET A LOT FROM BOOKS
JIM DAVIS 1-22
www.garfield.com
© 2010 PAWS, INC. All Rights Reserved.
FOR INSTANCE...
Distributed by Universal Press Syndicate
I'M NOW TALLER!

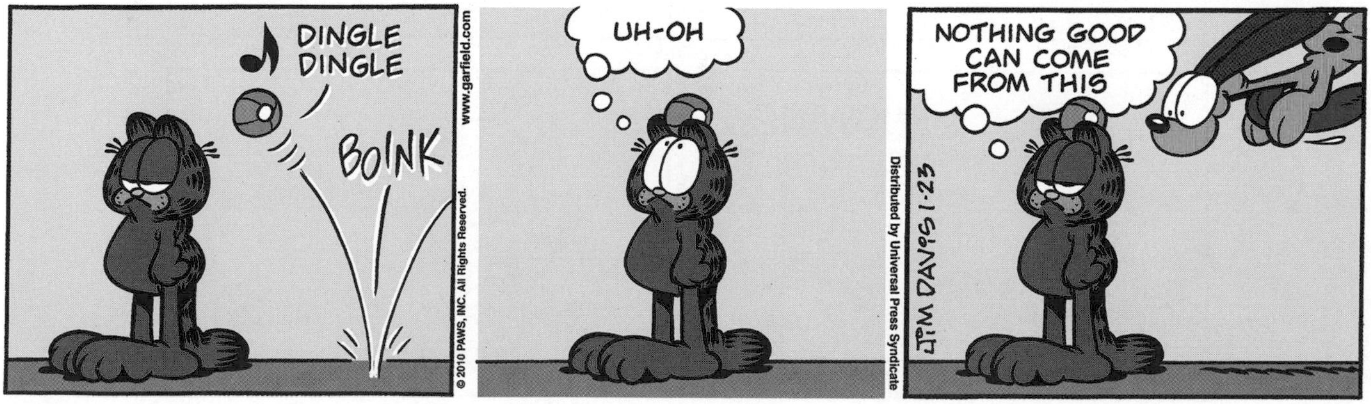
DINGLE DINGLE
BOINK
© 2010 PAWS, INC. All Rights Reserved.
www.garfield.com
UH-OH
Distributed by Universal Press Syndicate
NOTHING GOOD CAN COME FROM THIS
JIM DAVIS 1-23

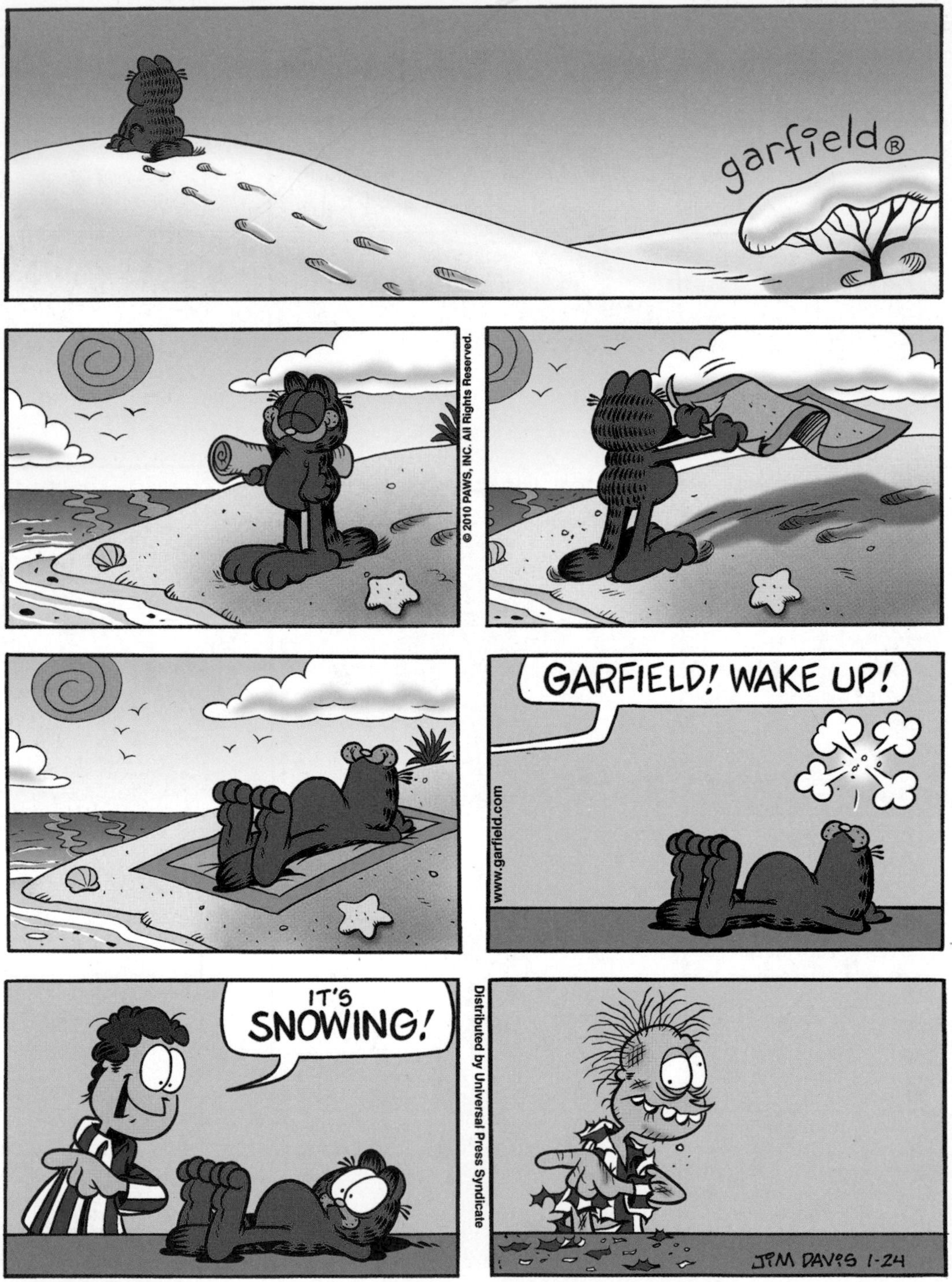
garfield®
© 2010 PAWS, INC. All Rights Reserved.
www.garfield.com
GARFIELD! WAKE UP!
Distributed by Universal Press Syndicate
IT'S SNOWING!
JIM DAVIS 1-24

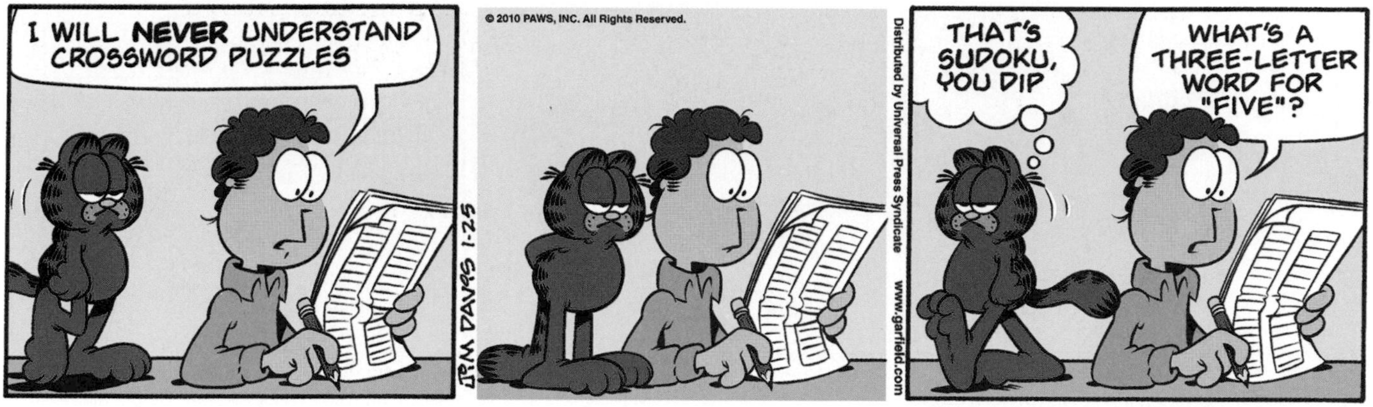
I WILL NEVER UNDERSTAND CROSSWORD PUZZLES
JIM DAVIS 1-25
© 2010 PAWS, INC. All Rights Reserved.
THAT'S SUDOKU, YOU DIP
WHAT'S A THREE-LETTER WORD FOR "FIVE"?
Distributed by Universal Press Syndicate www.garfield.com

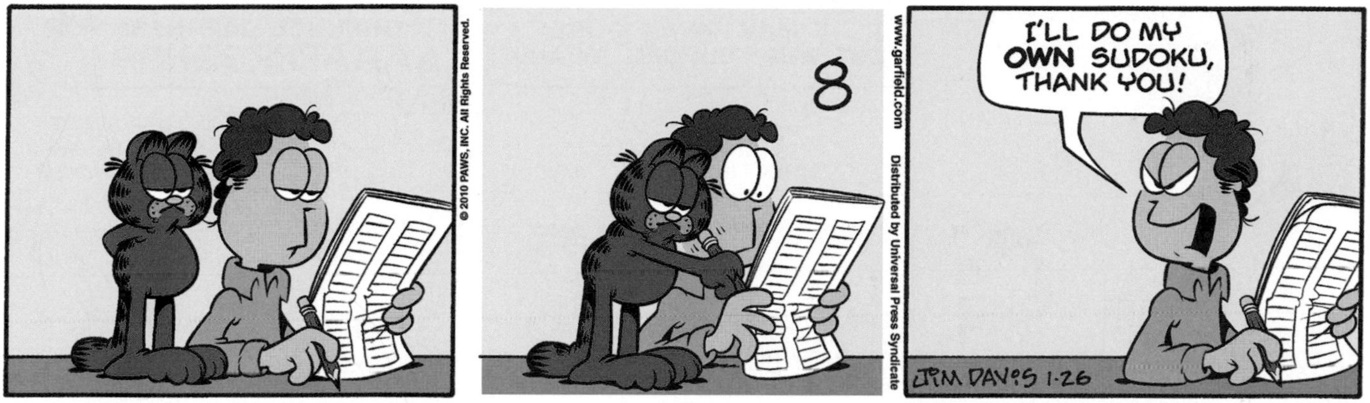
© 2010 PAWS, INC. All Rights Reserved.
8
www.garfield.com Distributed by Universal Press Syndicate
I'LL DO MY OWN SUDOKU, THANK YOU!
JIM DAVIS 1-26

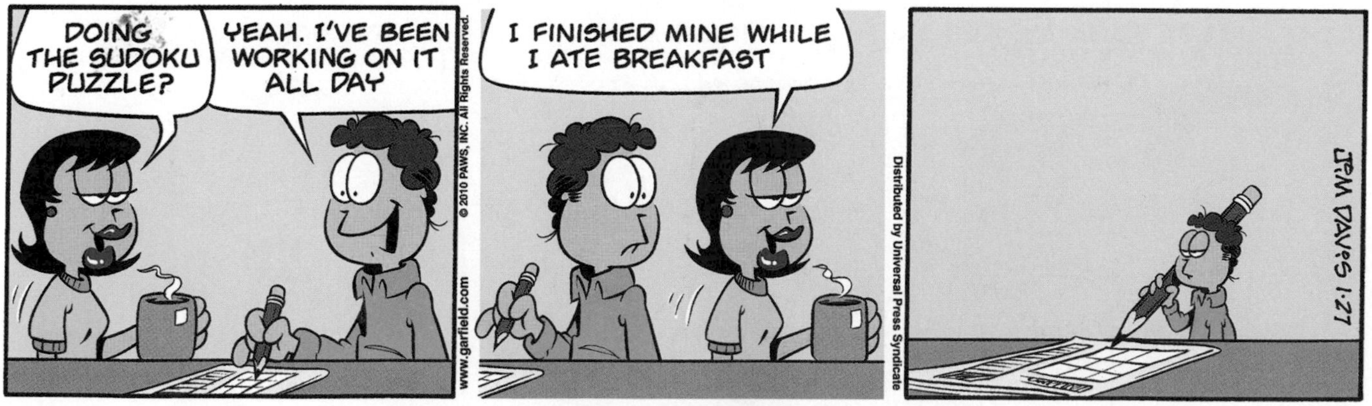
DOING THE SUDOKU PUZZLE?
YEAH. I'VE BEEN WORKING ON IT ALL DAY
© 2010 PAWS, INC. All Rights Reserved. www.garfield.com
I FINISHED MINE WHILE I ATE BREAKFAST
Distributed by Universal Press Syndicate
JIM DAVIS 1-27

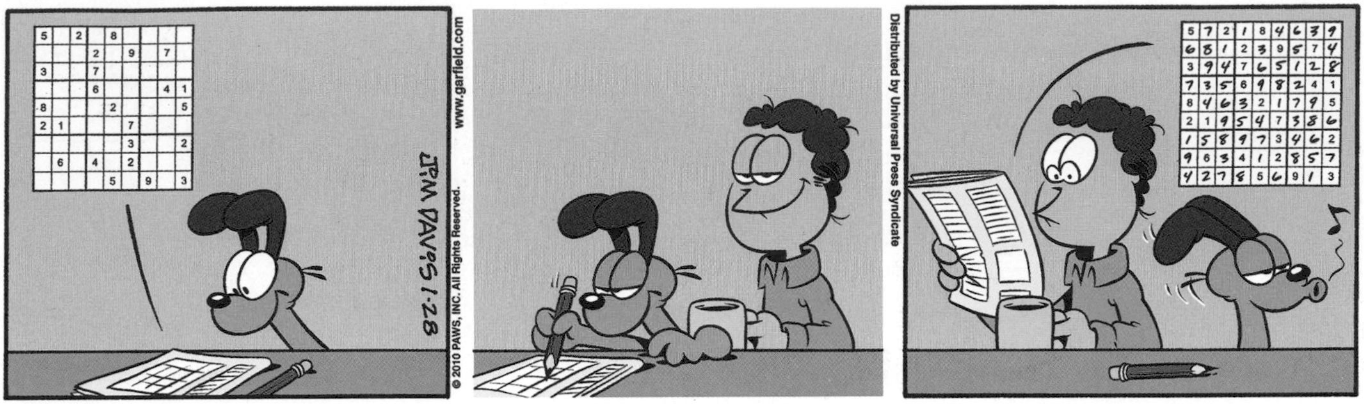

JIM DAVIS 1-28
© 2010 PAWS, INC. All Rights Reserved.
www.garfield.com
Distributed by Universal Press Syndicate

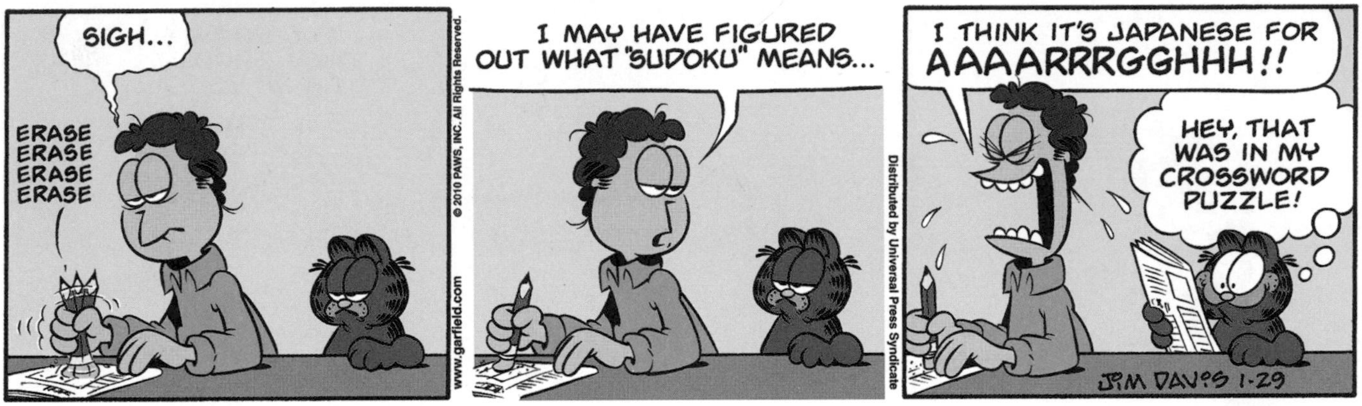

SIGH...
ERASE ERASE ERASE ERASE
I MAY HAVE FIGURED OUT WHAT "SUDOKU" MEANS...
I THINK IT'S JAPANESE FOR AAAARRRGGHHH!!
HEY, THAT WAS IN MY CROSSWORD PUZZLE!
JIM DAVIS 1-29
© 2010 PAWS, INC. All Rights Reserved.
www.garfield.com
Distributed by Universal Press Syndicate

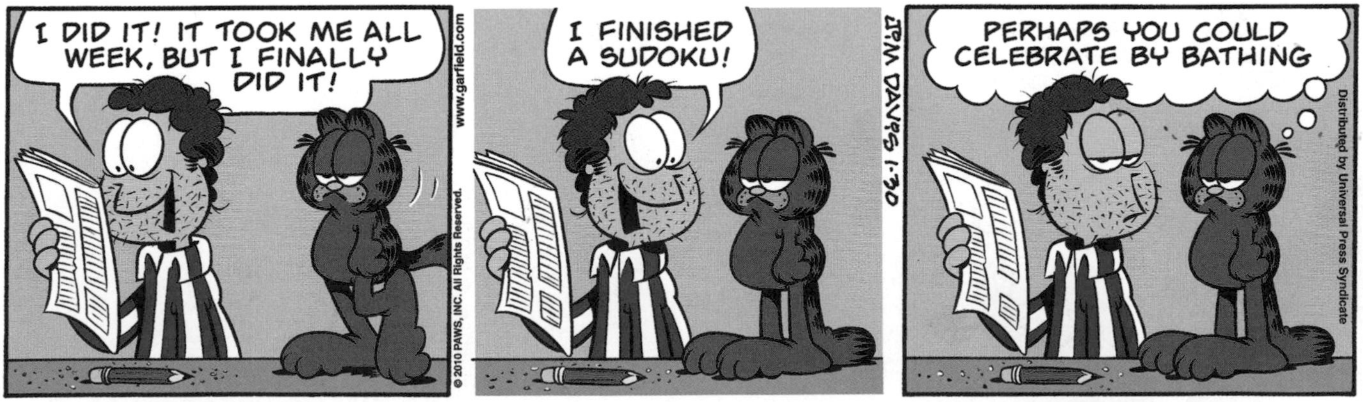

I DID IT! IT TOOK ME ALL WEEK, BUT I FINALLY DID IT!
I FINISHED A SUDOKU!
PERHAPS YOU COULD CELEBRATE BY BATHING
JIM DAVIS 1-30
© 2010 PAWS, INC. All Rights Reserved.
www.garfield.com
Distributed by Universal Press Syndicate

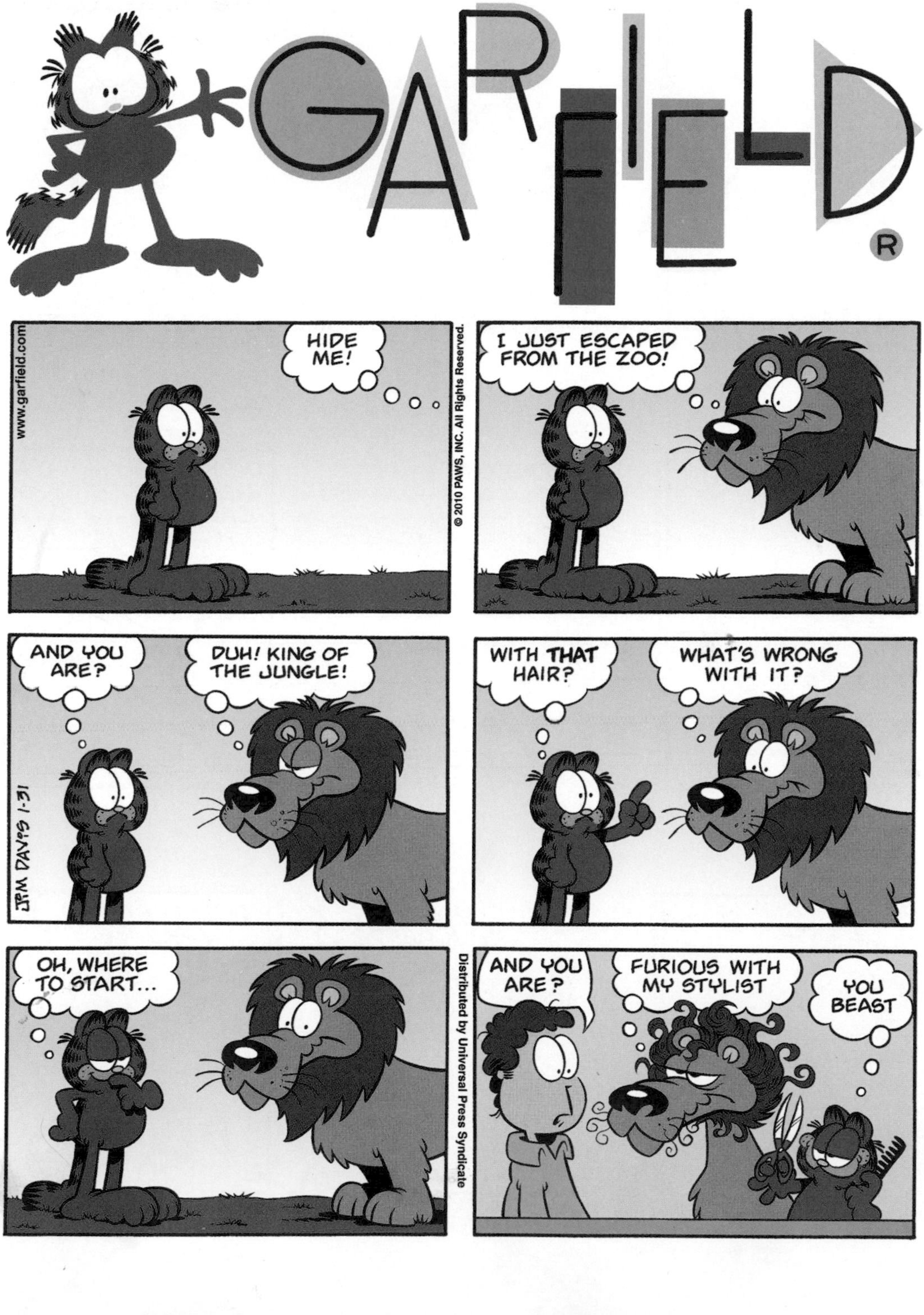
GARFIELD®
www.garfield.com
© 2010 PAWS, INC. All Rights Reserved.
HIDE ME!
I JUST ESCAPED FROM THE ZOO!
JIM DAVIS 1-31
AND YOU ARE?
DUH! KING OF THE JUNGLE!
WITH THAT HAIR?
WHAT'S WRONG WITH IT?
OH, WHERE TO START...
Distributed by Universal Press Syndicate
AND YOU ARE?
FURIOUS WITH MY STYLIST
YOU BEAST

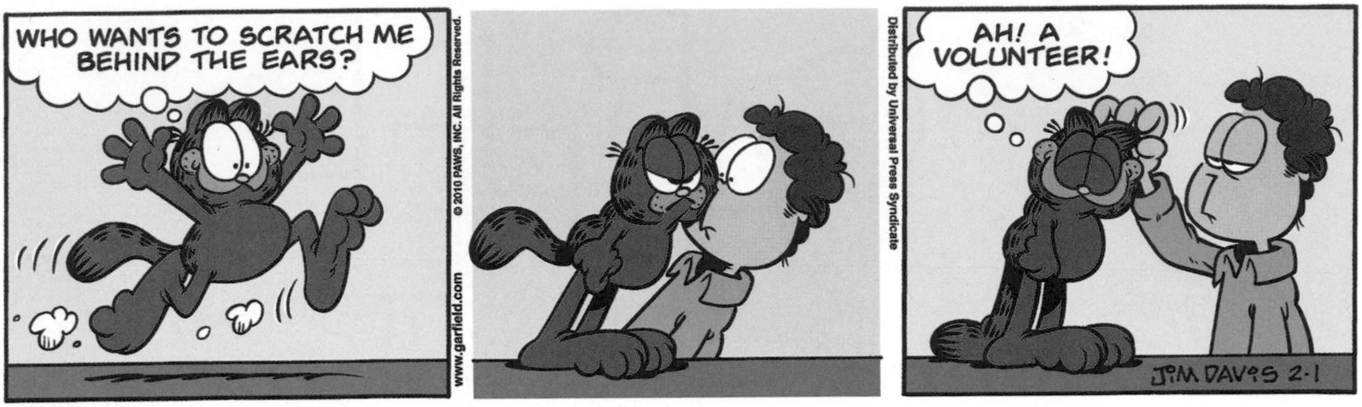
WHO WANTS TO SCRATCH ME BEHIND THE EARS?
AH! A VOLUNTEER!
JIM DAVIS 2·1
© 2010 PAWS, INC. All Rights Reserved.
www.garfield.com
Distributed by Universal Press Syndicate

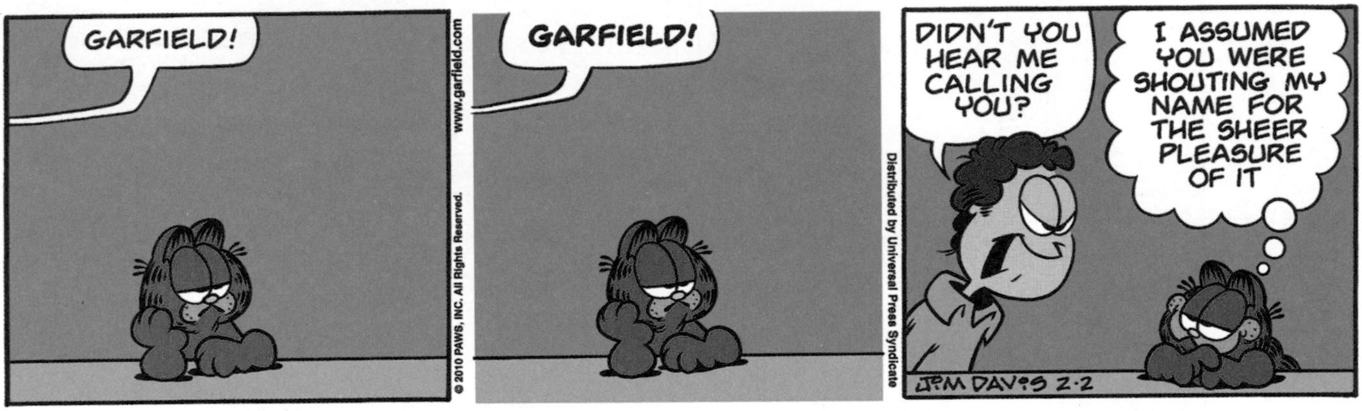
GARFIELD!
GARFIELD!
DIDN'T YOU HEAR ME CALLING YOU?
I ASSUMED YOU WERE SHOUTING MY NAME FOR THE SHEER PLEASURE OF IT
JIM DAVIS 2·2
© 2010 PAWS, INC. All Rights Reserved.
www.garfield.com
Distributed by Universal Press Syndicate

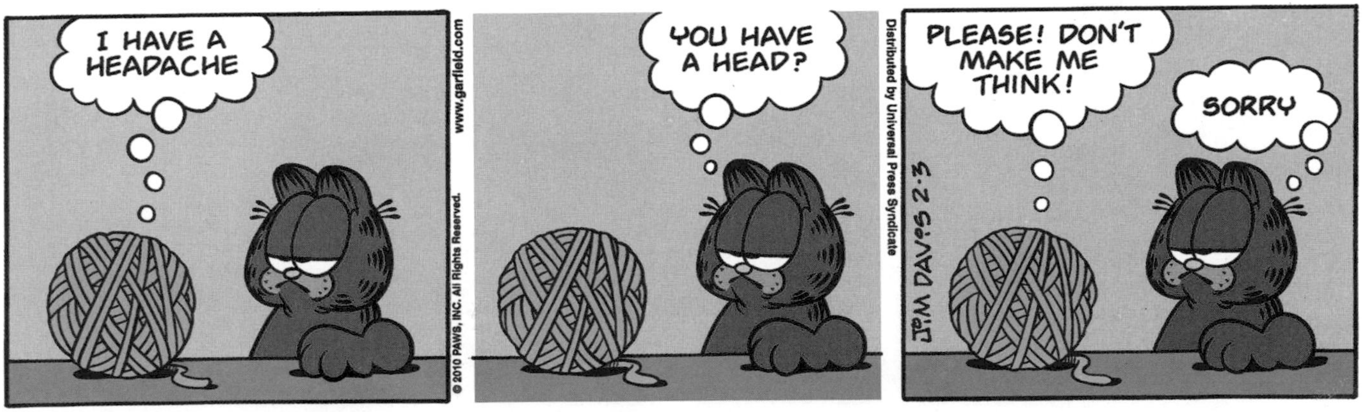
I HAVE A HEADACHE
YOU HAVE A HEAD?
PLEASE! DON'T MAKE ME THINK!
SORRY
JIM DAVIS 2·3
© 2010 PAWS, INC. All Rights Reserved.
www.garfield.com
Distributed by Universal Press Syndicate

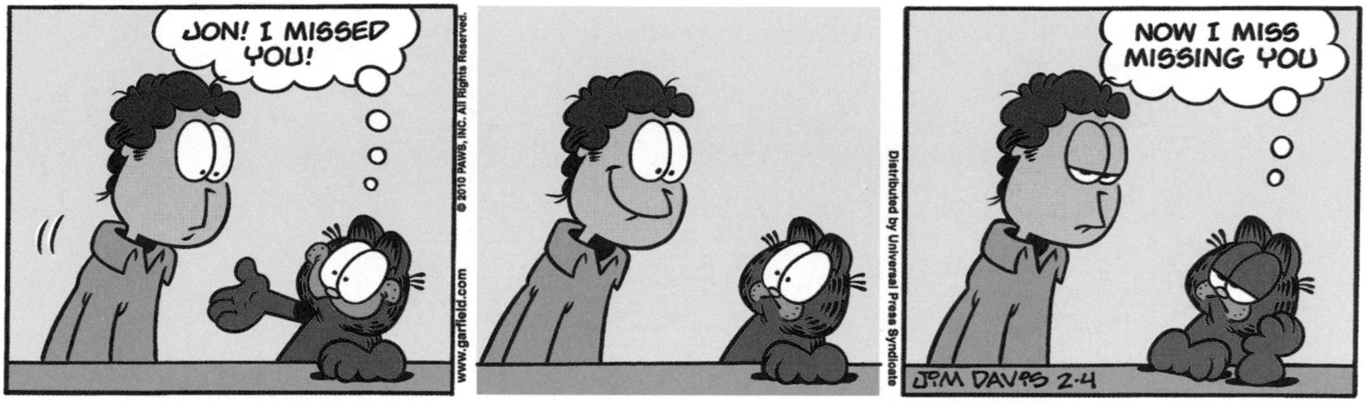
JON! I MISSED YOU!
NOW I MISS MISSING YOU
www.garfield.com
© 2010 PAWS, INC. All Rights Reserved.
Distributed by Universal Press Syndicate
JIM DAVIS 2-4

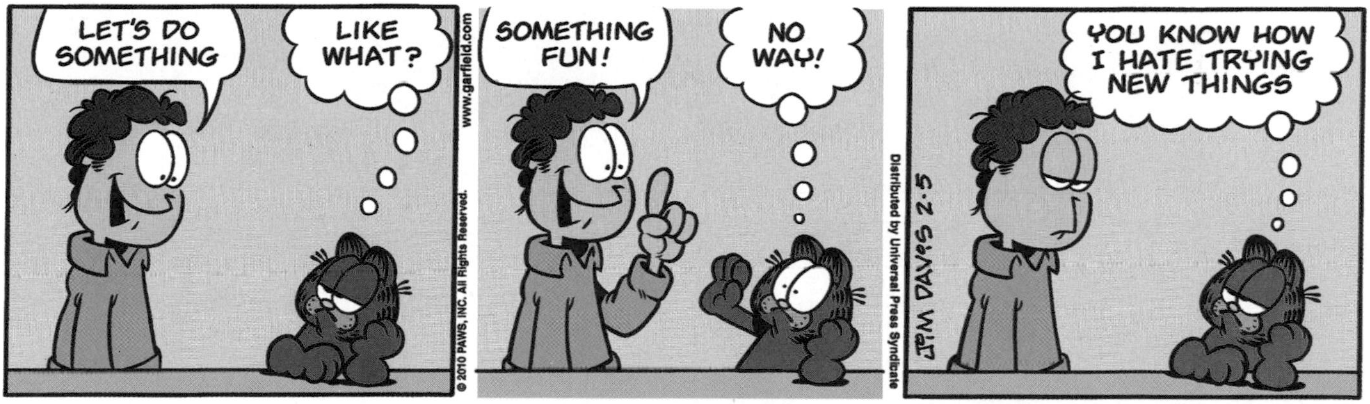
LET'S DO SOMETHING
LIKE WHAT?
SOMETHING FUN!
NO WAY!
YOU KNOW HOW I HATE TRYING NEW THINGS
© 2010 PAWS, INC. All Rights Reserved.
www.garfield.com
Distributed by Universal Press Syndicate
JIM DAVIS 2-5

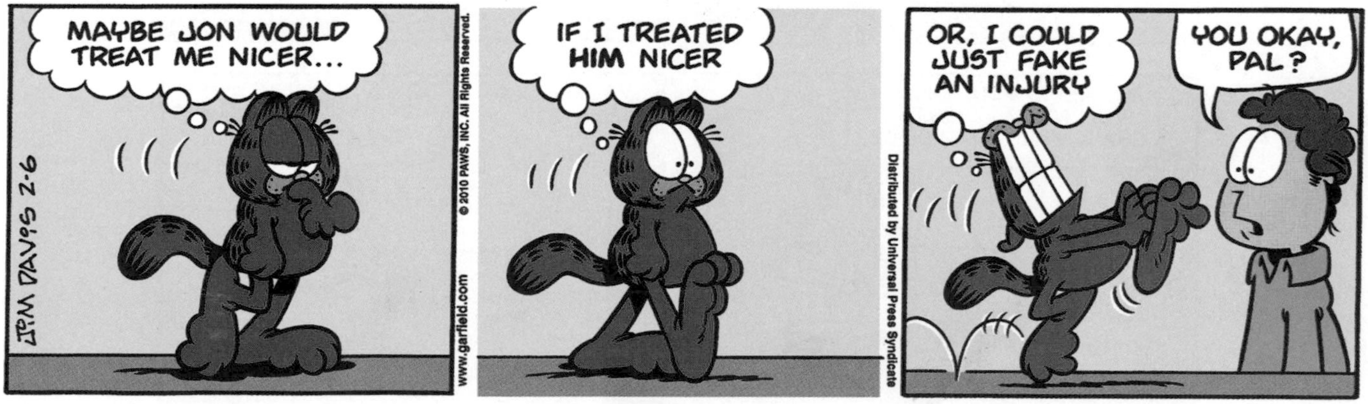
MAYBE JON WOULD TREAT ME NICER...
IF I TREATED HIM NICER
OR, I COULD JUST FAKE AN INJURY
YOU OKAY, PAL?
JIM DAVIS 2-6
www.garfield.com
© 2010 PAWS, INC. All Rights Reserved.
Distributed by Universal Press Syndicate

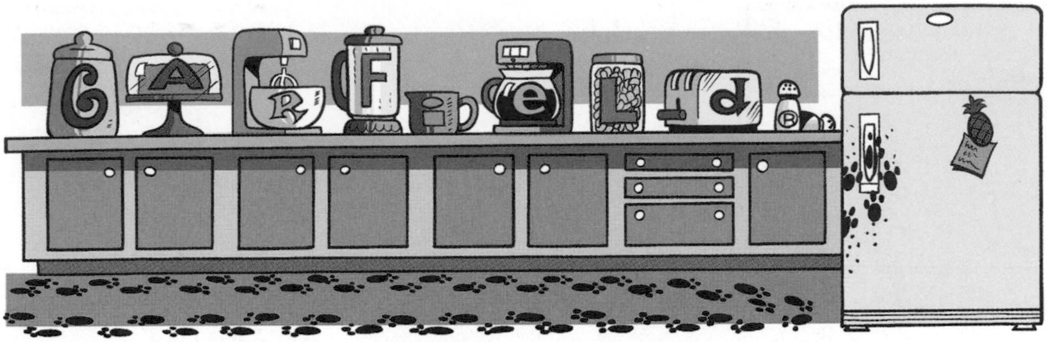
GARFIELD

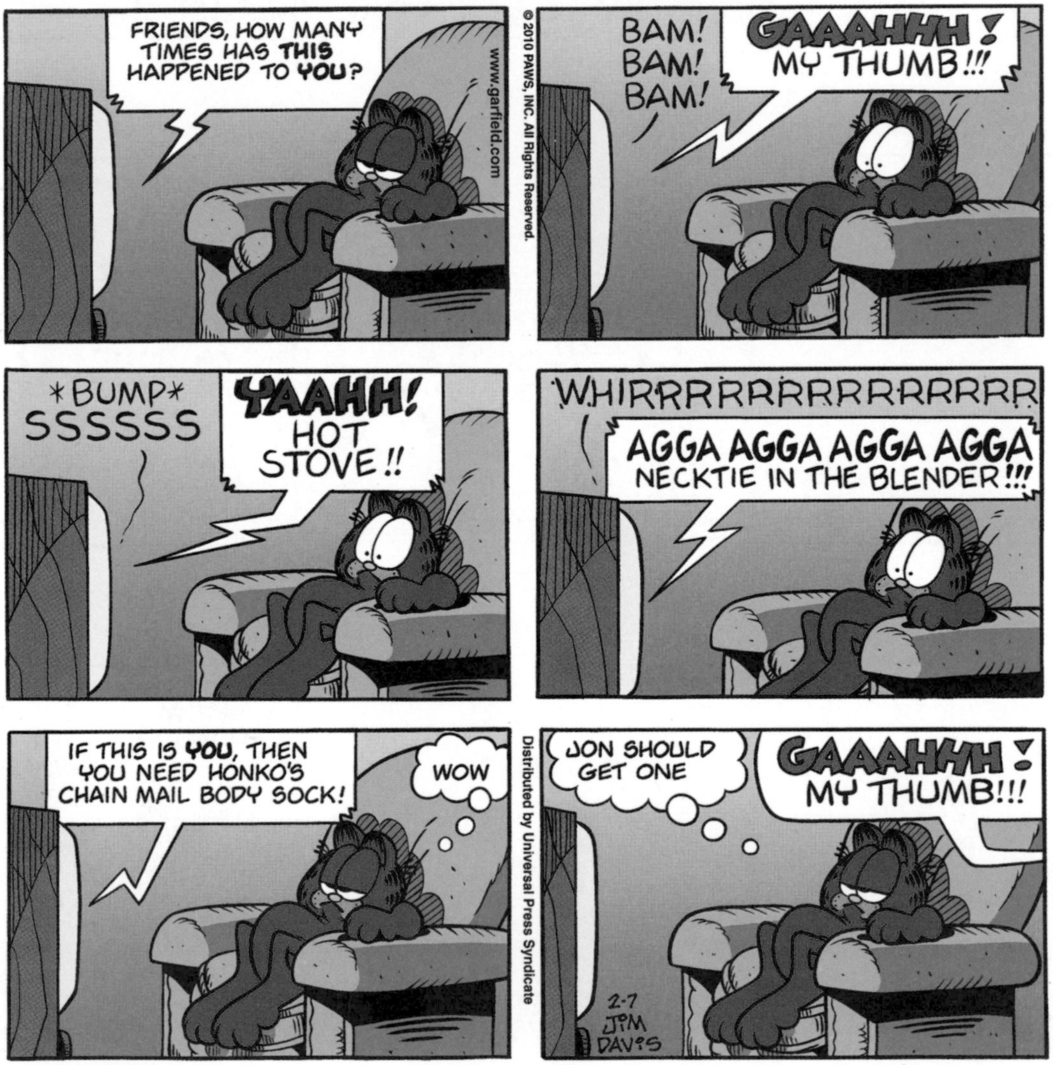
FRIENDS, HOW MANY TIMES HAS THIS HAPPENED TO YOU?
BAM! BAM! BAM!
GAAAHHH! MY THUMB!!!
BUMP SSSSSS
YAAHH! HOT STOVE!!
WHIRRRRRRRRRRRRRR
AGGA AGGA AGGA AGGA NECKTIE IN THE BLENDER!!!
IF THIS IS YOU, THEN YOU NEED HONKO'S CHAIN MAIL BODY SOCK!
WOW
JON SHOULD GET ONE
GAAAHHH! MY THUMB!!!
2-7 JIM DAVIS

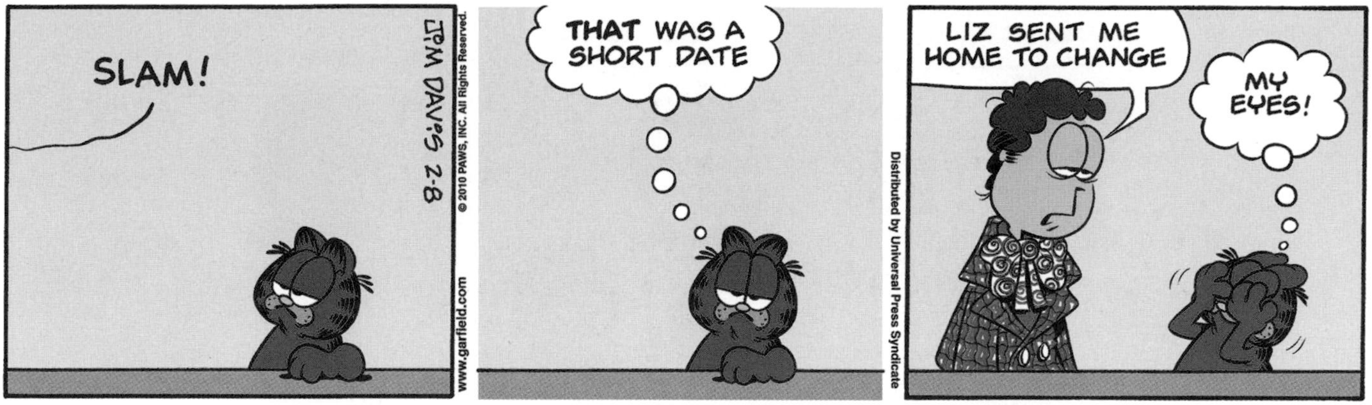
SLAM!
JIM DAVIS 2-8
© 2010 PAWS, INC. All Rights Reserved.
www.garfield.com
THAT WAS A SHORT DATE
Distributed by Universal Press Syndicate
LIZ SENT ME HOME TO CHANGE
MY EYES!

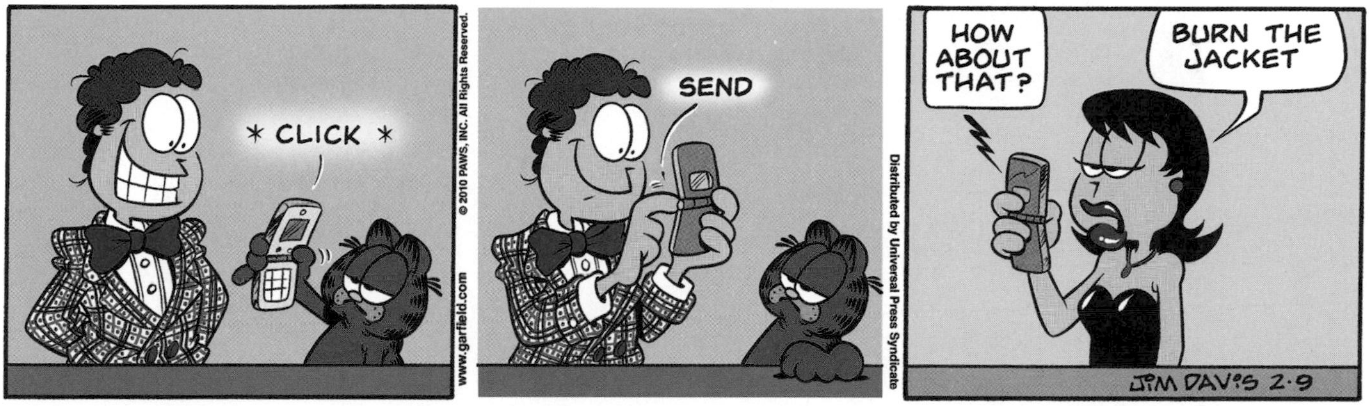
* CLICK *
© 2010 PAWS, INC. All Rights Reserved.
www.garfield.com
SEND
Distributed by Universal Press Syndicate
HOW ABOUT THAT?
BURN THE JACKET
JIM DAVIS 2-9

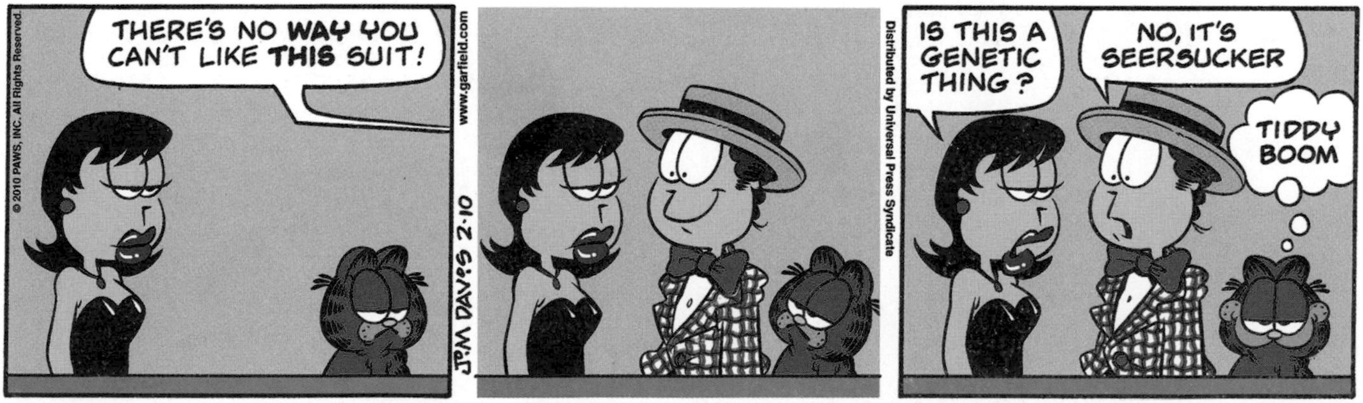
© 2010 PAWS, INC. All Rights Reserved.
THERE'S NO WAY YOU CAN'T LIKE THIS SUIT!
www.garfield.com
JIM DAVIS 2-10
Distributed by Universal Press Syndicate
IS THIS A GENETIC THING?
NO, IT'S SEERSUCKER
TIDDY BOOM

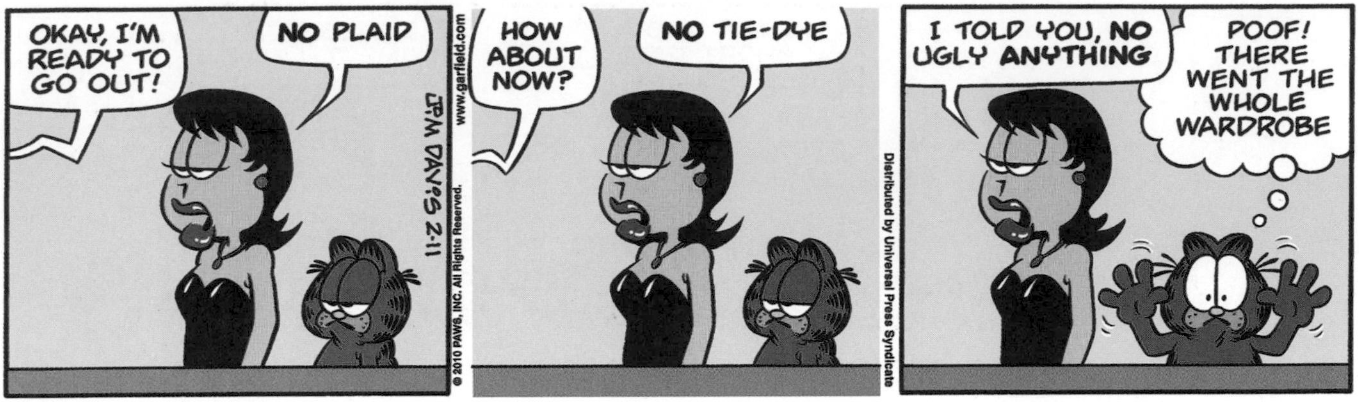
OKAY, I'M READY TO GO OUT!
NO PLAID
JIM DAVIS 2-11
© 2010 PAWS, INC. All Rights Reserved. www.garfield.com
HOW ABOUT NOW?
NO TIE-DYE
Distributed by Universal Press Syndicate
I TOLD YOU, NO UGLY ANYTHING
POOF! THERE WENT THE WHOLE WARDROBE

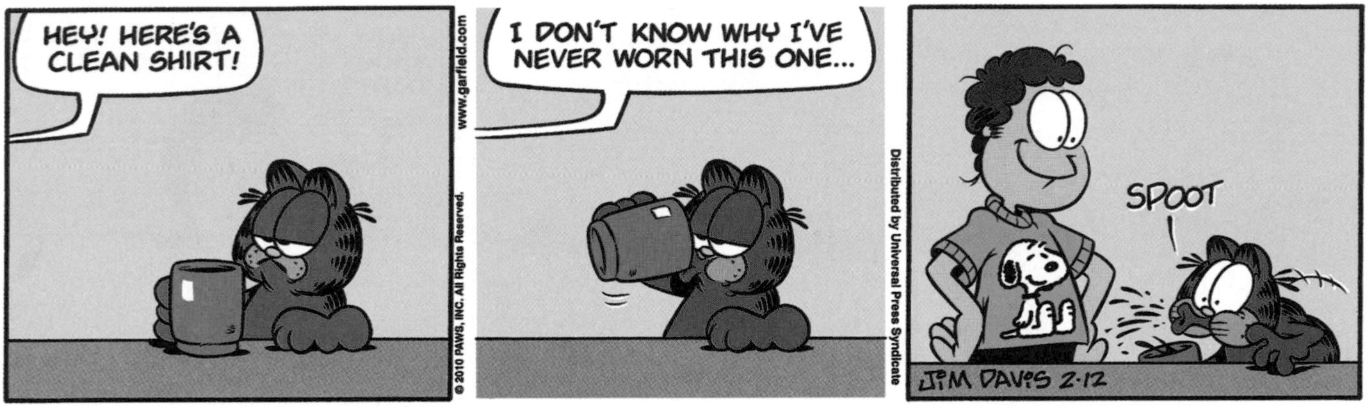
HEY! HERE'S A CLEAN SHIRT!
© 2010 PAWS, INC. All Rights Reserved. www.garfield.com
I DON'T KNOW WHY I'VE NEVER WORN THIS ONE...
Distributed by Universal Press Syndicate
SPOOT
JIM DAVIS 2-12

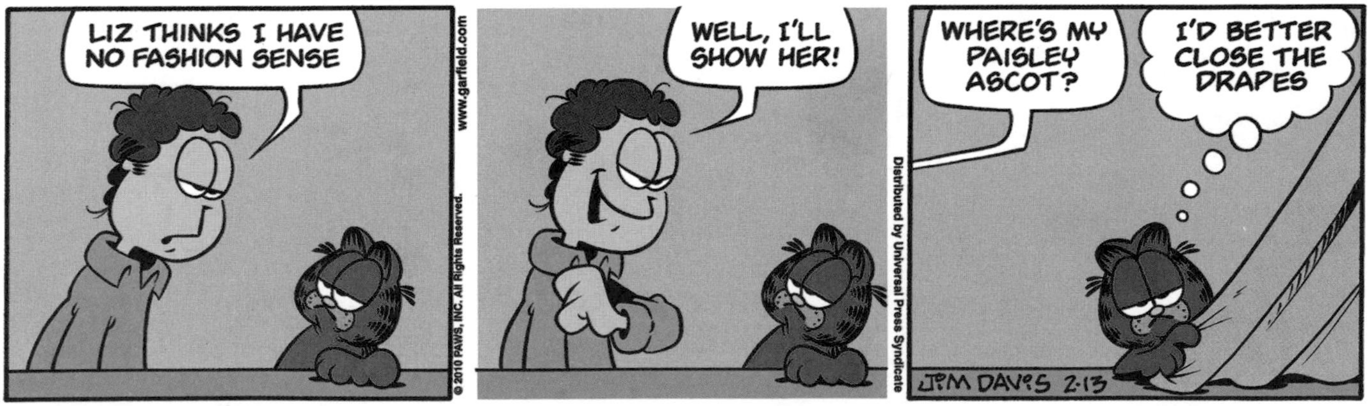
LIZ THINKS I HAVE NO FASHION SENSE
© 2010 PAWS, INC. All Rights Reserved. www.garfield.com
WELL, I'LL SHOW HER!
Distributed by Universal Press Syndicate
WHERE'S MY PAISLEY ASCOT?
I'D BETTER CLOSE THE DRAPES
JIM DAVIS 2-13

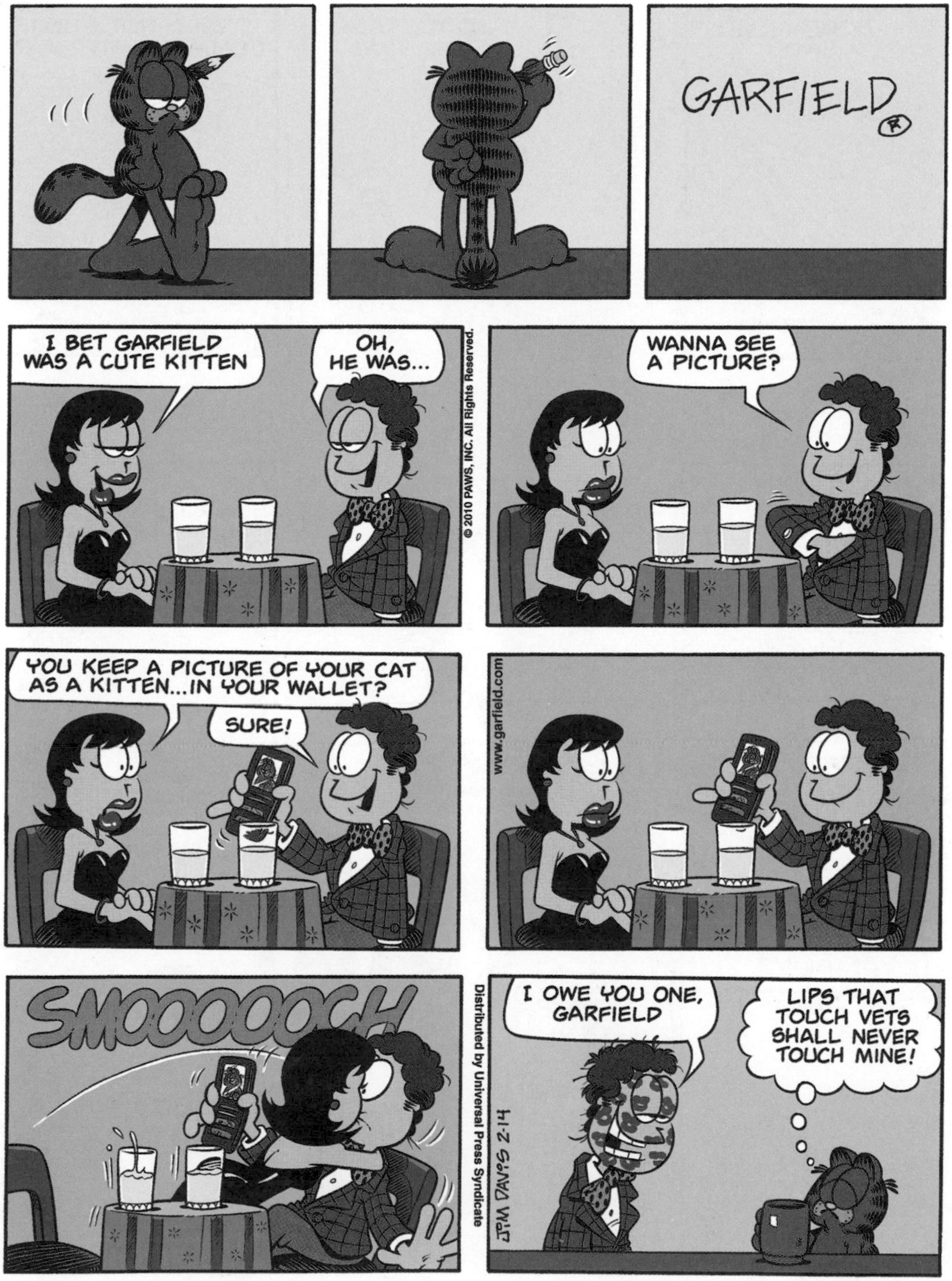
GARFIELD ®
I BET GARFIELD WAS A CUTE KITTEN
OH, HE WAS...
© 2010 PAWS, INC. All Rights Reserved.
WANNA SEE A PICTURE?
YOU KEEP A PICTURE OF YOUR CAT AS A KITTEN...IN YOUR WALLET?
SURE!
www.garfield.com
SMOOOOOCH
Distributed by Universal Press Syndicate
I OWE YOU ONE, GARFIELD
LIPS THAT TOUCH VETS SHALL NEVER TOUCH MINE!
JIM DAVIS 2-14

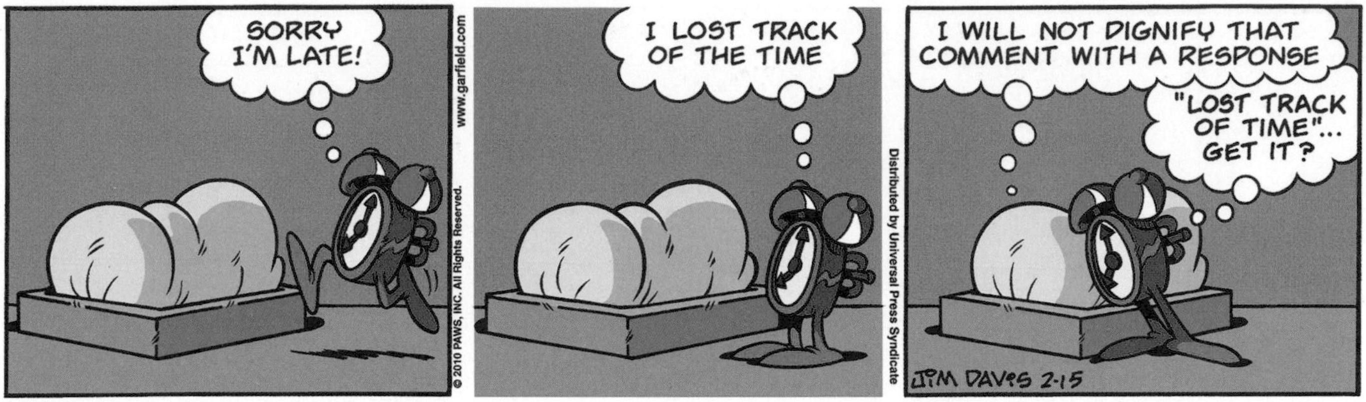
SORRY I'M LATE!
I LOST TRACK OF THE TIME
I WILL NOT DIGNIFY THAT COMMENT WITH A RESPONSE
"LOST TRACK OF TIME"... GET IT?
© 2010 PAWS, INC. All Rights Reserved. www.garfield.com
Distributed by Universal Press Syndicate
JIM DAVIS 2-15

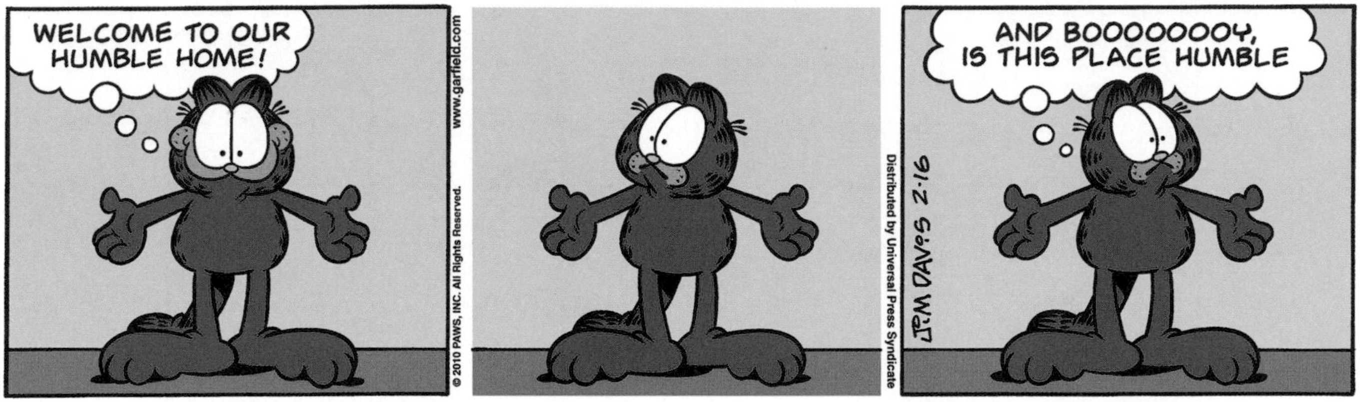
WELCOME TO OUR HUMBLE HOME!
AND BOOOOOOOY, IS THIS PLACE HUMBLE
© 2010 PAWS, INC. All Rights Reserved. www.garfield.com
Distributed by Universal Press Syndicate
JIM DAVIS 2-16

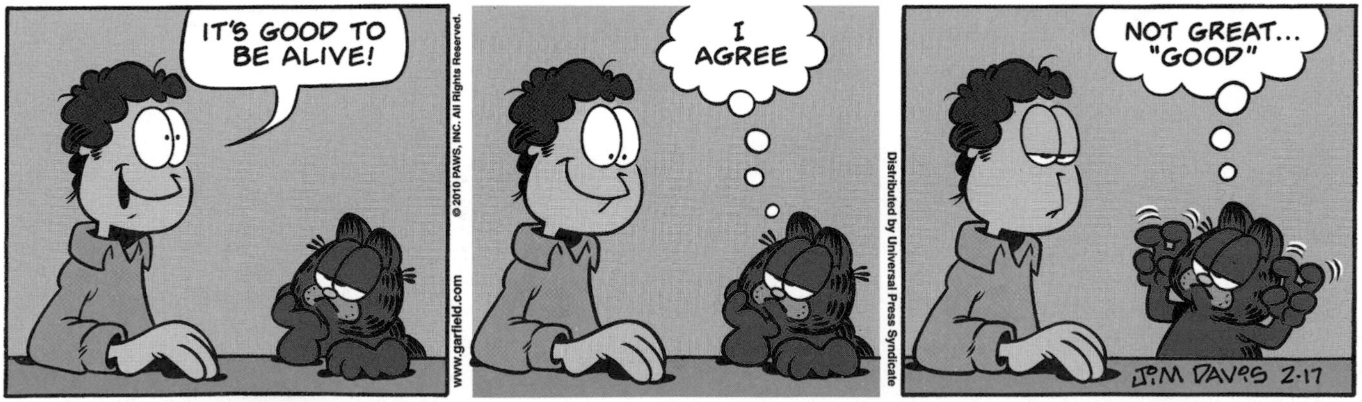
IT'S GOOD TO BE ALIVE!
I AGREE
NOT GREAT... "GOOD"
© 2010 PAWS, INC. All Rights Reserved. www.garfield.com
Distributed by Universal Press Syndicate
JIM DAVIS 2-17

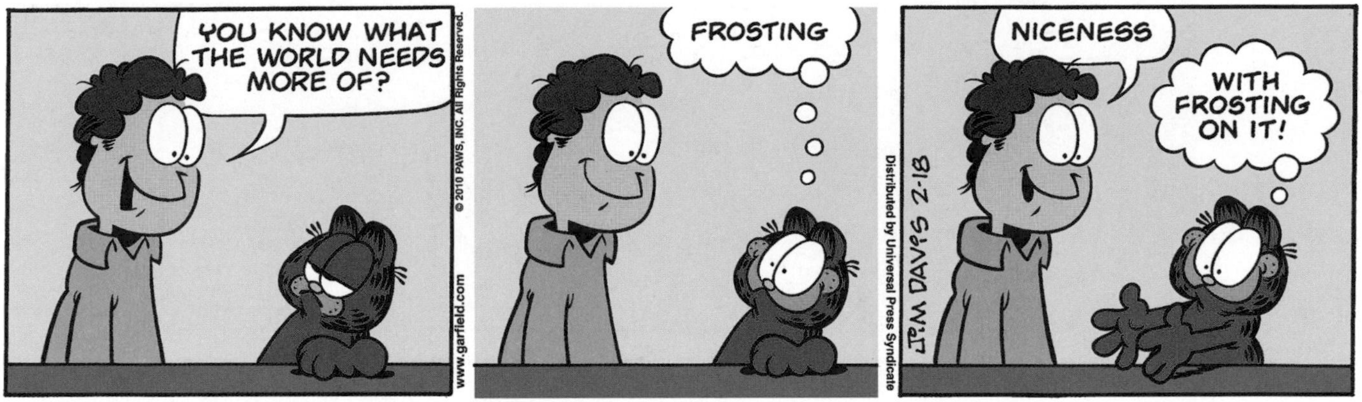
YOU KNOW WHAT THE WORLD NEEDS MORE OF?
FROSTING
NICENESS
WITH FROSTING ON IT!
© 2010 PAWS, INC. All Rights Reserved.
www.garfield.com
Distributed by Universal Press Syndicate
JIM DAVIS 2-18

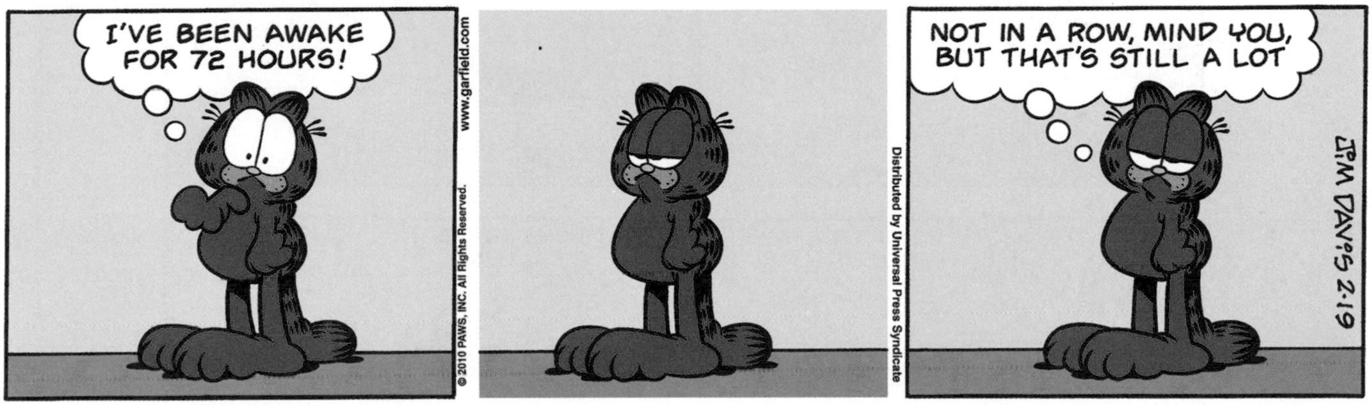
I'VE BEEN AWAKE FOR 72 HOURS!
NOT IN A ROW, MIND YOU, BUT THAT'S STILL A LOT
© 2010 PAWS, INC. All Rights Reserved.
www.garfield.com
Distributed by Universal Press Syndicate
JIM DAVIS 2-19

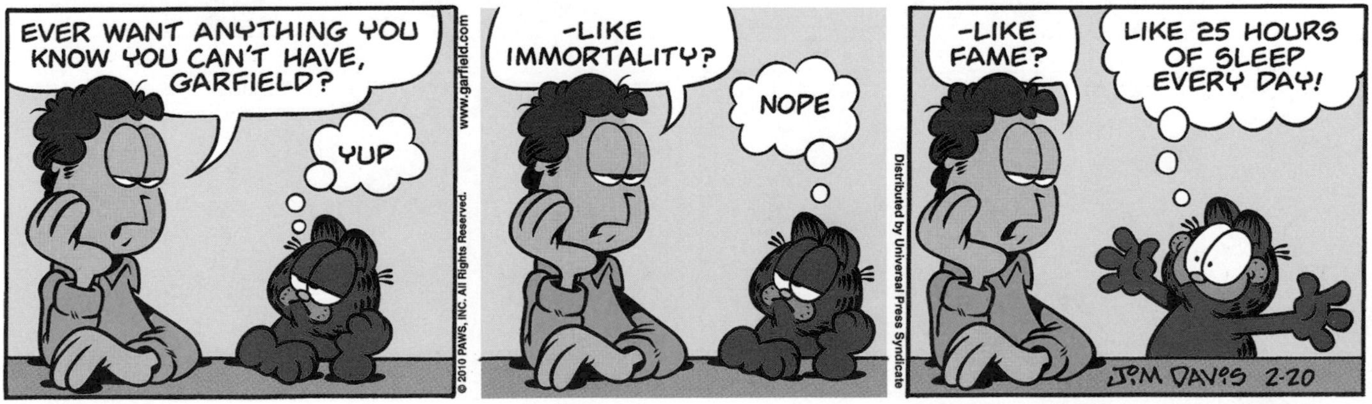
EVER WANT ANYTHING YOU KNOW YOU CAN'T HAVE, GARFIELD?
YUP
-LIKE IMMORTALITY?
NOPE
-LIKE FAME?
LIKE 25 HOURS OF SLEEP EVERY DAY!
© 2010 PAWS, INC. All Rights Reserved.
www.garfield.com
Distributed by Universal Press Syndicate
JIM DAVIS 2-20

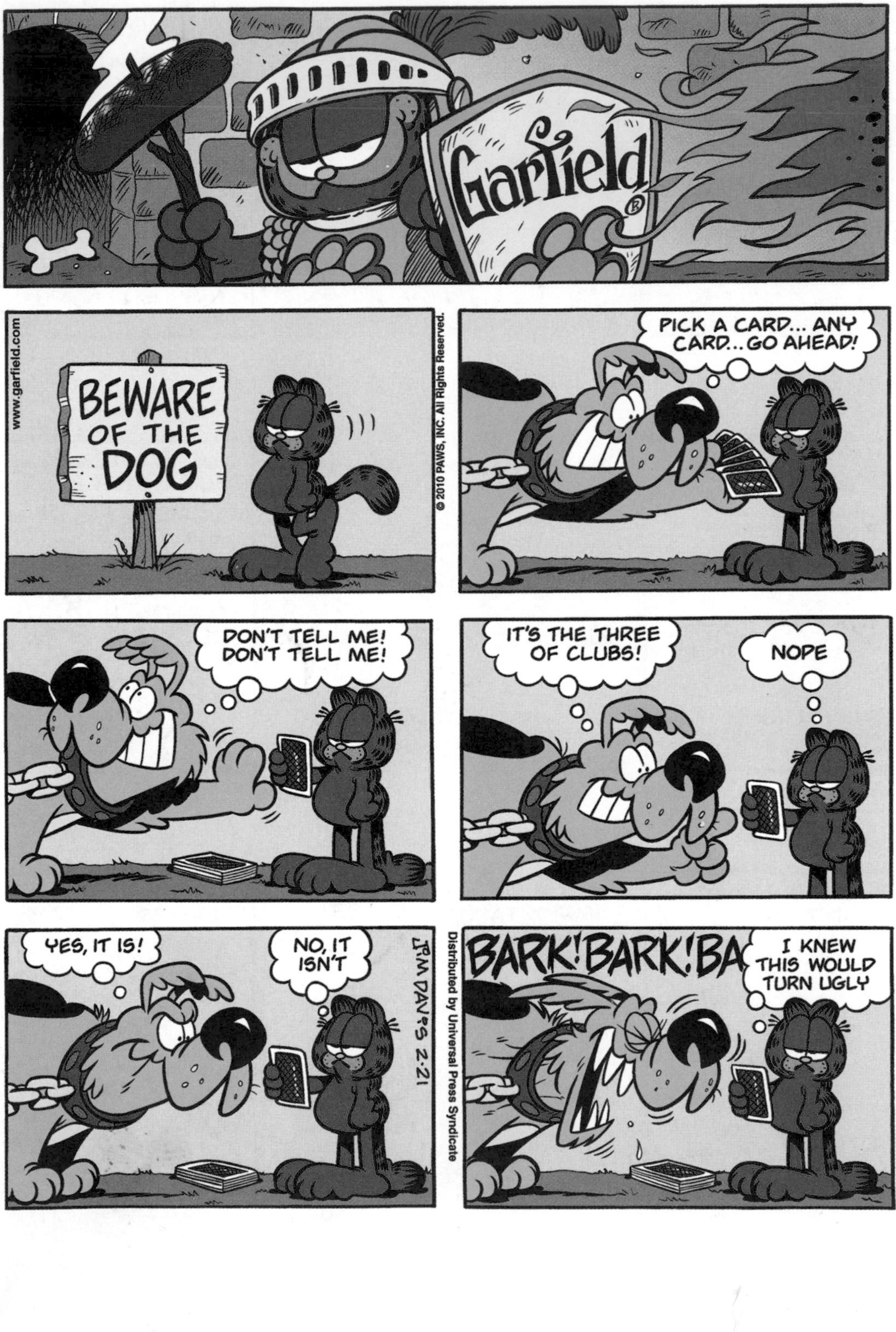
Garfield
www.garfield.com
© 2010 PAWS, INC. All Rights Reserved.
BEWARE OF THE DOG
PICK A CARD... ANY CARD...GO AHEAD!
DON'T TELL ME! DON'T TELL ME!
IT'S THE THREE OF CLUBS!
NOPE
YES, IT IS!
NO, IT ISN'T
JIM DAVIS 2-21
Distributed by Universal Press Syndicate
BARK!BARK!BA
I KNEW THIS WOULD TURN UGLY

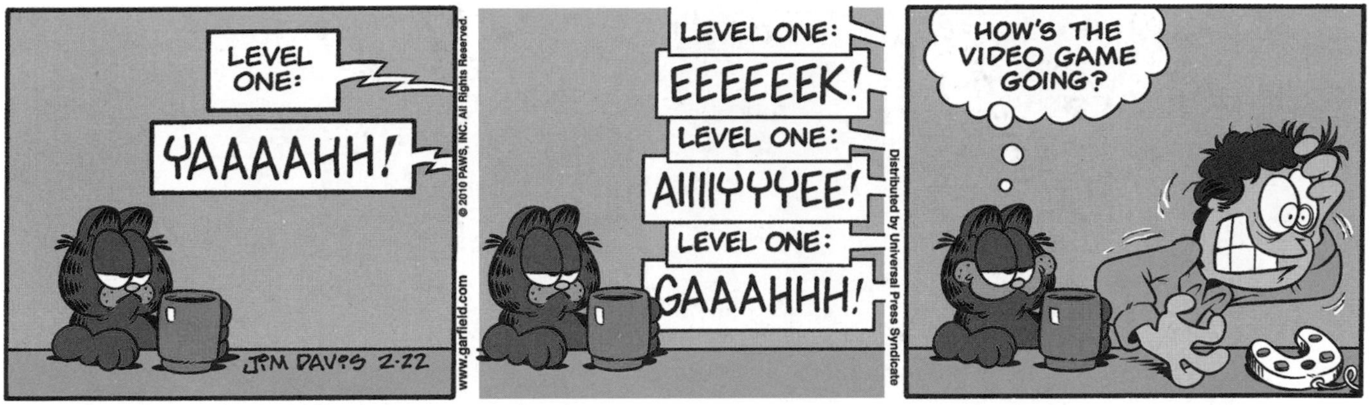
LEVEL ONE:
YAAAAHH!
JIM DAVIS 2-22
www.garfield.com
© 2010 PAWS, INC. All Rights Reserved.
LEVEL ONE:
EEEEEEK!
LEVEL ONE:
AIIIIYYYEE!
LEVEL ONE:
GAAAHHH!
Distributed by Universal Press Syndicate
HOW'S THE VIDEO GAME GOING?

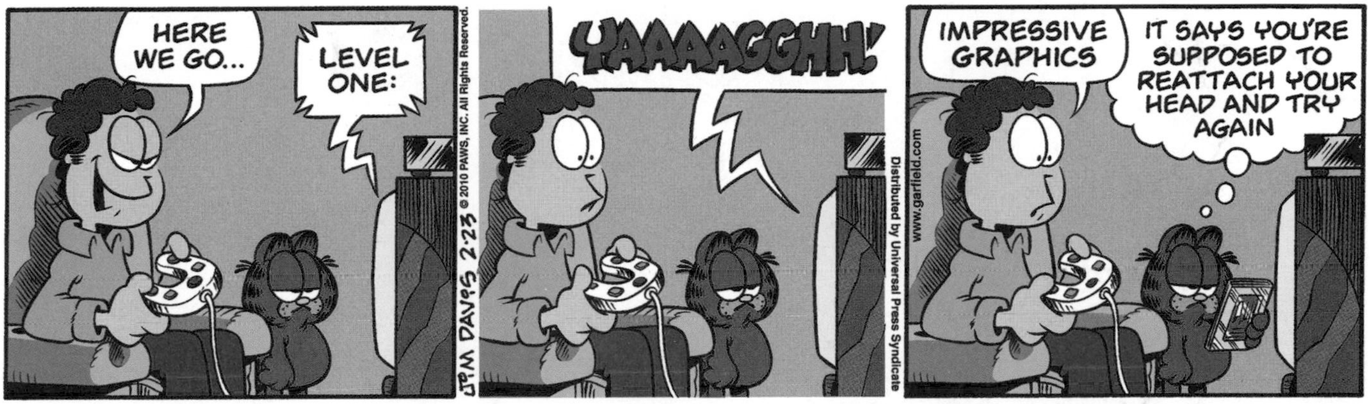
HERE WE GO...
LEVEL ONE:
JIM DAVIS 2-23
© 2010 PAWS, INC. All Rights Reserved.
YAAAAGGHH!
Distributed by Universal Press Syndicate
www.garfield.com
IMPRESSIVE GRAPHICS
IT SAYS YOU'RE SUPPOSED TO REATTACH YOUR HEAD AND TRY AGAIN

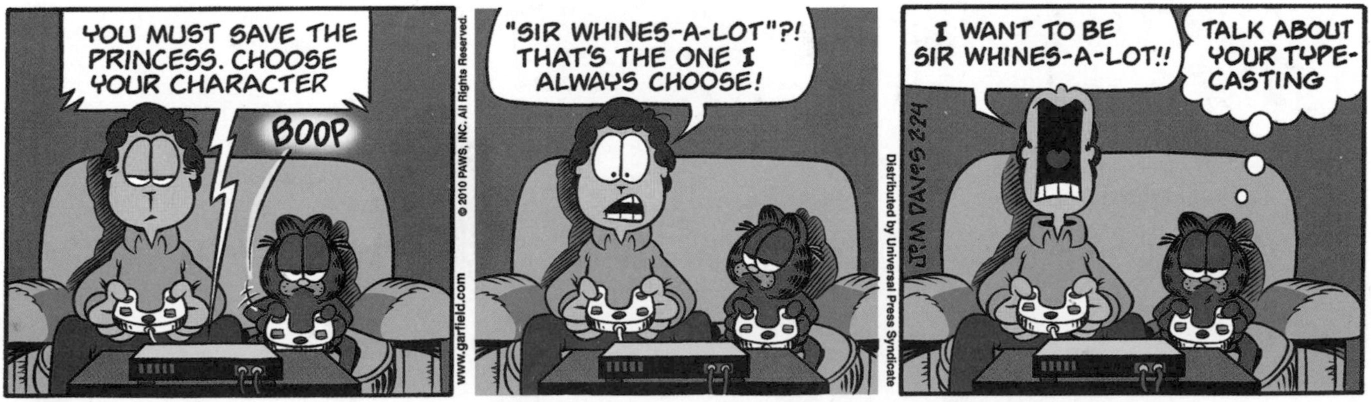
YOU MUST SAVE THE PRINCESS. CHOOSE YOUR CHARACTER
BOOP
www.garfield.com
© 2010 PAWS, INC. All Rights Reserved.
"SIR WHINES-A-LOT"?! THAT'S THE ONE I ALWAYS CHOOSE!
Distributed by Universal Press Syndicate
JIM DAVIS 2-24
I WANT TO BE SIR WHINES-A-LOT!!
TALK ABOUT YOUR TYPE-CASTING

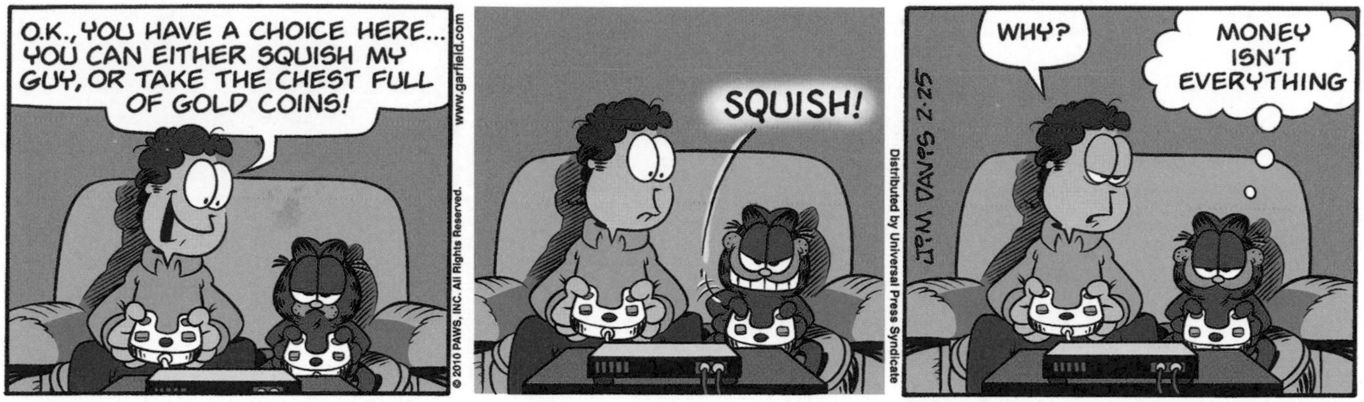
O.K., YOU HAVE A CHOICE HERE... YOU CAN EITHER SQUISH MY GUY, OR TAKE THE CHEST FULL OF GOLD COINS!
SQUISH!
WHY?
MONEY ISN'T EVERYTHING
JIM DAVIS 2-25
© 2010 PAWS, INC. All Rights Reserved.
www.garfield.com
Distributed by Universal Press Syndicate

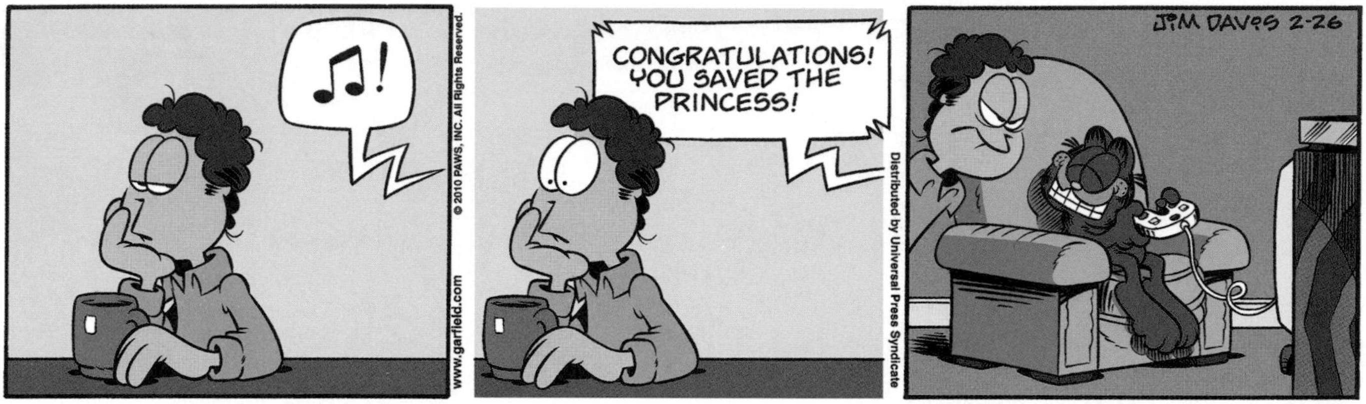
♫!
CONGRATULATIONS! YOU SAVED THE PRINCESS!
JIM DAVIS 2-26
© 2010 PAWS, INC. All Rights Reserved.
www.garfield.com
Distributed by Universal Press Syndicate

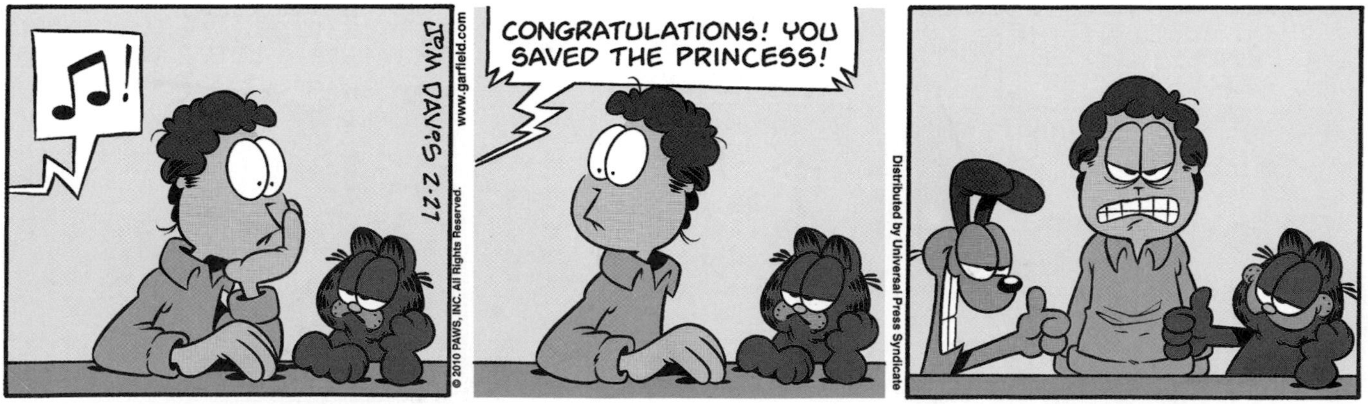
♫!
CONGRATULATIONS! YOU SAVED THE PRINCESS!
JIM DAVIS 2-27
© 2010 PAWS, INC. All Rights Reserved.
www.garfield.com
Distributed by Universal Press Syndicate

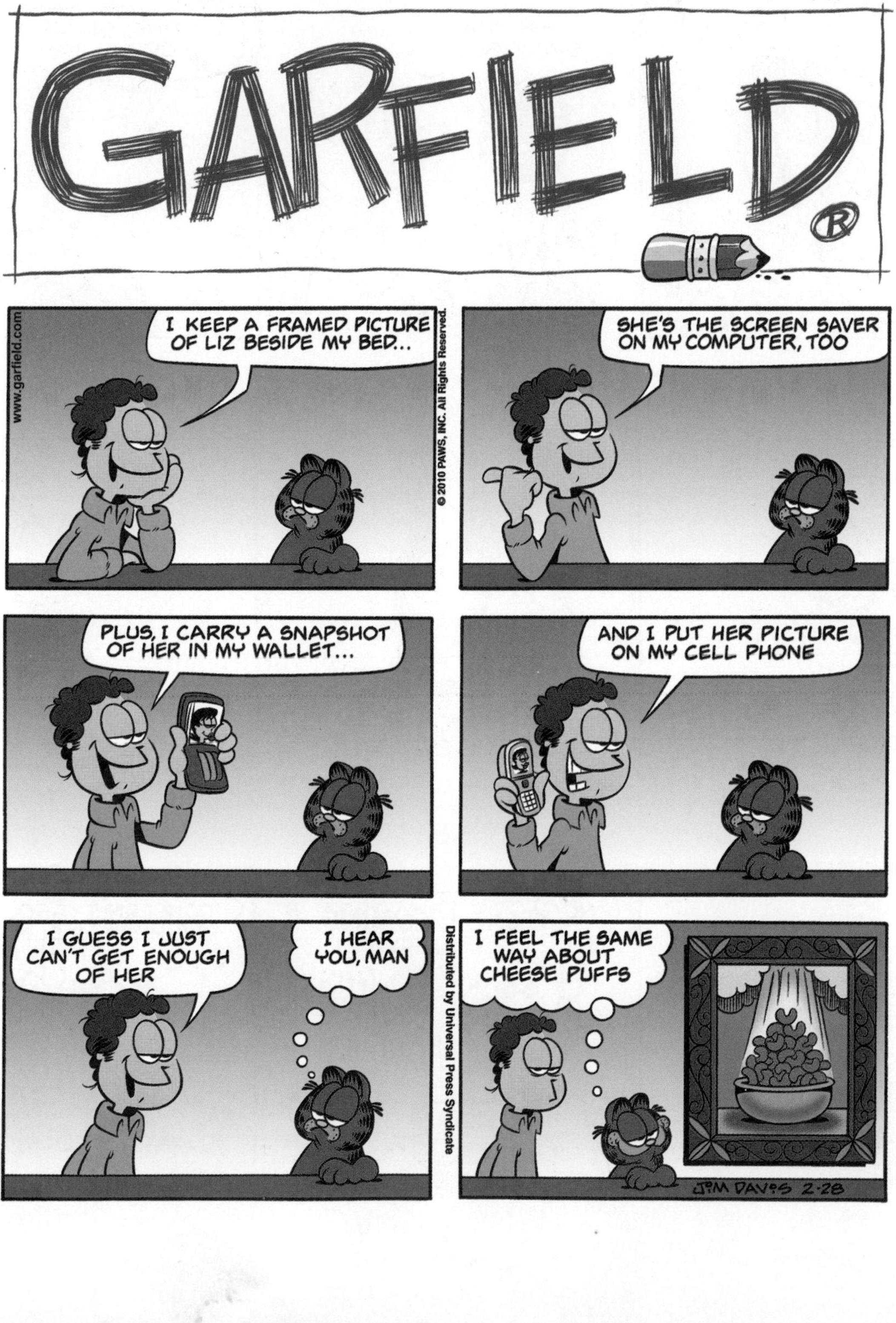
GARFIELD®
www.garfield.com
I KEEP A FRAMED PICTURE OF LIZ BESIDE MY BED...
© 2010 PAWS, INC. All Rights Reserved.
SHE'S THE SCREEN SAVER ON MY COMPUTER, TOO
PLUS, I CARRY A SNAPSHOT OF HER IN MY WALLET...
AND I PUT HER PICTURE ON MY CELL PHONE
I GUESS I JUST CAN'T GET ENOUGH OF HER
I HEAR YOU, MAN
Distributed by Universal Press Syndicate
I FEEL THE SAME WAY ABOUT CHEESE PUFFS
JIM DAVIS 2-28

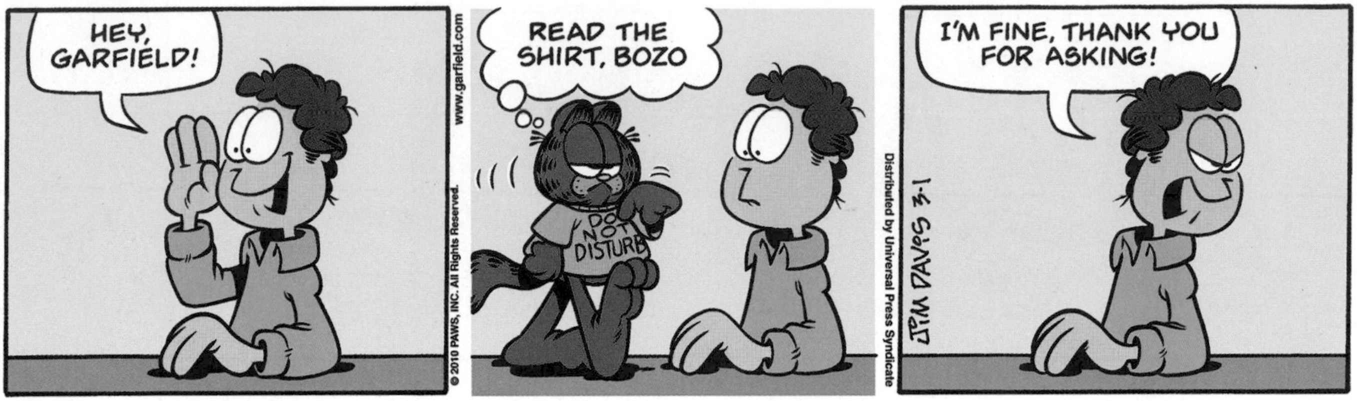
HEY, GARFIELD!
READ THE SHIRT, BOZO
DO NOT DISTURB
I'M FINE, THANK YOU FOR ASKING!
JPM DAVPS 3-1

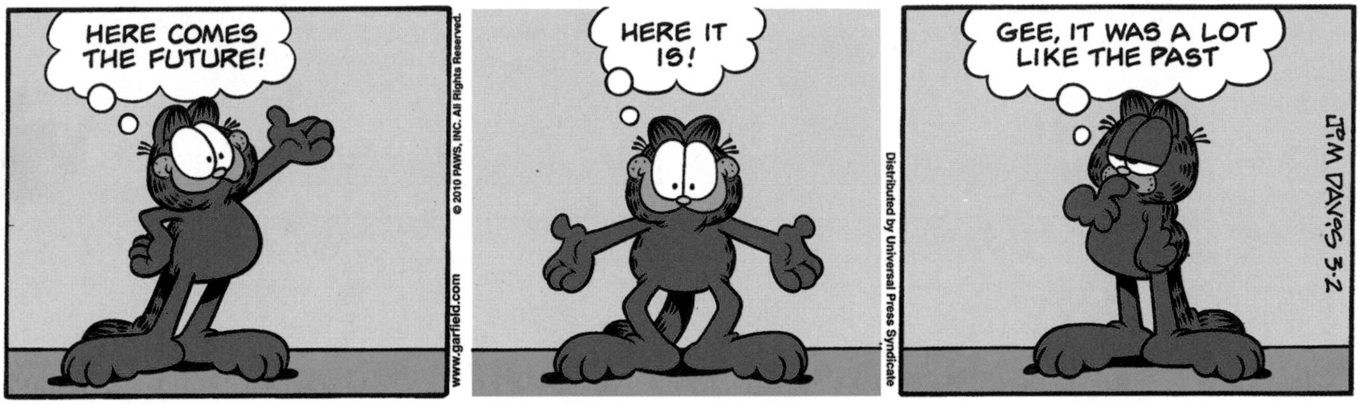
HERE COMES THE FUTURE!
HERE IT IS!
GEE, IT WAS A LOT LIKE THE PAST
JPM DAVPS 3-2

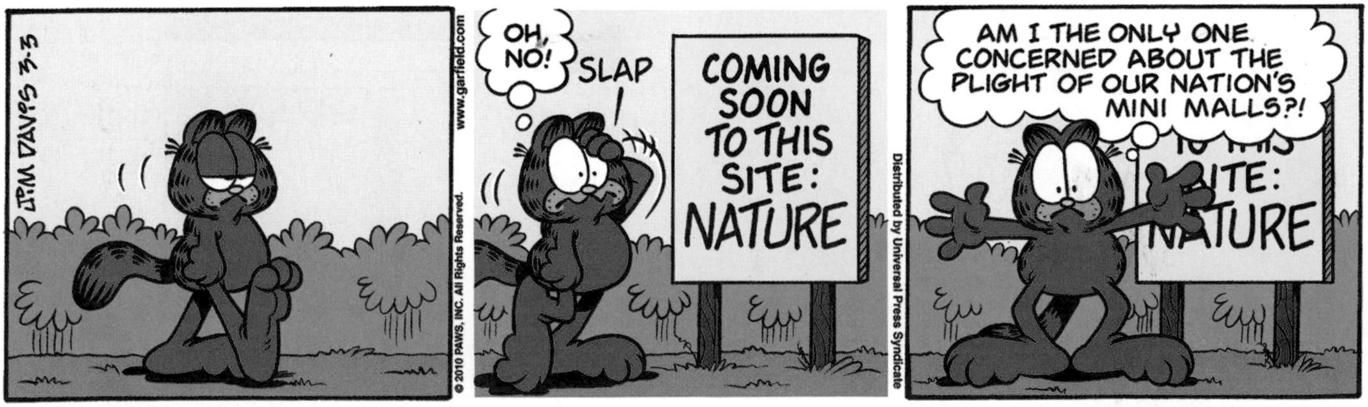
JPM DAVPS 3-3
OH, NO!
SLAP
COMING SOON TO THIS SITE: NATURE
AM I THE ONLY ONE CONCERNED ABOUT THE PLIGHT OF OUR NATION'S MINI MALLS?!

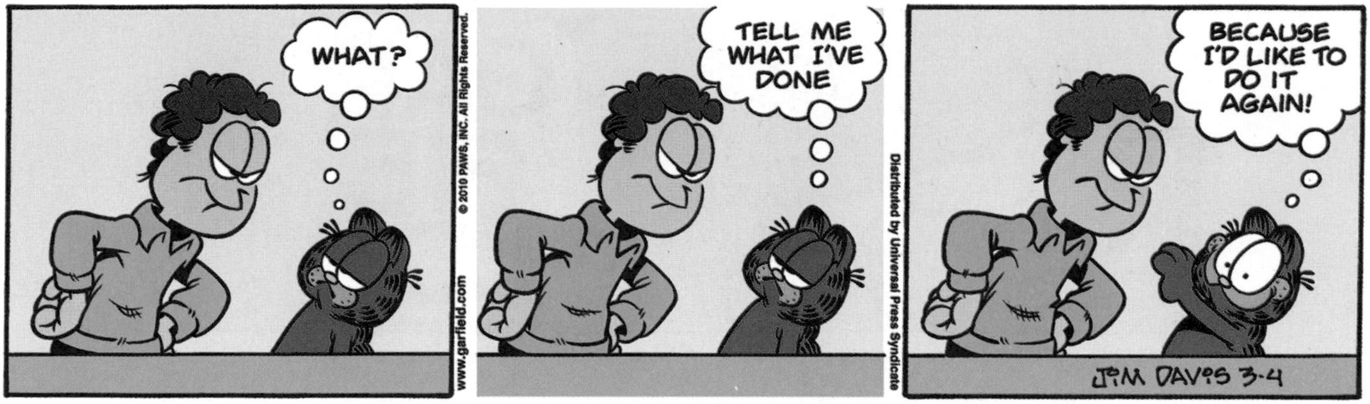
WHAT?
© 2010 PAWS, INC. All Rights Reserved.
www.garfield.com
TELL ME WHAT I'VE DONE
Distributed by Universal Press Syndicate
BECAUSE I'D LIKE TO DO IT AGAIN!
JIM DAVIS 3-4

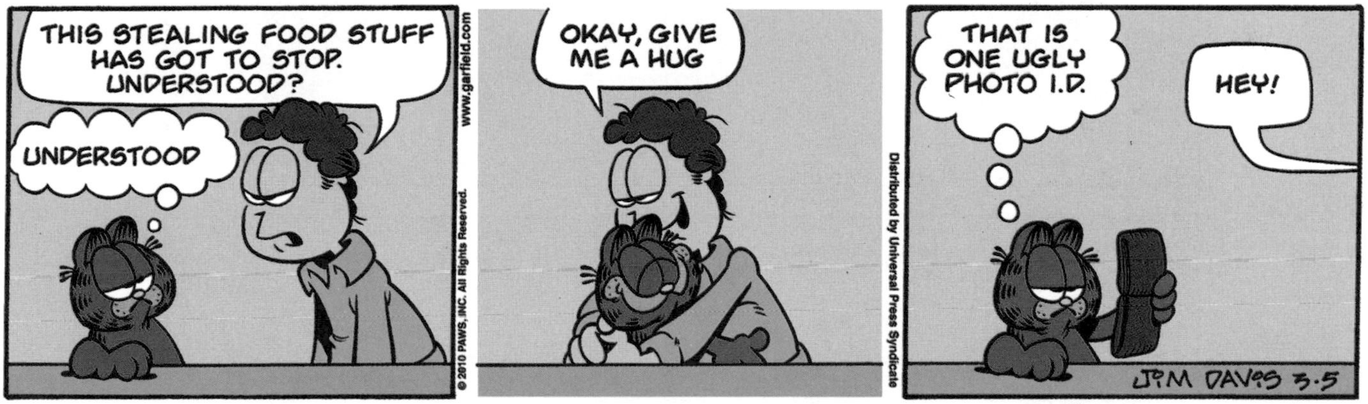
THIS STEALING FOOD STUFF HAS GOT TO STOP. UNDERSTOOD?
UNDERSTOOD
www.garfield.com
© 2010 PAWS, INC. All Rights Reserved.
OKAY, GIVE ME A HUG
Distributed by Universal Press Syndicate
THAT IS ONE UGLY PHOTO I.D.
HEY!
JIM DAVIS 3-5

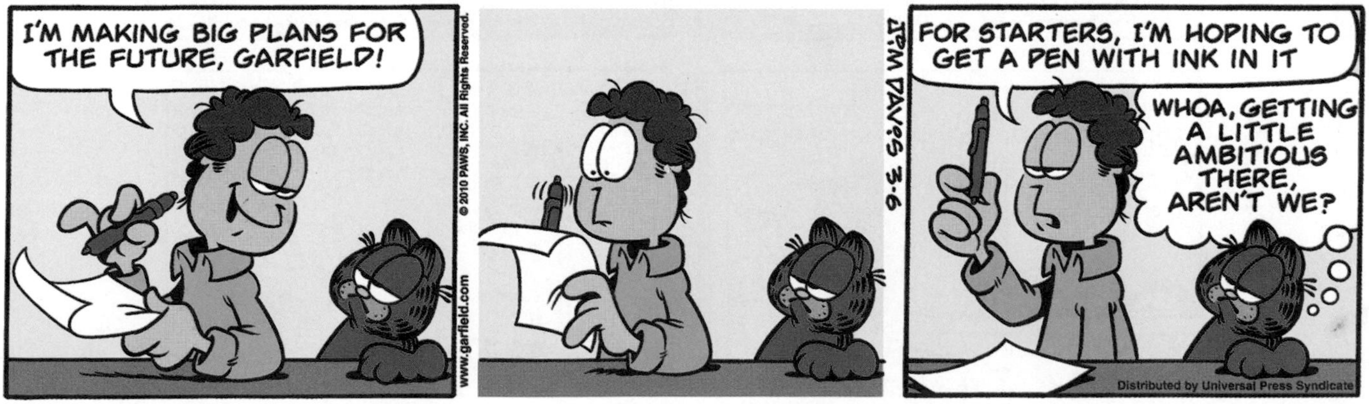
I'M MAKING BIG PLANS FOR THE FUTURE, GARFIELD!
© 2010 PAWS, INC. All Rights Reserved.
www.garfield.com
JIM DAVIS 3-6
FOR STARTERS, I'M HOPING TO GET A PEN WITH INK IN IT
WHOA, GETTING A LITTLE AMBITIOUS THERE, AREN'T WE?
Distributed by Universal Press Syndicate

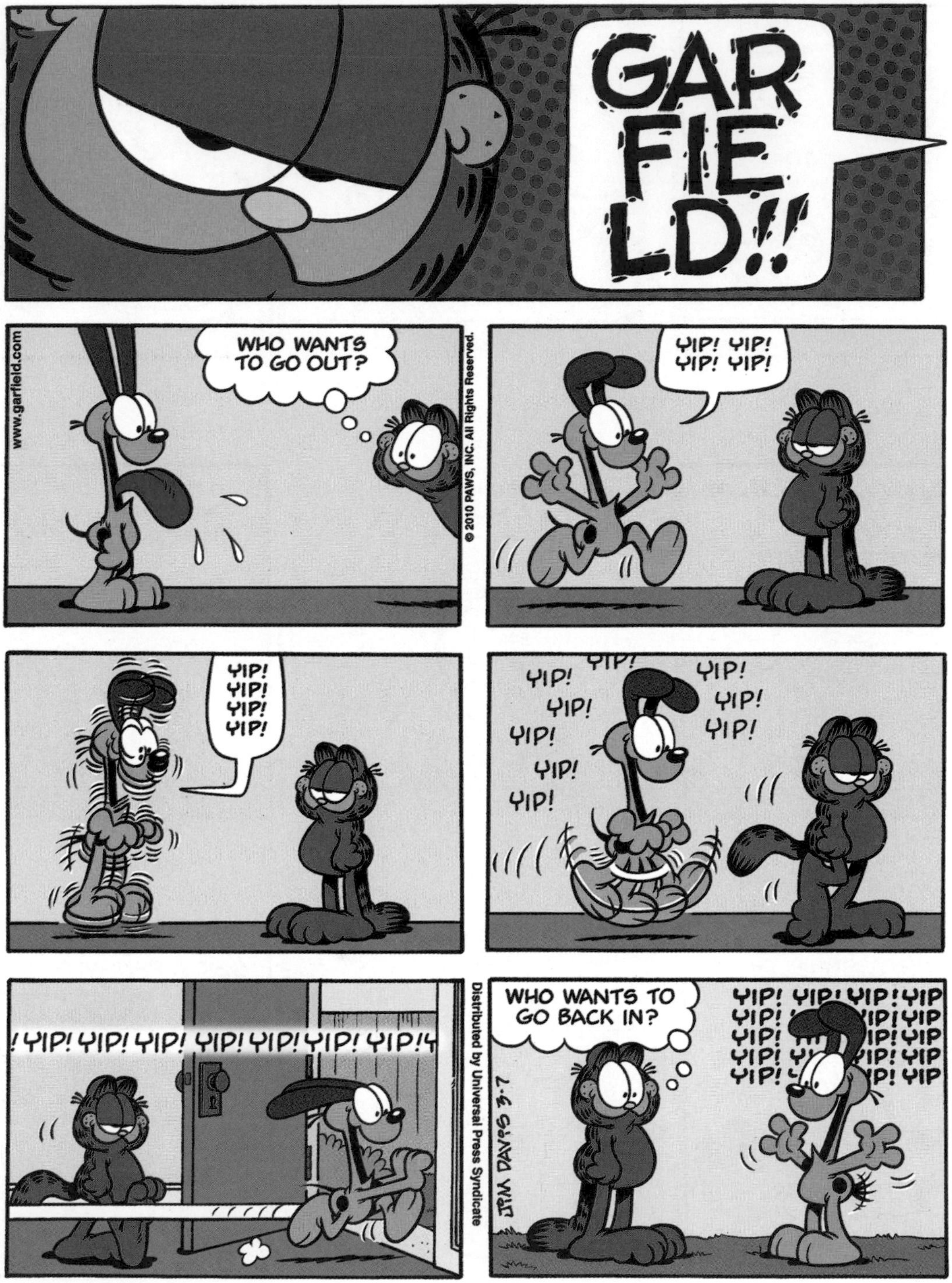
GARFIELD!!
www.garfield.com
WHO WANTS TO GO OUT?
© 2010 PAWS, INC. All Rights Reserved.
YIP! YIP! YIP! YIP!
YIP! YIP! YIP! YIP!
YIP! YIP! YIP! YIP! YIP! YIP! YIP! YIP! YIP! YIP!
YIP! YIP! YIP! YIP! YIP! YIP! YIP!
Distributed by Universal Press Syndicate
JPM DAVPS 3-7
WHO WANTS TO GO BACK IN?

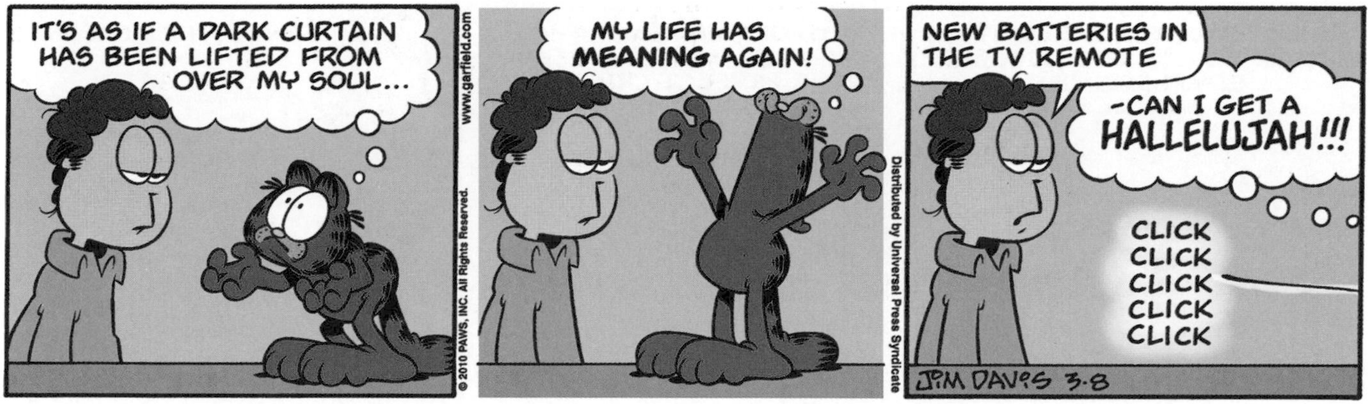
IT'S AS IF A DARK CURTAIN HAS BEEN LIFTED FROM OVER MY SOUL...
MY LIFE HAS MEANING AGAIN!
NEW BATTERIES IN THE TV REMOTE
-CAN I GET A HALLELUJAH!!!
CLICK CLICK CLICK CLICK CLICK
JIM DAVIS 3-8
© 2010 PAWS, INC. All Rights Reserved. www.garfield.com
Distributed by Universal Press Syndicate

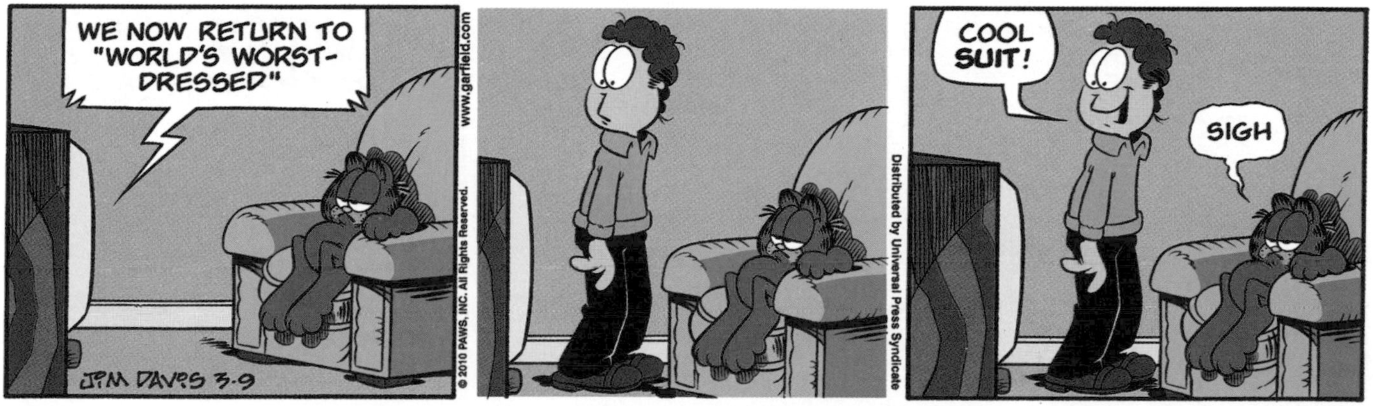
WE NOW RETURN TO "WORLD'S WORST-DRESSED"
COOL SUIT!
SIGH
JIM DAVIS 3-9
© 2010 PAWS, INC. All Rights Reserved. www.garfield.com
Distributed by Universal Press Syndicate

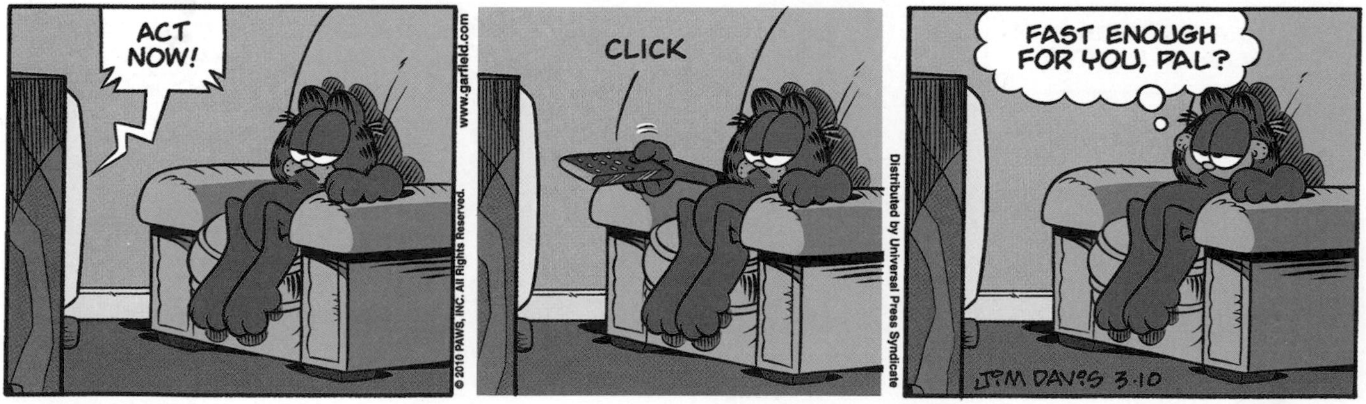
ACT NOW!
CLICK
FAST ENOUGH FOR YOU, PAL?
JIM DAVIS 3-10
© 2010 PAWS, INC. All Rights Reserved. www.garfield.com
Distributed by Universal Press Syndicate

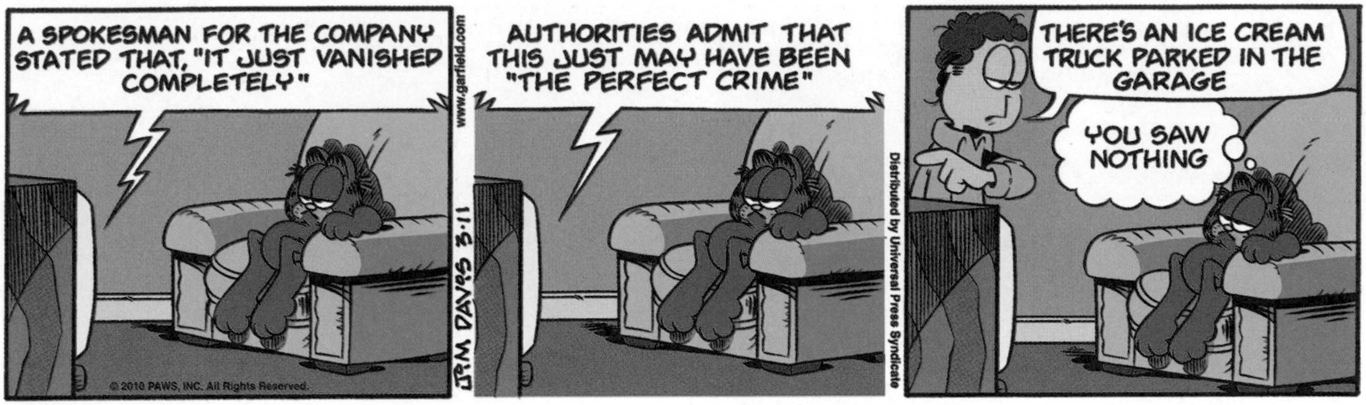
A SPOKESMAN FOR THE COMPANY STATED THAT, "IT JUST VANISHED COMPLETELY"
AUTHORITIES ADMIT THAT THIS JUST MAY HAVE BEEN "THE PERFECT CRIME"
THERE'S AN ICE CREAM TRUCK PARKED IN THE GARAGE
YOU SAW NOTHING
JPM DAVIS 3-11
www.garfield.com
© 2010 PAWS, INC. All Rights Reserved.
Distributed by Universal Press Syndicate

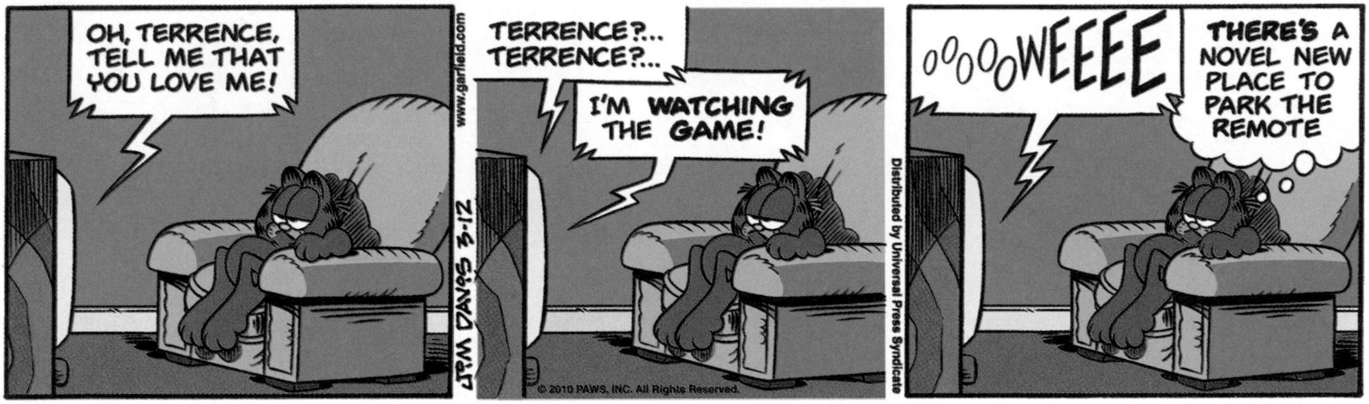
OH, TERRENCE, TELL ME THAT YOU LOVE ME!
TERRENCE?... TERRENCE?...
I'M WATCHING THE GAME!
OOOOOWEEEE
THERE'S A NOVEL NEW PLACE TO PARK THE REMOTE
JPM DAVIS 3-12
www.garfield.com
© 2010 PAWS, INC. All Rights Reserved.
Distributed by Universal Press Syndicate

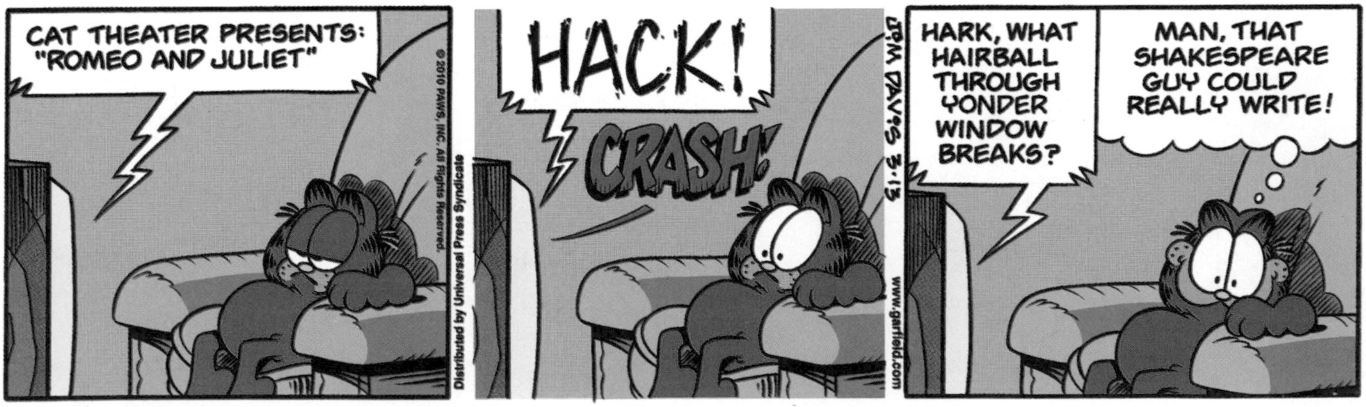
CAT THEATER PRESENTS: "ROMEO AND JULIET"
HACK!
CRASH!
HARK, WHAT HAIRBALL THROUGH YONDER WINDOW BREAKS?
MAN, THAT SHAKESPEARE GUY COULD REALLY WRITE!
JPM DAVIS 3-13
www.garfield.com
© 2010 PAWS, INC. All Rights Reserved.
Distributed by Universal Press Syndicate

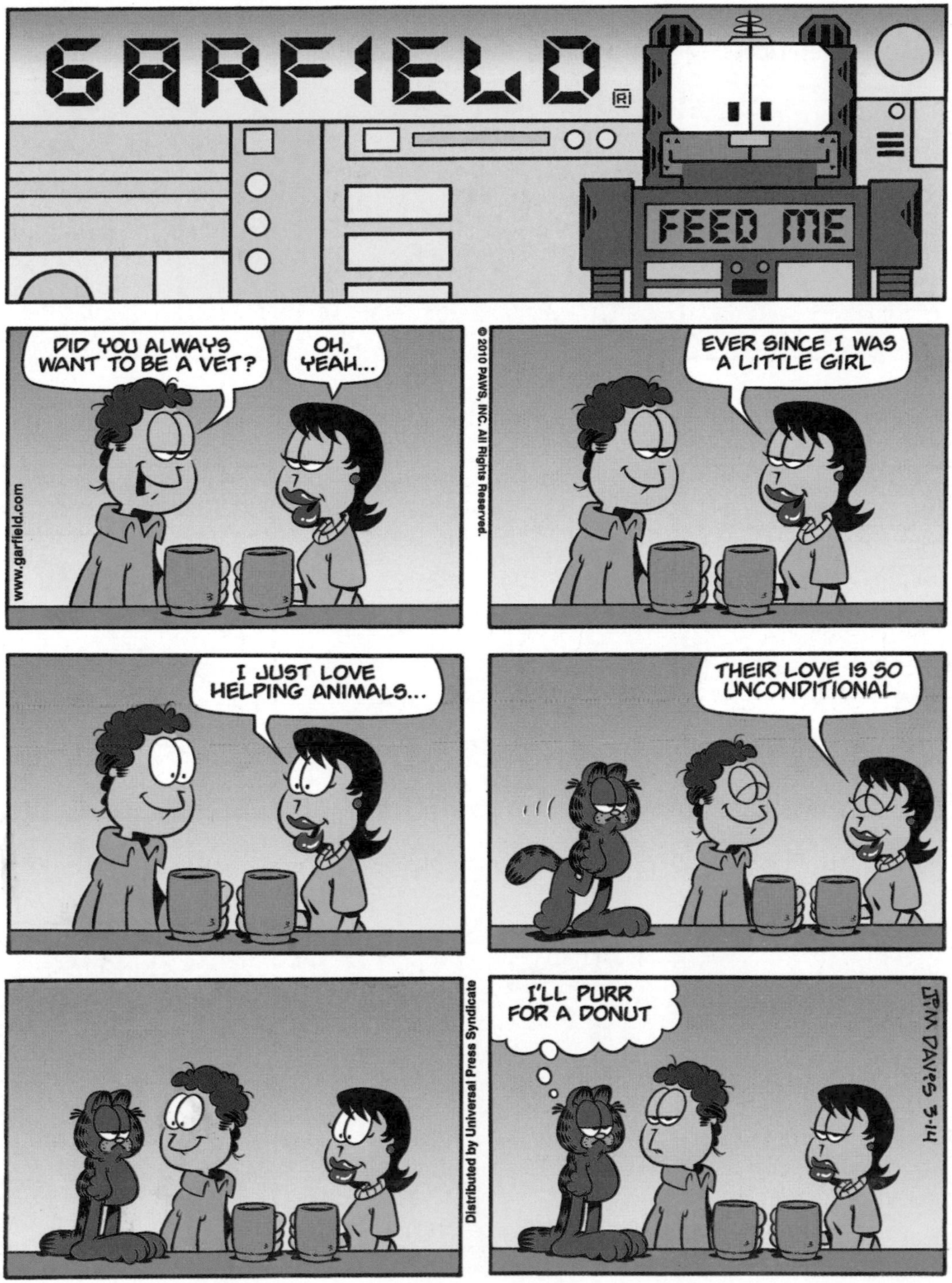
GARFIELD®
FEED ME
DID YOU ALWAYS WANT TO BE A VET?
OH, YEAH...
© 2010 PAWS, INC. All Rights Reserved.
www.garfield.com
EVER SINCE I WAS A LITTLE GIRL
I JUST LOVE HELPING ANIMALS...
THEIR LOVE IS SO UNCONDITIONAL
Distributed by Universal Press Syndicate
I'LL PURR FOR A DONUT
JIM DAVIS 3-14

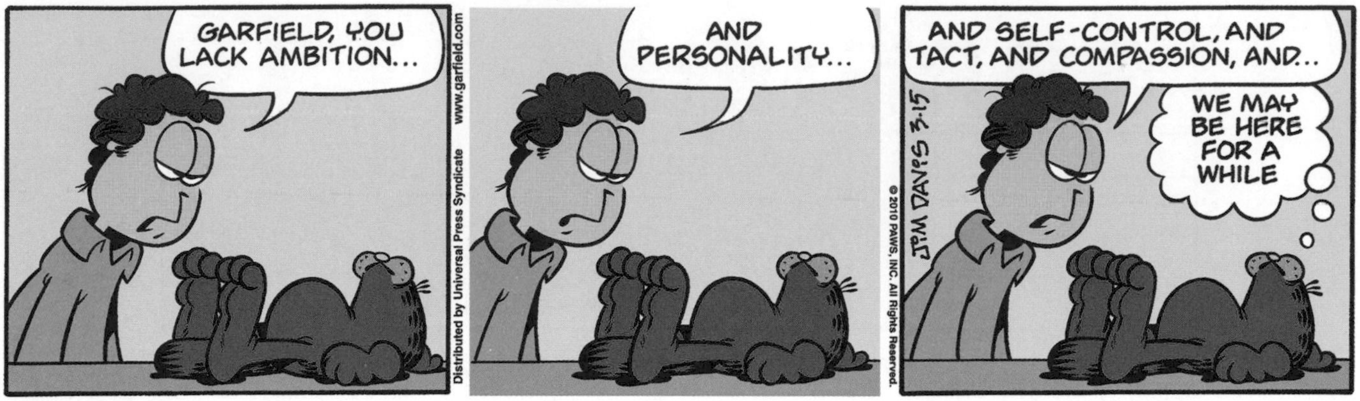
GARFIELD, YOU LACK AMBITION...
AND PERSONALITY...
AND SELF-CONTROL, AND TACT, AND COMPASSION, AND...
WE MAY BE HERE FOR A WHILE
JIM DAVIS 3-15
www.garfield.com
Distributed by Universal Press Syndicate
© 2010 PAWS, INC. All Rights Reserved.

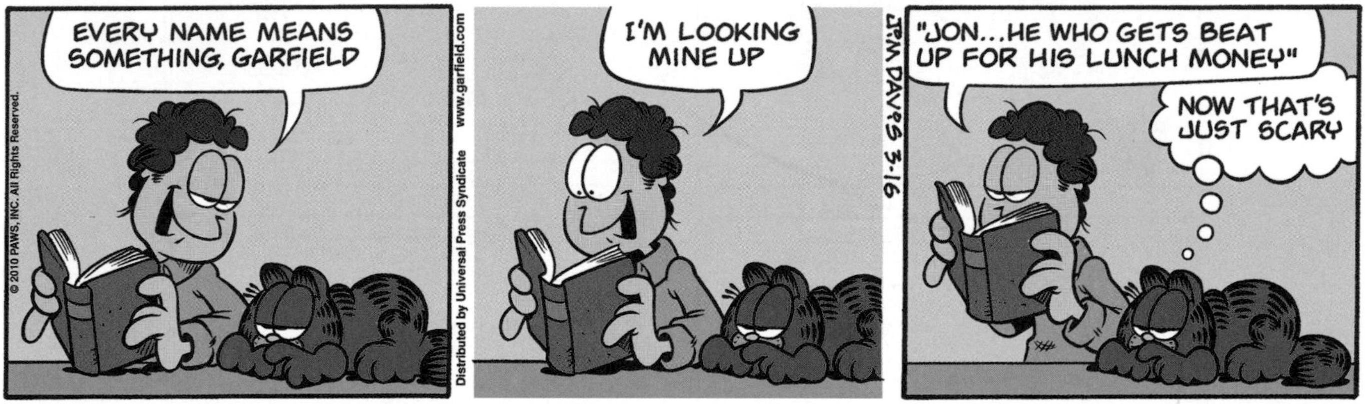
EVERY NAME MEANS SOMETHING, GARFIELD
I'M LOOKING MINE UP
"JON...HE WHO GETS BEAT UP FOR HIS LUNCH MONEY"
NOW THAT'S JUST SCARY
JIM DAVIS 3-16
© 2010 PAWS, INC. All Rights Reserved.
Distributed by Universal Press Syndicate
www.garfield.com

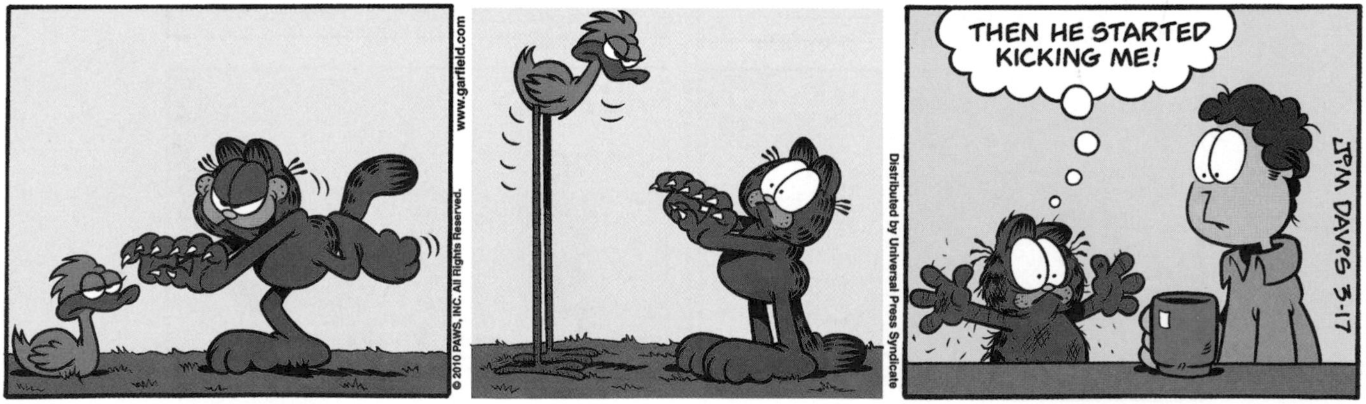
THEN HE STARTED KICKING ME!
JIM DAVIS 3-17
www.garfield.com
© 2010 PAWS, INC. All Rights Reserved.
Distributed by Universal Press Syndicate

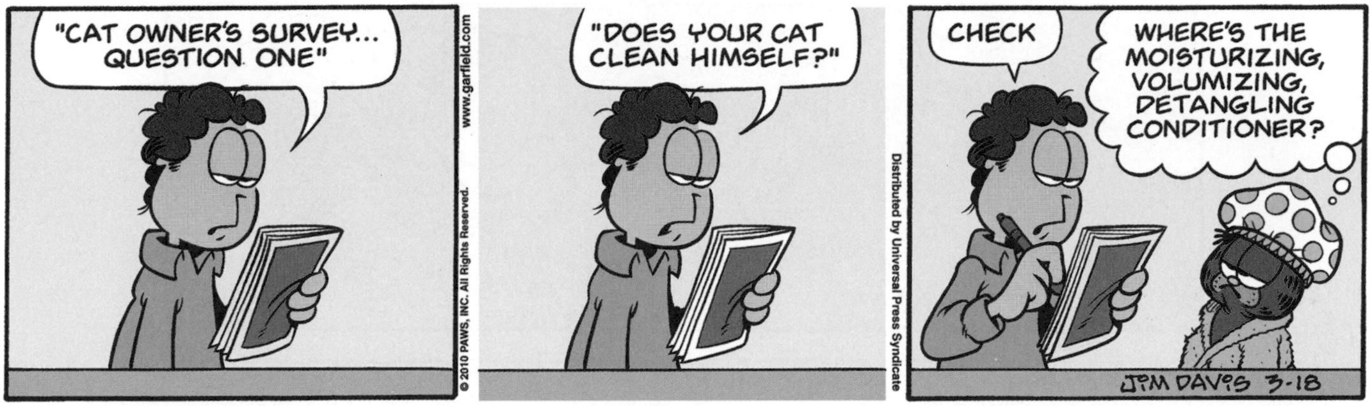
"CAT OWNER'S SURVEY... QUESTION ONE"
© 2010 PAWS, INC. All Rights Reserved. www.garfield.com
"DOES YOUR CAT CLEAN HIMSELF?"
Distributed by Universal Press Syndicate
CHECK
WHERE'S THE MOISTURIZING, VOLUMIZING, DETANGLING CONDITIONER?
JIM DAVIS 3-18

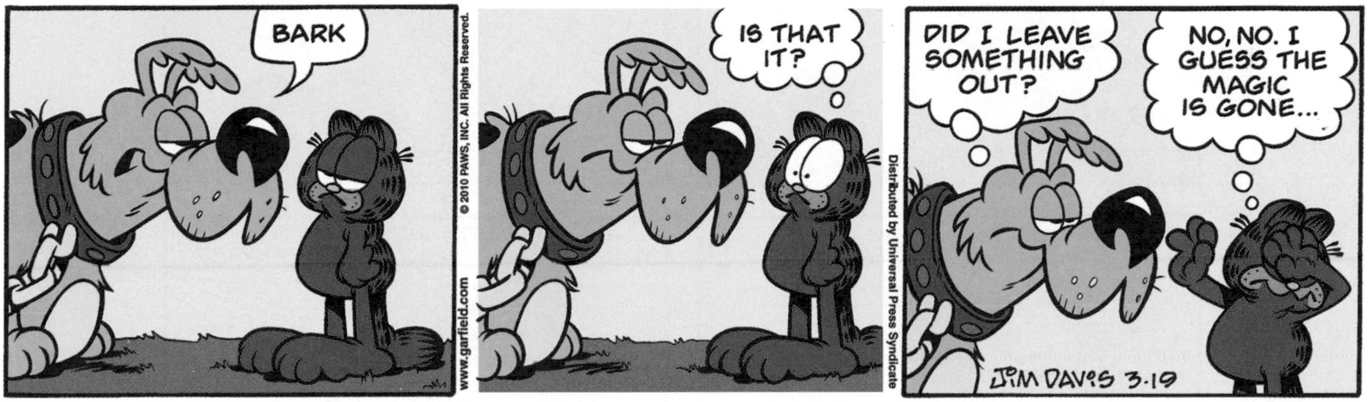
BARK
© 2010 PAWS, INC. All Rights Reserved. www.garfield.com
IS THAT IT?
Distributed by Universal Press Syndicate
DID I LEAVE SOMETHING OUT?
NO, NO. I GUESS THE MAGIC IS GONE...
JIM DAVIS 3-19

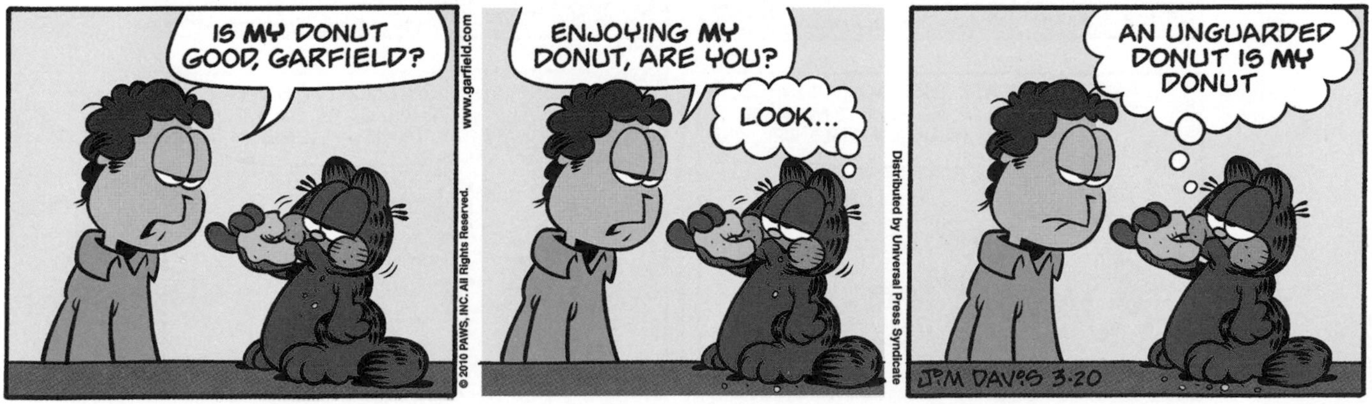
IS MY DONUT GOOD, GARFIELD?
© 2010 PAWS, INC. All Rights Reserved. www.garfield.com
ENJOYING MY DONUT, ARE YOU?
LOOK...
Distributed by Universal Press Syndicate
AN UNGUARDED DONUT IS MY DONUT
JIM DAVIS 3-20

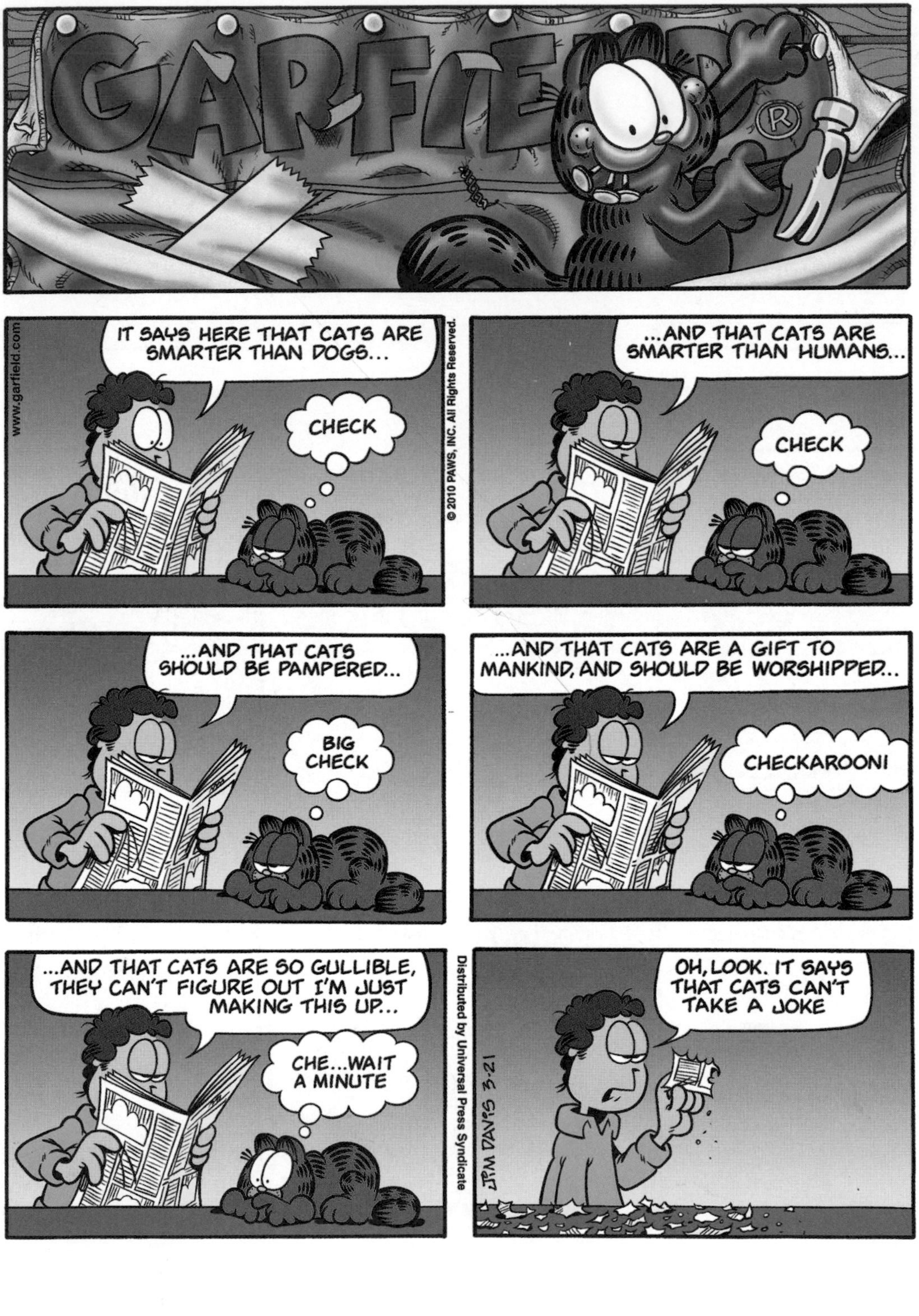
GARFIELD ®
www.garfield.com
IT SAYS HERE THAT CATS ARE SMARTER THAN DOGS...
CHECK
© 2010 PAWS, INC. All Rights Reserved.
...AND THAT CATS ARE SMARTER THAN HUMANS...
CHECK
...AND THAT CATS SHOULD BE PAMPERED...
BIG CHECK
...AND THAT CATS ARE A GIFT TO MANKIND, AND SHOULD BE WORSHIPPED...
CHECKAROONI
...AND THAT CATS ARE SO GULLIBLE, THEY CAN'T FIGURE OUT I'M JUST MAKING THIS UP...
CHE...WAIT A MINUTE
Distributed by Universal Press Syndicate
JPM DAVIS 3-21
OH, LOOK. IT SAYS THAT CATS CAN'T TAKE A JOKE

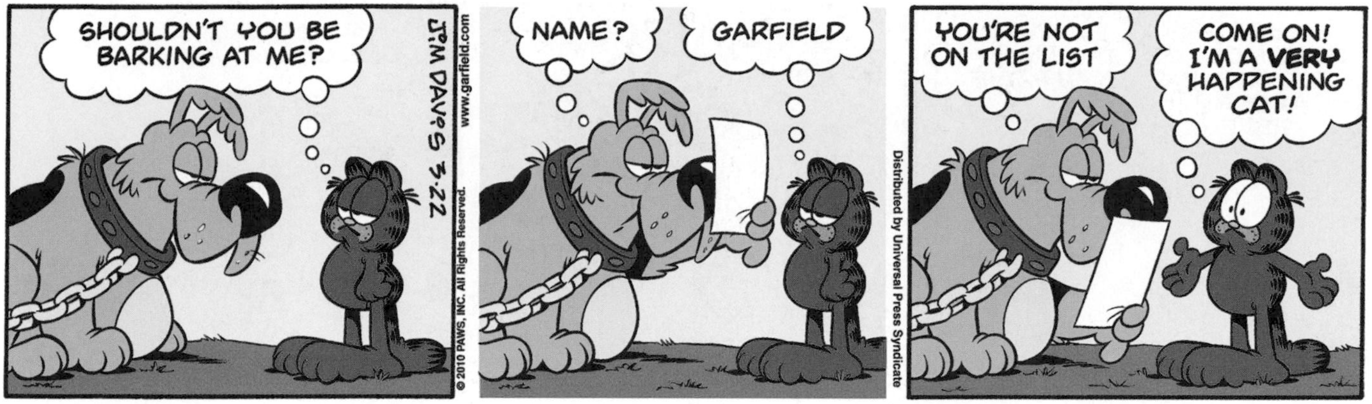
SHOULDN'T YOU BE BARKING AT ME?
JIM DAVIS 3·22
© 2010 PAWS, INC. All Rights Reserved. www.garfield.com
NAME?
GARFIELD
Distributed by Universal Press Syndicate
YOU'RE NOT ON THE LIST
COME ON! I'M A **VERY** HAPPENING CAT!

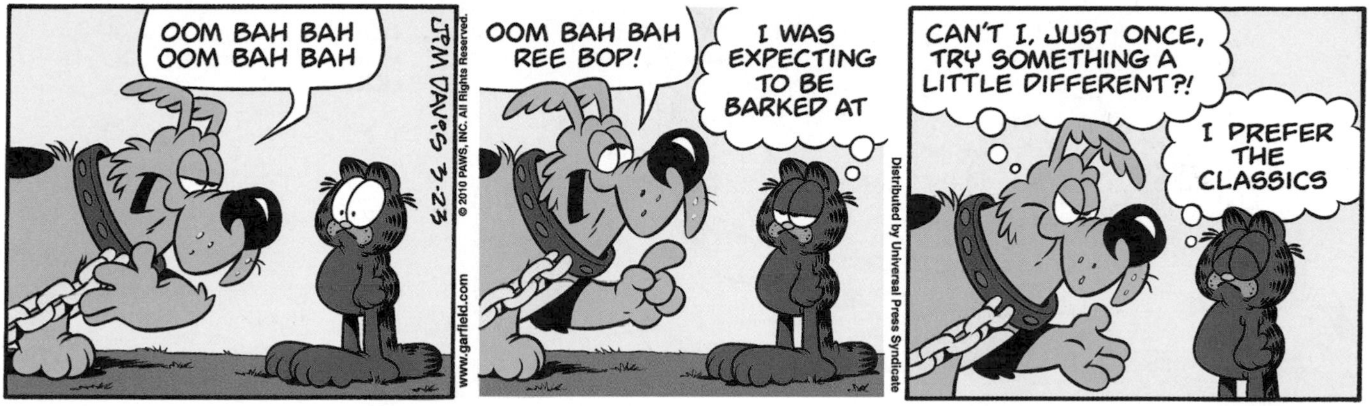
OOM BAH BAH OOM BAH BAH
JIM DAVIS 3·23
© 2010 PAWS, INC. All Rights Reserved. www.garfield.com
OOM BAH BAH REE BOP!
I WAS EXPECTING TO BE BARKED AT
Distributed by Universal Press Syndicate
CAN'T I, JUST ONCE, TRY SOMETHING A LITTLE DIFFERENT?!
I PREFER THE CLASSICS

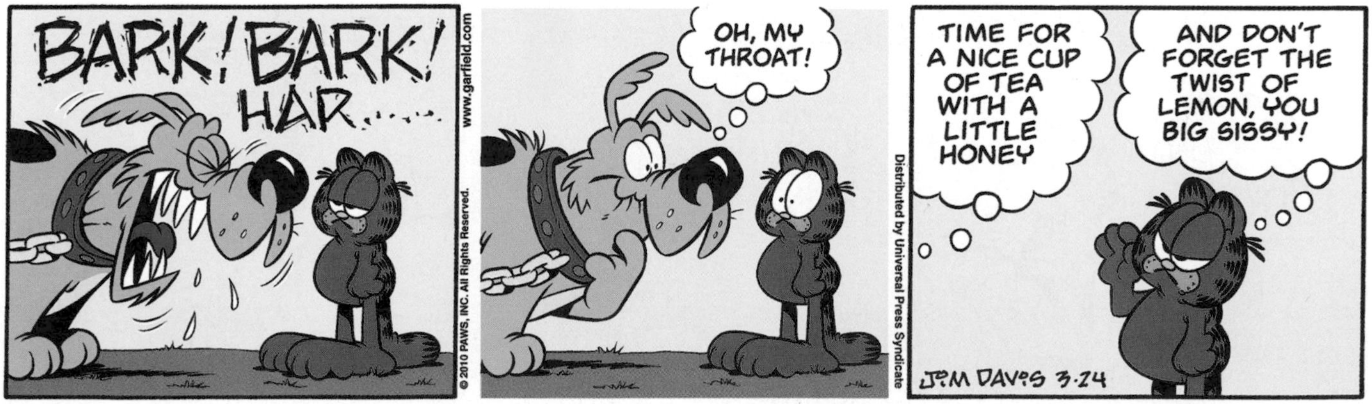
BARK! BARK! HAR......
© 2010 PAWS, INC. All Rights Reserved. www.garfield.com
OH, MY THROAT!
Distributed by Universal Press Syndicate
TIME FOR A NICE CUP OF TEA WITH A LITTLE HONEY
AND DON'T FORGET THE TWIST OF LEMON, YOU BIG SISSY!
JIM DAVIS 3·24

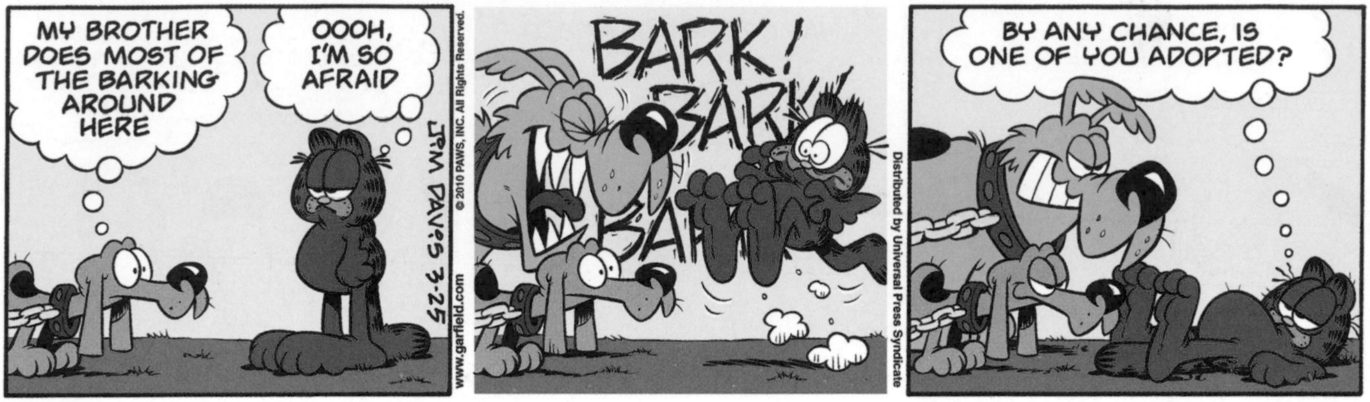
MY BROTHER DOES MOST OF THE BARKING AROUND HERE
OOOH, I'M SO AFRAID
JPM DAVIS 3-25
© 2010 PAWS, INC. All Rights Reserved.
www.garfield.com
BARK! BARK!
BY ANY CHANCE, IS ONE OF YOU ADOPTED?
Distributed by Universal Press Syndicate

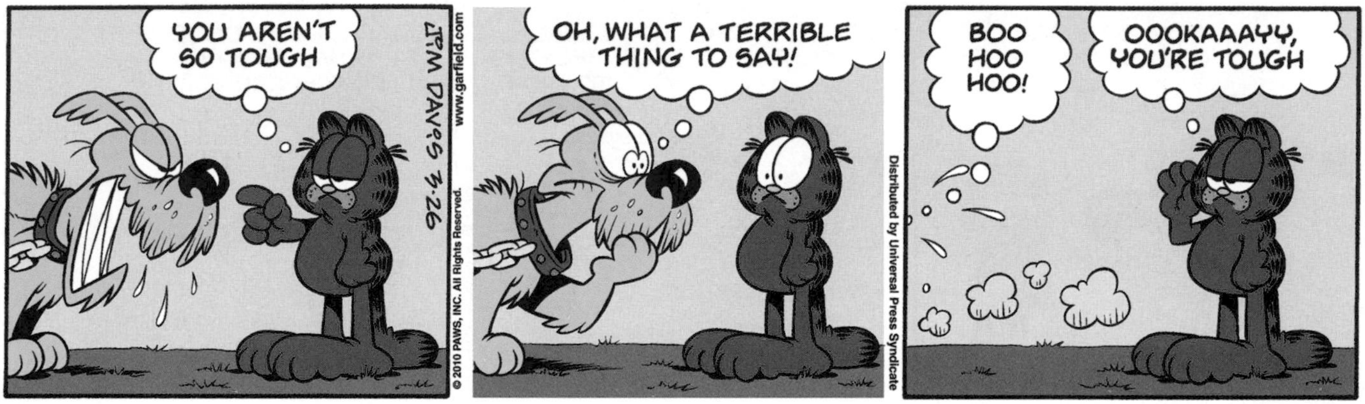
YOU AREN'T SO TOUGH
JPM DAVIS 3-26
www.garfield.com
© 2010 PAWS, INC. All Rights Reserved.
OH, WHAT A TERRIBLE THING TO SAY!
BOO HOO HOO!
OOOKAAAYY, YOU'RE TOUGH
Distributed by Universal Press Syndicate

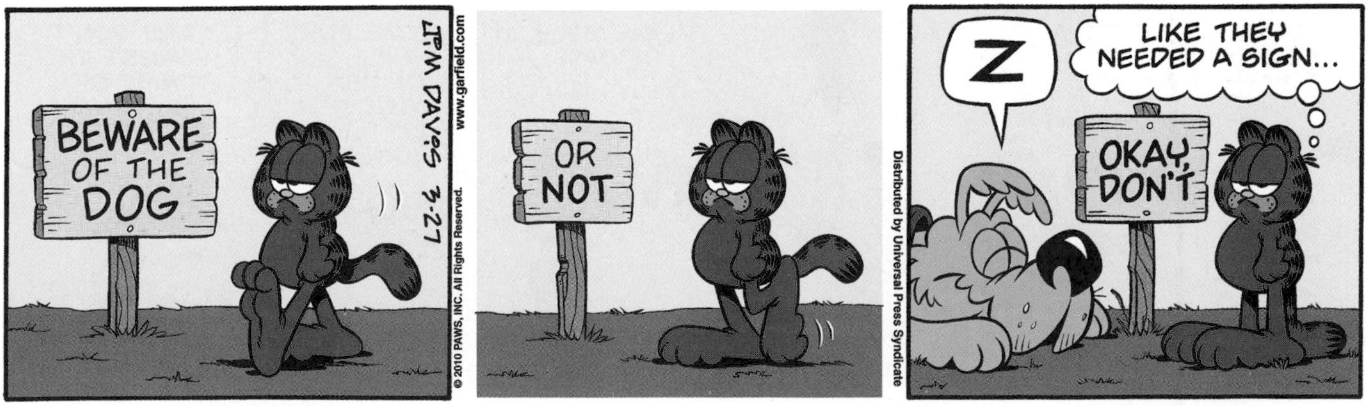
BEWARE OF THE DOG
JPM DAVIS 3-27
www.garfield.com
© 2010 PAWS, INC. All Rights Reserved.
OR NOT
Z
LIKE THEY NEEDED A SIGN...
OKAY, DON'T
Distributed by Universal Press Syndicate

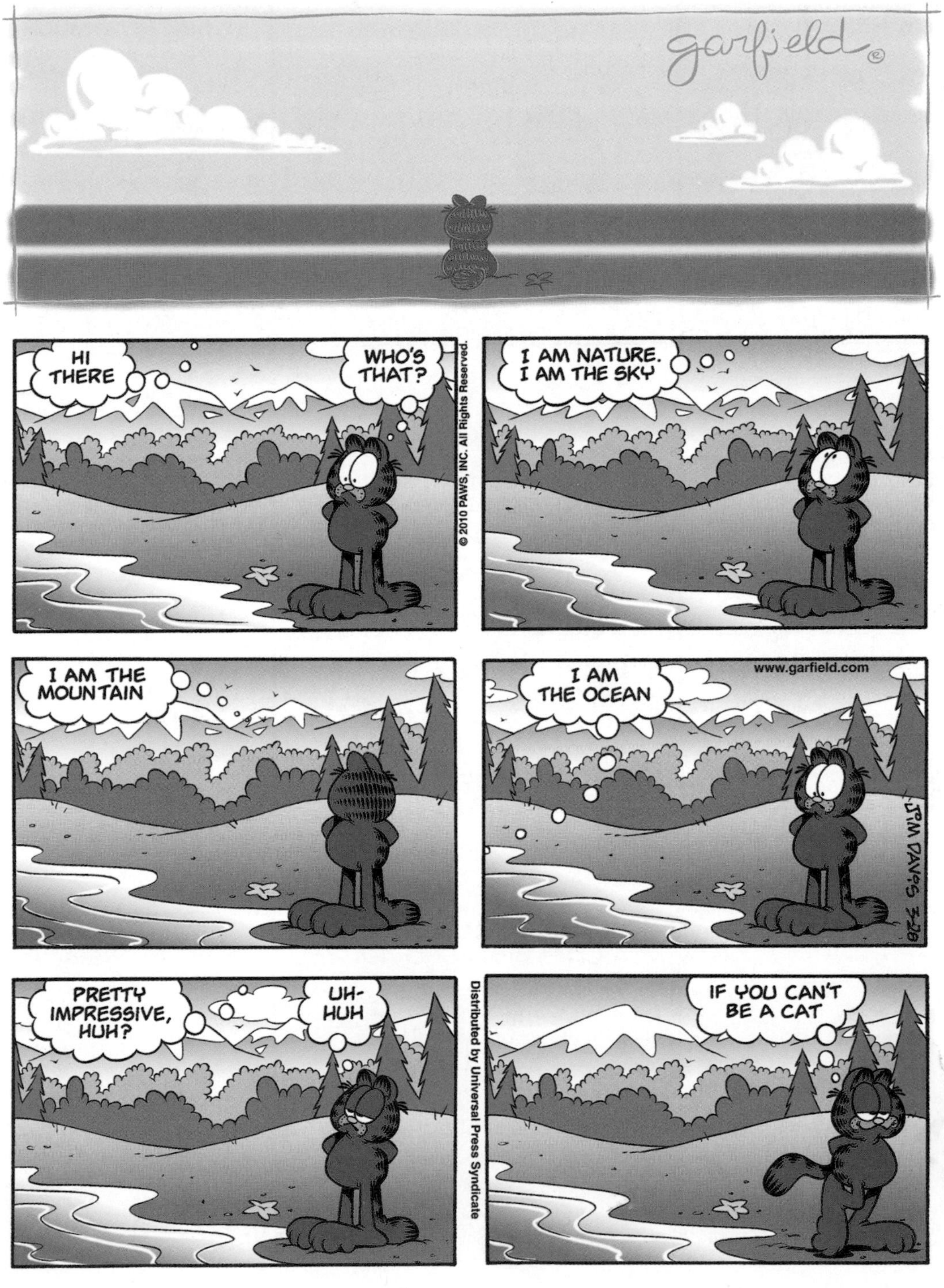
garfield
HI THERE
WHO'S THAT?
© 2010 PAWS, INC. All Rights Reserved.
I AM NATURE. I AM THE SKY
I AM THE MOUNTAIN
I AM THE OCEAN
www.garfield.com
JIM DAVIS 3-28
PRETTY IMPRESSIVE, HUH?
UH-HUH
Distributed by Universal Press Syndicate
IF YOU CAN'T BE A CAT

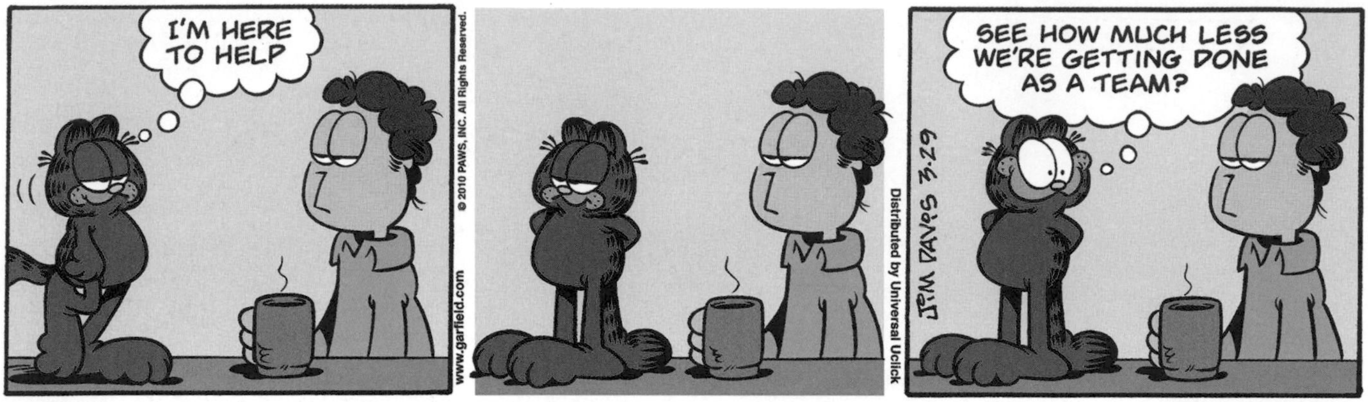
I'M HERE TO HELP
SEE HOW MUCH LESS WE'RE GETTING DONE AS A TEAM?
JIM DAVIS 3.29
© 2010 PAWS, INC. All Rights Reserved.
www.garfield.com
Distributed by Universal Uclick

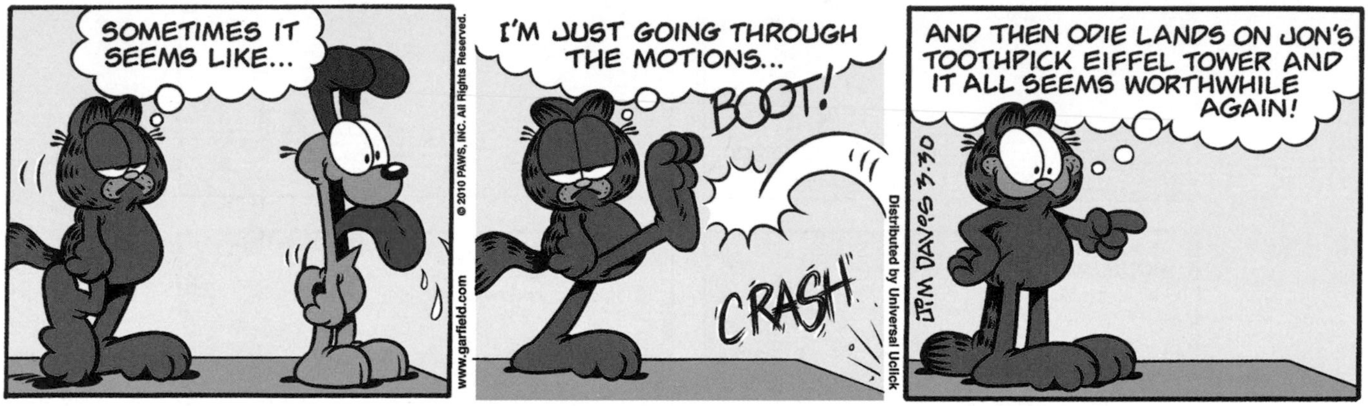
SOMETIMES IT SEEMS LIKE...
I'M JUST GOING THROUGH THE MOTIONS...
BOOT!
CRASH
AND THEN ODIE LANDS ON JON'S TOOTHPICK EIFFEL TOWER AND IT ALL SEEMS WORTHWHILE AGAIN!
JIM DAVIS 3.30
© 2010 PAWS, INC. All Rights Reserved.
www.garfield.com
Distributed by Universal Uclick

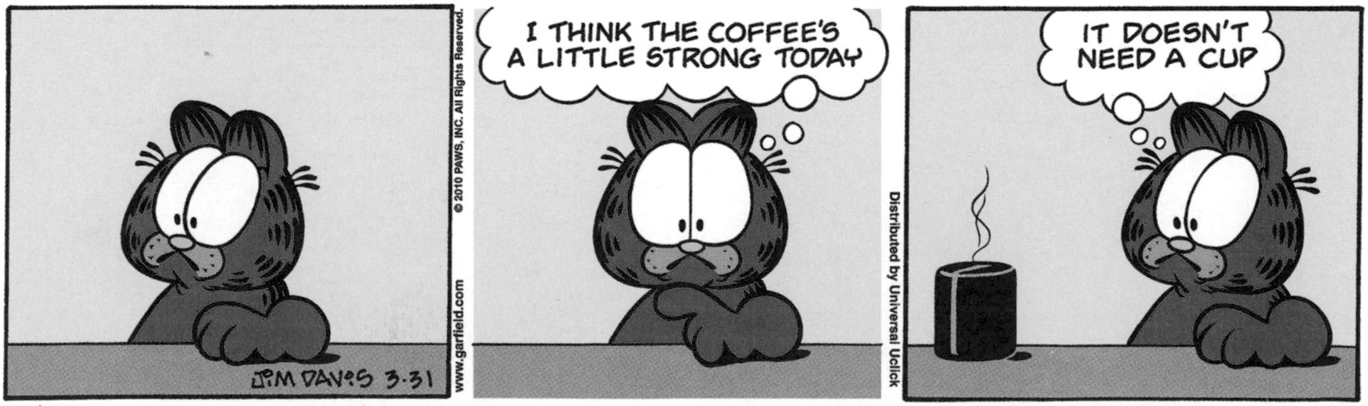
I THINK THE COFFEE'S A LITTLE STRONG TODAY
IT DOESN'T NEED A CUP
JIM DAVIS 3.31
© 2010 PAWS, INC. All Rights Reserved.
www.garfield.com
Distributed by Universal Uclick

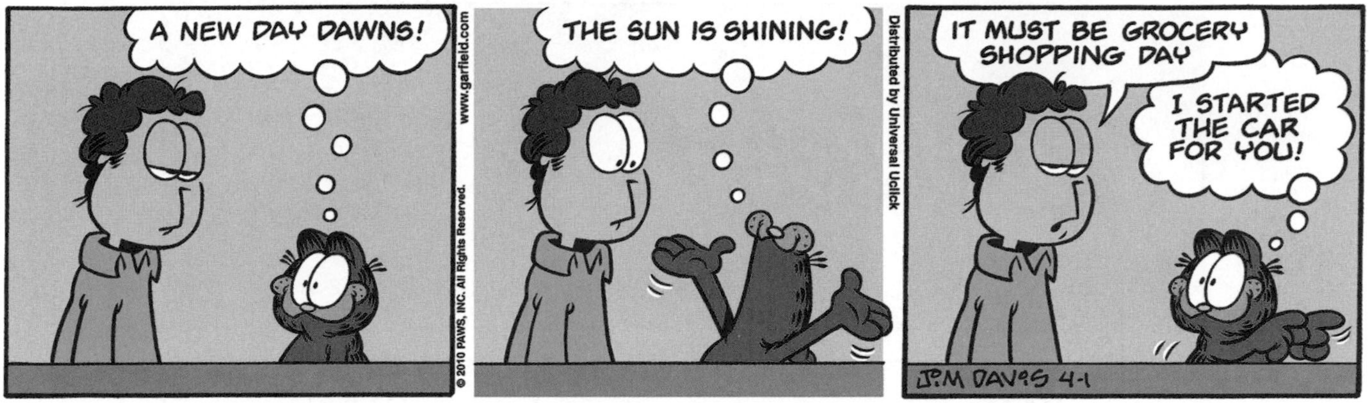
A NEW DAY DAWNS!
© 2010 PAWS, INC. All Rights Reserved. www.garfield.com
THE SUN IS SHINING!
Distributed by Universal Uclick
IT MUST BE GROCERY SHOPPING DAY
I STARTED THE CAR FOR YOU!
JIM DAVIS 4-1

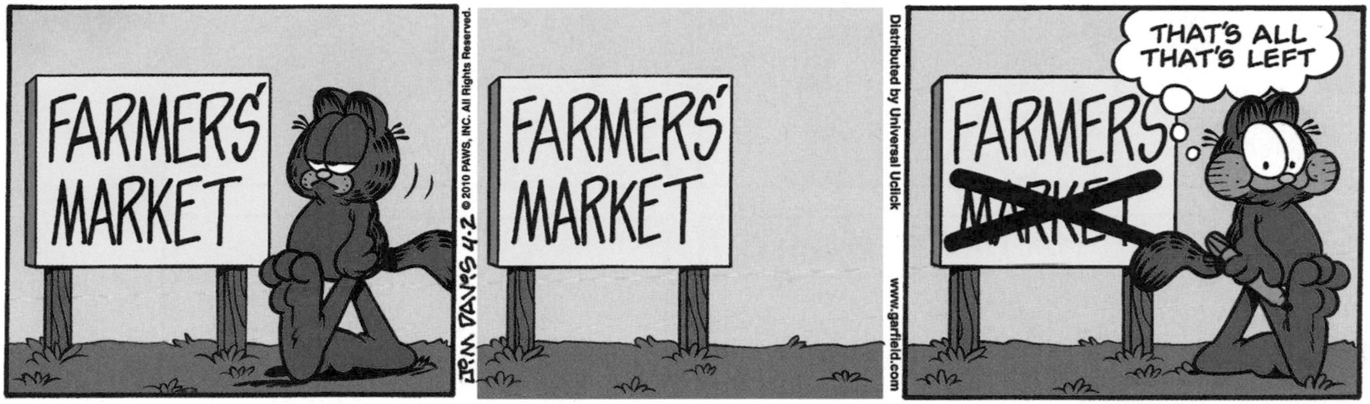
FARMERS' MARKET
JIM DAVIS 4-2 © 2010 PAWS, INC. All Rights Reserved.
FARMERS' MARKET
Distributed by Universal Uclick www.garfield.com
FARMERS' MARKET
THAT'S ALL THAT'S LEFT

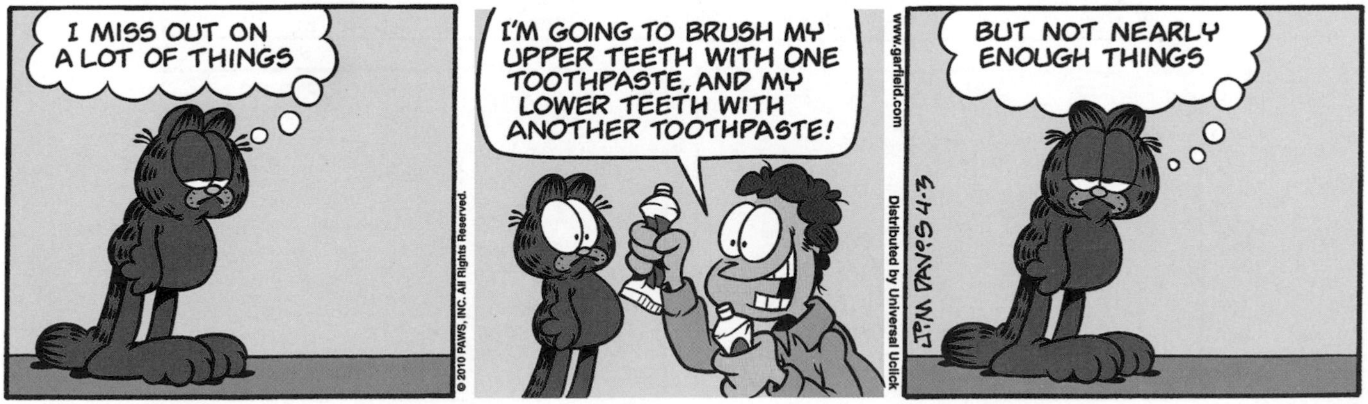
I MISS OUT ON A LOT OF THINGS
© 2010 PAWS, INC. All Rights Reserved.
I'M GOING TO BRUSH MY UPPER TEETH WITH ONE TOOTHPASTE, AND MY LOWER TEETH WITH ANOTHER TOOTHPASTE!
www.garfield.com Distributed by Universal Uclick
JIM DAVIS 4-3
BUT NOT NEARLY ENOUGH THINGS

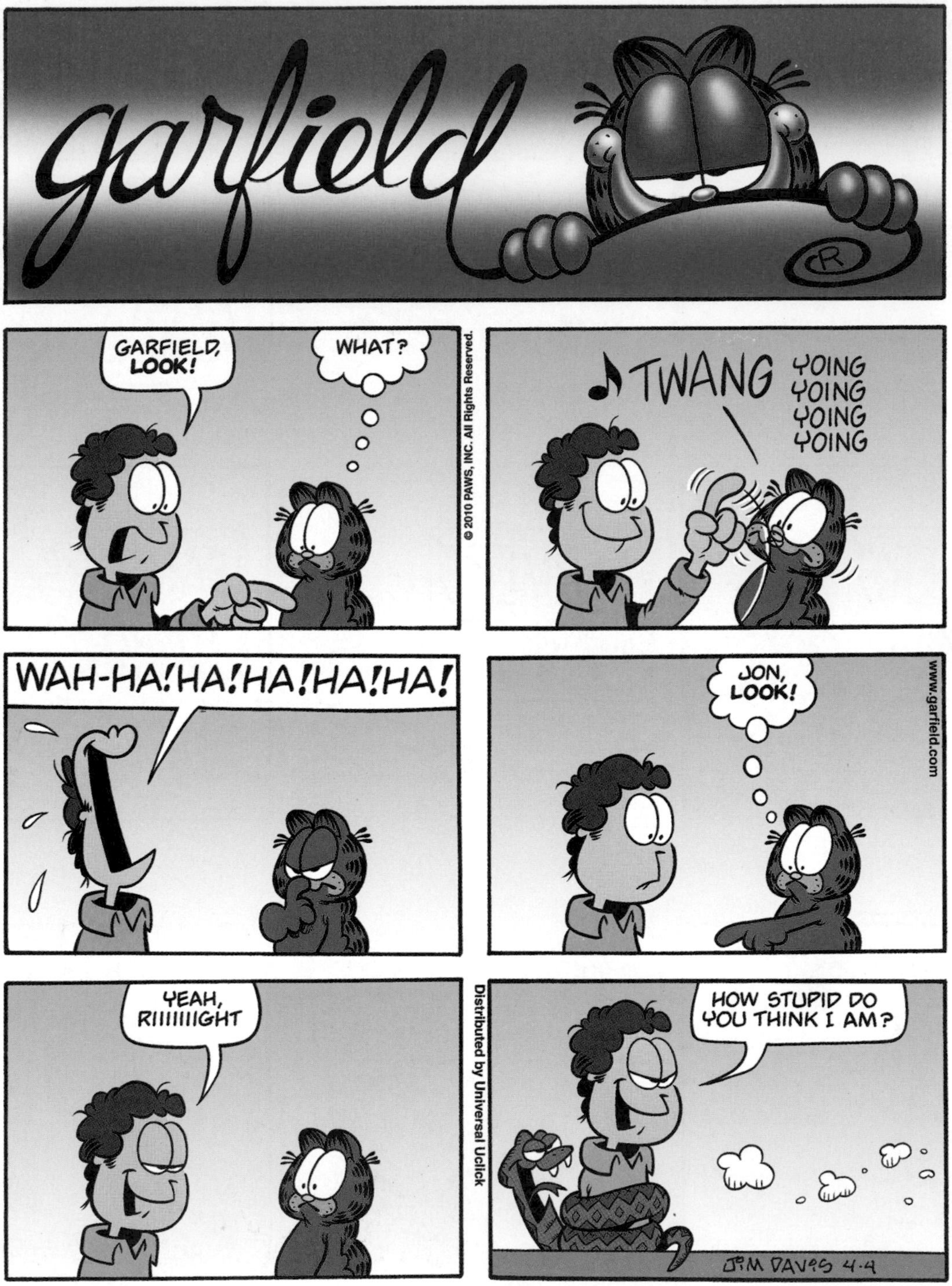
garfield
GARFIELD, LOOK!
WHAT?
© 2010 PAWS, INC. All Rights Reserved.
♪TWANG
YOING YOING YOING YOING
WAH-HA!HA!HA!HA!HA!
JON, LOOK!
www.garfield.com
YEAH, RIIIIIIIGHT
Distributed by Universal Uclick
HOW STUPID DO YOU THINK I AM?
JIM DAVIS 4-4

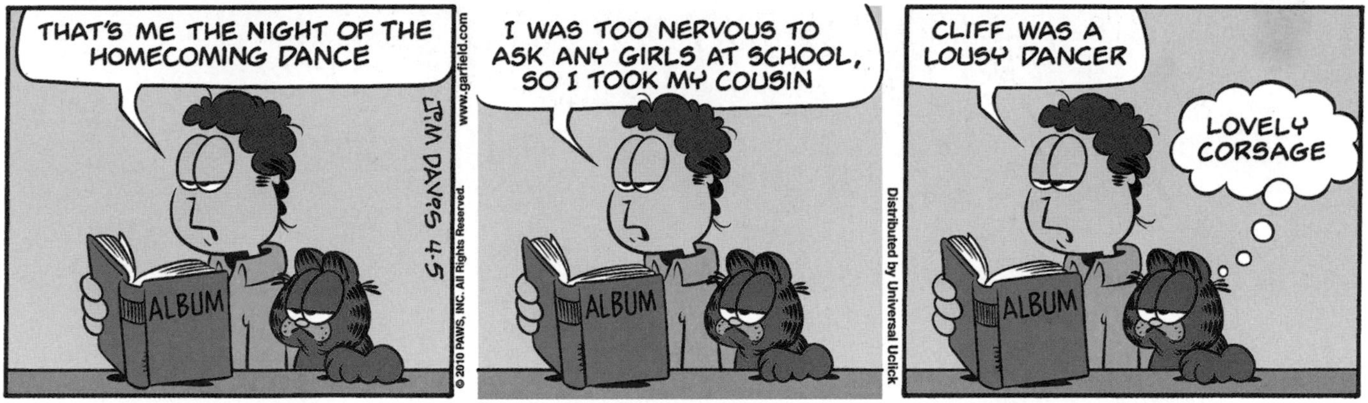
THAT'S ME THE NIGHT OF THE HOMECOMING DANCE
ALBUM
JIM DAVIS 4-5
© 2010 PAWS, INC. All Rights Reserved. www.garfield.com
I WAS TOO NERVOUS TO ASK ANY GIRLS AT SCHOOL, SO I TOOK MY COUSIN
ALBUM
Distributed by Universal Uclick
CLIFF WAS A LOUSY DANCER
LOVELY CORSAGE
ALBUM

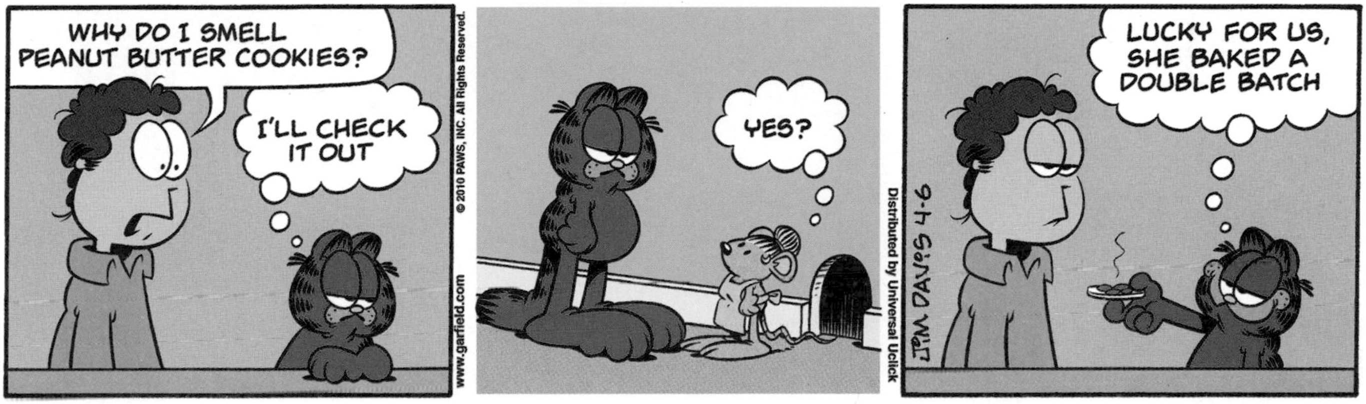
WHY DO I SMELL PEANUT BUTTER COOKIES?
I'LL CHECK IT OUT
© 2010 PAWS, INC. All Rights Reserved. www.garfield.com
YES?
Distributed by Universal Uclick
JIM DAVIS 4-6
LUCKY FOR US, SHE BAKED A DOUBLE BATCH

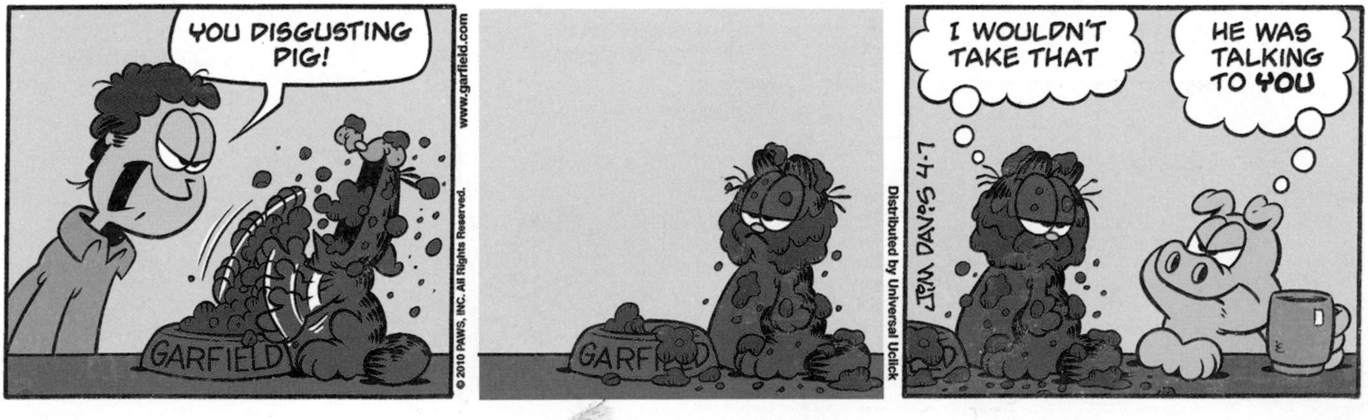
YOU DISGUSTING PIG!
GARFIELD
© 2010 PAWS, INC. All Rights Reserved. www.garfield.com
GARFIELD
Distributed by Universal Uclick
JIM DAVIS 4-7
I WOULDN'T TAKE THAT
HE WAS TALKING TO **YOU**

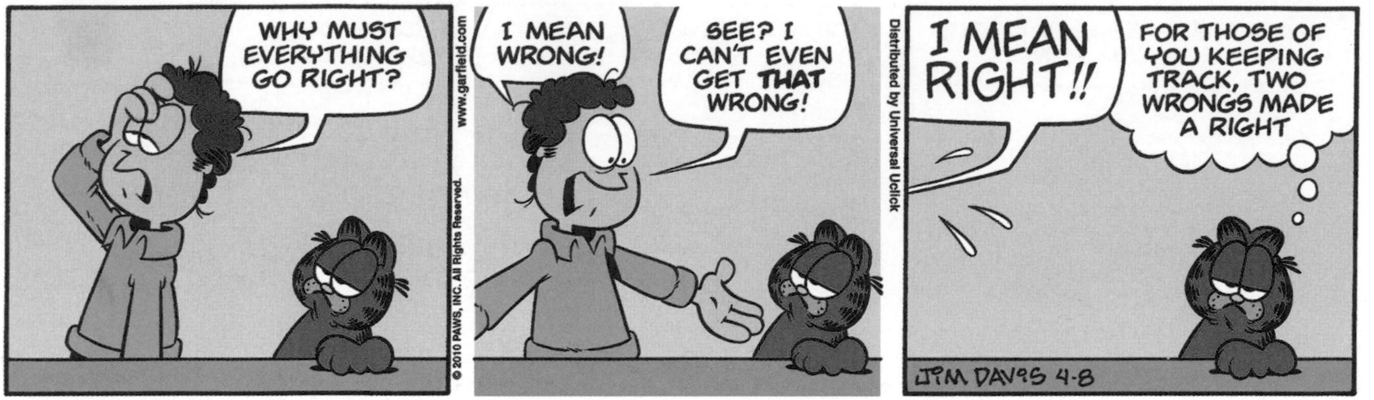
WHY MUST EVERYTHING GO RIGHT?
© 2010 PAWS, INC. All Rights Reserved. www.garfield.com
I MEAN WRONG!
SEE? I CAN'T EVEN GET THAT WRONG!
Distributed by Universal Uclick
I MEAN RIGHT!!
FOR THOSE OF YOU KEEPING TRACK, TWO WRONGS MADE A RIGHT
JIM DAVIS 4-8

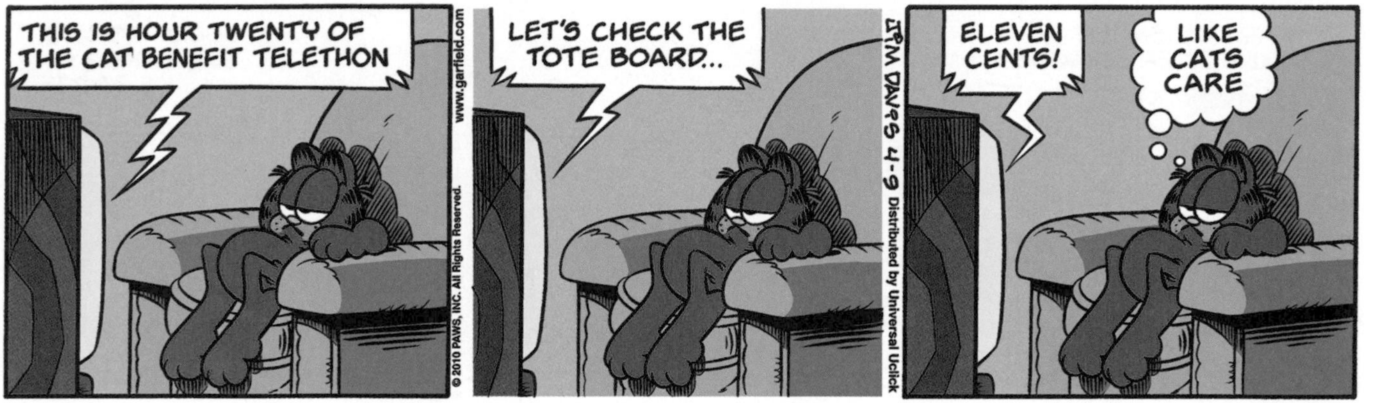
THIS IS HOUR TWENTY OF THE CAT BENEFIT TELETHON
© 2010 PAWS, INC. All Rights Reserved. www.garfield.com
LET'S CHECK THE TOTE BOARD...
JIM DAVIS 4-9 Distributed by Universal Uclick
ELEVEN CENTS!
LIKE CATS CARE

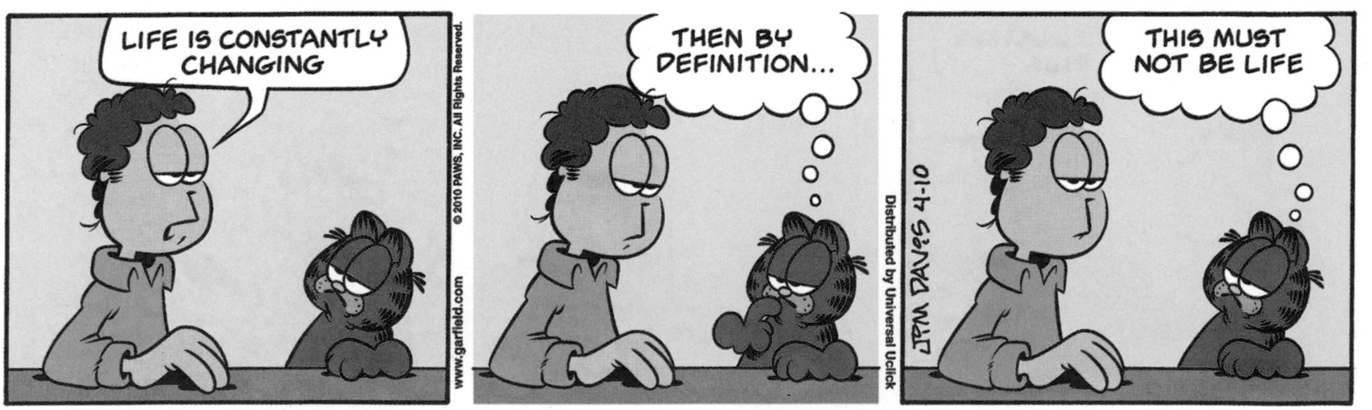
LIFE IS CONSTANTLY CHANGING
© 2010 PAWS, INC. All Rights Reserved. www.garfield.com
THEN BY DEFINITION...
Distributed by Universal Uclick
THIS MUST NOT BE LIFE
JIM DAVIS 4-10

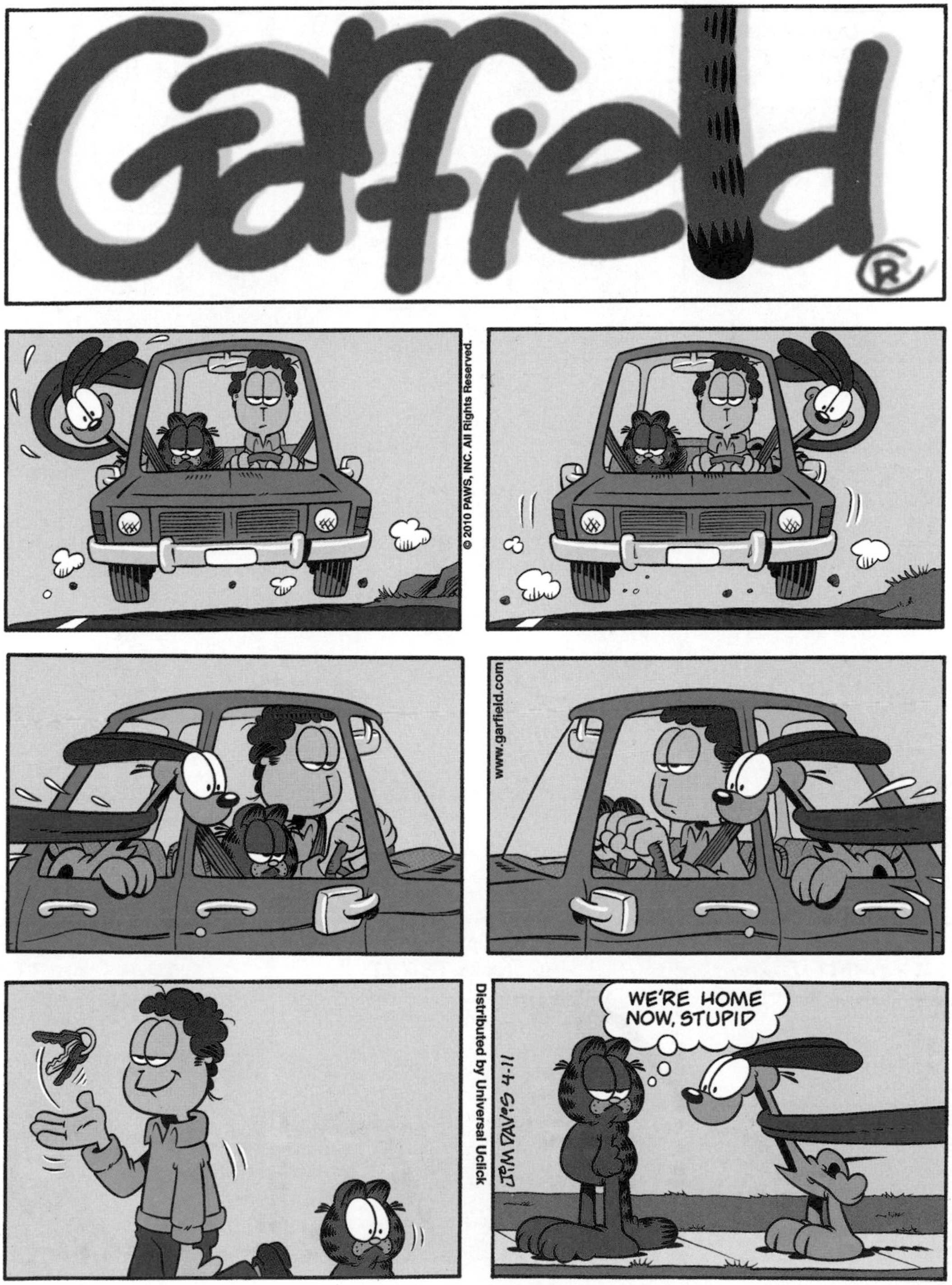
Garfield
© 2010 PAWS, INC. All Rights Reserved.
www.garfield.com
Distributed by Universal Uclick
WE'RE HOME NOW, STUPID

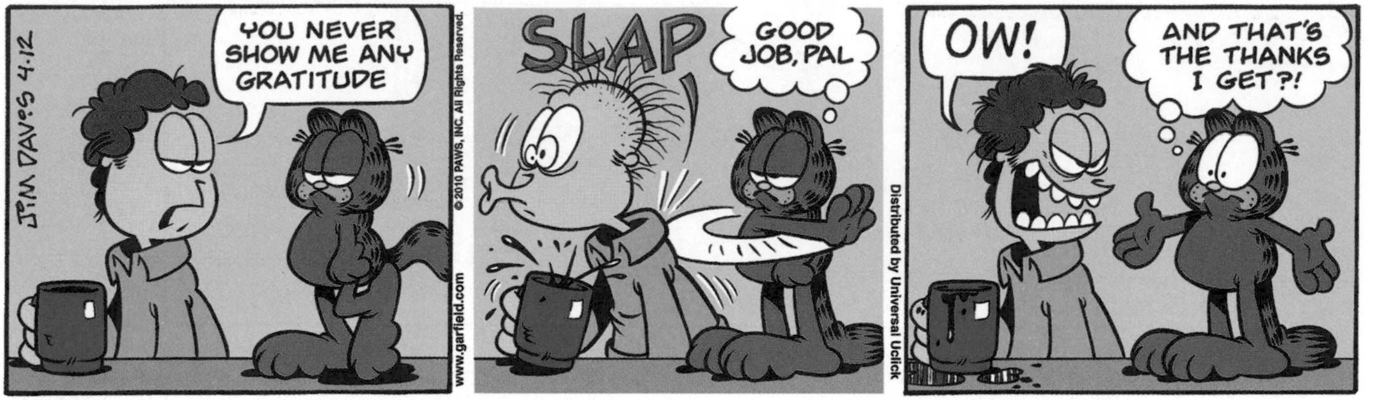
JIM DAVIS 4·12
YOU NEVER SHOW ME ANY GRATITUDE
© 2010 PAWS, INC. All Rights Reserved.
www.garfield.com
SLAP
GOOD JOB, PAL
Distributed by Universal Uclick
OW!
AND THAT'S THE THANKS I GET?!

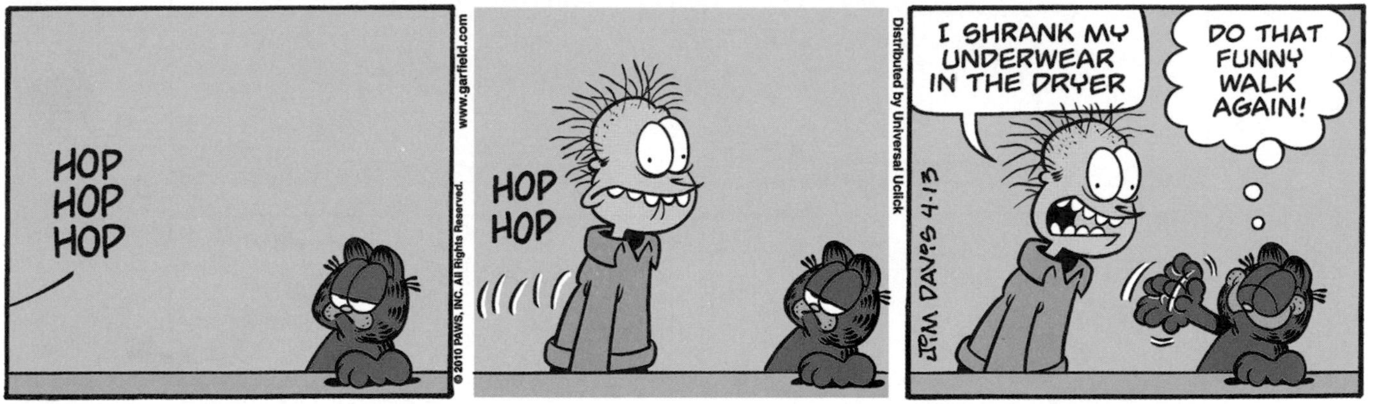
HOP
HOP
HOP
© 2010 PAWS, INC. All Rights Reserved.
www.garfield.com
HOP
HOP
Distributed by Universal Uclick
I SHRANK MY UNDERWEAR IN THE DRYER
DO THAT FUNNY WALK AGAIN!
JIM DAVIS 4·13

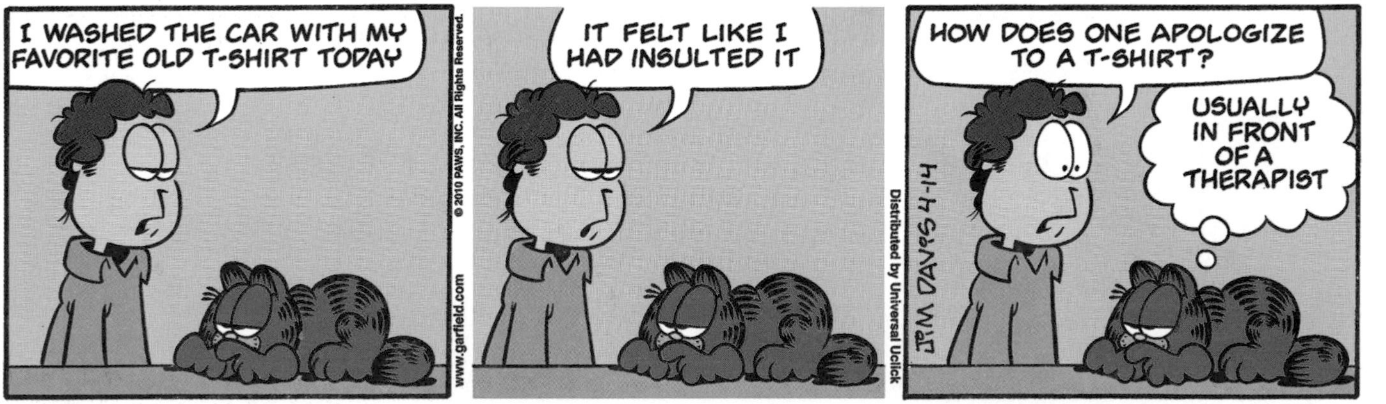
I WASHED THE CAR WITH MY FAVORITE OLD T-SHIRT TODAY
© 2010 PAWS, INC. All Rights Reserved.
www.garfield.com
IT FELT LIKE I HAD INSULTED IT
Distributed by Universal Uclick
HOW DOES ONE APOLOGIZE TO A T-SHIRT?
USUALLY IN FRONT OF A THERAPIST
JIM DAVIS 4·14

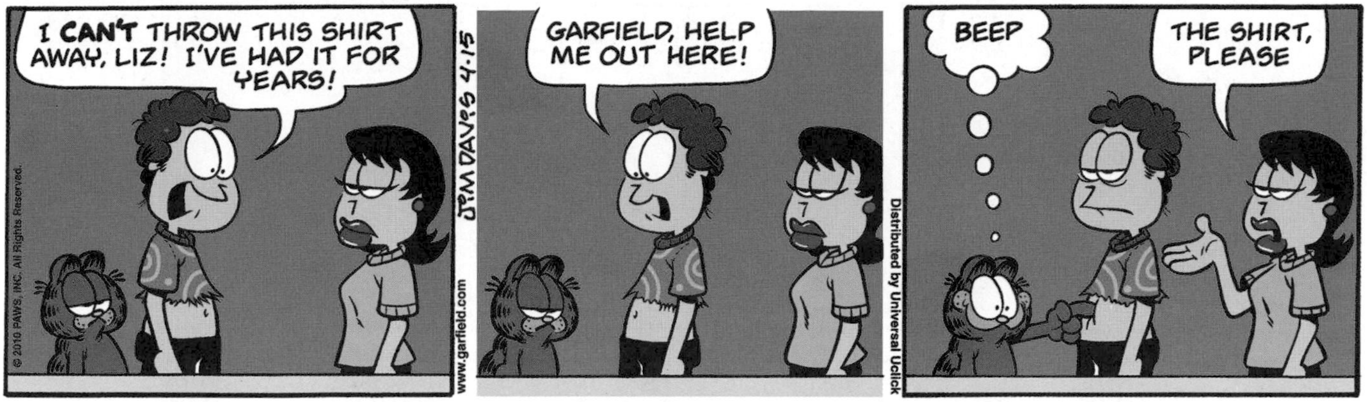
I CAN'T THROW THIS SHIRT AWAY, LIZ! I'VE HAD IT FOR YEARS!
© 2010 PAWS, INC. All Rights Reserved.
JPM DAVPS 4-15
www.garfield.com
GARFIELD, HELP ME OUT HERE!
Distributed by Universal Uclick
BEEP
THE SHIRT, PLEASE

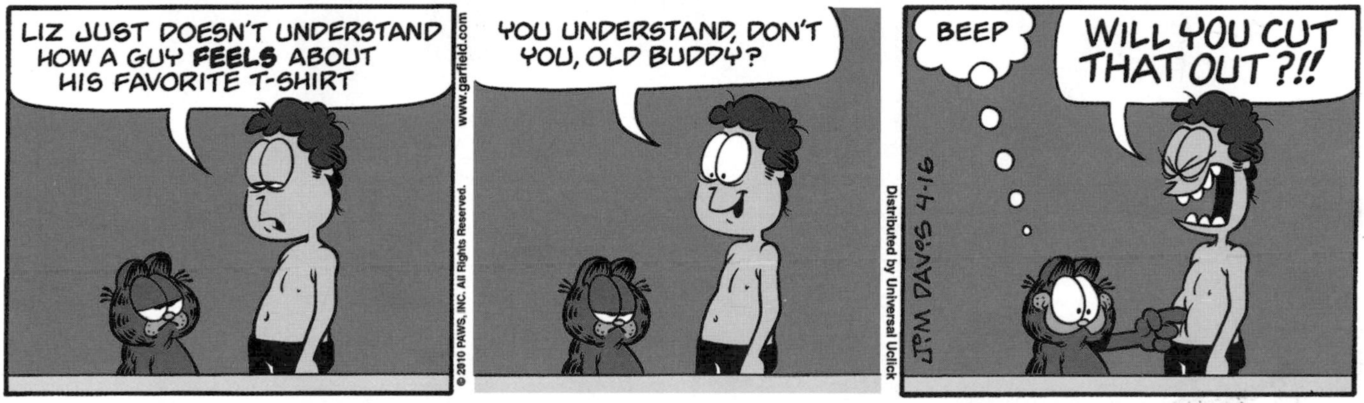
LIZ JUST DOESN'T UNDERSTAND HOW A GUY FEELS ABOUT HIS FAVORITE T-SHIRT
www.garfield.com
© 2010 PAWS, INC. All Rights Reserved.
YOU UNDERSTAND, DON'T YOU, OLD BUDDY?
Distributed by Universal Uclick
BEEP
WILL YOU CUT THAT OUT?!!
JPM DAVPS 4-16

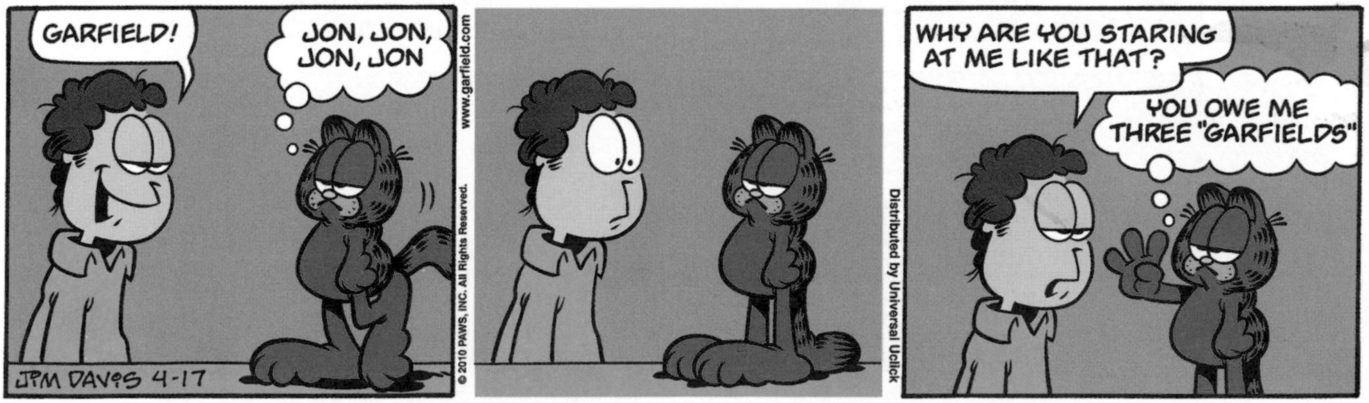
GARFIELD!
JON, JON, JON, JON
JPM DAVPS 4-17
www.garfield.com
© 2010 PAWS, INC. All Rights Reserved.
Distributed by Universal Uclick
WHY ARE YOU STARING AT ME LIKE THAT?
YOU OWE ME THREE "GARFIELDS"

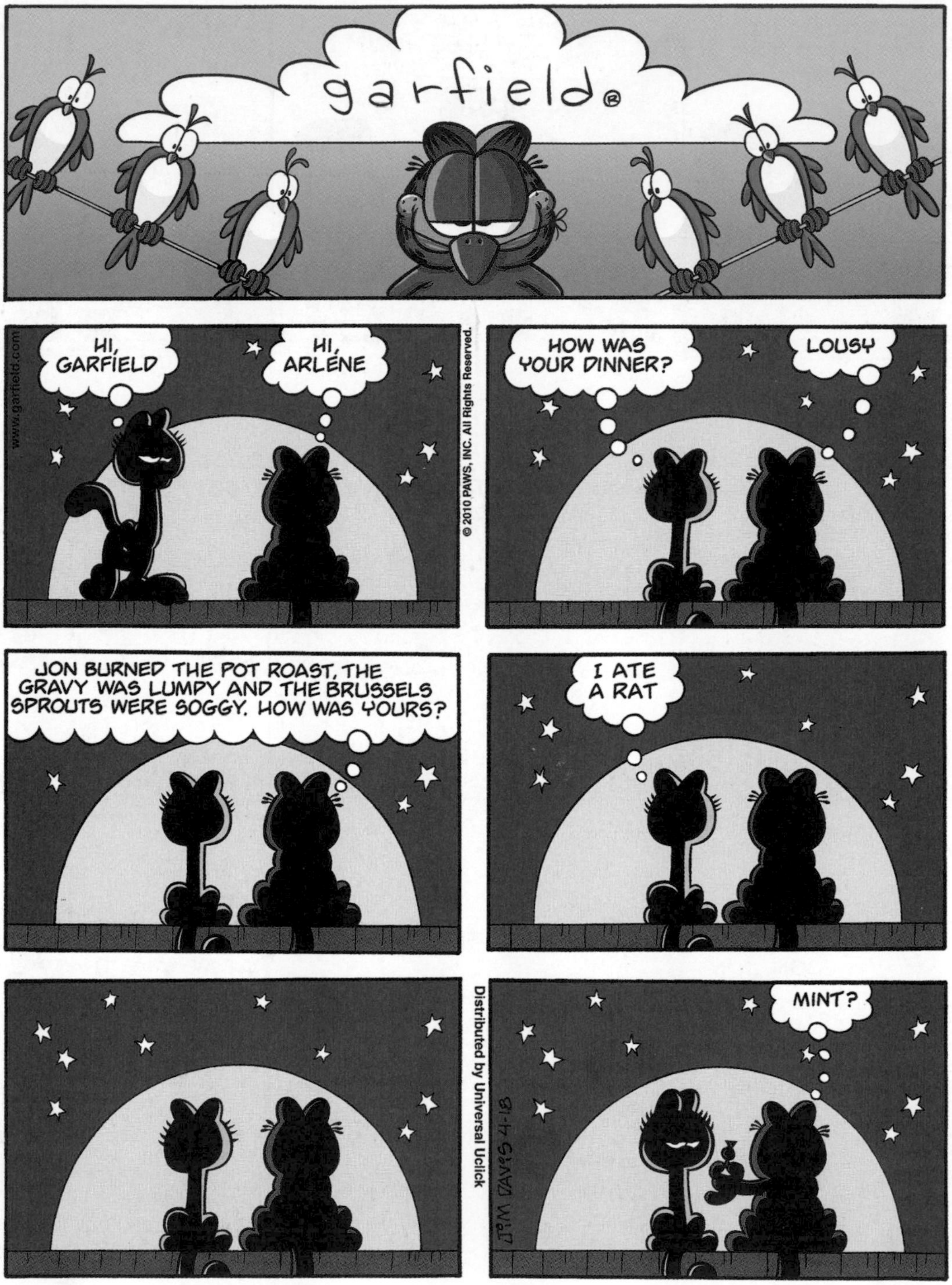
garfield®
www.garfield.com
HI, GARFIELD
HI, ARLENE
© 2010 PAWS, INC. All Rights Reserved.
HOW WAS YOUR DINNER?
LOUSY
JON BURNED THE POT ROAST, THE GRAVY WAS LUMPY AND THE BRUSSELS SPROUTS WERE SOGGY. HOW WAS YOURS?
I ATE A RAT
Distributed by Universal Uclick
JPM DAVIS 4-18
MINT?

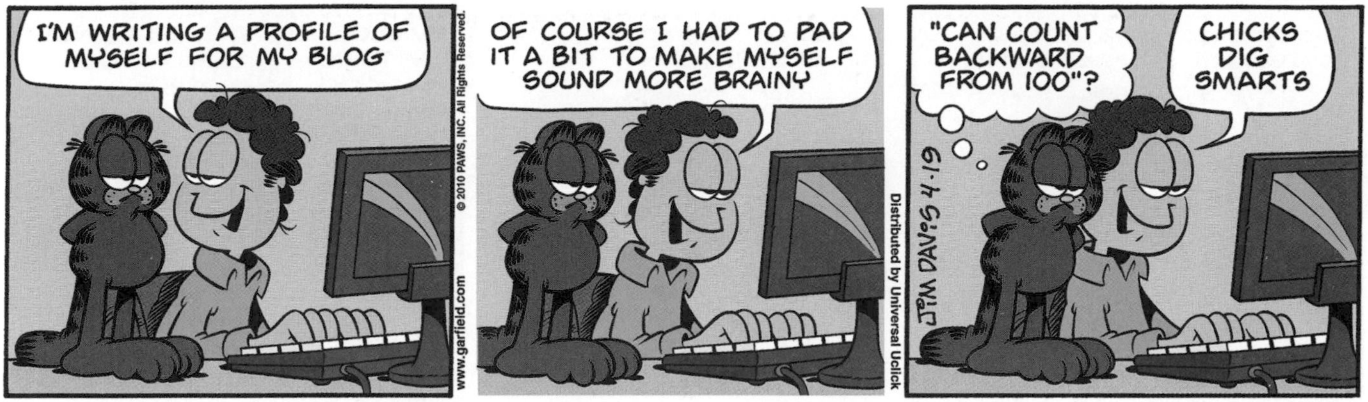
I'M WRITING A PROFILE OF MYSELF FOR MY BLOG
© 2010 PAWS, INC. All Rights Reserved.
www.garfield.com
OF COURSE I HAD TO PAD IT A BIT TO MAKE MYSELF SOUND MORE BRAINY
Distributed by Universal Uclick
JIM DAVIS 4·19
"CAN COUNT BACKWARD FROM 100"?
CHICKS DIG SMARTS

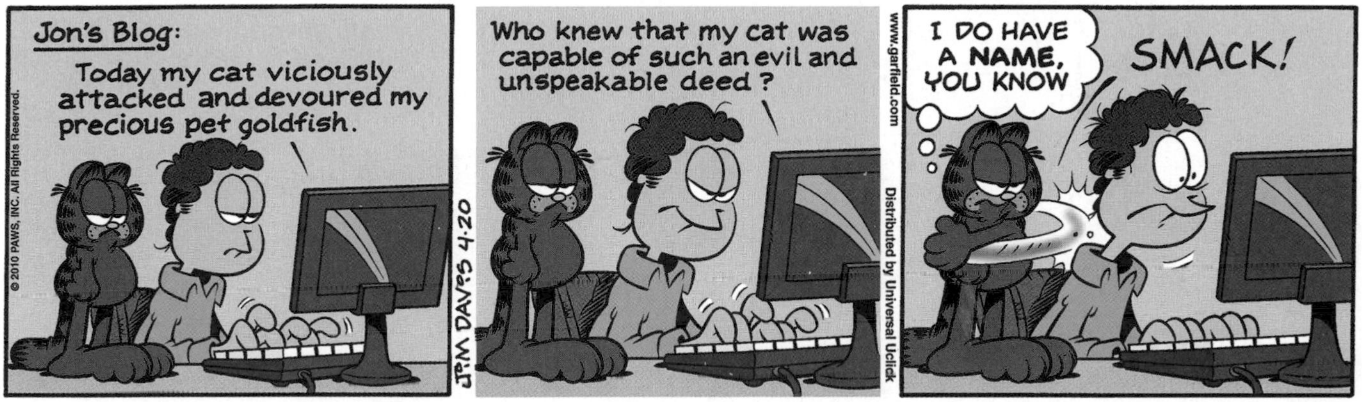
Jon's Blog:
Today my cat viciously attacked and devoured my precious pet goldfish.
© 2010 PAWS, INC. All Rights Reserved.
JIM DAVIS 4·20
Who knew that my cat was capable of such an evil and unspeakable deed?
www.garfield.com
Distributed by Universal Uclick
I DO HAVE A **NAME**, YOU KNOW
SMACK!

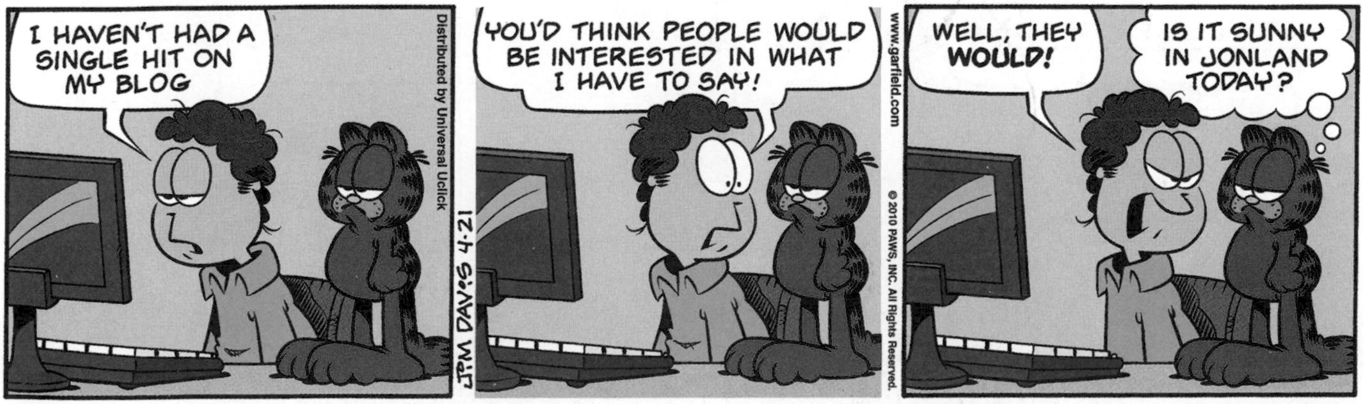
I HAVEN'T HAD A SINGLE HIT ON MY BLOG
Distributed by Universal Uclick
JIM DAVIS 4·21
YOU'D THINK PEOPLE WOULD BE INTERESTED IN WHAT I HAVE TO SAY!
www.garfield.com
© 2010 PAWS, INC. All Rights Reserved.
WELL, THEY **WOULD!**
IS IT SUNNY IN JONLAND TODAY?

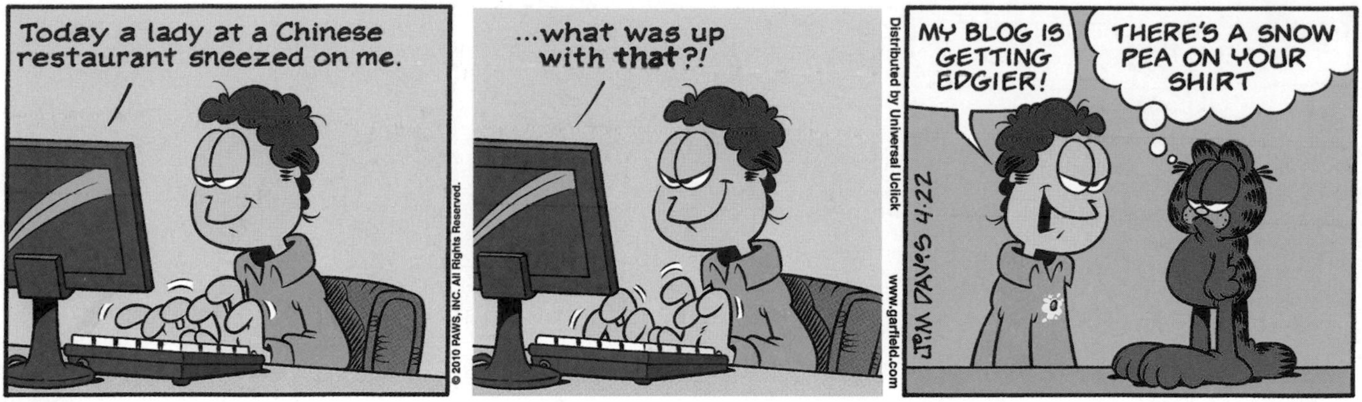
Today a lady at a Chinese restaurant sneezed on me.
© 2010 PAWS, INC. All Rights Reserved.
...what was up with that?!
Distributed by Universal Uclick
www.garfield.com
JIM DAVIS 4·22
MY BLOG IS GETTING EDGIER!
THERE'S A SNOW PEA ON YOUR SHIRT

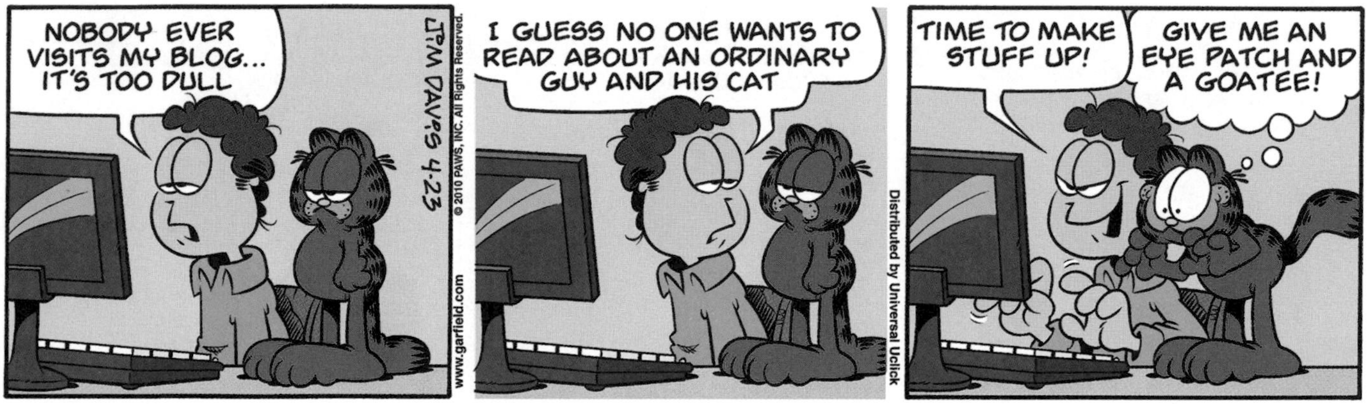
NOBODY EVER VISITS MY BLOG... IT'S TOO DULL
JIM DAVIS 4·23
© 2010 PAWS, INC. All Rights Reserved.
www.garfield.com
I GUESS NO ONE WANTS TO READ ABOUT AN ORDINARY GUY AND HIS CAT
Distributed by Universal Uclick
TIME TO MAKE STUFF UP!
GIVE ME AN EYE PATCH AND A GOATEE!

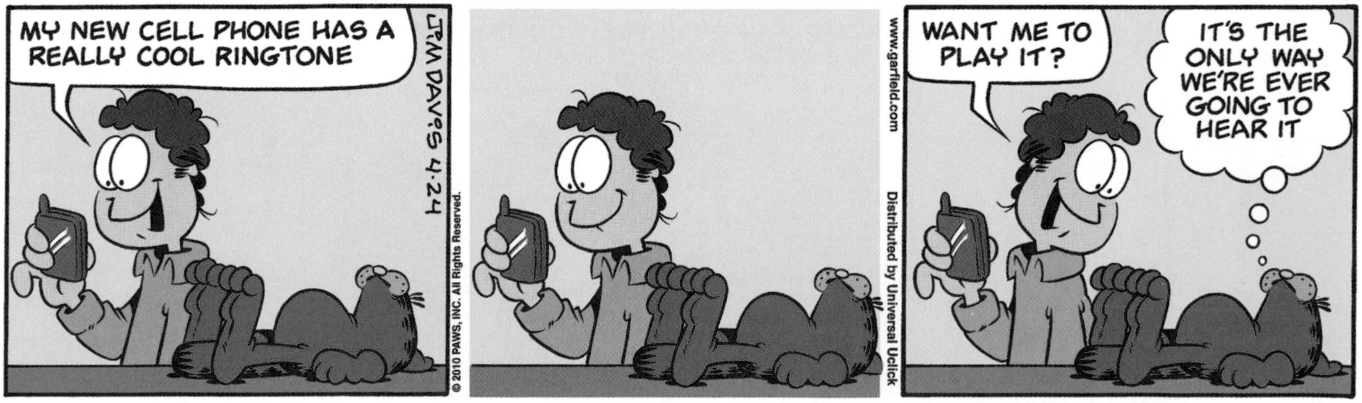
MY NEW CELL PHONE HAS A REALLY COOL RINGTONE
JIM DAVIS 4·24
© 2010 PAWS, INC. All Rights Reserved.
www.garfield.com
Distributed by Universal Uclick
WANT ME TO PLAY IT?
IT'S THE ONLY WAY WE'RE EVER GOING TO HEAR IT

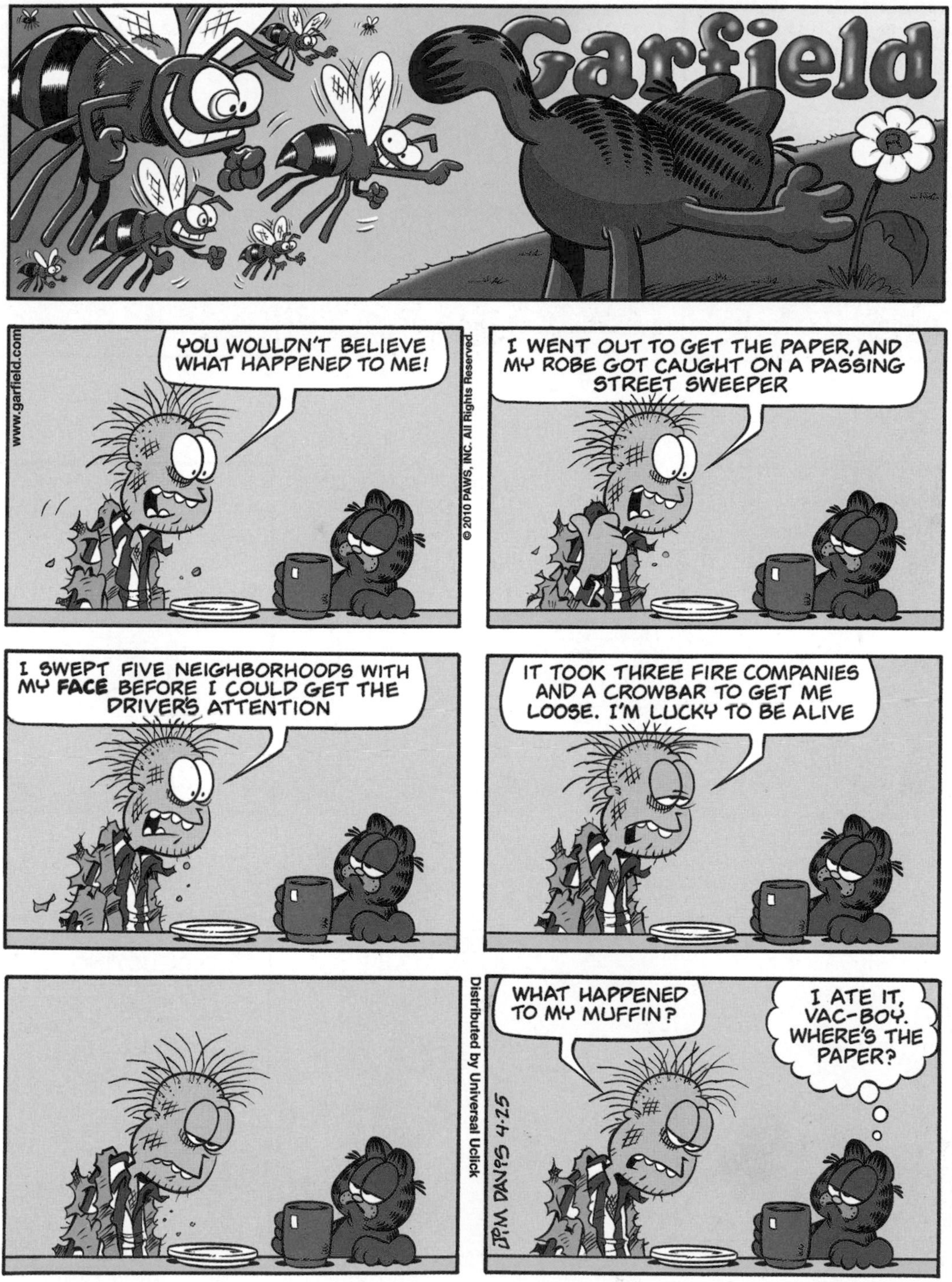

Garfield
www.garfield.com
© 2010 PAWS, INC. All Rights Reserved.
YOU WOULDN'T BELIEVE WHAT HAPPENED TO ME!
I WENT OUT TO GET THE PAPER, AND MY ROBE GOT CAUGHT ON A PASSING STREET SWEEPER
I SWEPT FIVE NEIGHBORHOODS WITH MY FACE BEFORE I COULD GET THE DRIVER'S ATTENTION
IT TOOK THREE FIRE COMPANIES AND A CROWBAR TO GET ME LOOSE. I'M LUCKY TO BE ALIVE
Distributed by Universal Uclick
JPM DAVIS 4-25
WHAT HAPPENED TO MY MUFFIN?
I ATE IT, VAC-BOY. WHERE'S THE PAPER?

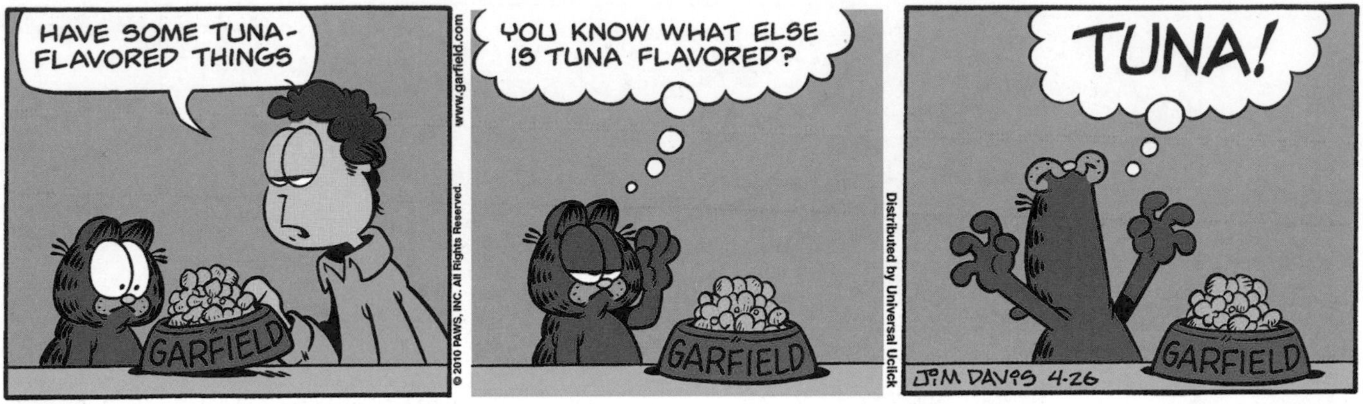
HAVE SOME TUNA-FLAVORED THINGS
© 2010 PAWS, INC. All Rights Reserved.
www.garfield.com
YOU KNOW WHAT ELSE IS TUNA FLAVORED?
Distributed by Universal Uclick
TUNA!
GARFIELD
JIM DAVIS 4-26

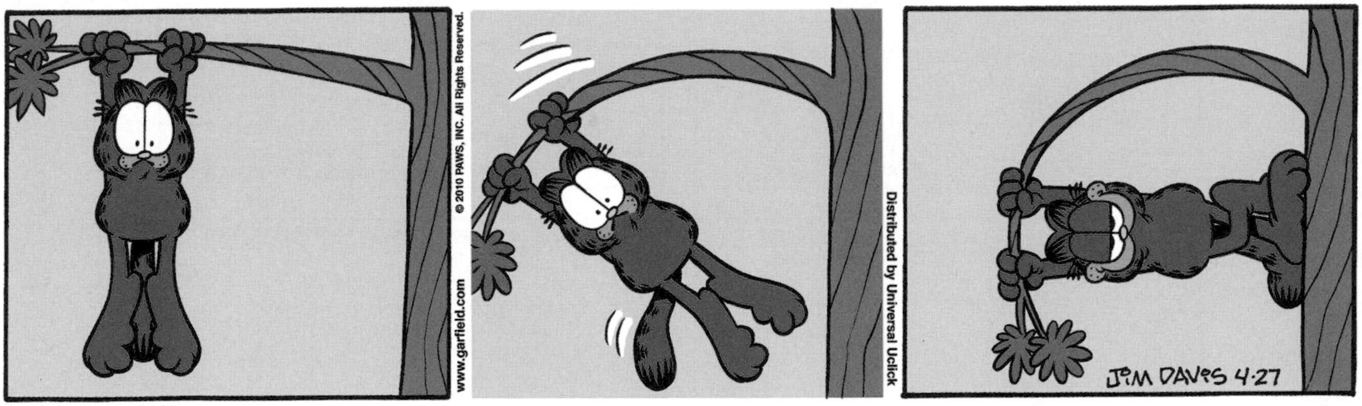
© 2010 PAWS, INC. All Rights Reserved.
www.garfield.com
Distributed by Universal Uclick
JIM DAVIS 4-27

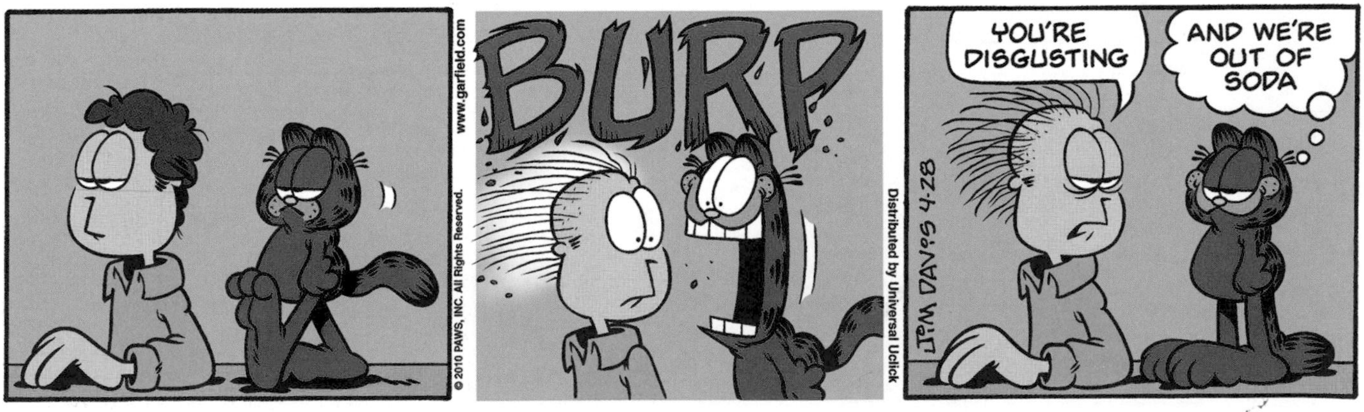
© 2010 PAWS, INC. All Rights Reserved.
www.garfield.com
BURP
Distributed by Universal Uclick
YOU'RE DISGUSTING
AND WE'RE OUT OF SODA
JIM DAVIS 4-28

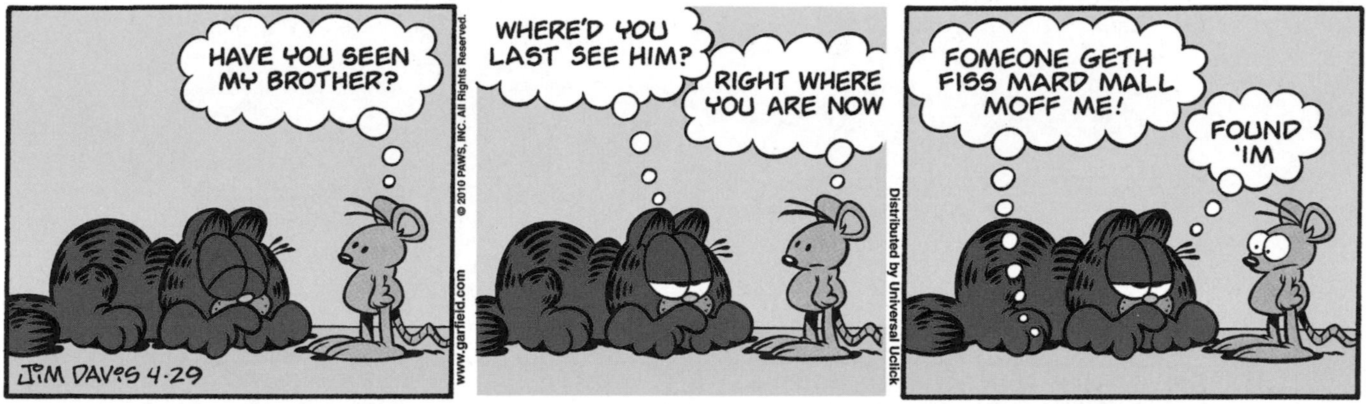
HAVE YOU SEEN MY BROTHER?
JIM DAVIS 4-29
© 2010 PAWS, INC. All Rights Reserved.
www.garfield.com
WHERE'D YOU LAST SEE HIM?
RIGHT WHERE YOU ARE NOW
Distributed by Universal Uclick
FOMEONE GETH FISS MARD MALL MOFF ME!
FOUND 'IM

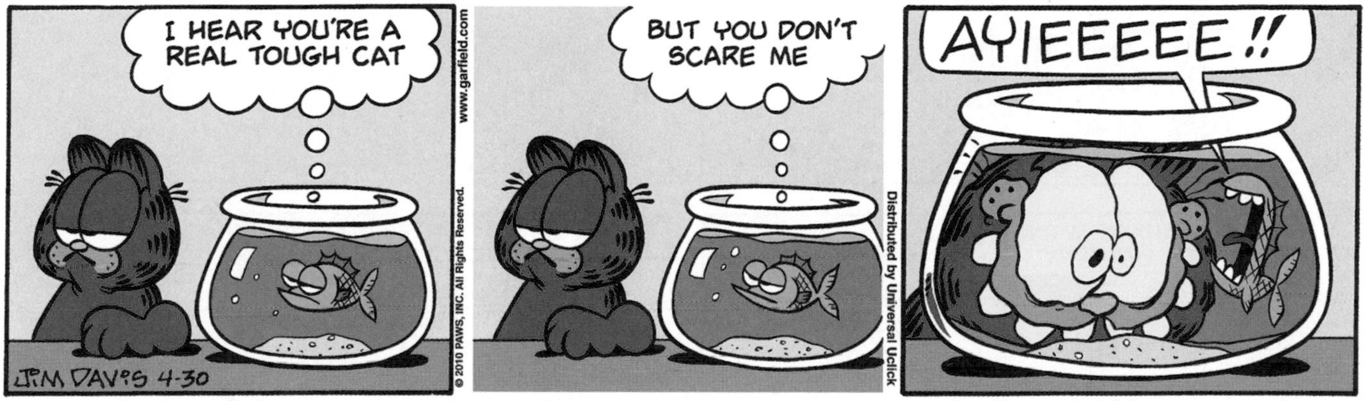
I HEAR YOU'RE A REAL TOUGH CAT
JIM DAVIS 4-30
www.garfield.com
© 2010 PAWS, INC. All Rights Reserved.
BUT YOU DON'T SCARE ME
Distributed by Universal Uclick
AYIEEEEEE!!

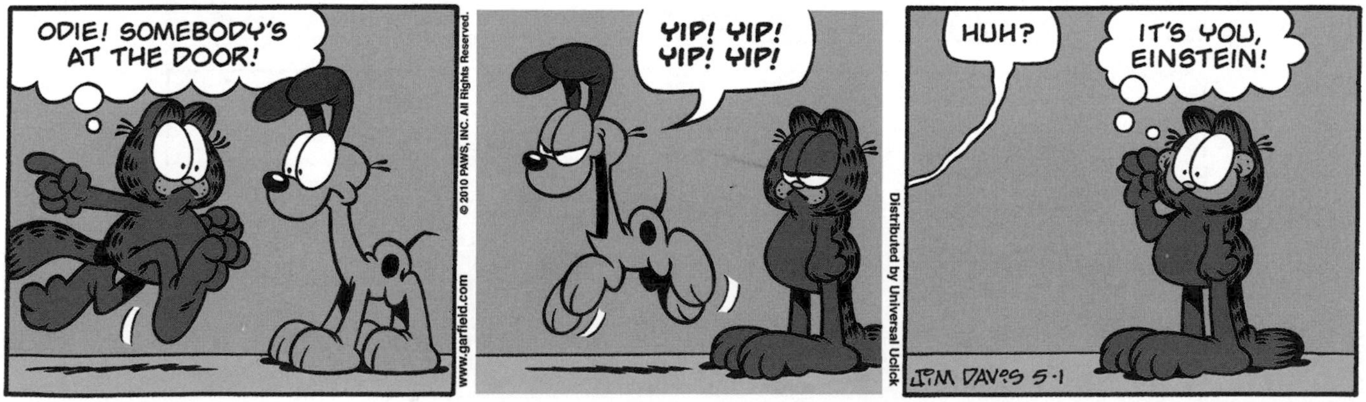
ODIE! SOMEBODY'S AT THE DOOR!
© 2010 PAWS, INC. All Rights Reserved.
www.garfield.com
YIP! YIP! YIP! YIP!
Distributed by Universal Uclick
HUH?
IT'S YOU, EINSTEIN!
JIM DAVIS 5-1

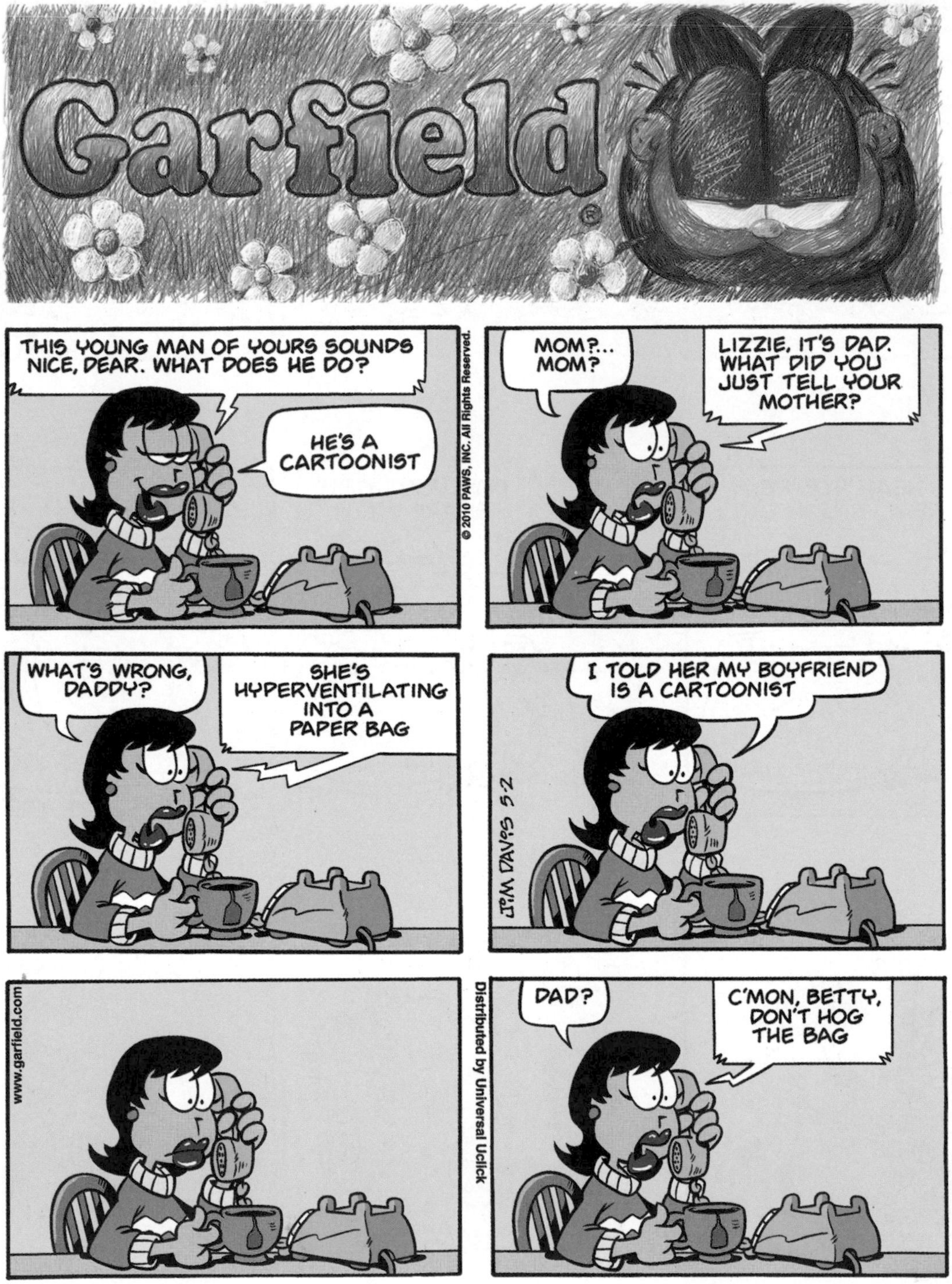
Garfield®
THIS YOUNG MAN OF YOURS SOUNDS NICE, DEAR. WHAT DOES HE DO?
HE'S A CARTOONIST
© 2010 PAWS, INC. All Rights Reserved.
MOM?... MOM?
LIZZIE, IT'S DAD. WHAT DID YOU JUST TELL YOUR MOTHER?
WHAT'S WRONG, DADDY?
SHE'S HYPERVENTILATING INTO A PAPER BAG
I TOLD HER MY BOYFRIEND IS A CARTOONIST
JPM DAVPS 5-2
www.garfield.com
Distributed by Universal Uclick
DAD?
C'MON, BETTY, DON'T HOG THE BAG

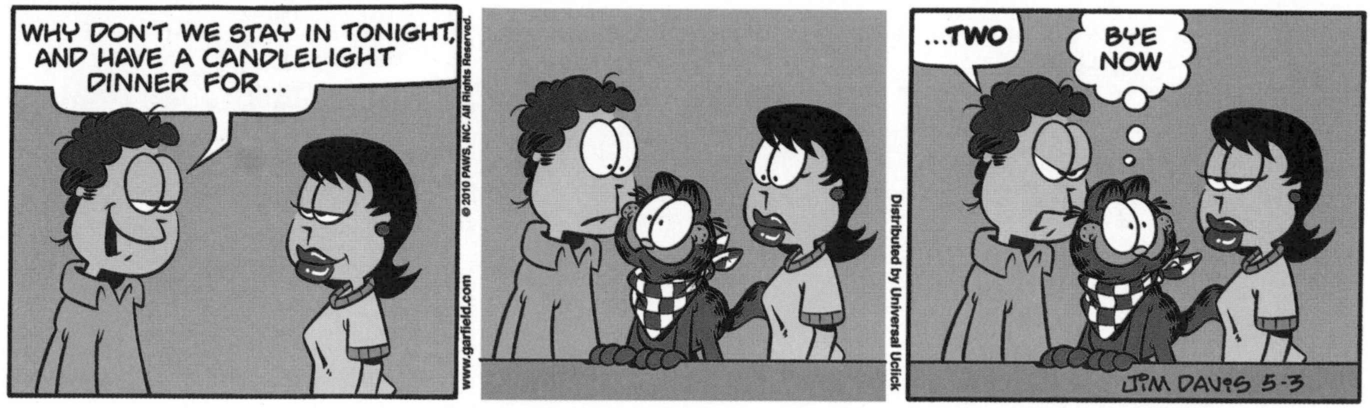
WHY DON'T WE STAY IN TONIGHT, AND HAVE A CANDLELIGHT DINNER FOR...
...TWO
BYE NOW
JIM DAVIS 5-3

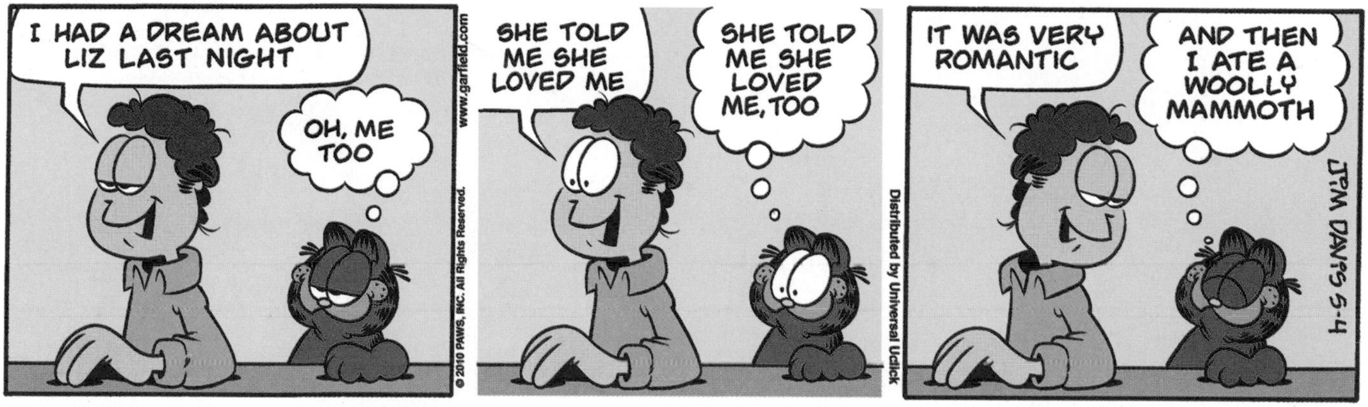
I HAD A DREAM ABOUT LIZ LAST NIGHT
OH, ME TOO
SHE TOLD ME SHE LOVED ME
SHE TOLD ME SHE LOVED ME, TOO
IT WAS VERY ROMANTIC
AND THEN I ATE A WOOLLY MAMMOTH
JIM DAVIS 5-4
© 2010 PAWS, INC. All Rights Reserved.
www.garfield.com
Distributed by Universal Uclick

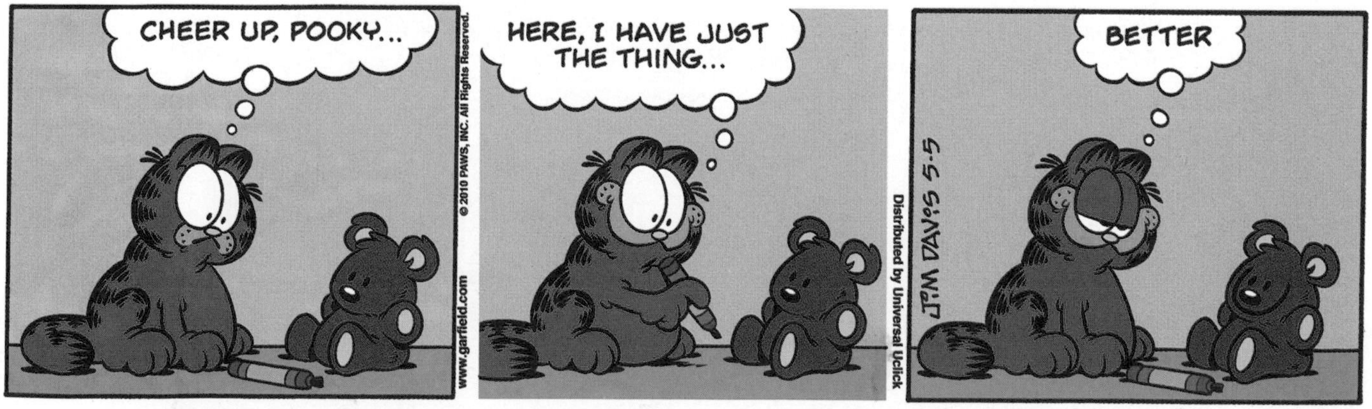
CHEER UP, POOKY...
HERE, I HAVE JUST THE THING...
BETTER
JIM DAVIS 5-5
© 2010 PAWS, INC. All Rights Reserved.
www.garfield.com
Distributed by Universal Uclick

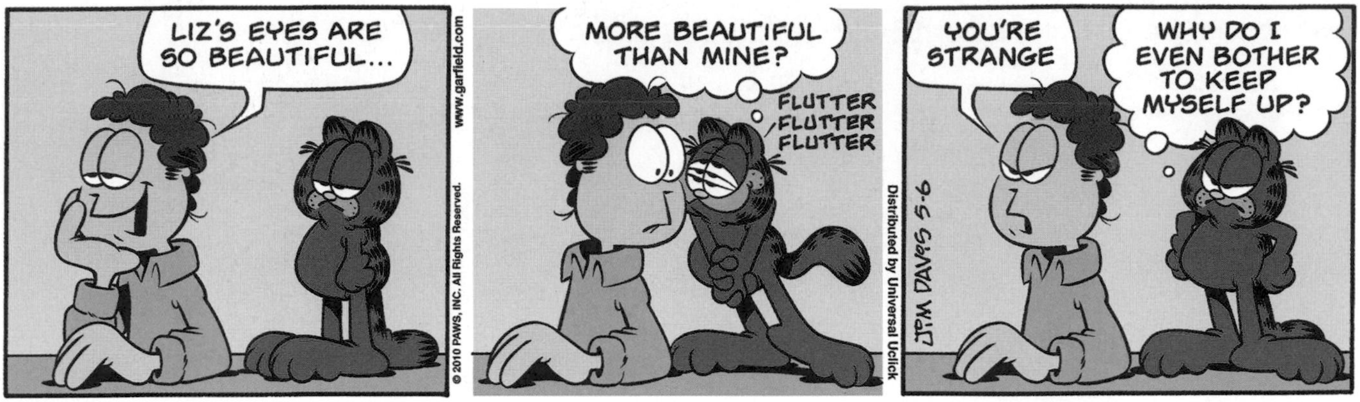
LIZ'S EYES ARE SO BEAUTIFUL...
www.garfield.com
© 2010 PAWS, INC. All Rights Reserved.
MORE BEAUTIFUL THAN MINE?
FLUTTER FLUTTER FLUTTER
Distributed by Universal Uclick
JIM DAVIS 5-6
YOU'RE STRANGE
WHY DO I EVEN BOTHER TO KEEP MYSELF UP?

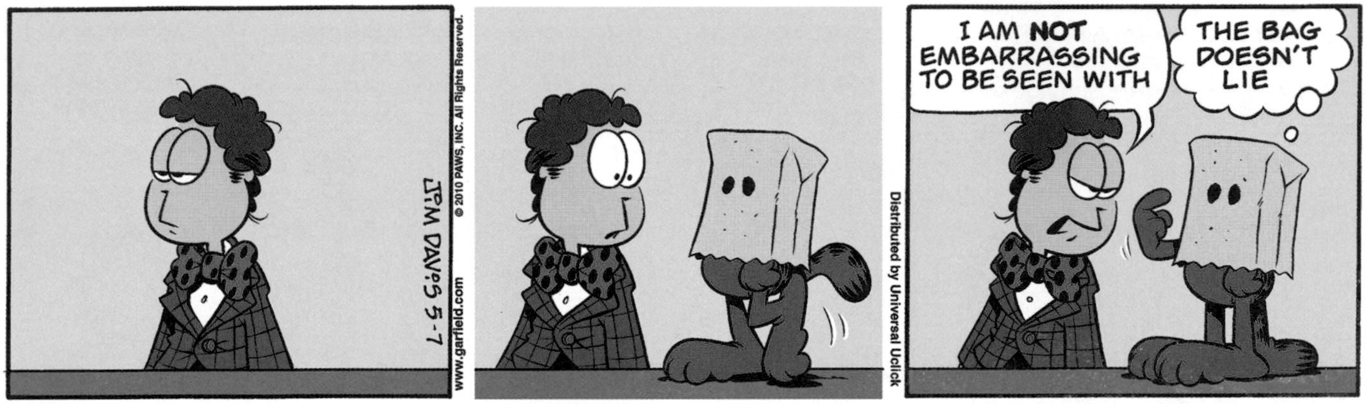
JIM DAVIS 5-7
www.garfield.com
© 2010 PAWS, INC. All Rights Reserved.
Distributed by Universal Uclick
I AM **NOT** EMBARRASSING TO BE SEEN WITH
THE BAG DOESN'T LIE

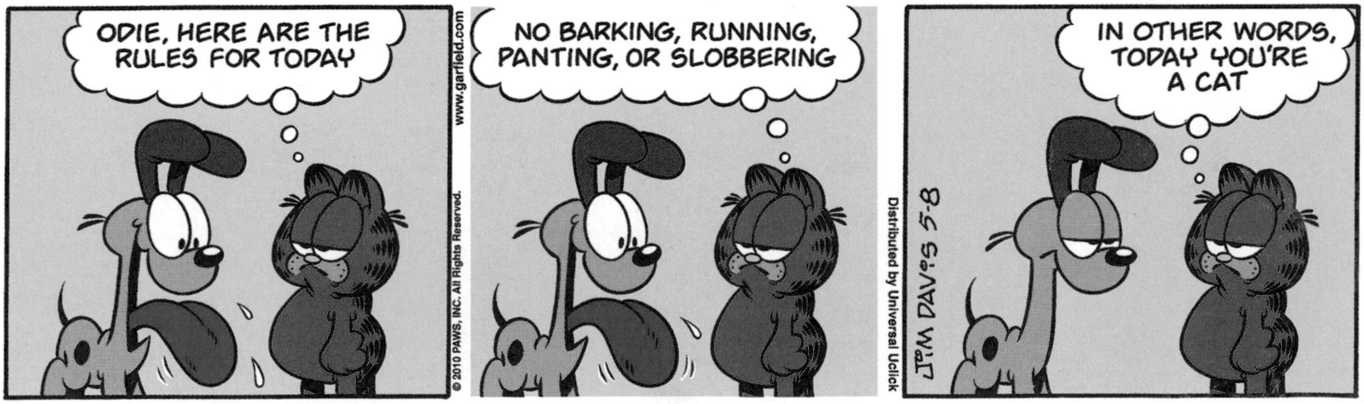
ODIE, HERE ARE THE RULES FOR TODAY
www.garfield.com
© 2010 PAWS, INC. All Rights Reserved.
NO BARKING, RUNNING, PANTING, OR SLOBBERING
Distributed by Universal Uclick
JIM DAVIS 5-8
IN OTHER WORDS, TODAY YOU'RE A CAT

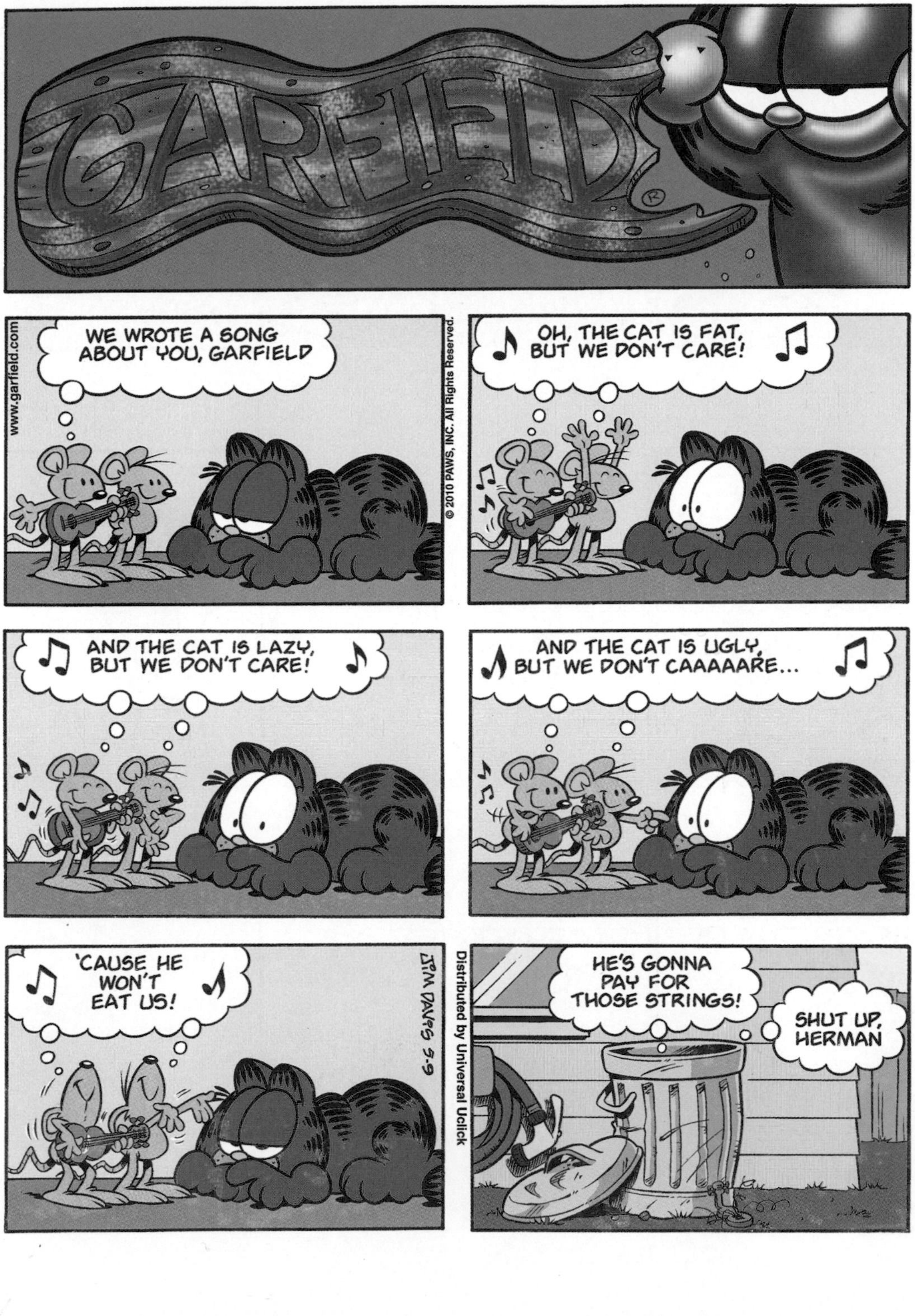
GARFIELD
www.garfield.com
© 2010 PAWS, INC. All Rights Reserved.
WE WROTE A SONG ABOUT YOU, GARFIELD
OH, THE CAT IS FAT, BUT WE DON'T CARE!
AND THE CAT IS LAZY, BUT WE DON'T CARE!
AND THE CAT IS UGLY, BUT WE DON'T CAAAAARE...
'CAUSE HE WON'T EAT US!
JIM DAVIS 5-9
Distributed by Universal Uclick
HE'S GONNA PAY FOR THOSE STRINGS!
SHUT UP, HERMAN

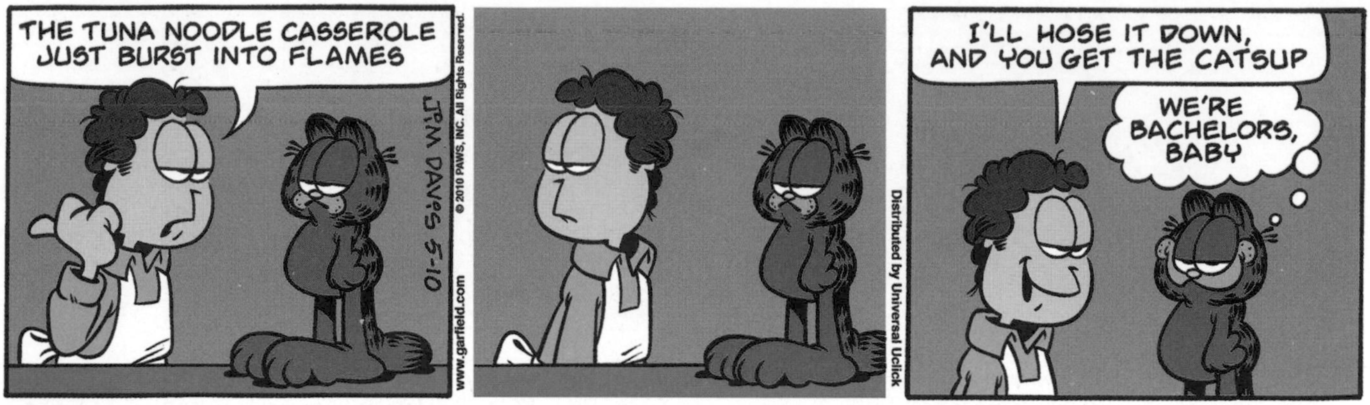
THE TUNA NOODLE CASSEROLE JUST BURST INTO FLAMES
JIM DAVIS 5-10
© 2010 PAWS, INC. All Rights Reserved.
www.garfield.com
Distributed by Universal Uclick
I'LL HOSE IT DOWN, AND YOU GET THE CATSUP
WE'RE BACHELORS, BABY

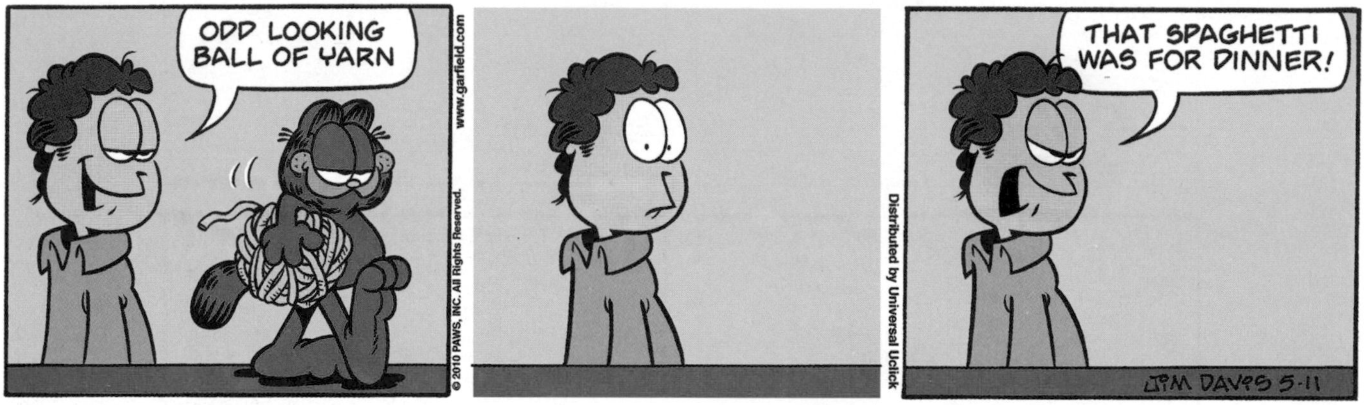
ODD LOOKING BALL OF YARN
www.garfield.com
© 2010 PAWS, INC. All Rights Reserved.
Distributed by Universal Uclick
THAT SPAGHETTI WAS FOR DINNER!
JIM DAVIS 5-11

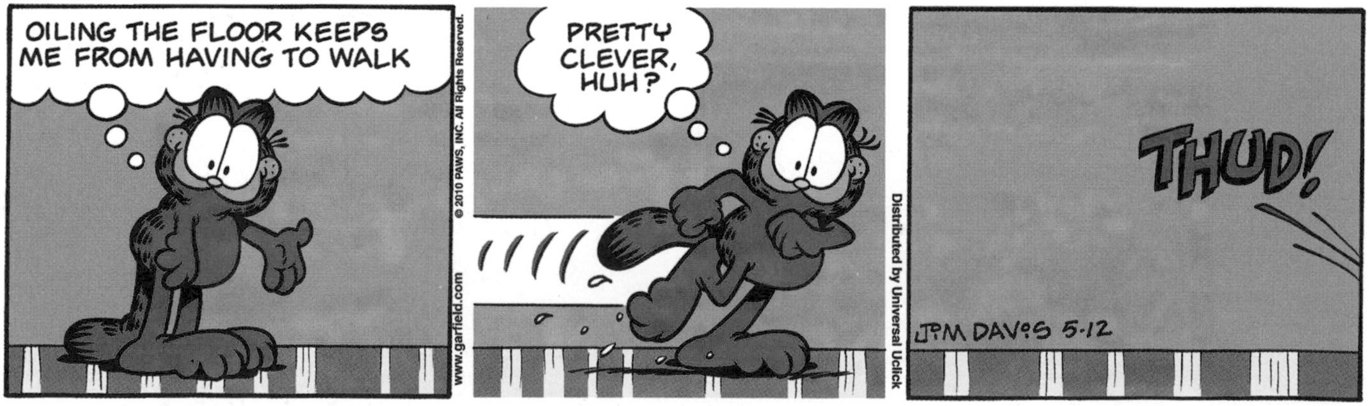
OILING THE FLOOR KEEPS ME FROM HAVING TO WALK
© 2010 PAWS, INC. All Rights Reserved.
www.garfield.com
PRETTY CLEVER, HUH?
Distributed by Universal Uclick
THUD!
JIM DAVIS 5-12

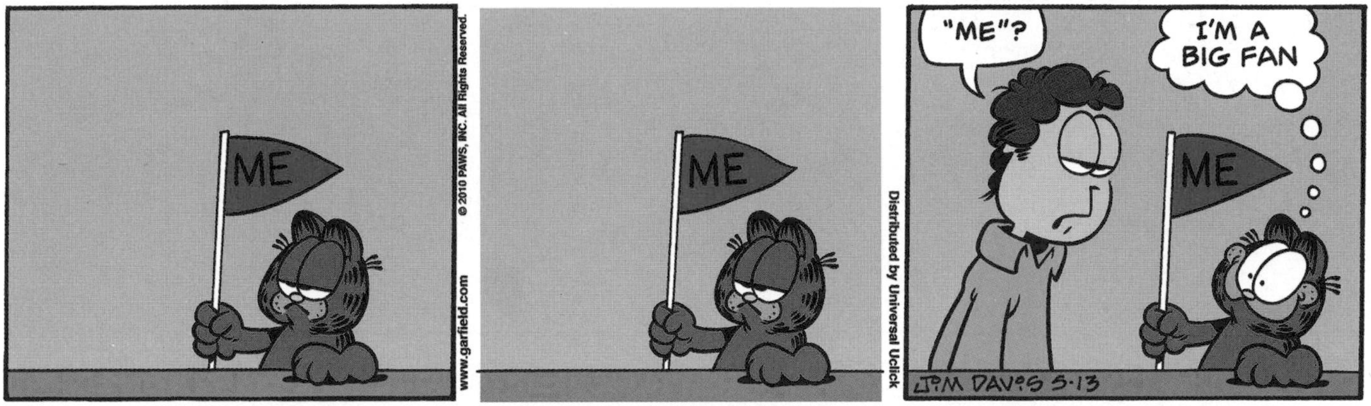
ME
ME
"ME"?
ME
I'M A BIG FAN
JIM DAVIS 5-13
© 2010 PAWS, INC. All Rights Reserved.
www.garfield.com
Distributed by Universal Uclick

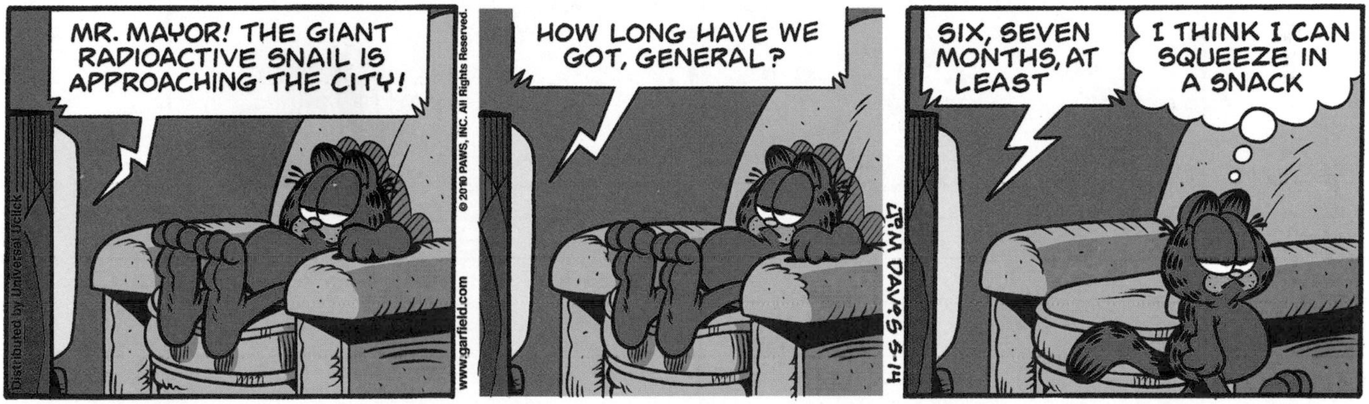
MR. MAYOR! THE GIANT RADIOACTIVE SNAIL IS APPROACHING THE CITY!
HOW LONG HAVE WE GOT, GENERAL?
SIX, SEVEN MONTHS, AT LEAST
I THINK I CAN SQUEEZE IN A SNACK
JIM DAVIS 5-14
Distributed by Universal Uclick
© 2010 PAWS, INC. All Rights Reserved.
www.garfield.com

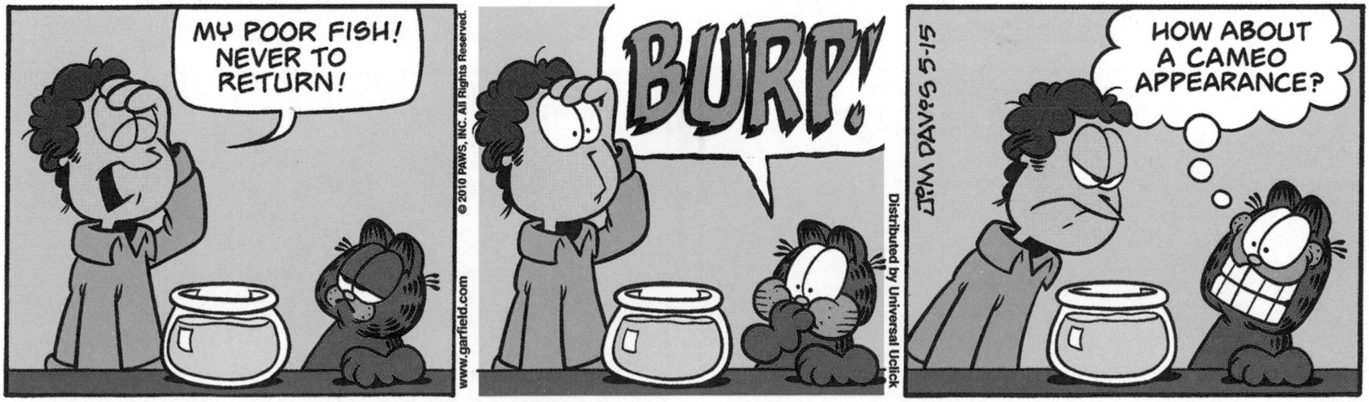
MY POOR FISH! NEVER TO RETURN!
BURP!
HOW ABOUT A CAMEO APPEARANCE?
JIM DAVIS 5-15
© 2010 PAWS, INC. All Rights Reserved.
www.garfield.com
Distributed by Universal Uclick

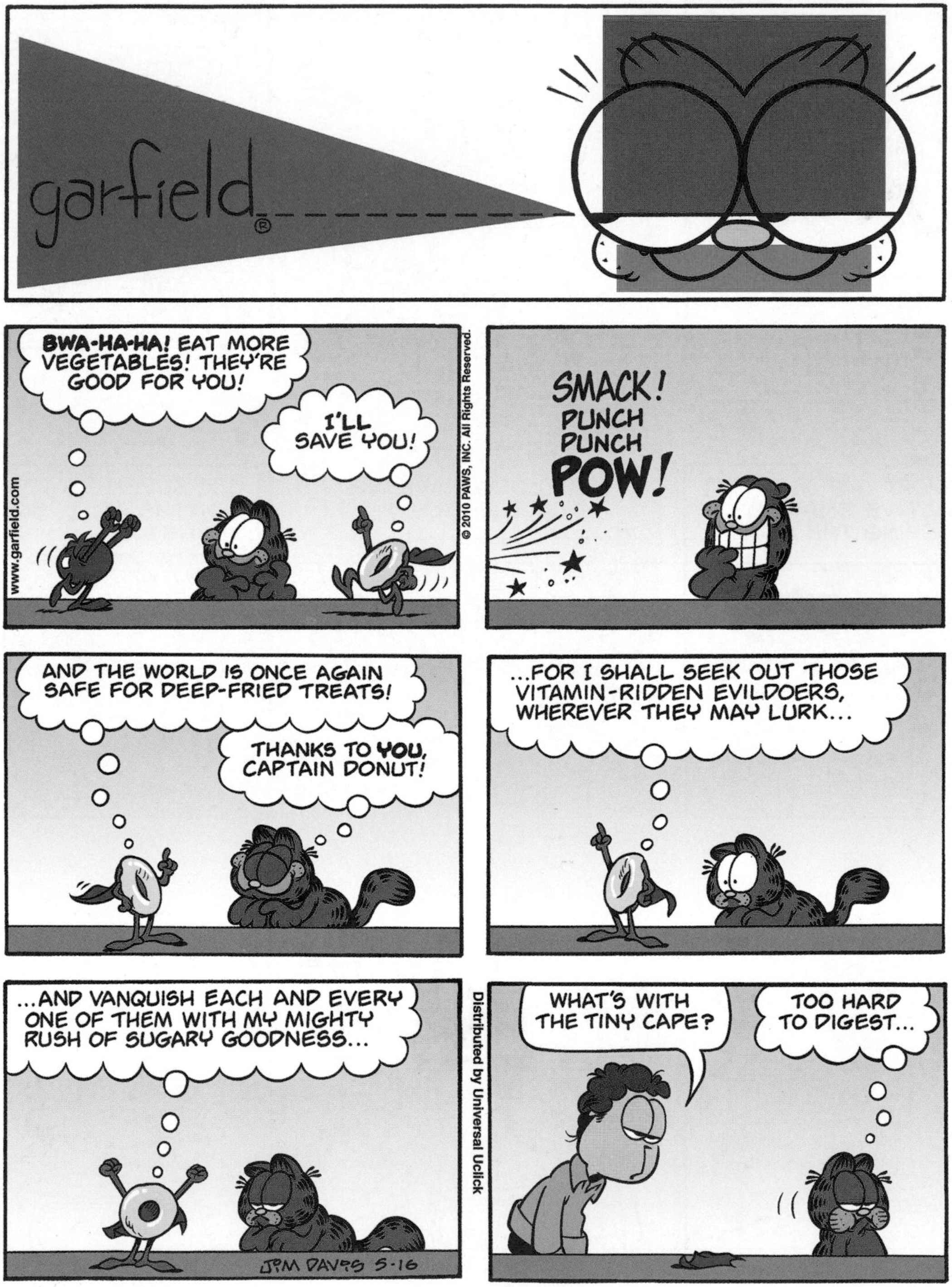
garfield
BWA-HA-HA! EAT MORE VEGETABLES! THEY'RE GOOD FOR YOU!
I'LL SAVE YOU!
www.garfield.com
© 2010 PAWS, INC. All Rights Reserved.
SMACK! PUNCH PUNCH POW!
AND THE WORLD IS ONCE AGAIN SAFE FOR DEEP-FRIED TREATS!
THANKS TO YOU, CAPTAIN DONUT!
...FOR I SHALL SEEK OUT THOSE VITAMIN-RIDDEN EVILDOERS, WHEREVER THEY MAY LURK...
...AND VANQUISH EACH AND EVERY ONE OF THEM WITH MY MIGHTY RUSH OF SUGARY GOODNESS...
JIM DAVIS 5-16
Distributed by Universal Uclick
WHAT'S WITH THE TINY CAPE?
TOO HARD TO DIGEST...

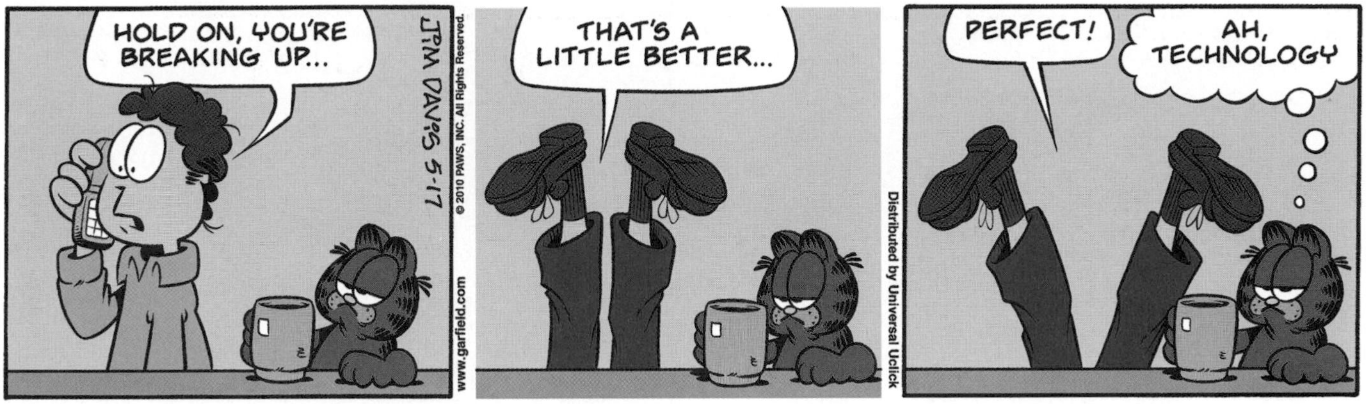
HOLD ON, YOU'RE BREAKING UP...
JIM DAVIS 5-17
© 2010 PAWS, INC. All Rights Reserved.
www.garfield.com
THAT'S A LITTLE BETTER...
Distributed by Universal Uclick
PERFECT!
AH, TECHNOLOGY

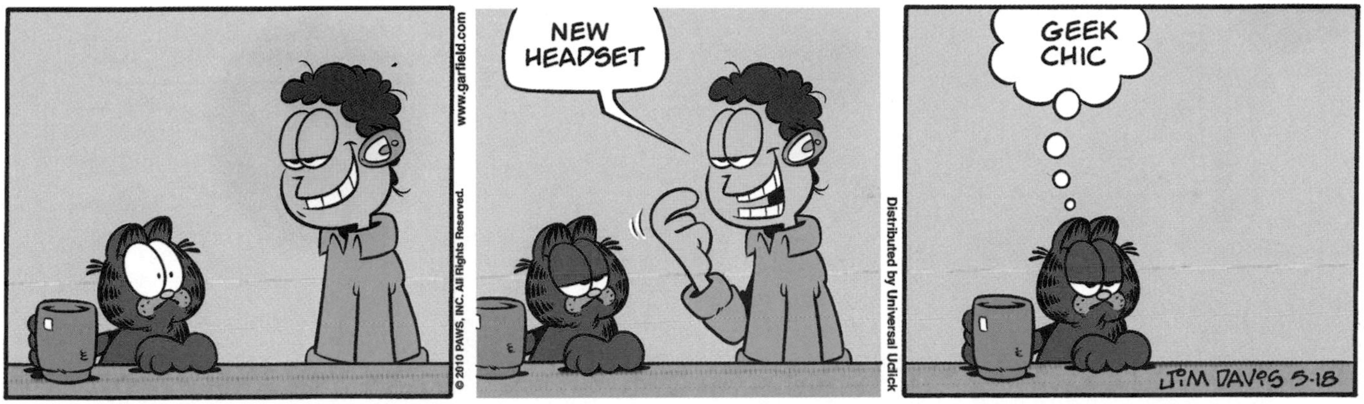
© 2010 PAWS, INC. All Rights Reserved.
www.garfield.com
NEW HEADSET
Distributed by Universal Uclick
GEEK CHIC
JIM DAVIS 5-18

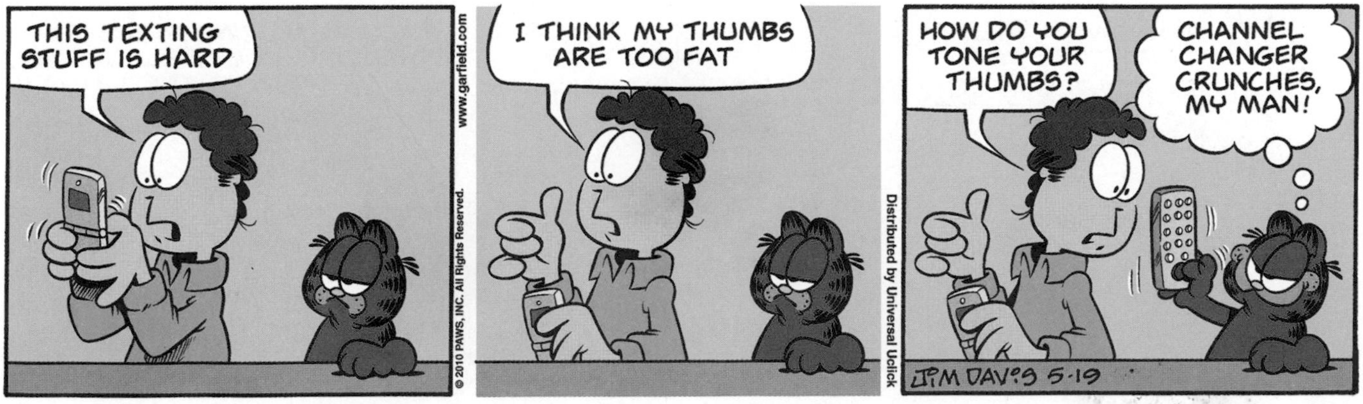
THIS TEXTING STUFF IS HARD
© 2010 PAWS, INC. All Rights Reserved.
www.garfield.com
I THINK MY THUMBS ARE TOO FAT
Distributed by Universal Uclick
HOW DO YOU TONE YOUR THUMBS?
CHANNEL CHANGER CRUNCHES, MY MAN!
JIM DAVIS 5-19

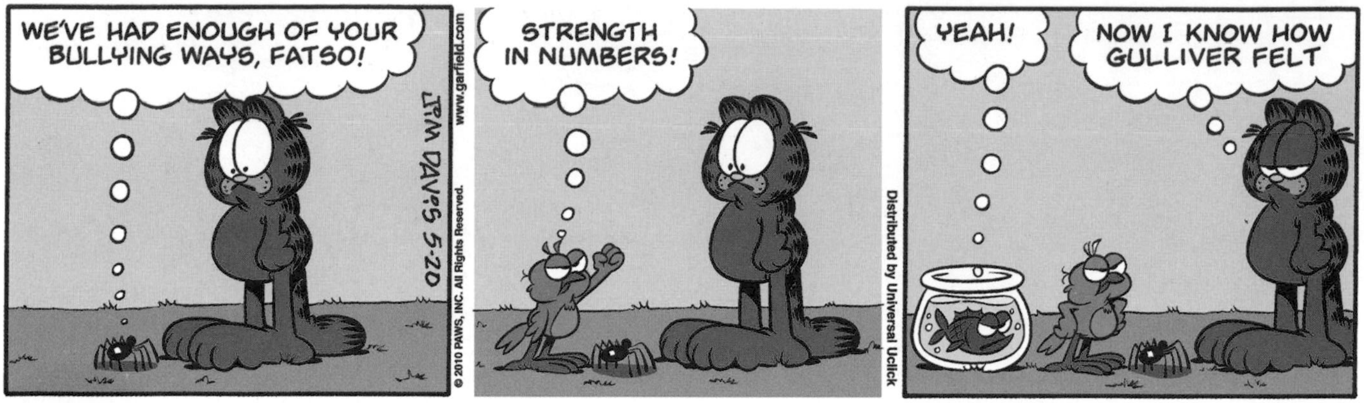
WE'VE HAD ENOUGH OF YOUR BULLYING WAYS, FATSO!
STRENGTH IN NUMBERS!
YEAH!
NOW I KNOW HOW GULLIVER FELT
JIM DAVIS 5-20
© 2010 PAWS, INC. All Rights Reserved. www.garfield.com
Distributed by Universal Uclick

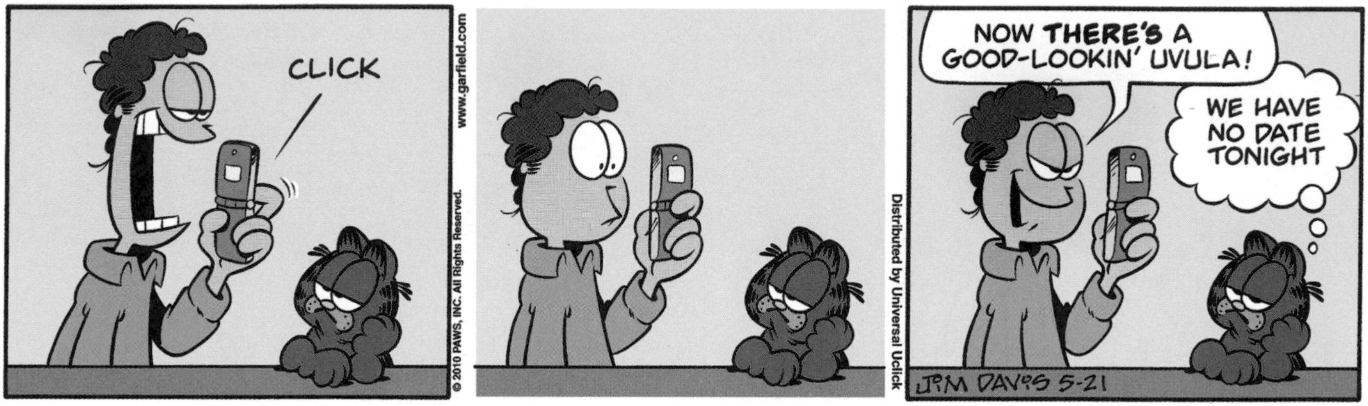
CLICK
NOW THERE'S A GOOD-LOOKIN' UVULA!
WE HAVE NO DATE TONIGHT
JIM DAVIS 5-21
© 2010 PAWS, INC. All Rights Reserved. www.garfield.com
Distributed by Universal Uclick

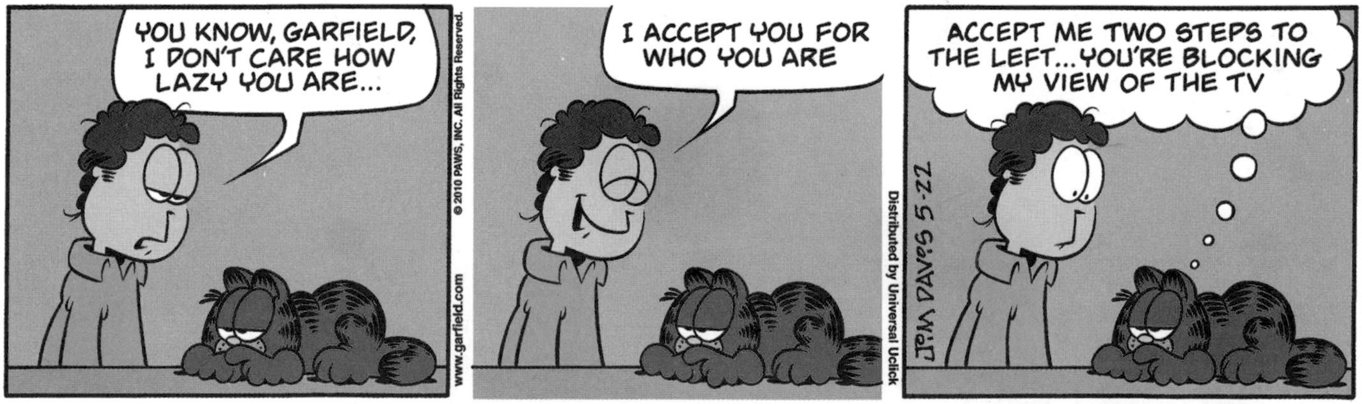
YOU KNOW, GARFIELD, I DON'T CARE HOW LAZY YOU ARE...
I ACCEPT YOU FOR WHO YOU ARE
ACCEPT ME TWO STEPS TO THE LEFT...YOU'RE BLOCKING MY VIEW OF THE TV
JIM DAVIS 5-22
© 2010 PAWS, INC. All Rights Reserved. www.garfield.com
Distributed by Universal Uclick

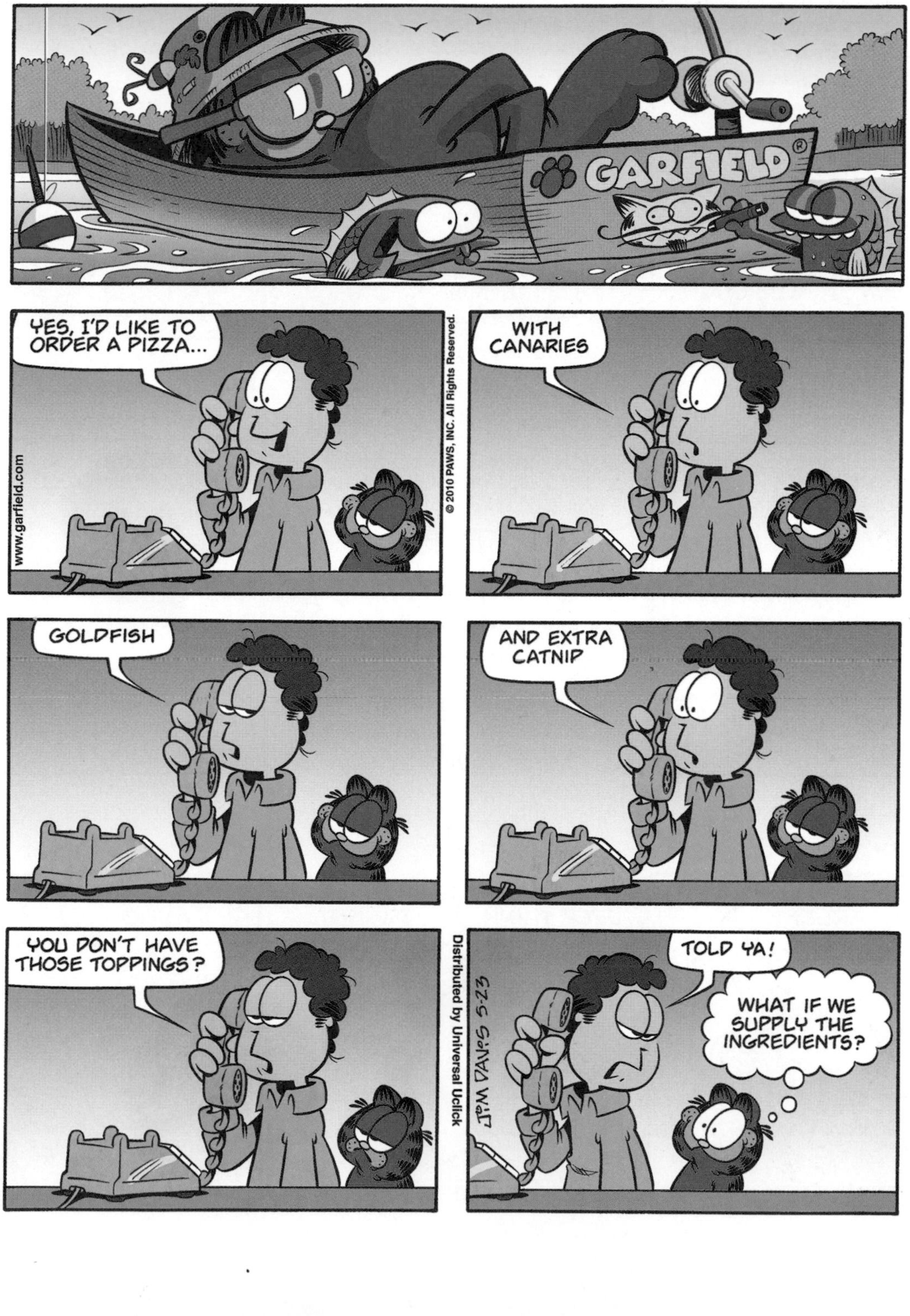
GARFIELD®
www.garfield.com
YES, I'D LIKE TO ORDER A PIZZA...
© 2010 PAWS, INC. All Rights Reserved.
WITH CANARIES
GOLDFISH
AND EXTRA CATNIP
YOU DON'T HAVE THOSE TOPPINGS?
Distributed by Universal Uclick
JIM DAVIS 5-23
TOLD YA!
WHAT IF WE SUPPLY THE INGREDIENTS?

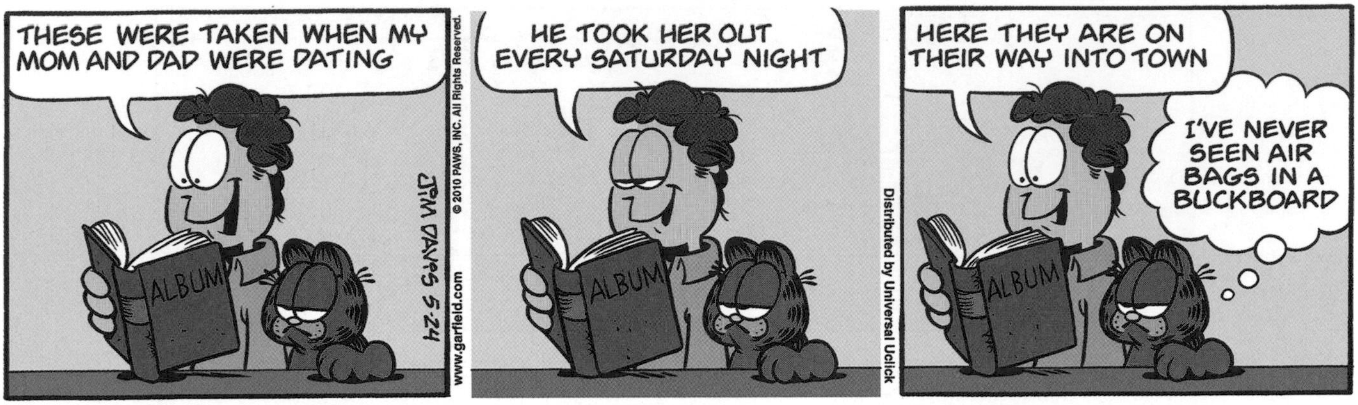
THESE WERE TAKEN WHEN MY MOM AND DAD WERE DATING
HE TOOK HER OUT EVERY SATURDAY NIGHT
HERE THEY ARE ON THEIR WAY INTO TOWN
I'VE NEVER SEEN AIR BAGS IN A BUCKBOARD
ALBUM
JIM DAVIS 5-24
© 2010 PAWS, INC. All Rights Reserved.
www.garfield.com
Distributed by Universal Uclick

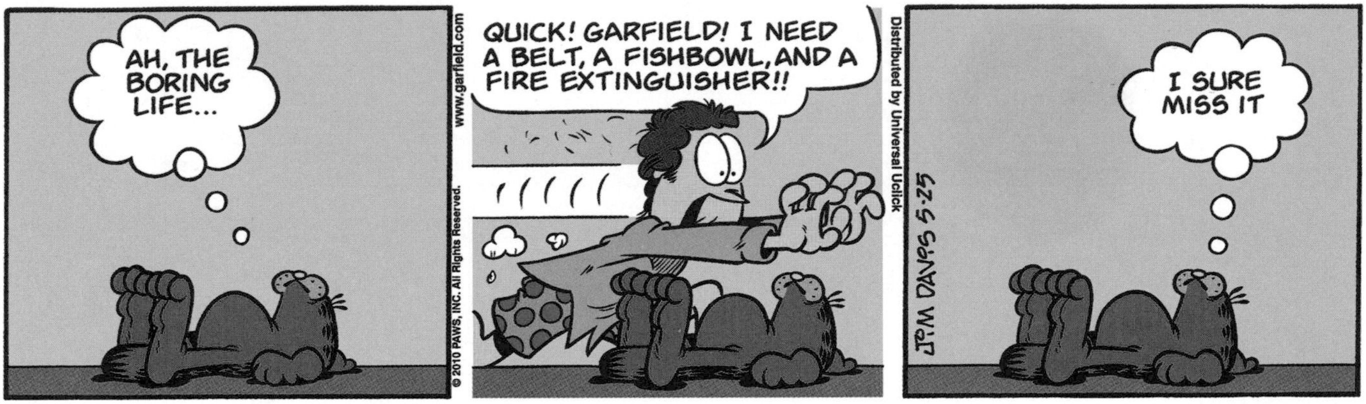
AH, THE BORING LIFE...
QUICK! GARFIELD! I NEED A BELT, A FISHBOWL, AND A FIRE EXTINGUISHER!!
I SURE MISS IT
JIM DAVIS 5-25
© 2010 PAWS, INC. All Rights Reserved.
www.garfield.com
Distributed by Universal Uclick

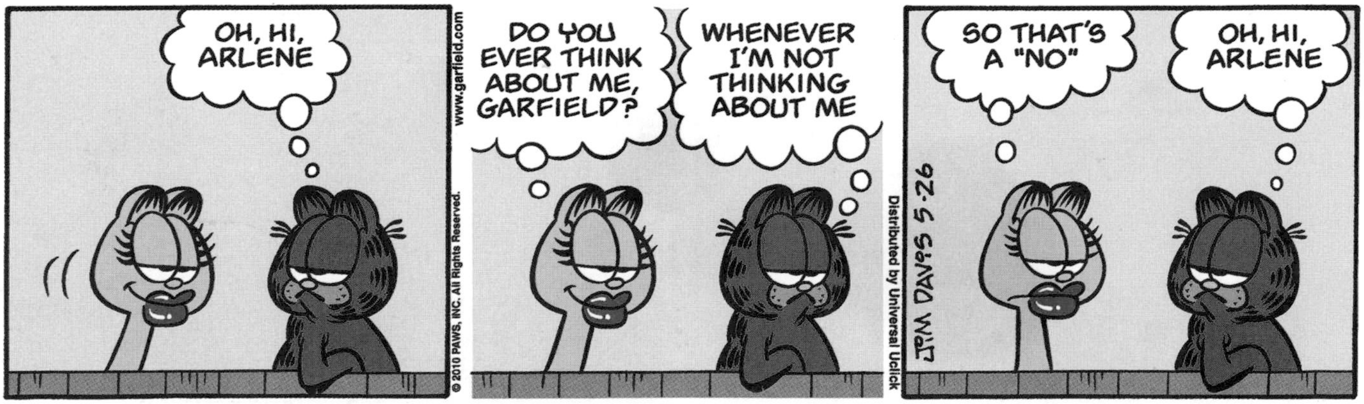
OH, HI, ARLENE
DO YOU EVER THINK ABOUT ME, GARFIELD?
WHENEVER I'M NOT THINKING ABOUT ME
SO THAT'S A "NO"
OH, HI, ARLENE
JIM DAVIS 5-26
© 2010 PAWS, INC. All Rights Reserved.
www.garfield.com
Distributed by Universal Uclick

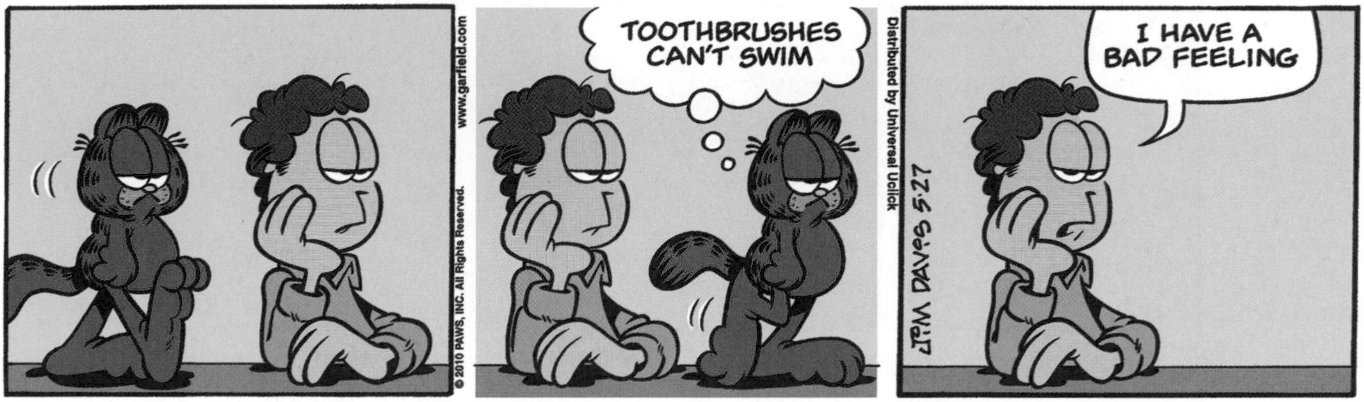
© 2010 PAWS, INC. All Rights Reserved.
www.garfield.com
TOOTHBRUSHES CAN'T SWIM
Distributed by Universal Uclick
JIM DAVIS 5-27
I HAVE A BAD FEELING

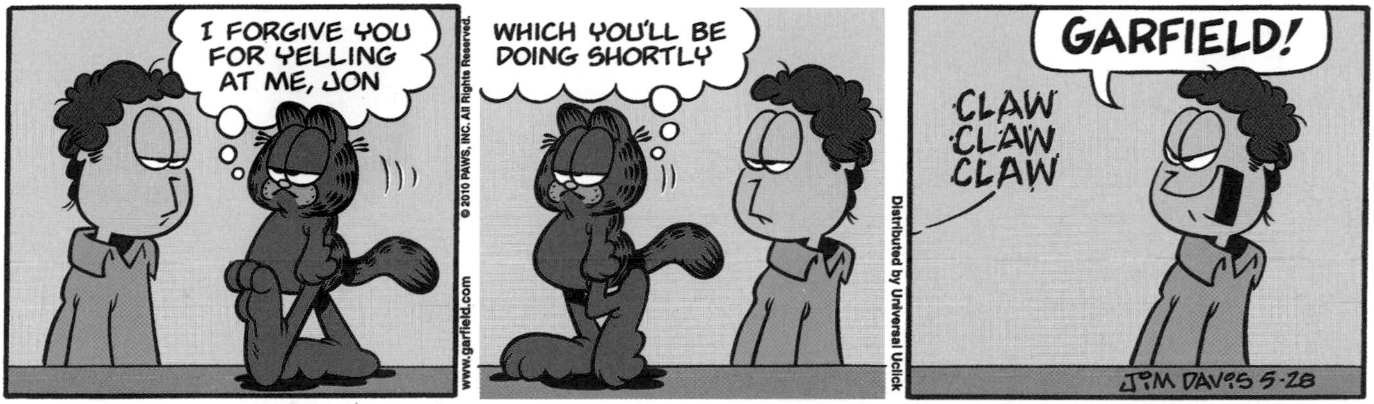
I FORGIVE YOU FOR YELLING AT ME, JON
www.garfield.com
© 2010 PAWS, INC. All Rights Reserved.
WHICH YOU'LL BE DOING SHORTLY
Distributed by Universal Uclick
CLAW CLAW CLAW
GARFIELD!
JIM DAVIS 5-28

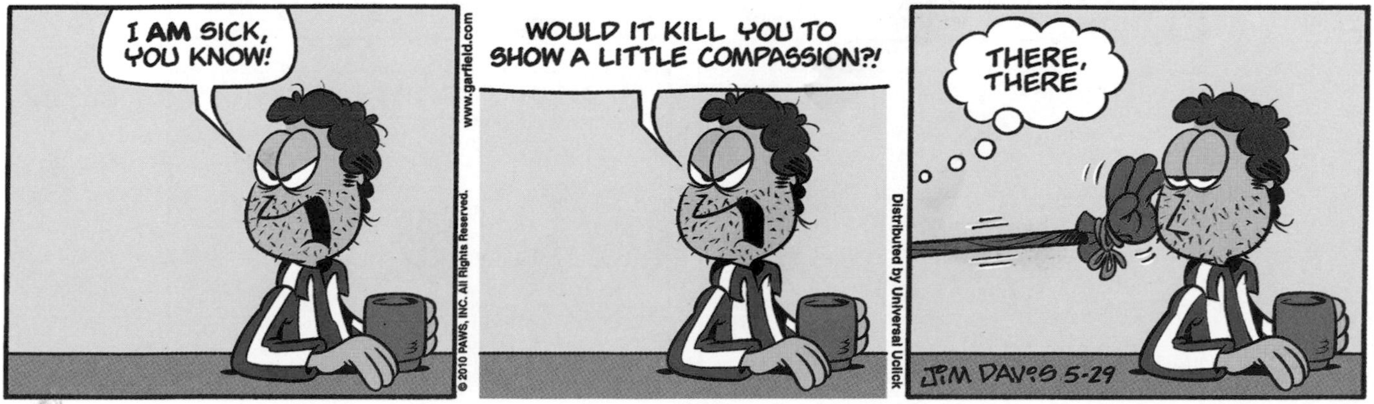
I AM SICK, YOU KNOW!
© 2010 PAWS, INC. All Rights Reserved.
www.garfield.com
WOULD IT KILL YOU TO SHOW A LITTLE COMPASSION?!
Distributed by Universal Uclick
THERE, THERE
JIM DAVIS 5-29

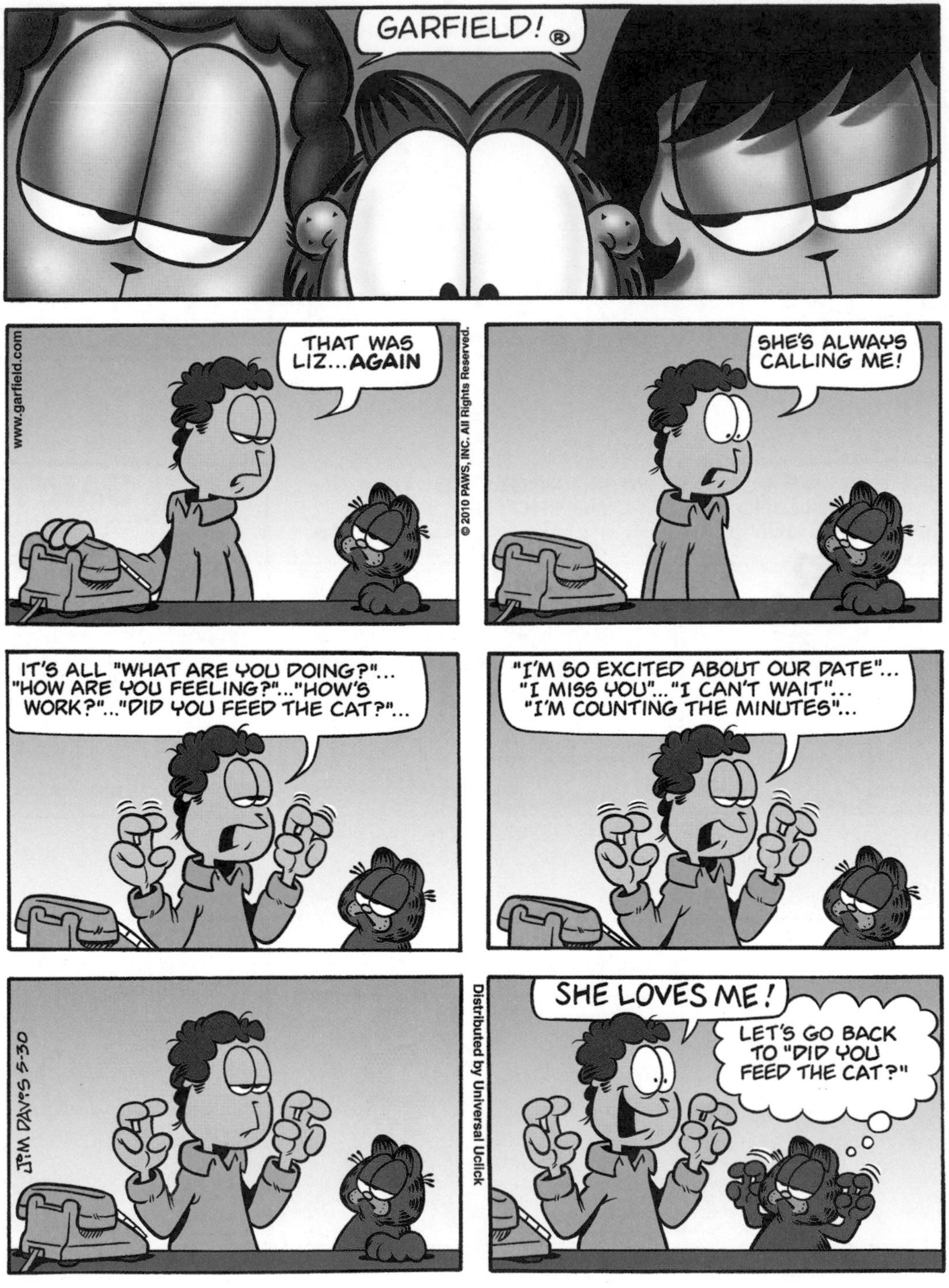
GARFIELD!®
www.garfield.com
THAT WAS LIZ...AGAIN
© 2010 PAWS, INC. All Rights Reserved.
SHE'S ALWAYS CALLING ME!
IT'S ALL "WHAT ARE YOU DOING?"... "HOW ARE YOU FEELING?"..."HOW'S WORK?"..."DID YOU FEED THE CAT?"...
"I'M SO EXCITED ABOUT OUR DATE"... "I MISS YOU"..."I CAN'T WAIT"... "I'M COUNTING THE MINUTES"...
JIM DAVIS 5-30
Distributed by Universal Uclick
SHE LOVES ME!
LET'S GO BACK TO "DID YOU FEED THE CAT?"

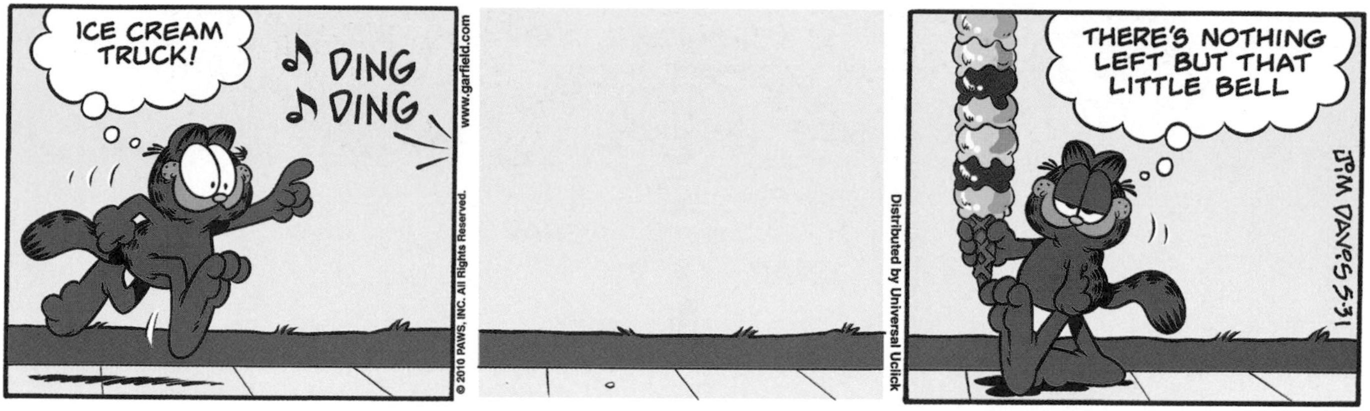
ICE CREAM TRUCK!
DING
DING
© 2010 PAWS, INC. All Rights Reserved. www.garfield.com
Distributed by Universal Uclick
THERE'S NOTHING LEFT BUT THAT LITTLE BELL
JIM DAVIS 5-31

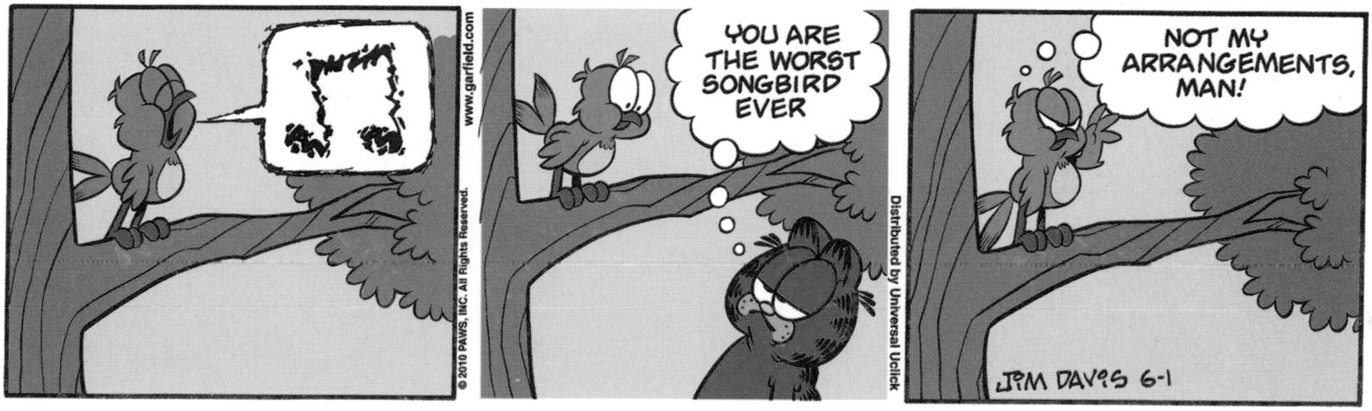
© 2010 PAWS, INC. All Rights Reserved. www.garfield.com
YOU ARE THE WORST SONGBIRD EVER
Distributed by Universal Uclick
NOT MY ARRANGEMENTS, MAN!
JIM DAVIS 6-1

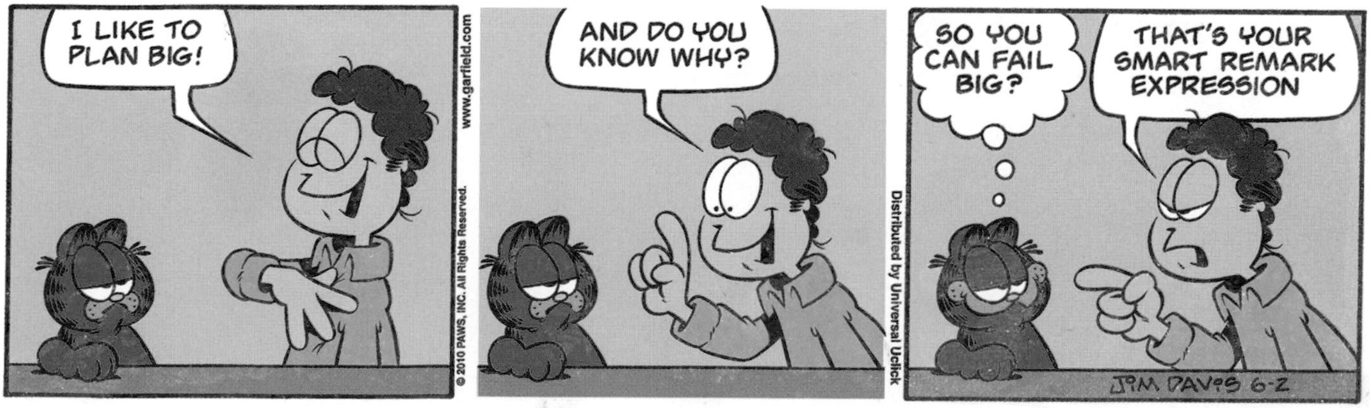
I LIKE TO PLAN BIG!
© 2010 PAWS, INC. All Rights Reserved. www.garfield.com
AND DO YOU KNOW WHY?
Distributed by Universal Uclick
SO YOU CAN FAIL BIG?
THAT'S YOUR SMART REMARK EXPRESSION
JIM DAVIS 6-2

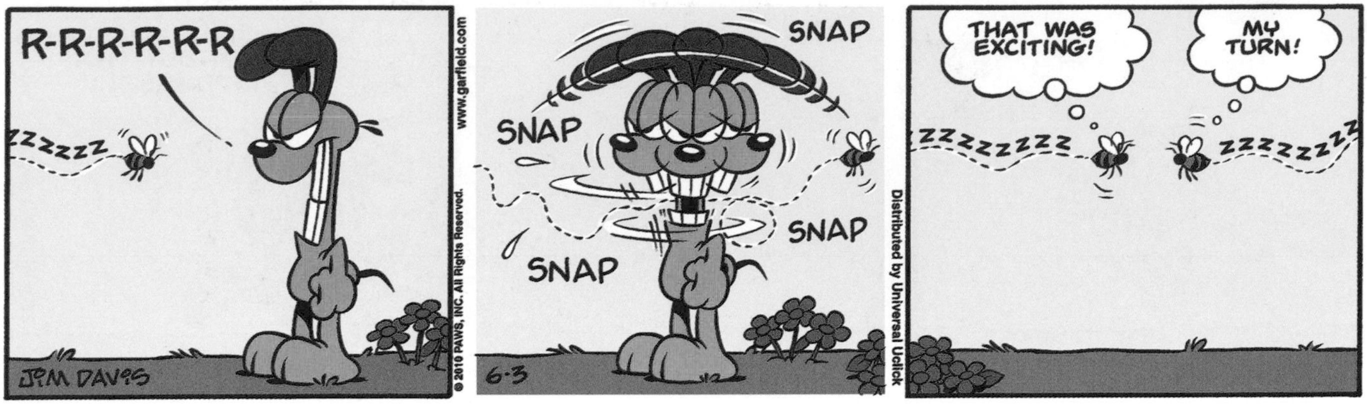
R-R-R-R-R-R
ZZZZZZ
JIM DAVIS
www.garfield.com
© 2010 PAWS, INC. All Rights Reserved.
SNAP
SNAP
SNAP
SNAP
6-3
Distributed by Universal Uclick
THAT WAS EXCITING!
MY TURN!
ZZZZZZZZ
ZZZZZZZZ

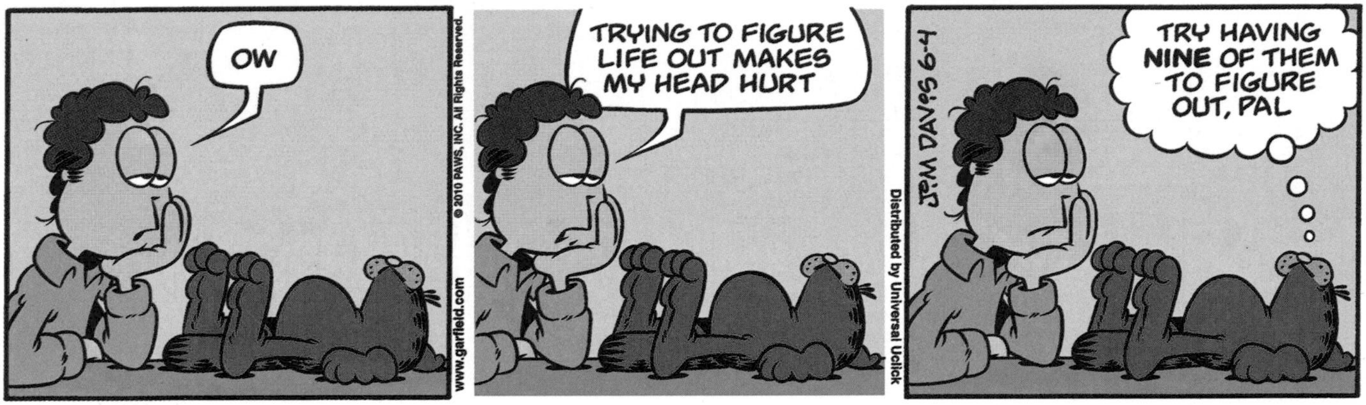
OW
© 2010 PAWS, INC. All Rights Reserved.
www.garfield.com
TRYING TO FIGURE LIFE OUT MAKES MY HEAD HURT
JIM DAVIS 6-4
Distributed by Universal Uclick
TRY HAVING NINE OF THEM TO FIGURE OUT, PAL

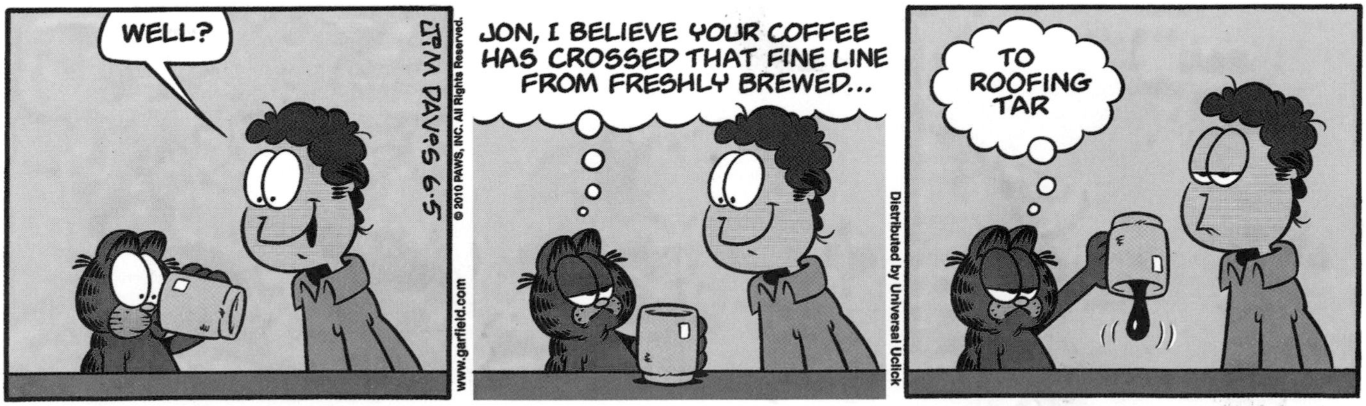
WELL?
JIM DAVIS 6-5
© 2010 PAWS, INC. All Rights Reserved.
www.garfield.com
JON, I BELIEVE YOUR COFFEE HAS CROSSED THAT FINE LINE FROM FRESHLY BREWED...
Distributed by Universal Uclick
TO ROOFING TAR

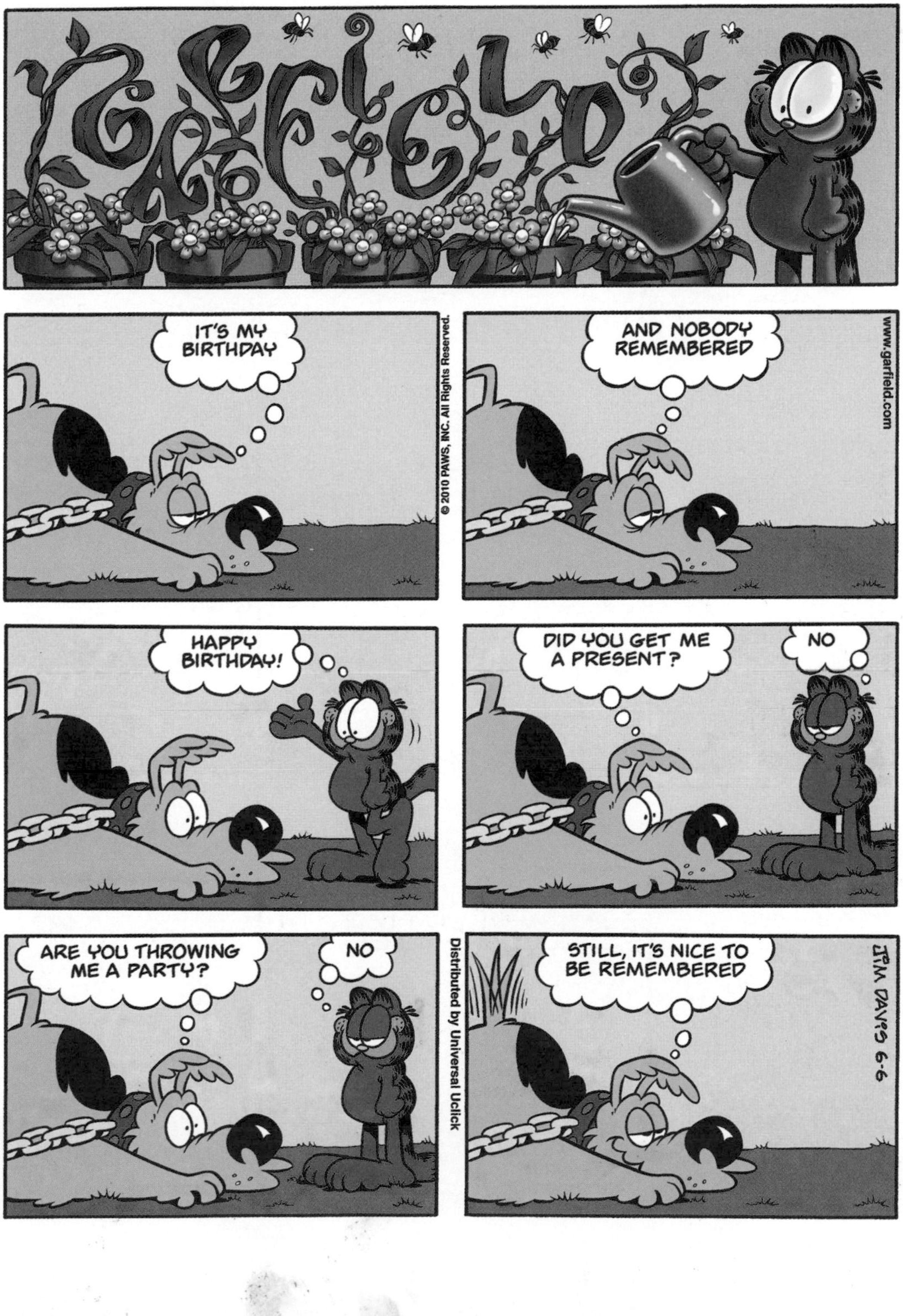
GARFIELD
IT'S MY BIRTHDAY
AND NOBODY REMEMBERED
HAPPY BIRTHDAY!
DID YOU GET ME A PRESENT?
NO
ARE YOU THROWING ME A PARTY?
NO
STILL, IT'S NICE TO BE REMEMBERED
JIM DAVIS 6-6

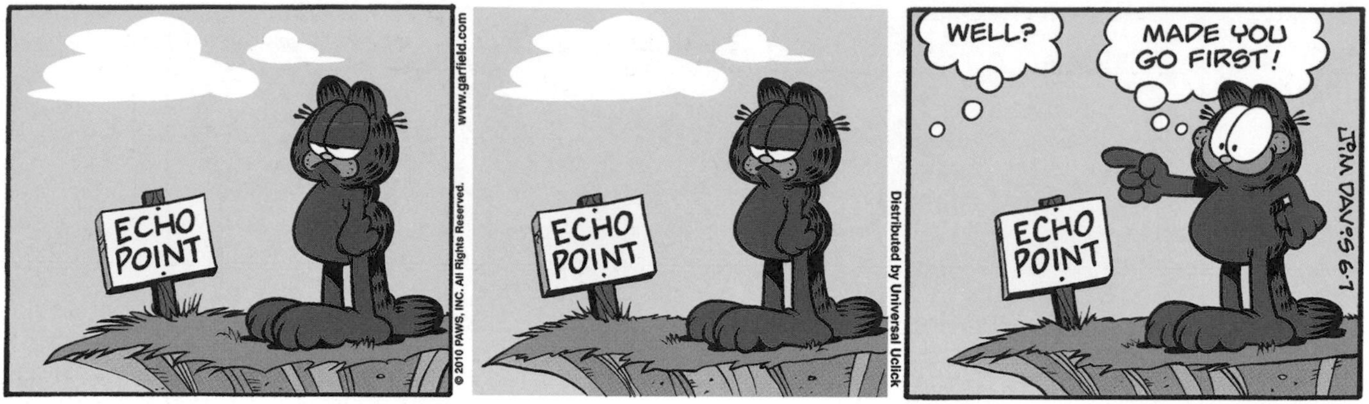
ECHO POINT
© 2010 PAWS, INC. All Rights Reserved. www.garfield.com
Distributed by Universal Uclick
WELL?
MADE YOU GO FIRST!
JPM DAVPS 6-7

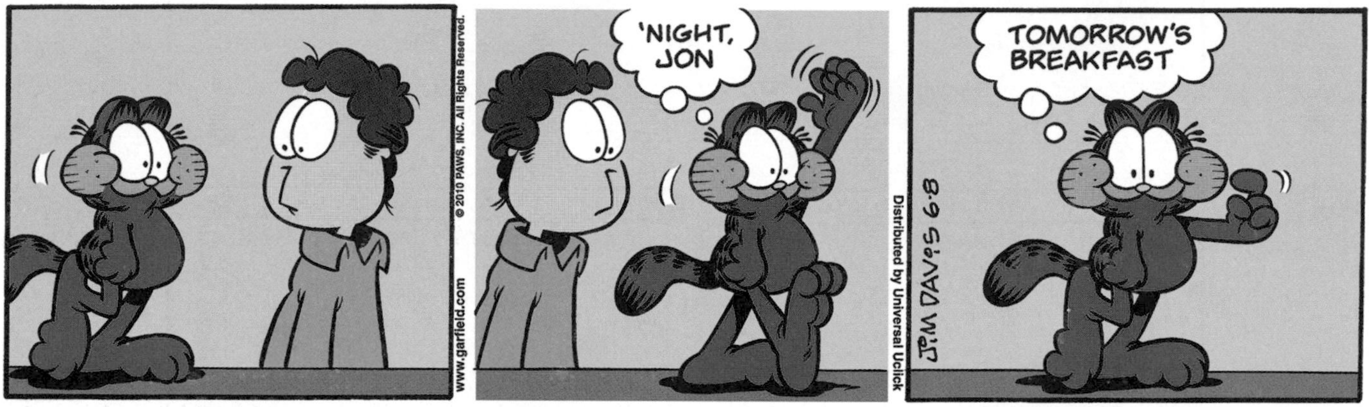
© 2010 PAWS, INC. All Rights Reserved. www.garfield.com
'NIGHT, JON
Distributed by Universal Uclick
TOMORROW'S BREAKFAST
JPM DAVPS 6-8

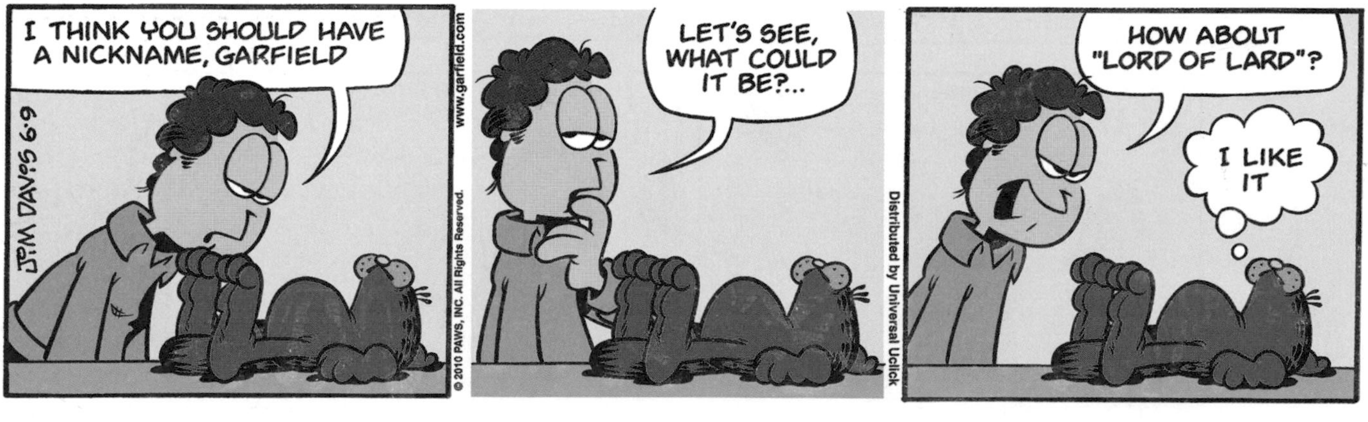
I THINK YOU SHOULD HAVE A NICKNAME, GARFIELD
JPM DAVPS 6-9
© 2010 PAWS, INC. All Rights Reserved. www.garfield.com
LET'S SEE, WHAT COULD IT BE?...
Distributed by Universal Uclick
HOW ABOUT "LORD OF LARD"?
I LIKE IT

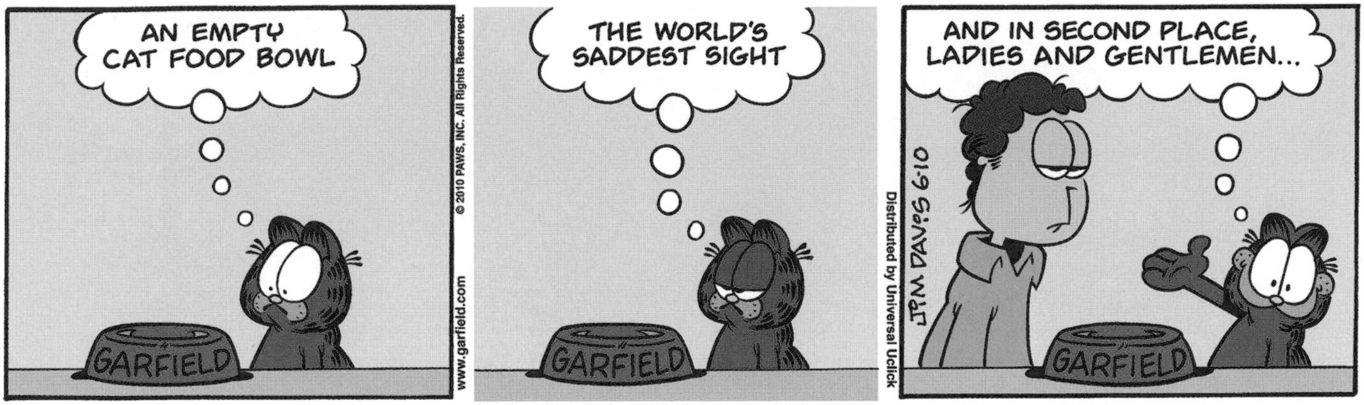
AN EMPTY CAT FOOD BOWL
GARFIELD
© 2010 PAWS, INC. All Rights Reserved.
www.garfield.com
THE WORLD'S SADDEST SIGHT
GARFIELD
Distributed by Universal Uclick
AND IN SECOND PLACE, LADIES AND GENTLEMEN...
JIM DAVIS 6·10
GARFIELD

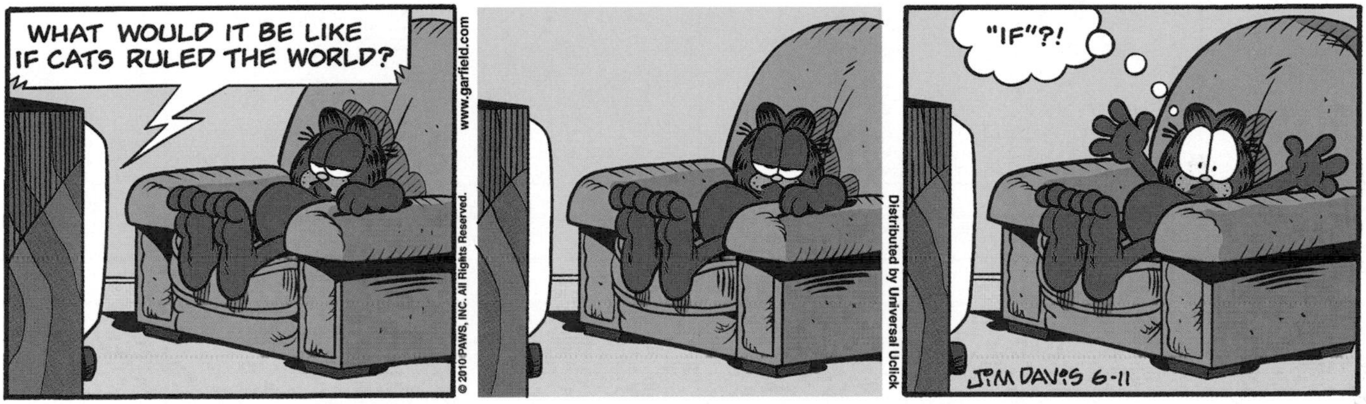
WHAT WOULD IT BE LIKE IF CATS RULED THE WORLD?
www.garfield.com
© 2010 PAWS, INC. All Rights Reserved.
Distributed by Universal Uclick
"IF"?!
JIM DAVIS 6-11

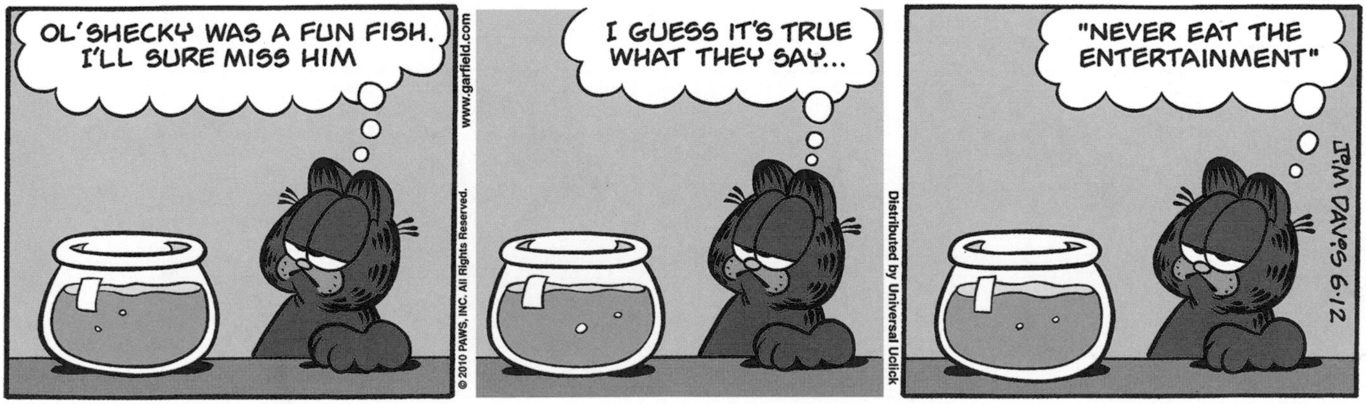
OL' SHECKY WAS A FUN FISH. I'LL SURE MISS HIM
www.garfield.com
© 2010 PAWS, INC. All Rights Reserved.
I GUESS IT'S TRUE WHAT THEY SAY...
Distributed by Universal Uclick
"NEVER EAT THE ENTERTAINMENT"
JIM DAVIS 6·12

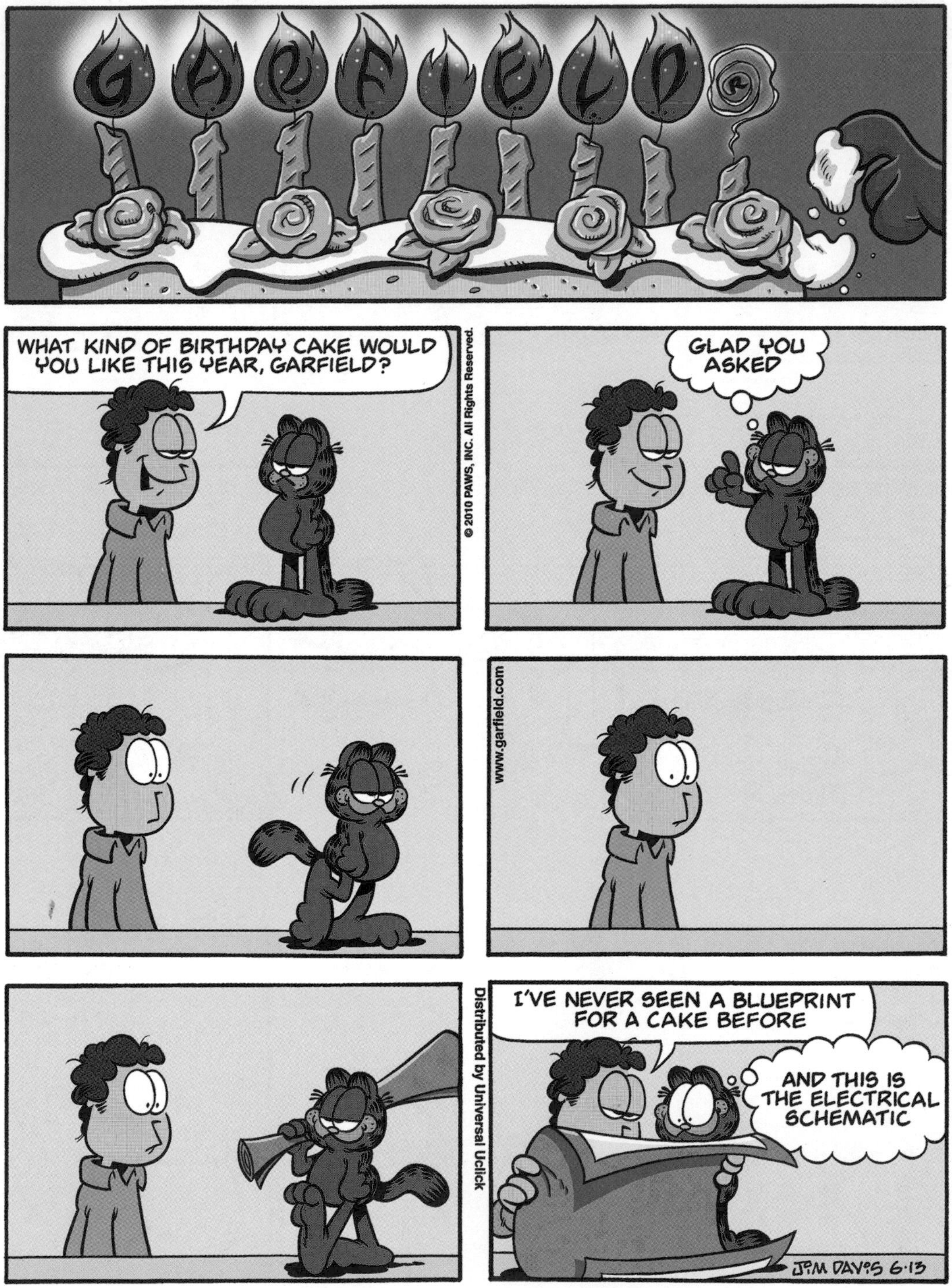
GARFIELD®
WHAT KIND OF BIRTHDAY CAKE WOULD YOU LIKE THIS YEAR, GARFIELD?
© 2010 PAWS, INC. All Rights Reserved.
GLAD YOU ASKED
www.garfield.com
Distributed by Universal Uclick
I'VE NEVER SEEN A BLUEPRINT FOR A CAKE BEFORE
AND THIS IS THE ELECTRICAL SCHEMATIC
JIM DAVIS 6-13

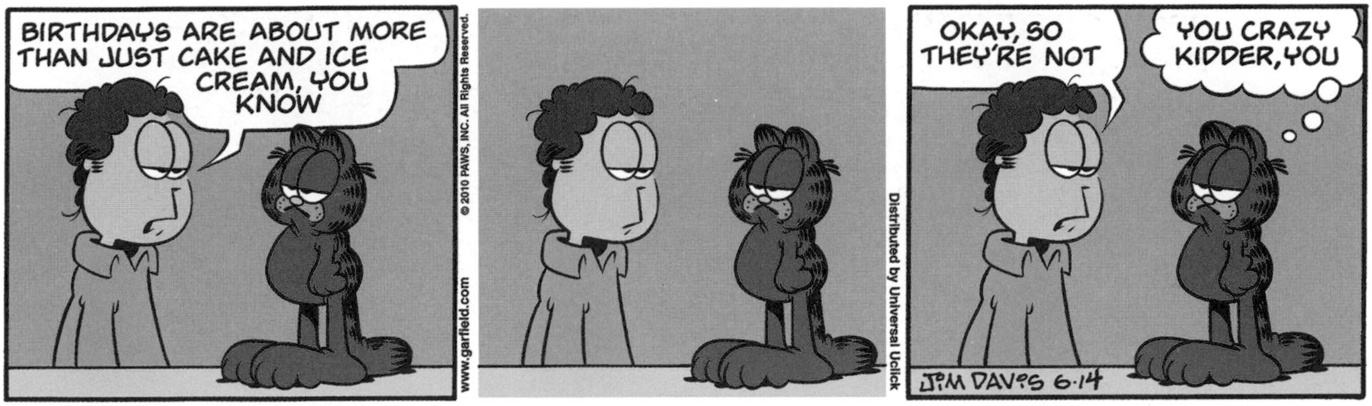
BIRTHDAYS ARE ABOUT MORE THAN JUST CAKE AND ICE CREAM, YOU KNOW
OKAY, SO THEY'RE NOT
YOU CRAZY KIDDER, YOU
JIM DAVIS 6-14
© 2010 PAWS, INC. All Rights Reserved.
www.garfield.com
Distributed by Universal Uclick

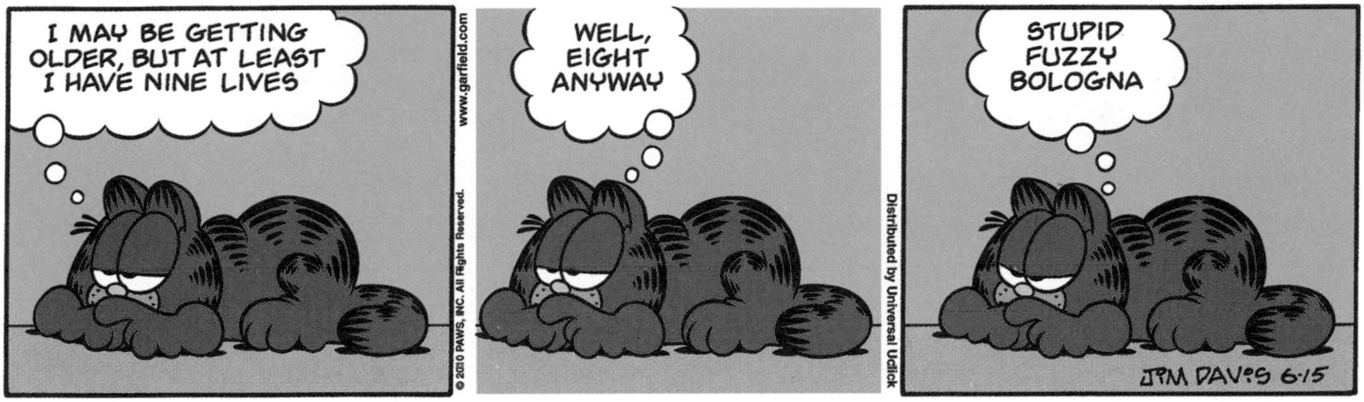
I MAY BE GETTING OLDER, BUT AT LEAST I HAVE NINE LIVES
WELL, EIGHT ANYWAY
STUPID FUZZY BOLOGNA
JIM DAVIS 6-15
www.garfield.com
© 2010 PAWS, INC. All Rights Reserved.
Distributed by Universal Uclick

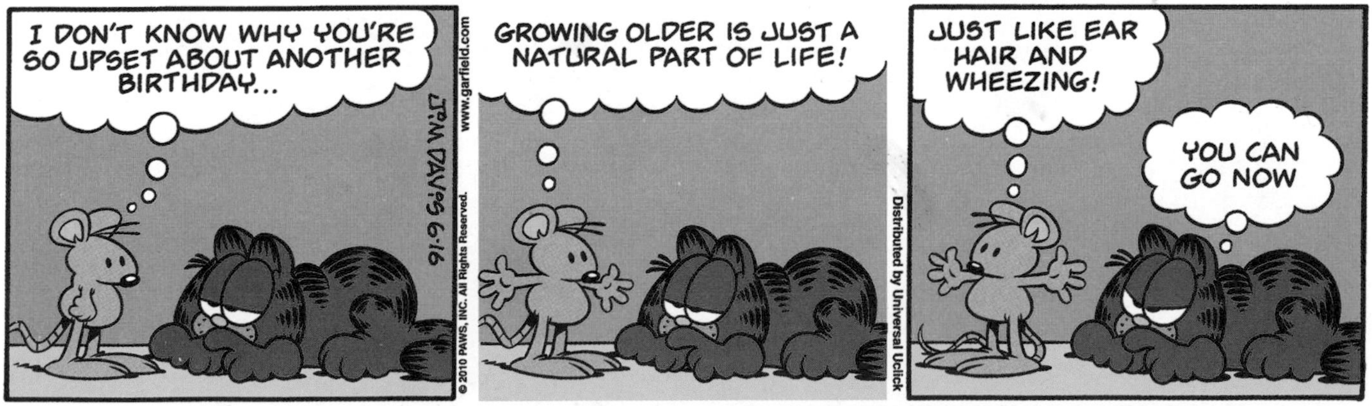
I DON'T KNOW WHY YOU'RE SO UPSET ABOUT ANOTHER BIRTHDAY...
GROWING OLDER IS JUST A NATURAL PART OF LIFE!
JUST LIKE EAR HAIR AND WHEEZING!
YOU CAN GO NOW
JIM DAVIS 6-16
www.garfield.com
© 2010 PAWS, INC. All Rights Reserved.
Distributed by Universal Uclick

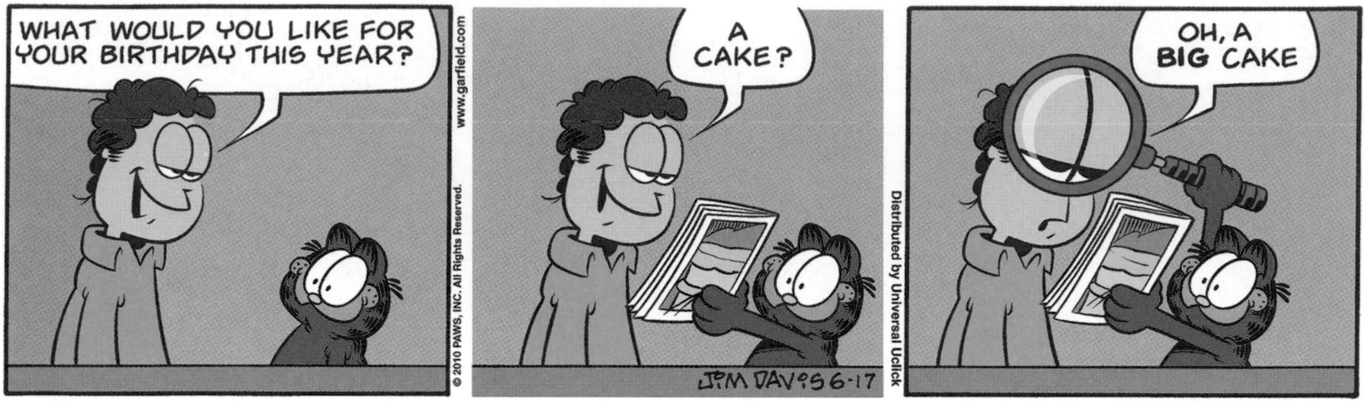
WHAT WOULD YOU LIKE FOR YOUR BIRTHDAY THIS YEAR?
A CAKE?
OH, A **BIG** CAKE
JIM DAVIS 6-17
© 2010 PAWS, INC. All Rights Reserved.
www.garfield.com
Distributed by Universal Uclick

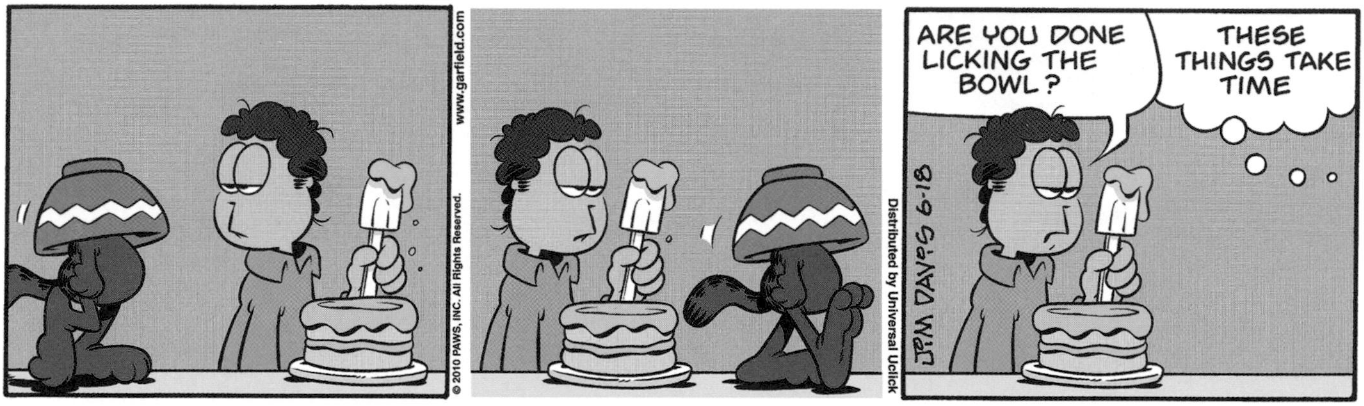
ARE YOU DONE LICKING THE BOWL?
THESE THINGS TAKE TIME
JIM DAVIS 6-18
© 2010 PAWS, INC. All Rights Reserved.
www.garfield.com
Distributed by Universal Uclick

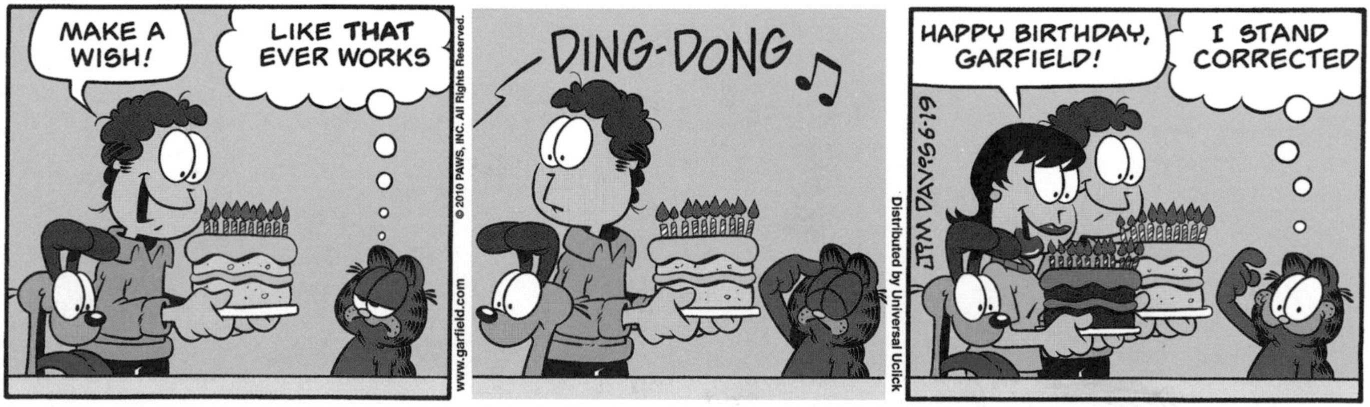
MAKE A WISH!
LIKE **THAT** EVER WORKS
DING-DONG
HAPPY BIRTHDAY, GARFIELD!
I STAND CORRECTED
JIM DAVIS 6-19
© 2010 PAWS, INC. All Rights Reserved.
www.garfield.com
Distributed by Universal Uclick

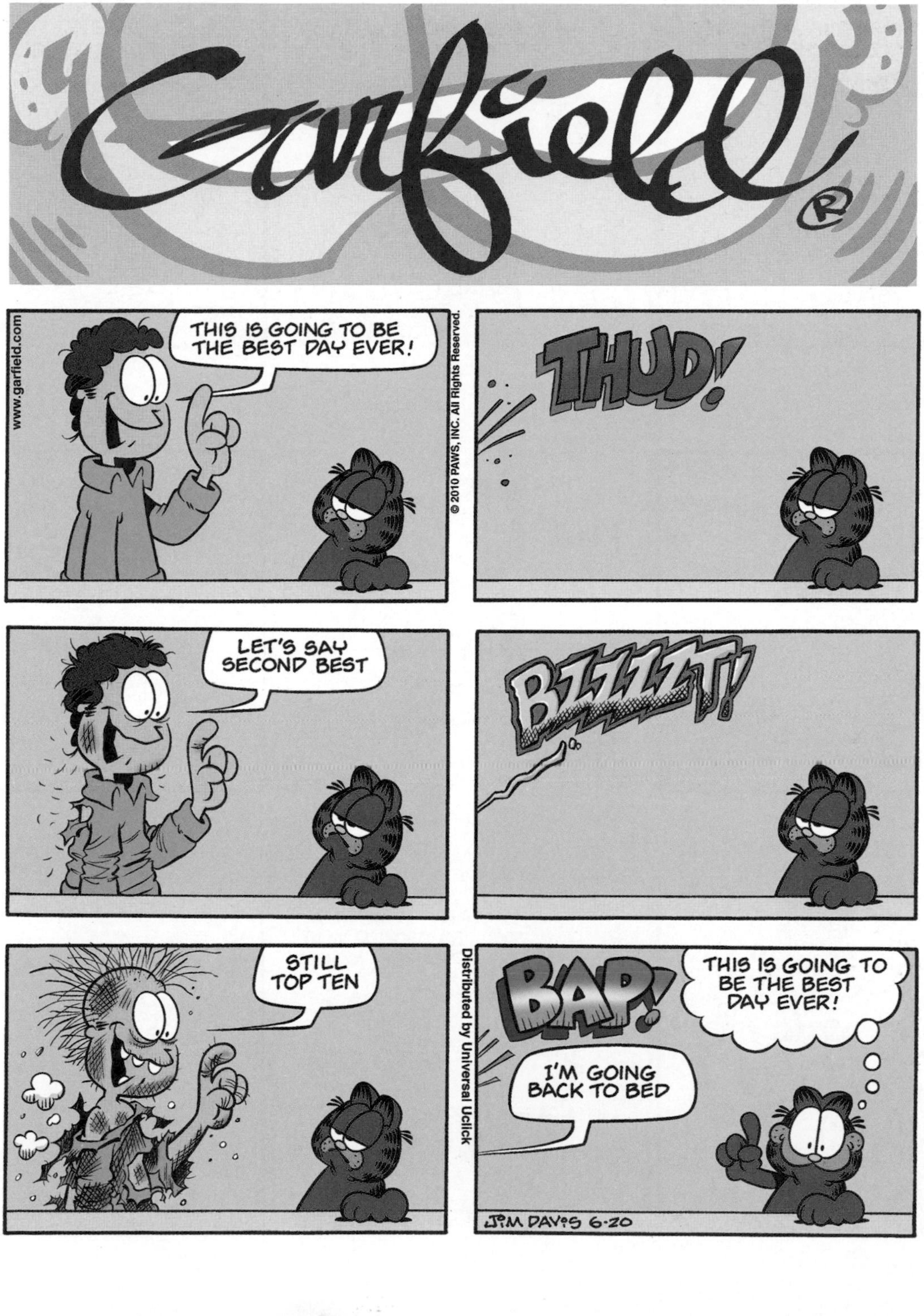
Garfield®
www.garfield.com
© 2010 PAWS, INC. All Rights Reserved.
THIS IS GOING TO BE THE BEST DAY EVER!
THUD!
LET'S SAY SECOND BEST
BZZZT!
STILL TOP TEN
Distributed by Universal Uclick
BAP!
I'M GOING BACK TO BED
THIS IS GOING TO BE THE BEST DAY EVER!
JIM DAVIS 6-20

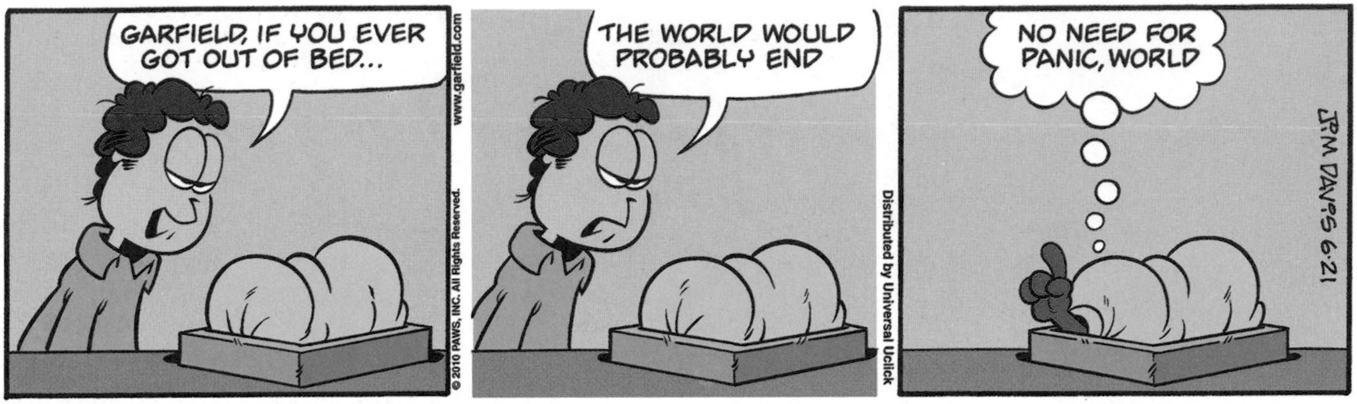
GARFIELD, IF YOU EVER GOT OUT OF BED...
THE WORLD WOULD PROBABLY END
NO NEED FOR PANIC, WORLD
JIM DAVIS 6-21
© 2010 PAWS, INC. All Rights Reserved.
www.garfield.com
Distributed by Universal Uclick

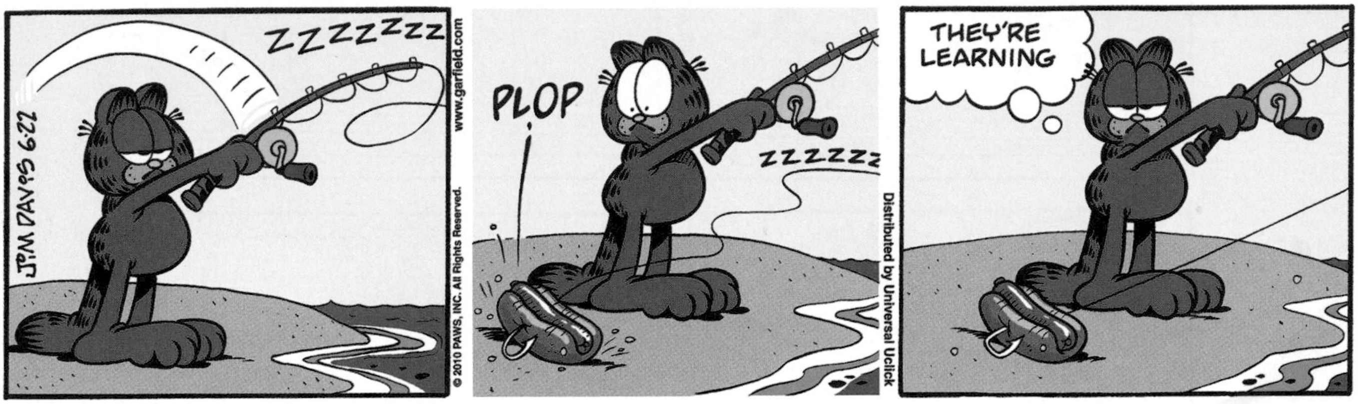
ZZZZZZZ
JIM DAVIS 6-22
PLOP
ZZZZZZ
THEY'RE LEARNING
© 2010 PAWS, INC. All Rights Reserved.
www.garfield.com
Distributed by Universal Uclick

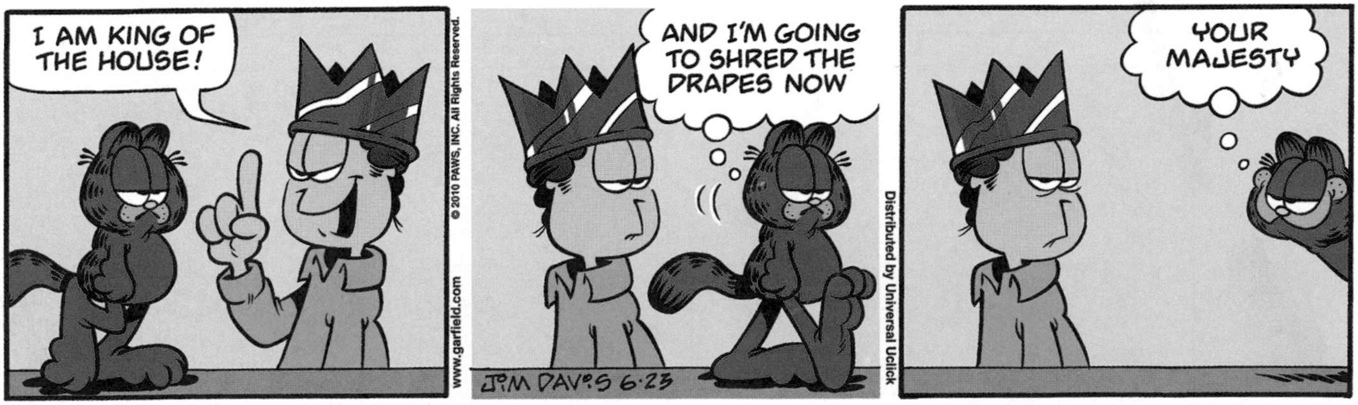
I AM KING OF THE HOUSE!
AND I'M GOING TO SHRED THE DRAPES NOW
YOUR MAJESTY
JIM DAVIS 6-23
© 2010 PAWS, INC. All Rights Reserved.
www.garfield.com
Distributed by Universal Uclick

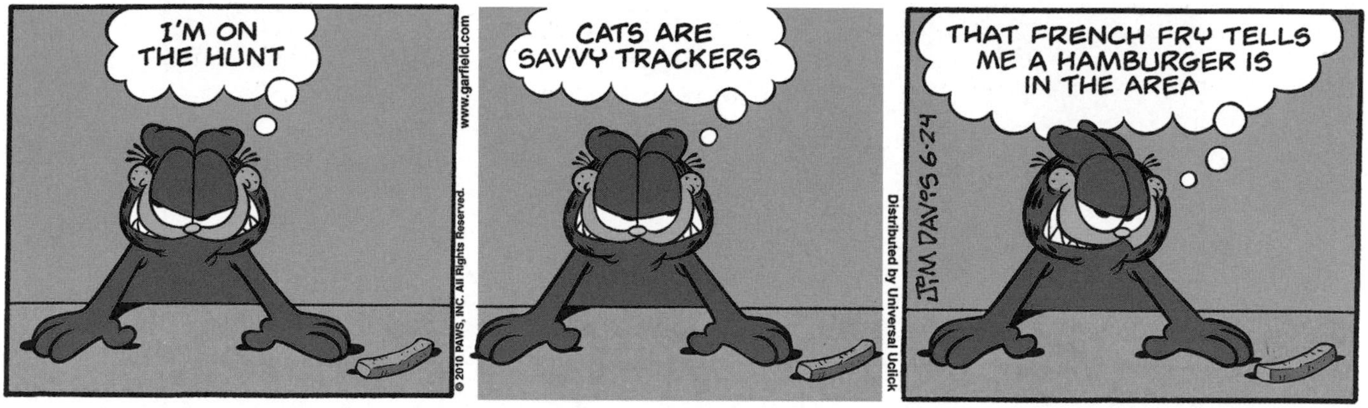
I'M ON THE HUNT
www.garfield.com
© 2010 PAWS, INC. All Rights Reserved.
CATS ARE SAVVY TRACKERS
Distributed by Universal Uclick
THAT FRENCH FRY TELLS ME A HAMBURGER IS IN THE AREA
JIM DAVIS 6·24

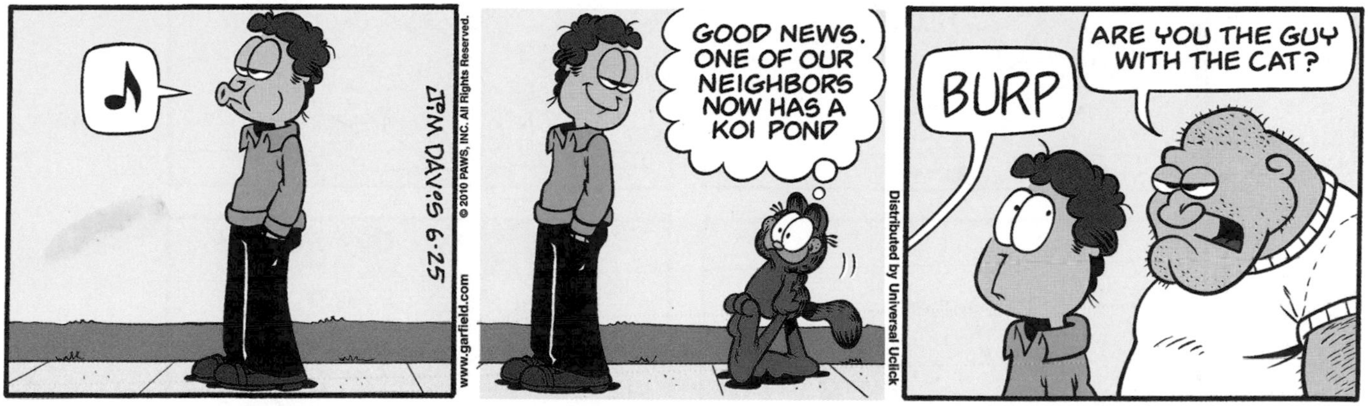
♪
JIM DAVIS 6·25
© 2010 PAWS, INC. All Rights Reserved.
www.garfield.com
GOOD NEWS. ONE OF OUR NEIGHBORS NOW HAS A KOI POND
Distributed by Universal Uclick
BURP
ARE YOU THE GUY WITH THE CAT?

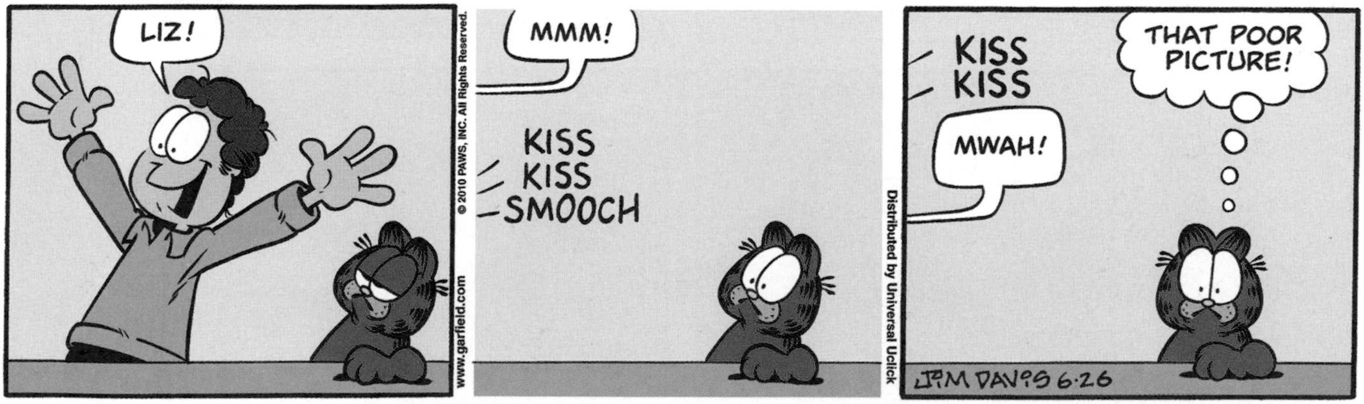
LIZ!
© 2010 PAWS, INC. All Rights Reserved.
www.garfield.com
MMM!
KISS
KISS
SMOOCH
Distributed by Universal Uclick
KISS
KISS
MWAH!
THAT POOR PICTURE!
JIM DAVIS 6·26

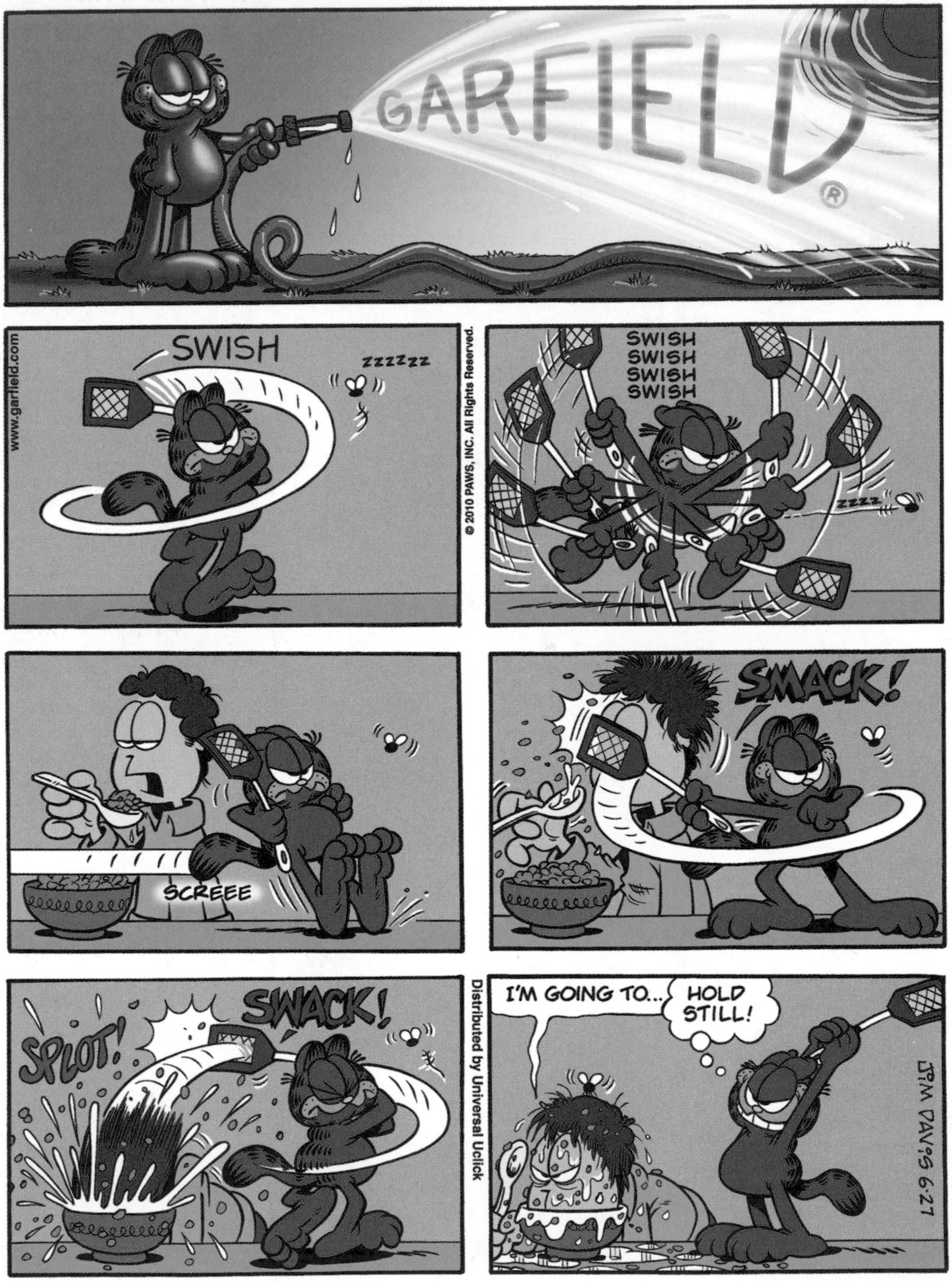
GARFIELD®
www.garfield.com
SWISH
ZZZZZZ
SWISH
SWISH
SWISH
SWISH
ZZZZ
© 2010 PAWS, INC. All Rights Reserved.
SCREEE
SMACK!
Distributed by Universal Uclick
SPLOT!
SWACK!
I'M GOING TO...
HOLD STILL!
JIM DAVIS 6-27

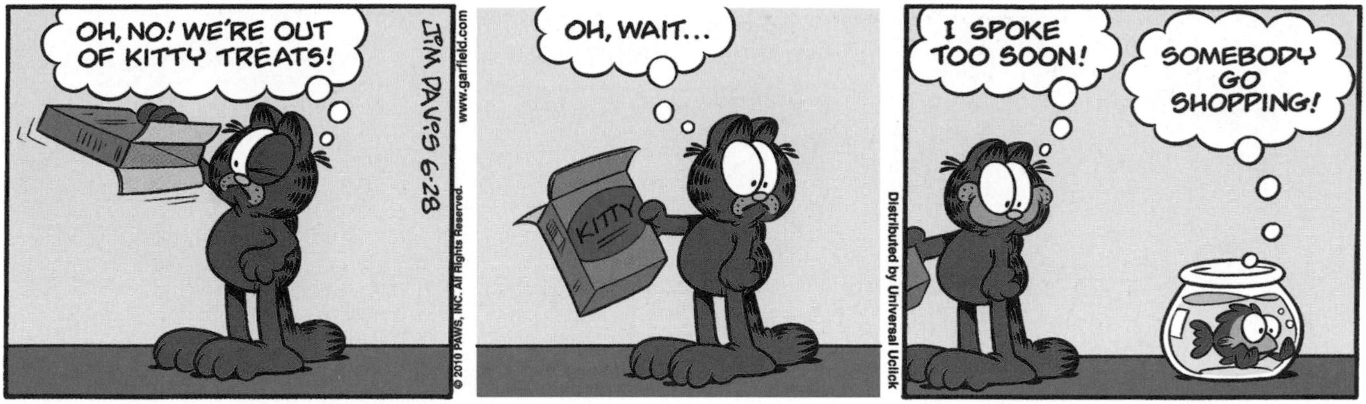
OH, NO! WE'RE OUT OF KITTY TREATS!
JIM DAVIS 6-28
© 2010 PAWS, INC. All Rights Reserved.
www.garfield.com
OH, WAIT...
KITTY
Distributed by Universal Uclick
I SPOKE TOO SOON!
SOMEBODY GO SHOPPING!

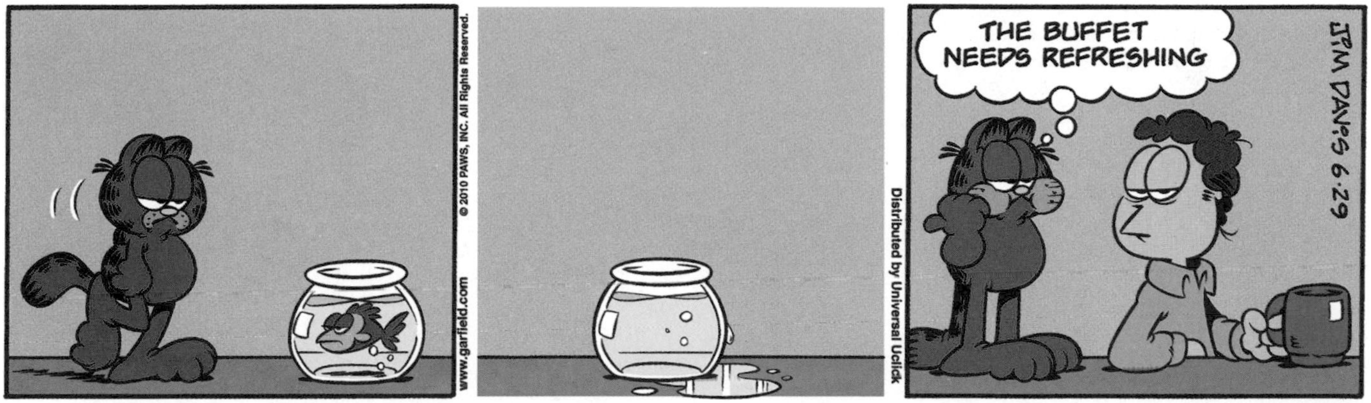
© 2010 PAWS, INC. All Rights Reserved.
www.garfield.com
Distributed by Universal Uclick
THE BUFFET NEEDS REFRESHING
JIM DAVIS 6-29

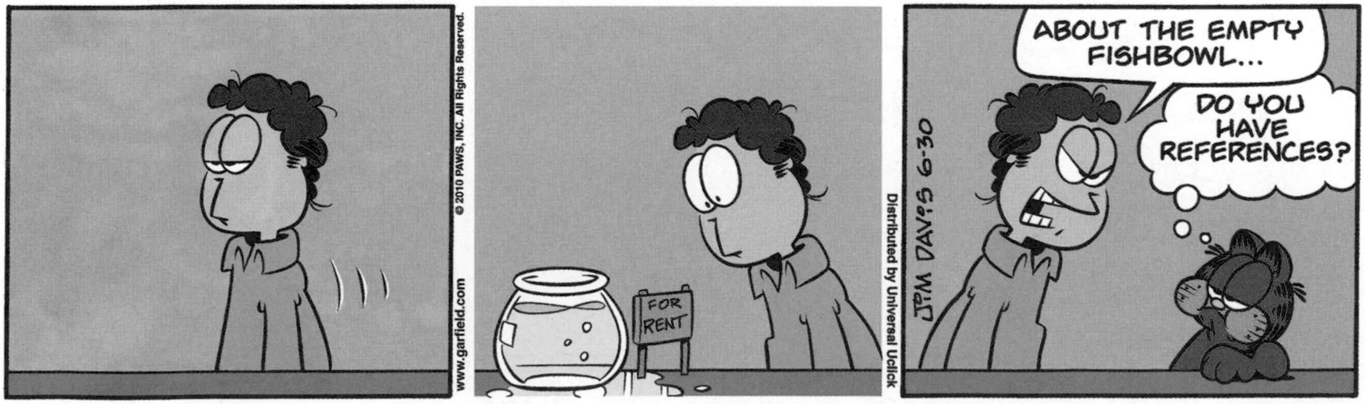
© 2010 PAWS, INC. All Rights Reserved.
www.garfield.com
FOR RENT
Distributed by Universal Uclick
JIM DAVIS 6-30
ABOUT THE EMPTY FISHBOWL...
DO YOU HAVE REFERENCES?

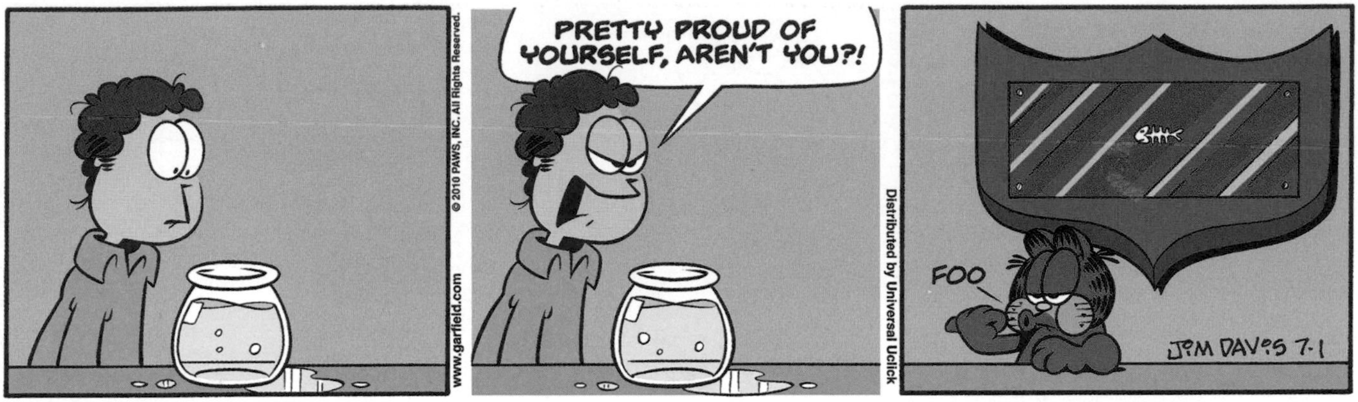
© 2010 PAWS, INC. All Rights Reserved.
www.garfield.com
PRETTY PROUD OF YOURSELF, AREN'T YOU?!
Distributed by Universal Uclick
FOO
JIM DAVIS 7-1

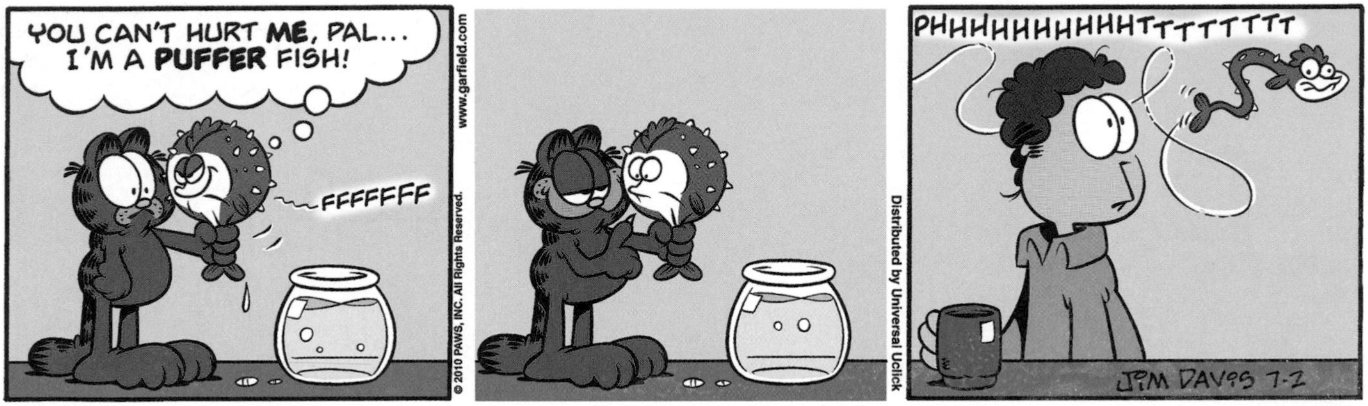
YOU CAN'T HURT **ME**, PAL... I'M A **PUFFER** FISH!
FFFFFFF
www.garfield.com
© 2010 PAWS, INC. All Rights Reserved.
Distributed by Universal Uclick
PHHHHHHHHHHTTTTTTT
JIM DAVIS 7-2

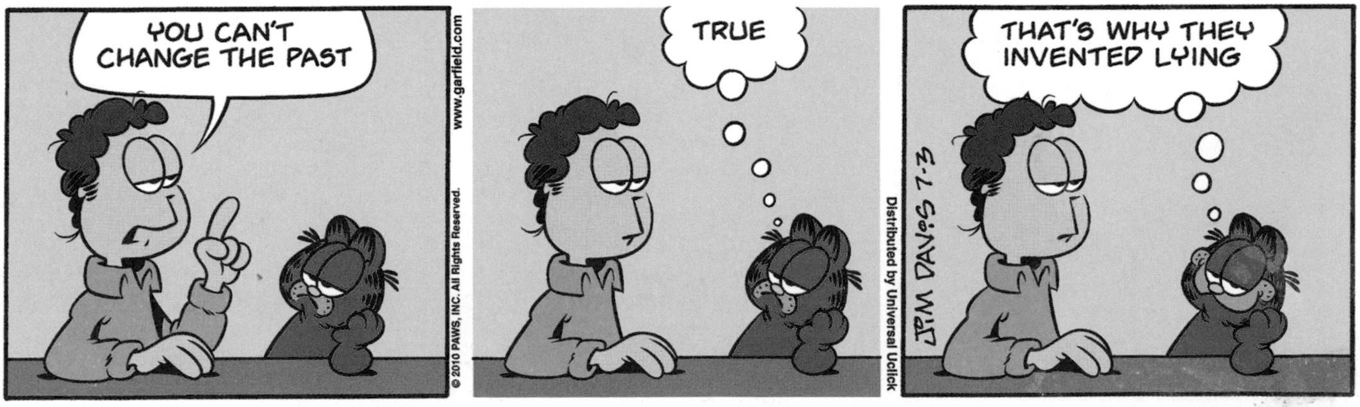
YOU CAN'T CHANGE THE PAST
www.garfield.com
© 2010 PAWS, INC. All Rights Reserved.
TRUE
Distributed by Universal Uclick
JIM DAVIS 7-3
THAT'S WHY THEY INVENTED LYING

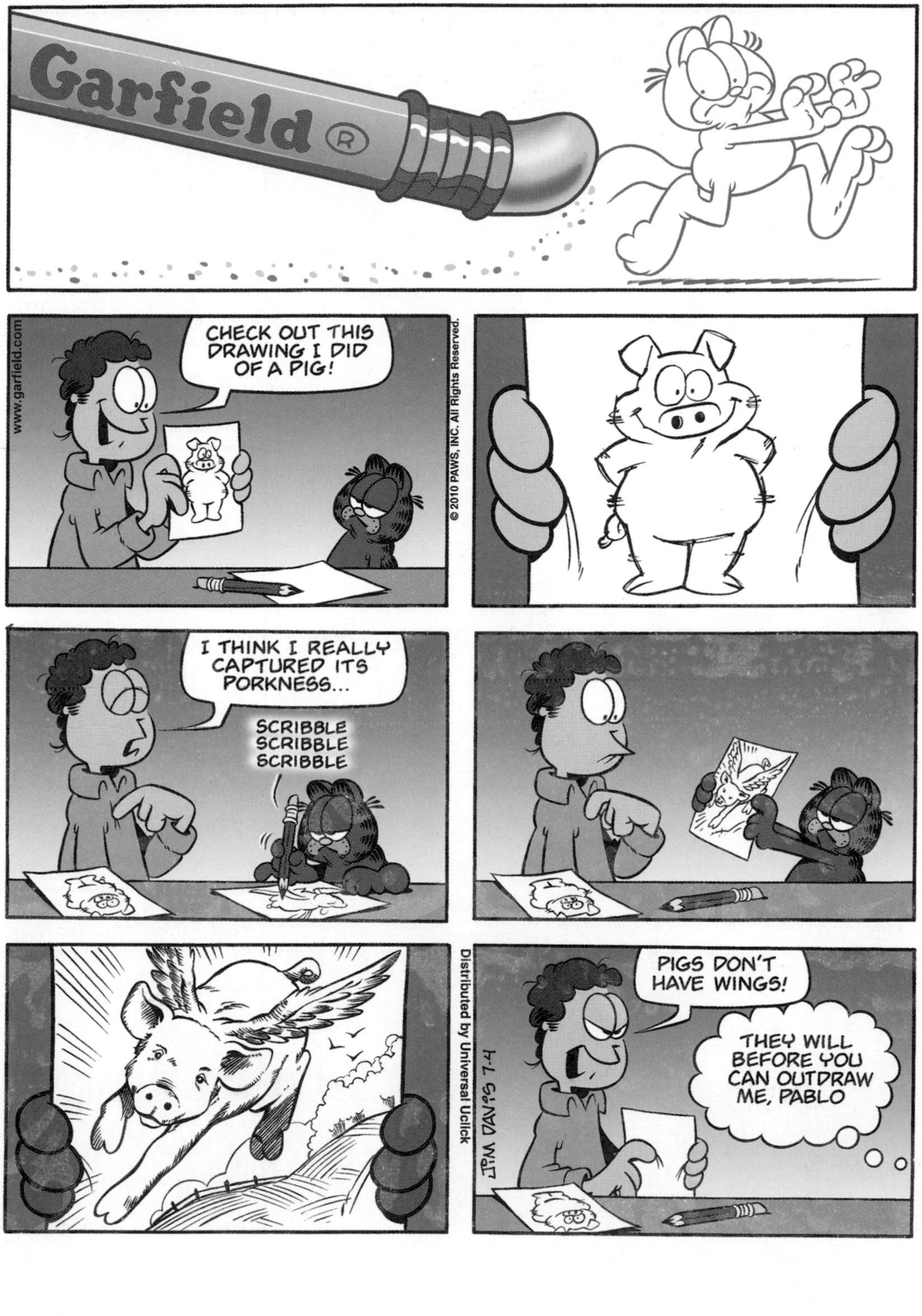
Garfield ®
www.garfield.com
CHECK OUT THIS DRAWING I DID OF A PIG!
© 2010 PAWS, INC. All Rights Reserved.
I THINK I REALLY CAPTURED ITS PORKNESS...
SCRIBBLE SCRIBBLE SCRIBBLE
Distributed by Universal Uclick
JIM DAVIS 7-4
PIGS DON'T HAVE WINGS!
THEY WILL BEFORE YOU CAN OUTDRAW ME, PABLO

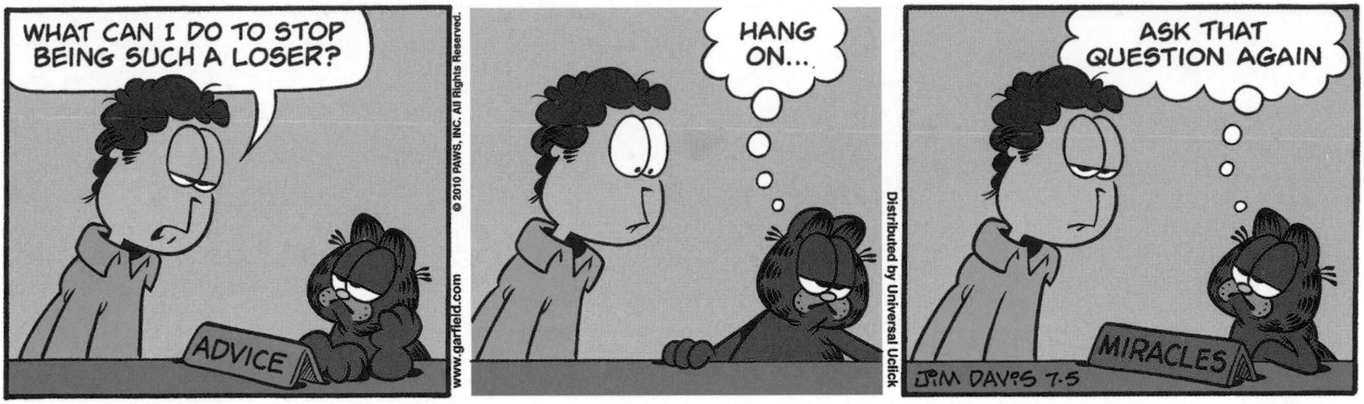
WHAT CAN I DO TO STOP BEING SUCH A LOSER?
ADVICE
© 2010 PAWS, INC. All Rights Reserved. www.garfield.com
HANG ON...
Distributed by Universal Uclick
ASK THAT QUESTION AGAIN
MIRACLES
JIM DAVIS 7-5

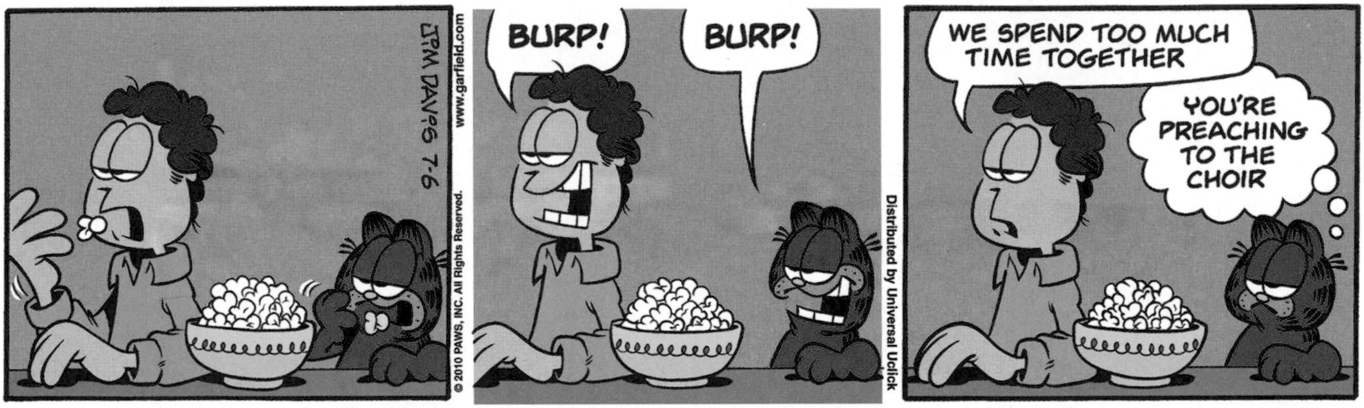
JIM DAVIS 7-6
© 2010 PAWS, INC. All Rights Reserved. www.garfield.com
BURP!
BURP!
Distributed by Universal Uclick
WE SPEND TOO MUCH TIME TOGETHER
YOU'RE PREACHING TO THE CHOIR

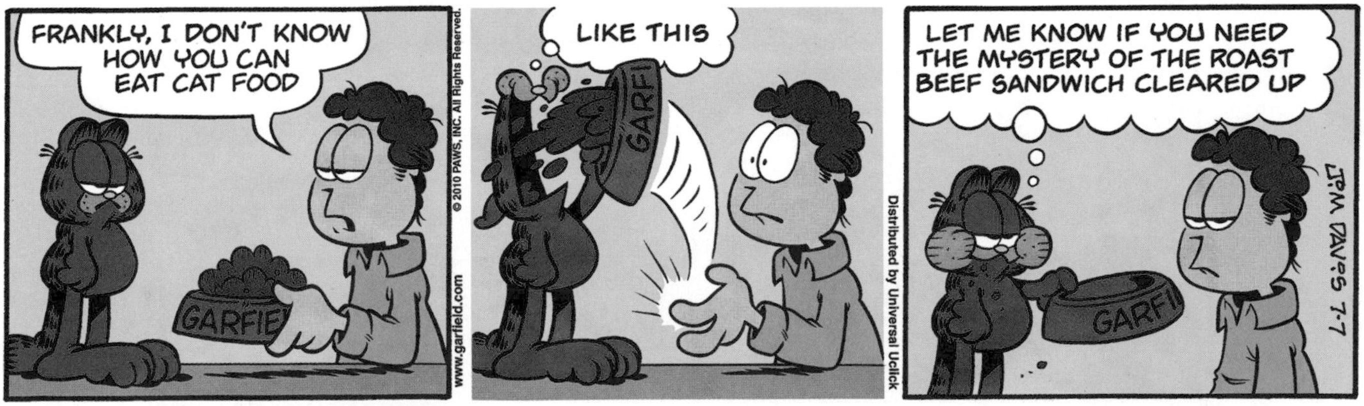
FRANKLY, I DON'T KNOW HOW YOU CAN EAT CAT FOOD
GARFIE
© 2010 PAWS, INC. All Rights Reserved. www.garfield.com
LIKE THIS
GARFI
Distributed by Universal Uclick
LET ME KNOW IF YOU NEED THE MYSTERY OF THE ROAST BEEF SANDWICH CLEARED UP
GARFI
JIM DAVIS 7-7

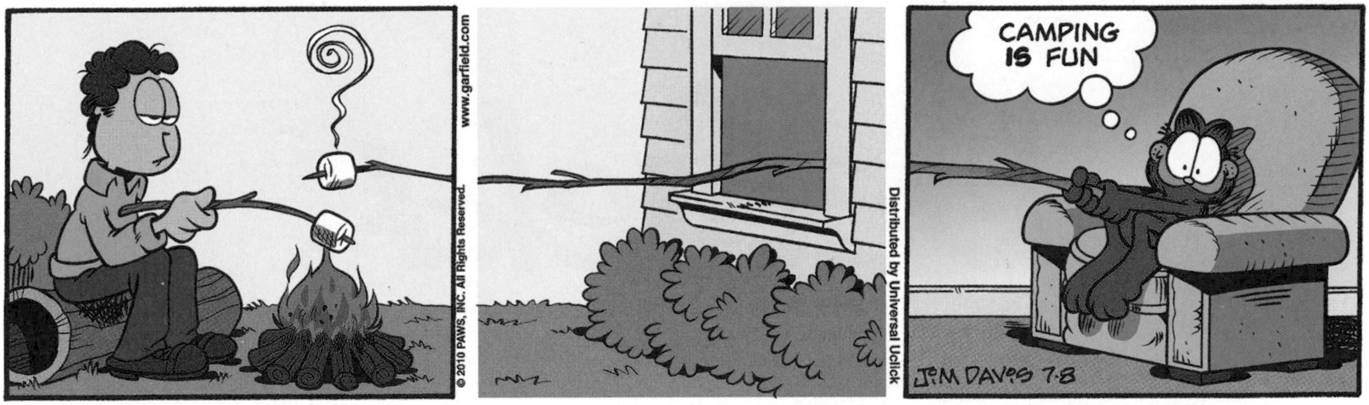
www.garfield.com
© 2010 PAWS, INC. All Rights Reserved.
Distributed by Universal Uclick
CAMPING IS FUN
JIM DAVIS 7-8

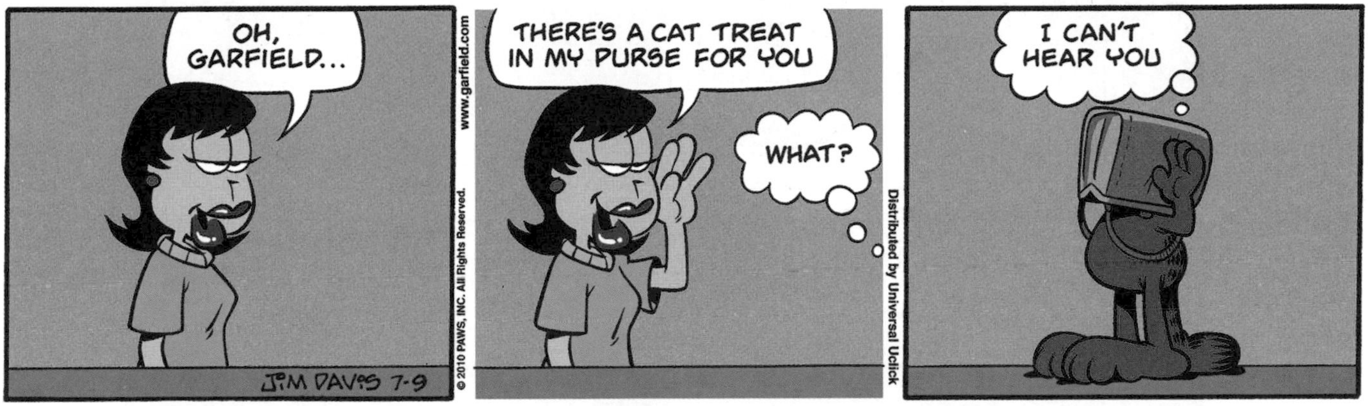
OH, GARFIELD...
JIM DAVIS 7-9
www.garfield.com
© 2010 PAWS, INC. All Rights Reserved.
THERE'S A CAT TREAT IN MY PURSE FOR YOU
WHAT?
Distributed by Universal Uclick
I CAN'T HEAR YOU

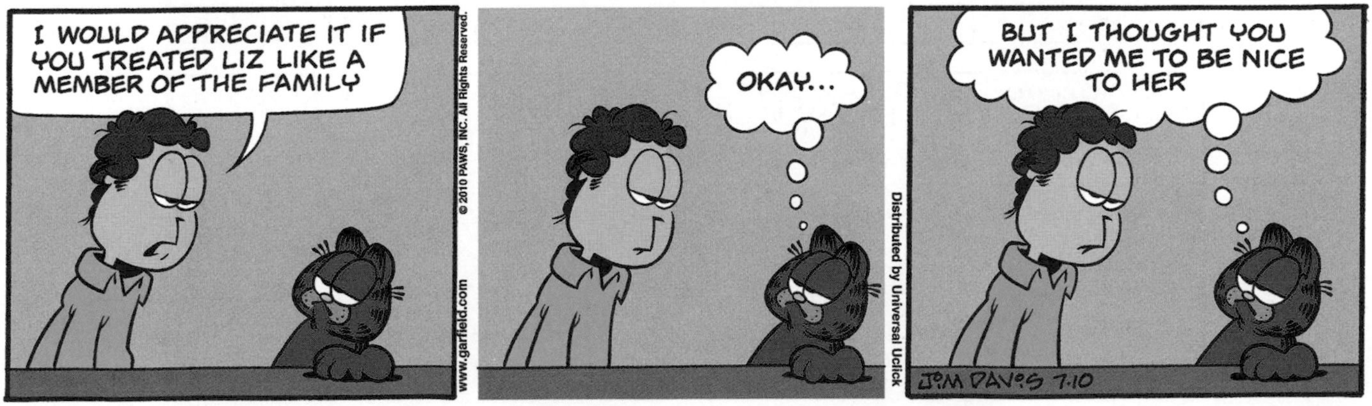
I WOULD APPRECIATE IT IF YOU TREATED LIZ LIKE A MEMBER OF THE FAMILY
© 2010 PAWS, INC. All Rights Reserved.
www.garfield.com
OKAY...
Distributed by Universal Uclick
BUT I THOUGHT YOU WANTED ME TO BE NICE TO HER
JIM DAVIS 7-10

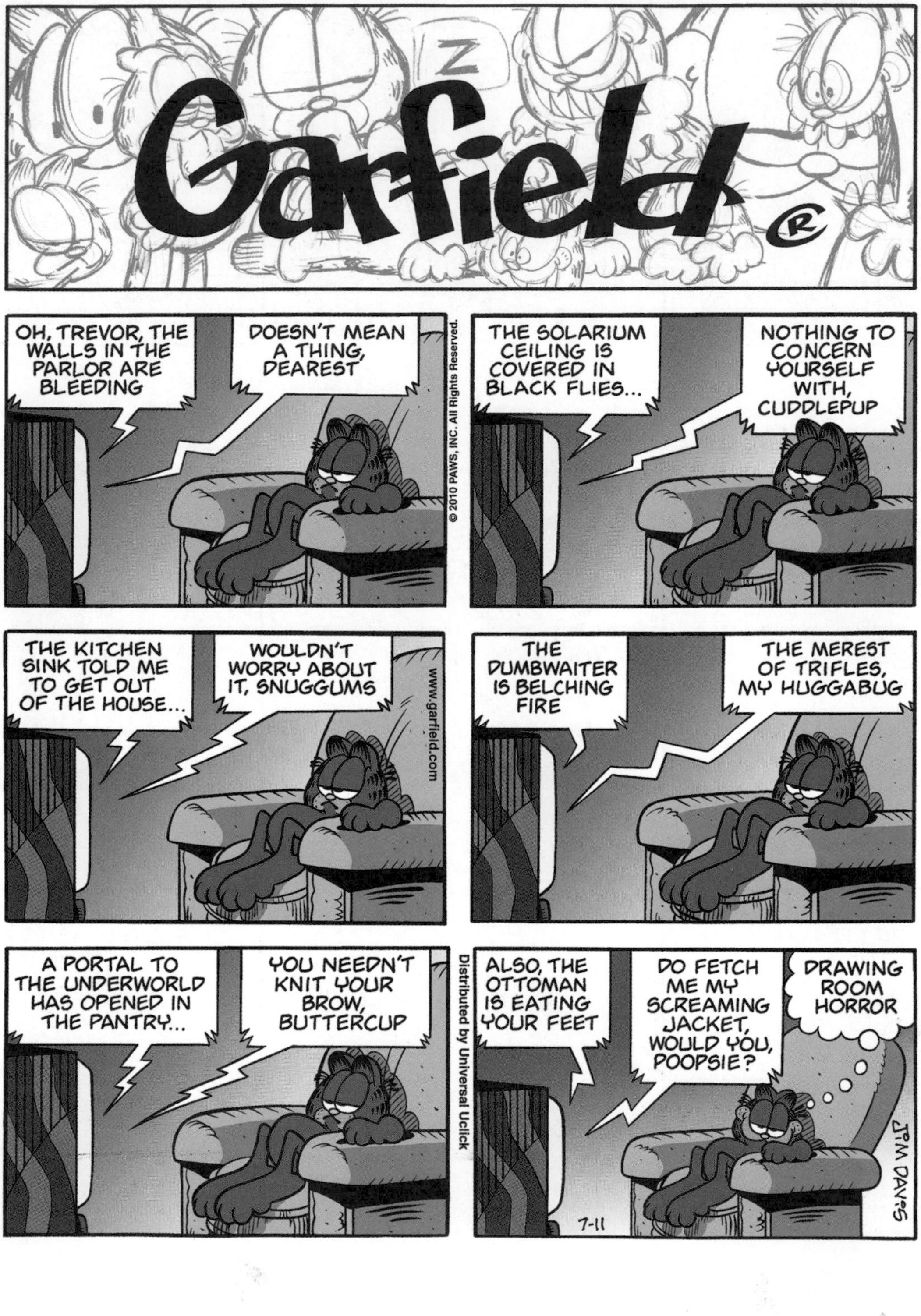
Garfield®
OH, TREVOR, THE WALLS IN THE PARLOR ARE BLEEDING
DOESN'T MEAN A THING, DEAREST
© 2010 PAWS, INC. All Rights Reserved.
THE SOLARIUM CEILING IS COVERED IN BLACK FLIES...
NOTHING TO CONCERN YOURSELF WITH, CUDDLEPUP
THE KITCHEN SINK TOLD ME TO GET OUT OF THE HOUSE...
WOULDN'T WORRY ABOUT IT, SNUGGUMS
www.garfield.com
THE DUMBWAITER IS BELCHING FIRE
THE MEREST OF TRIFLES, MY HUGGABUG
A PORTAL TO THE UNDERWORLD HAS OPENED IN THE PANTRY...
YOU NEEDN'T KNIT YOUR BROW, BUTTERCUP
Distributed by Universal Uclick
ALSO, THE OTTOMAN IS EATING YOUR FEET
DO FETCH ME MY SCREAMING JACKET, WOULD YOU, POOPSIE?
DRAWING ROOM HORROR
7-11
JIM DAVIS

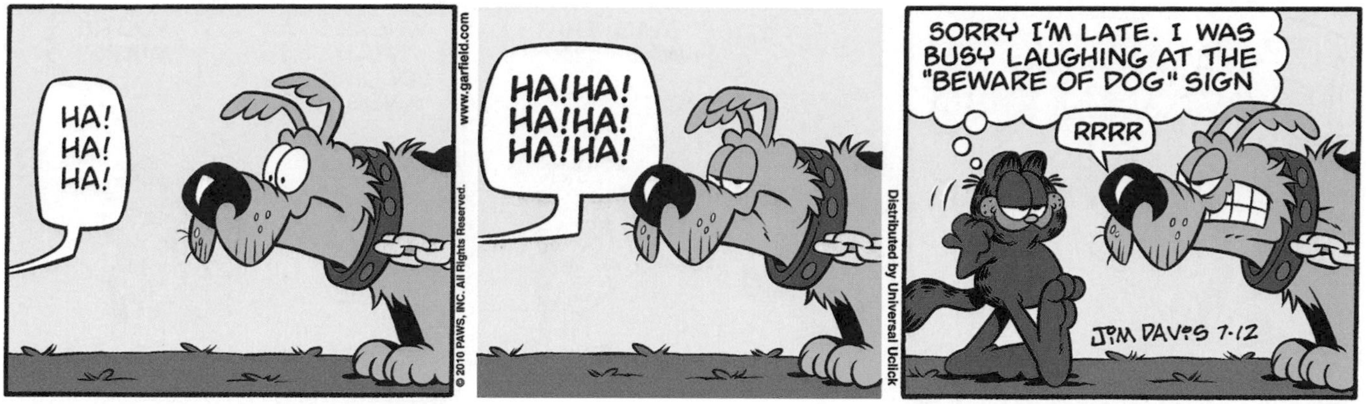
HA! HA! HA!
HA!HA! HA!HA! HA!HA!
SORRY I'M LATE. I WAS BUSY LAUGHING AT THE "BEWARE OF DOG" SIGN
RRRR
JIM DAVIS 7-12
© 2010 PAWS, INC. All Rights Reserved. www.garfield.com
Distributed by Universal Uclick

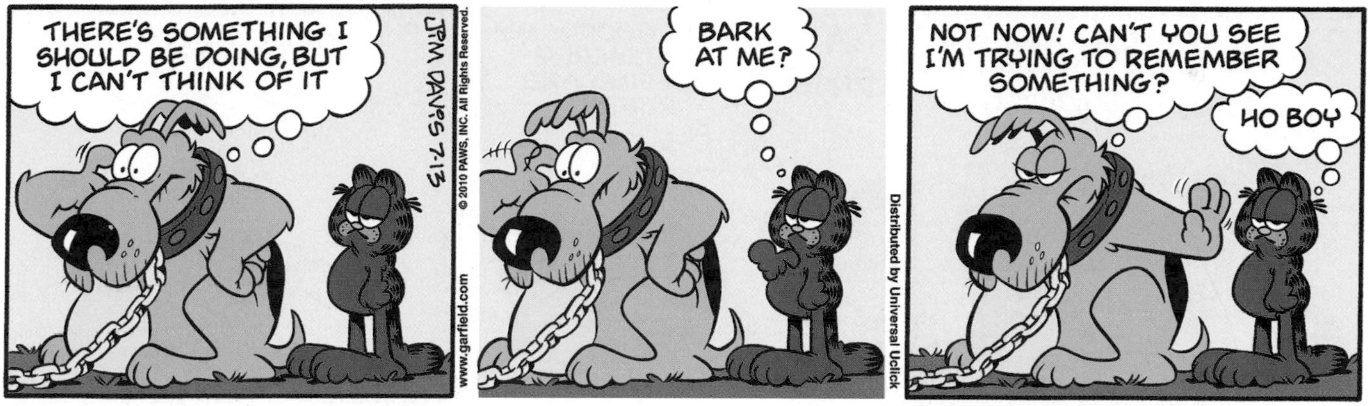
THERE'S SOMETHING I SHOULD BE DOING, BUT I CAN'T THINK OF IT
JIM DAVIS 7-13
BARK AT ME?
NOT NOW! CAN'T YOU SEE I'M TRYING TO REMEMBER SOMETHING?
HO BOY
© 2010 PAWS, INC. All Rights Reserved. www.garfield.com
Distributed by Universal Uclick

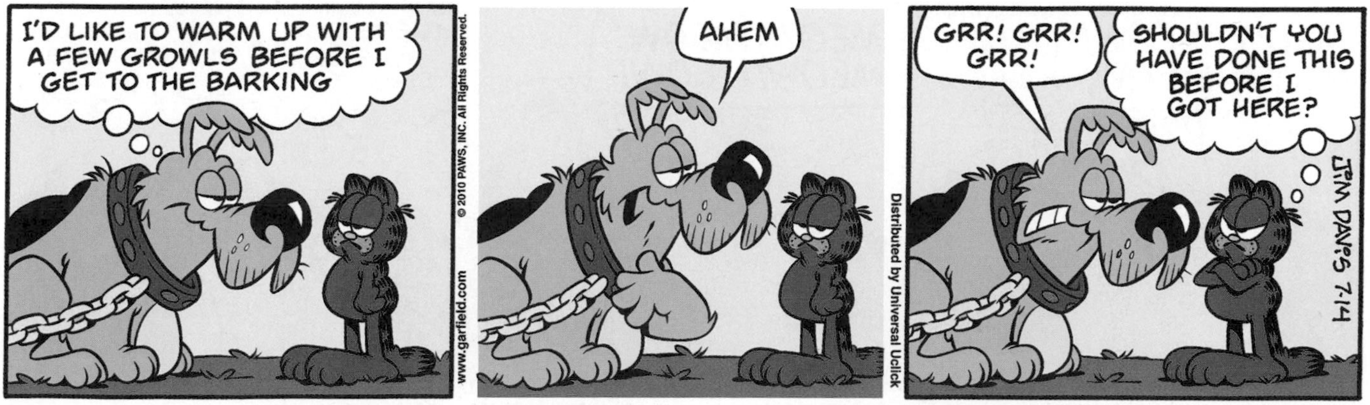
I'D LIKE TO WARM UP WITH A FEW GROWLS BEFORE I GET TO THE BARKING
AHEM
GRR! GRR! GRR!
SHOULDN'T YOU HAVE DONE THIS BEFORE I GOT HERE?
JIM DAVIS 7-14
© 2010 PAWS, INC. All Rights Reserved. www.garfield.com
Distributed by Universal Uclick

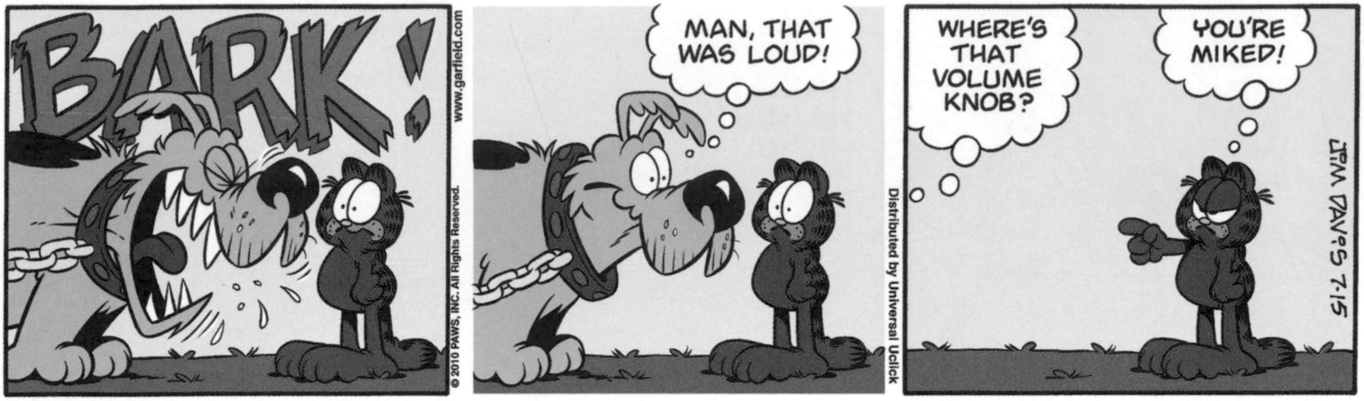
BARK!
MAN, THAT WAS LOUD!
WHERE'S THAT VOLUME KNOB?
YOU'RE MIKED!
© 2010 PAWS, INC. All Rights Reserved.
www.garfield.com
Distributed by Universal Uclick
JIM DAVIS 7-15

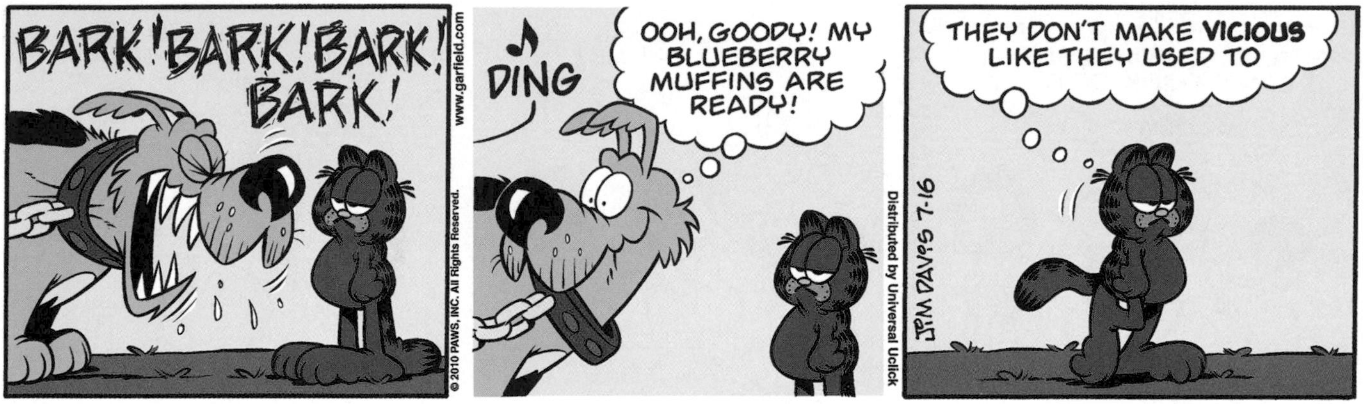
BARK! BARK! BARK! BARK!
DING
OOH, GOODY! MY BLUEBERRY MUFFINS ARE READY!
THEY DON'T MAKE **VICIOUS** LIKE THEY USED TO
© 2010 PAWS, INC. All Rights Reserved.
www.garfield.com
Distributed by Universal Uclick
JIM DAVIS 7-16

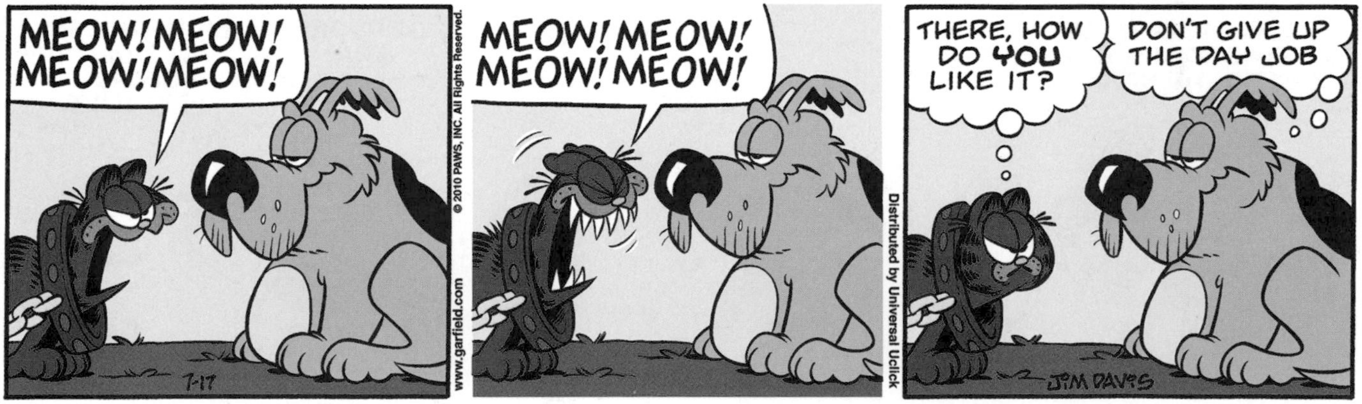
MEOW! MEOW! MEOW! MEOW!
MEOW! MEOW! MEOW! MEOW!
THERE, HOW DO **YOU** LIKE IT?
DON'T GIVE UP THE DAY JOB
7-17
© 2010 PAWS, INC. All Rights Reserved.
www.garfield.com
Distributed by Universal Uclick
JIM DAVIS

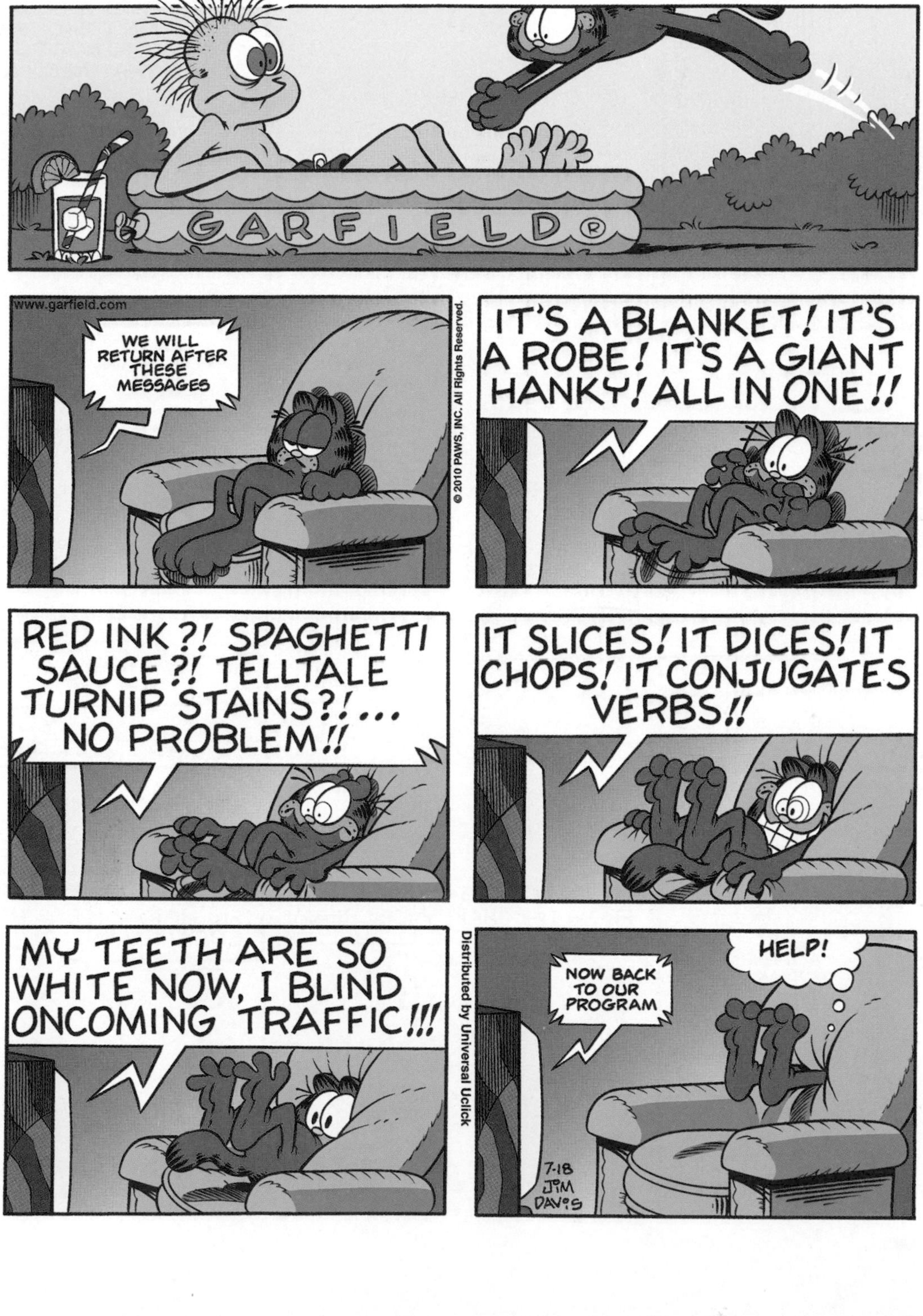
GARFIELD®
www.garfield.com
WE WILL RETURN AFTER THESE MESSAGES
IT'S A BLANKET! IT'S A ROBE! IT'S A GIANT HANKY! ALL IN ONE!!
RED INK?! SPAGHETTI SAUCE?! TELLTALE TURNIP STAINS?!... NO PROBLEM!!
IT SLICES! IT DICES! IT CHOPS! IT CONJUGATES VERBS!!
MY TEETH ARE SO WHITE NOW, I BLIND ONCOMING TRAFFIC!!!
NOW BACK TO OUR PROGRAM
HELP!
7-18 JIM DAVIS

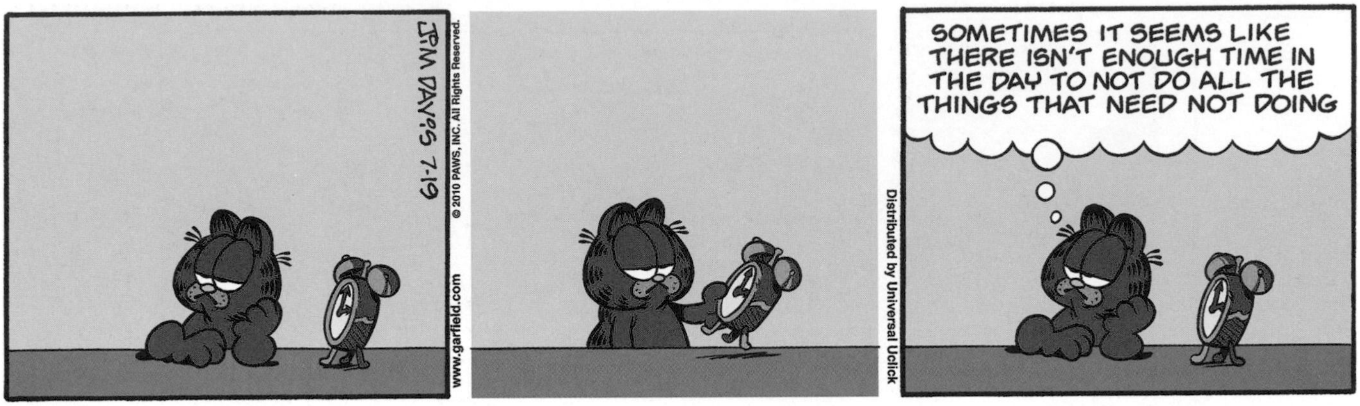
JIM DAVIS 7-19
© 2010 PAWS, INC. All Rights Reserved.
www.garfield.com
Distributed by Universal Uclick
SOMETIMES IT SEEMS LIKE THERE ISN'T ENOUGH TIME IN THE DAY TO NOT DO ALL THE THINGS THAT NEED NOT DOING

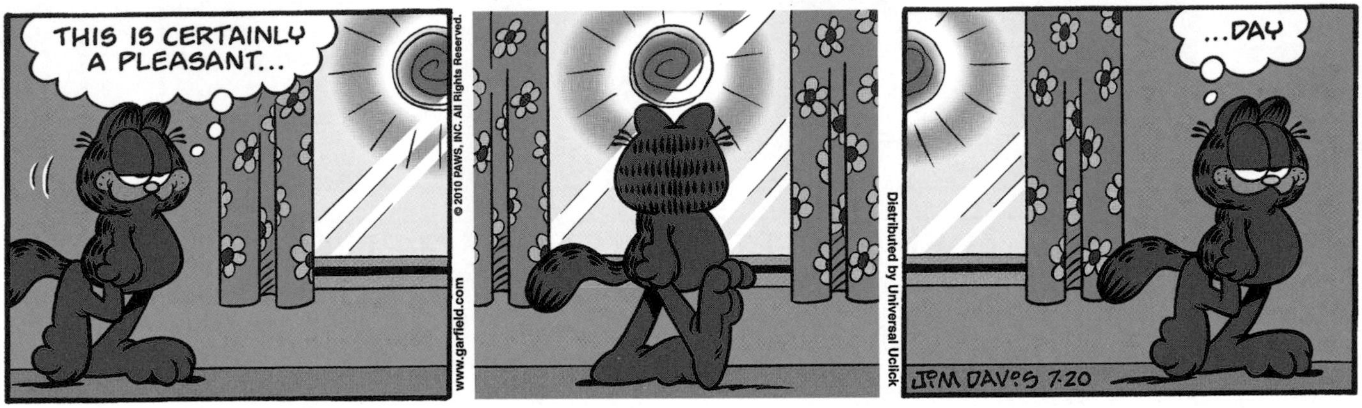
THIS IS CERTAINLY A PLEASANT...
© 2010 PAWS, INC. All Rights Reserved.
www.garfield.com
Distributed by Universal Uclick
...DAY
JIM DAVIS 7-20

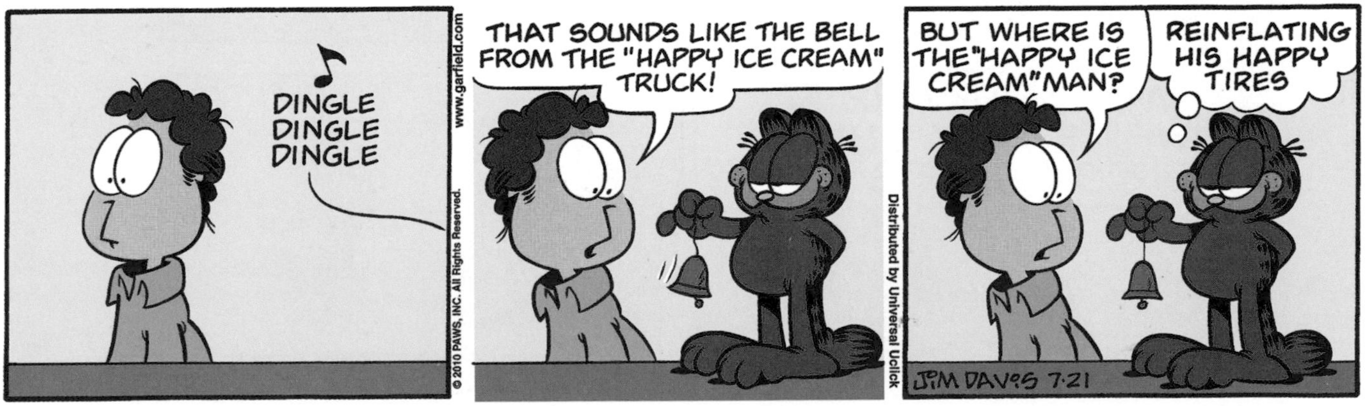
DINGLE DINGLE DINGLE
www.garfield.com
© 2010 PAWS, INC. All Rights Reserved.
THAT SOUNDS LIKE THE BELL FROM THE "HAPPY ICE CREAM" TRUCK!
Distributed by Universal Uclick
BUT WHERE IS THE "HAPPY ICE CREAM" MAN?
REINFLATING HIS HAPPY TIRES
JIM DAVIS 7-21

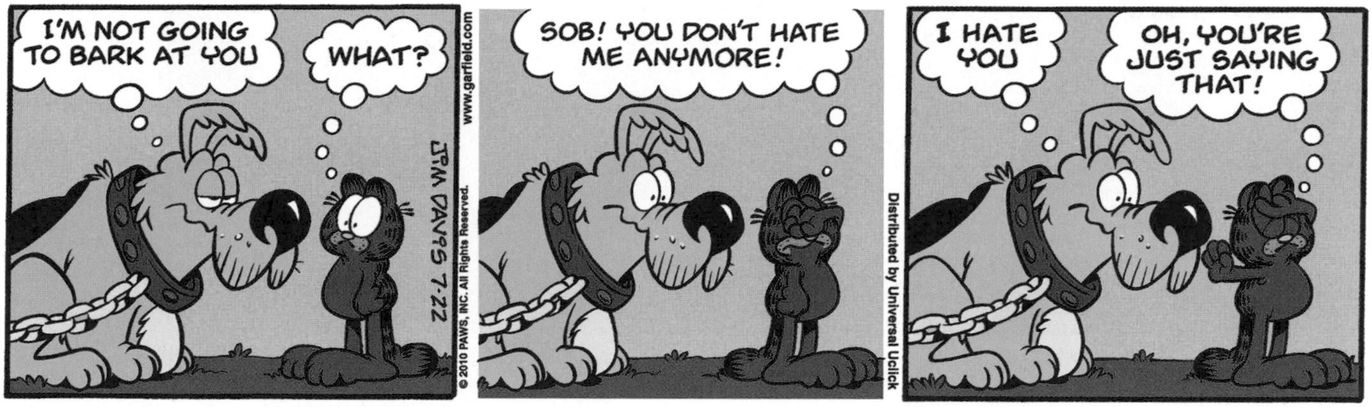
I'M NOT GOING TO BARK AT YOU
WHAT?
JIM DAVIS 7·22
© 2010 PAWS, INC. All Rights Reserved. www.garfield.com
SOB! YOU DON'T HATE ME ANYMORE!
Distributed by Universal Uclick
I HATE YOU
OH, YOU'RE JUST SAYING THAT!

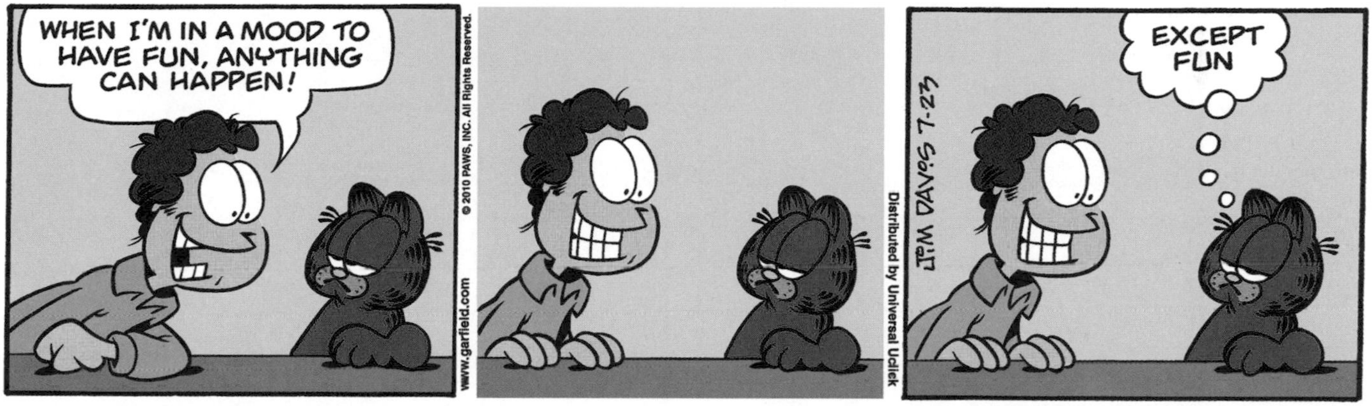
WHEN I'M IN A MOOD TO HAVE FUN, ANYTHING CAN HAPPEN!
© 2010 PAWS, INC. All Rights Reserved. www.garfield.com
Distributed by Universal Uclick
JIM DAVIS 7·23
EXCEPT FUN

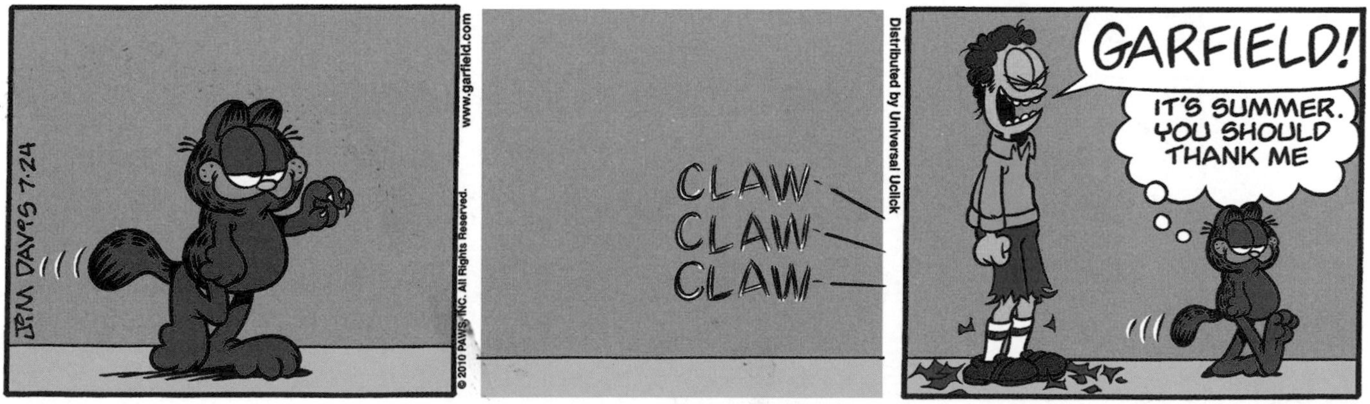
JIM DAVIS 7·24
© 2010 PAWS, INC. All Rights Reserved. www.garfield.com
CLAW
CLAW
CLAW
Distributed by Universal Uclick
GARFIELD!
IT'S SUMMER. YOU SHOULD THANK ME

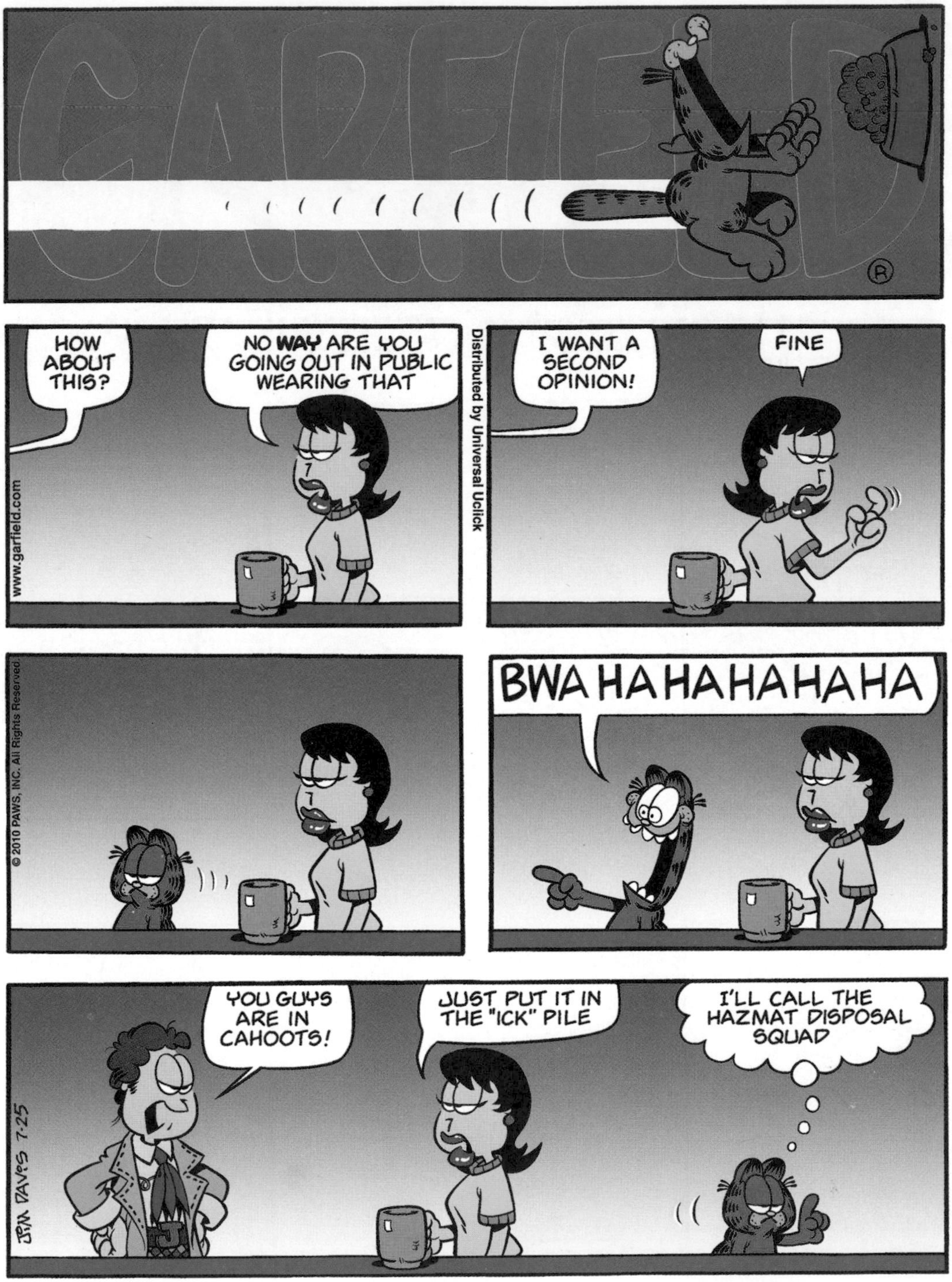
GARFIELD
HOW ABOUT THIS?
NO WAY ARE YOU GOING OUT IN PUBLIC WEARING THAT
www.garfield.com
Distributed by Universal Uclick
I WANT A SECOND OPINION!
FINE
© 2010 PAWS, INC. All Rights Reserved.
BWA HA HA HA HA HA HA
YOU GUYS ARE IN CAHOOTS!
JUST PUT IT IN THE "ICK" PILE
I'LL CALL THE HAZMAT DISPOSAL SQUAD
JPM DAVIS 7-25

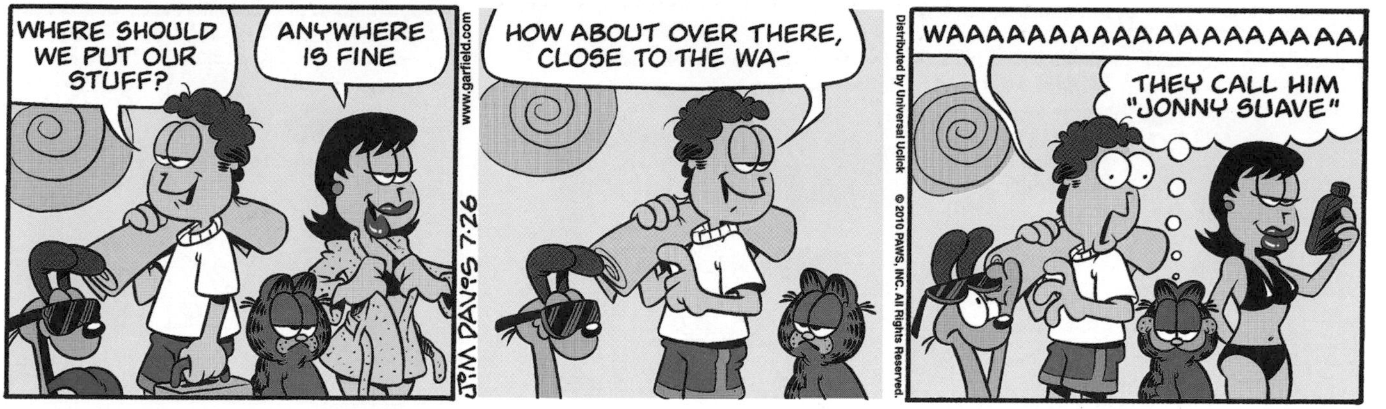
WHERE SHOULD WE PUT OUR STUFF?
ANYWHERE IS FINE
JIM DAVIS 7.26
www.garfield.com
HOW ABOUT OVER THERE, CLOSE TO THE WA-
Distributed by Universal Uclick
© 2010 PAWS, INC. All Rights Reserved.
WAAAAAAAAAAAAAAAAAAA
THEY CALL HIM "JONNY SUAVE"

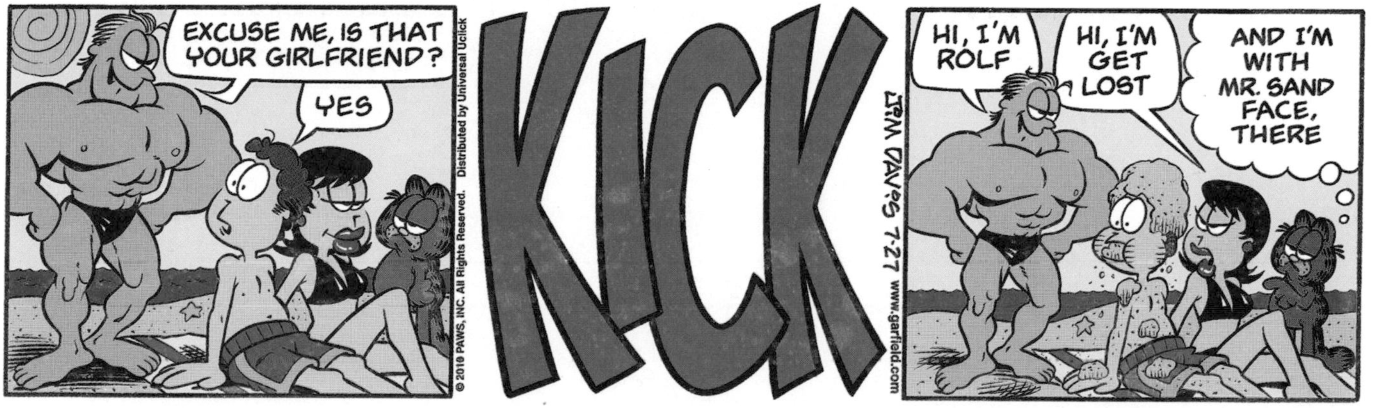
EXCUSE ME, IS THAT YOUR GIRLFRIEND?
YES
© 2010 PAWS, INC. All Rights Reserved. Distributed by Universal Uclick
KICK
JIM DAVIS 7.27
www.garfield.com
HI, I'M ROLF
HI, I'M GET LOST
AND I'M WITH MR. SAND FACE, THERE

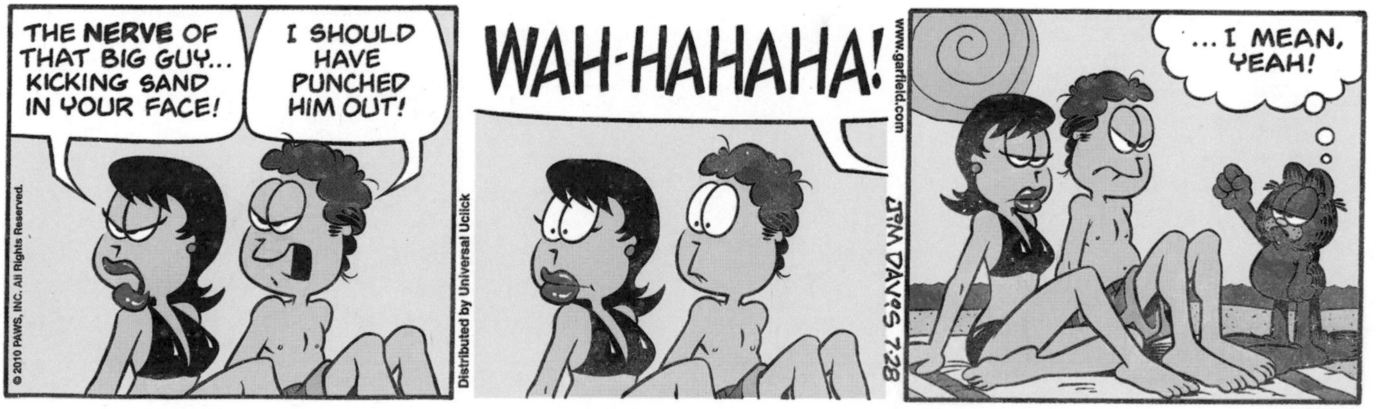
THE NERVE OF THAT BIG GUY... KICKING SAND IN YOUR FACE!
I SHOULD HAVE PUNCHED HIM OUT!
© 2010 PAWS, INC. All Rights Reserved.
Distributed by Universal Uclick
WAH-HAHAHA!
www.garfield.com
JIM DAVIS 7.28
...I MEAN, YEAH!

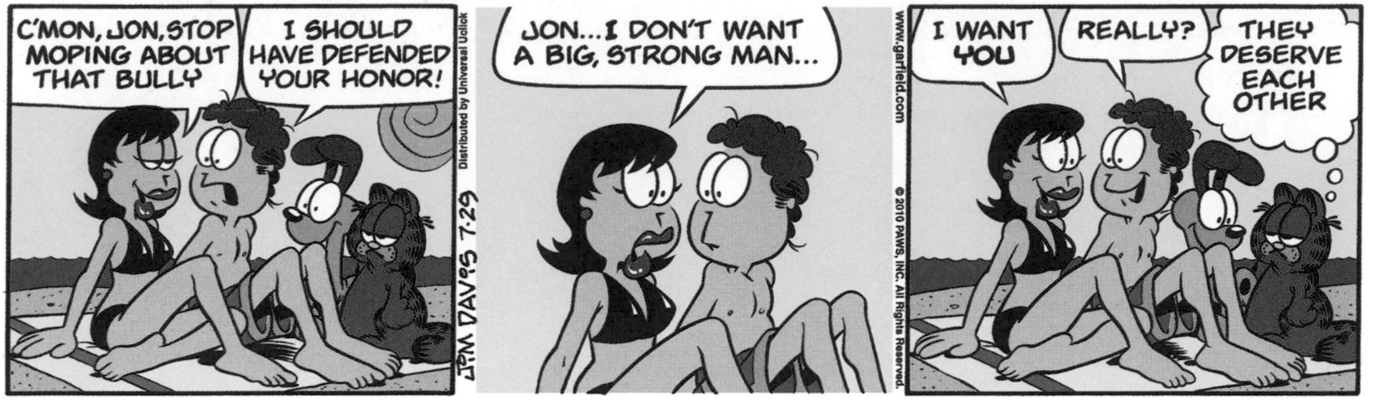
C'MON, JON, STOP MOPING ABOUT THAT BULLY
I SHOULD HAVE DEFENDED YOUR HONOR!
JON... I DON'T WANT A BIG, STRONG MAN...
I WANT YOU
REALLY?
THEY DESERVE EACH OTHER
JIM DAVIS 7-29
Distributed by Universal Uclick
www.garfield.com
© 2010 PAWS, INC. All Rights Reserved.

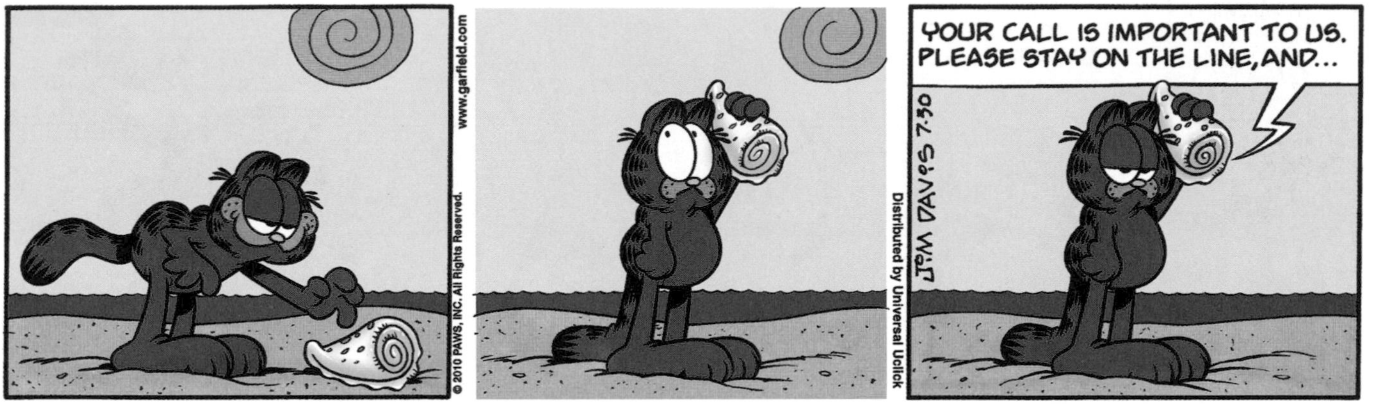
YOUR CALL IS IMPORTANT TO US. PLEASE STAY ON THE LINE, AND...
JIM DAVIS 7-30
© 2010 PAWS, INC. All Rights Reserved.
www.garfield.com
Distributed by Universal Uclick

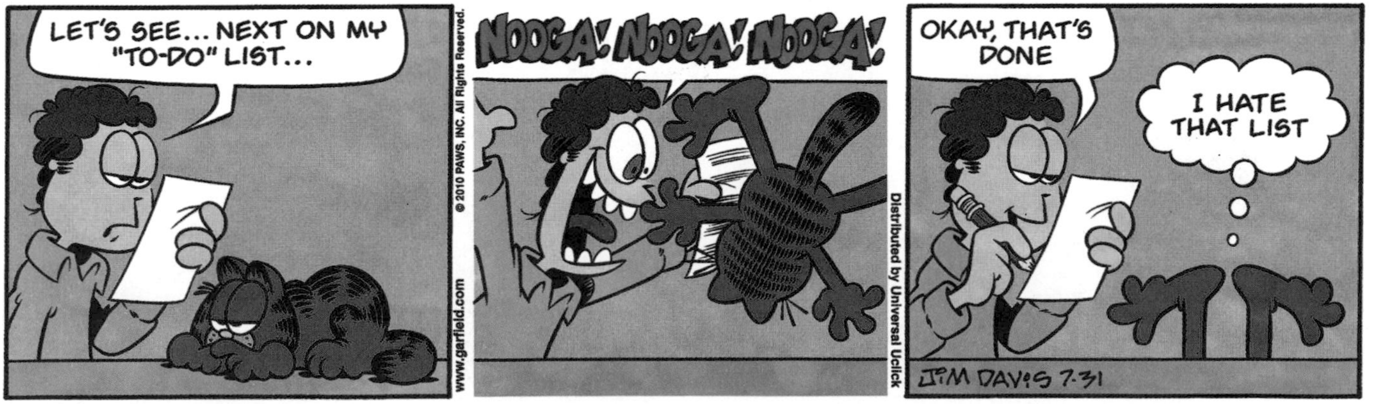
LET'S SEE... NEXT ON MY "TO-DO" LIST...
NOOGA! NOOGA! NOOGA!
OKAY, THAT'S DONE
I HATE THAT LIST
JIM DAVIS 7-31
© 2010 PAWS, INC. All Rights Reserved.
www.garfield.com
Distributed by Universal Uclick

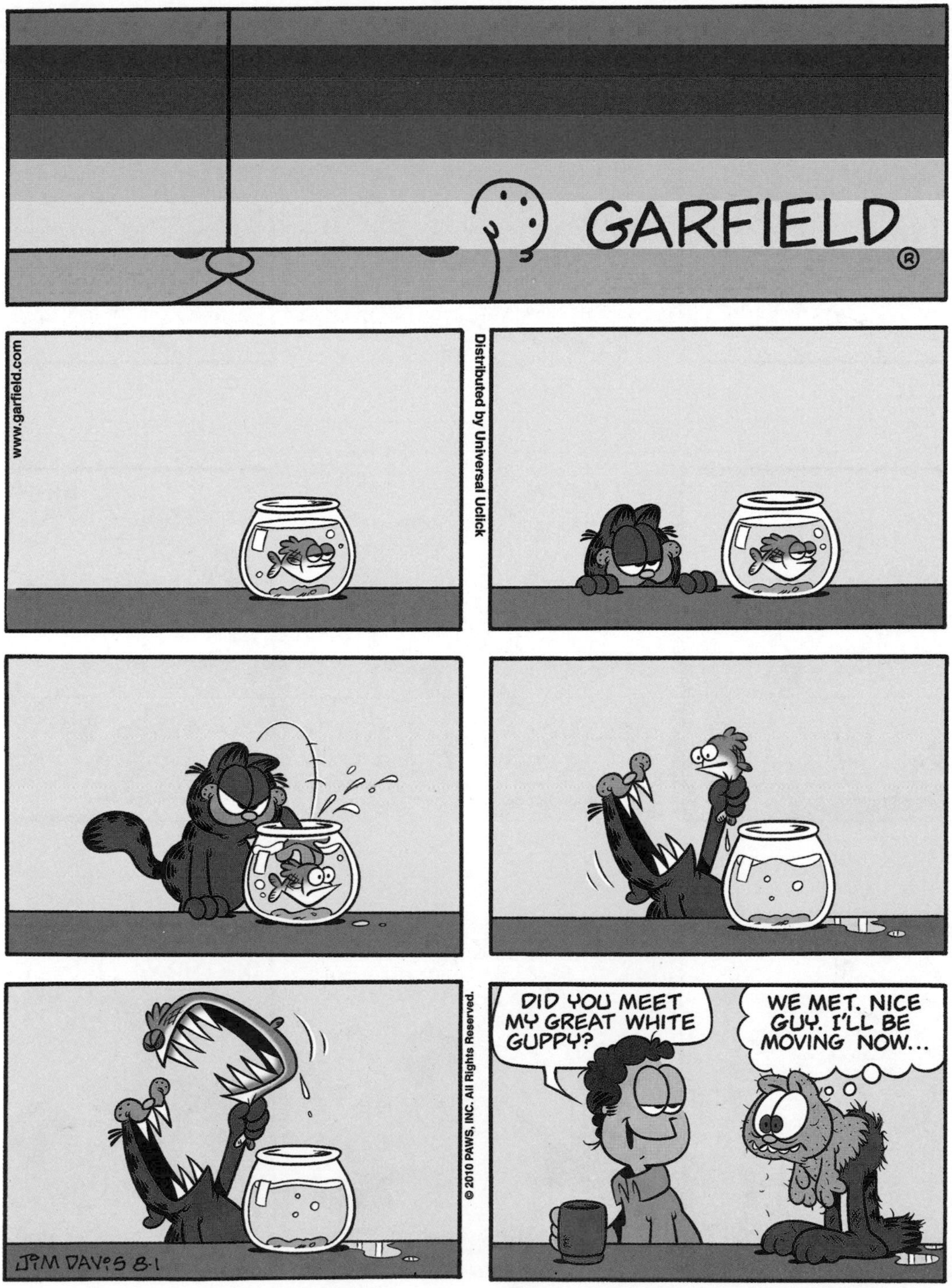
GARFIELD®
www.garfield.com
Distributed by Universal Uclick
DID YOU MEET MY GREAT WHITE GUPPY?
WE MET. NICE GUY. I'LL BE MOVING NOW...
© 2010 PAWS, INC. All Rights Reserved.
JIM DAVIS 8-1

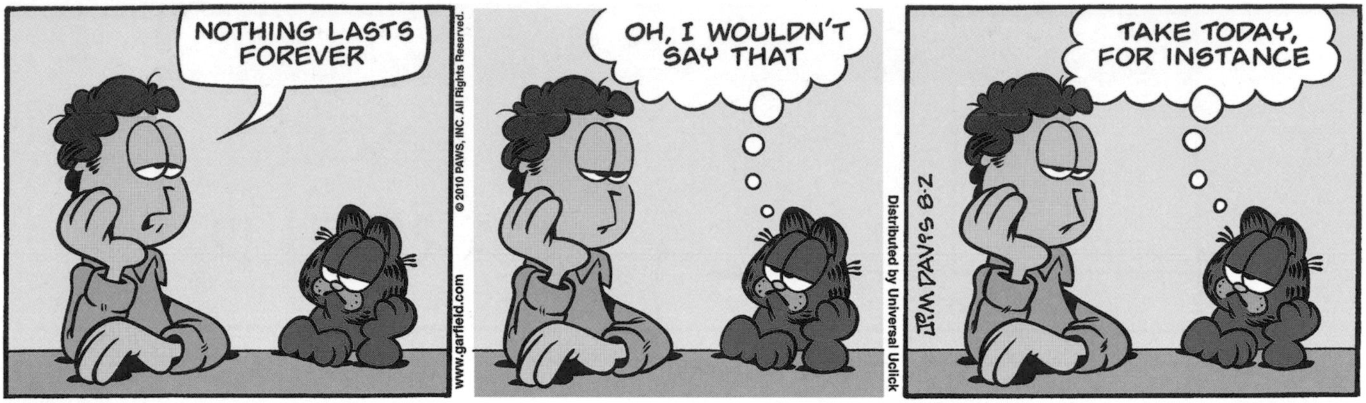
NOTHING LASTS FOREVER
OH, I WOULDN'T SAY THAT
TAKE TODAY, FOR INSTANCE
JIM DAVIS 8-2
© 2010 PAWS, INC. All Rights Reserved.
www.garfield.com
Distributed by Universal Uclick

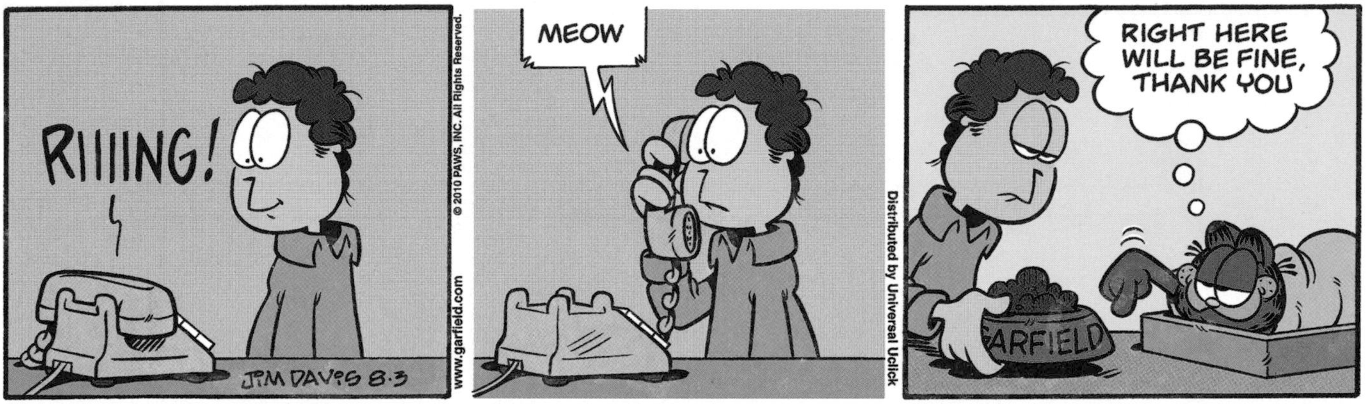
RIIIING!
JIM DAVIS 8-3
MEOW
RIGHT HERE WILL BE FINE, THANK YOU
GARFIELD
© 2010 PAWS, INC. All Rights Reserved.
www.garfield.com
Distributed by Universal Uclick

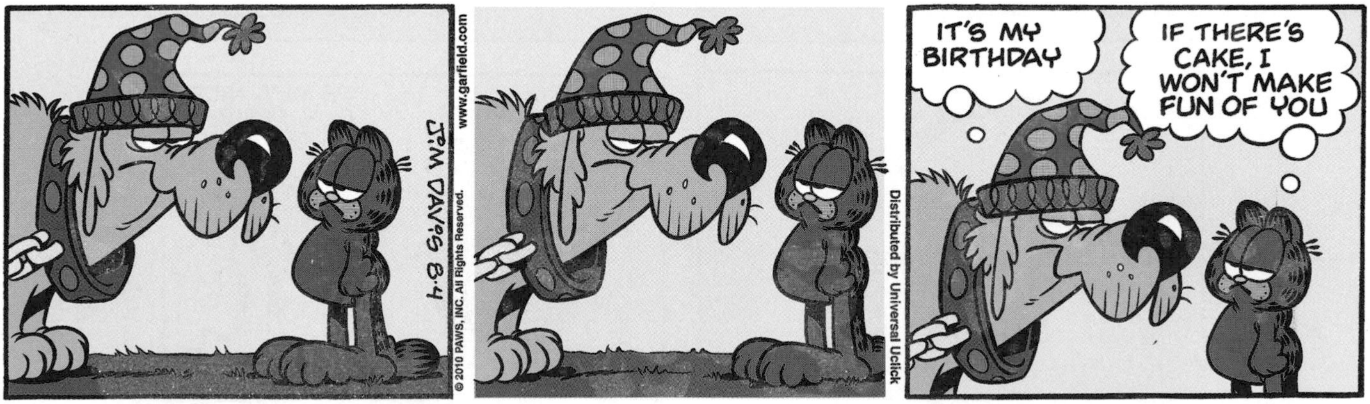
JIM DAVIS 8-4
IT'S MY BIRTHDAY
IF THERE'S CAKE, I WON'T MAKE FUN OF YOU
© 2010 PAWS, INC. All Rights Reserved.
www.garfield.com
Distributed by Universal Uclick

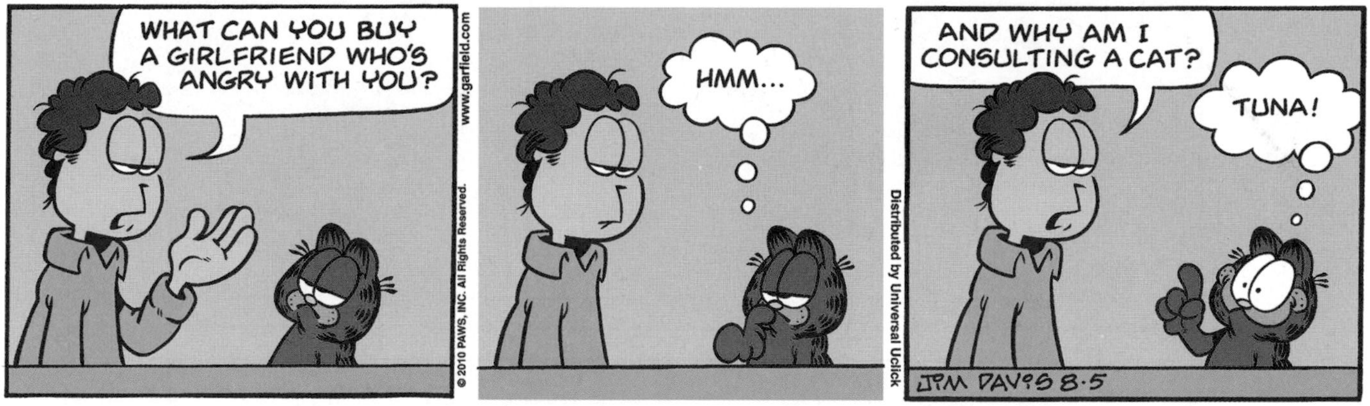
WHAT CAN YOU BUY A GIRLFRIEND WHO'S ANGRY WITH YOU?
© 2010 PAWS, INC. All Rights Reserved. www.garfield.com
HMM...
Distributed by Universal Uclick
AND WHY AM I CONSULTING A CAT?
TUNA!
JIM DAVIS 8·5

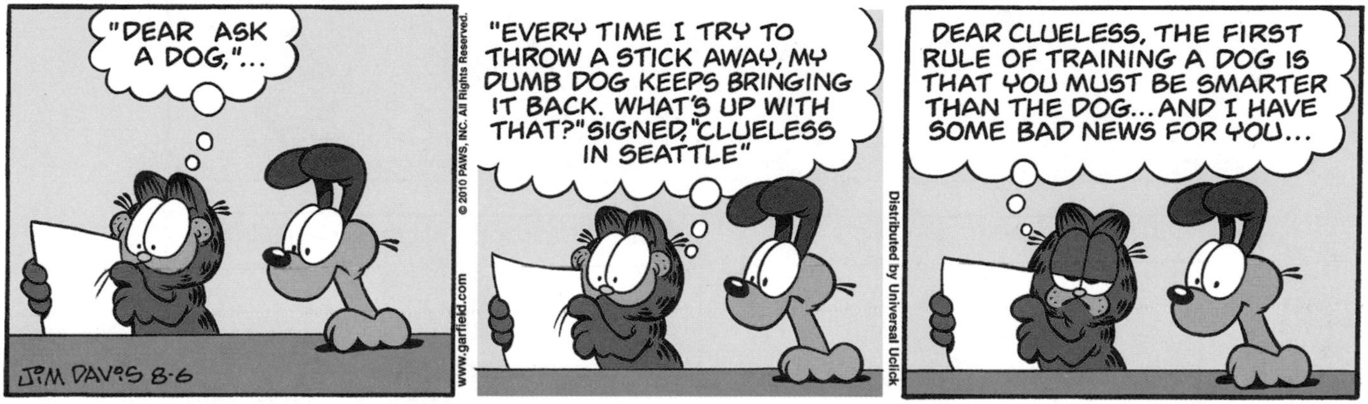
"DEAR ASK A DOG,"...
JIM DAVIS 8·6
www.garfield.com © 2010 PAWS, INC. All Rights Reserved.
"EVERY TIME I TRY TO THROW A STICK AWAY, MY DUMB DOG KEEPS BRINGING IT BACK. WHAT'S UP WITH THAT?" SIGNED, "CLUELESS IN SEATTLE"
Distributed by Universal Uclick
DEAR CLUELESS, THE FIRST RULE OF TRAINING A DOG IS THAT YOU MUST BE SMARTER THAN THE DOG... AND I HAVE SOME BAD NEWS FOR YOU...

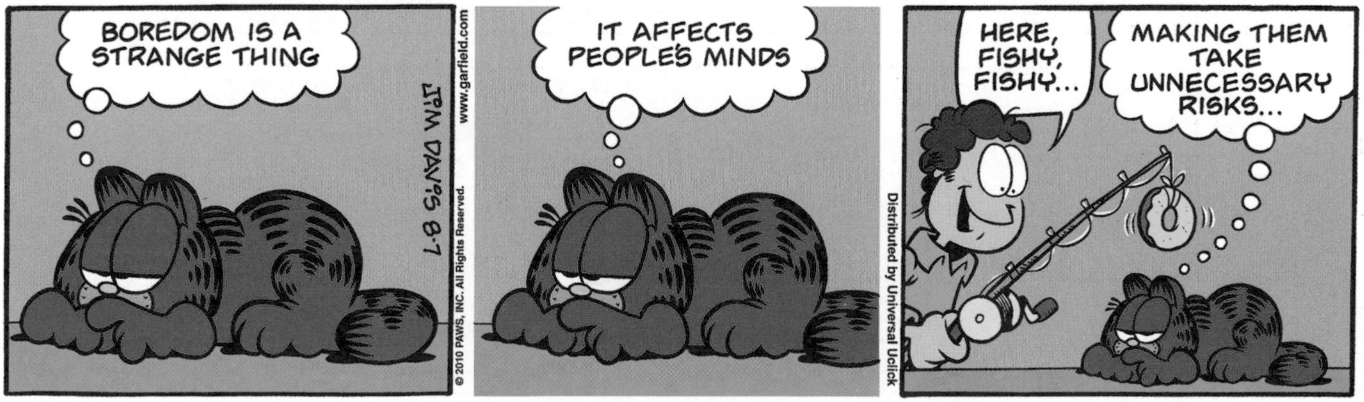
BOREDOM IS A STRANGE THING
JIM DAVIS 8·7
© 2010 PAWS, INC. All Rights Reserved. www.garfield.com
IT AFFECTS PEOPLE'S MINDS
Distributed by Universal Uclick
HERE, FISHY, FISHY...
MAKING THEM TAKE UNNECESSARY RISKS...

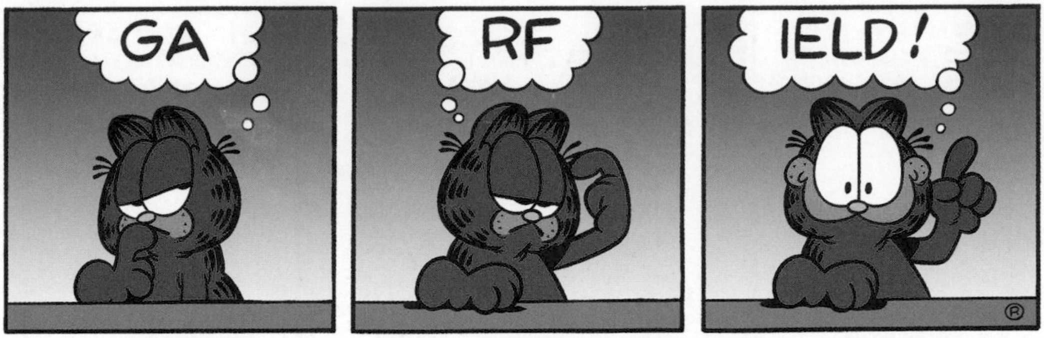
GA
RF
IELD!

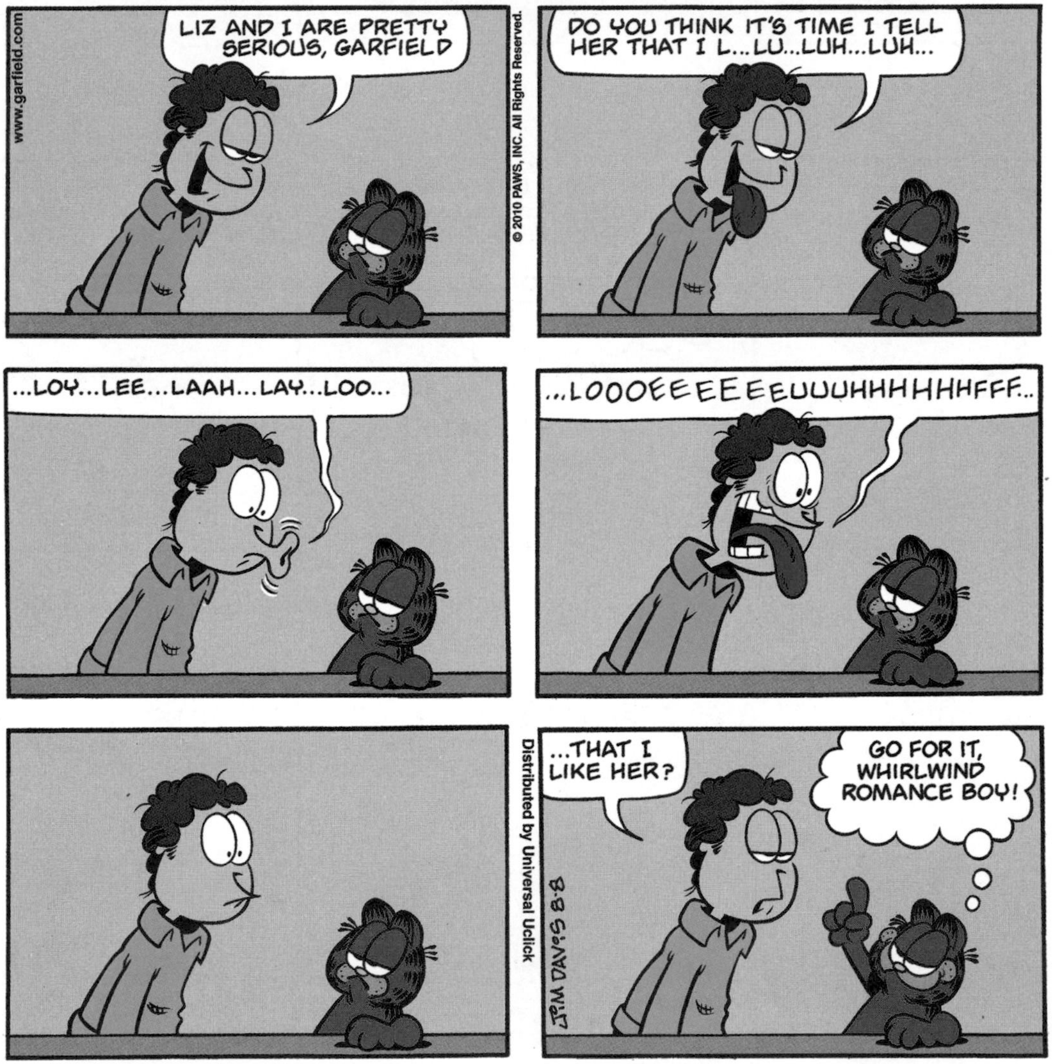
www.garfield.com
LIZ AND I ARE PRETTY SERIOUS, GARFIELD
© 2010 PAWS, INC. All Rights Reserved.
DO YOU THINK IT'S TIME I TELL HER THAT I L...LU...LUH...LUH...
...LOY...LEE...LAAH...LAY...LOO...
...LOOOEEEEEEEUUUHHHHHHHFFF...
Distributed by Universal Uclick
JPM DAVIS 8-8
...THAT I LIKE HER?
GO FOR IT, WHIRLWIND ROMANCE BOY!

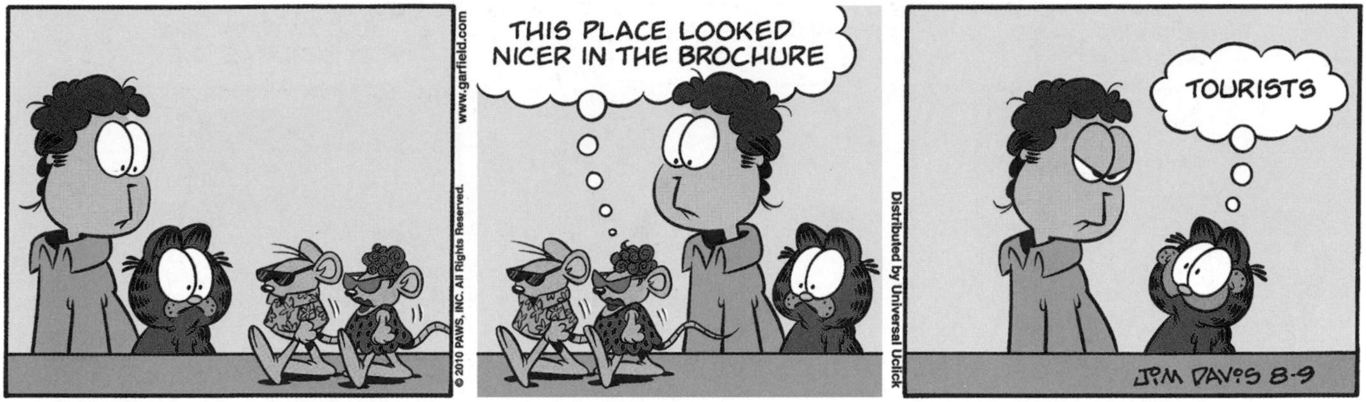
© 2010 PAWS, INC. All Rights Reserved. www.garfield.com
THIS PLACE LOOKED NICER IN THE BROCHURE
Distributed by Universal Uclick
TOURISTS
JIM DAVIS 8-9

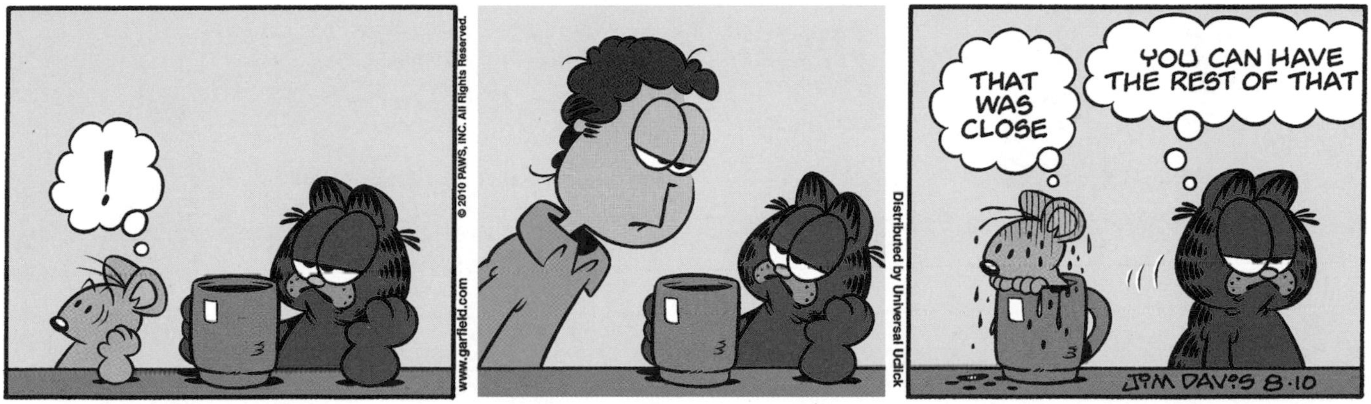
!
© 2010 PAWS, INC. All Rights Reserved. www.garfield.com
Distributed by Universal Uclick
THAT WAS CLOSE
YOU CAN HAVE THE REST OF THAT
JIM DAVIS 8·10

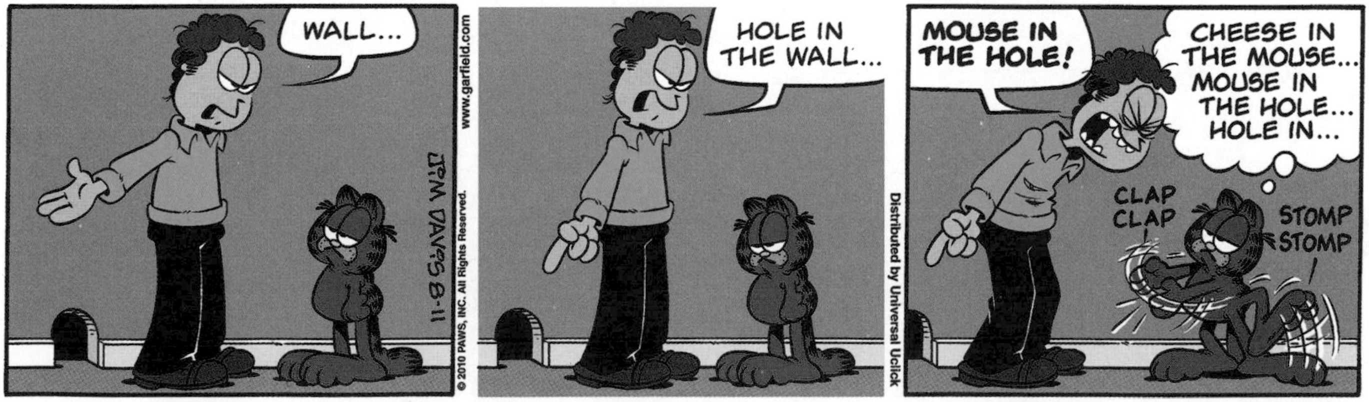
WALL...
JIM DAVIS 8-11
© 2010 PAWS, INC. All Rights Reserved. www.garfield.com
HOLE IN THE WALL...
Distributed by Universal Uclick
MOUSE IN THE HOLE!
CHEESE IN THE MOUSE... MOUSE IN THE HOLE... HOLE IN...
CLAP CLAP
STOMP STOMP

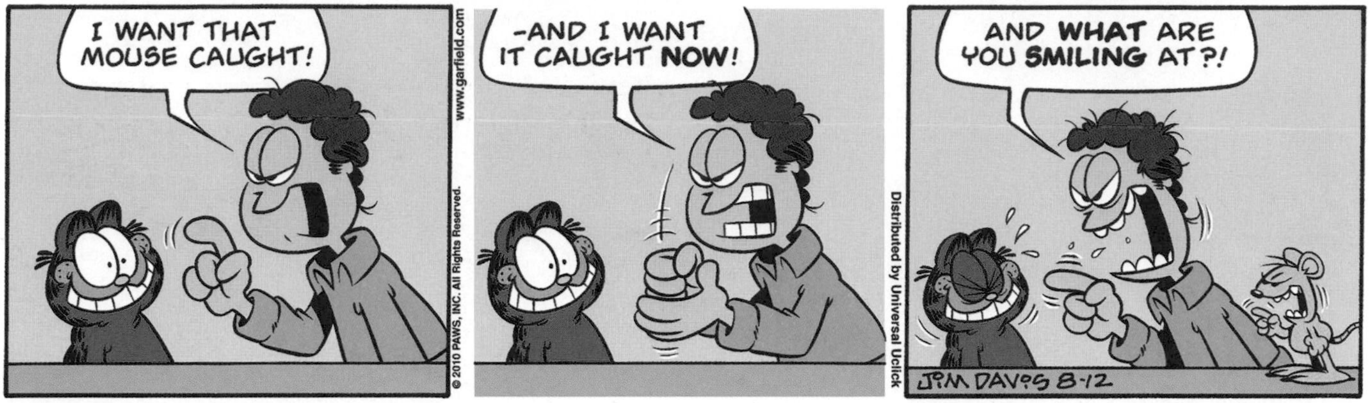
I WANT THAT MOUSE CAUGHT!
© 2010 PAWS, INC. All Rights Reserved. www.garfield.com
-AND I WANT IT CAUGHT NOW!
Distributed by Universal Uclick
AND WHAT ARE YOU SMILING AT?!
JIM DAVIS 8-12

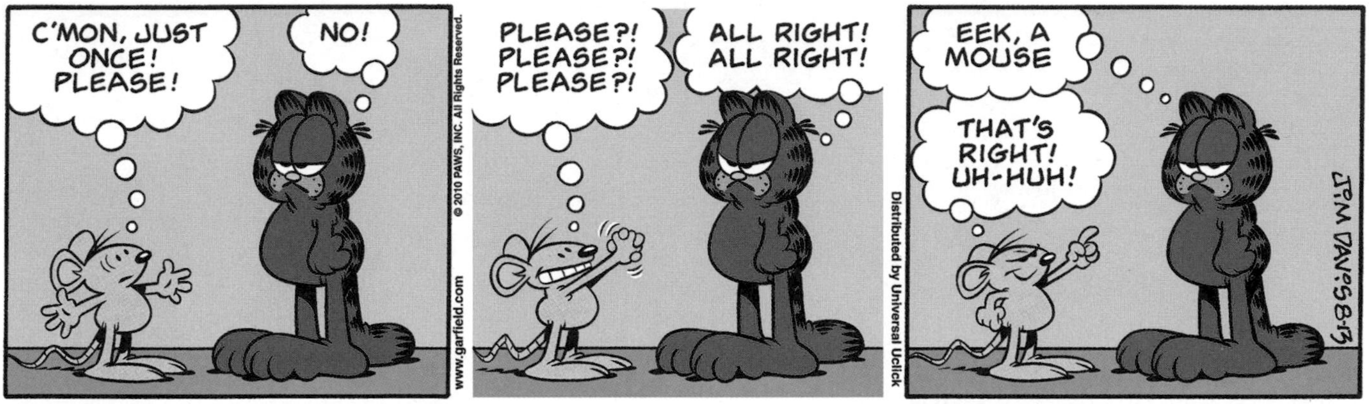
C'MON, JUST ONCE! PLEASE!
NO!
www.garfield.com © 2010 PAWS, INC. All Rights Reserved.
PLEASE?! PLEASE?! PLEASE?!
ALL RIGHT! ALL RIGHT!
Distributed by Universal Uclick
EEK, A MOUSE
THAT'S RIGHT! UH-HUH!
JIM DAVIS 8-13

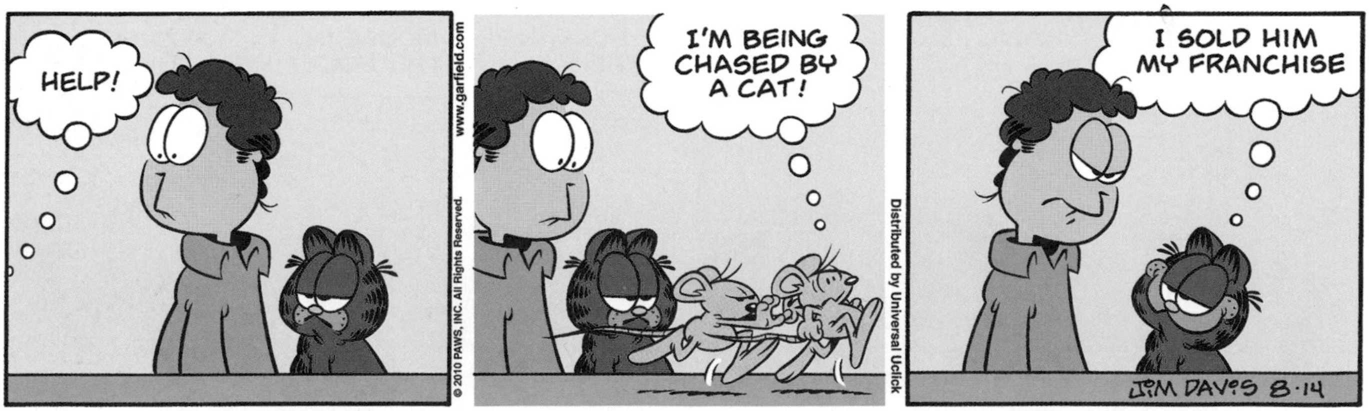
HELP!
© 2010 PAWS, INC. All Rights Reserved. www.garfield.com
I'M BEING CHASED BY A CAT!
Distributed by Universal Uclick
I SOLD HIM MY FRANCHISE
JIM DAVIS 8-14

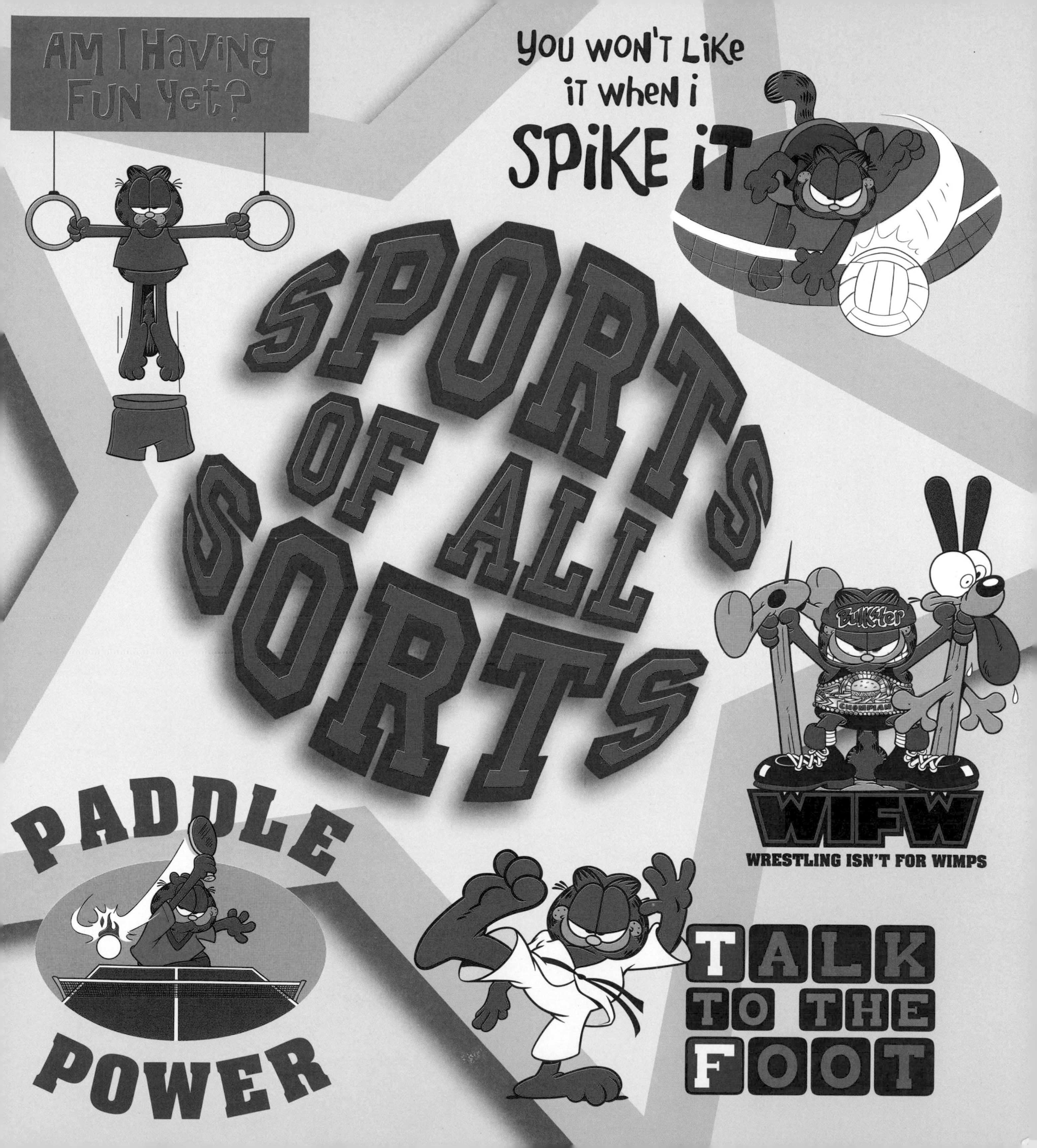
AM I Having FUN Yet?
YOU WON'T LIKE IT WHEN I SPIKE IT
SPORTS OF ALL SORTS
Bulkster
CHOMPIAN
WIFW
WRESTLING ISN'T FOR WIMPS
PADDLE POWER
TALK TO THE FOOT

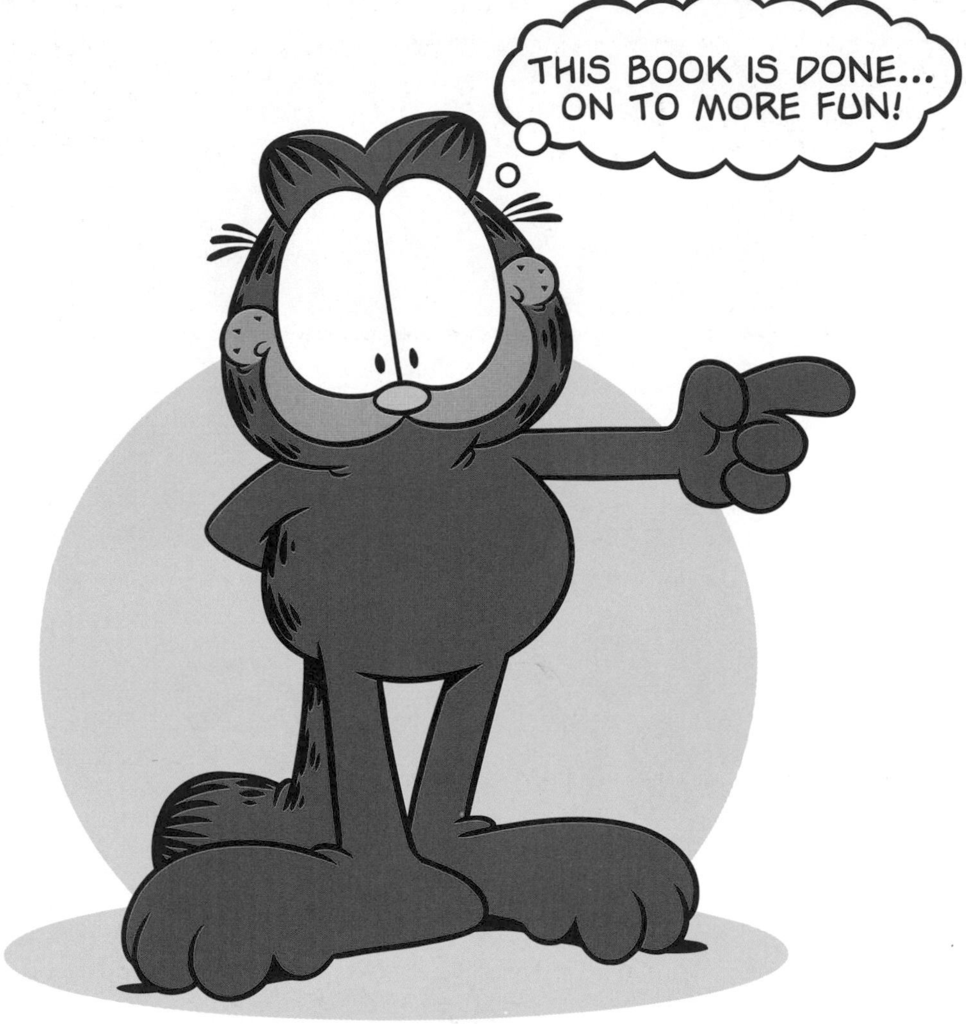
THIS BOOK IS DONE... ON TO MORE FUN!

Garfield
CAUTION:
WIDE LOAD

BY JIM DAVIS

Ballantine Books • **New York**

NOT-SO-SUPER SUPERHEROES

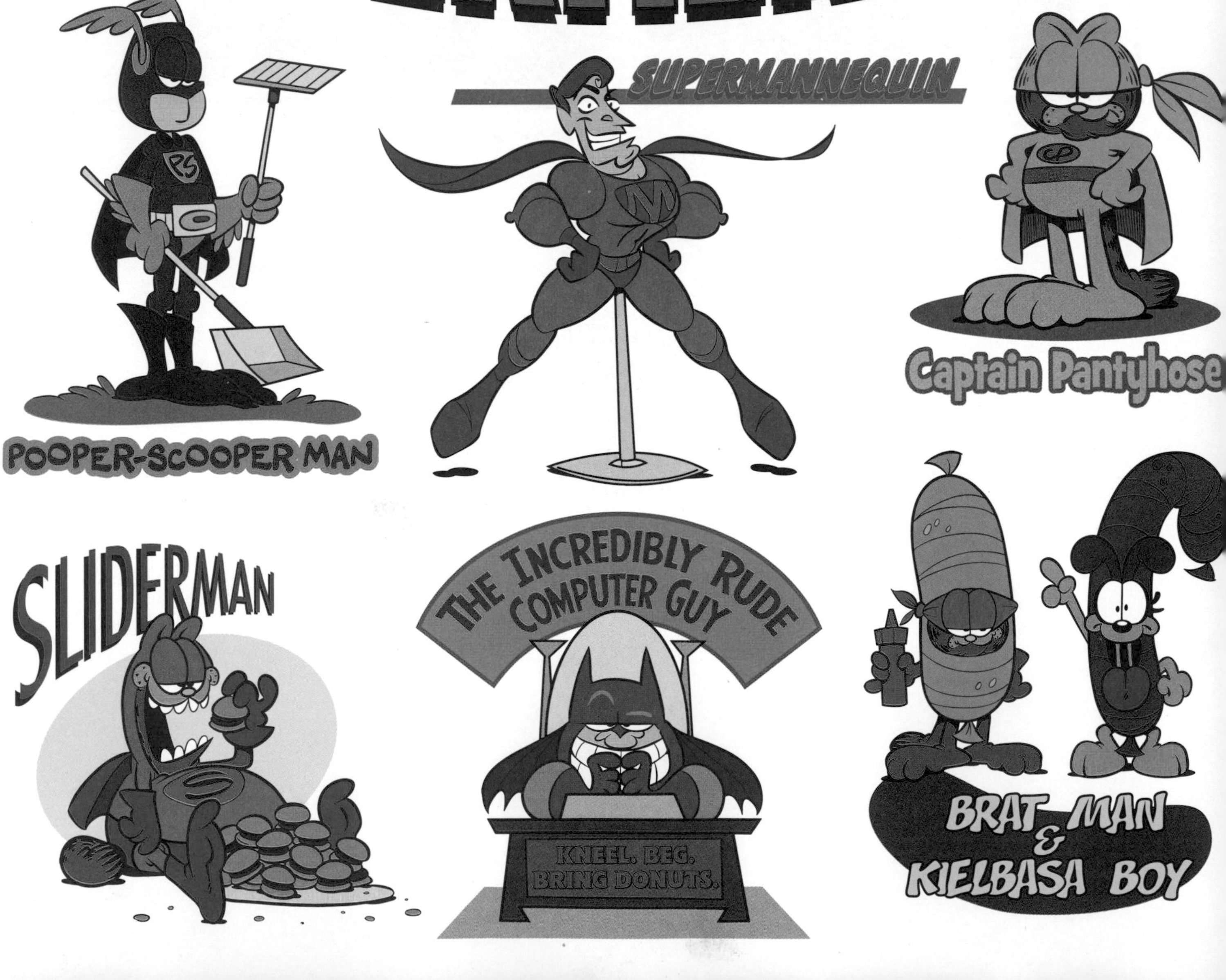
SUPERMANNEQUIN
POOPER-SCOOPER MAN
Captain Pantyhose
SLIDERMAN
THE INCREDIBLY RUDE COMPUTER GUY
KNEEL. BEG. BRING DONUTS.
BRAT MAN & KIELBASA BOY

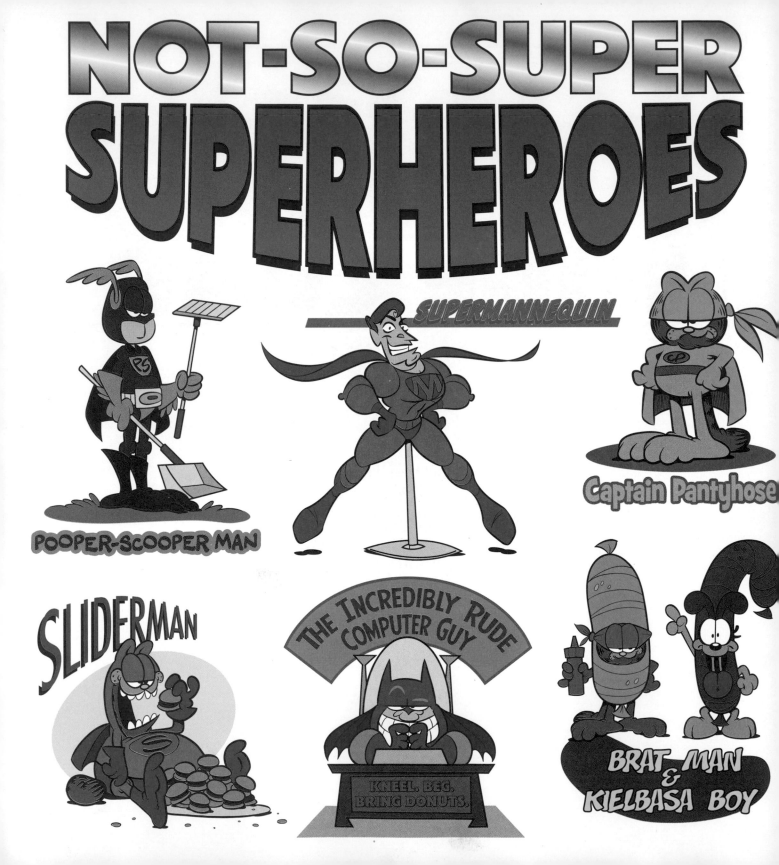

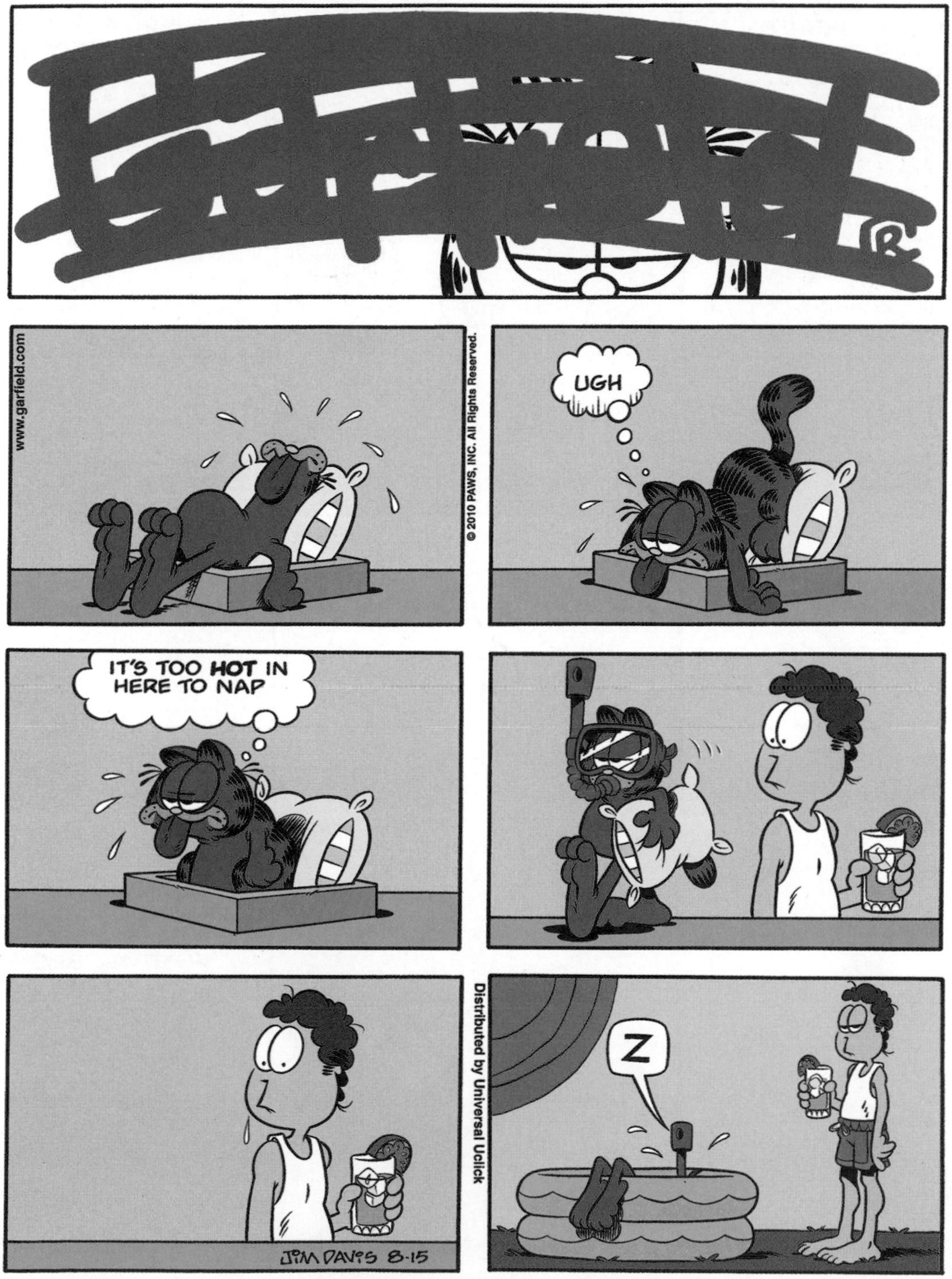
www.garfield.com
© 2010 PAWS, INC. All Rights Reserved.
UGH
IT'S TOO HOT IN HERE TO NAP
Z
JIM DAVIS 8-15
Distributed by Universal Uclick

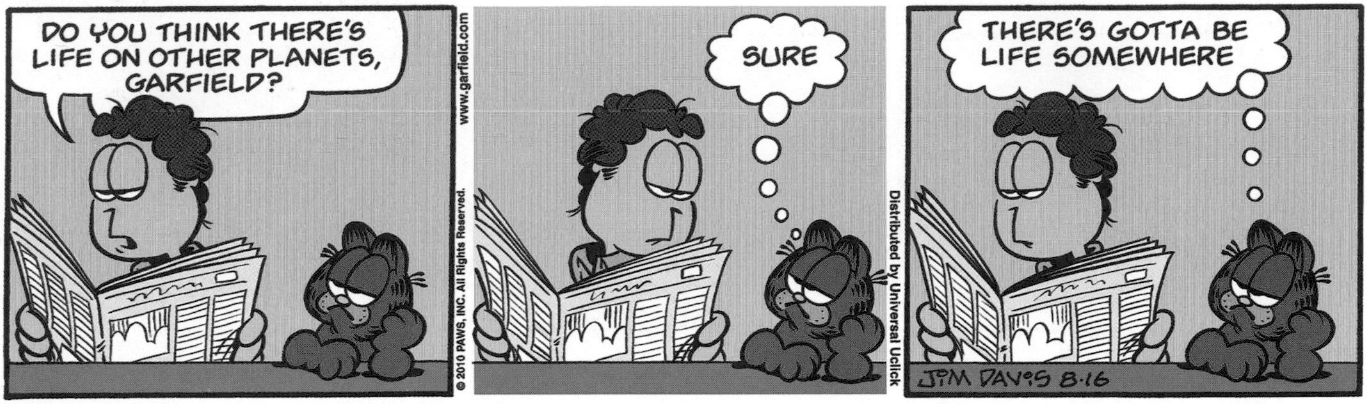
DO YOU THINK THERE'S LIFE ON OTHER PLANETS, GARFIELD?
© 2010 PAWS, INC. All Rights Reserved. www.garfield.com
SURE
Distributed by Universal Uclick
THERE'S GOTTA BE LIFE SOMEWHERE
JIM DAVIS 8-16

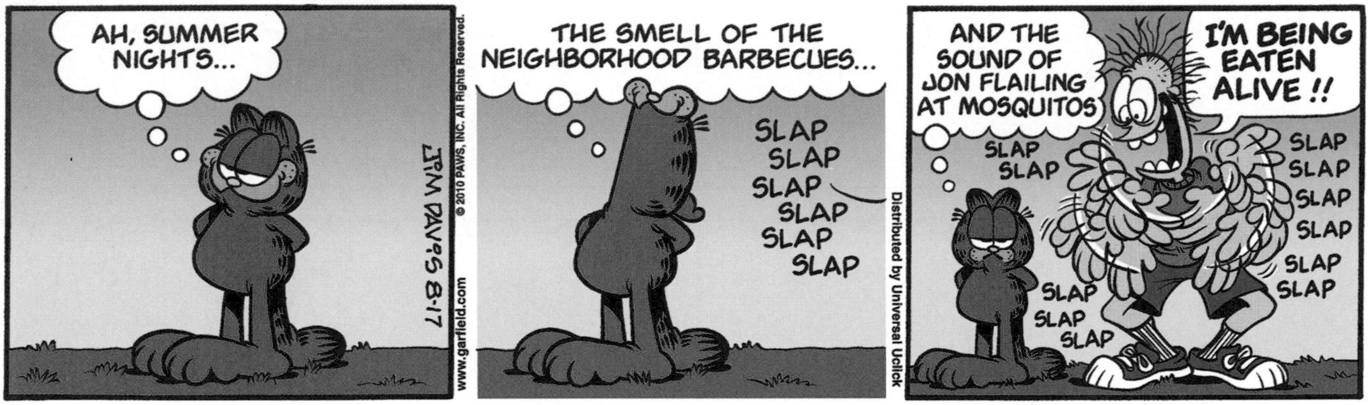
AH, SUMMER NIGHTS...
JIM DAVIS 8-17
© 2010 PAWS, INC. All Rights Reserved. www.garfield.com
THE SMELL OF THE NEIGHBORHOOD BARBECUES...
SLAP SLAP SLAP SLAP SLAP SLAP
Distributed by Universal Uclick
AND THE SOUND OF JON FLAILING AT MOSQUITOS
I'M BEING EATEN ALIVE !!
SLAP SLAP
SLAP SLAP SLAP SLAP SLAP SLAP
SLAP SLAP SLAP

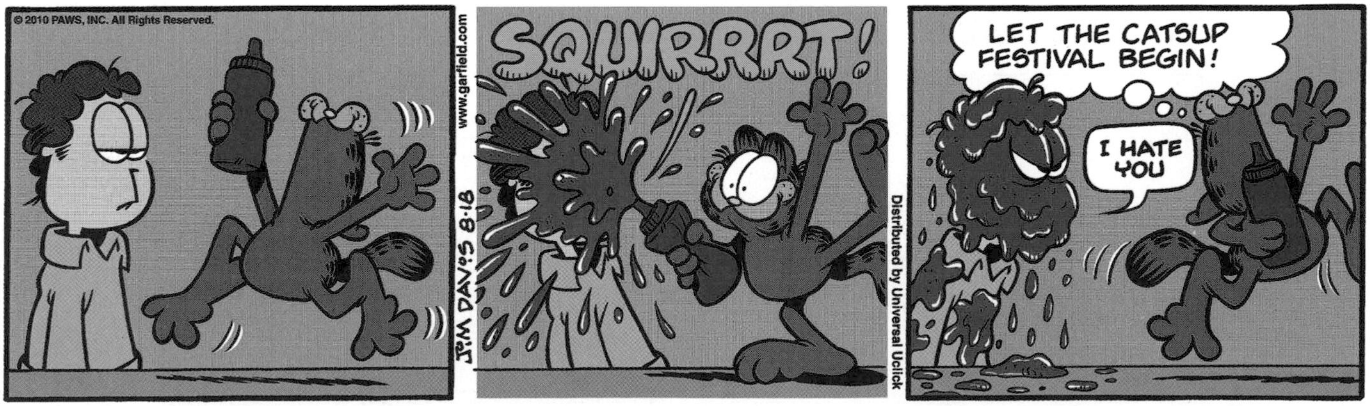
© 2010 PAWS, INC. All Rights Reserved.
www.garfield.com
JIM DAVIS 8-18
SQUIRRRT!
Distributed by Universal Uclick
LET THE CATSUP FESTIVAL BEGIN!
I HATE YOU

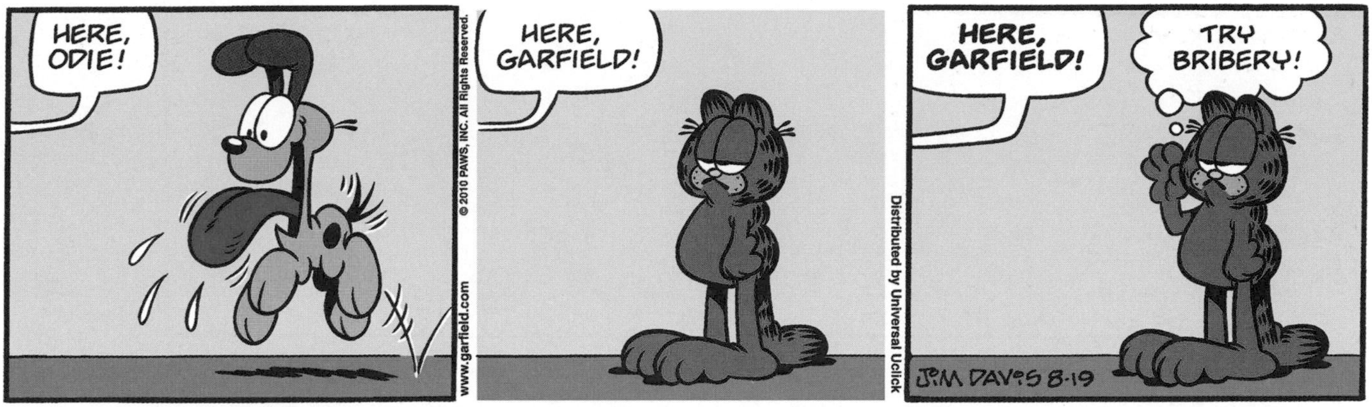
HERE, ODIE!
© 2010 PAWS, INC. All Rights Reserved. www.garfield.com
HERE, GARFIELD!
Distributed by Universal Uclick
HERE, GARFIELD!
TRY BRIBERY!
JIM DAVIS 8·19

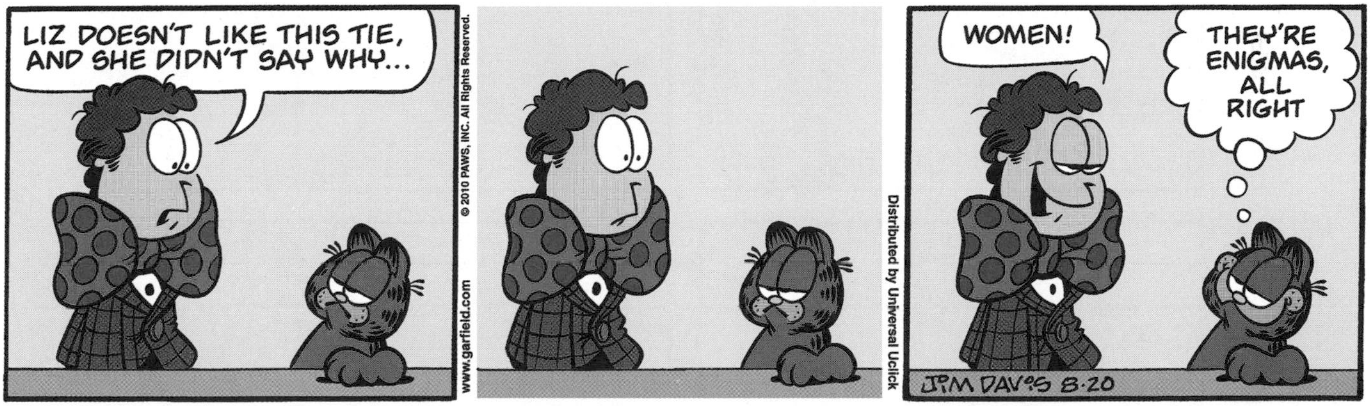
LIZ DOESN'T LIKE THIS TIE, AND SHE DIDN'T SAY WHY...
© 2010 PAWS, INC. All Rights Reserved. www.garfield.com
Distributed by Universal Uclick
WOMEN!
THEY'RE ENIGMAS, ALL RIGHT
JIM DAVIS 8·20

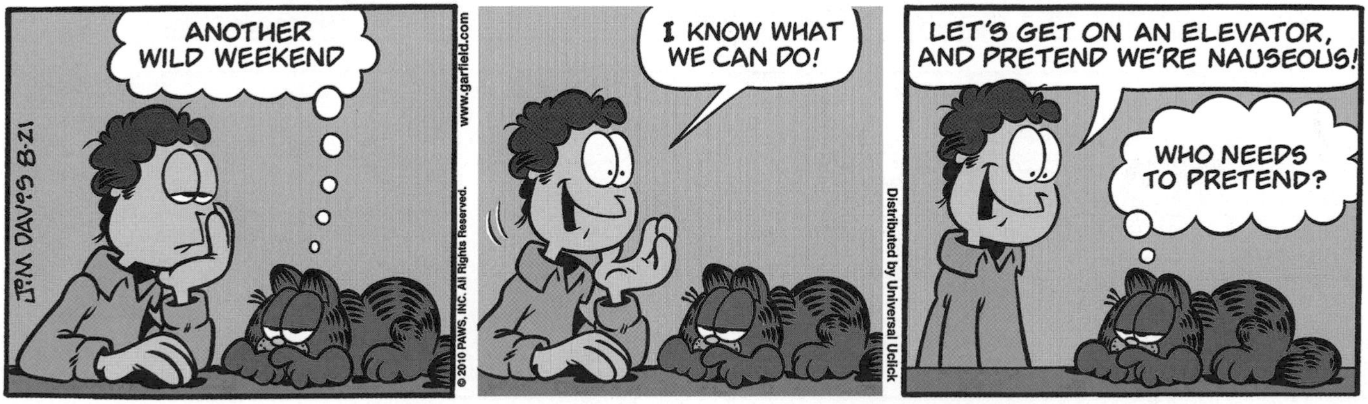
ANOTHER WILD WEEKEND
JIM DAVIS 8·21
www.garfield.com © 2010 PAWS, INC. All Rights Reserved.
I KNOW WHAT WE CAN DO!
Distributed by Universal Uclick
LET'S GET ON AN ELEVATOR, AND PRETEND WE'RE NAUSEOUS!
WHO NEEDS TO PRETEND?

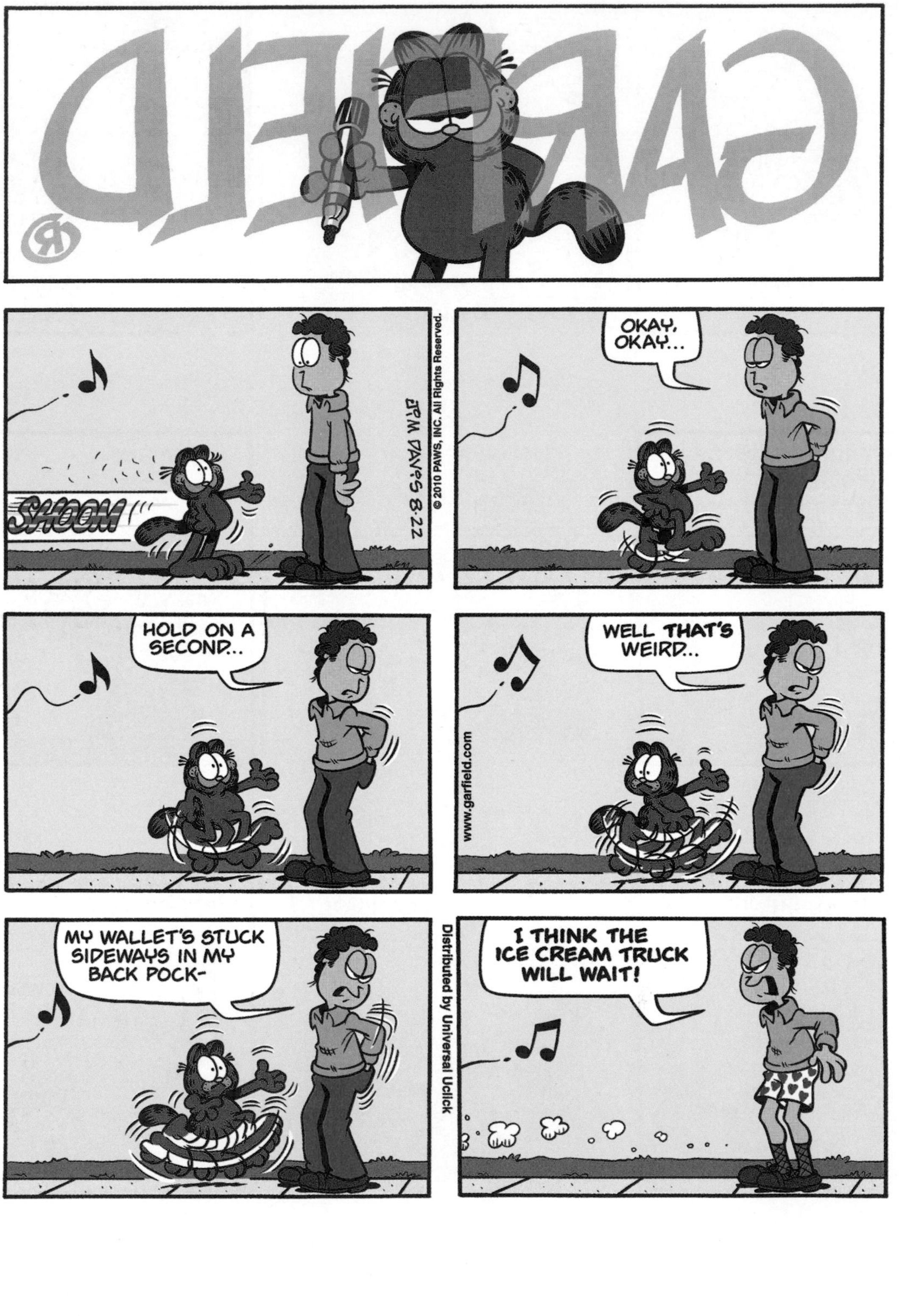
GARFIELD
SHOOM
JIM DAVIS 8-22
© 2010 PAWS, INC. All Rights Reserved.
OKAY, OKAY...
HOLD ON A SECOND...
WELL THAT'S WEIRD...
www.garfield.com
MY WALLET'S STUCK SIDEWAYS IN MY BACK POCK-
Distributed by Universal Uclick
I THINK THE ICE CREAM TRUCK WILL WAIT!

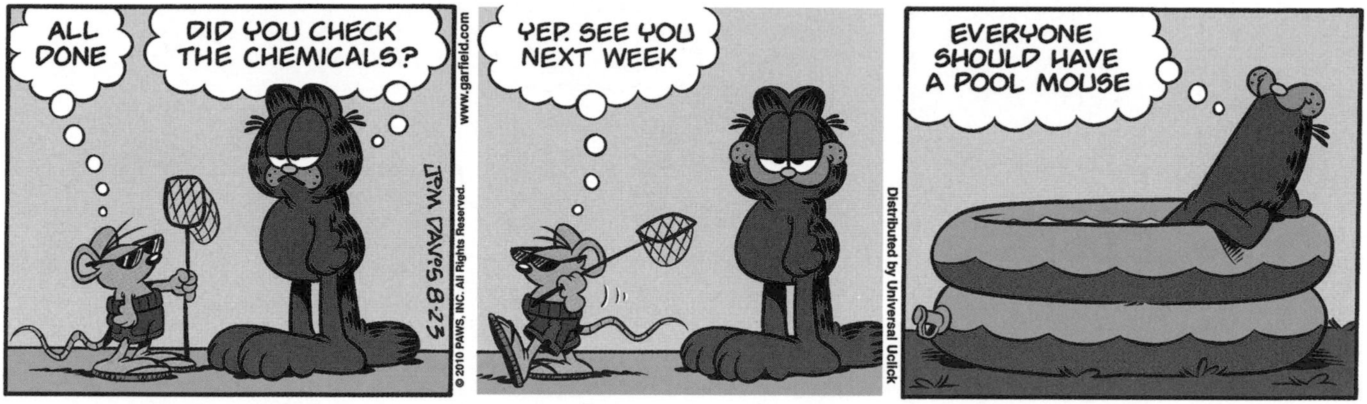
ALL DONE
DID YOU CHECK THE CHEMICALS?
JPM DAVPS 8-23
© 2010 PAWS, INC. All Rights Reserved. www.garfield.com
YEP. SEE YOU NEXT WEEK
Distributed by Universal Uclick
EVERYONE SHOULD HAVE A POOL MOUSE

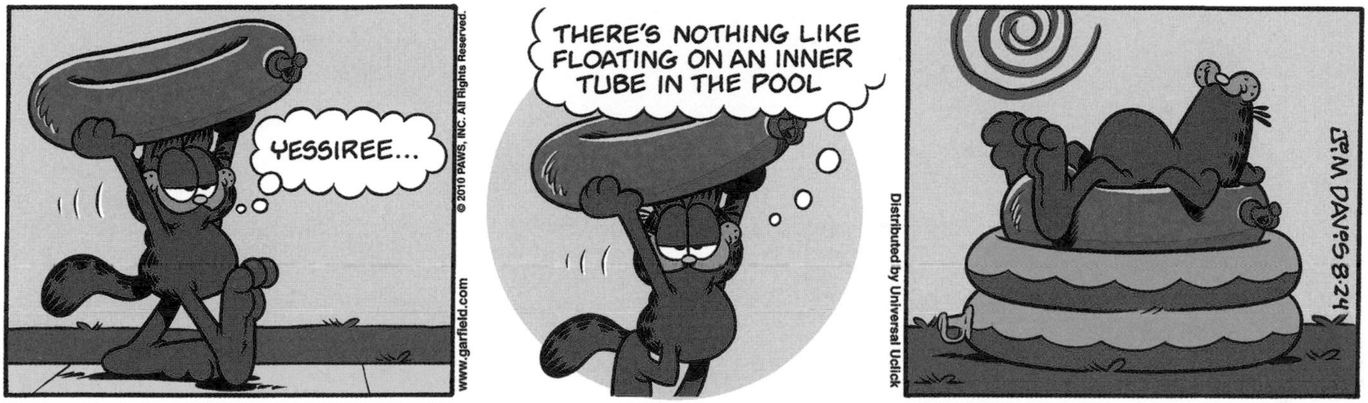
YESSIREE...
www.garfield.com © 2010 PAWS, INC. All Rights Reserved.
THERE'S NOTHING LIKE FLOATING ON AN INNER TUBE IN THE POOL
Distributed by Universal Uclick
JPM DAVPS 8-24

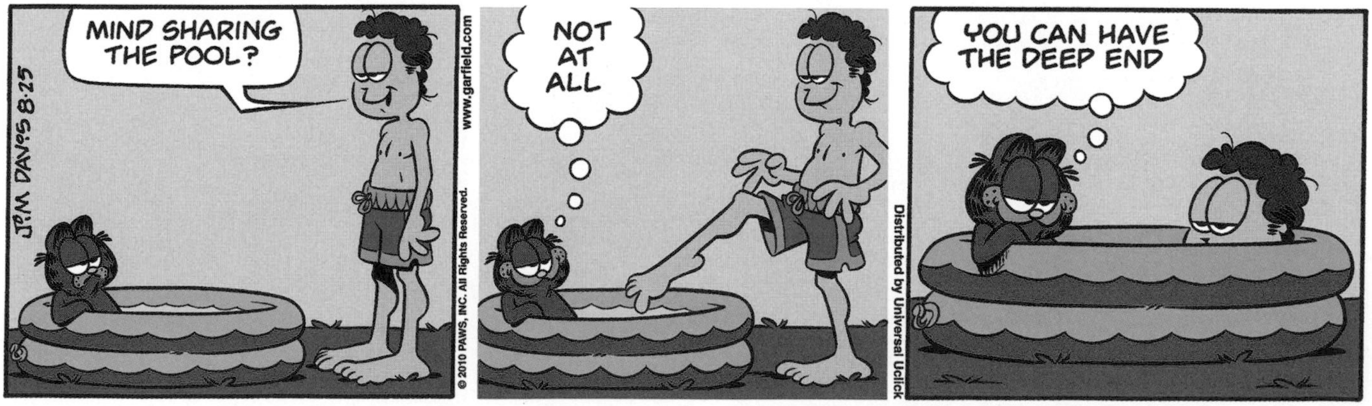
JPM DAVPS 8-25
MIND SHARING THE POOL?
© 2010 PAWS, INC. All Rights Reserved. www.garfield.com
NOT AT ALL
Distributed by Universal Uclick
YOU CAN HAVE THE DEEP END

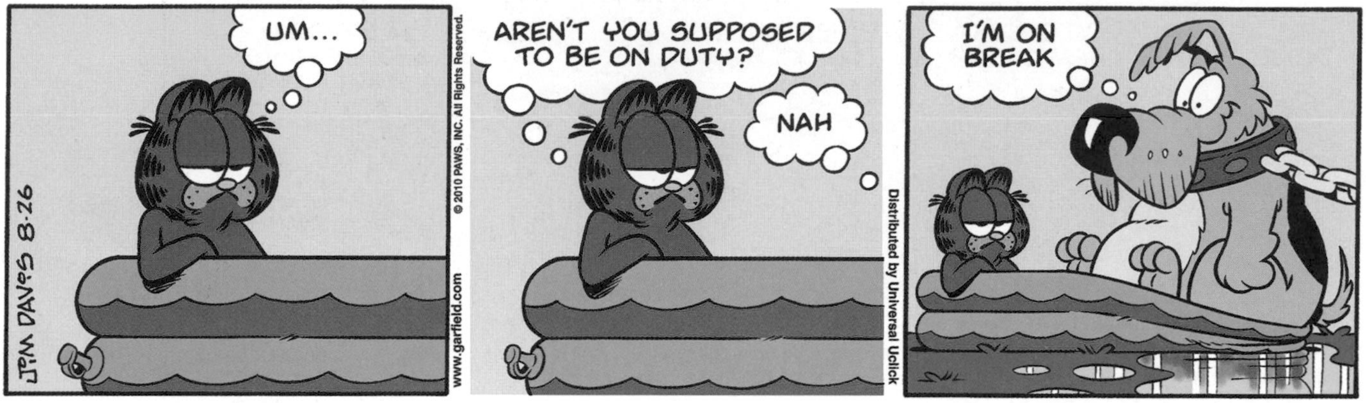
UM...
AREN'T YOU SUPPOSED TO BE ON DUTY?
NAH
I'M ON BREAK
© 2010 PAWS, INC. All Rights Reserved.
www.garfield.com
Distributed by Universal Uclick

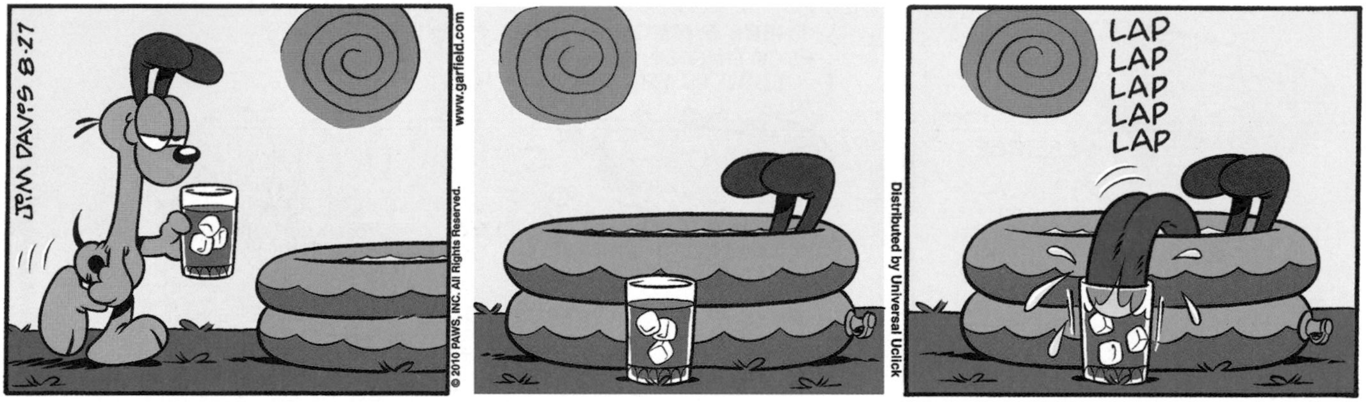
LAP
LAP
LAP
LAP
LAP
© 2010 PAWS, INC. All Rights Reserved.
www.garfield.com
Distributed by Universal Uclick

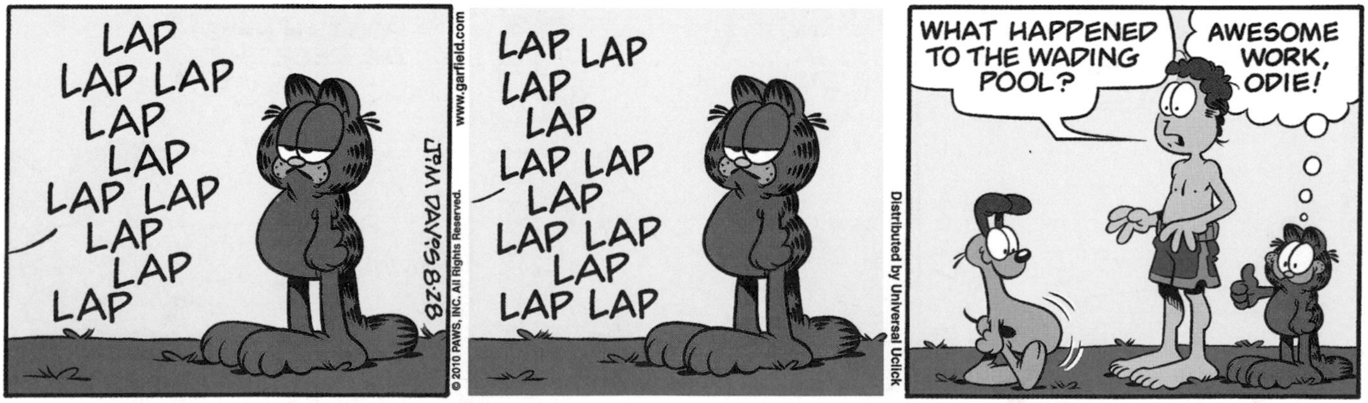
LAP
LAP LAP
LAP
LAP
LAP LAP
LAP
LAP
LAP
LAP LAP
LAP
LAP
LAP LAP
LAP
LAP LAP
LAP
LAP LAP
WHAT HAPPENED TO THE WADING POOL?
AWESOME WORK, ODIE!
© 2010 PAWS, INC. All Rights Reserved.
www.garfield.com
Distributed by Universal Uclick

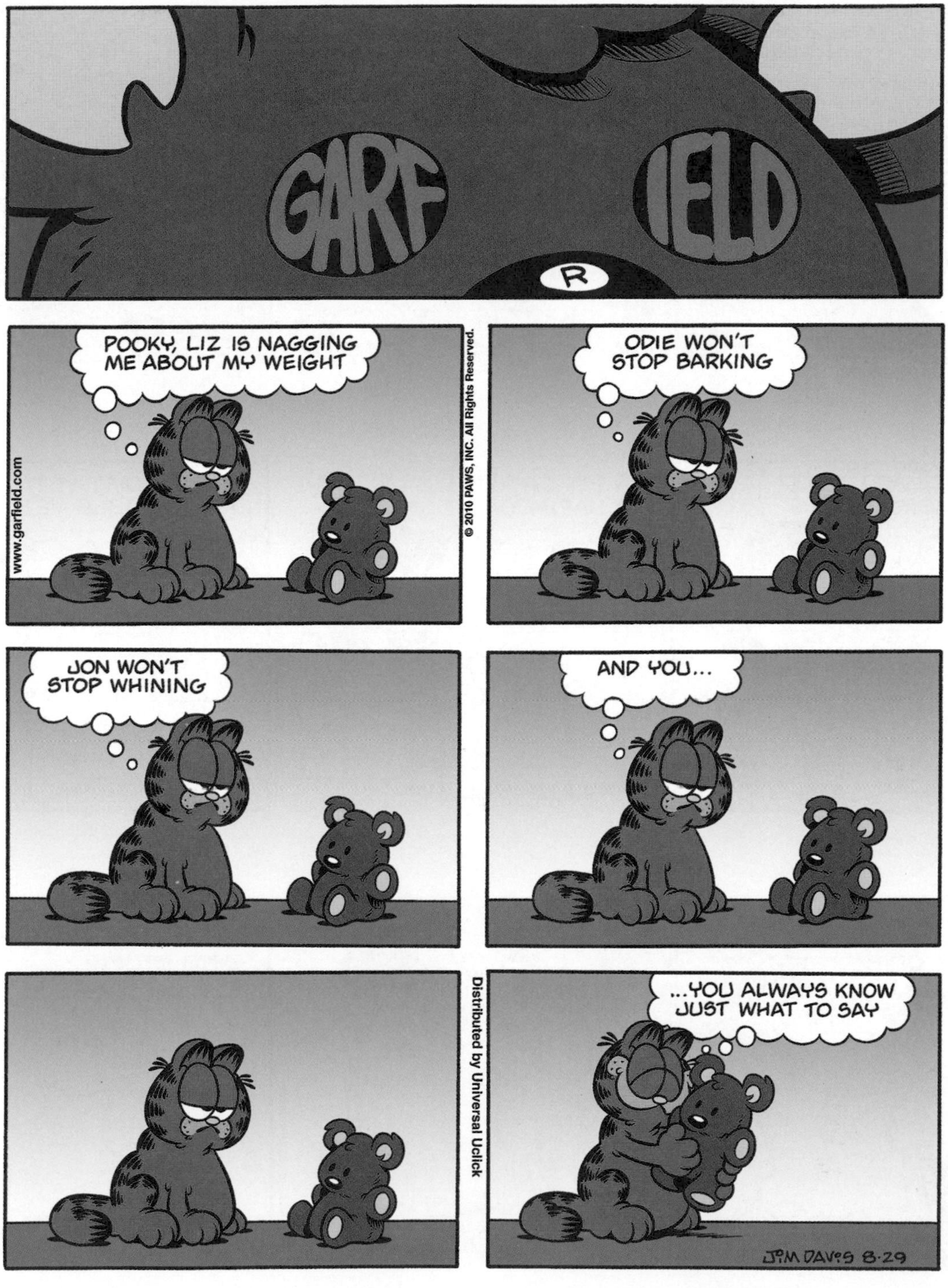
GARFIELD
POOKY, LIZ IS NAGGING ME ABOUT MY WEIGHT
ODIE WON'T STOP BARKING
JON WON'T STOP WHINING
AND YOU...
...YOU ALWAYS KNOW JUST WHAT TO SAY
JIM DAVIS 8-29
www.garfield.com
© 2010 PAWS, INC. All Rights Reserved.
Distributed by Universal Uclick

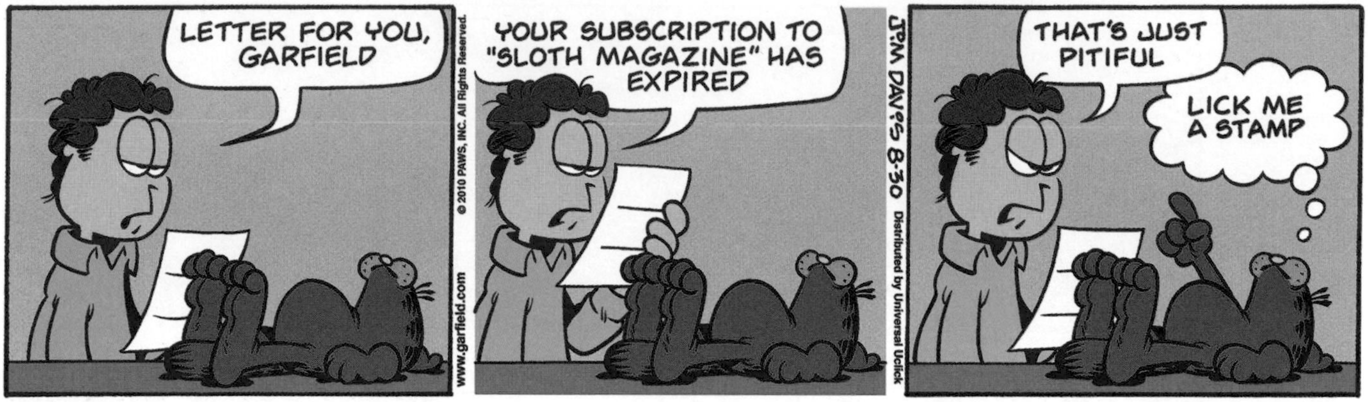
LETTER FOR YOU, GARFIELD
© 2010 PAWS, INC. All Rights Reserved.
www.garfield.com
YOUR SUBSCRIPTION TO "SLOTH MAGAZINE" HAS EXPIRED
JIM DAVIS 8-30
Distributed by Universal Uclick
THAT'S JUST PITIFUL
LICK ME A STAMP

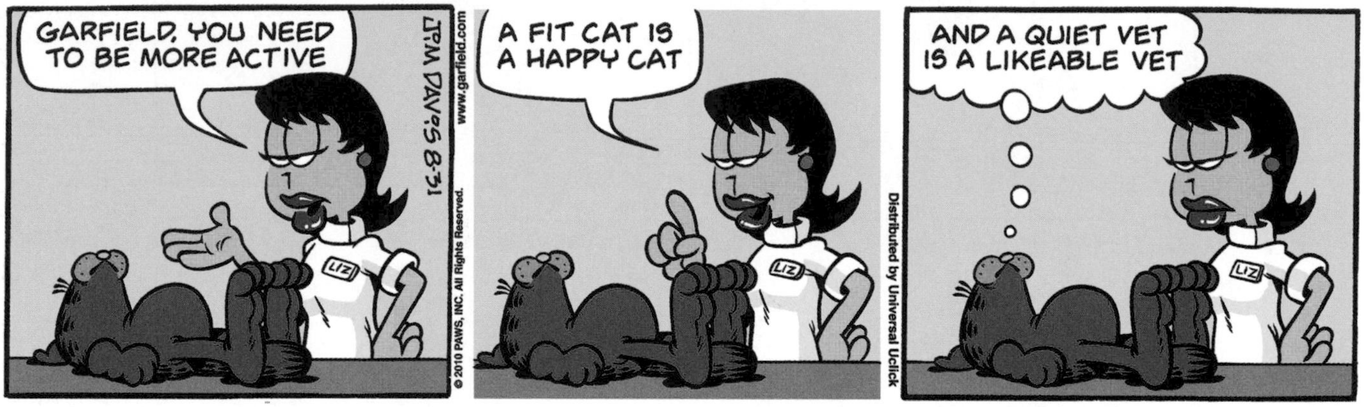
GARFIELD, YOU NEED TO BE MORE ACTIVE
LIZ
JIM DAVIS 8-31
© 2010 PAWS, INC. All Rights Reserved.
www.garfield.com
A FIT CAT IS A HAPPY CAT
Distributed by Universal Uclick
AND A QUIET VET IS A LIKEABLE VET

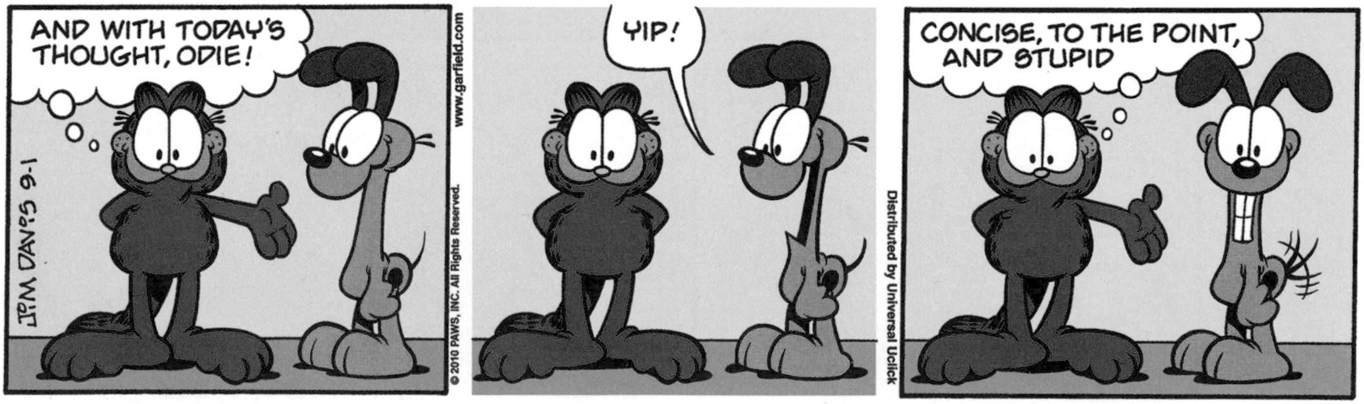
AND WITH TODAY'S THOUGHT, ODIE!
JIM DAVIS 9-1
www.garfield.com
© 2010 PAWS, INC. All Rights Reserved.
YIP!
Distributed by Universal Uclick
CONCISE, TO THE POINT, AND STUPID

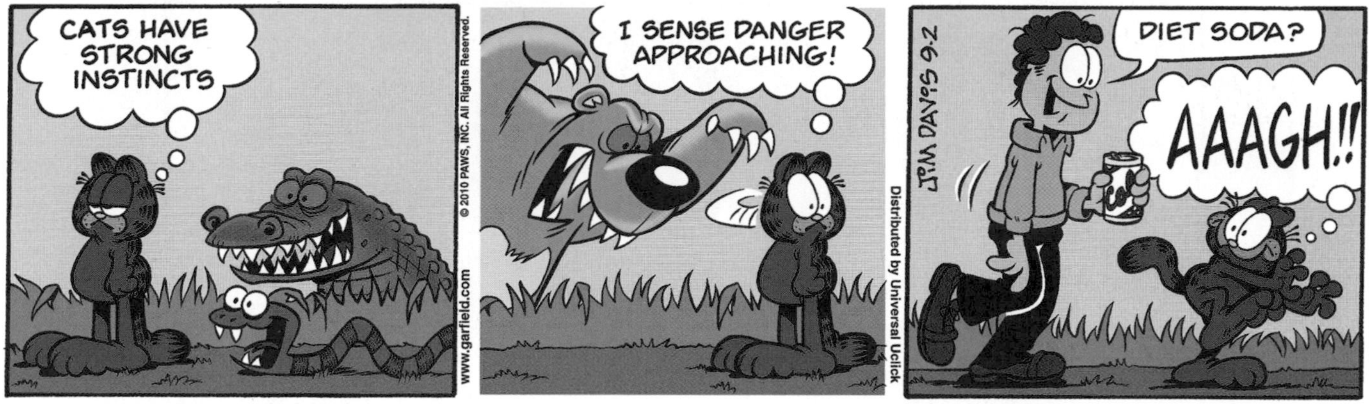
CATS HAVE STRONG INSTINCTS
© 2010 PAWS, INC. All Rights Reserved.
www.garfield.com
I SENSE DANGER APPROACHING!
Distributed by Universal Uclick
JIM DAVIS 9-2
DIET SODA?
AAAGH!!

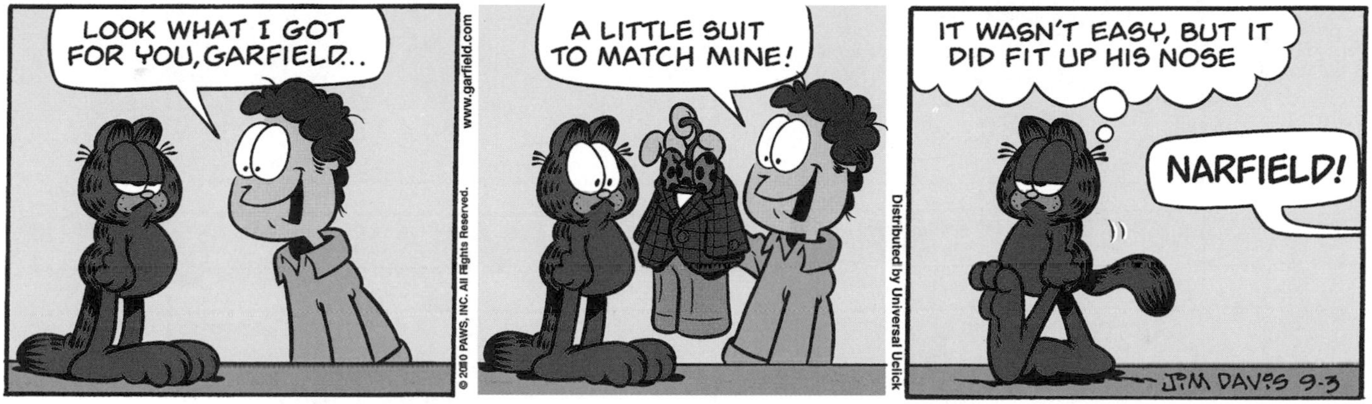
LOOK WHAT I GOT FOR YOU, GARFIELD...
www.garfield.com
© 2010 PAWS, INC. All Rights Reserved.
A LITTLE SUIT TO MATCH MINE!
Distributed by Universal Uclick
IT WASN'T EASY, BUT IT DID FIT UP HIS NOSE
NARFIELD!
JIM DAVIS 9-3

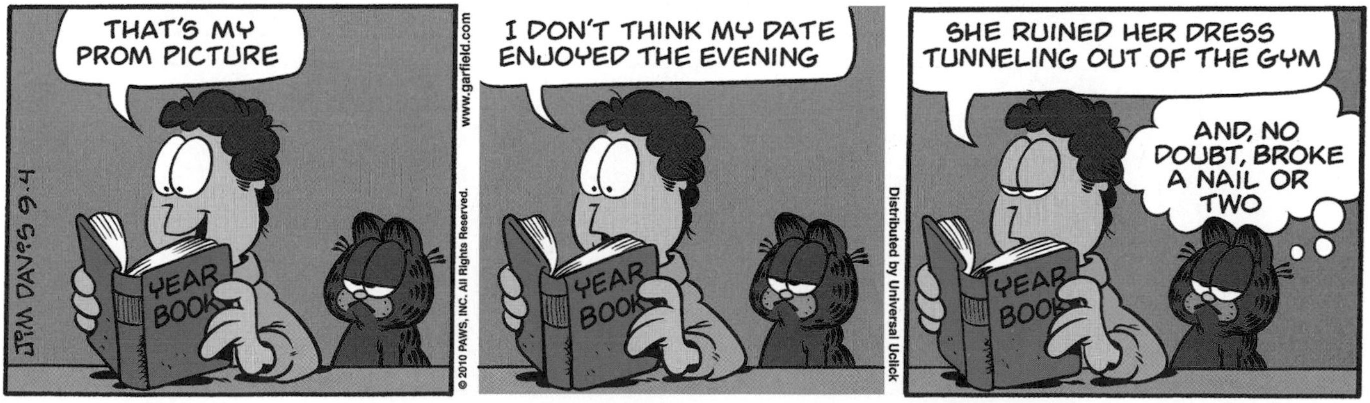
THAT'S MY PROM PICTURE
JIM DAVIS 9-4
YEAR BOOK
www.garfield.com
© 2010 PAWS, INC. All Rights Reserved.
I DON'T THINK MY DATE ENJOYED THE EVENING
Distributed by Universal Uclick
SHE RUINED HER DRESS TUNNELING OUT OF THE GYM
AND, NO DOUBT, BROKE A NAIL OR TWO

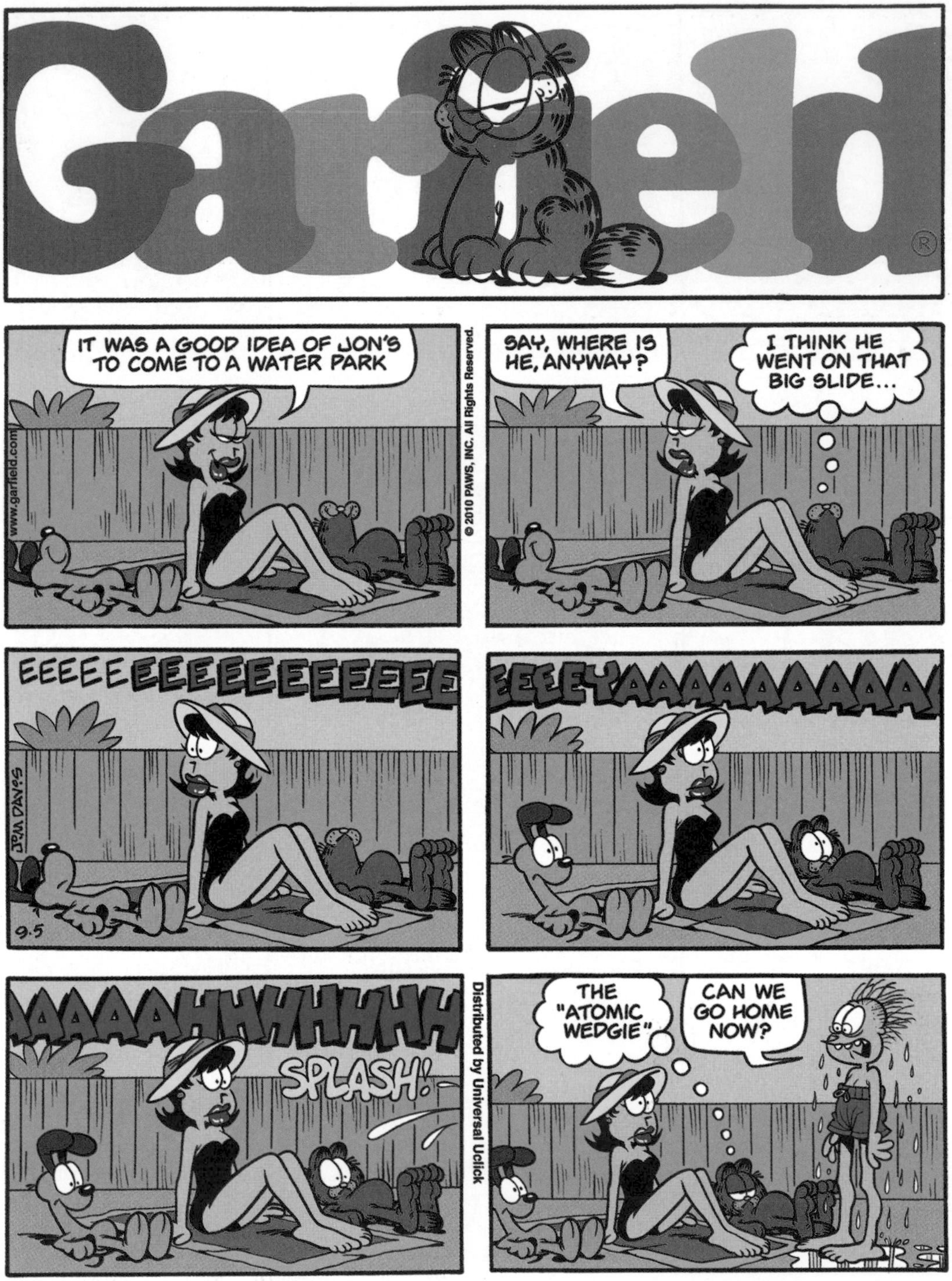
Garfield
IT WAS A GOOD IDEA OF JON'S TO COME TO A WATER PARK
www.garfield.com
© 2010 PAWS, INC. All Rights Reserved.
SAY, WHERE IS HE, ANYWAY?
I THINK HE WENT ON THAT BIG SLIDE...
EEEEEEEEEEEEEEEE
JPM DAVIS
9.5
EEEEYAAAAAAAAAA
AAAAAHHHHHHH
SPLASH!
Distributed by Universal Uclick
THE "ATOMIC WEDGIE"
CAN WE GO HOME NOW?

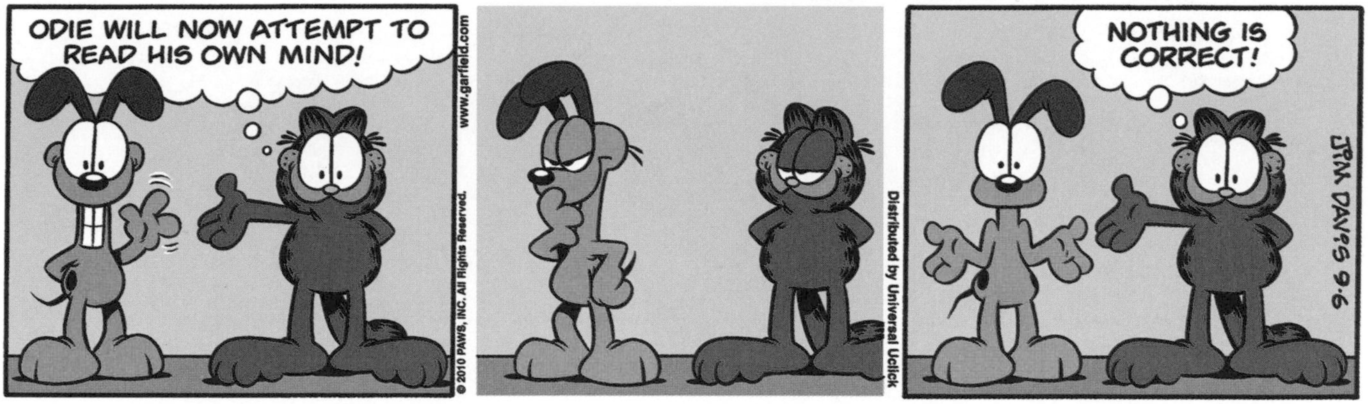
ODIE WILL NOW ATTEMPT TO READ HIS OWN MIND!
NOTHING IS CORRECT!
JIM DAVIS 9-6
www.garfield.com
© 2010 PAWS, INC. All Rights Reserved.
Distributed by Universal Uclick

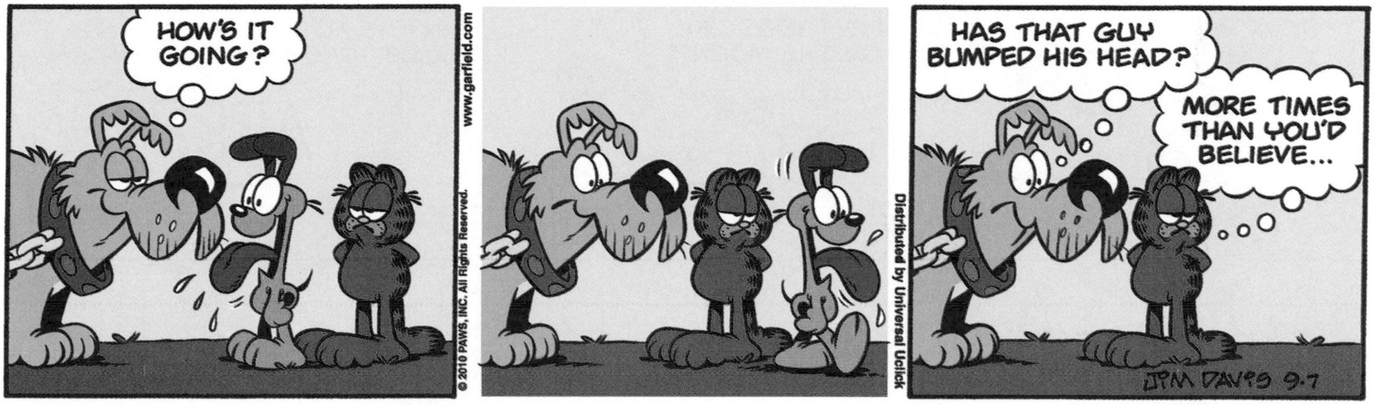
HOW'S IT GOING?
HAS THAT GUY BUMPED HIS HEAD?
MORE TIMES THAN YOU'D BELIEVE...
JIM DAVIS 9-7
www.garfield.com
© 2010 PAWS, INC. All Rights Reserved.
Distributed by Universal Uclick

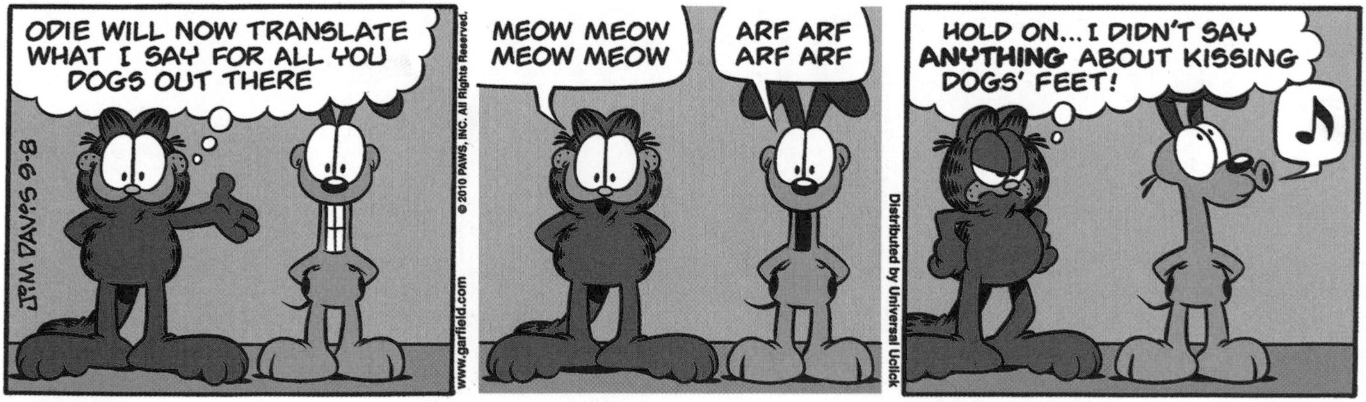
ODIE WILL NOW TRANSLATE WHAT I SAY FOR ALL YOU DOGS OUT THERE
MEOW MEOW MEOW MEOW
ARF ARF ARF ARF
HOLD ON... I DIDN'T SAY **ANYTHING** ABOUT KISSING DOGS' FEET!
JIM DAVIS 9-8
www.garfield.com
© 2010 PAWS, INC. All Rights Reserved.
Distributed by Universal Uclick

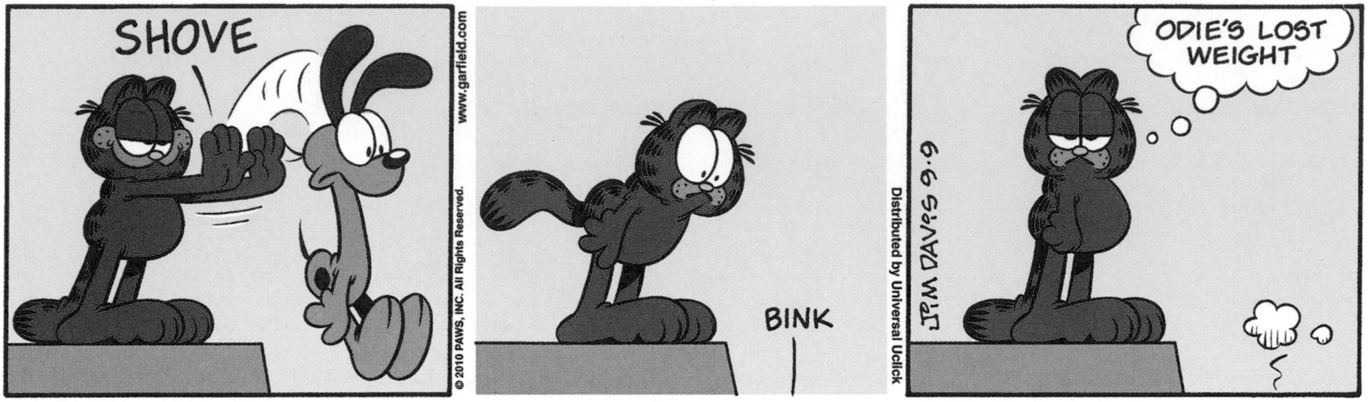
SHOVE
© 2010 PAWS, INC. All Rights Reserved.
www.garfield.com
BINK
Distributed by Universal Uclick
JIM DAVIS 9-9
ODIE'S LOST WEIGHT

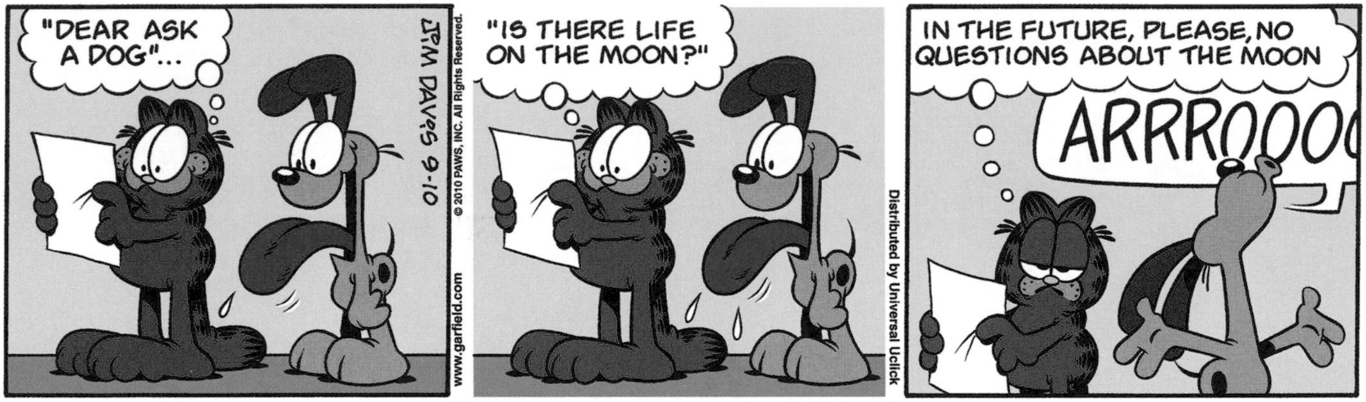
"DEAR ASK A DOG"...
JIM DAVIS 9-10
© 2010 PAWS, INC. All Rights Reserved.
www.garfield.com
"IS THERE LIFE ON THE MOON?"
Distributed by Universal Uclick
IN THE FUTURE, PLEASE, NO QUESTIONS ABOUT THE MOON
ARRROOOO

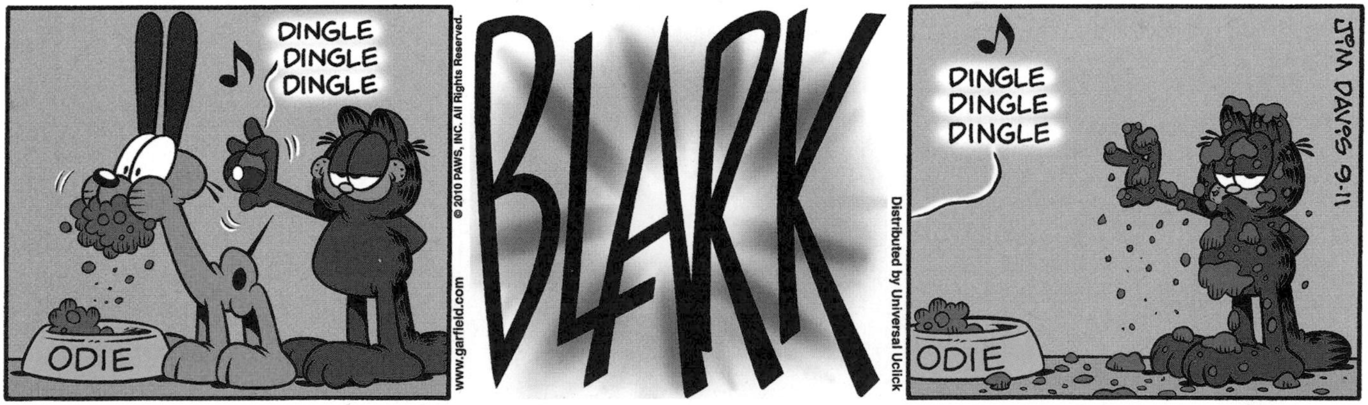
DINGLE DINGLE DINGLE
ODIE
© 2010 PAWS, INC. All Rights Reserved.
www.garfield.com
BLARK
Distributed by Universal Uclick
DINGLE DINGLE DINGLE
ODIE
JIM DAVIS 9-11

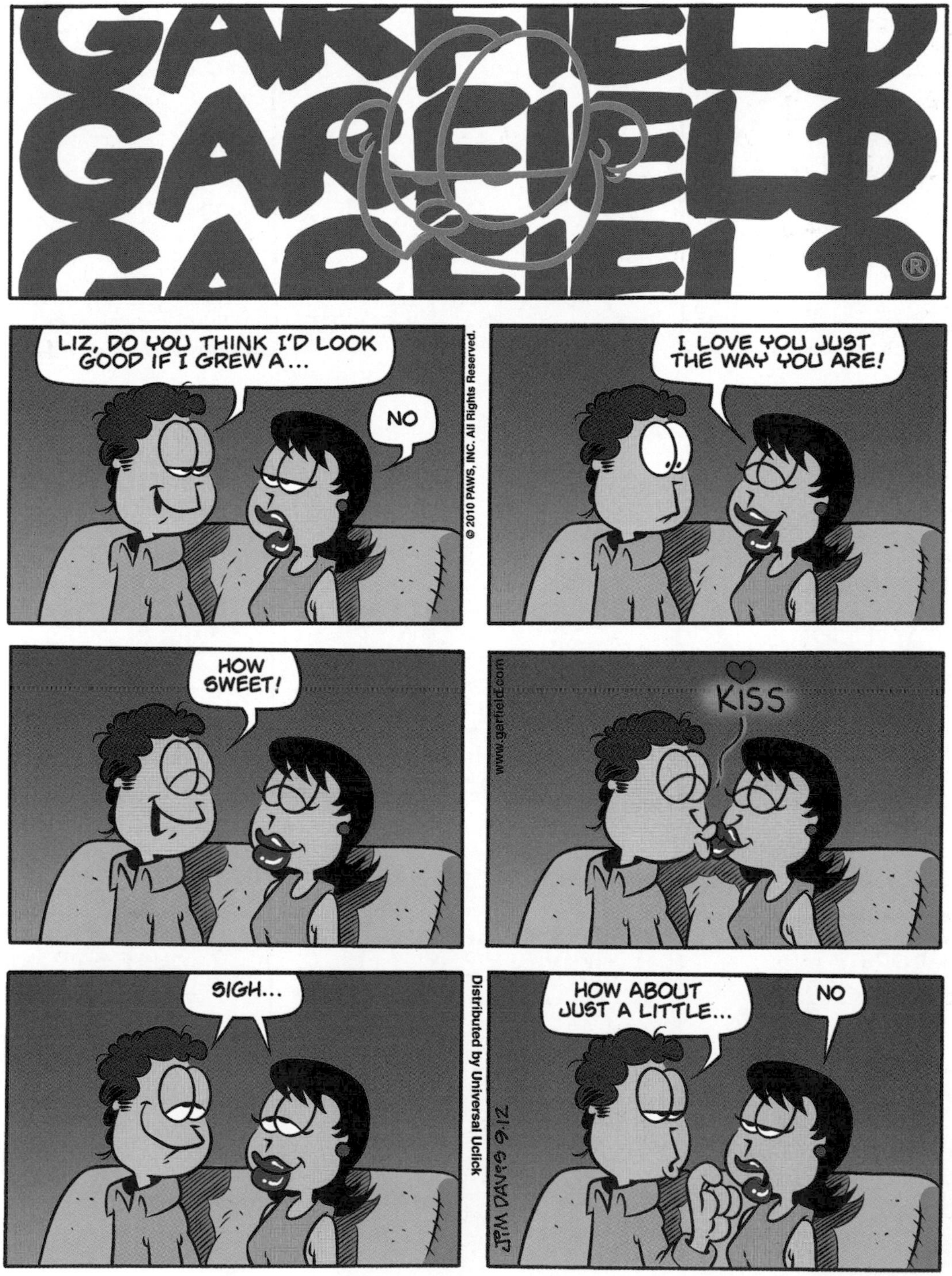
GARFIELD
LIZ, DO YOU THINK I'D LOOK GOOD IF I GREW A...
NO
I LOVE YOU JUST THE WAY YOU ARE!
HOW SWEET!
KISS
SIGH...
HOW ABOUT JUST A LITTLE...
NO
© 2010 PAWS, INC. All Rights Reserved.
www.garfield.com
Distributed by Universal Uclick
JPM DAVPS 9.12

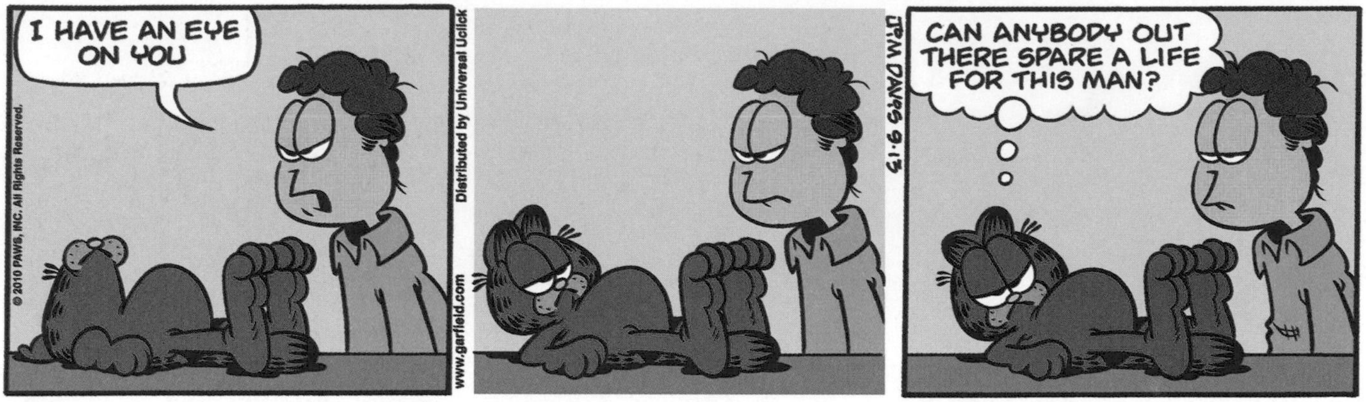
I HAVE AN EYE ON YOU
CAN ANYBODY OUT THERE SPARE A LIFE FOR THIS MAN?
© 2010 PAWS, INC. All Rights Reserved.
www.garfield.com
Distributed by Universal Uclick
JPM DAVPS 9·13

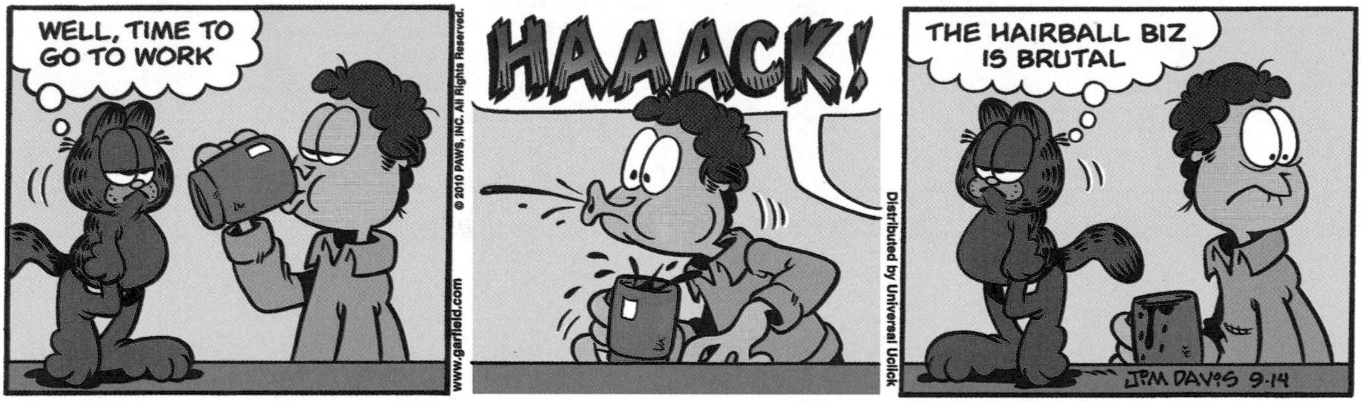
WELL, TIME TO GO TO WORK
HAAACK!
THE HAIRBALL BIZ IS BRUTAL
© 2010 PAWS, INC. All Rights Reserved.
www.garfield.com
Distributed by Universal Uclick
JPM DAVPS 9·14

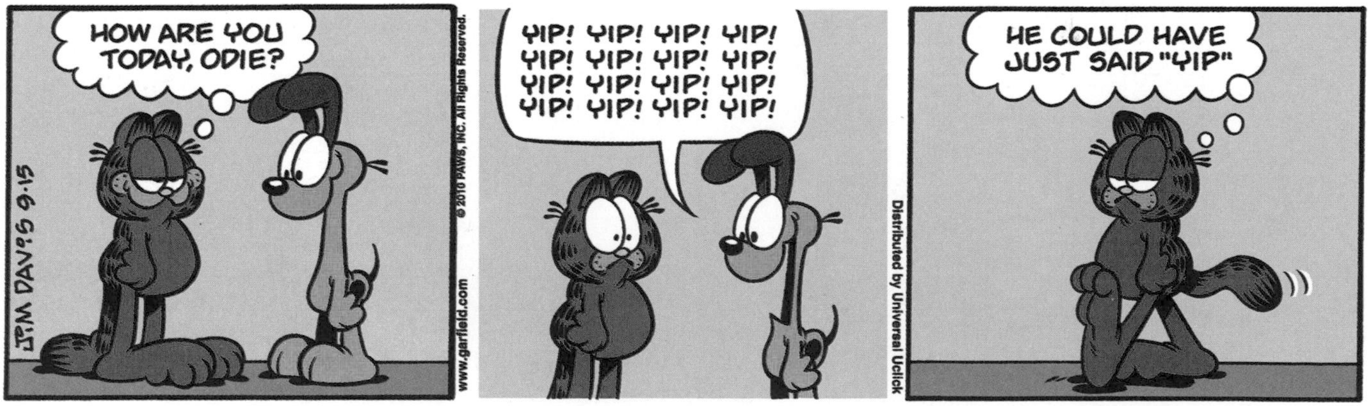
HOW ARE YOU TODAY, ODIE?
YIP! YIP! YIP! YIP! YIP! YIP! YIP! YIP! YIP! YIP! YIP! YIP! YIP! YIP! YIP! YIP!
HE COULD HAVE JUST SAID "YIP"
JPM DAVPS 9·15
© 2010 PAWS, INC. All Rights Reserved.
www.garfield.com
Distributed by Universal Uclick

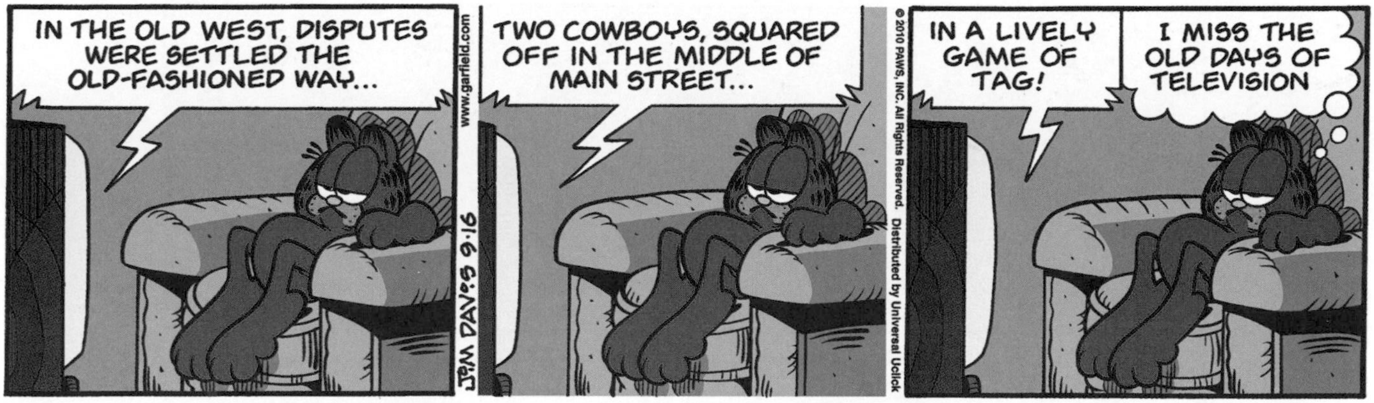
IN THE OLD WEST, DISPUTES WERE SETTLED THE OLD-FASHIONED WAY...
TWO COWBOYS, SQUARED OFF IN THE MIDDLE OF MAIN STREET...
IN A LIVELY GAME OF TAG!
I MISS THE OLD DAYS OF TELEVISION
JIM DAVIS 9·16
www.garfield.com
© 2010 PAWS, INC. All Rights Reserved. Distributed by Universal Uclick

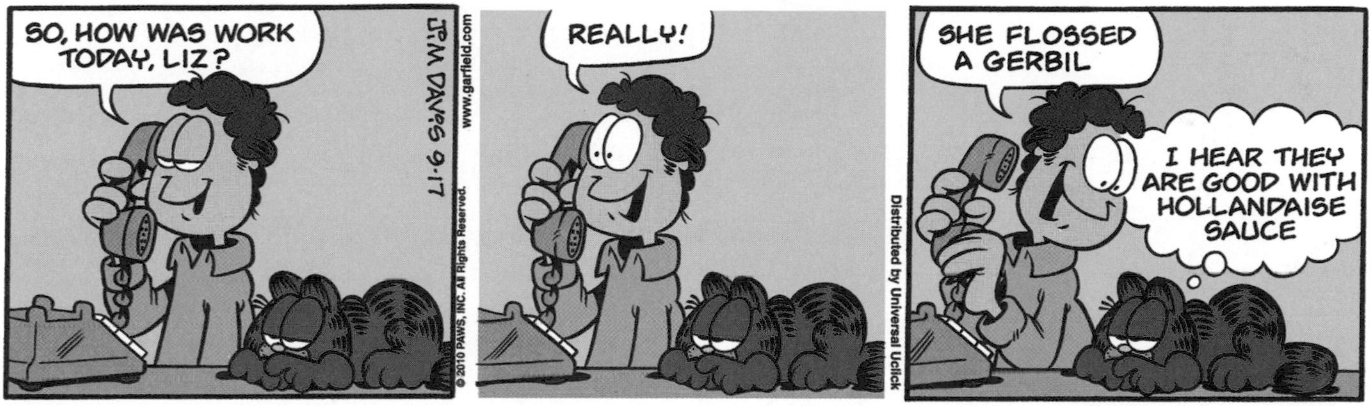
SO, HOW WAS WORK TODAY, LIZ?
REALLY!
SHE FLOSSED A GERBIL
I HEAR THEY ARE GOOD WITH HOLLANDAISE SAUCE
JIM DAVIS 9·17
www.garfield.com
© 2010 PAWS, INC. All Rights Reserved.
Distributed by Universal Uclick

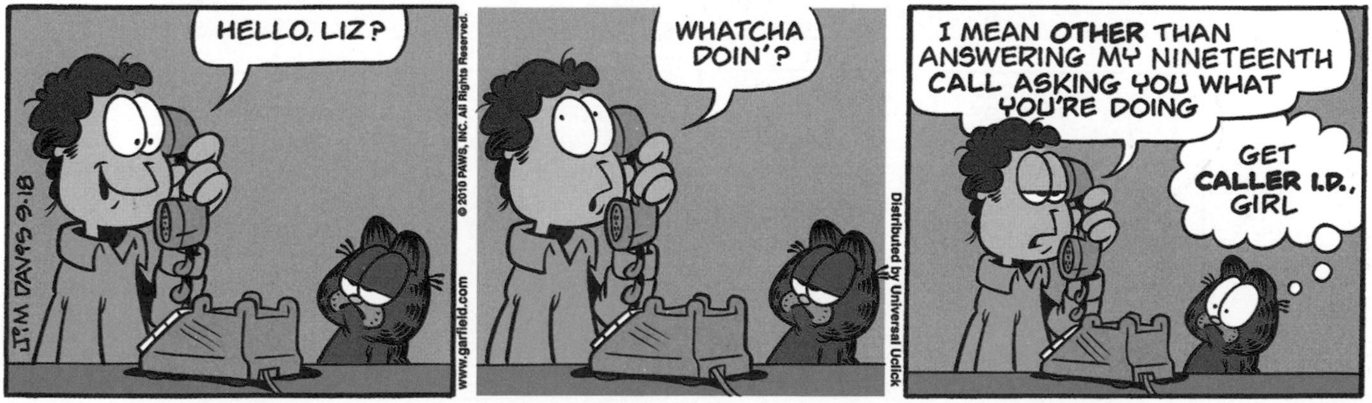
HELLO, LIZ?
WHATCHA DOIN'?
I MEAN OTHER THAN ANSWERING MY NINETEENTH CALL ASKING YOU WHAT YOU'RE DOING
GET CALLER I.D., GIRL
JIM DAVIS 9·18
www.garfield.com
© 2010 PAWS, INC. All Rights Reserved.
Distributed by Universal Uclick

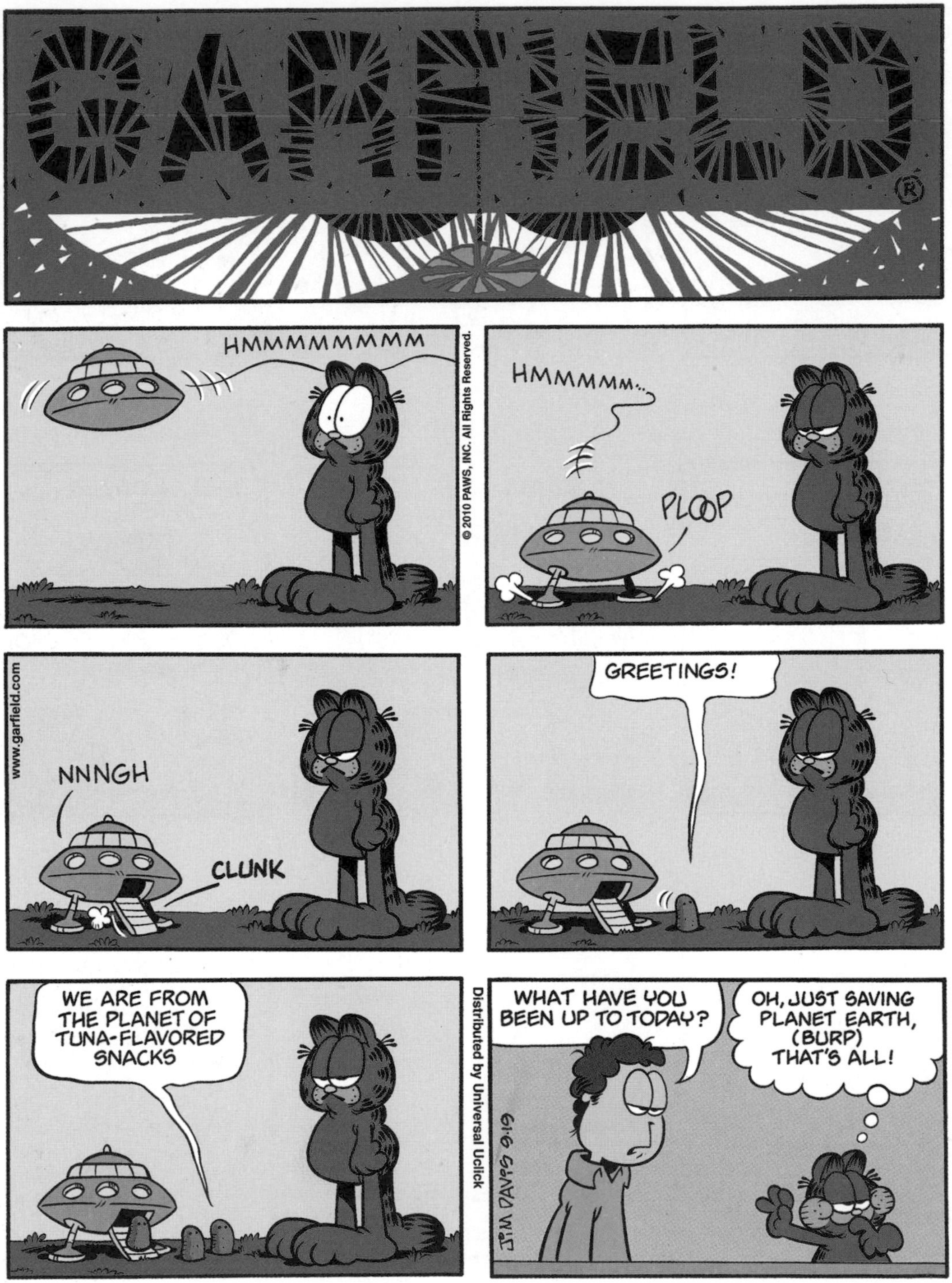
GARFIELD®
HMMMMMMMMM
© 2010 PAWS, INC. All Rights Reserved.
HMMMMM...
PLOOP
www.garfield.com
NNNGH
CLUNK
GREETINGS!
WE ARE FROM THE PLANET OF TUNA-FLAVORED SNACKS
Distributed by Universal Uclick
JIM DAVIS 9-19
WHAT HAVE YOU BEEN UP TO TODAY?
OH, JUST SAVING PLANET EARTH, (BURP) THAT'S ALL!

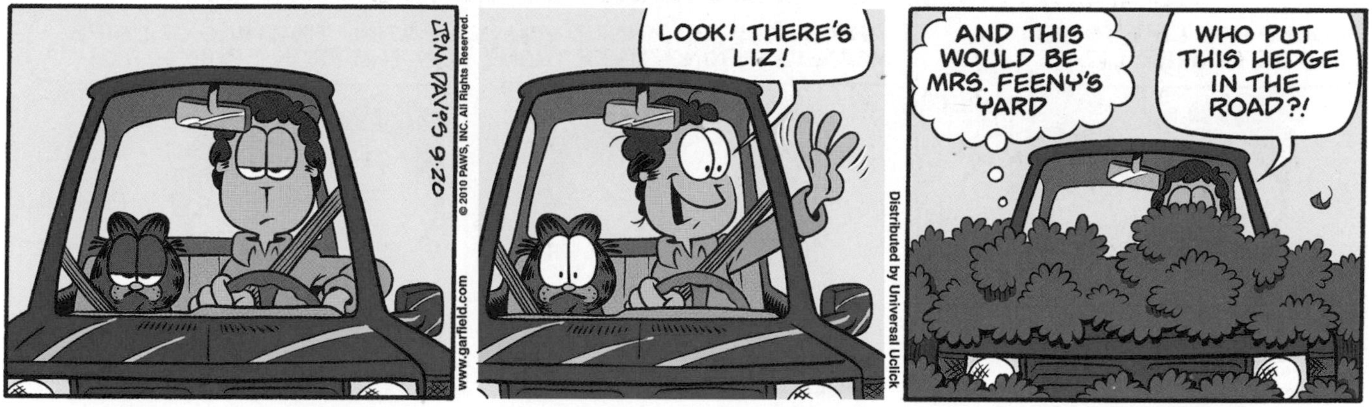
JIM DAVIS 9·20
© 2010 PAWS, INC. All Rights Reserved.
www.garfield.com
LOOK! THERE'S LIZ!
Distributed by Universal Uclick
AND THIS WOULD BE MRS. FEENY'S YARD
WHO PUT THIS HEDGE IN THE ROAD?!

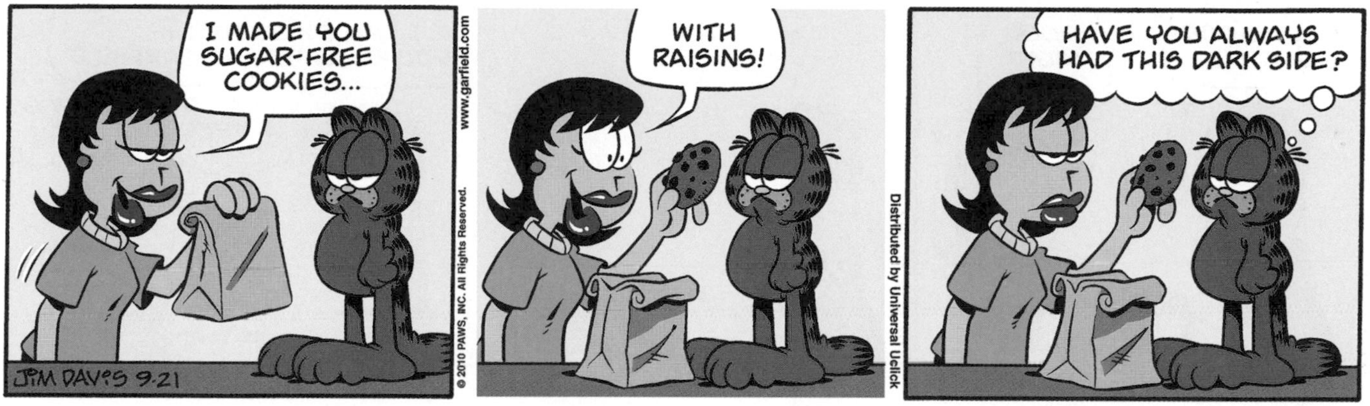
I MADE YOU SUGAR-FREE COOKIES...
JIM DAVIS 9·21
www.garfield.com
© 2010 PAWS, INC. All Rights Reserved.
WITH RAISINS!
Distributed by Universal Uclick
HAVE YOU ALWAYS HAD THIS DARK SIDE?

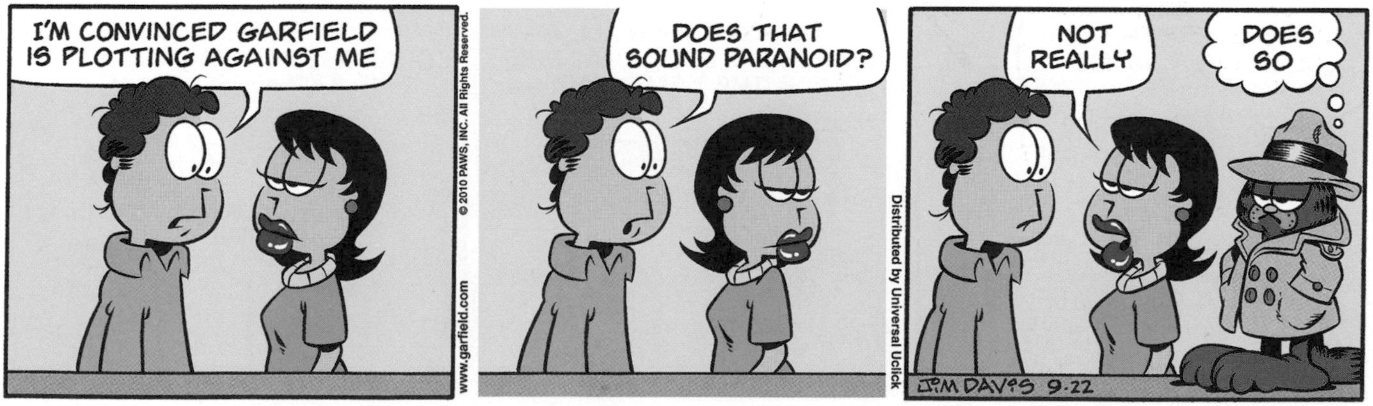
I'M CONVINCED GARFIELD IS PLOTTING AGAINST ME
© 2010 PAWS, INC. All Rights Reserved.
www.garfield.com
DOES THAT SOUND PARANOID?
Distributed by Universal Uclick
NOT REALLY
DOES SO
JIM DAVIS 9·22

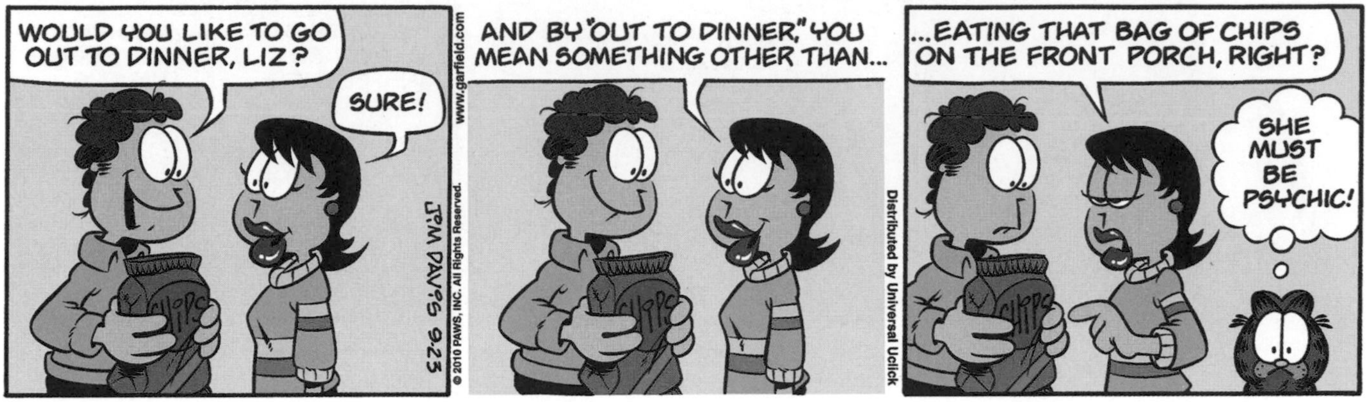
WOULD YOU LIKE TO GO OUT TO DINNER, LIZ?
SURE!
JIM DAVIS 9.23
www.garfield.com
© 2010 PAWS, INC. All Rights Reserved.
AND BY "OUT TO DINNER," YOU MEAN SOMETHING OTHER THAN...
Distributed by Universal Uclick
...EATING THAT BAG OF CHIPS ON THE FRONT PORCH, RIGHT?
SHE MUST BE PSYCHIC!
CHIPS

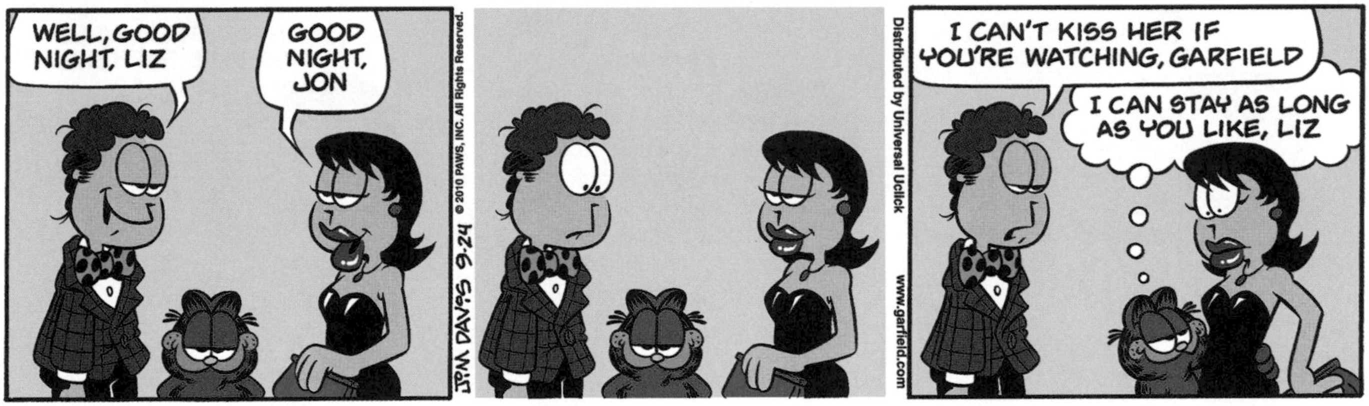
WELL, GOOD NIGHT, LIZ
GOOD NIGHT, JON
JIM DAVIS 9.24
© 2010 PAWS, INC. All Rights Reserved.
Distributed by Universal Uclick
www.garfield.com
I CAN'T KISS HER IF YOU'RE WATCHING, GARFIELD
I CAN STAY AS LONG AS YOU LIKE, LIZ

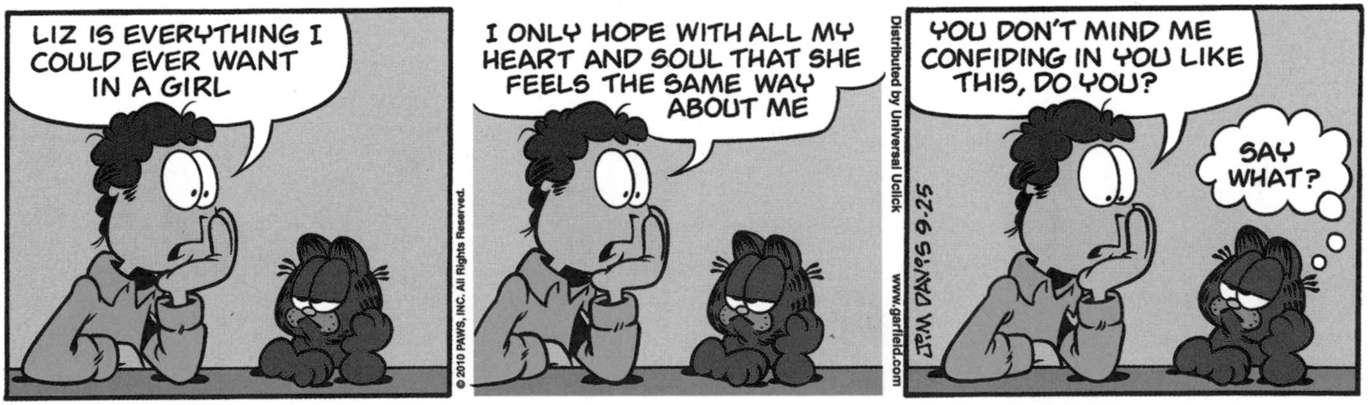
LIZ IS EVERYTHING I COULD EVER WANT IN A GIRL
© 2010 PAWS, INC. All Rights Reserved.
I ONLY HOPE WITH ALL MY HEART AND SOUL THAT SHE FEELS THE SAME WAY ABOUT ME
Distributed by Universal Uclick
www.garfield.com
JIM DAVIS 9.25
YOU DON'T MIND ME CONFIDING IN YOU LIKE THIS, DO YOU?
SAY WHAT?

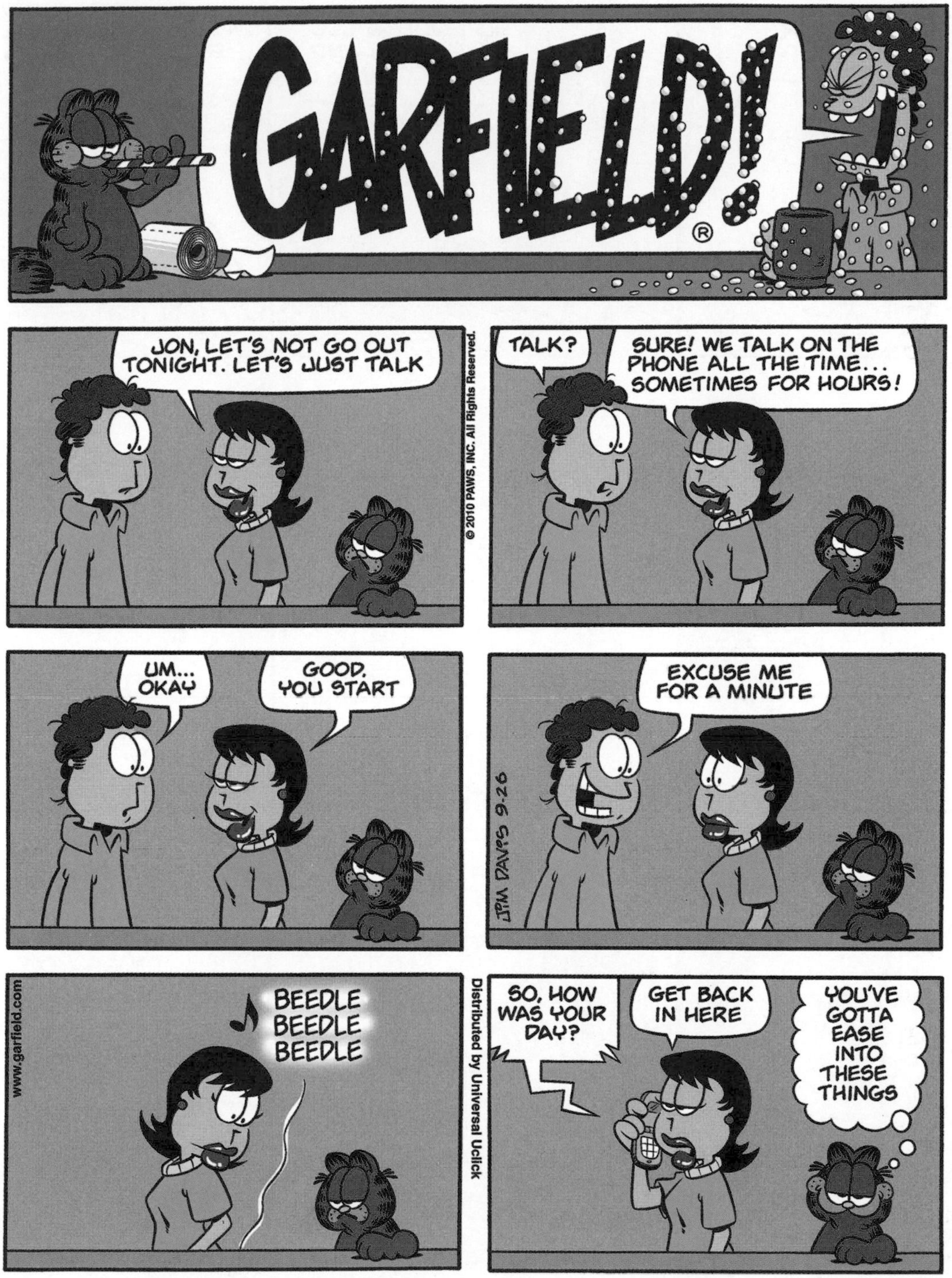
GARFIELD!
JON, LET'S NOT GO OUT TONIGHT. LET'S JUST TALK
TALK?
SURE! WE TALK ON THE PHONE ALL THE TIME... SOMETIMES FOR HOURS!
UM... OKAY
GOOD. YOU START
EXCUSE ME FOR A MINUTE
JPM DAVIS 9-26
BEEDLE BEEDLE BEEDLE
SO, HOW WAS YOUR DAY?
GET BACK IN HERE
YOU'VE GOTTA EASE INTO THESE THINGS
© 2010 PAWS, INC. All Rights Reserved.
www.garfield.com
Distributed by Universal Uclick

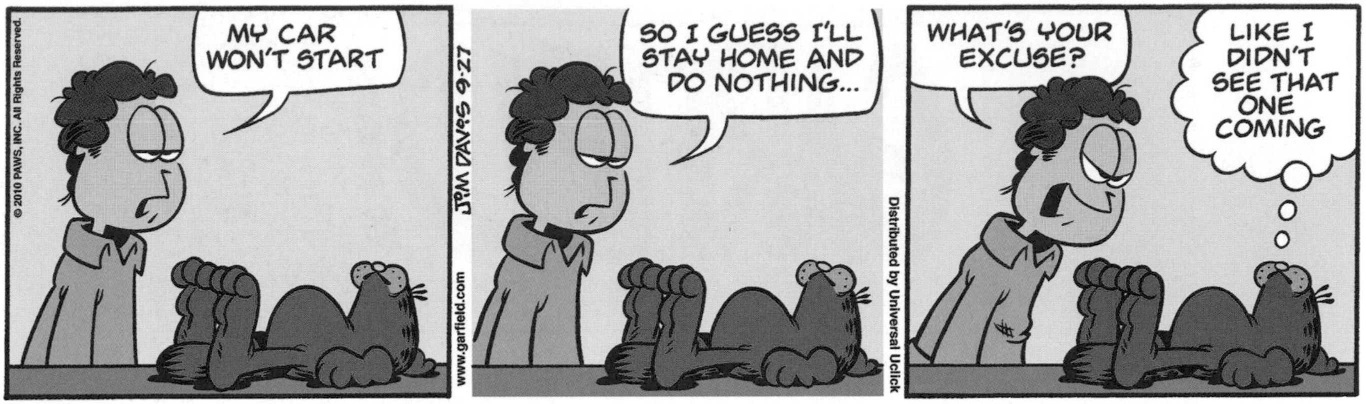
MY CAR WON'T START
SO I GUESS I'LL STAY HOME AND DO NOTHING...
WHAT'S YOUR EXCUSE?
LIKE I DIDN'T SEE THAT ONE COMING
© 2010 PAWS, INC. All Rights Reserved.
www.garfield.com
JIM DAVIS 9-27
Distributed by Universal Uclick

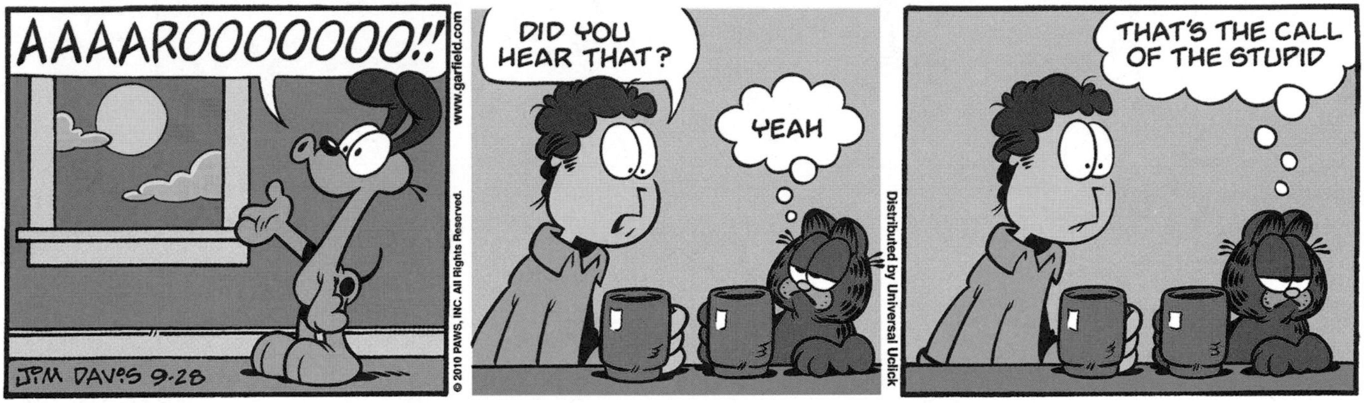
AAAAROOOOOOOO!!
JIM DAVIS 9-28
© 2010 PAWS, INC. All Rights Reserved.
www.garfield.com
DID YOU HEAR THAT?
YEAH
THAT'S THE CALL OF THE STUPID
Distributed by Universal Uclick

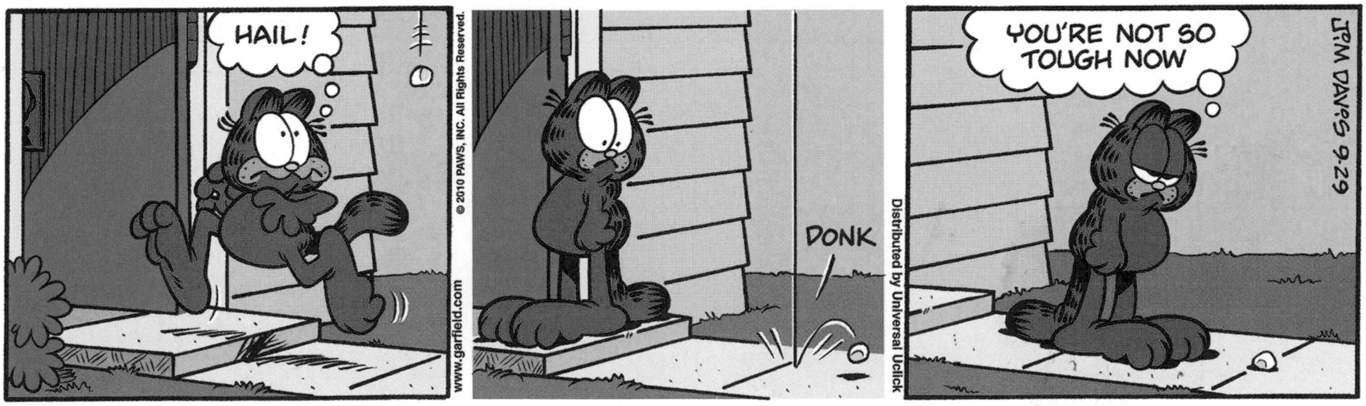
HAIL!
© 2010 PAWS, INC. All Rights Reserved.
www.garfield.com
DONK
YOU'RE NOT SO TOUGH NOW
JIM DAVIS 9-29
Distributed by Universal Uclick

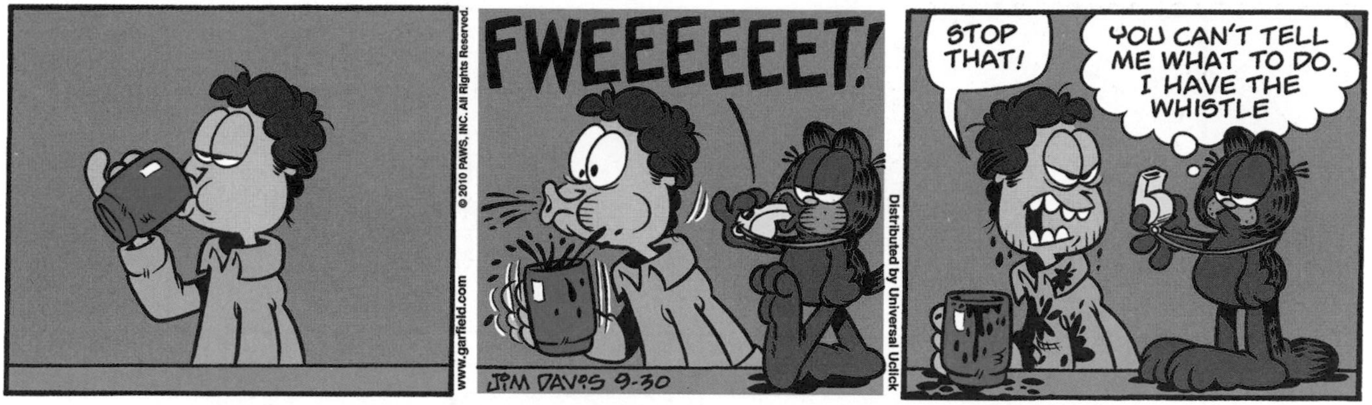
FWEEEEEEET!
STOP THAT!
YOU CAN'T TELL ME WHAT TO DO. I HAVE THE WHISTLE
JIM DAVIS 9-30

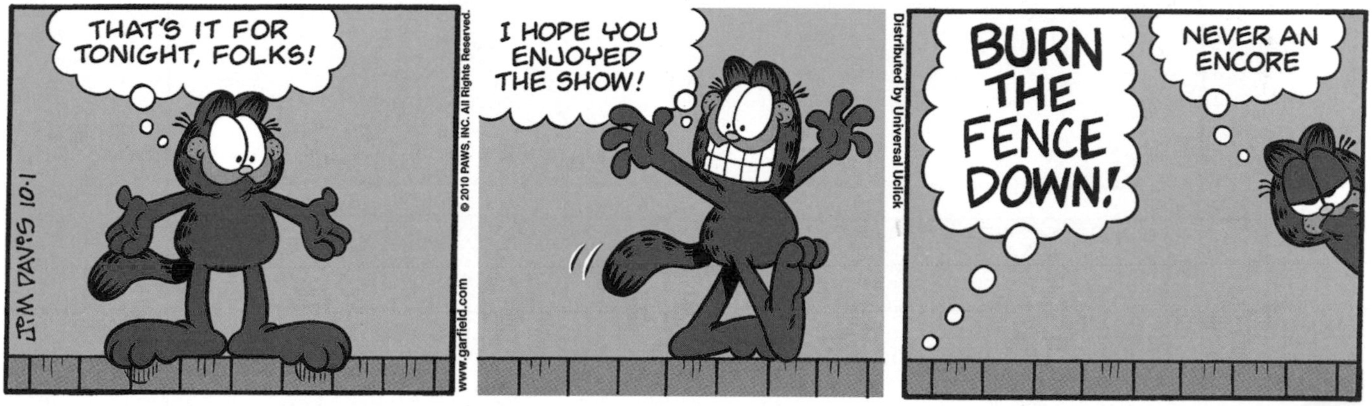
THAT'S IT FOR TONIGHT, FOLKS!
JIM DAVIS 10-1
I HOPE YOU ENJOYED THE SHOW!
BURN THE FENCE DOWN!
NEVER AN ENCORE

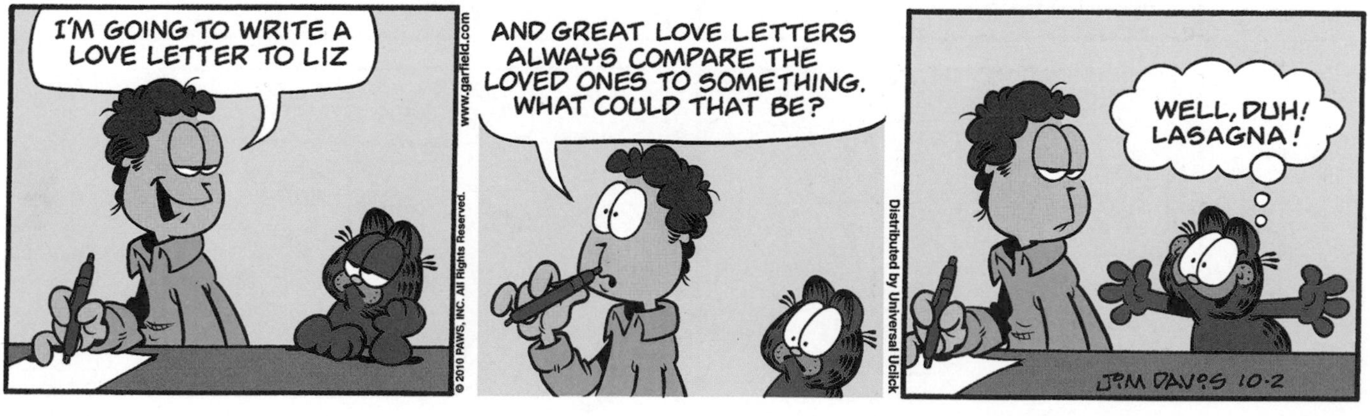
I'M GOING TO WRITE A LOVE LETTER TO LIZ
AND GREAT LOVE LETTERS ALWAYS COMPARE THE LOVED ONES TO SOMETHING. WHAT COULD THAT BE?
WELL, DUH! LASAGNA!
JIM DAVIS 10-2

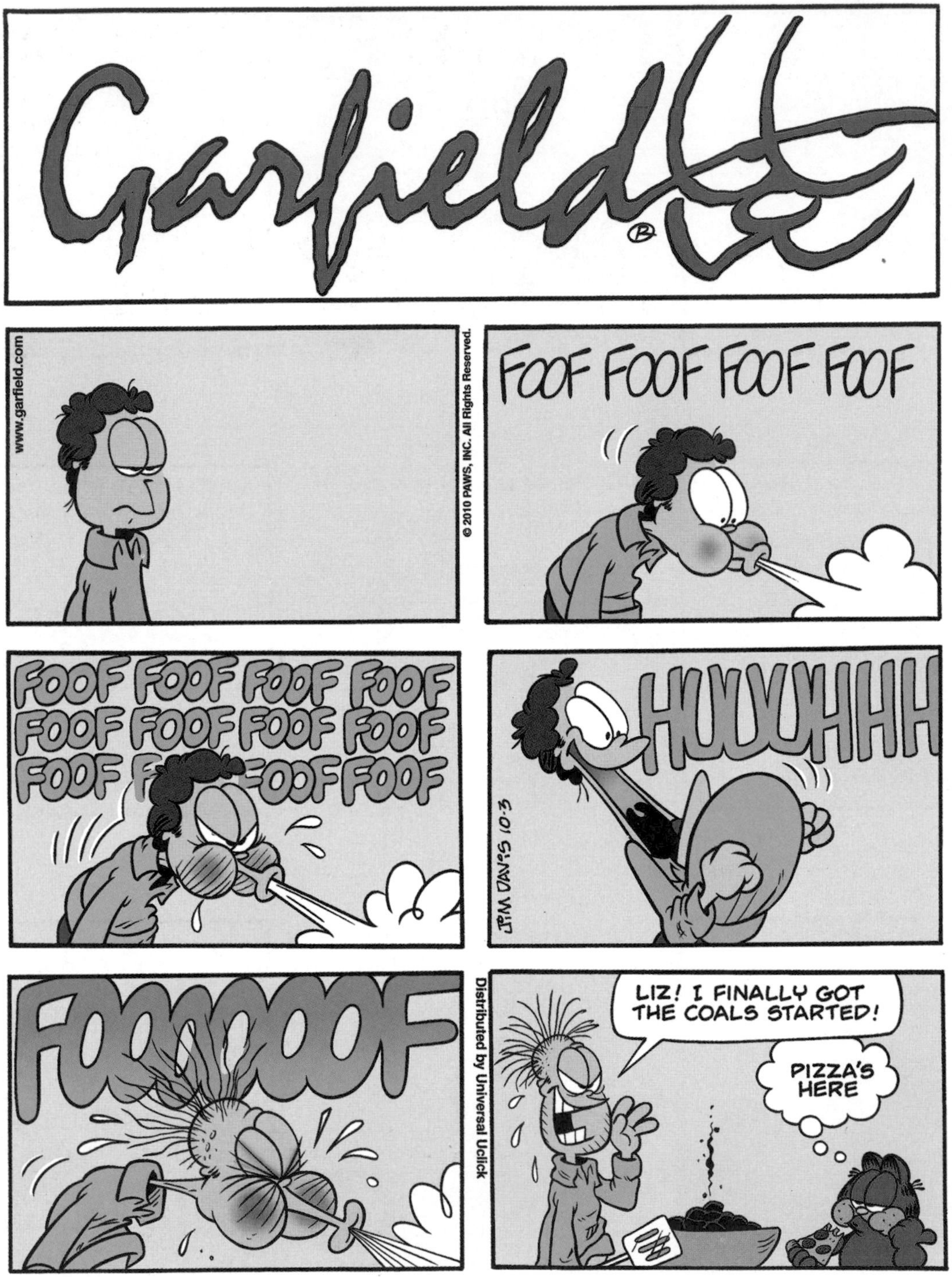
Garfield®
www.garfield.com
© 2010 PAWS, INC. All Rights Reserved.
FOOF FOOF FOOF FOOF
FOOF FOOF FOOF FOOF
FOOF FOOF FOOF FOOF
FOOF FOOF
HUUUHHH
JPM DAVIS 10-3
FOOOOOOF
Distributed by Universal Uclick
LIZ! I FINALLY GOT THE COALS STARTED!
PIZZA'S HERE

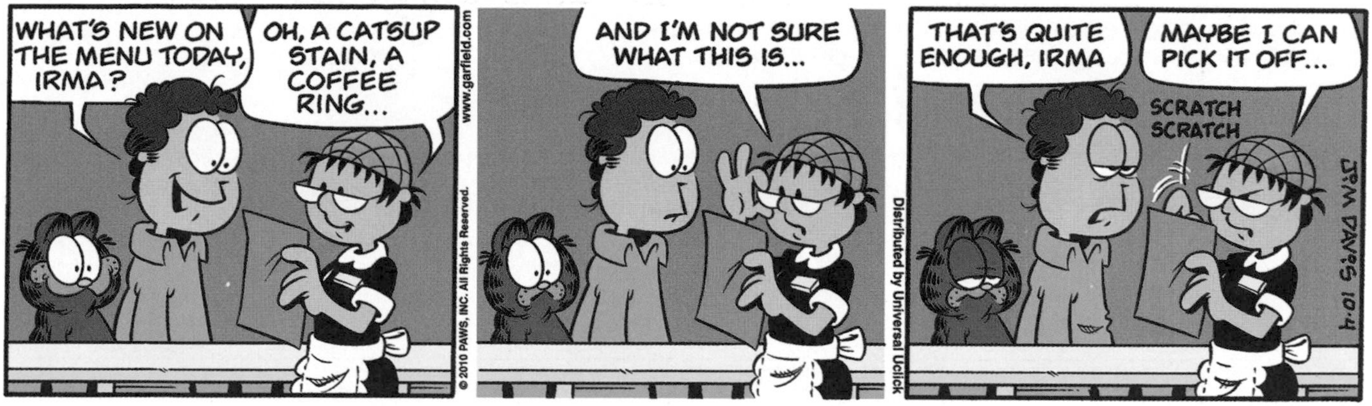
WHAT'S NEW ON THE MENU TODAY, IRMA?
OH, A CATSUP STAIN, A COFFEE RING...
© 2010 PAWS, INC. All Rights Reserved.
www.garfield.com
AND I'M NOT SURE WHAT THIS IS...
Distributed by Universal Uclick
THAT'S QUITE ENOUGH, IRMA
MAYBE I CAN PICK IT OFF...
SCRATCH SCRATCH
JIM DAVIS 10-4

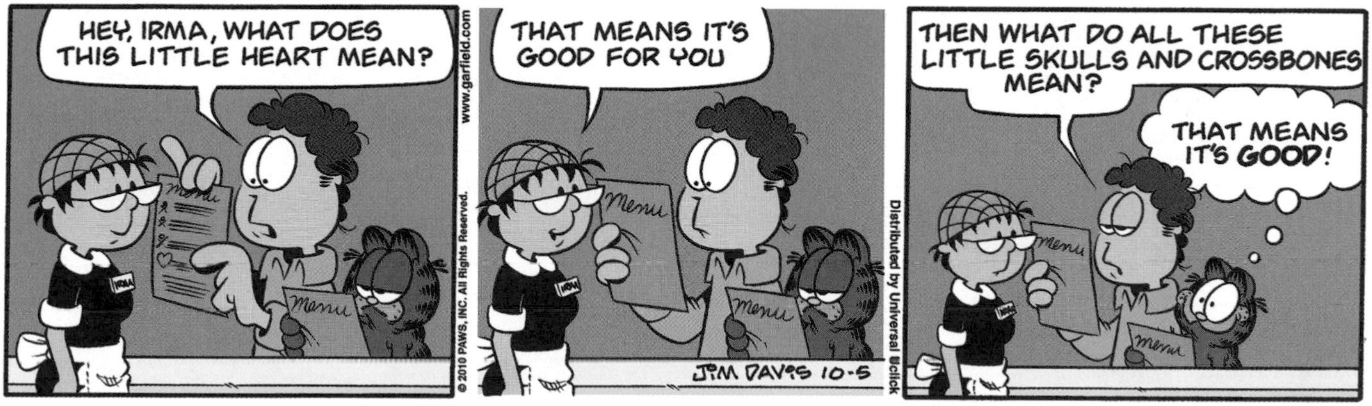
HEY, IRMA, WHAT DOES THIS LITTLE HEART MEAN?
© 2010 PAWS, INC. All Rights Reserved.
www.garfield.com
THAT MEANS IT'S GOOD FOR YOU
JIM DAVIS 10-5
Distributed by Universal Uclick
THEN WHAT DO ALL THESE LITTLE SKULLS AND CROSSBONES MEAN?
THAT MEANS IT'S **GOOD**!

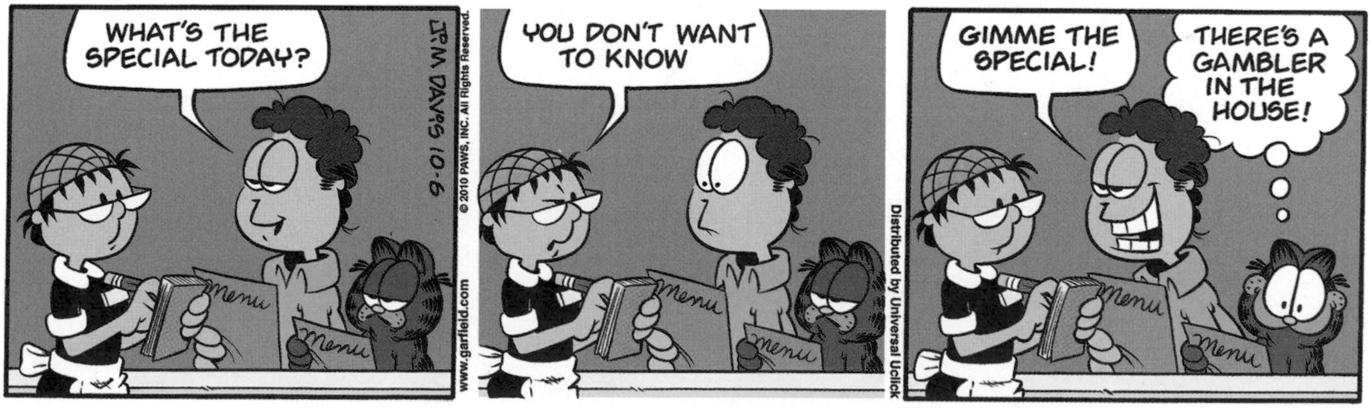
WHAT'S THE SPECIAL TODAY?
JIM DAVIS 10-6
© 2010 PAWS, INC. All Rights Reserved.
www.garfield.com
YOU DON'T WANT TO KNOW
Distributed by Universal Uclick
GIMME THE SPECIAL!
THERE'S A GAMBLER IN THE HOUSE!

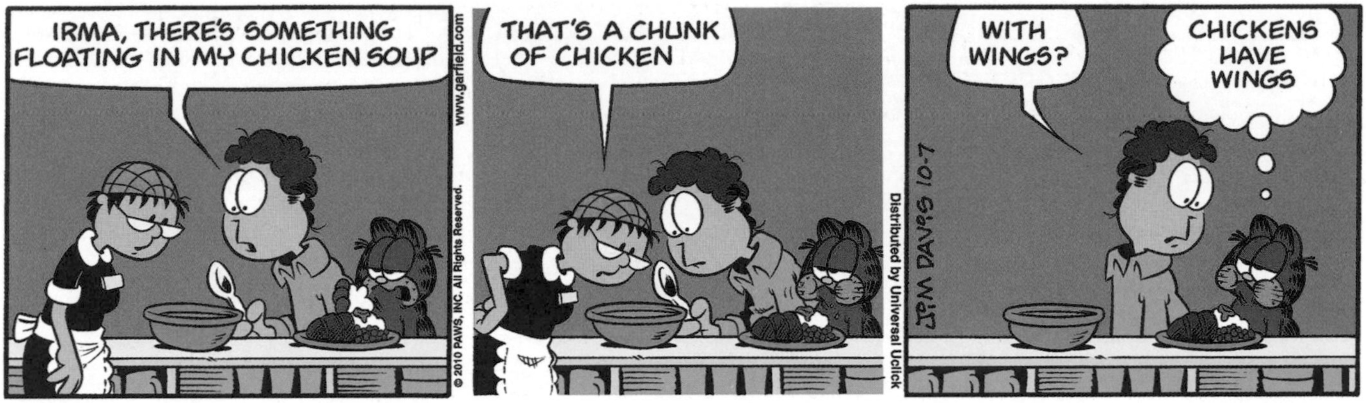
IRMA, THERE'S SOMETHING FLOATING IN MY CHICKEN SOUP
THAT'S A CHUNK OF CHICKEN
WITH WINGS?
CHICKENS HAVE WINGS
www.garfield.com
© 2010 PAWS, INC. All Rights Reserved.
Distributed by Universal Uclick
JIM DAVIS 10-7

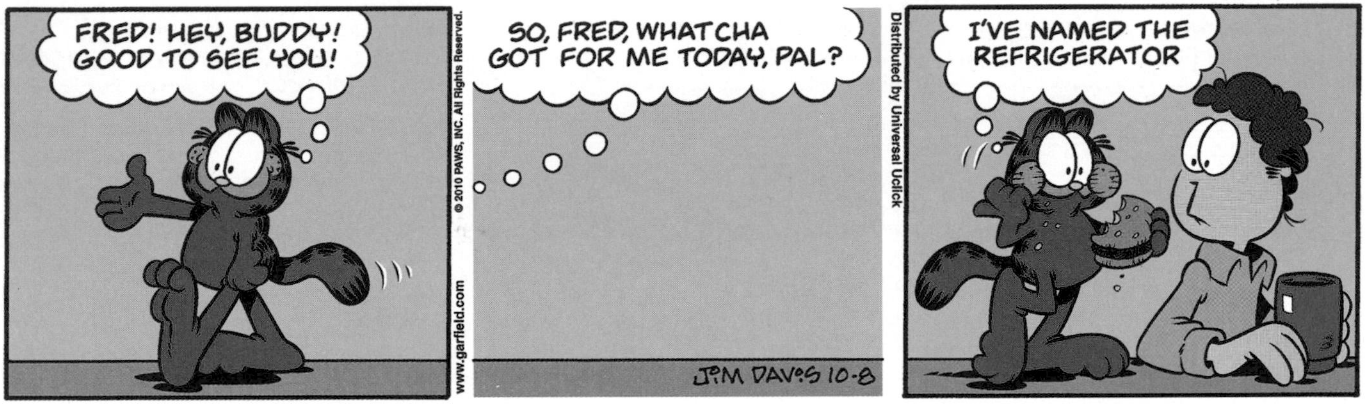
FRED! HEY, BUDDY! GOOD TO SEE YOU!
SO, FRED, WHATCHA GOT FOR ME TODAY, PAL?
I'VE NAMED THE REFRIGERATOR
www.garfield.com
© 2010 PAWS, INC. All Rights Reserved.
Distributed by Universal Uclick
JIM DAVIS 10-8

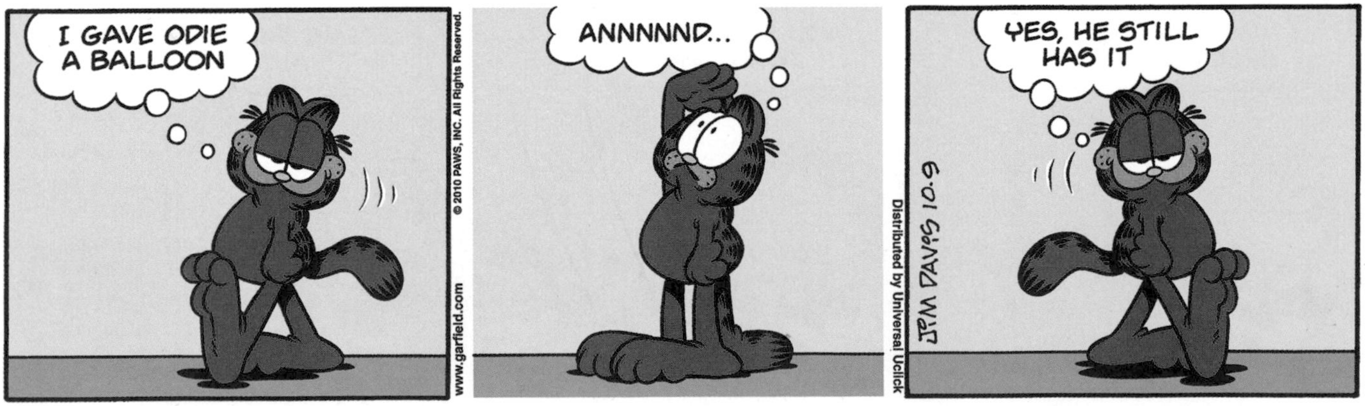
I GAVE ODIE A BALLOON
ANNNNND...
YES, HE STILL HAS IT
www.garfield.com
© 2010 PAWS, INC. All Rights Reserved.
Distributed by Universal Uclick
JIM DAVIS 10-9

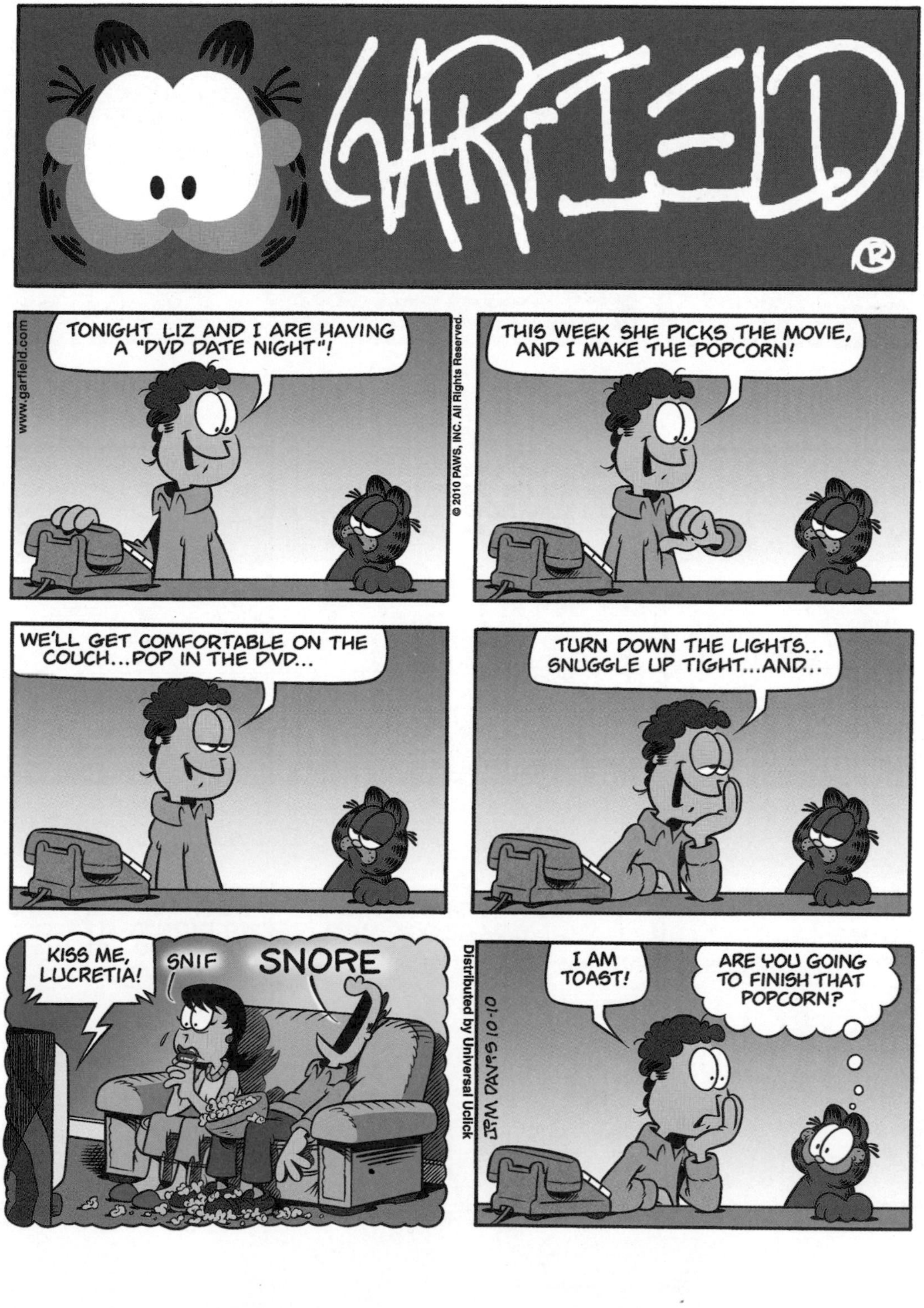
GARFIELD
www.garfield.com
© 2010 PAWS, INC. All Rights Reserved.
TONIGHT LIZ AND I ARE HAVING A "DVD DATE NIGHT"!
THIS WEEK SHE PICKS THE MOVIE, AND I MAKE THE POPCORN!
WE'LL GET COMFORTABLE ON THE COUCH...POP IN THE DVD...
TURN DOWN THE LIGHTS... SNUGGLE UP TIGHT...AND...
KISS ME, LUCRETIA!
SNIF
SNORE
Distributed by Universal Uclick
JIM DAVIS 10-10
I AM TOAST!
ARE YOU GOING TO FINISH THAT POPCORN?

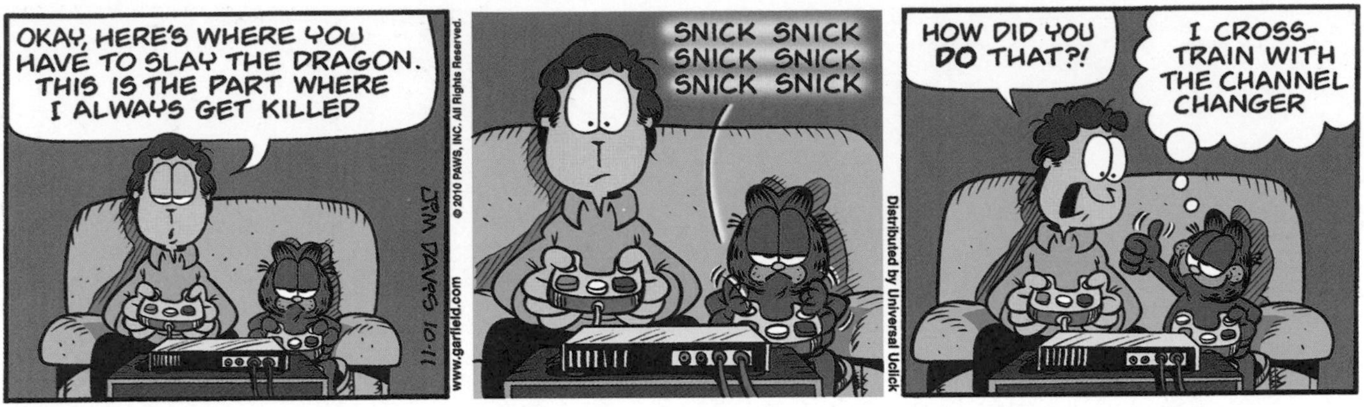
OKAY, HERE'S WHERE YOU HAVE TO SLAY THE DRAGON. THIS IS THE PART WHERE I ALWAYS GET KILLED
JIM DAVIS 10-11
© 2010 PAWS, INC. All Rights Reserved.
www.garfield.com
SNICK SNICK SNICK SNICK SNICK SNICK
Distributed by Universal Uclick
HOW DID YOU DO THAT?!
I CROSS-TRAIN WITH THE CHANNEL CHANGER

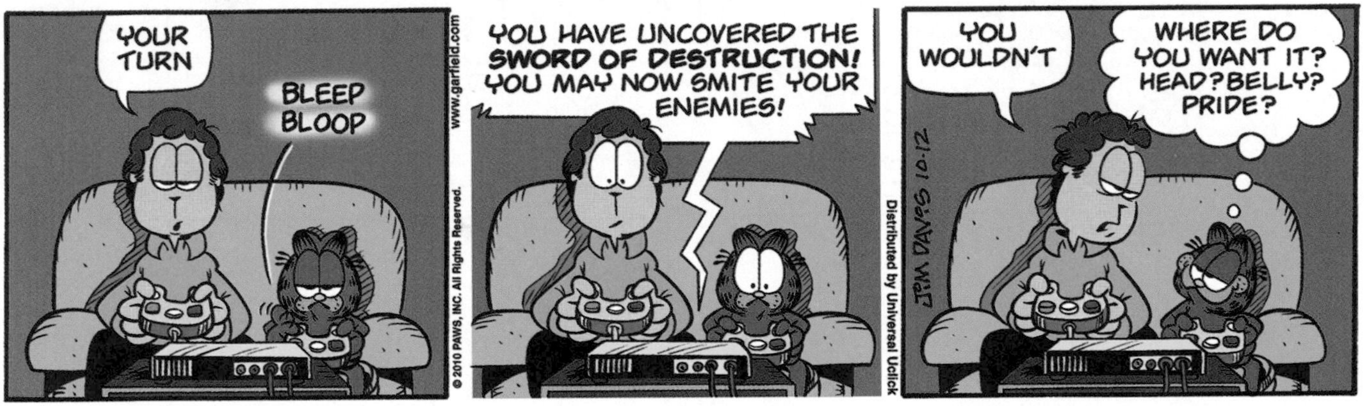
YOUR TURN
BLEEP BLOOP
www.garfield.com
© 2010 PAWS, INC. All Rights Reserved.
YOU HAVE UNCOVERED THE SWORD OF DESTRUCTION! YOU MAY NOW SMITE YOUR ENEMIES!
Distributed by Universal Uclick
YOU WOULDN'T
WHERE DO YOU WANT IT? HEAD? BELLY? PRIDE?
JIM DAVIS 10-12

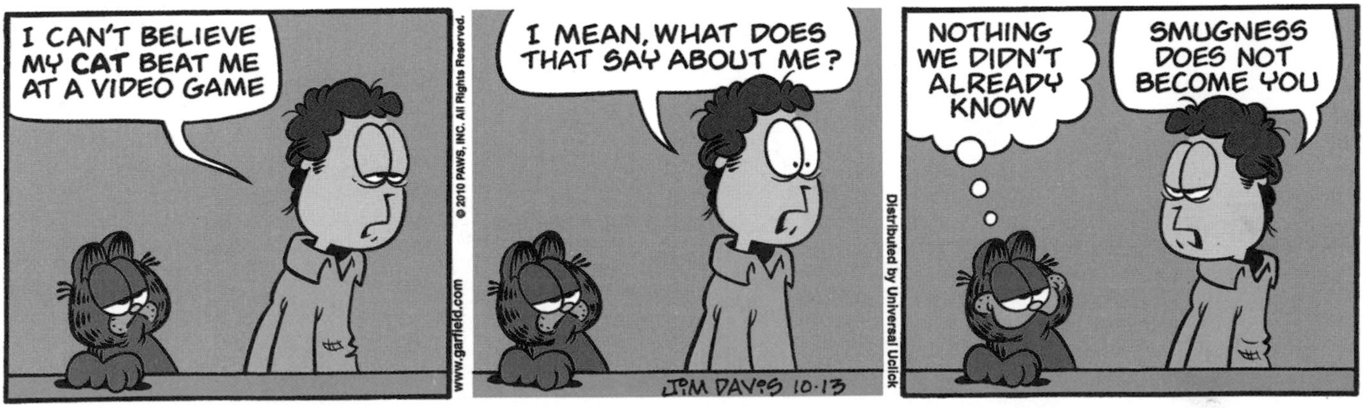
I CAN'T BELIEVE MY CAT BEAT ME AT A VIDEO GAME
© 2010 PAWS, INC. All Rights Reserved.
www.garfield.com
I MEAN, WHAT DOES THAT SAY ABOUT ME?
JIM DAVIS 10-13
Distributed by Universal Uclick
NOTHING WE DIDN'T ALREADY KNOW
SMUGNESS DOES NOT BECOME YOU

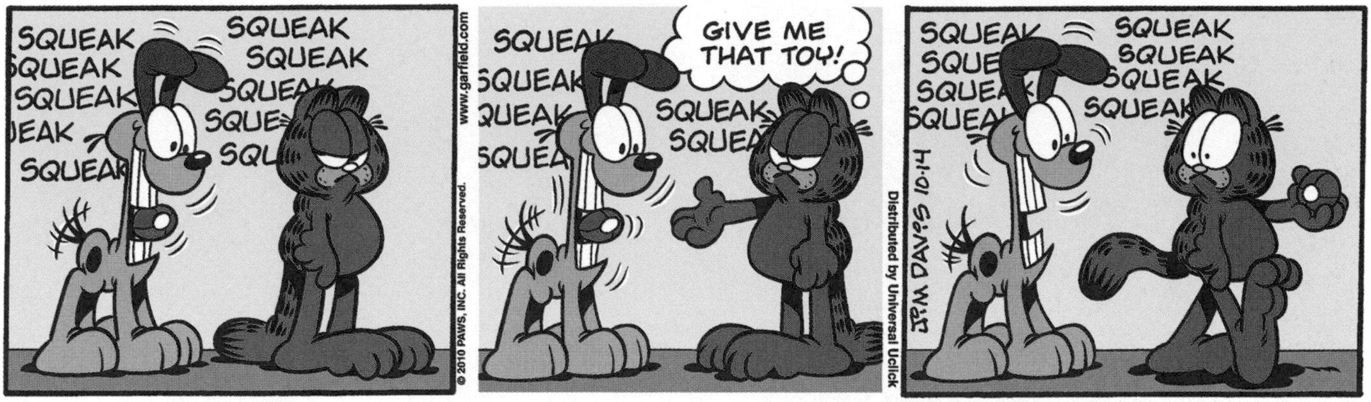
SQUEAK
SQUEAK
SQUEAK
SQUEAK
SQUEAK
SQUEAK
SQUEAK
GIVE ME THAT TOY!
SQUEAK
SQUEAK
SQUEAK
SQUEAK
SQUEAK
SQUEAK
SQUEAK
© 2010 PAWS, INC. All Rights Reserved. www.garfield.com
Distributed by Universal Uclick
JIM DAVIS 10-14

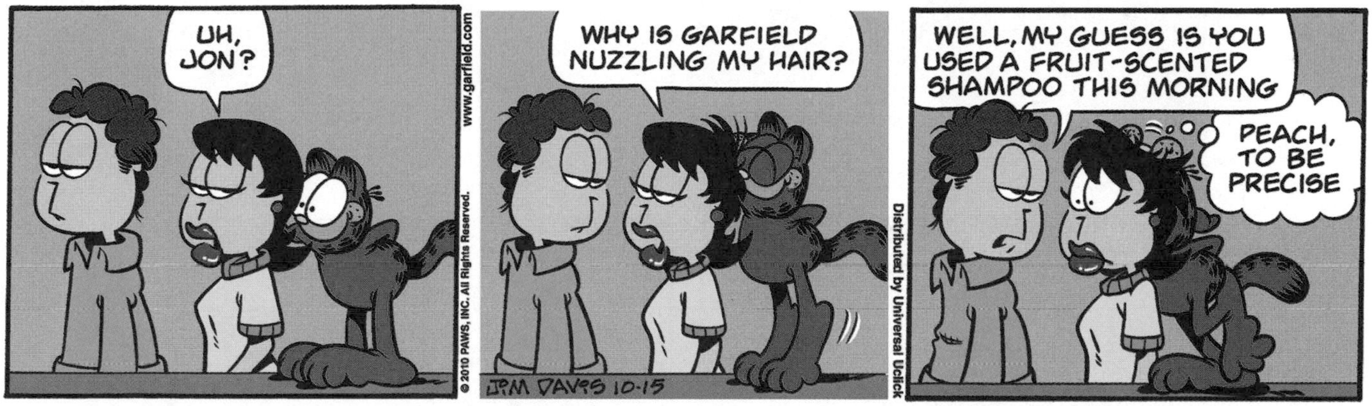
UH, JON?
WHY IS GARFIELD NUZZLING MY HAIR?
WELL, MY GUESS IS YOU USED A FRUIT-SCENTED SHAMPOO THIS MORNING
PEACH, TO BE PRECISE
© 2010 PAWS, INC. All Rights Reserved. www.garfield.com
Distributed by Universal Uclick
JIM DAVIS 10-15

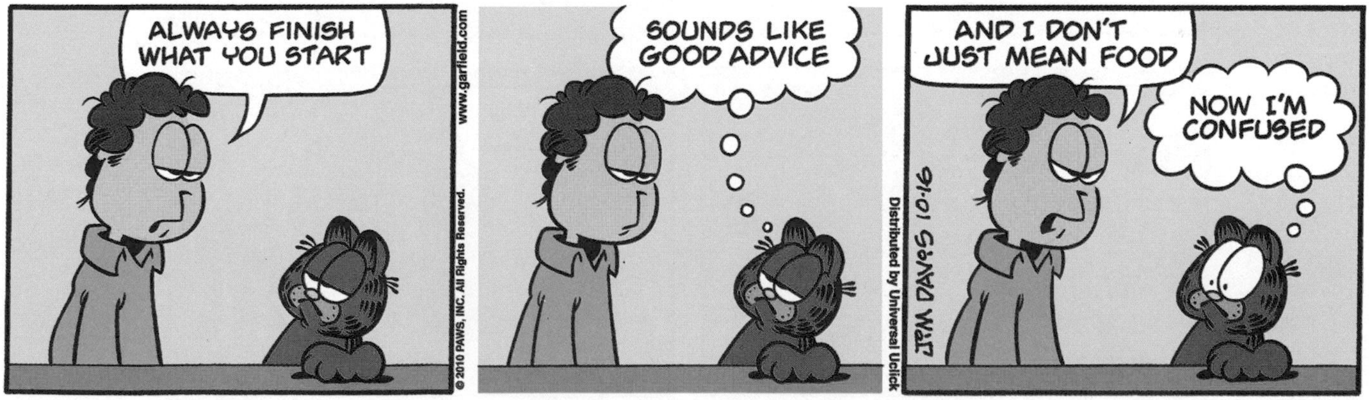
ALWAYS FINISH WHAT YOU START
SOUNDS LIKE GOOD ADVICE
AND I DON'T JUST MEAN FOOD
NOW I'M CONFUSED
© 2010 PAWS, INC. All Rights Reserved. www.garfield.com
Distributed by Universal Uclick
JIM DAVIS 10-16

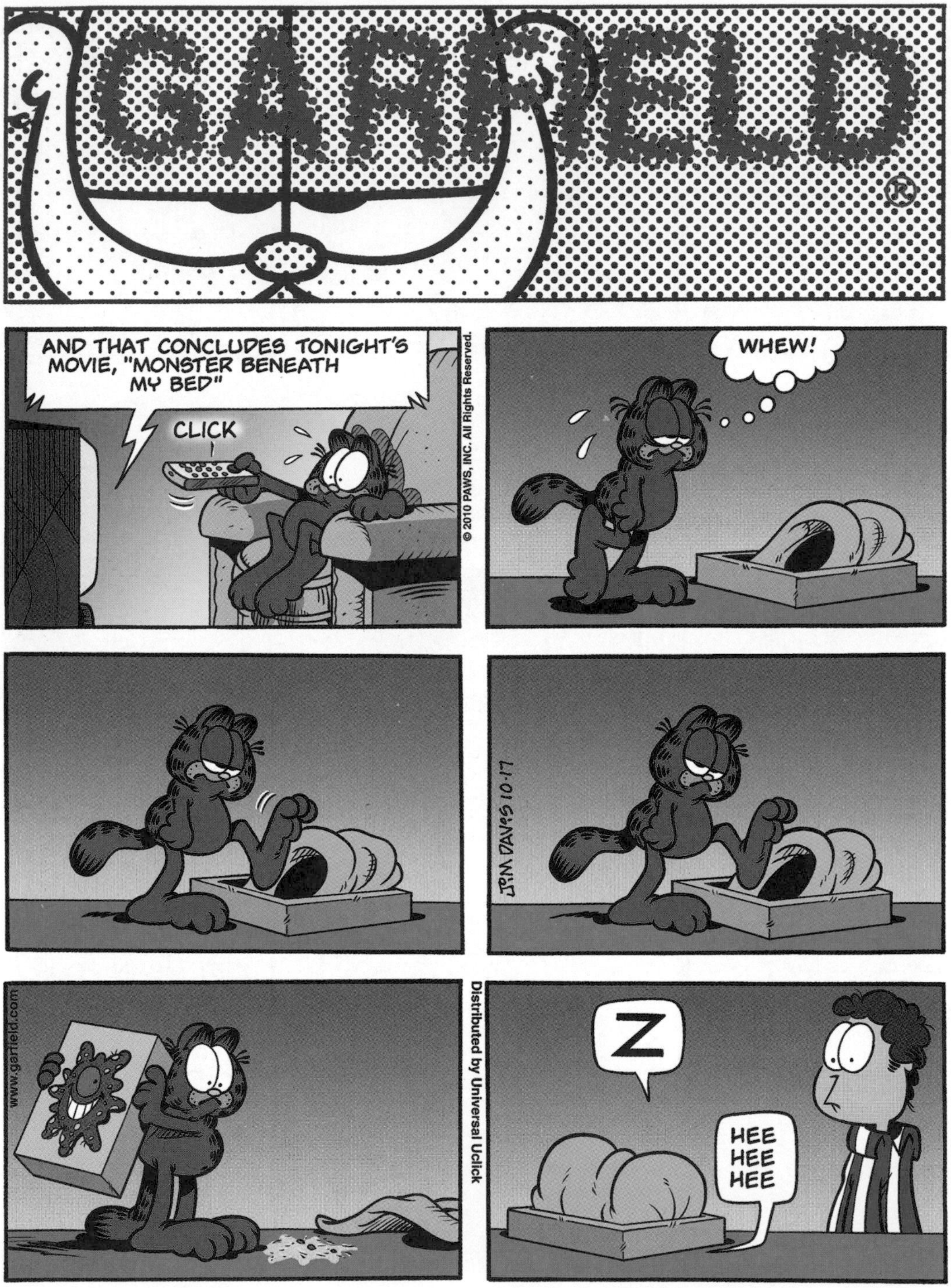
GARFIELD
AND THAT CONCLUDES TONIGHT'S MOVIE, "MONSTER BENEATH MY BED"
CLICK
© 2010 PAWS, INC. All Rights Reserved.
WHEW!
JPM DAVPS 10-17
www.garfield.com
Distributed by Universal Uclick
Z
HEE HEE HEE

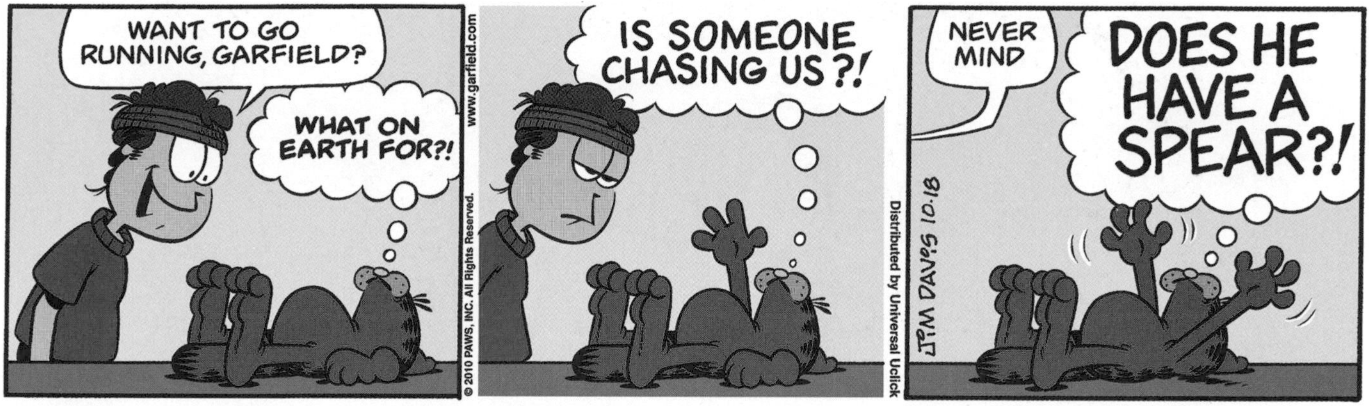
WANT TO GO RUNNING, GARFIELD?
WHAT ON EARTH FOR?!
IS SOMEONE CHASING US?!
NEVER MIND
DOES HE HAVE A SPEAR?!
www.garfield.com
© 2010 PAWS, INC. All Rights Reserved.
Distributed by Universal Uclick
JIM DAVIS 10-18

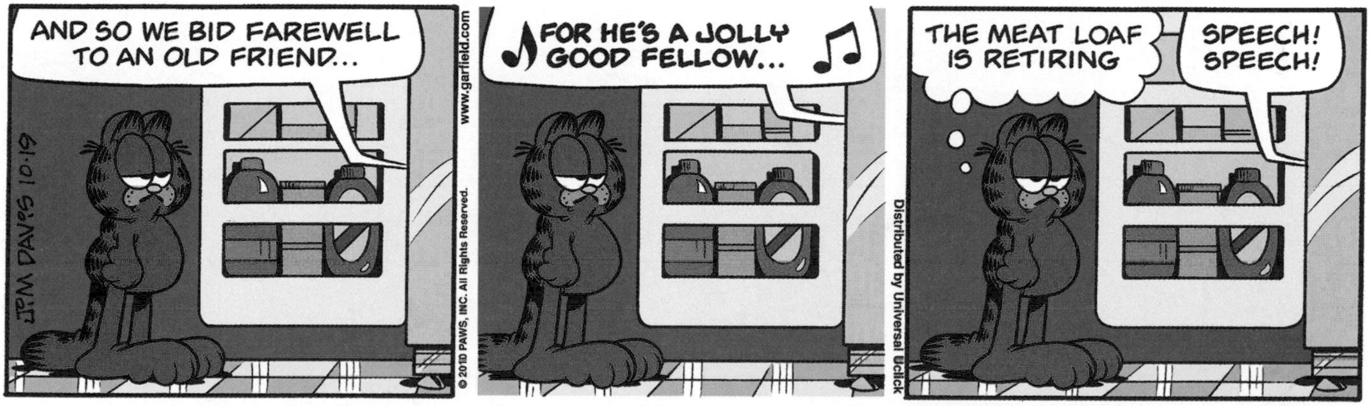
AND SO WE BID FAREWELL TO AN OLD FRIEND...
FOR HE'S A JOLLY GOOD FELLOW...
THE MEAT LOAF IS RETIRING
SPEECH! SPEECH!
JIM DAVIS 10-19
www.garfield.com
© 2010 PAWS, INC. All Rights Reserved.
Distributed by Universal Uclick

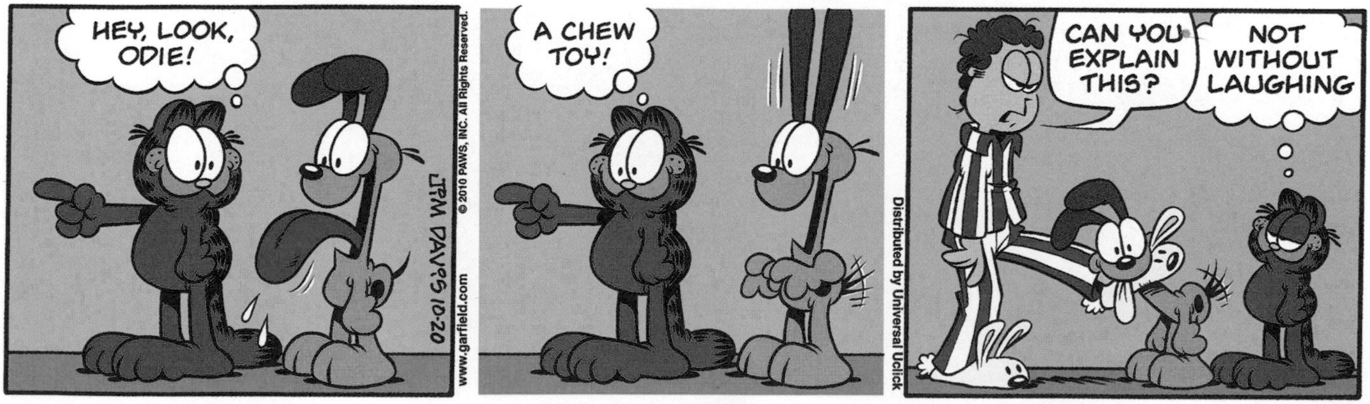
HEY, LOOK, ODIE!
A CHEW TOY!
CAN YOU EXPLAIN THIS?
NOT WITHOUT LAUGHING
JIM DAVIS 10-20
© 2010 PAWS, INC. All Rights Reserved.
www.garfield.com
Distributed by Universal Uclick

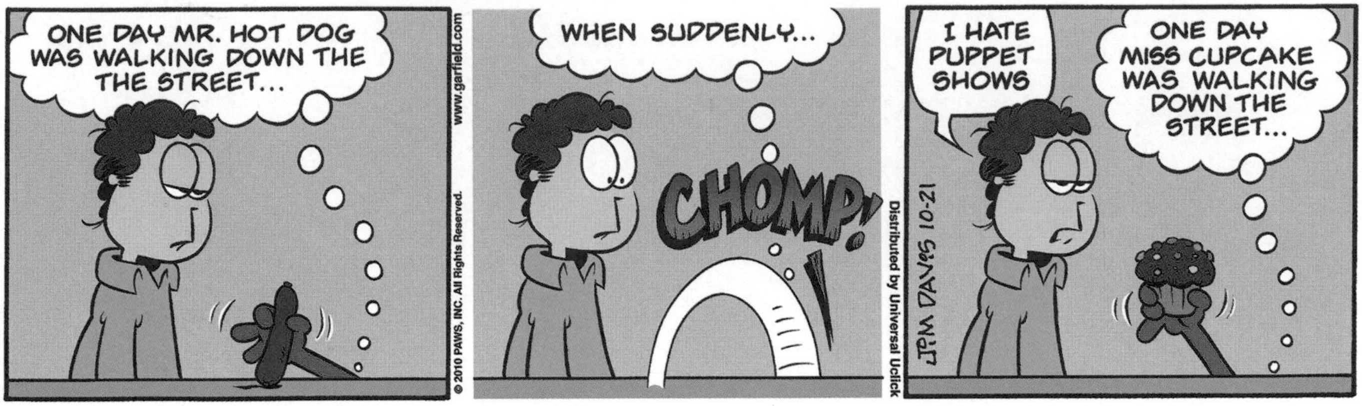
ONE DAY MR. HOT DOG WAS WALKING DOWN THE THE STREET...
WHEN SUDDENLY...
CHOMP!
I HATE PUPPET SHOWS
ONE DAY MISS CUPCAKE WAS WALKING DOWN THE STREET...
JPM DAVPS 10-21
© 2010 PAWS, INC. All Rights Reserved. www.garfield.com
Distributed by Universal Uclick

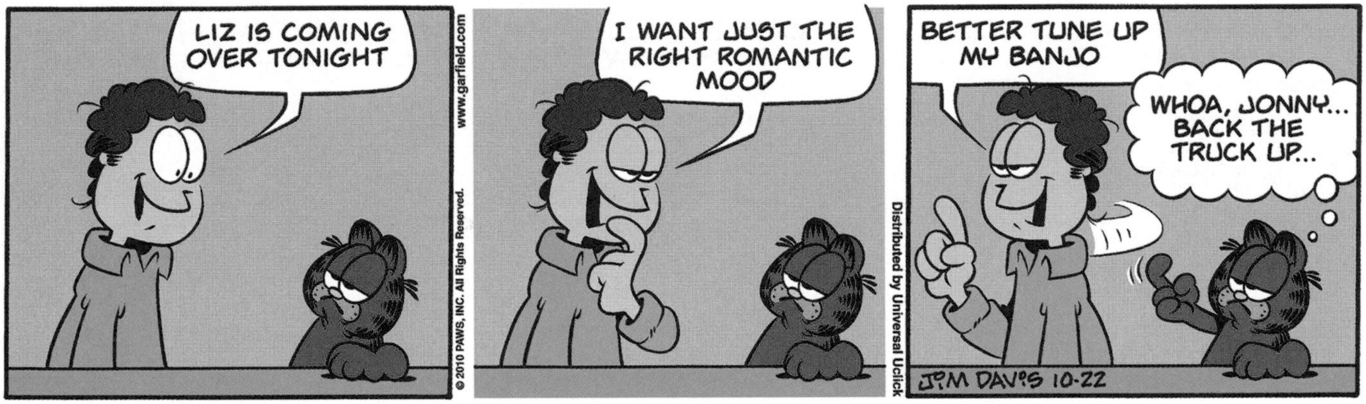
LIZ IS COMING OVER TONIGHT
I WANT JUST THE RIGHT ROMANTIC MOOD
BETTER TUNE UP MY BANJO
WHOA, JONNY... BACK THE TRUCK UP...
JPM DAVPS 10-22
© 2010 PAWS, INC. All Rights Reserved. www.garfield.com
Distributed by Universal Uclick

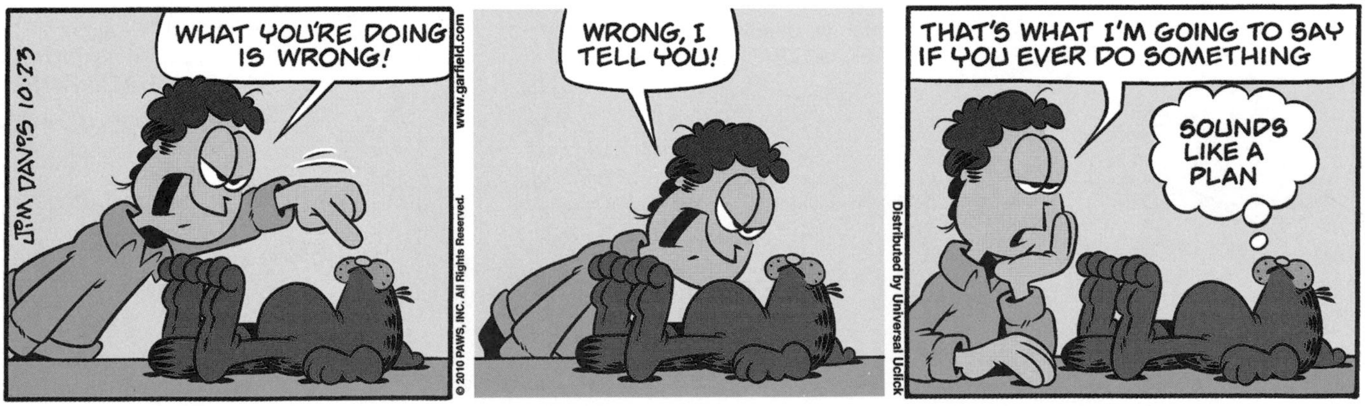
WHAT YOU'RE DOING IS WRONG!
WRONG, I TELL YOU!
THAT'S WHAT I'M GOING TO SAY IF YOU EVER DO SOMETHING
SOUNDS LIKE A PLAN
JPM DAVPS 10-23
© 2010 PAWS, INC. All Rights Reserved. www.garfield.com
Distributed by Universal Uclick

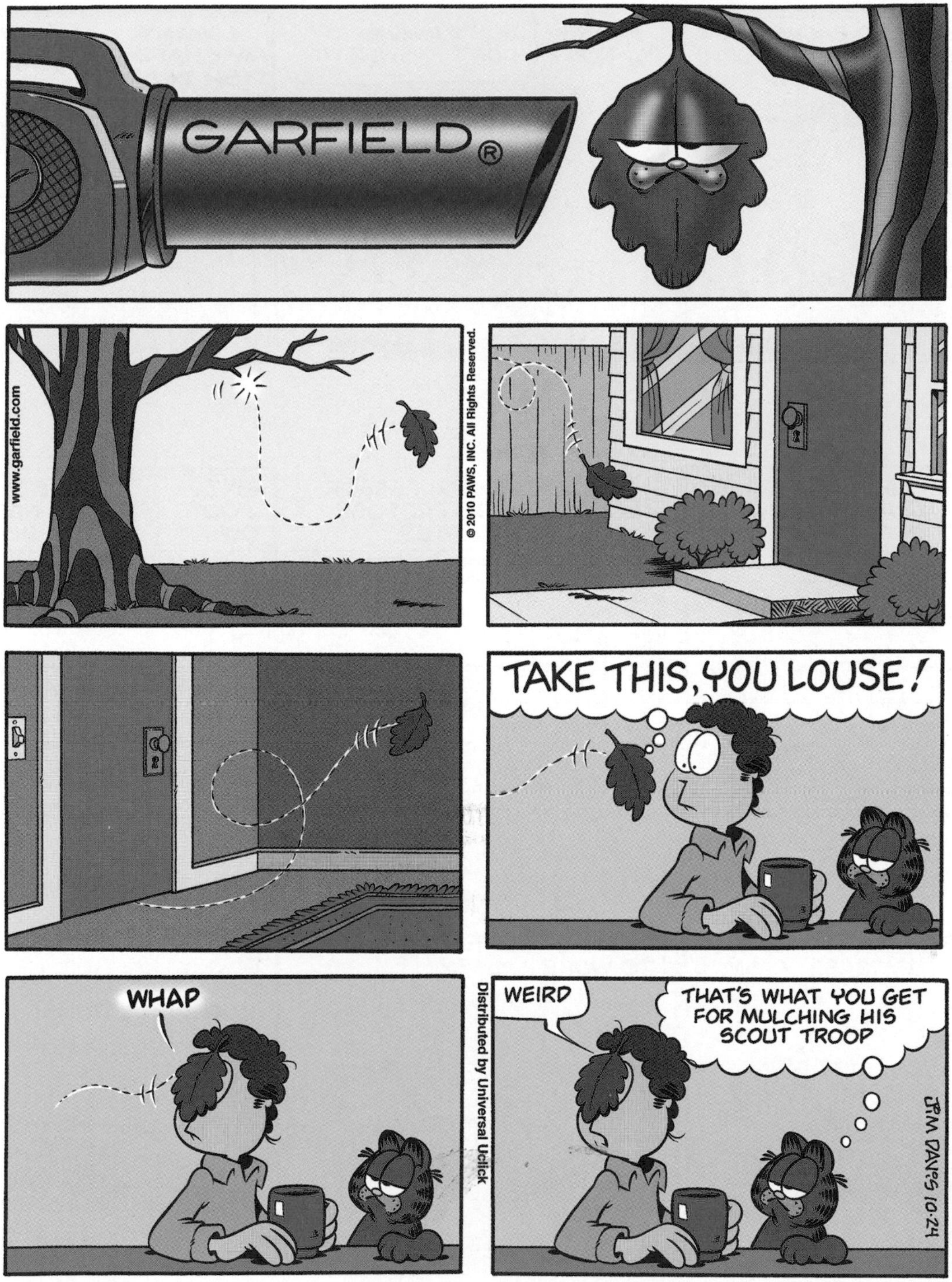
GARFIELD®
www.garfield.com
© 2010 PAWS, INC. All Rights Reserved.
TAKE THIS, YOU LOUSE!
WHAP
Distributed by Universal Uclick
WEIRD
THAT'S WHAT YOU GET FOR MULCHING HIS SCOUT TROOP
JPM DAVIS 10-24

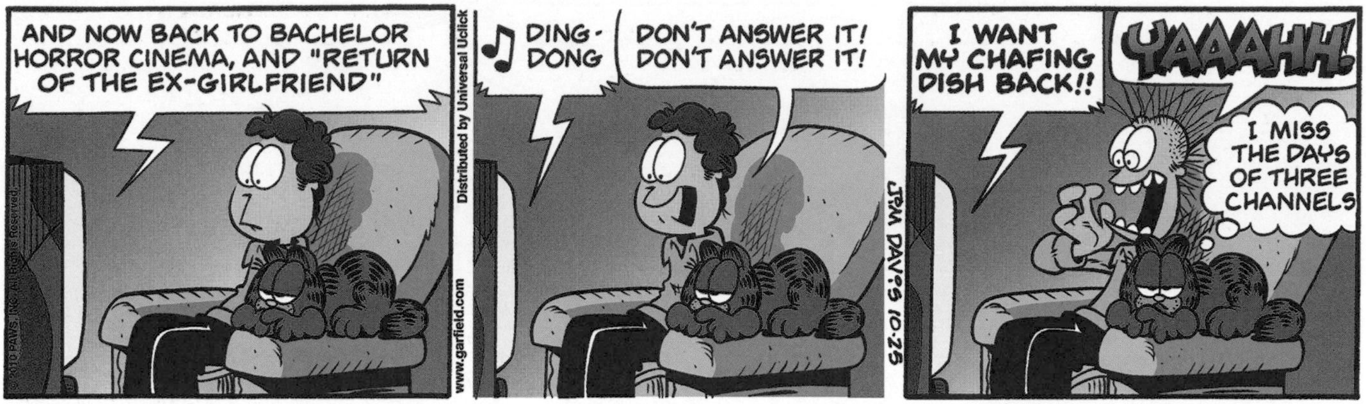
AND NOW BACK TO BACHELOR HORROR CINEMA, AND "RETURN OF THE EX-GIRLFRIEND"
Distributed by Universal Uclick
www.garfield.com
DING-DONG
DON'T ANSWER IT! DON'T ANSWER IT!
JPM DAVIS 10-25
I WANT MY CHAFING DISH BACK!!
YAAAHH!
I MISS THE DAYS OF THREE CHANNELS

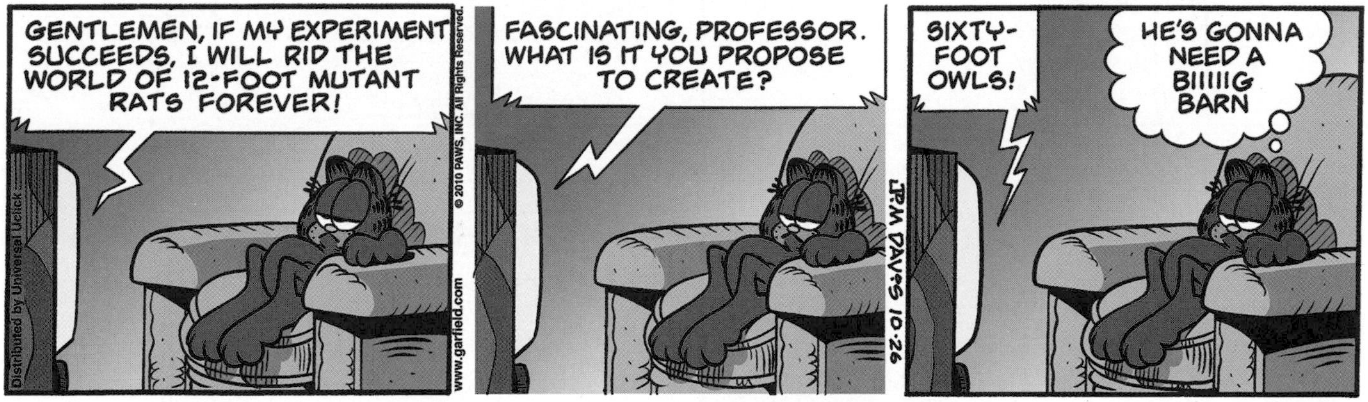
GENTLEMEN, IF MY EXPERIMENT SUCCEEDS, I WILL RID THE WORLD OF 12-FOOT MUTANT RATS FOREVER!
Distributed by Universal Uclick
www.garfield.com
© 2010 PAWS, INC. All Rights Reserved.
FASCINATING, PROFESSOR. WHAT IS IT YOU PROPOSE TO CREATE?
JPM DAVIS 10-26
SIXTY-FOOT OWLS!
HE'S GONNA NEED A BIIIIIG BARN

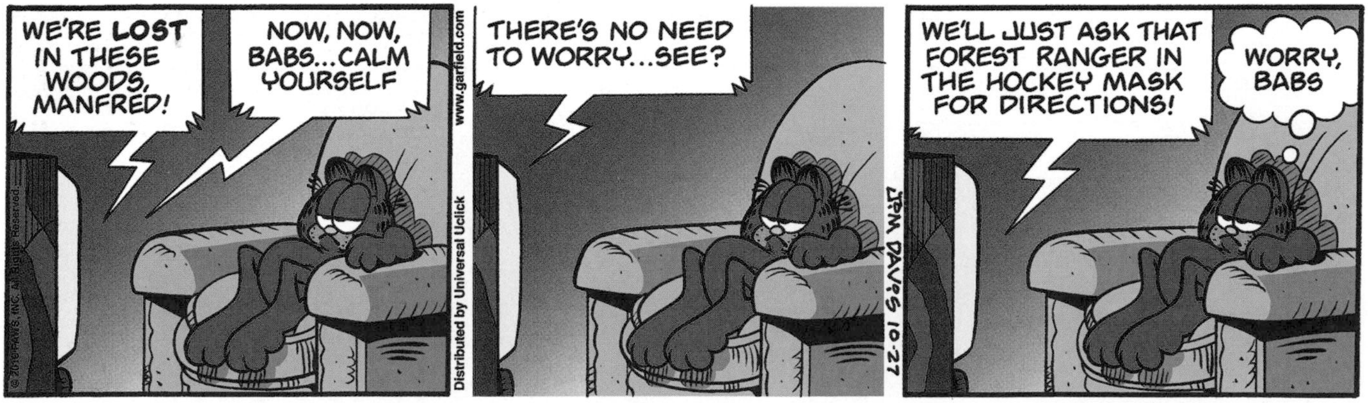
WE'RE **LOST** IN THESE WOODS, MANFRED!
NOW, NOW, BABS...CALM YOURSELF
www.garfield.com
Distributed by Universal Uclick
THERE'S NO NEED TO WORRY...SEE?
JPM DAVIS 10-27
WE'LL JUST ASK THAT FOREST RANGER IN THE HOCKEY MASK FOR DIRECTIONS!
WORRY, BABS

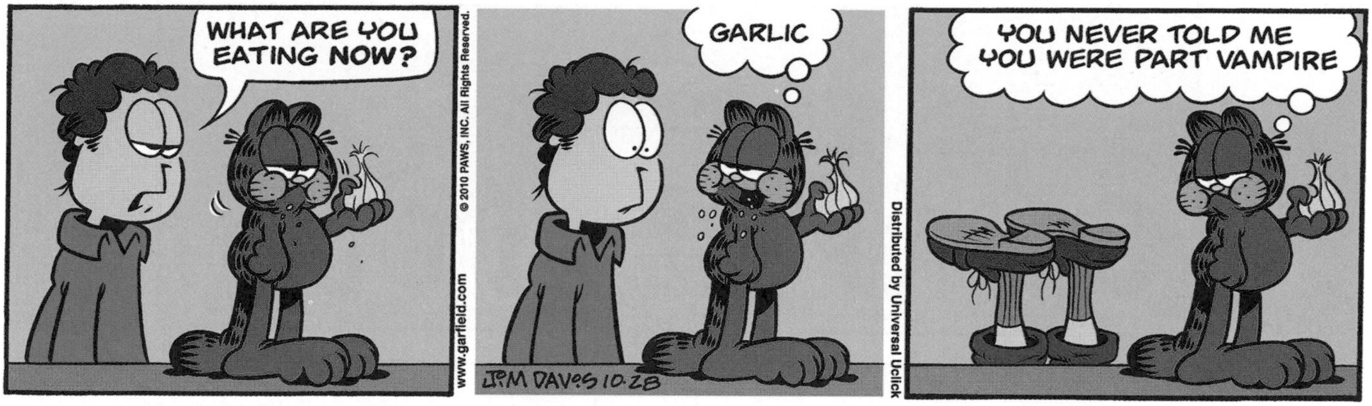

WHAT ARE YOU EATING NOW?
© 2010 PAWS, INC. All Rights Reserved.
www.garfield.com
GARLIC
JIM DAVIS 10-28
Distributed by Universal Uclick
YOU NEVER TOLD ME YOU WERE PART VAMPIRE

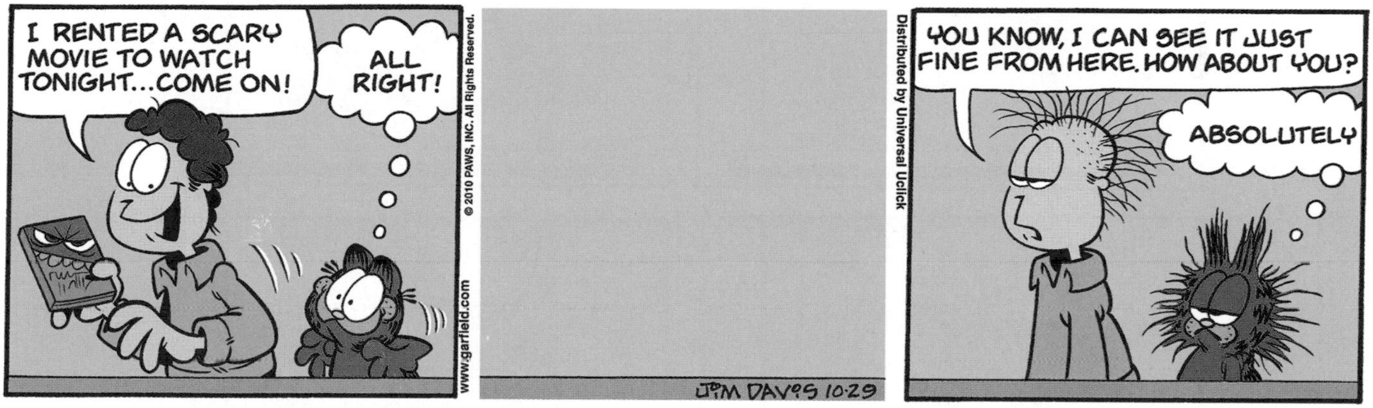

I RENTED A SCARY MOVIE TO WATCH TONIGHT...COME ON!
ALL RIGHT!
© 2010 PAWS, INC. All Rights Reserved.
www.garfield.com
JIM DAVIS 10-29
Distributed by Universal Uclick
YOU KNOW, I CAN SEE IT JUST FINE FROM HERE. HOW ABOUT YOU?
ABSOLUTELY

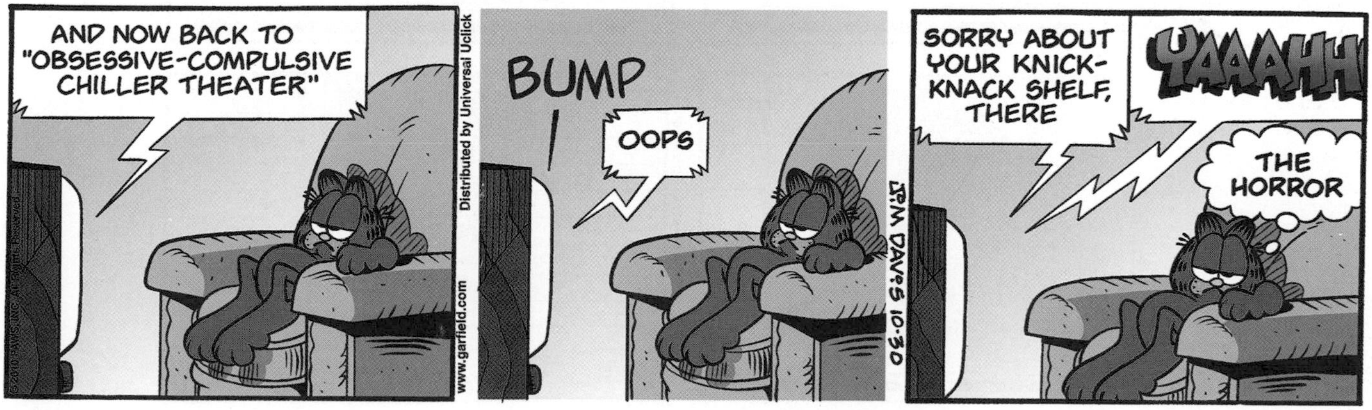

AND NOW BACK TO "OBSESSIVE-COMPULSIVE CHILLER THEATER"
Distributed by Universal Uclick
www.garfield.com
BUMP
OOPS
JIM DAVIS 10-30
SORRY ABOUT YOUR KNICK-KNACK SHELF, THERE
YAAAHH
THE HORROR

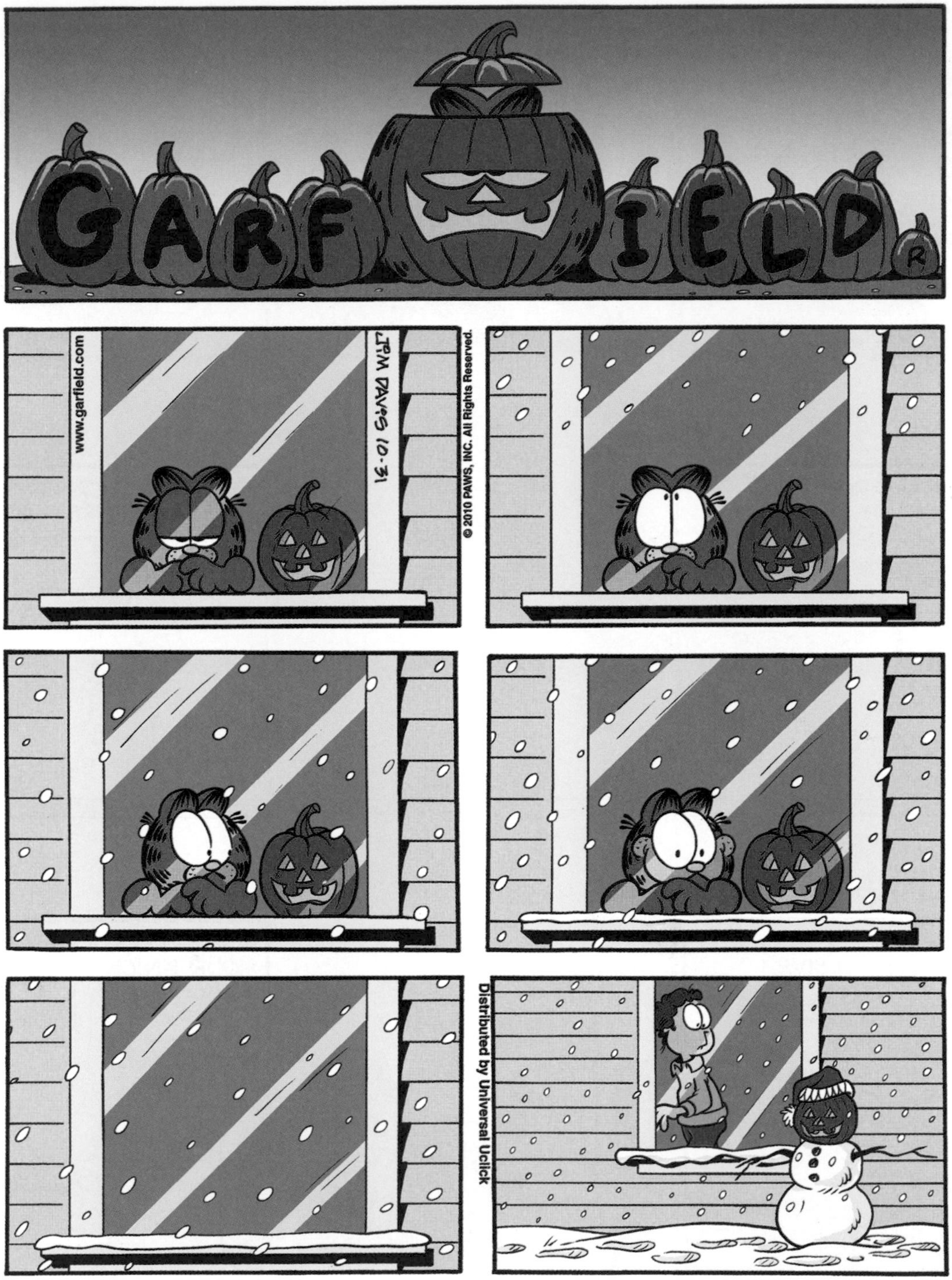
GARFIELD
www.garfield.com
JPM DAVIS 10-31
© 2010 PAWS, INC. All Rights Reserved.
Distributed by Universal Uclick

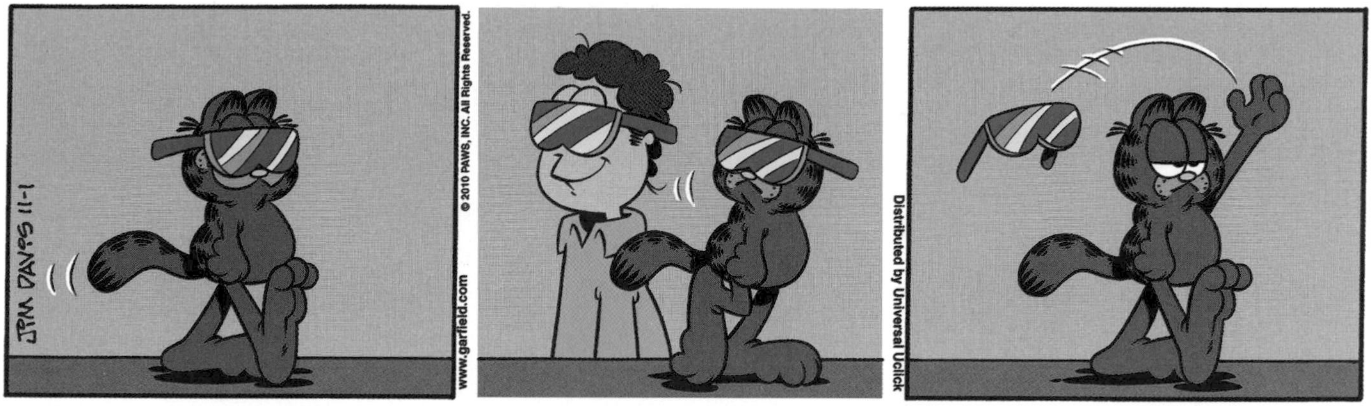
JIM DAVIS 11-1
© 2010 PAWS, INC. All Rights Reserved.
www.garfield.com
Distributed by Universal Uclick

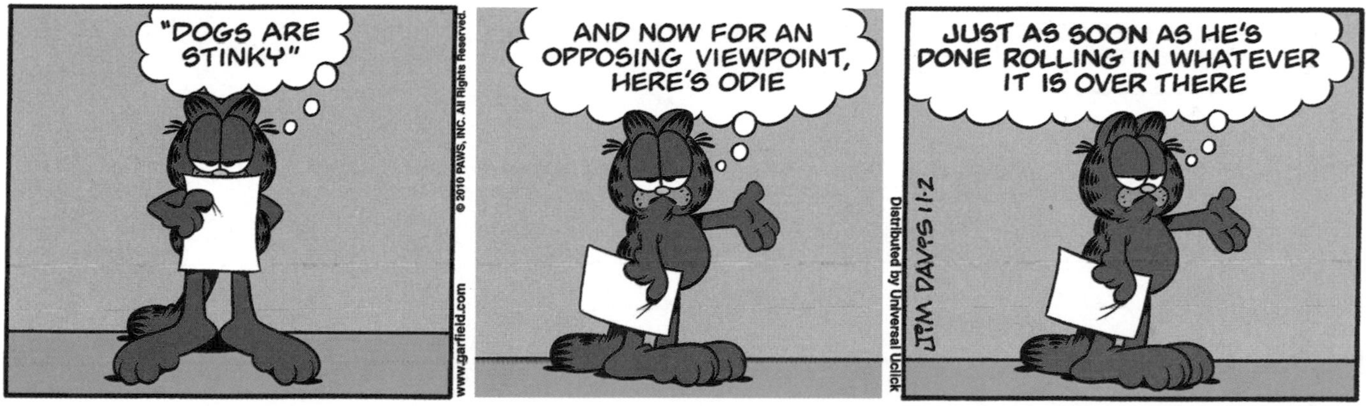
"DOGS ARE STINKY"
AND NOW FOR AN OPPOSING VIEWPOINT, HERE'S ODIE
JUST AS SOON AS HE'S DONE ROLLING IN WHATEVER IT IS OVER THERE
JIM DAVIS 11-2
© 2010 PAWS, INC. All Rights Reserved.
www.garfield.com
Distributed by Universal Uclick

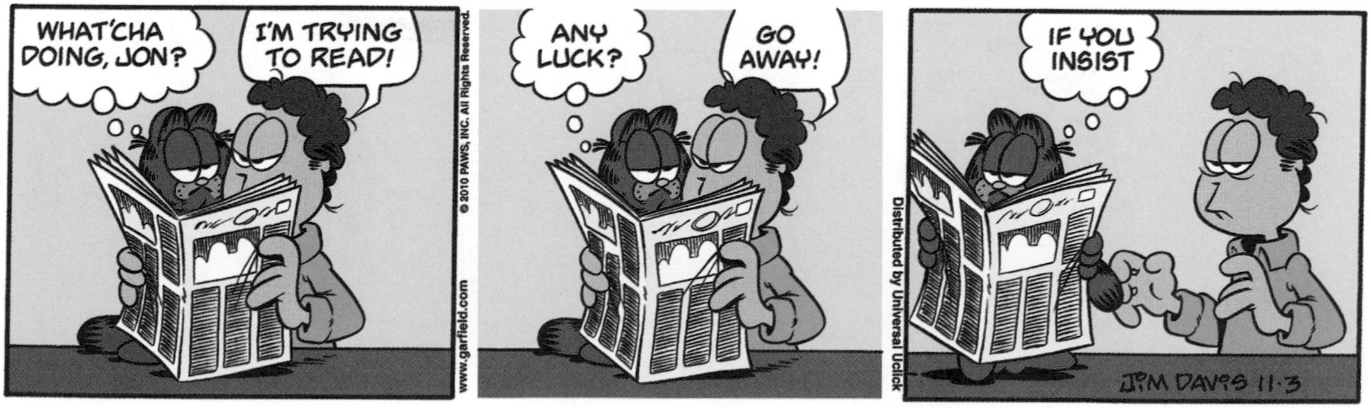
WHAT'CHA DOING, JON?
I'M TRYING TO READ!
ANY LUCK?
GO AWAY!
IF YOU INSIST
JIM DAVIS 11-3
© 2010 PAWS, INC. All Rights Reserved.
www.garfield.com
Distributed by Universal Uclick

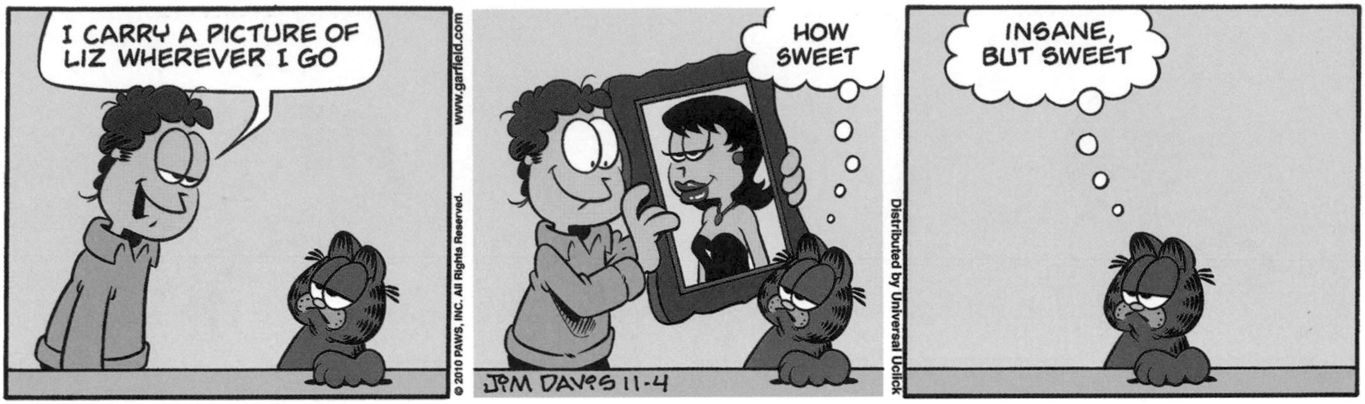
I CARRY A PICTURE OF LIZ WHEREVER I GO
HOW SWEET
INSANE, BUT SWEET
JIM DAVIS 11-4
© 2010 PAWS, INC. All Rights Reserved.
www.garfield.com
Distributed by Universal Uclick

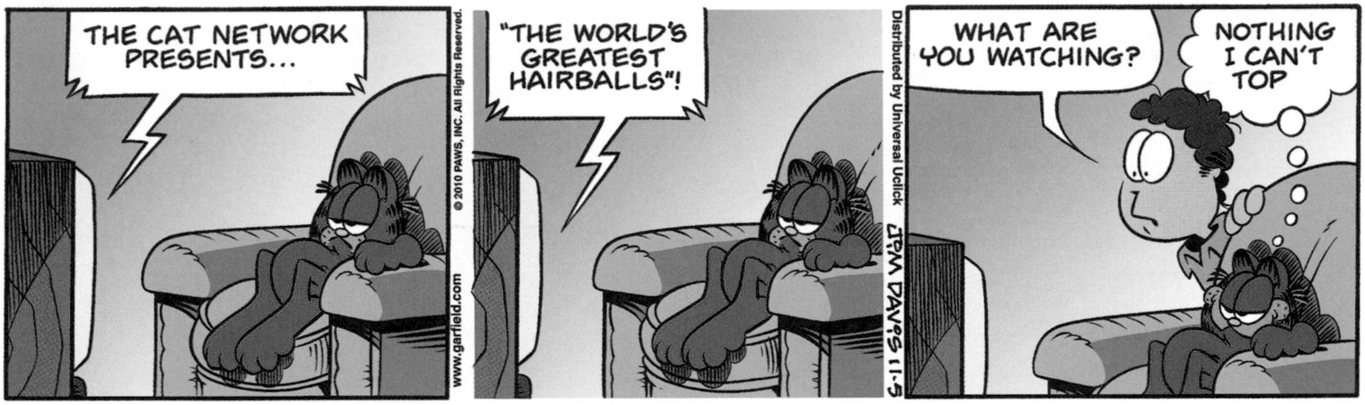
THE CAT NETWORK PRESENTS...
"THE WORLD'S GREATEST HAIRBALLS"!
WHAT ARE YOU WATCHING?
NOTHING I CAN'T TOP
JIM DAVIS 11-5
© 2010 PAWS, INC. All Rights Reserved.
www.garfield.com
Distributed by Universal Uclick

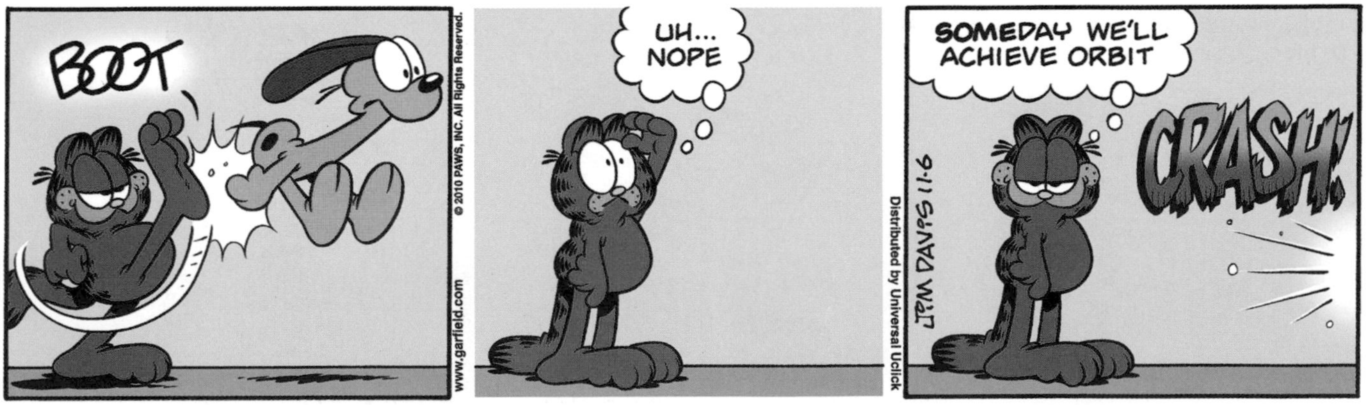
BOOT
UH... NOPE
SOMEDAY WE'LL ACHIEVE ORBIT
CRASH!
JIM DAVIS 11-6
© 2010 PAWS, INC. All Rights Reserved.
www.garfield.com
Distributed by Universal Uclick

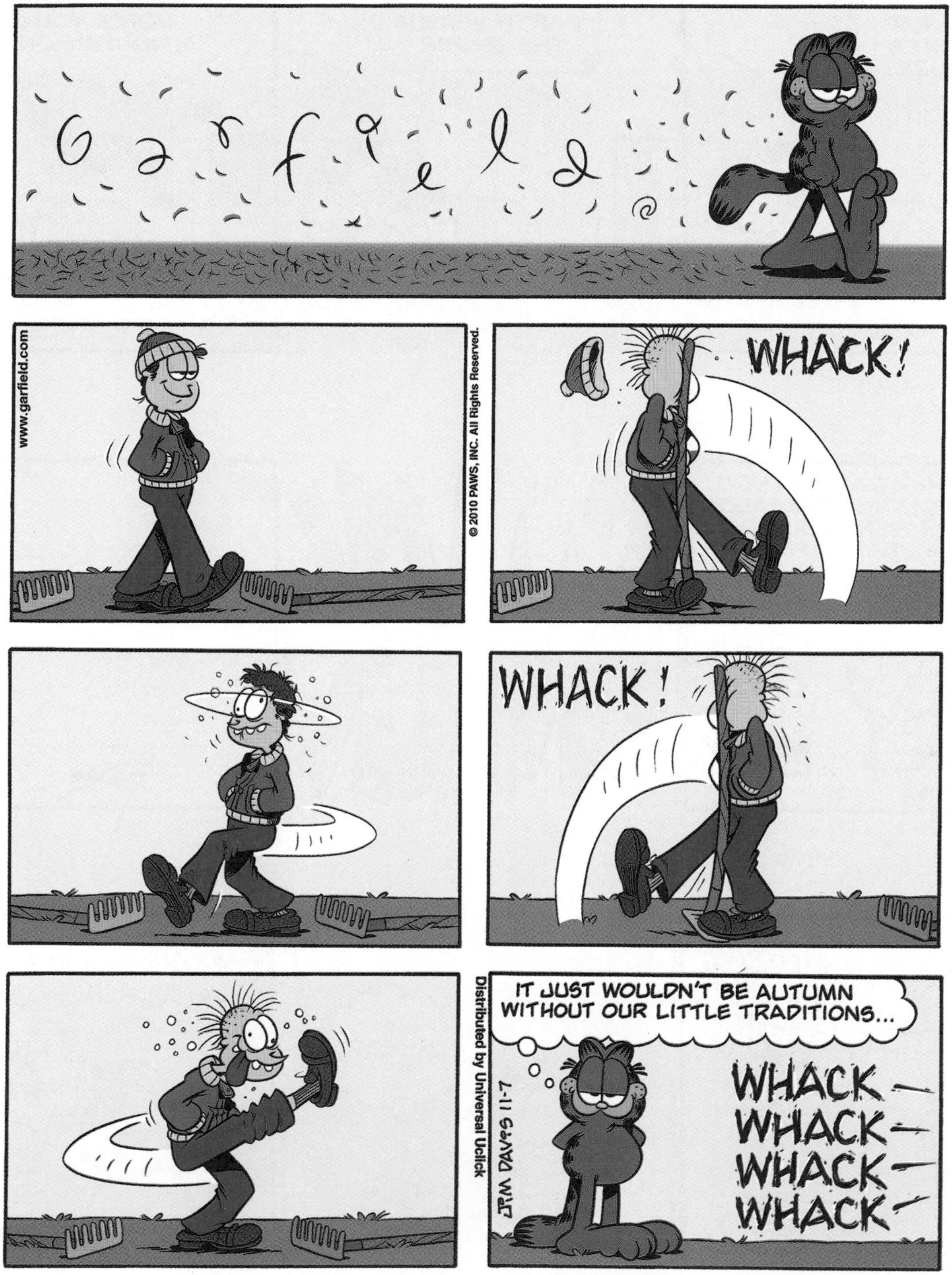
garfield
www.garfield.com
© 2010 PAWS, INC. All Rights Reserved.
WHACK!
WHACK!
IT JUST WOULDN'T BE AUTUMN WITHOUT OUR LITTLE TRADITIONS...
WHACK
WHACK
WHACK
WHACK
JPM DAVPS 11-7
Distributed by Universal Uclick

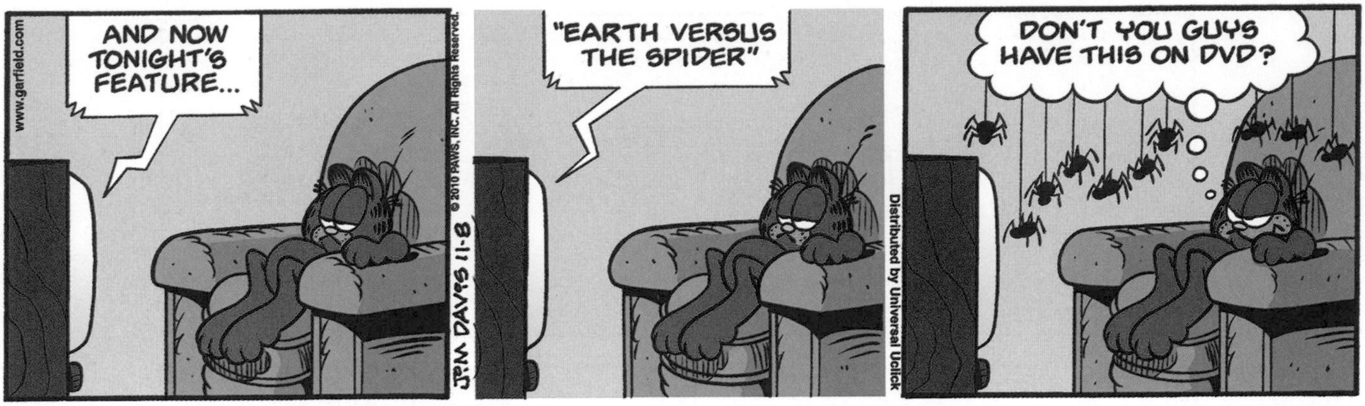
AND NOW TONIGHT'S FEATURE...
"EARTH VERSUS THE SPIDER"
DON'T YOU GUYS HAVE THIS ON DVD?
www.garfield.com
© 2010 PAWS, INC. All Rights Reserved.
JIM DAVIS 11-8
Distributed by Universal Uclick

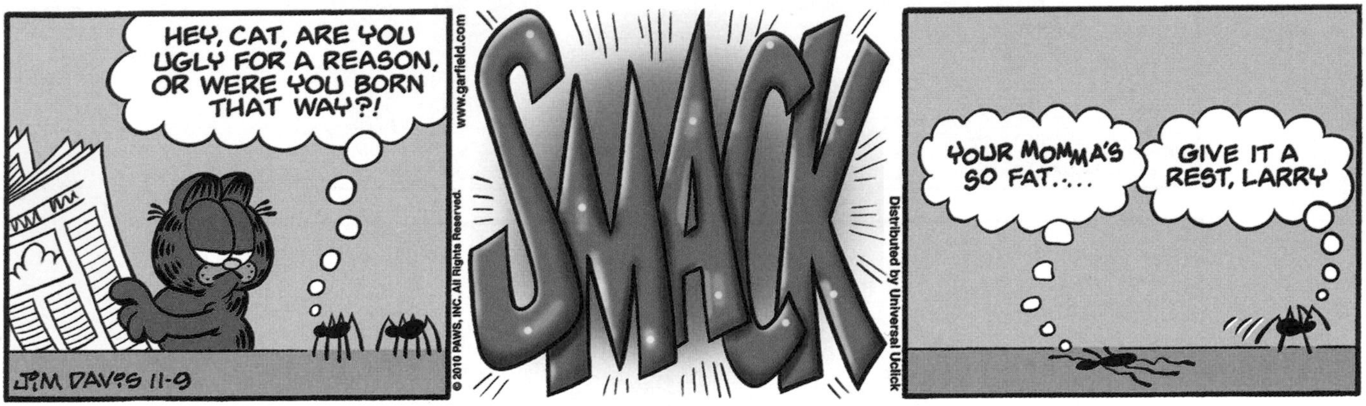
HEY, CAT, ARE YOU UGLY FOR A REASON, OR WERE YOU BORN THAT WAY?!
JIM DAVIS 11-9
SMACK
YOUR MOMMA'S SO FAT.....
GIVE IT A REST, LARRY
www.garfield.com
© 2010 PAWS, INC. All Rights Reserved.
Distributed by Universal Uclick

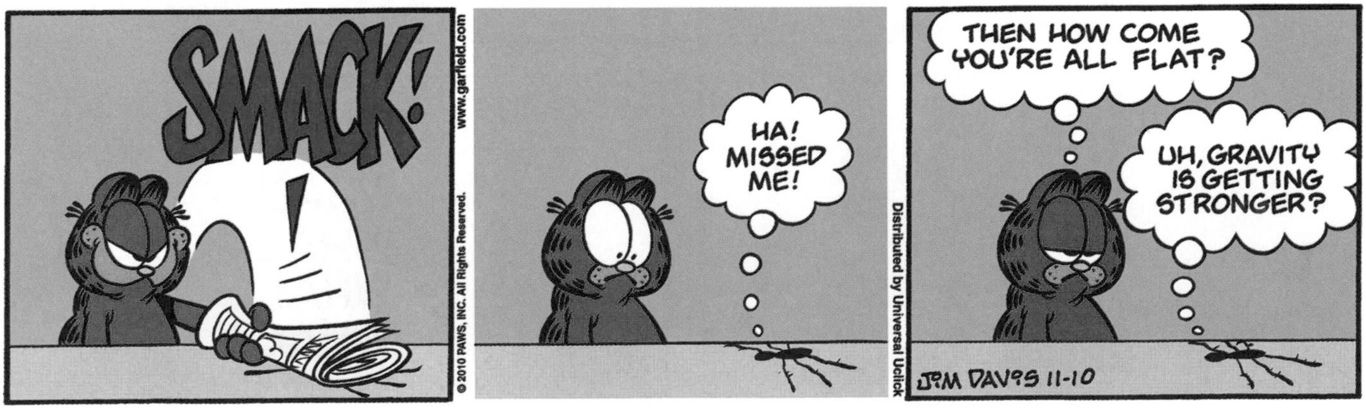
SMACK!
HA! MISSED ME!
THEN HOW COME YOU'RE ALL FLAT?
UH, GRAVITY IS GETTING STRONGER?
JIM DAVIS 11-10
www.garfield.com
© 2010 PAWS, INC. All Rights Reserved.
Distributed by Universal Uclick

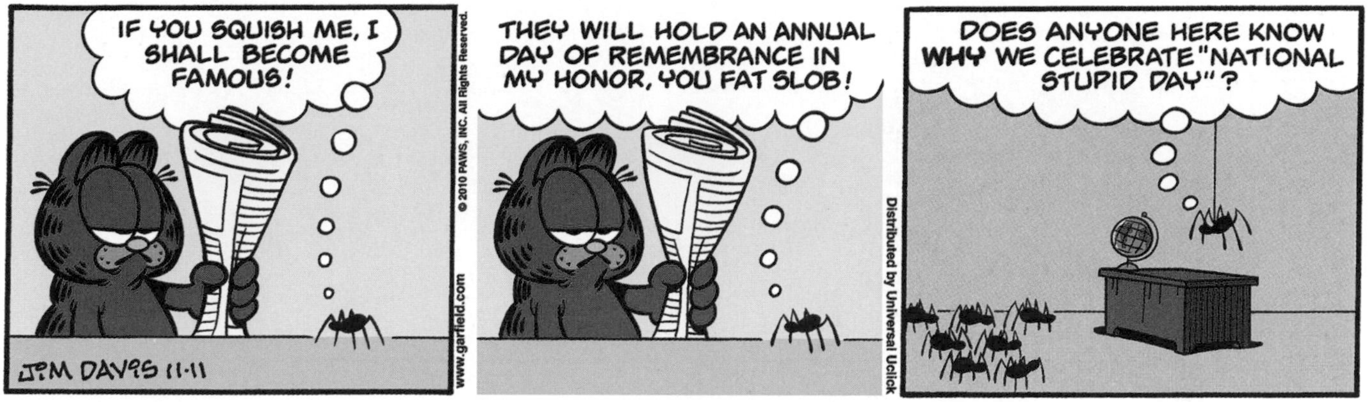
IF YOU SQUISH ME, I SHALL BECOME FAMOUS!
JIM DAVIS 11-11
© 2010 PAWS, INC. All Rights Reserved.
www.garfield.com
THEY WILL HOLD AN ANNUAL DAY OF REMEMBRANCE IN MY HONOR, YOU FAT SLOB!
Distributed by Universal Uclick
DOES ANYONE HERE KNOW WHY WE CELEBRATE "NATIONAL STUPID DAY"?

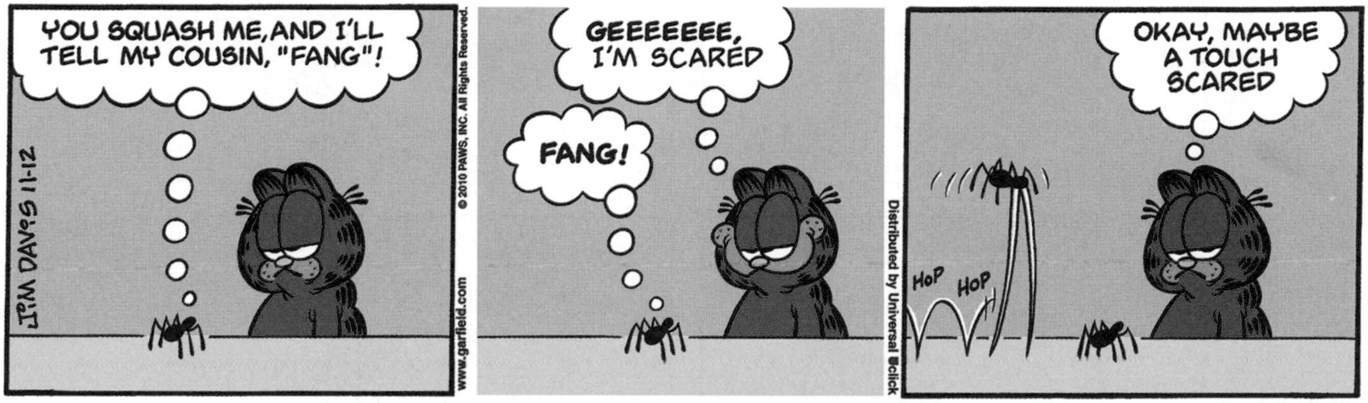
YOU SQUASH ME, AND I'LL TELL MY COUSIN, "FANG"!
JIM DAVIS 11-12
© 2010 PAWS, INC. All Rights Reserved.
www.garfield.com
GEEEEEEE, I'M SCARED
FANG!
Distributed by Universal Uclick
HOP
HOP
OKAY, MAYBE A TOUCH SCARED

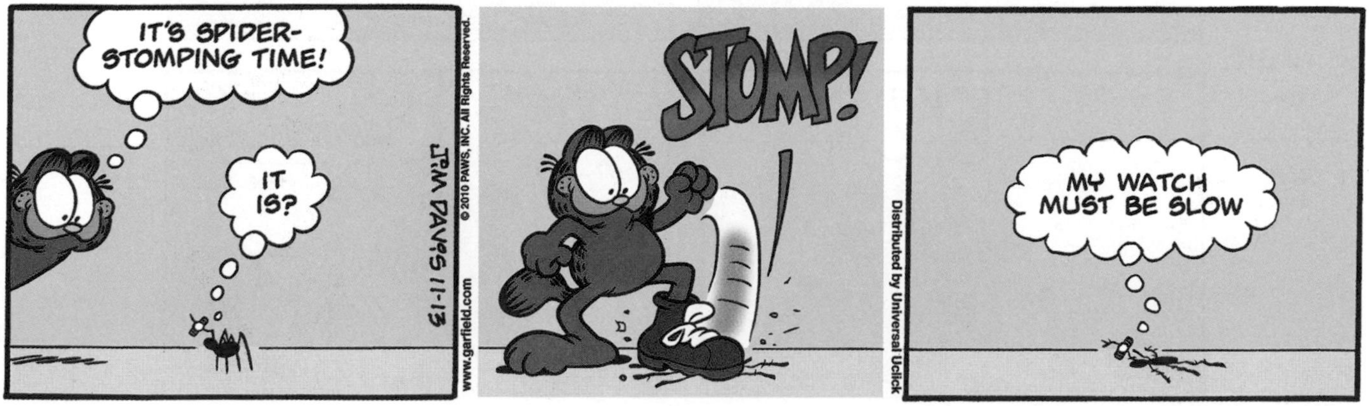
IT'S SPIDER-STOMPING TIME!
IT IS?
JIM DAVIS 11-13
© 2010 PAWS, INC. All Rights Reserved.
www.garfield.com
STOMP!
Distributed by Universal Uclick
MY WATCH MUST BE SLOW

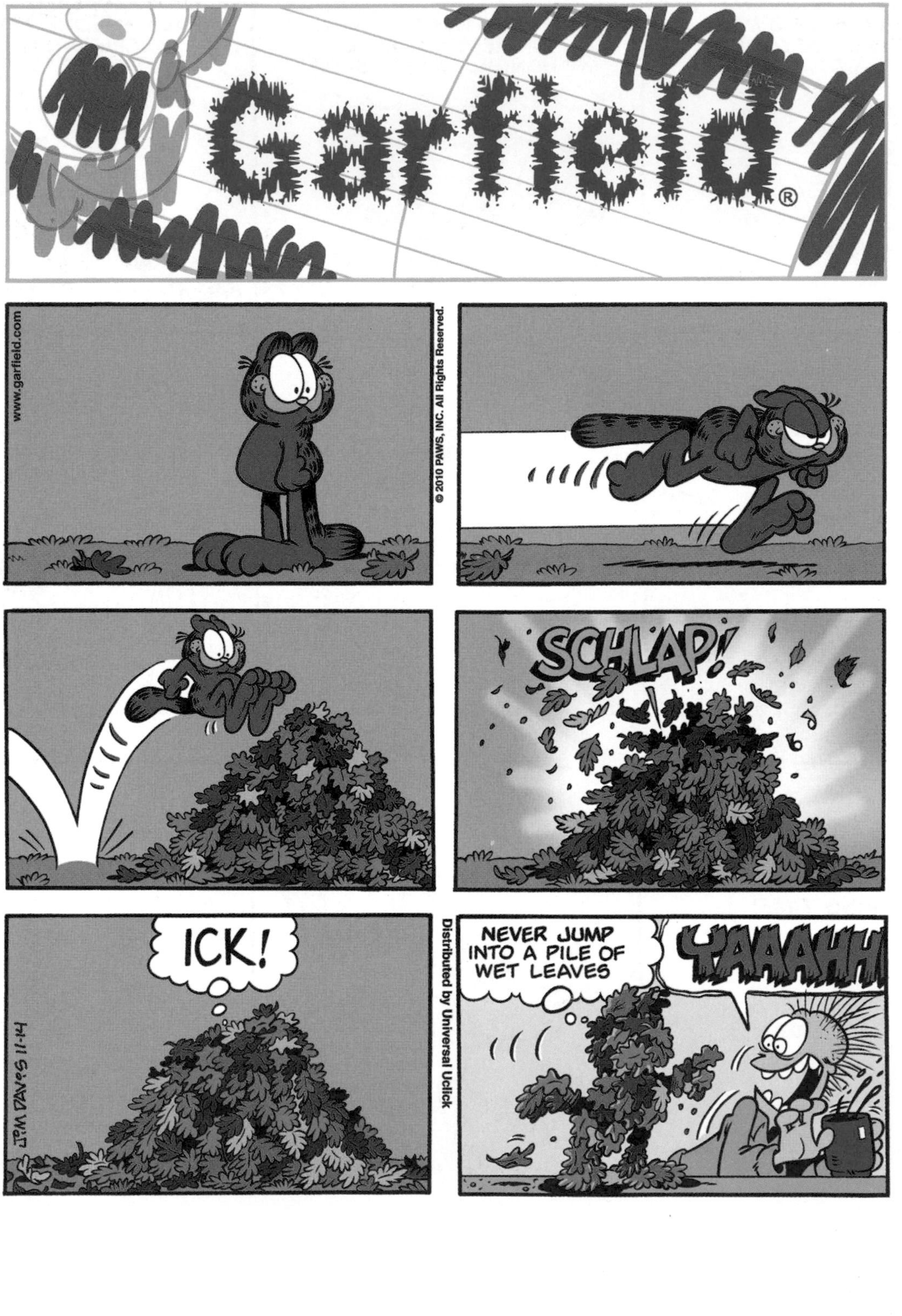
Garfield®
www.garfield.com
© 2010 PAWS, INC. All Rights Reserved.
SCHLAP!
ICK!
JPM DAVIS 11-14
Distributed by Universal Uclick
NEVER JUMP INTO A PILE OF WET LEAVES
YAAAHH

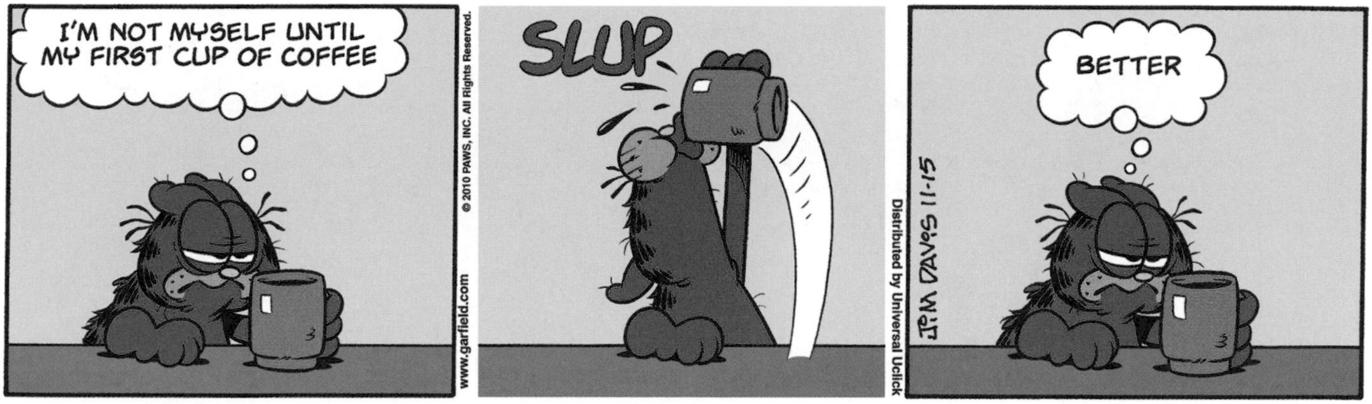
I'M NOT MYSELF UNTIL MY FIRST CUP OF COFFEE
SLUP
BETTER
JIM DAVIS 11-15
www.garfield.com
© 2010 PAWS, INC. All Rights Reserved.
Distributed by Universal Uclick

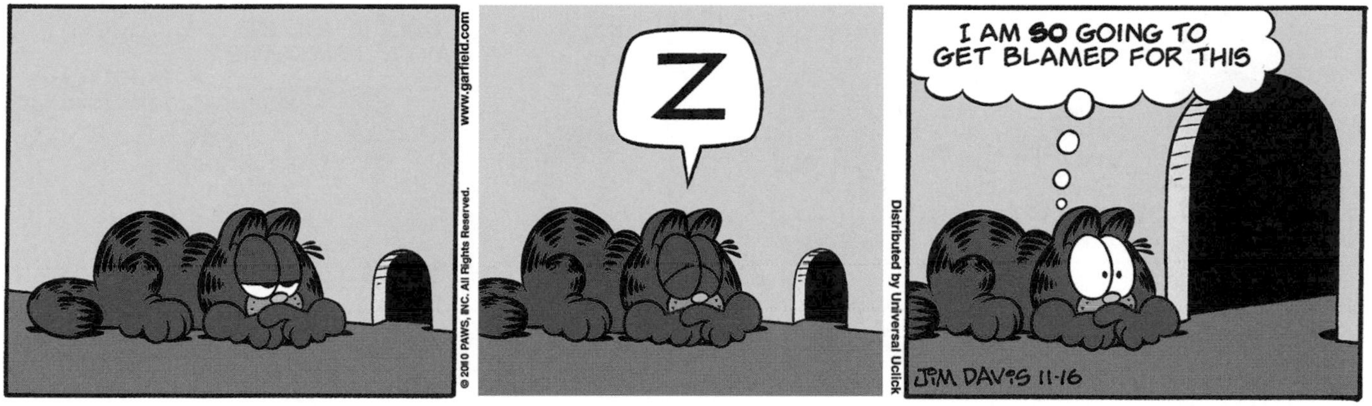
Z
I AM **SO** GOING TO GET BLAMED FOR THIS
JIM DAVIS 11-16
www.garfield.com
© 2010 PAWS, INC. All Rights Reserved.
Distributed by Universal Uclick

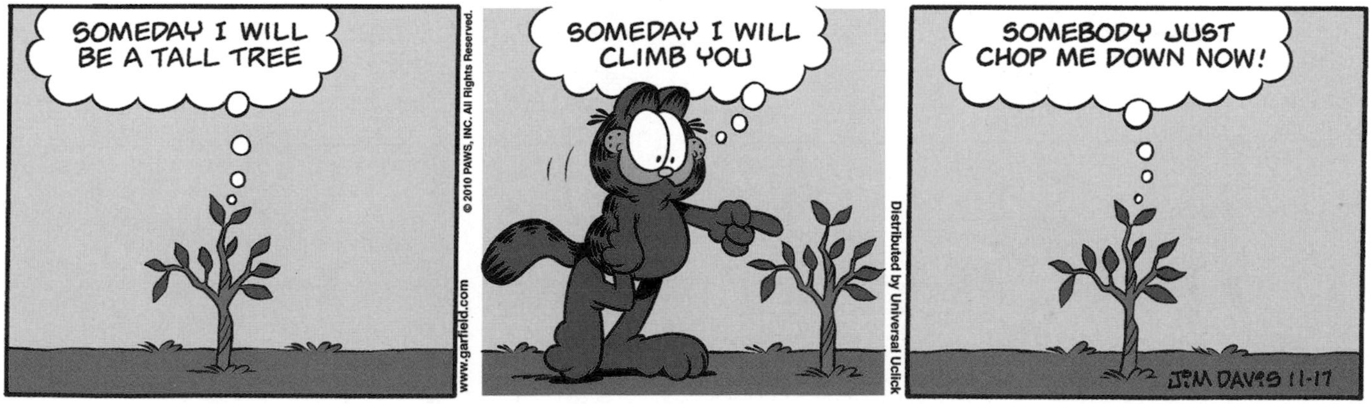
SOMEDAY I WILL BE A TALL TREE
SOMEDAY I WILL CLIMB YOU
SOMEBODY JUST CHOP ME DOWN NOW!
JIM DAVIS 11-17
www.garfield.com
© 2010 PAWS, INC. All Rights Reserved.
Distributed by Universal Uclick

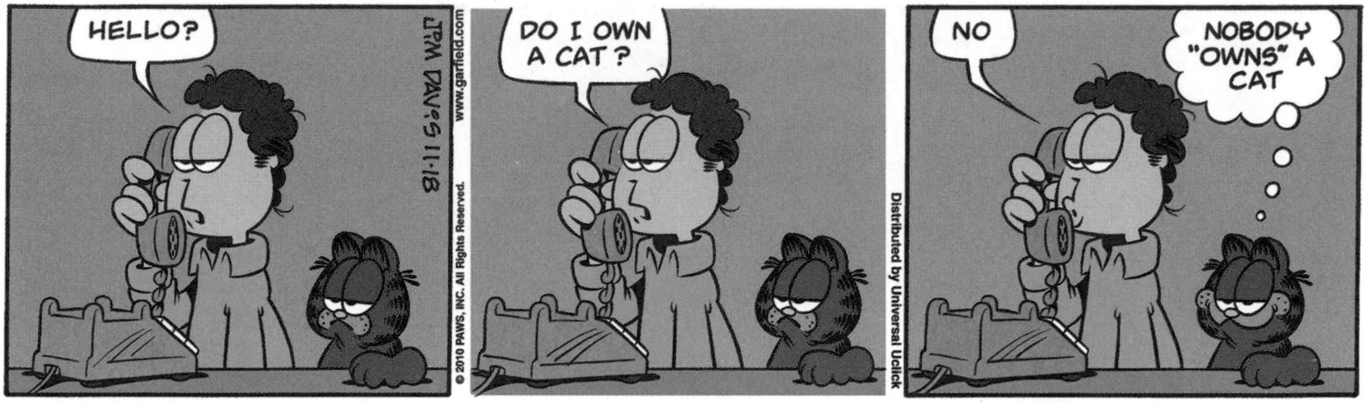
HELLO?
JIM DAVIS 11-18
DO I OWN A CAT?
NO
NOBODY "OWNS" A CAT
© 2010 PAWS, INC. All Rights Reserved.
www.garfield.com
Distributed by Universal Uclick

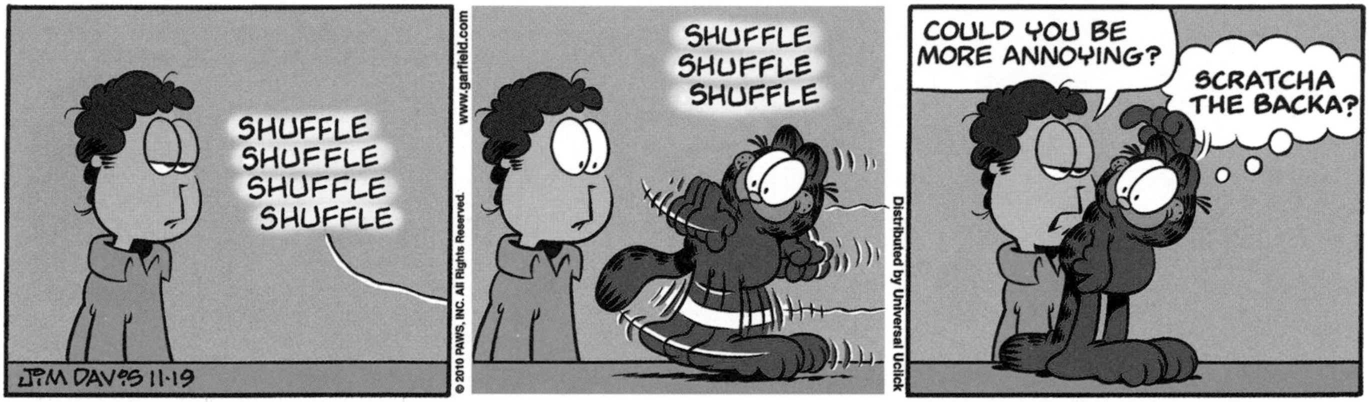
SHUFFLE SHUFFLE SHUFFLE SHUFFLE
JIM DAVIS 11-19
SHUFFLE SHUFFLE SHUFFLE
COULD YOU BE MORE ANNOYING?
SCRATCHA THE BACKA?
© 2010 PAWS, INC. All Rights Reserved.
www.garfield.com
Distributed by Universal Uclick

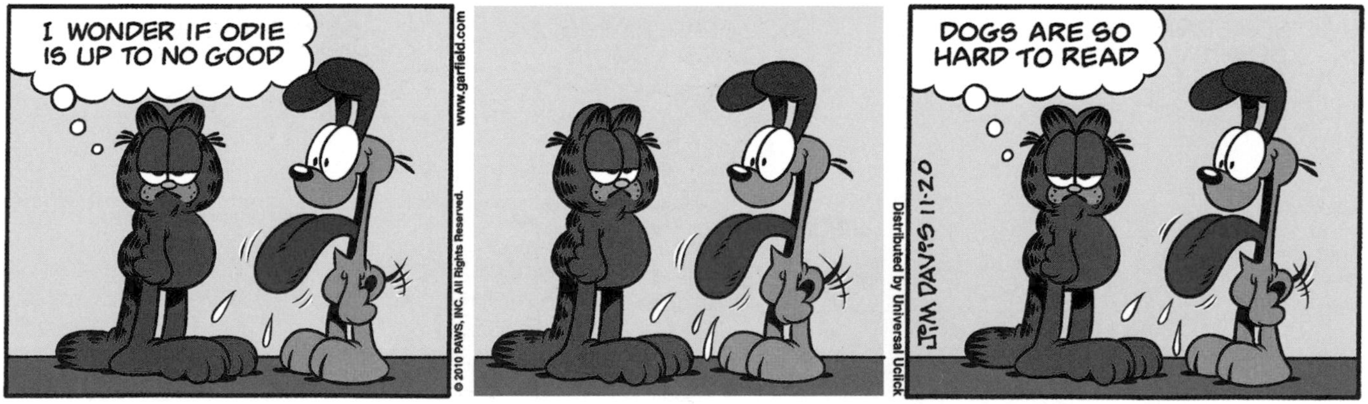
I WONDER IF ODIE IS UP TO NO GOOD
DOGS ARE SO HARD TO READ
JIM DAVIS 11-20
© 2010 PAWS, INC. All Rights Reserved.
www.garfield.com
Distributed by Universal Uclick

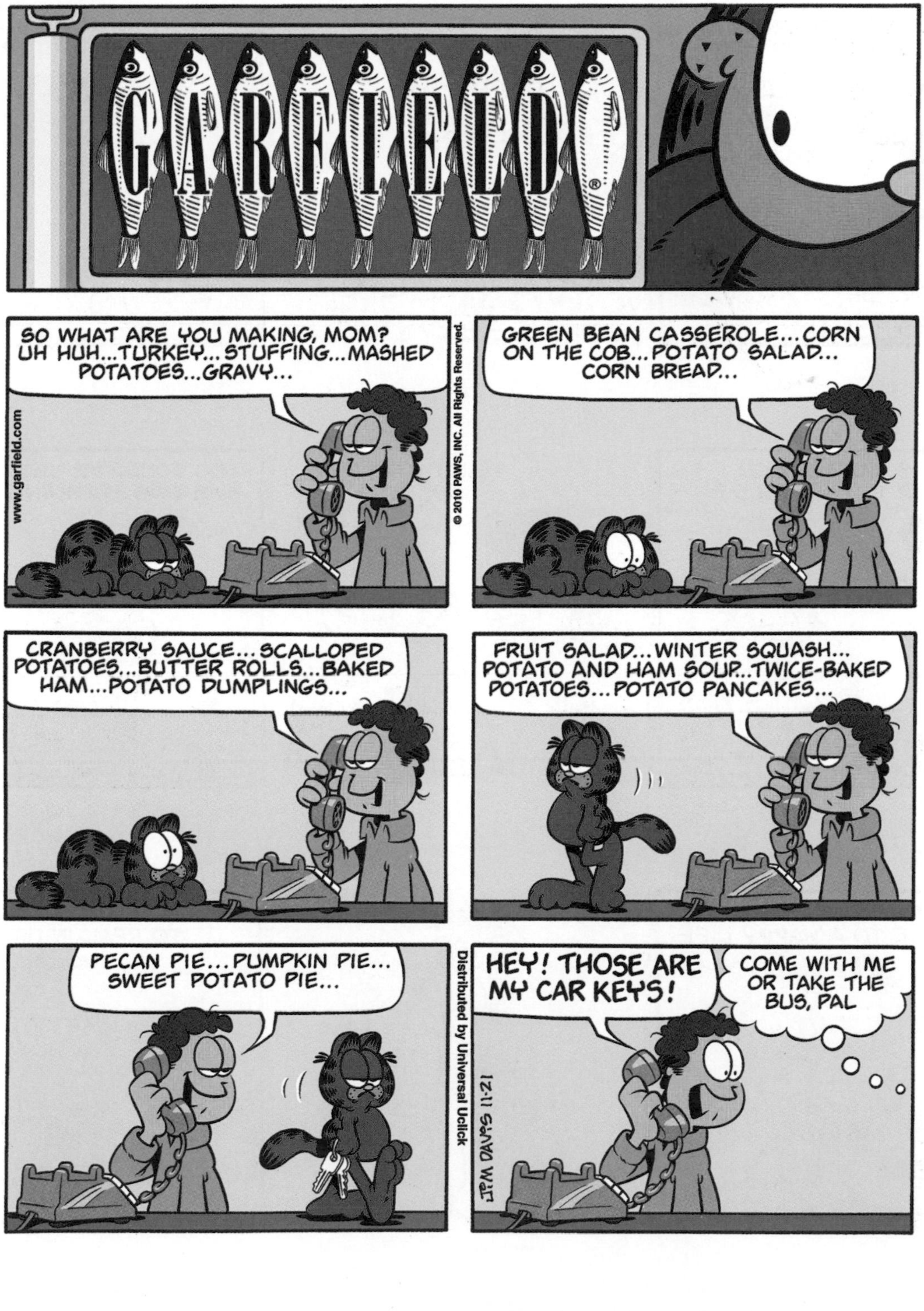
GARFIELD®
www.garfield.com
© 2010 PAWS, INC. All Rights Reserved.
SO WHAT ARE YOU MAKING, MOM? UH HUH...TURKEY... STUFFING...MASHED POTATOES...GRAVY...
GREEN BEAN CASSEROLE...CORN ON THE COB...POTATO SALAD... CORN BREAD...
CRANBERRY SAUCE... SCALLOPED POTATOES...BUTTER ROLLS...BAKED HAM...POTATO DUMPLINGS...
FRUIT SALAD...WINTER SQUASH... POTATO AND HAM SOUP...TWICE-BAKED POTATOES...POTATO PANCAKES...
PECAN PIE...PUMPKIN PIE... SWEET POTATO PIE...
Distributed by Universal Uclick
JPM DAVIS 11-21
HEY! THOSE ARE MY CAR KEYS!
COME WITH ME OR TAKE THE BUS, PAL

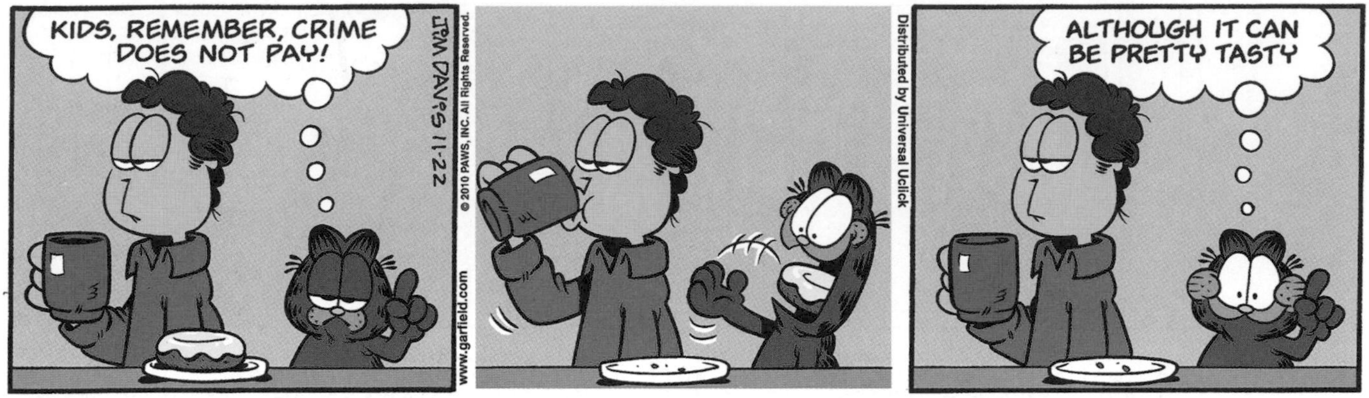
KIDS, REMEMBER, CRIME DOES NOT PAY!
JPM DAVIS 11-22
© 2010 PAWS, INC. All Rights Reserved.
www.garfield.com
Distributed by Universal Uclick
ALTHOUGH IT CAN BE PRETTY TASTY

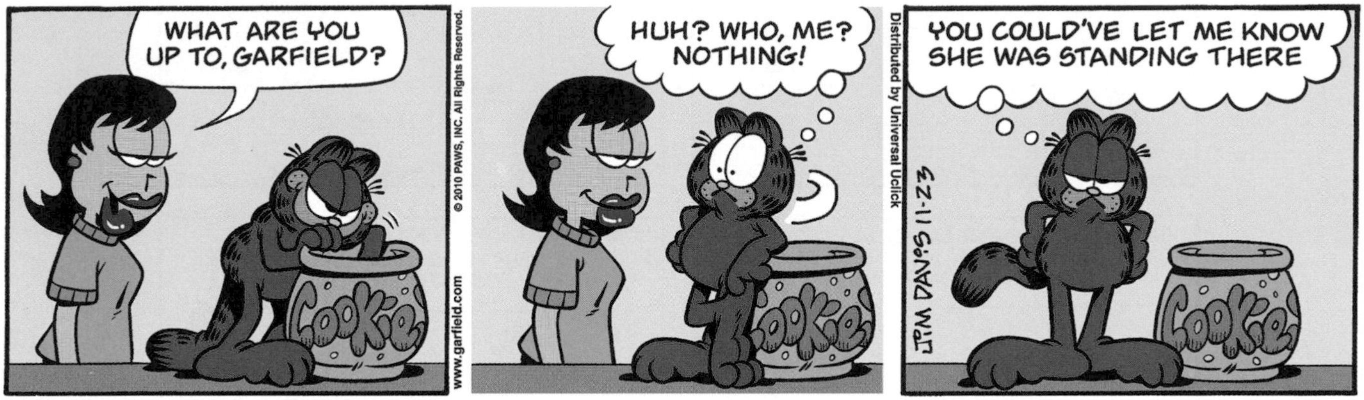
WHAT ARE YOU UP TO, GARFIELD?
© 2010 PAWS, INC. All Rights Reserved.
www.garfield.com
HUH? WHO, ME? NOTHING!
Distributed by Universal Uclick
YOU COULD'VE LET ME KNOW SHE WAS STANDING THERE
JPM DAVIS 11-23

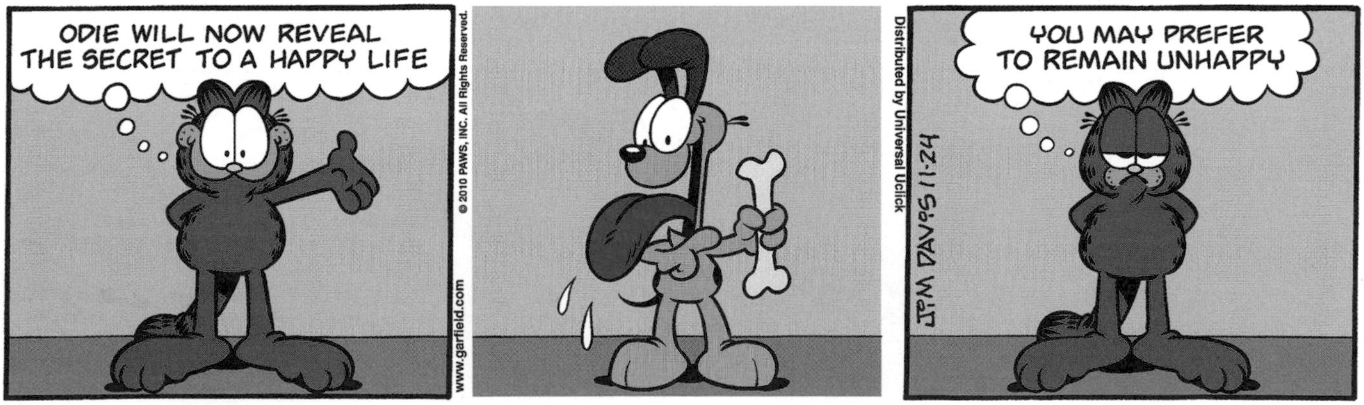
ODIE WILL NOW REVEAL THE SECRET TO A HAPPY LIFE
© 2010 PAWS, INC. All Rights Reserved.
www.garfield.com
Distributed by Universal Uclick
JPM DAVIS 11-24
YOU MAY PREFER TO REMAIN UNHAPPY

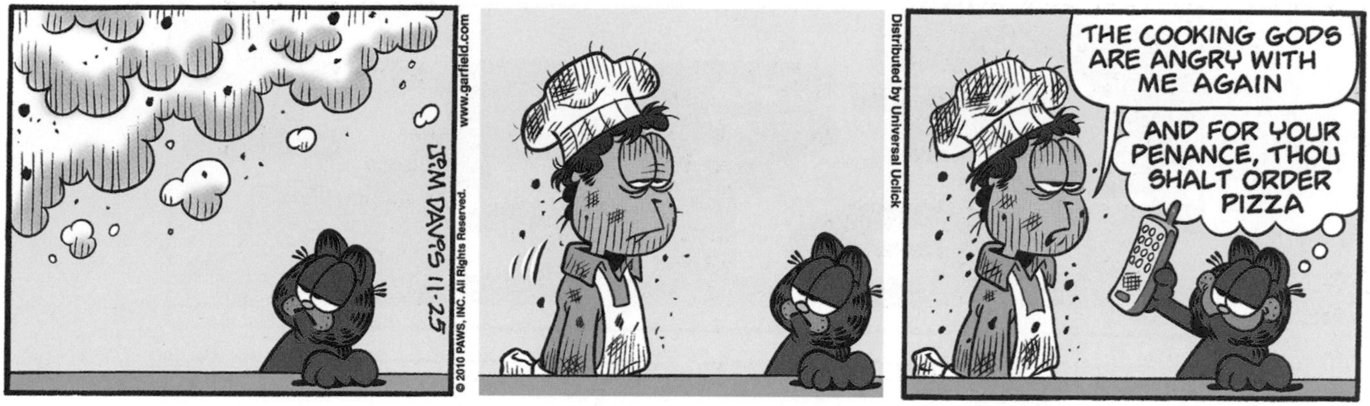
JIM DAVIS 11-25
© 2010 PAWS, INC. All Rights Reserved. www.garfield.com
Distributed by Universal Uclick
THE COOKING GODS ARE ANGRY WITH ME AGAIN
AND FOR YOUR PENANCE, THOU SHALT ORDER PIZZA

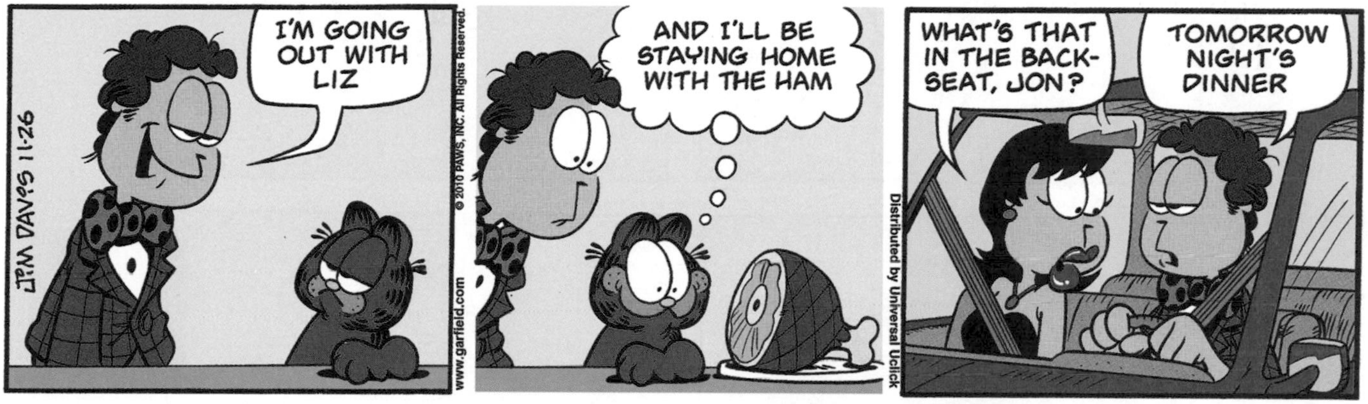
JIM DAVIS 11-26
I'M GOING OUT WITH LIZ
© 2010 PAWS, INC. All Rights Reserved. www.garfield.com
AND I'LL BE STAYING HOME WITH THE HAM
Distributed by Universal Uclick
WHAT'S THAT IN THE BACK-SEAT, JON?
TOMORROW NIGHT'S DINNER

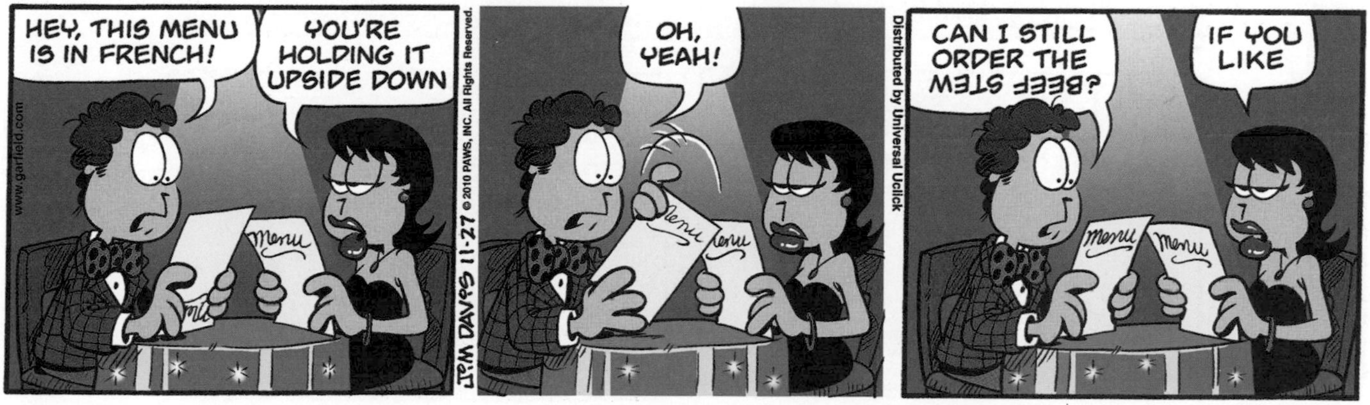
www.garfield.com
HEY, THIS MENU IS IN FRENCH!
YOU'RE HOLDING IT UPSIDE DOWN
Menu
JIM DAVIS 11-27
© 2010 PAWS, INC. All Rights Reserved.
OH, YEAH!
Distributed by Universal Uclick
CAN I STILL ORDER THE BEEF STEW?
IF YOU LIKE

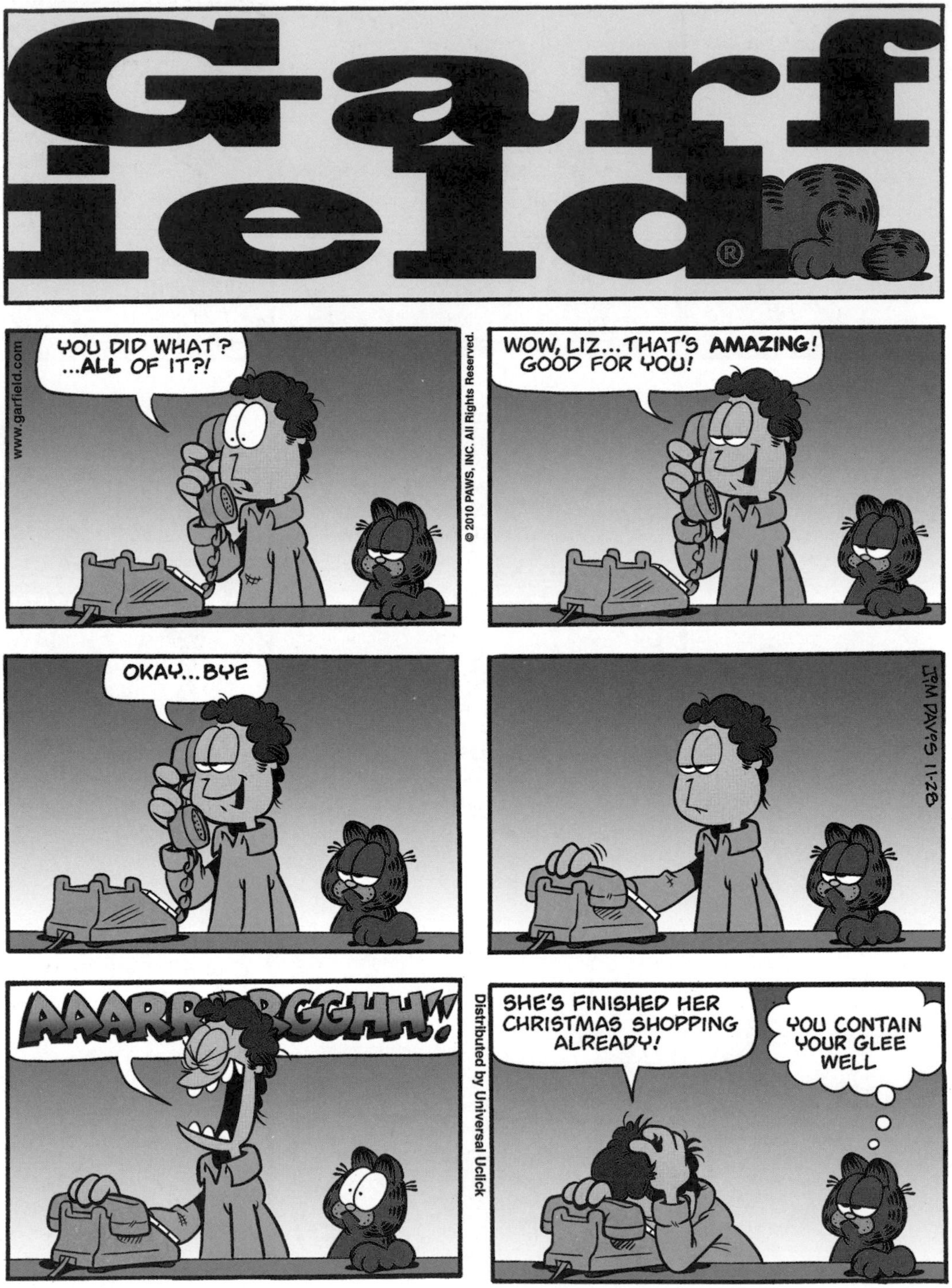
Garfield®
www.garfield.com
YOU DID WHAT? ...ALL OF IT?!
© 2010 PAWS, INC. All Rights Reserved.
WOW, LIZ... THAT'S AMAZING! GOOD FOR YOU!
OKAY... BYE
JIM DAVIS 11-28
AAARR RGGHH!!
Distributed by Universal Uclick
SHE'S FINISHED HER CHRISTMAS SHOPPING ALREADY!
YOU CONTAIN YOUR GLEE WELL

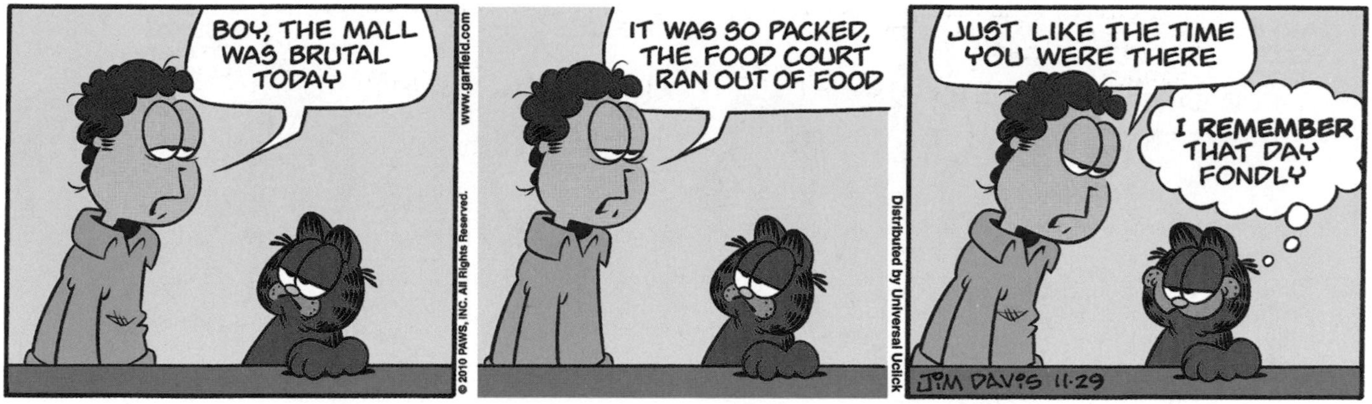
BOY, THE MALL WAS BRUTAL TODAY
IT WAS SO PACKED, THE FOOD COURT RAN OUT OF FOOD
JUST LIKE THE TIME YOU WERE THERE
I REMEMBER THAT DAY FONDLY
www.garfield.com
© 2010 PAWS, INC. All Rights Reserved.
Distributed by Universal Uclick
JIM DAVIS 11-29

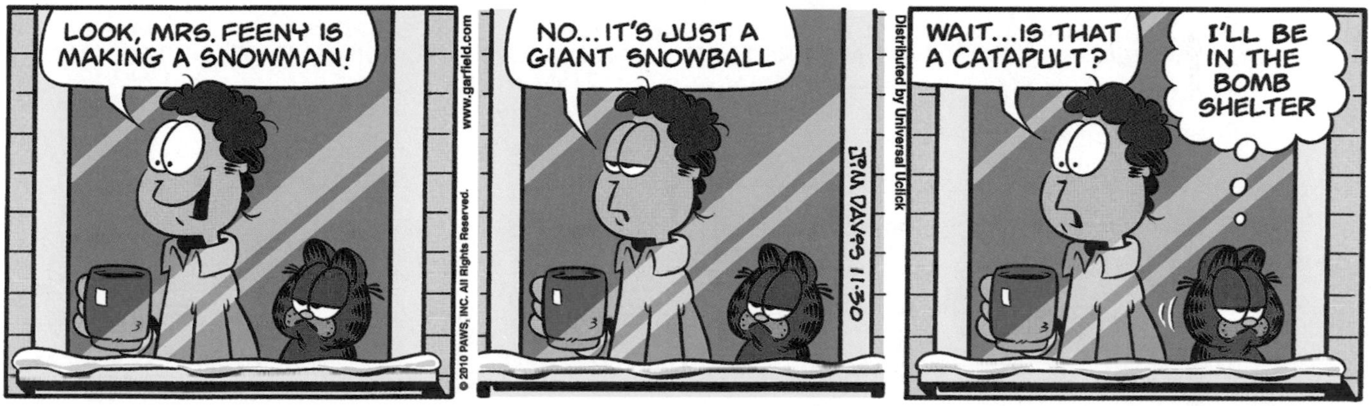
LOOK, MRS. FEENY IS MAKING A SNOWMAN!
NO... IT'S JUST A GIANT SNOWBALL
WAIT... IS THAT A CATAPULT?
I'LL BE IN THE BOMB SHELTER
www.garfield.com
© 2010 PAWS, INC. All Rights Reserved.
Distributed by Universal Uclick
JIM DAVIS 11-30

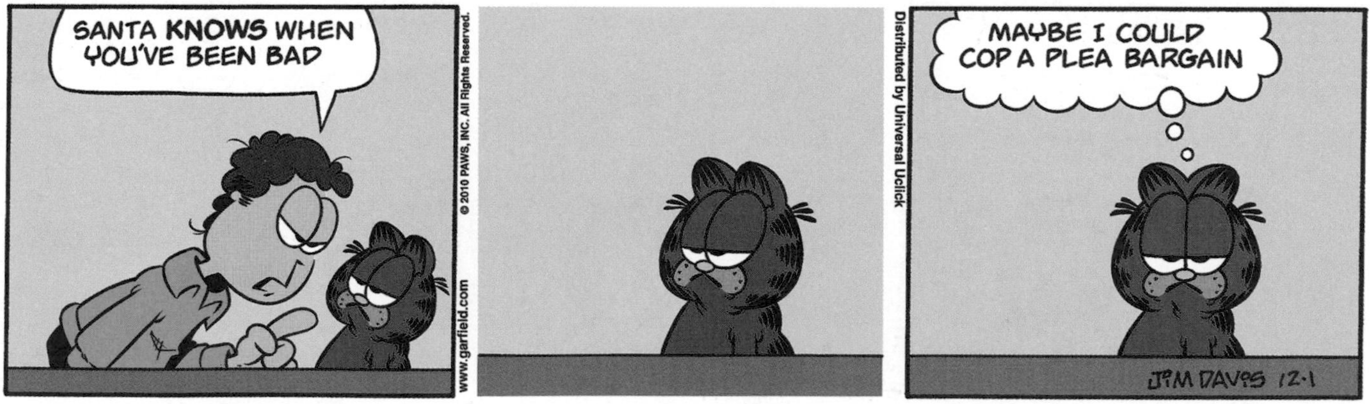
SANTA KNOWS WHEN YOU'VE BEEN BAD
MAYBE I COULD COP A PLEA BARGAIN
© 2010 PAWS, INC. All Rights Reserved.
www.garfield.com
Distributed by Universal Uclick
JIM DAVIS 12-1

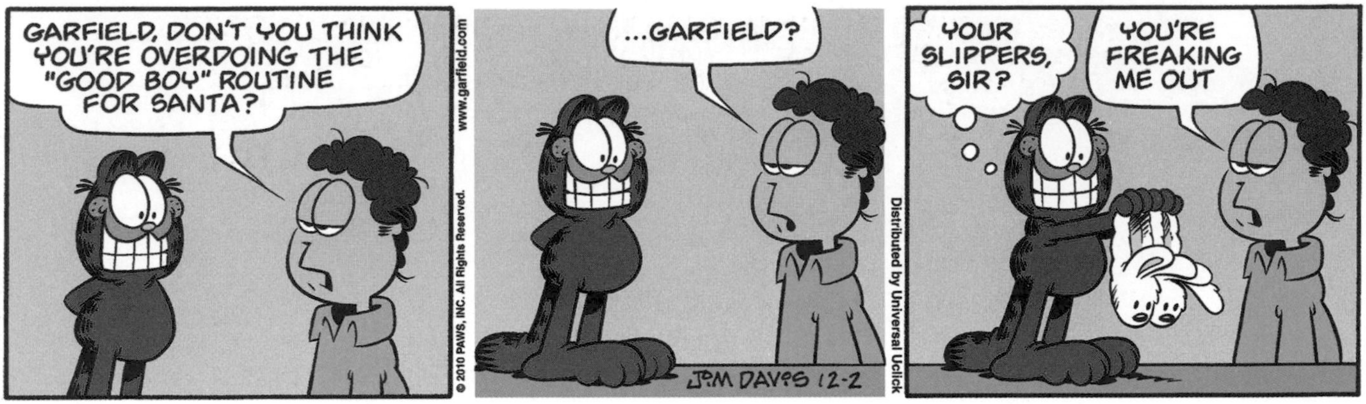
GARFIELD, DON'T YOU THINK YOU'RE OVERDOING THE "GOOD BOY" ROUTINE FOR SANTA?
...GARFIELD?
YOUR SLIPPERS, SIR?
YOU'RE FREAKING ME OUT
JIM DAVIS 12-2
© 2010 PAWS, INC. All Rights Reserved. www.garfield.com
Distributed by Universal Uclick

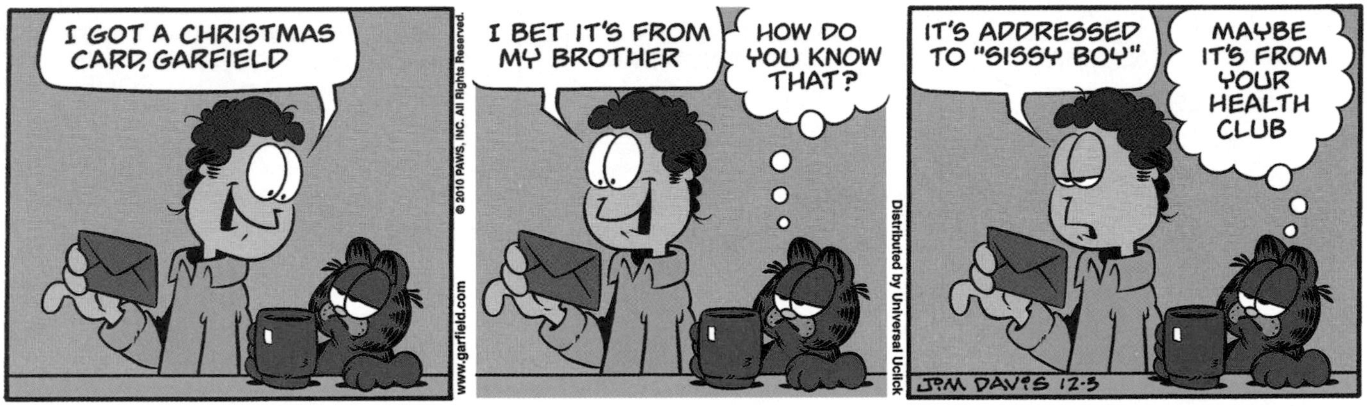
I GOT A CHRISTMAS CARD, GARFIELD
I BET IT'S FROM MY BROTHER
HOW DO YOU KNOW THAT?
IT'S ADDRESSED TO "SISSY BOY"
MAYBE IT'S FROM YOUR HEALTH CLUB
JIM DAVIS 12-3
© 2010 PAWS, INC. All Rights Reserved. www.garfield.com
Distributed by Universal Uclick

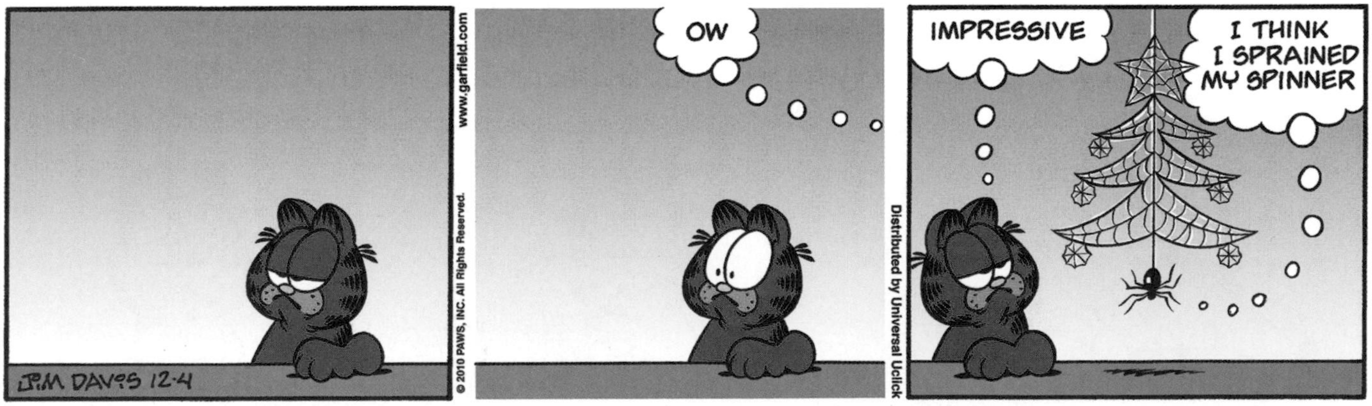
JIM DAVIS 12-4
OW
IMPRESSIVE
I THINK I SPRAINED MY SPINNER
© 2010 PAWS, INC. All Rights Reserved. www.garfield.com
Distributed by Universal Uclick

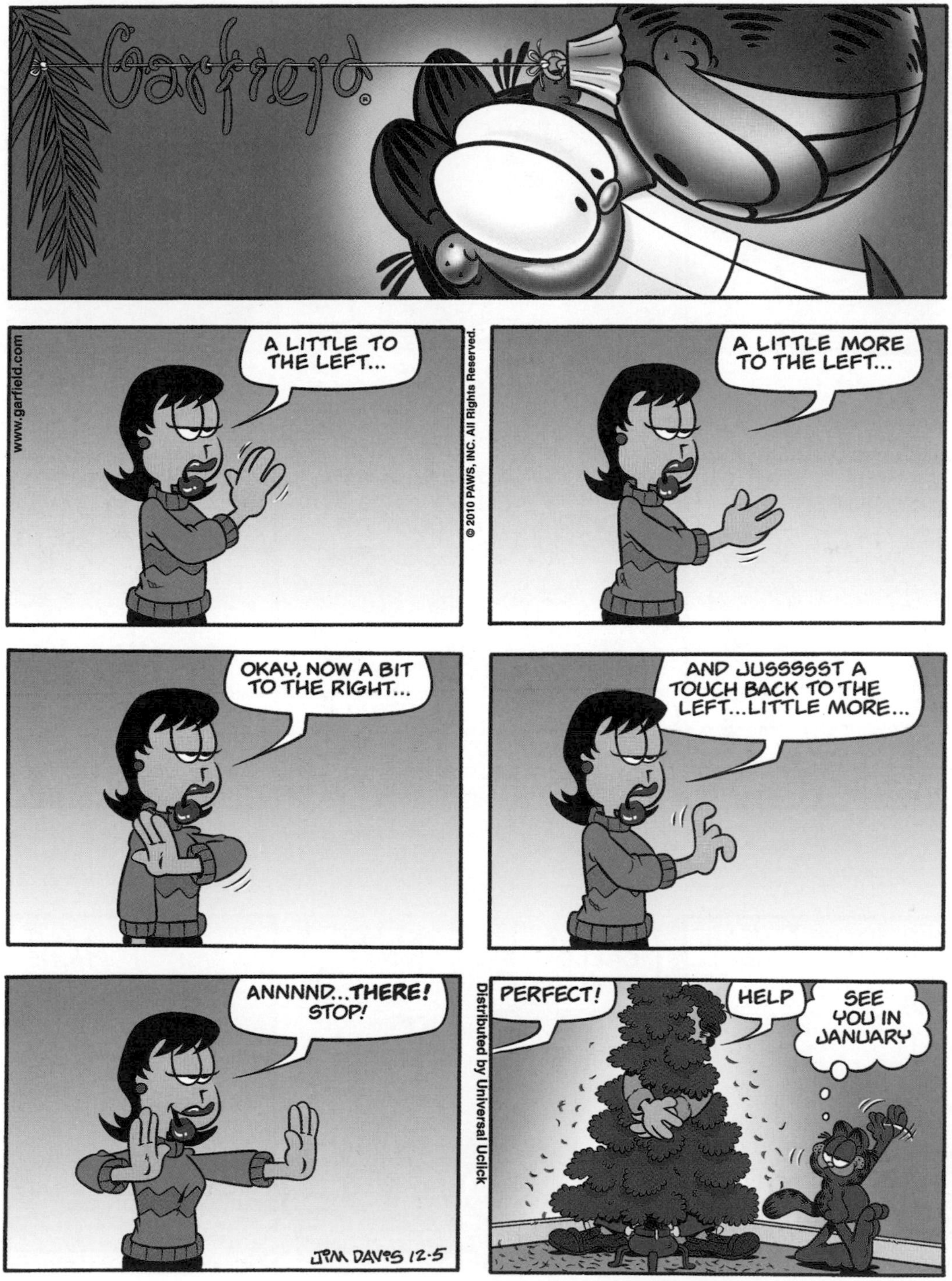
Garfield®
www.garfield.com
© 2010 PAWS, INC. All Rights Reserved.
A LITTLE TO THE LEFT...
A LITTLE MORE TO THE LEFT...
OKAY, NOW A BIT TO THE RIGHT...
AND JUSSSSST A TOUCH BACK TO THE LEFT...LITTLE MORE...
ANNNND...THERE! STOP!
JIM DAVIS 12-5
Distributed by Universal Uclick
PERFECT!
HELP
SEE YOU IN JANUARY

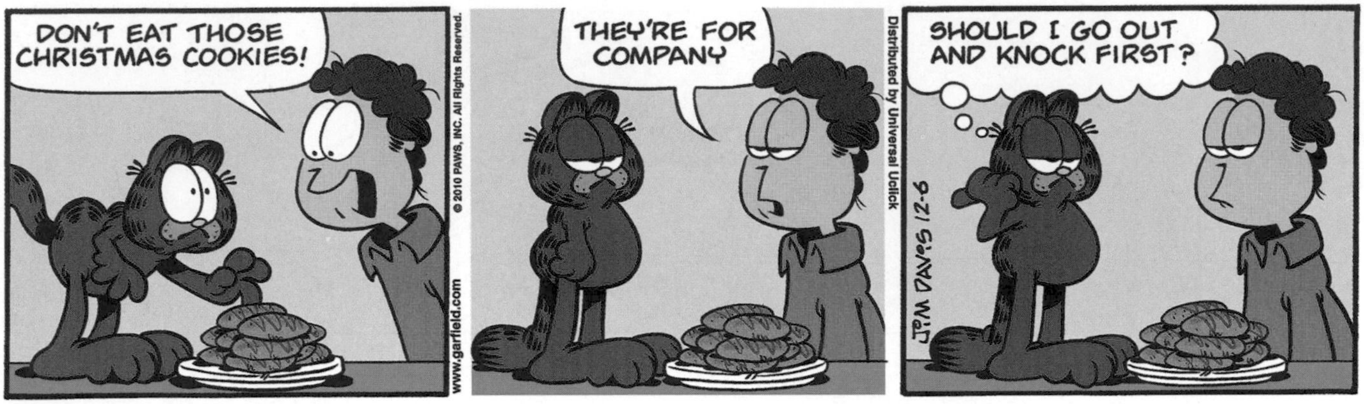
DON'T EAT THOSE CHRISTMAS COOKIES!
THEY'RE FOR COMPANY
SHOULD I GO OUT AND KNOCK FIRST?
JIM DAVIS 12-6
© 2010 PAWS, INC. All Rights Reserved. www.garfield.com
Distributed by Universal Uclick

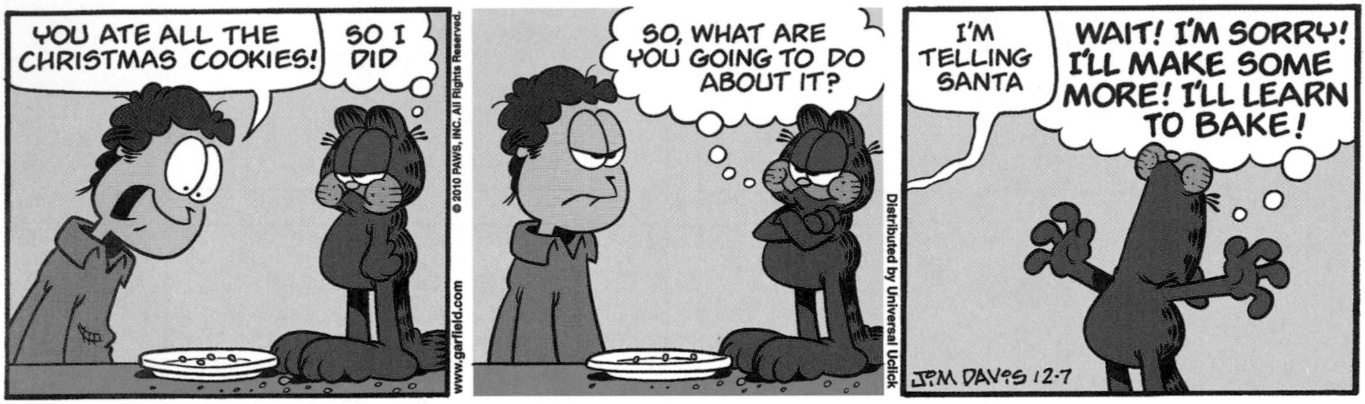
YOU ATE ALL THE CHRISTMAS COOKIES!
SO I DID
SO, WHAT ARE YOU GOING TO DO ABOUT IT?
I'M TELLING SANTA
WAIT! I'M SORRY! I'LL MAKE SOME MORE! I'LL LEARN TO BAKE!
JIM DAVIS 12-7
© 2010 PAWS, INC. All Rights Reserved. www.garfield.com
Distributed by Universal Uclick

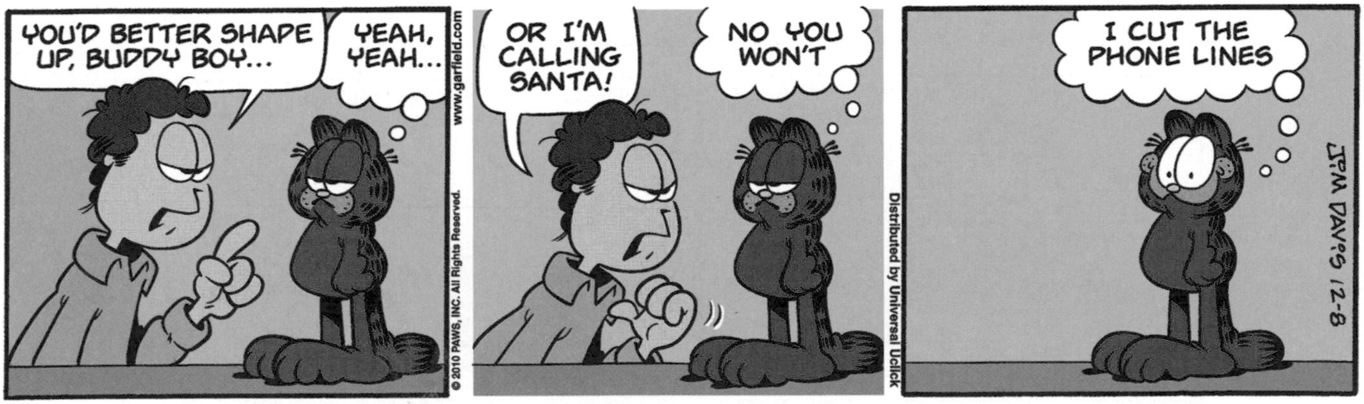
YOU'D BETTER SHAPE UP, BUDDY BOY...
YEAH, YEAH...
OR I'M CALLING SANTA!
NO YOU WON'T
I CUT THE PHONE LINES
JIM DAVIS 12-8
© 2010 PAWS, INC. All Rights Reserved. www.garfield.com
Distributed by Universal Uclick

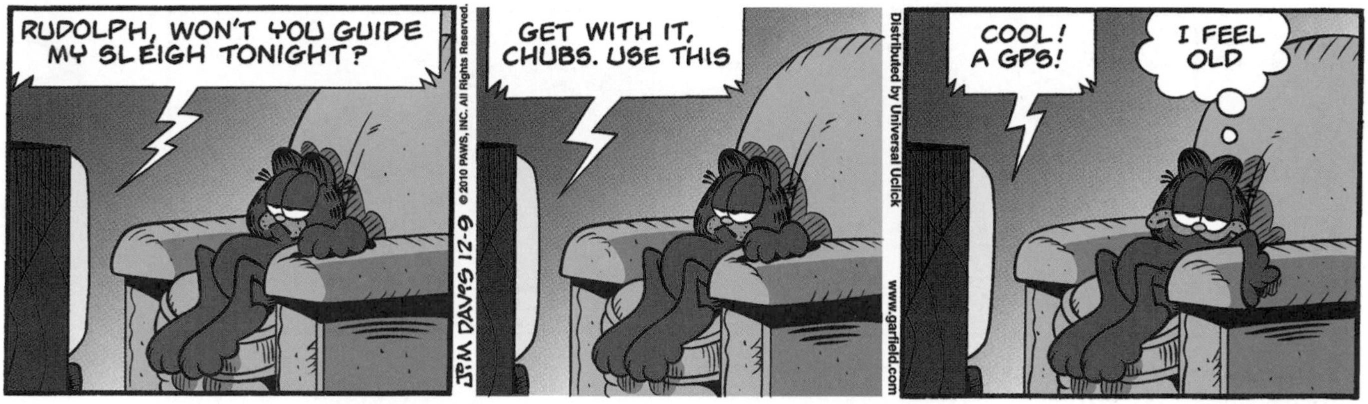
RUDOLPH, WON'T YOU GUIDE MY SLEIGH TONIGHT?
JIM DAVIS 12-9
© 2010 PAWS, INC. All Rights Reserved.
GET WITH IT, CHUBS. USE THIS
Distributed by Universal Uclick
www.garfield.com
COOL! A GPS!
I FEEL OLD

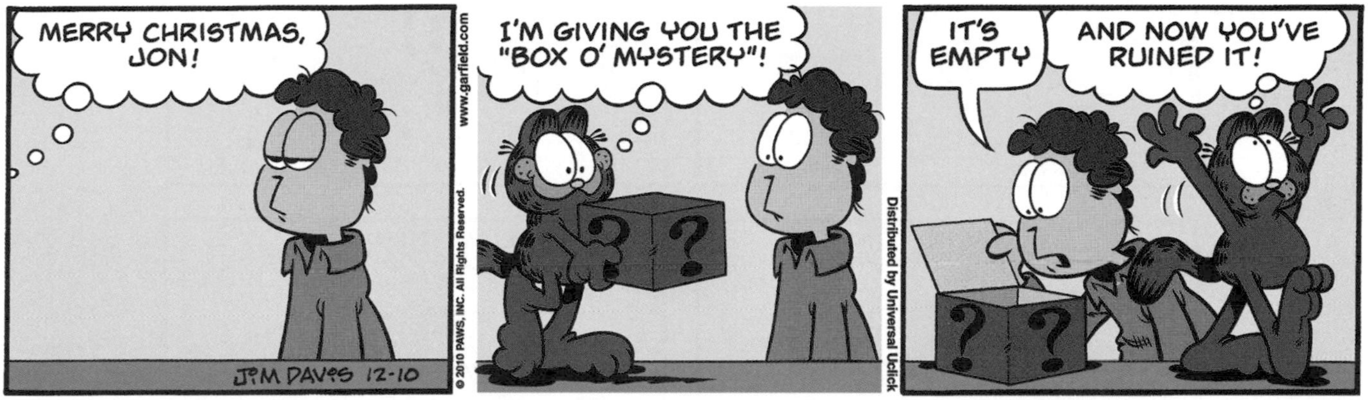
MERRY CHRISTMAS, JON!
JIM DAVIS 12-10
www.garfield.com
© 2010 PAWS, INC. All Rights Reserved.
I'M GIVING YOU THE "BOX O' MYSTERY"!
Distributed by Universal Uclick
IT'S EMPTY
AND NOW YOU'VE RUINED IT!

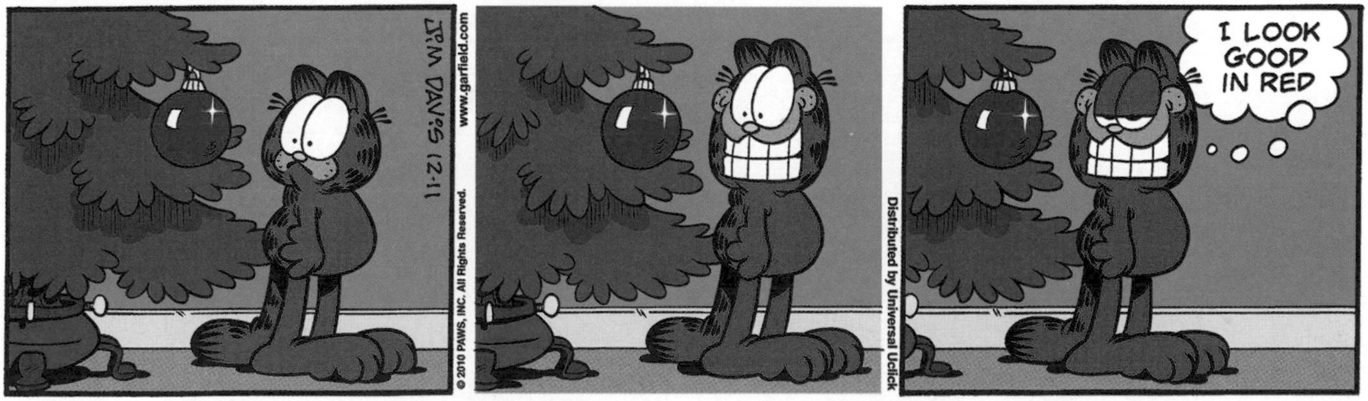
JIM DAVIS 12-11
www.garfield.com
© 2010 PAWS, INC. All Rights Reserved.
Distributed by Universal Uclick
I LOOK GOOD IN RED

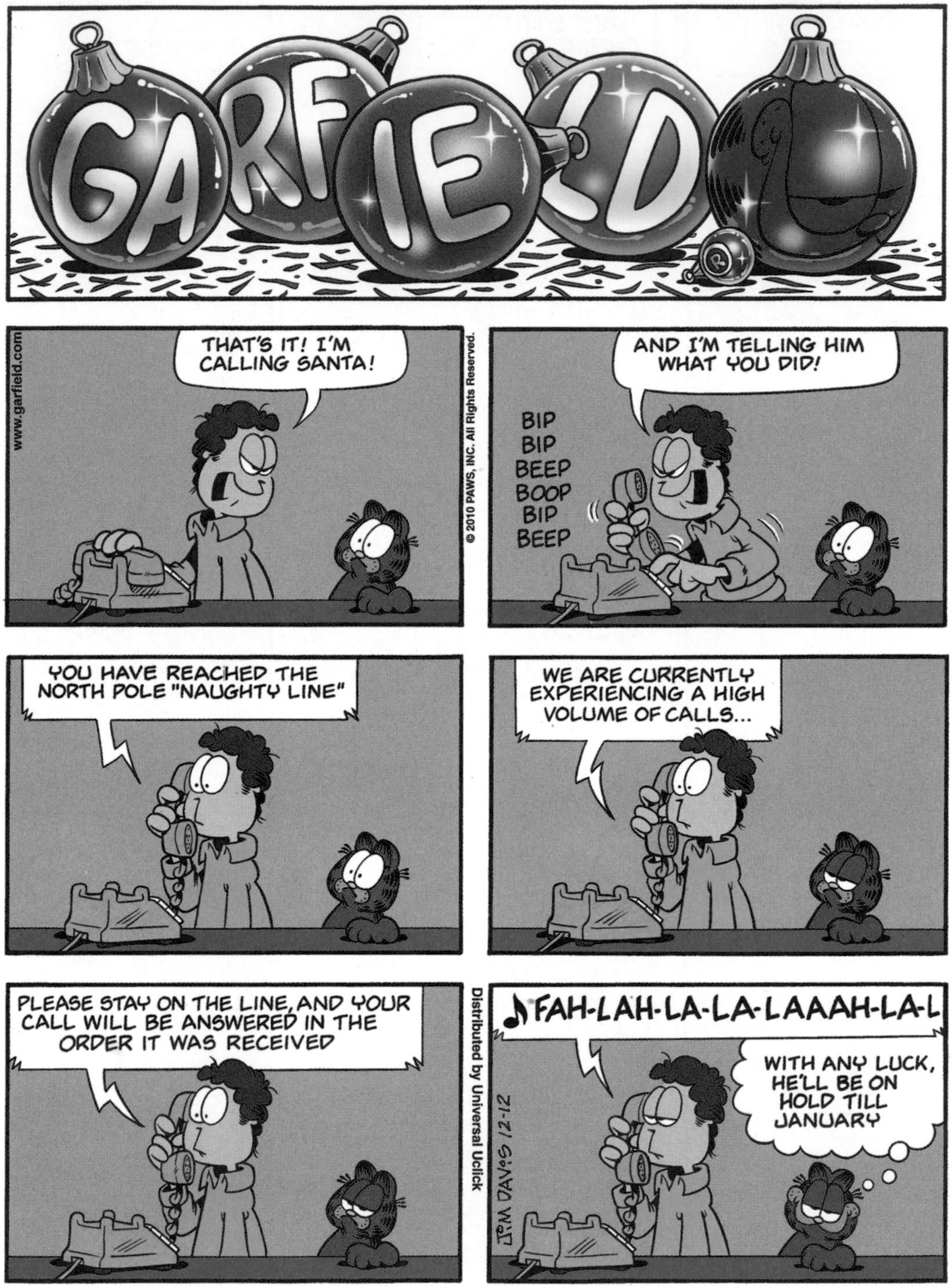
GARFIELD
www.garfield.com
THAT'S IT! I'M CALLING SANTA!
© 2010 PAWS, INC. All Rights Reserved.
AND I'M TELLING HIM WHAT YOU DID!
BIP BIP BEEP BOOP BIP BEEP
YOU HAVE REACHED THE NORTH POLE "NAUGHTY LINE"
WE ARE CURRENTLY EXPERIENCING A HIGH VOLUME OF CALLS...
PLEASE STAY ON THE LINE, AND YOUR CALL WILL BE ANSWERED IN THE ORDER IT WAS RECEIVED
Distributed by Universal Uclick
FAH-LAH-LA-LA-LAAAH-LA-L
WITH ANY LUCK, HE'LL BE ON HOLD TILL JANUARY
JIM DAVIS 12-12

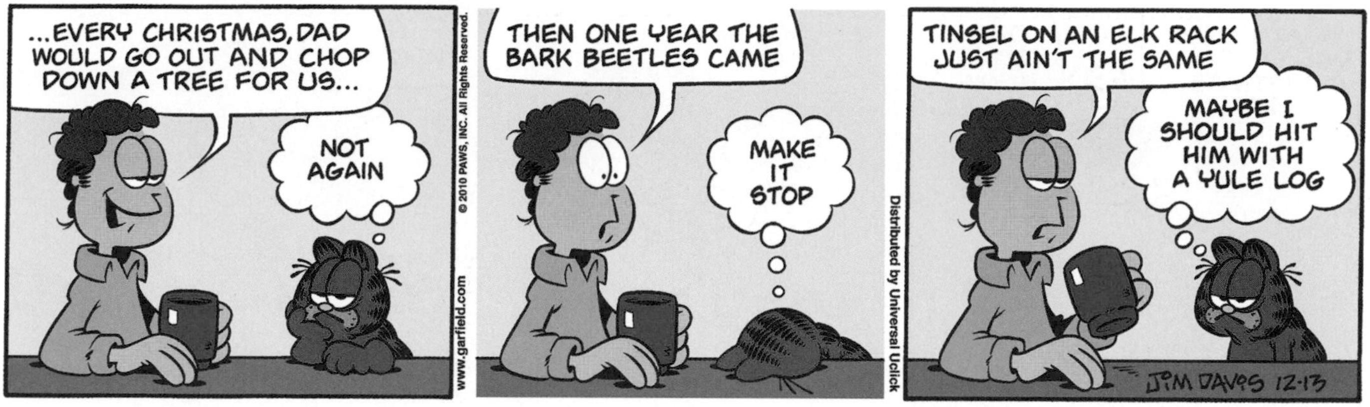
...EVERY CHRISTMAS, DAD WOULD GO OUT AND CHOP DOWN A TREE FOR US...
NOT AGAIN
THEN ONE YEAR THE BARK BEETLES CAME
MAKE IT STOP
TINSEL ON AN ELK RACK JUST AIN'T THE SAME
MAYBE I SHOULD HIT HIM WITH A YULE LOG
JIM DAVIS 12-13
www.garfield.com
© 2010 PAWS, INC. All Rights Reserved.
Distributed by Universal Uclick

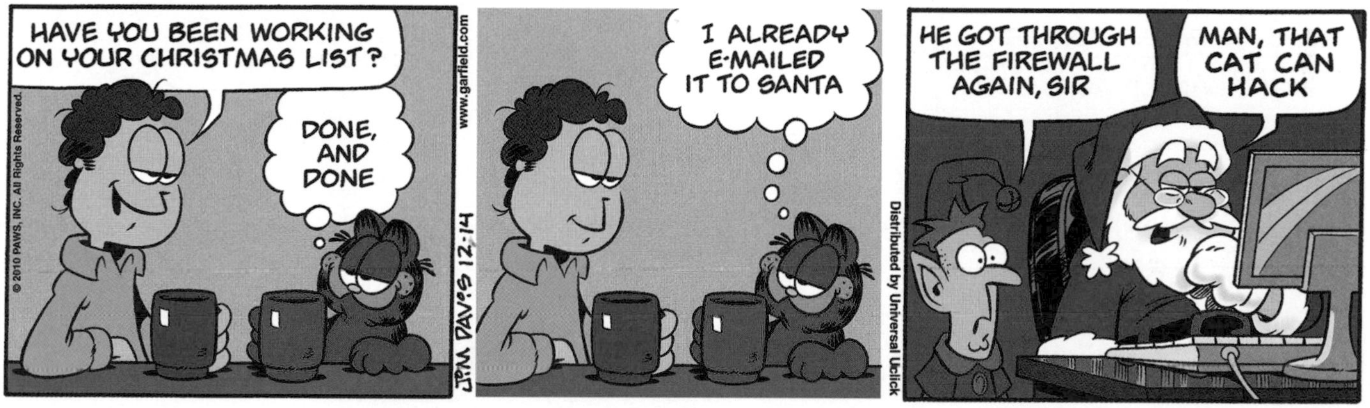
HAVE YOU BEEN WORKING ON YOUR CHRISTMAS LIST?
DONE, AND DONE
I ALREADY E-MAILED IT TO SANTA
HE GOT THROUGH THE FIREWALL AGAIN, SIR
MAN, THAT CAT CAN HACK
JIM DAVIS 12-14
© 2010 PAWS, INC. All Rights Reserved.
www.garfield.com
Distributed by Universal Uclick

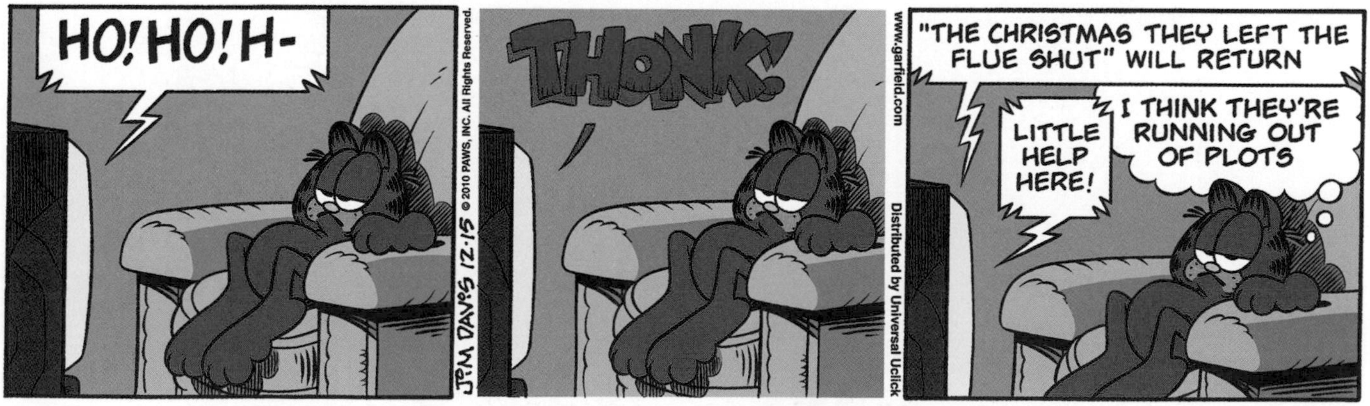
HO! HO! H-
THONK!
"THE CHRISTMAS THEY LEFT THE FLUE SHUT" WILL RETURN
LITTLE HELP HERE!
I THINK THEY'RE RUNNING OUT OF PLOTS
JIM DAVIS 12-15
© 2010 PAWS, INC. All Rights Reserved.
www.garfield.com
Distributed by Universal Uclick

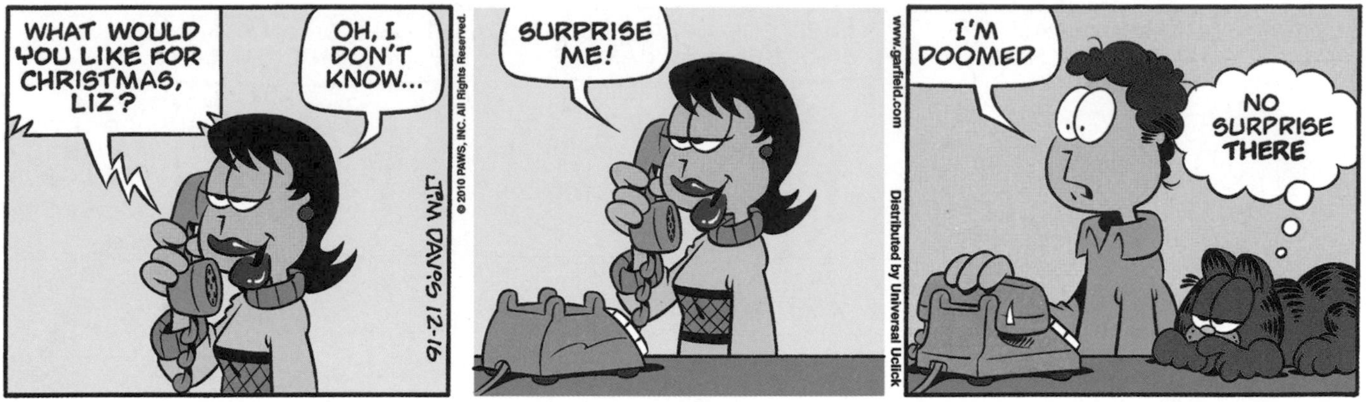
WHAT WOULD YOU LIKE FOR CHRISTMAS, LIZ?
OH, I DON'T KNOW...
JPM DAVPS 12-16
© 2010 PAWS, INC. All Rights Reserved.
SURPRISE ME!
www.garfield.com
Distributed by Universal Uclick
I'M DOOMED
NO SURPRISE THERE

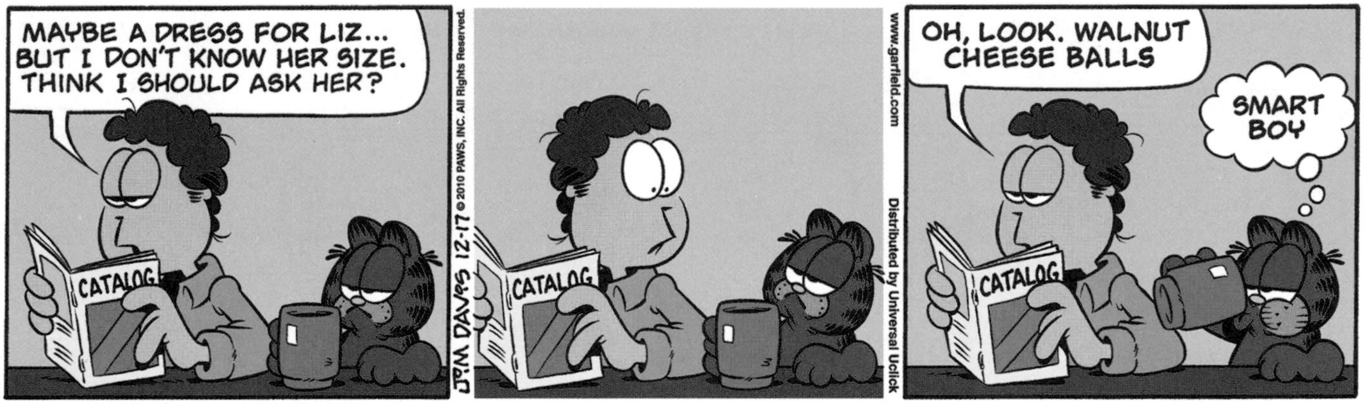
MAYBE A DRESS FOR LIZ... BUT I DON'T KNOW HER SIZE. THINK I SHOULD ASK HER?
CATALOG
JPM DAVPS 12-17
© 2010 PAWS, INC. All Rights Reserved.
CATALOG
www.garfield.com
Distributed by Universal Uclick
OH, LOOK. WALNUT CHEESE BALLS
SMART BOY
CATALOG

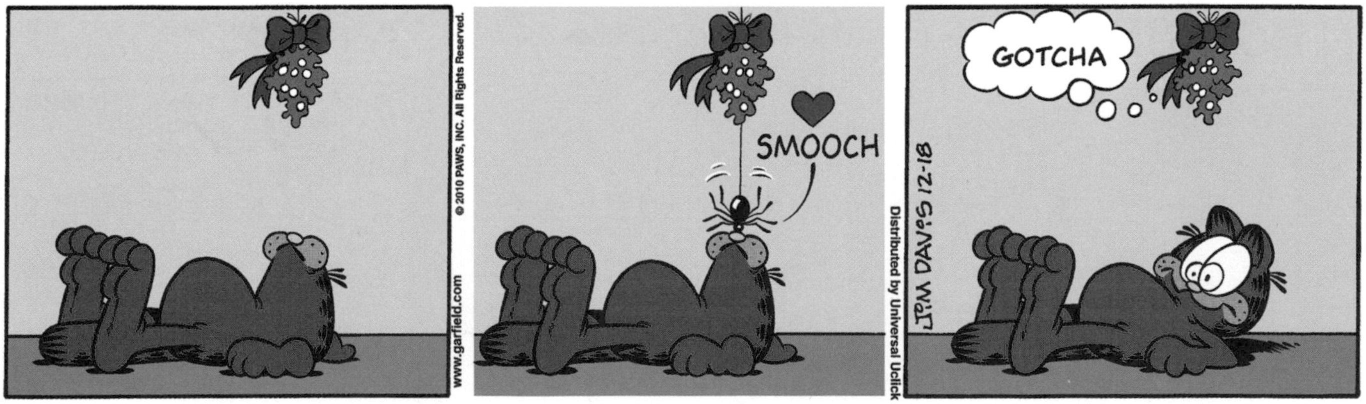
© 2010 PAWS, INC. All Rights Reserved.
www.garfield.com
SMOOCH
JPM DAVPS 12-18
Distributed by Universal Uclick
GOTCHA

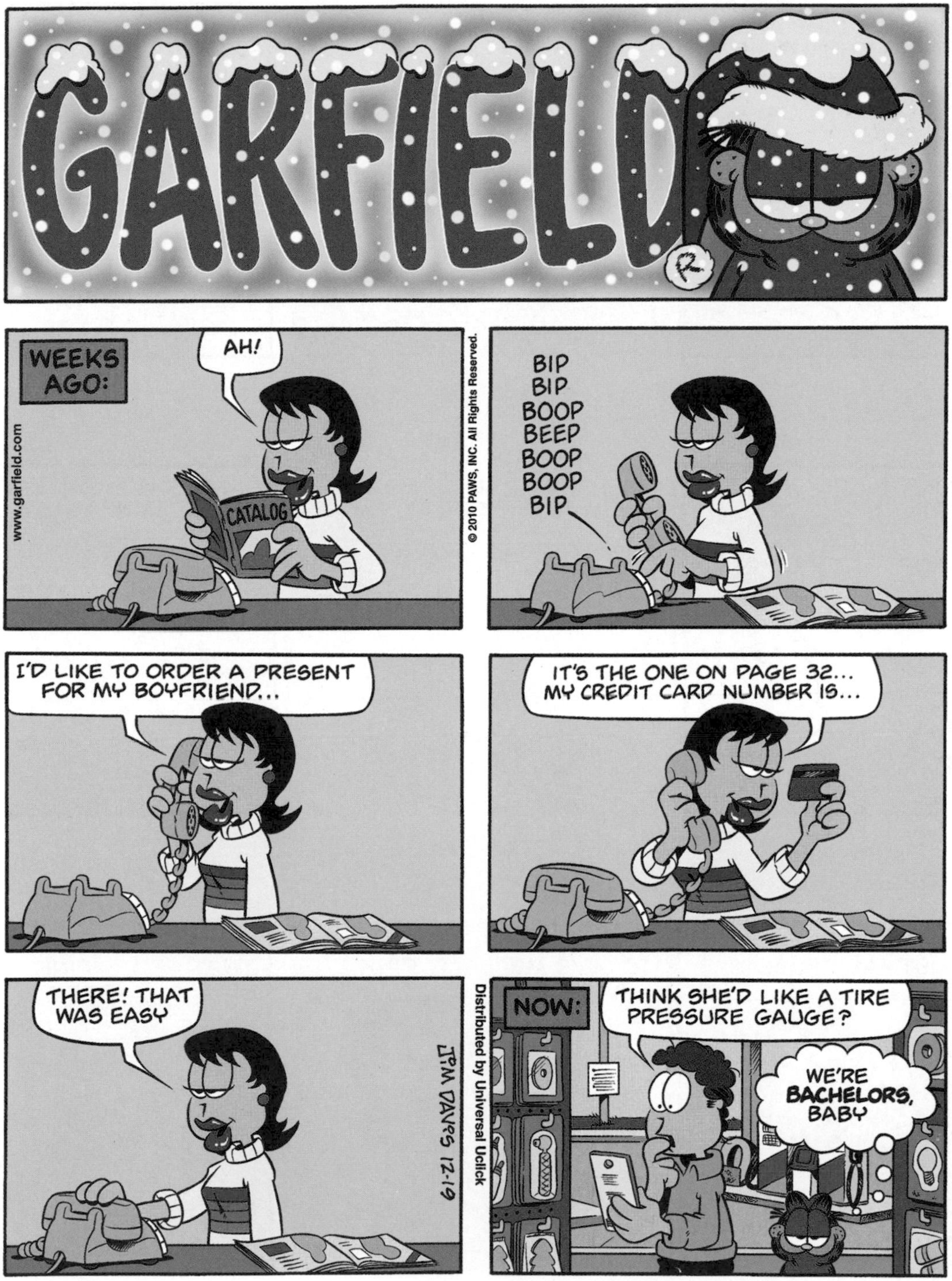
GARFIELD
WEEKS AGO:
AH!
CATALOG
www.garfield.com
© 2010 PAWS, INC. All Rights Reserved.
BIP BIP BOOP BEEP BOOP BOOP BIP
I'D LIKE TO ORDER A PRESENT FOR MY BOYFRIEND...
IT'S THE ONE ON PAGE 32... MY CREDIT CARD NUMBER IS...
THERE! THAT WAS EASY
JPM DAVIS 12-19
Distributed by Universal Uclick
NOW:
THINK SHE'D LIKE A TIRE PRESSURE GAUGE?
WE'RE BACHELORS, BABY

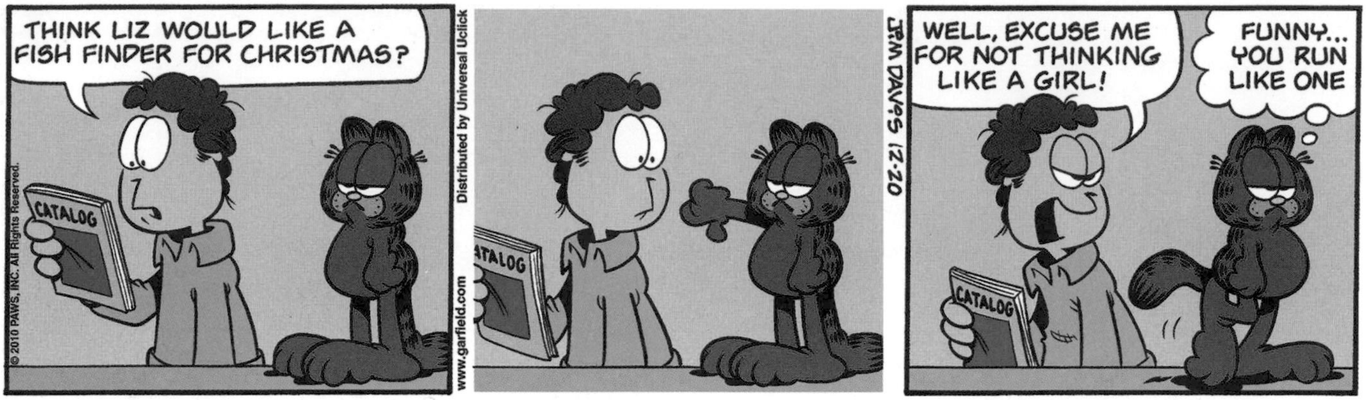
THINK LIZ WOULD LIKE A FISH FINDER FOR CHRISTMAS?
© 2010 PAWS, INC. All Rights Reserved.
www.garfield.com
Distributed by Universal Uclick
JIM DAVIS 12-20
WELL, EXCUSE ME FOR NOT THINKING LIKE A GIRL!
FUNNY... YOU RUN LIKE ONE
CATALOG

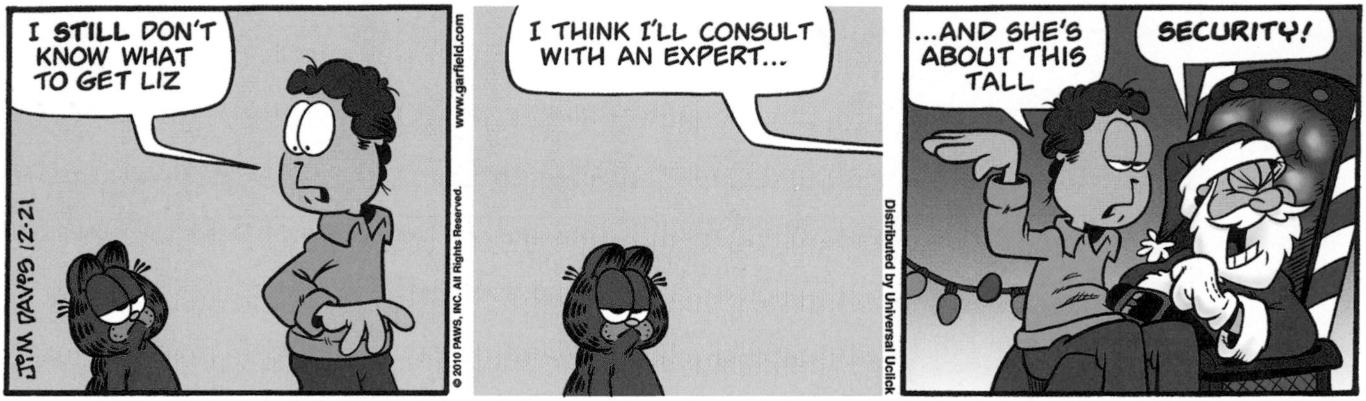
I **STILL** DON'T KNOW WHAT TO GET LIZ
JIM DAVIS 12-21
www.garfield.com
© 2010 PAWS, INC. All Rights Reserved.
I THINK I'LL CONSULT WITH AN EXPERT...
Distributed by Universal Uclick
...AND SHE'S ABOUT THIS TALL
SECURITY!

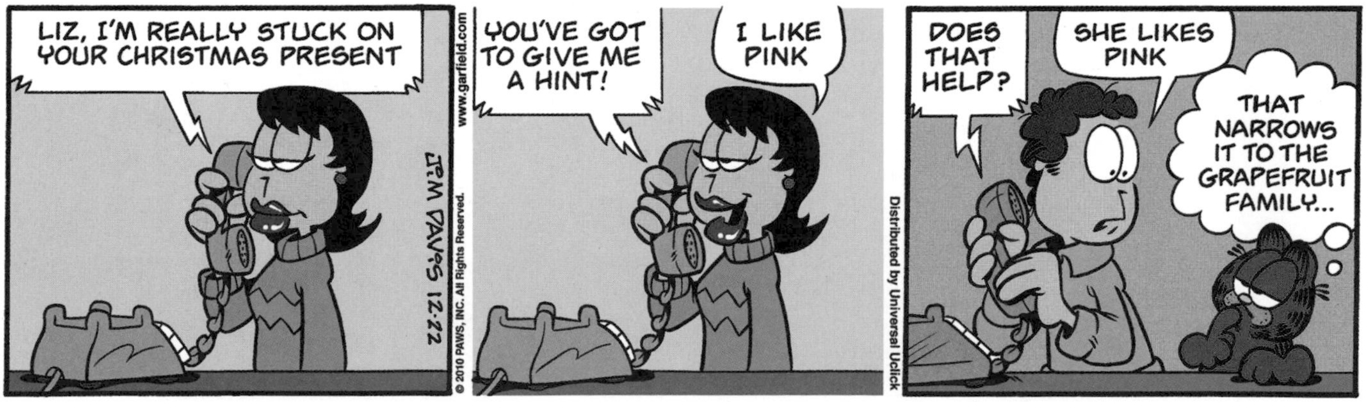
LIZ, I'M REALLY STUCK ON YOUR CHRISTMAS PRESENT
JIM DAVIS 12-22
www.garfield.com
© 2010 PAWS, INC. All Rights Reserved.
YOU'VE GOT TO GIVE ME A HINT!
I LIKE PINK
Distributed by Universal Uclick
DOES THAT HELP?
SHE LIKES PINK
THAT NARROWS IT TO THE GRAPEFRUIT FAMILY...

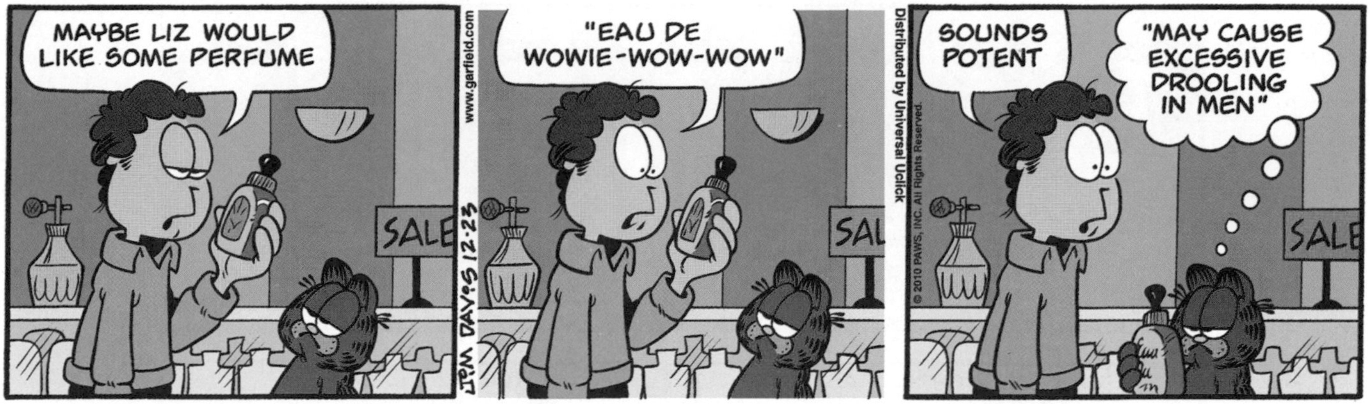
MAYBE LIZ WOULD LIKE SOME PERFUME
"EAU DE WOWIE-WOW-WOW"
SOUNDS POTENT
"MAY CAUSE EXCESSIVE DROOLING IN MEN"
JPM DAVIS 12-23
www.garfield.com
Distributed by Universal Uclick
© 2010 PAWS, INC. All Rights Reserved.

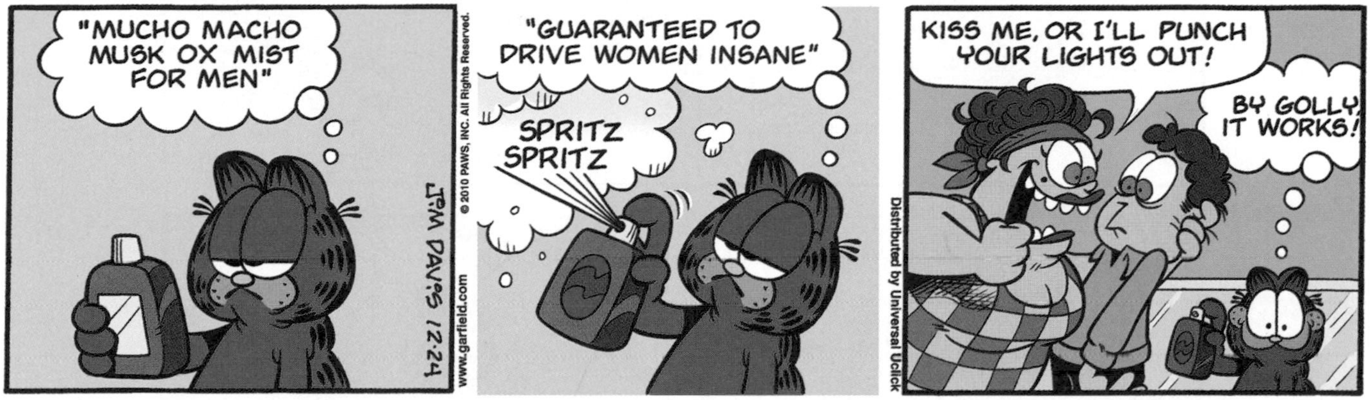
"MUCHO MACHO MUSK OX MIST FOR MEN"
JPM DAVIS 12-24
"GUARANTEED TO DRIVE WOMEN INSANE"
SPRITZ SPRITZ
KISS ME, OR I'LL PUNCH YOUR LIGHTS OUT!
BY GOLLY, IT WORKS!
© 2010 PAWS, INC. All Rights Reserved.
www.garfield.com
Distributed by Universal Uclick

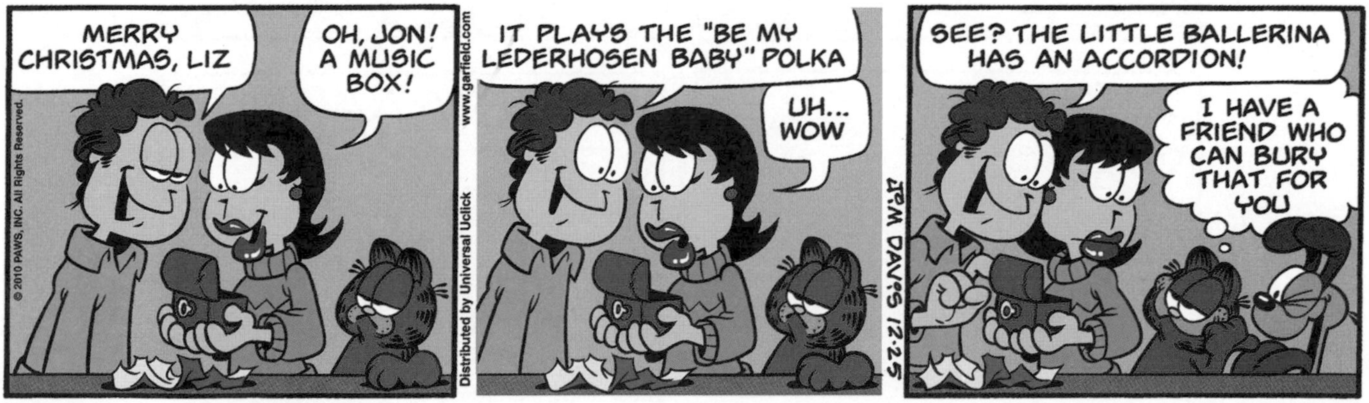
MERRY CHRISTMAS, LIZ
OH, JON! A MUSIC BOX!
IT PLAYS THE "BE MY LEDERHOSEN BABY" POLKA
UH... WOW
SEE? THE LITTLE BALLERINA HAS AN ACCORDION!
I HAVE A FRIEND WHO CAN BURY THAT FOR YOU
JPM DAVIS 12-25
© 2010 PAWS, INC. All Rights Reserved.
www.garfield.com
Distributed by Universal Uclick

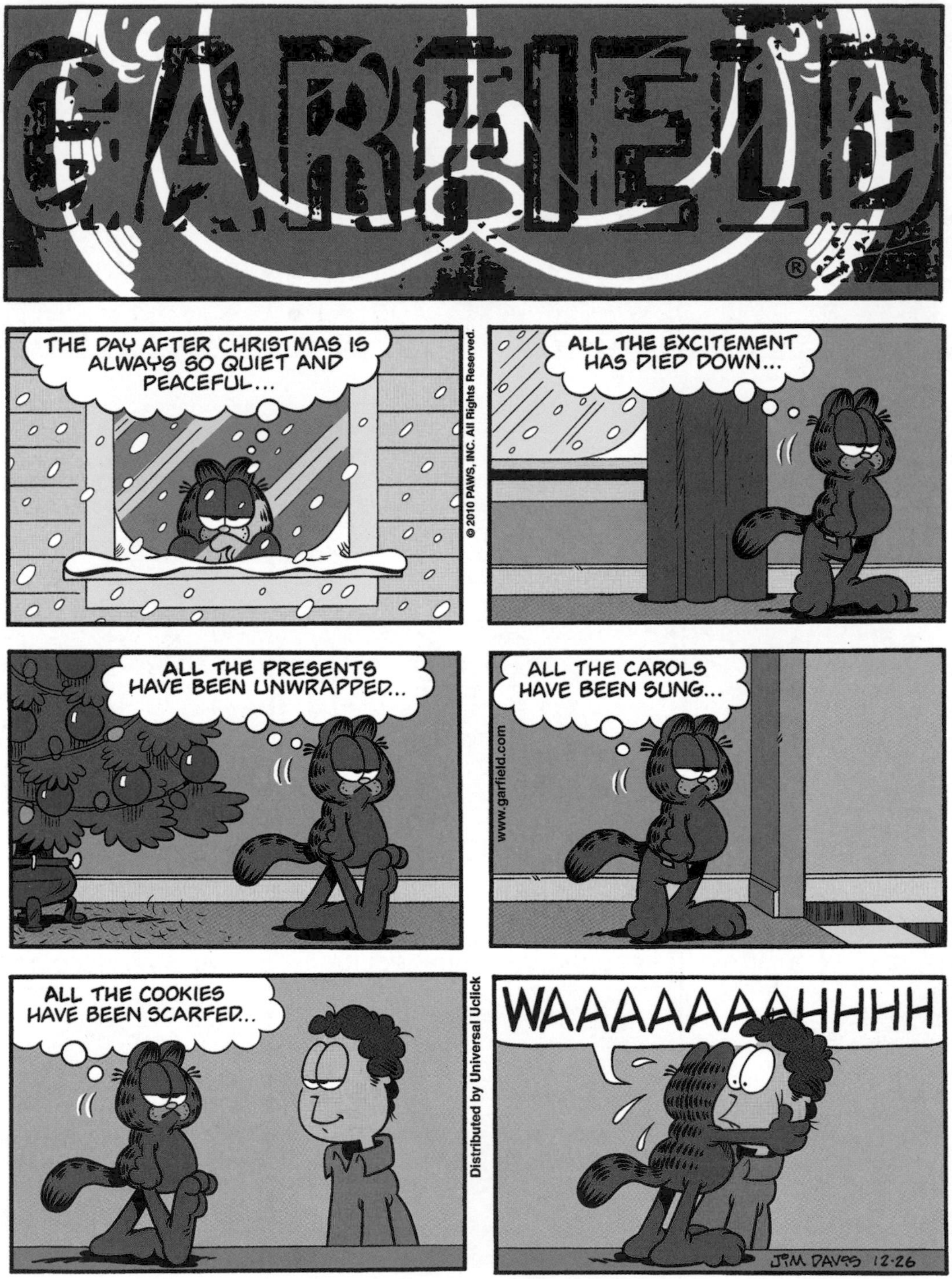
GARFIELD®
THE DAY AFTER CHRISTMAS IS ALWAYS SO QUIET AND PEACEFUL...
© 2010 PAWS, INC. All Rights Reserved.
ALL THE EXCITEMENT HAS DIED DOWN...
ALL THE PRESENTS HAVE BEEN UNWRAPPED...
ALL THE CAROLS HAVE BEEN SUNG...
www.garfield.com
ALL THE COOKIES HAVE BEEN SCARFED...
Distributed by Universal Uclick
WAAAAAAAHHHH
JIM DAVIS 12-26

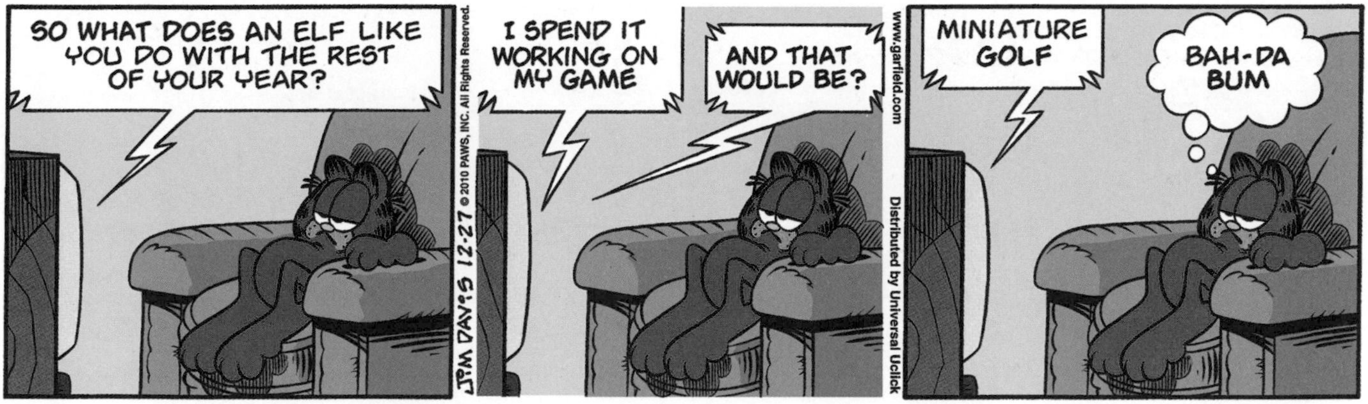
SO WHAT DOES AN ELF LIKE YOU DO WITH THE REST OF YOUR YEAR?
I SPEND IT WORKING ON MY GAME
AND THAT WOULD BE?
MINIATURE GOLF
BAH-DA BUM
JIM DAVIS 12-27
© 2010 PAWS, INC. All Rights Reserved.
www.garfield.com
Distributed by Universal Uclick

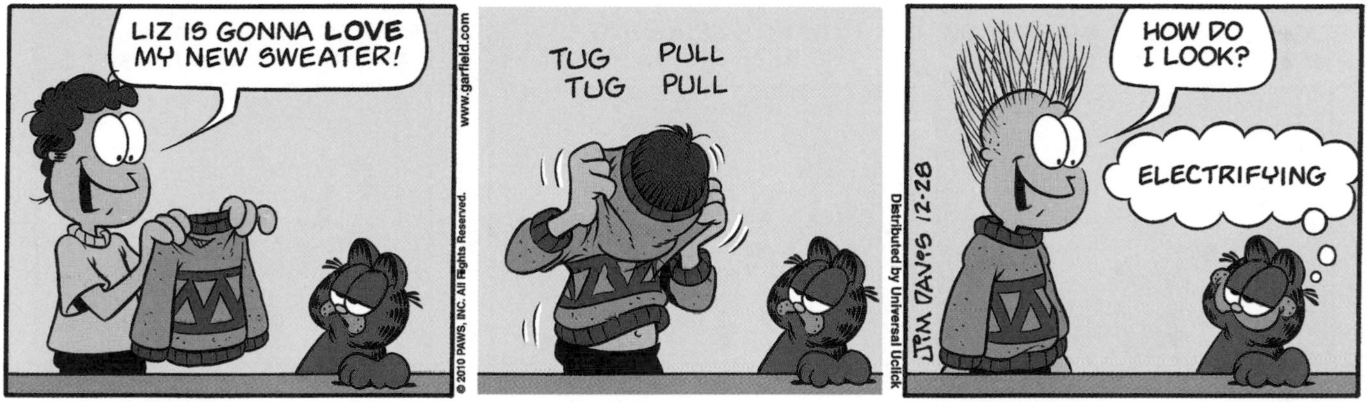
LIZ IS GONNA LOVE MY NEW SWEATER!
TUG TUG
PULL PULL
HOW DO I LOOK?
ELECTRIFYING
JIM DAVIS 12-28
© 2010 PAWS, INC. All Rights Reserved.
www.garfield.com
Distributed by Universal Uclick

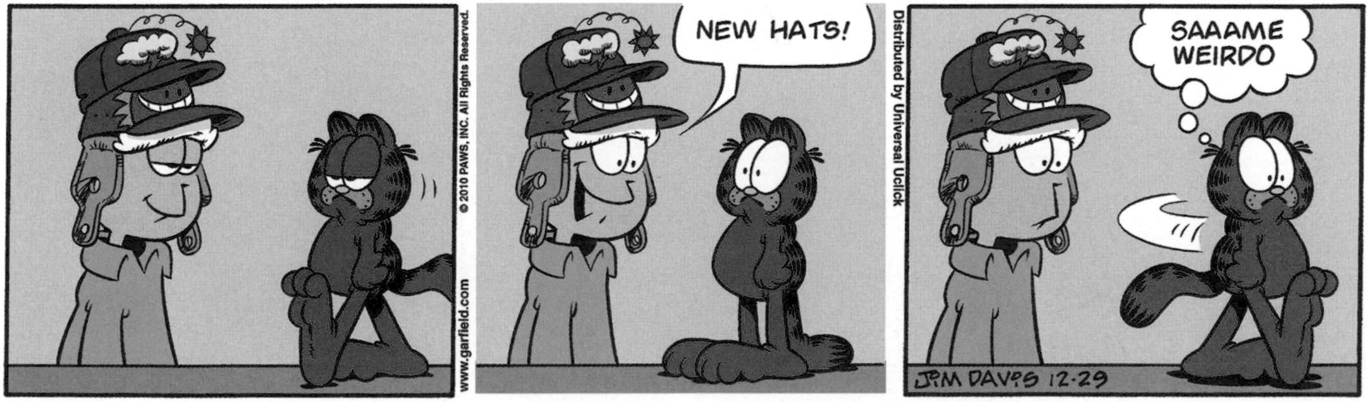
NEW HATS!
SAAAME WEIRDO
JIM DAVIS 12-29
© 2010 PAWS, INC. All Rights Reserved.
www.garfield.com
Distributed by Universal Uclick

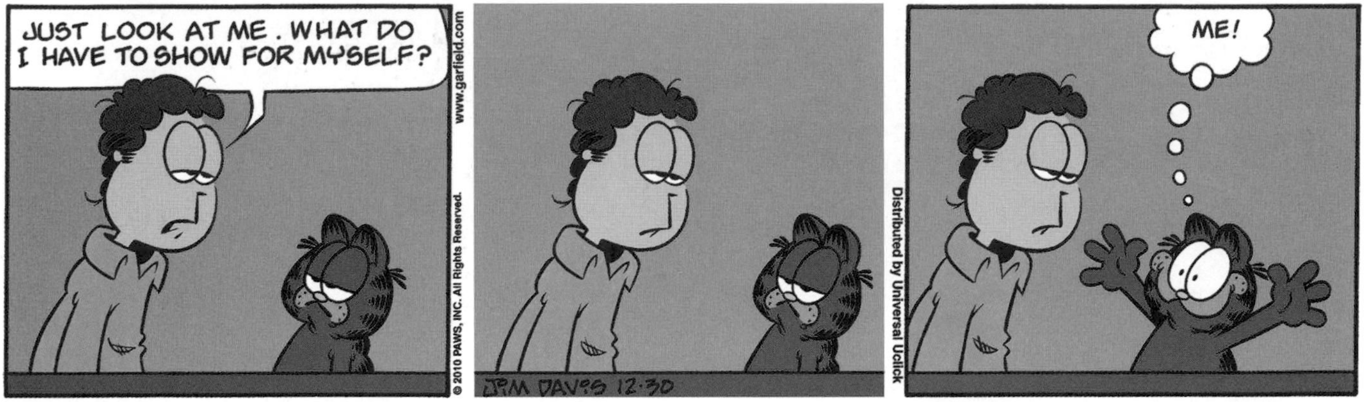
JUST LOOK AT ME. WHAT DO I HAVE TO SHOW FOR MYSELF?
ME!
© 2010 PAWS, INC. All Rights Reserved.
www.garfield.com
Distributed by Universal Uclick

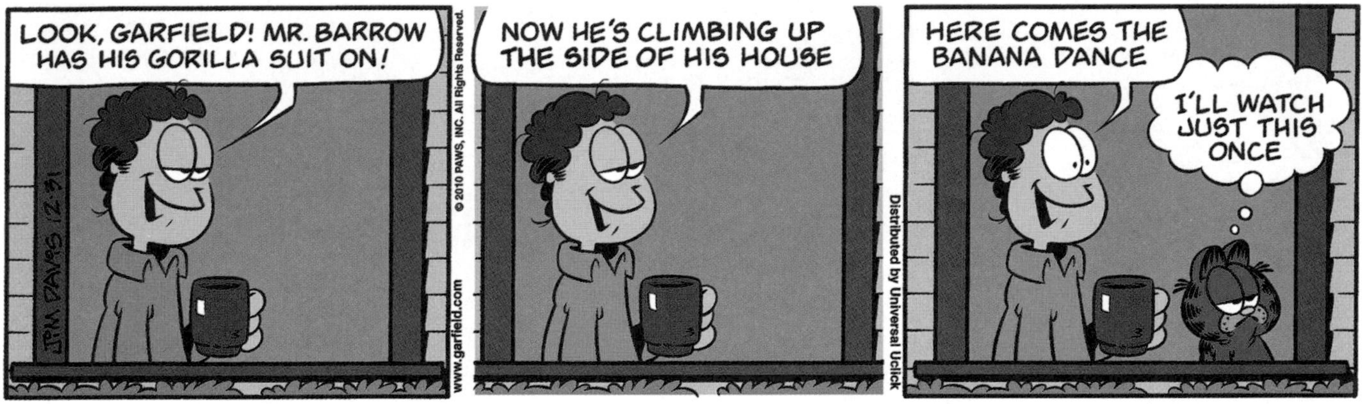
LOOK, GARFIELD! MR. BARROW HAS HIS GORILLA SUIT ON!
NOW HE'S CLIMBING UP THE SIDE OF HIS HOUSE
HERE COMES THE BANANA DANCE
I'LL WATCH JUST THIS ONCE
© 2010 PAWS, INC. All Rights Reserved.
www.garfield.com
Distributed by Universal Uclick

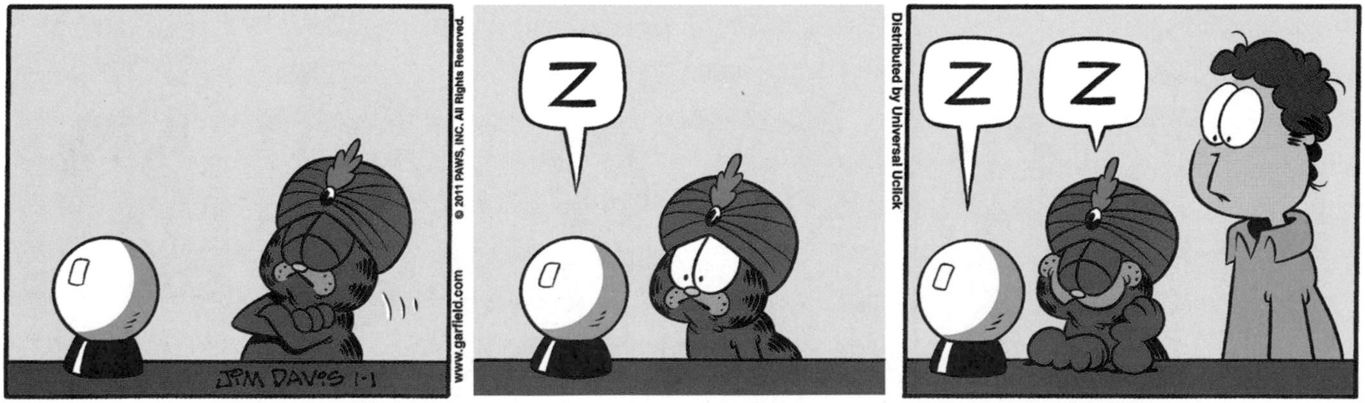
Z
Z
Z
© 2011 PAWS, INC. All Rights Reserved.
www.garfield.com
Distributed by Universal Uclick

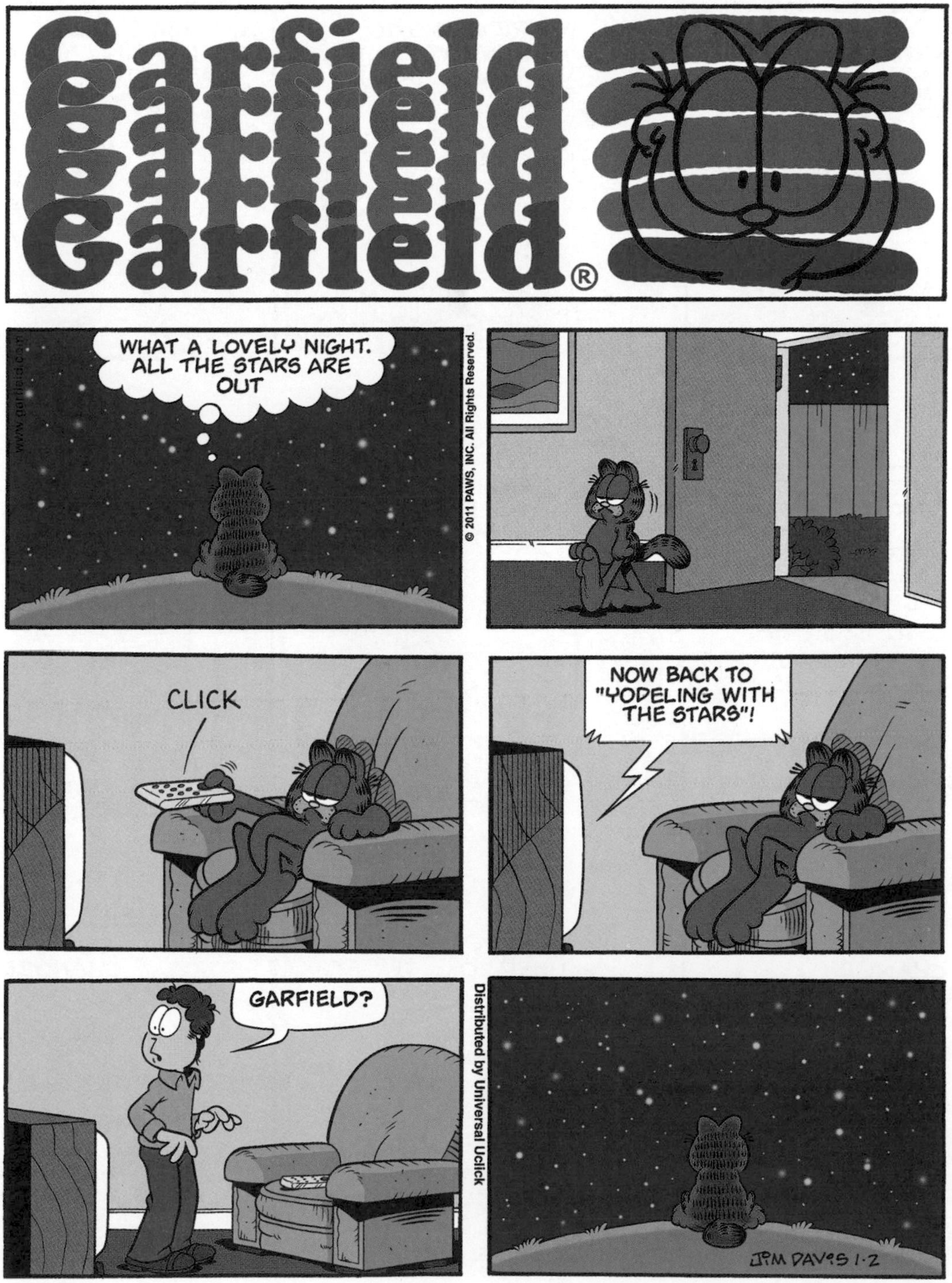
Garfield®
WHAT A LOVELY NIGHT. ALL THE STARS ARE OUT
www.garfield.com
© 2011 PAWS, INC. All Rights Reserved.
CLICK
NOW BACK TO "YODELING WITH THE STARS"!
GARFIELD?
Distributed by Universal Uclick
JIM DAVIS 1·2

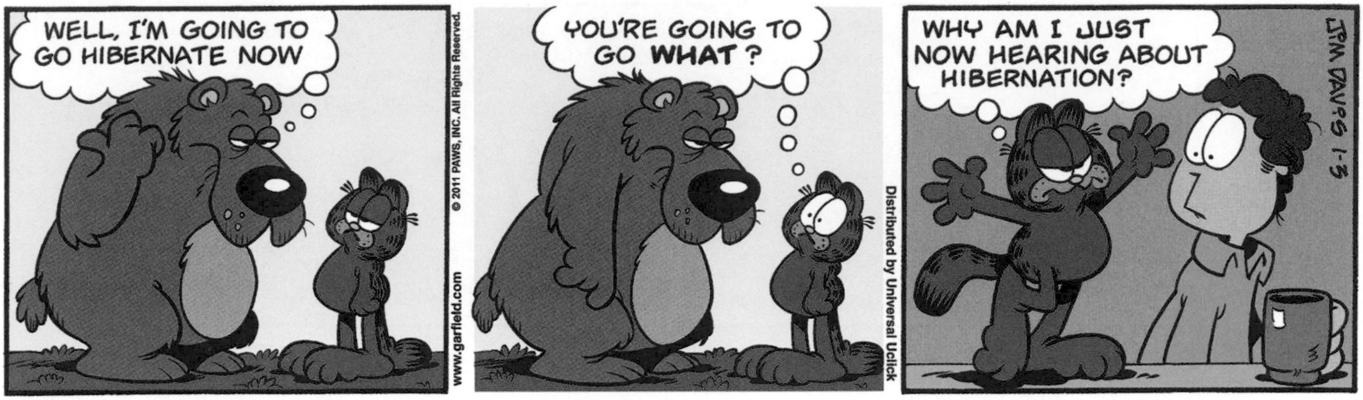
WELL, I'M GOING TO GO HIBERNATE NOW
© 2011 PAWS, INC. All Rights Reserved.
www.garfield.com
YOU'RE GOING TO GO **WHAT**?
Distributed by Universal Uclick
WHY AM I JUST NOW HEARING ABOUT HIBERNATION?
JPM DAVPS 1-3

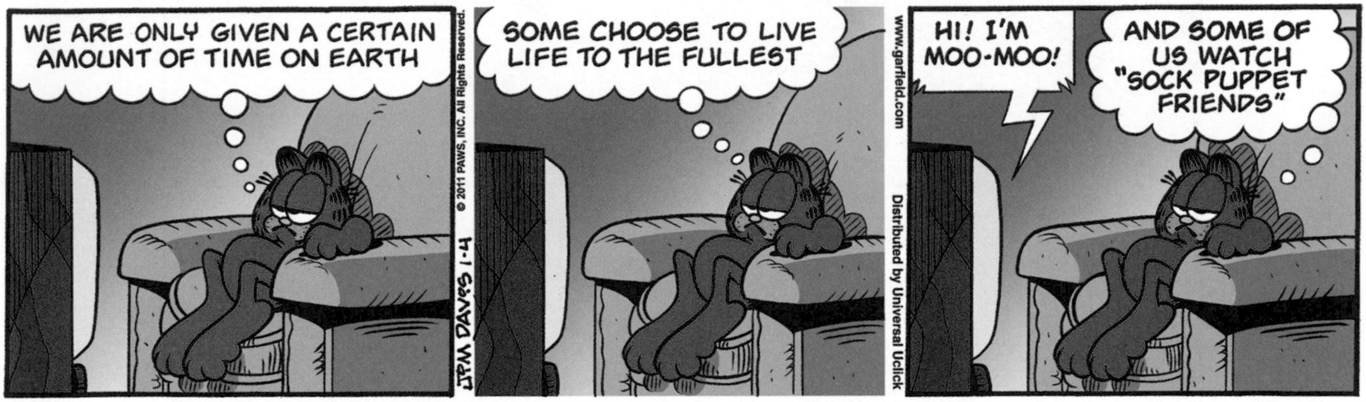
WE ARE ONLY GIVEN A CERTAIN AMOUNT OF TIME ON EARTH
© 2011 PAWS, INC. All Rights Reserved.
JPM DAVPS 1-4
SOME CHOOSE TO LIVE LIFE TO THE FULLEST
www.garfield.com
Distributed by Universal Uclick
HI! I'M MOO-MOO!
AND SOME OF US WATCH "SOCK PUPPET FRIENDS"

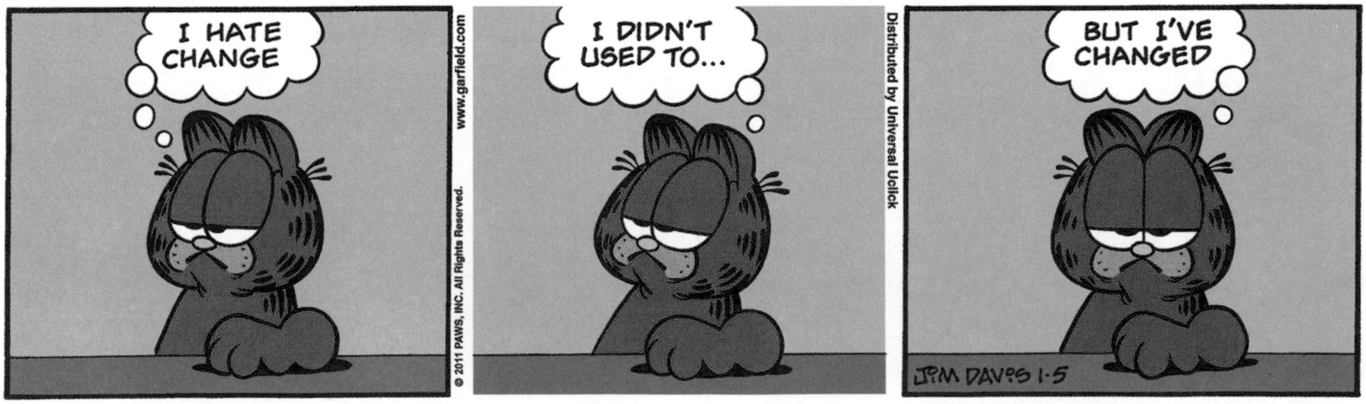
I HATE CHANGE
www.garfield.com
© 2011 PAWS, INC. All Rights Reserved.
I DIDN'T USED TO...
Distributed by Universal Uclick
BUT I'VE CHANGED
JPM DAVPS 1-5

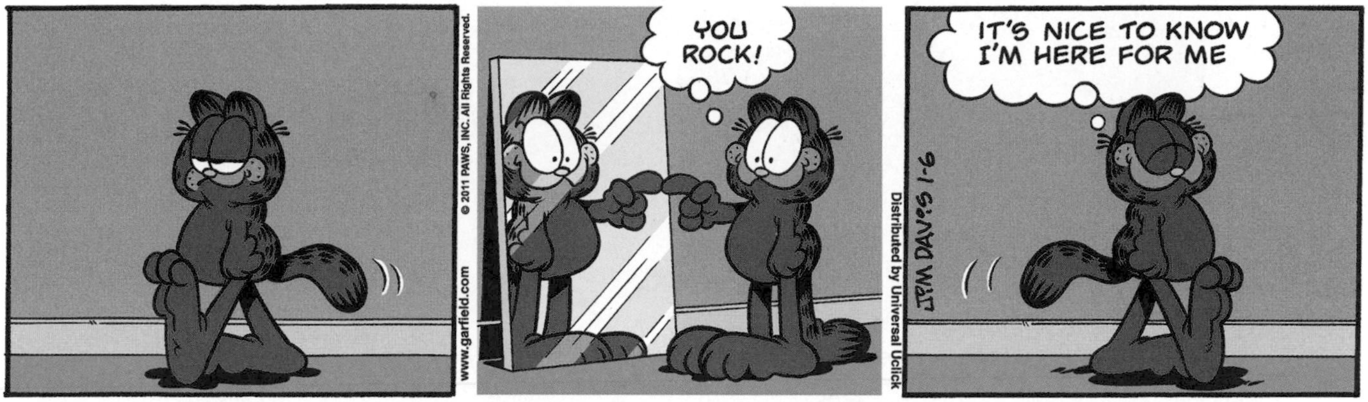
© 2011 PAWS, INC. All Rights Reserved.
www.garfield.com
YOU ROCK!
Distributed by Universal Uclick
JIM DAVIS 1-6
IT'S NICE TO KNOW I'M HERE FOR ME

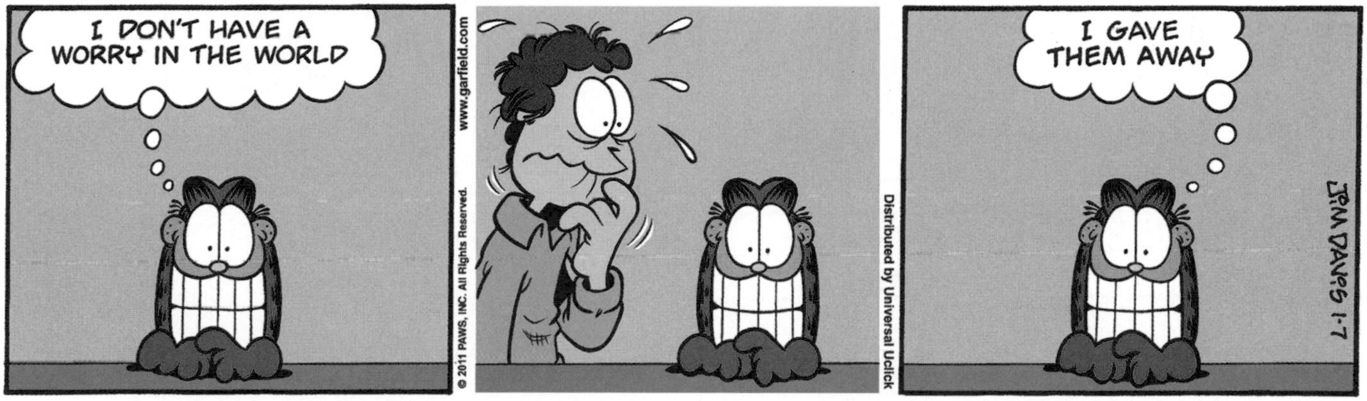
I DON'T HAVE A WORRY IN THE WORLD
© 2011 PAWS, INC. All Rights Reserved.
www.garfield.com
Distributed by Universal Uclick
I GAVE THEM AWAY
JIM DAVIS 1-7

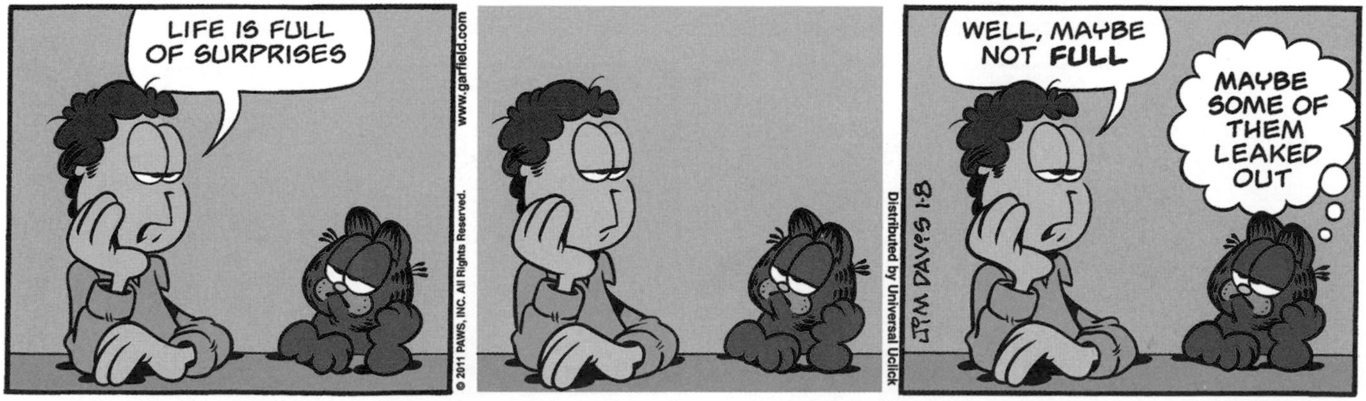
LIFE IS FULL OF SURPRISES
© 2011 PAWS, INC. All Rights Reserved.
www.garfield.com
Distributed by Universal Uclick
JIM DAVIS 1-8
WELL, MAYBE NOT **FULL**
MAYBE SOME OF THEM LEAKED OUT

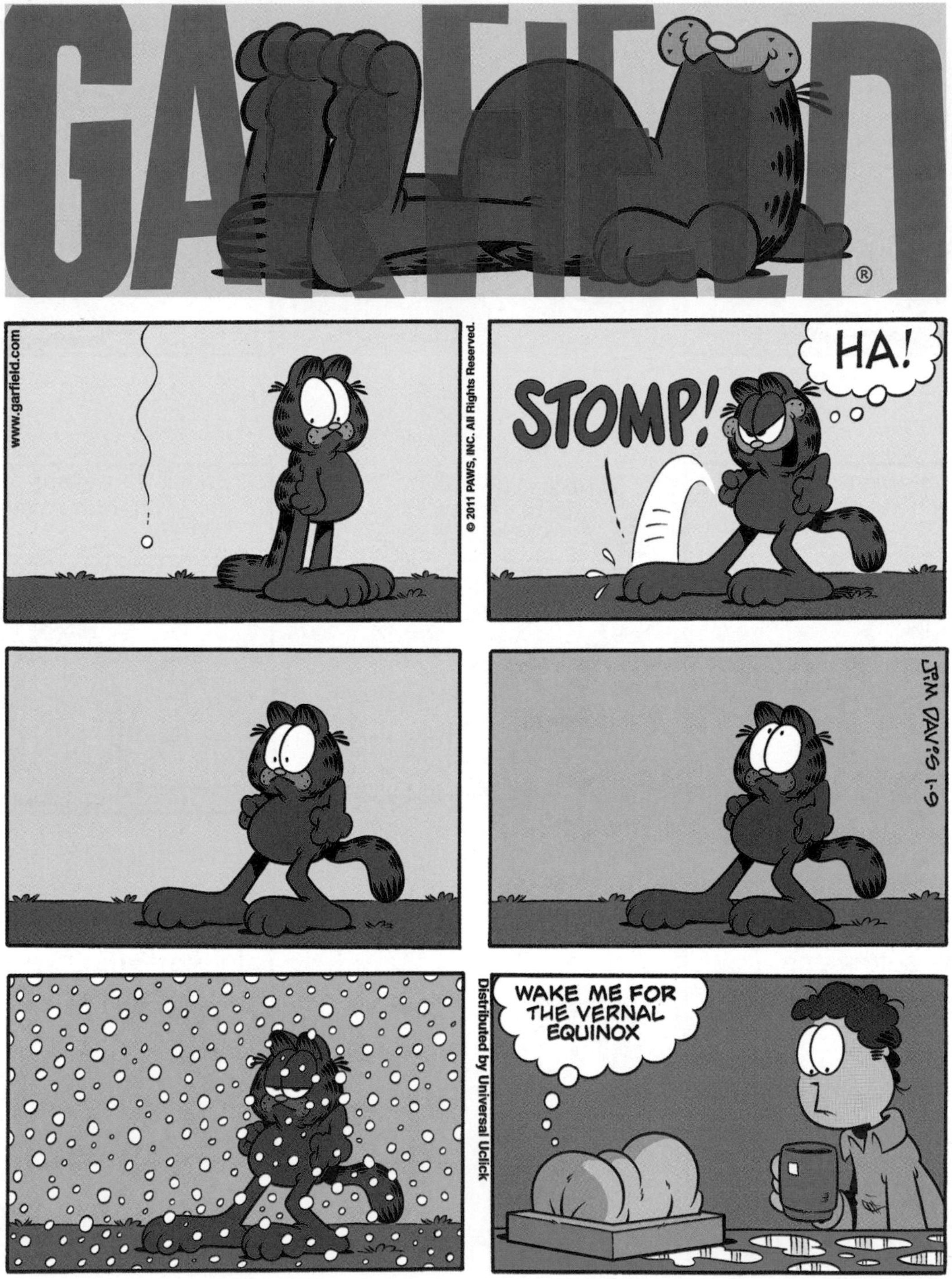
GARFIELD®
www.garfield.com
© 2011 PAWS, INC. All Rights Reserved.
STOMP!
HA!
JIM DAVIS 1-9
Distributed by Universal Uclick
WAKE ME FOR THE VERNAL EQUINOX

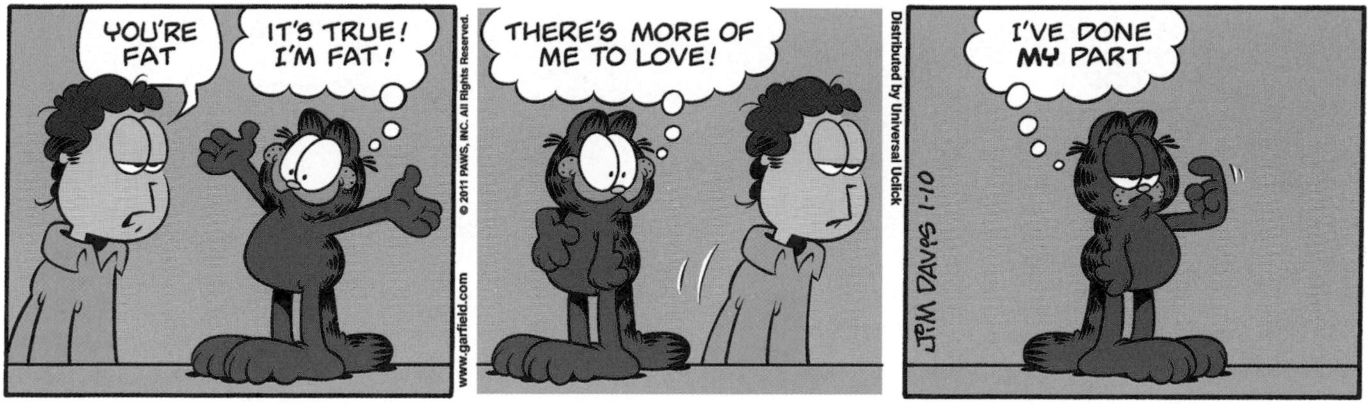
YOU'RE FAT
IT'S TRUE! I'M FAT!
© 2011 PAWS, INC. All Rights Reserved.
www.garfield.com
THERE'S MORE OF ME TO LOVE!
Distributed by Universal Uclick
JIM DAVIS 1-10
I'VE DONE **MY** PART

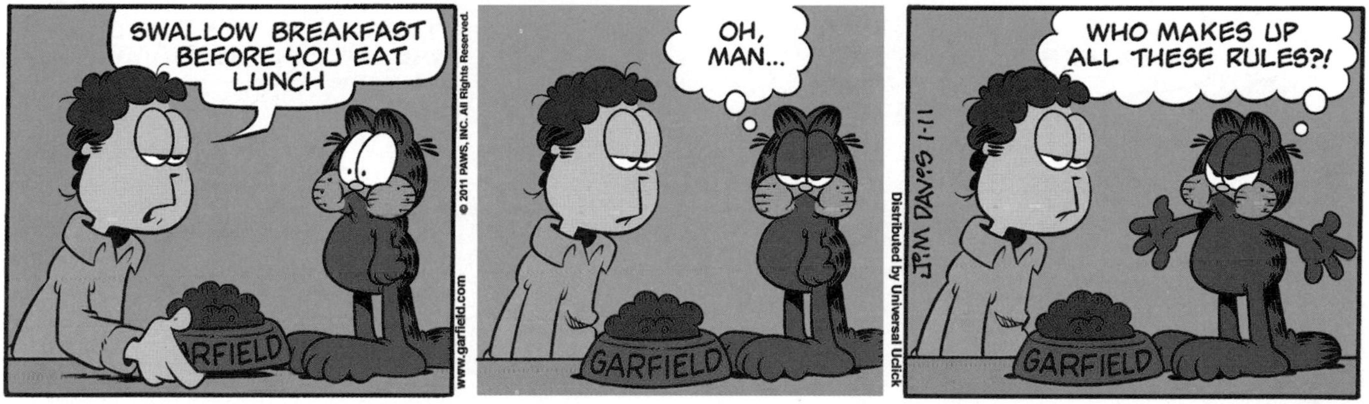
SWALLOW BREAKFAST BEFORE YOU EAT LUNCH
RFIELD
© 2011 PAWS, INC. All Rights Reserved.
www.garfield.com
OH, MAN...
GARFIELD
JIM DAVIS 1-11
Distributed by Universal Uclick
WHO MAKES UP ALL THESE RULES?!
GARFIELD

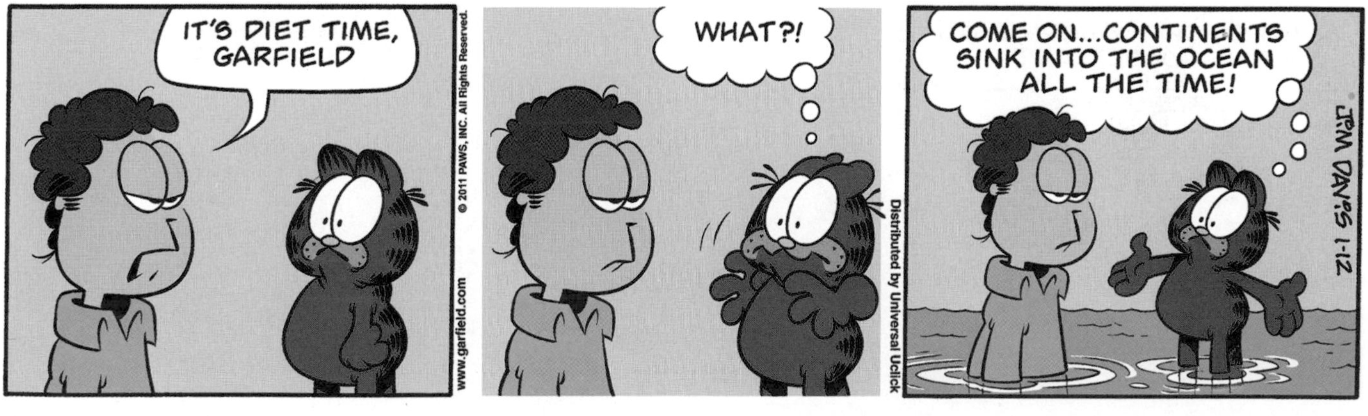
IT'S DIET TIME, GARFIELD
© 2011 PAWS, INC. All Rights Reserved.
www.garfield.com
WHAT?!
Distributed by Universal Uclick
COME ON...CONTINENTS SINK INTO THE OCEAN ALL THE TIME!
JIM DAVIS 1-12

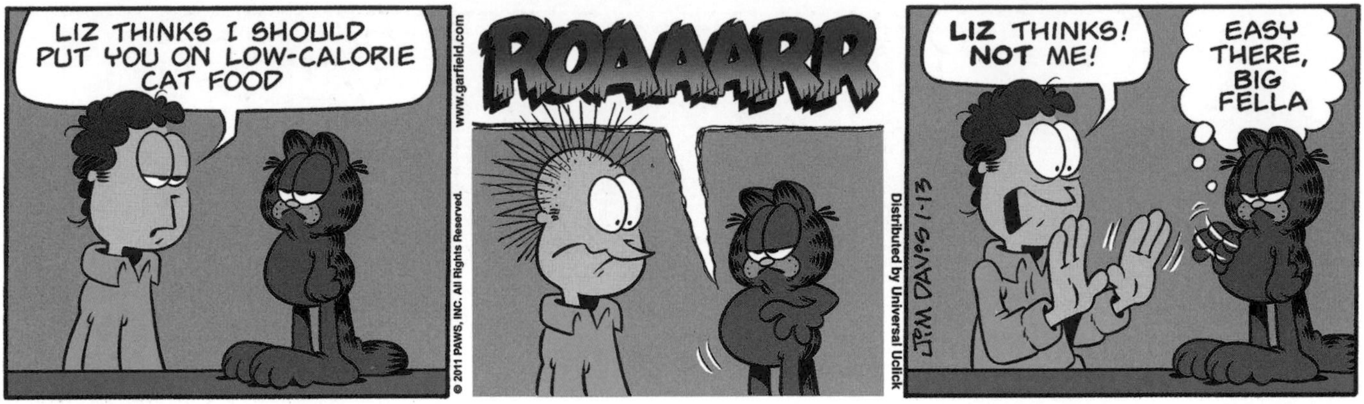
LIZ THINKS I SHOULD PUT YOU ON LOW-CALORIE CAT FOOD
www.garfield.com
© 2011 PAWS, INC. All Rights Reserved.
ROAAAARR
Distributed by Universal Uclick
JIM DAVIS 1-13
LIZ THINKS! NOT ME!
EASY THERE, BIG FELLA

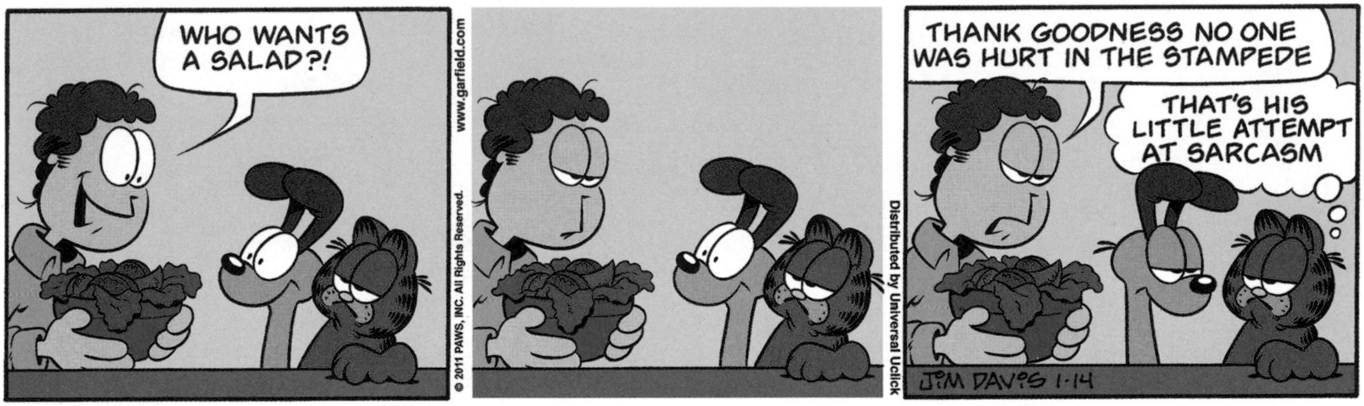
WHO WANTS A SALAD?!
www.garfield.com
© 2011 PAWS, INC. All Rights Reserved.
Distributed by Universal Uclick
THANK GOODNESS NO ONE WAS HURT IN THE STAMPEDE
THAT'S HIS LITTLE ATTEMPT AT SARCASM
JIM DAVIS 1-14

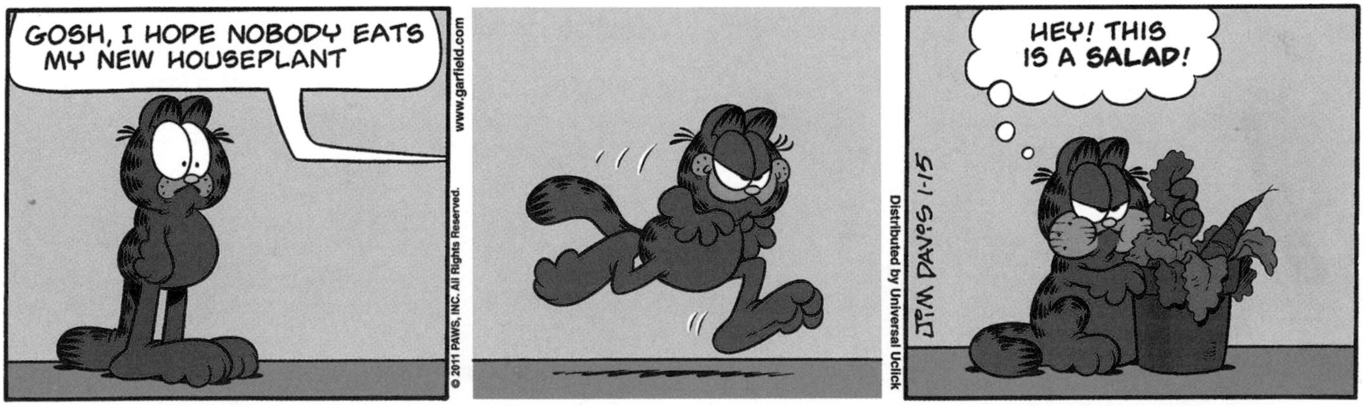
GOSH, I HOPE NOBODY EATS MY NEW HOUSEPLANT
www.garfield.com
© 2011 PAWS, INC. All Rights Reserved.
Distributed by Universal Uclick
JIM DAVIS 1-15
HEY! THIS IS A SALAD!

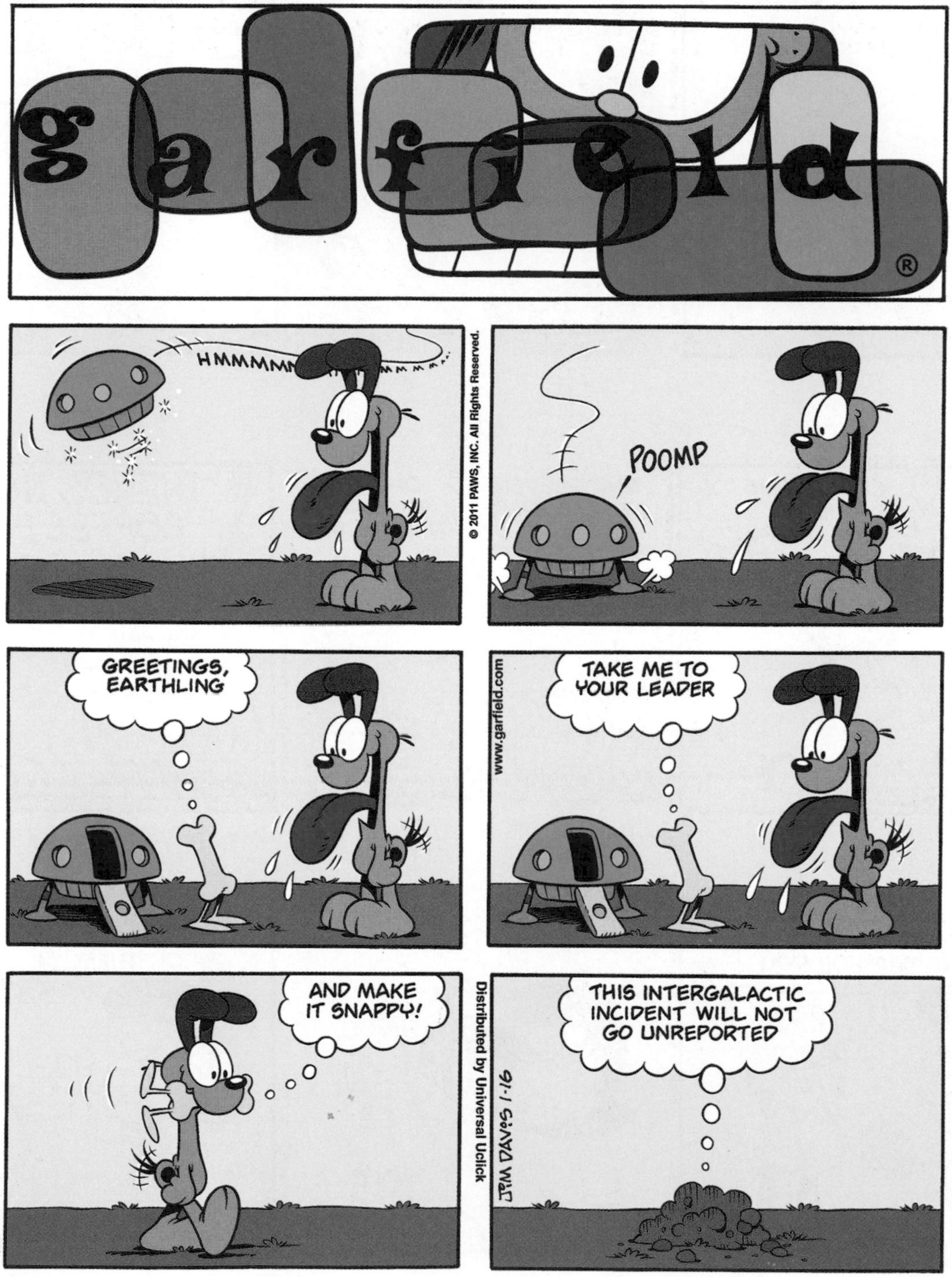
garfield®
HMMMMMMMMMMMM
© 2011 PAWS, INC. All Rights Reserved.
POOMP
GREETINGS, EARTHLING
www.garfield.com
TAKE ME TO YOUR LEADER
AND MAKE IT SNAPPY!
Distributed by Universal Uclick
JPM DAVIS 9-1
THIS INTERGALACTIC INCIDENT WILL NOT GO UNREPORTED

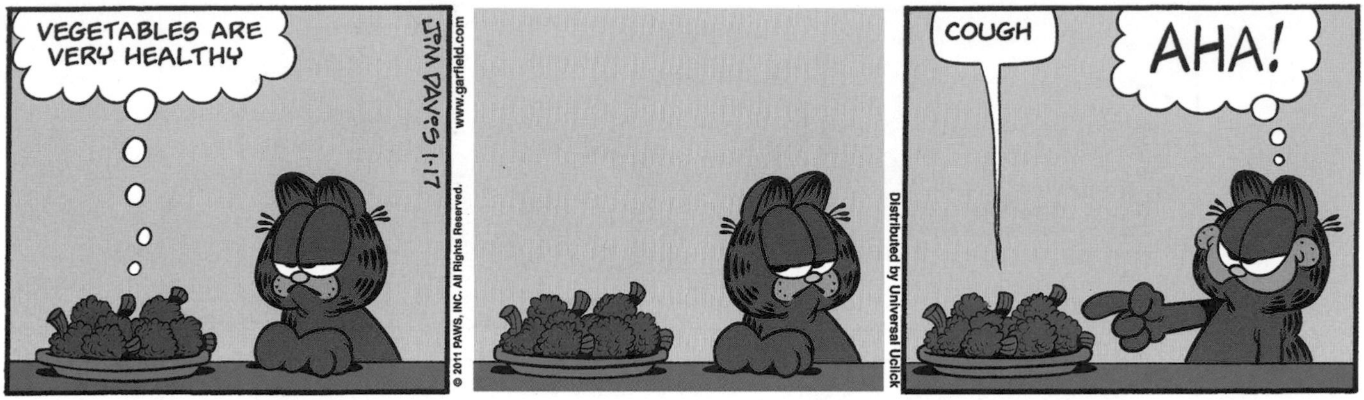
VEGETABLES ARE VERY HEALTHY
JIM DAVIS 1-17
www.garfield.com
© 2011 PAWS, INC. All Rights Reserved.
Distributed by Universal Uclick
COUGH
AHA!

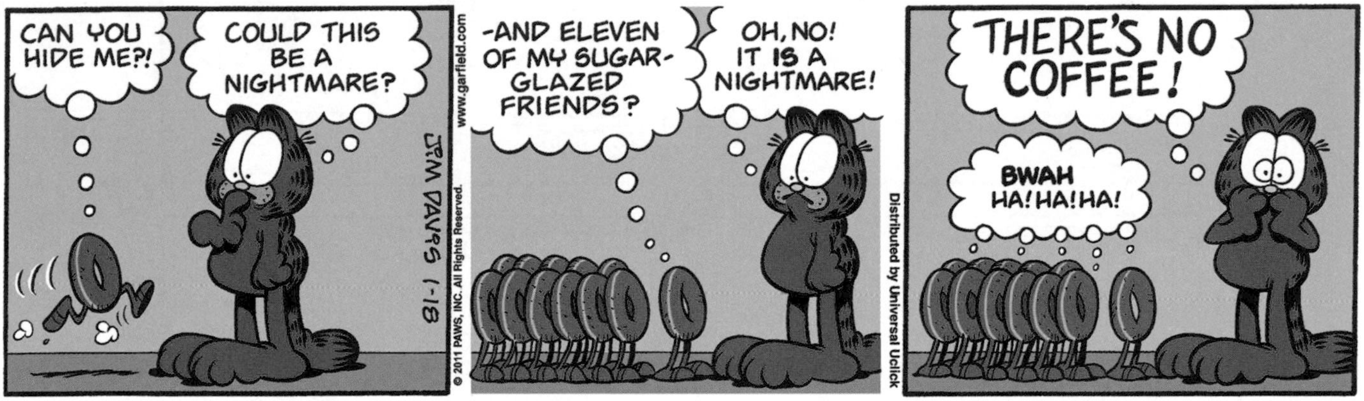
CAN YOU HIDE ME?!
COULD THIS BE A NIGHTMARE?
JIM DAVIS 1-18
www.garfield.com
© 2011 PAWS, INC. All Rights Reserved.
-AND ELEVEN OF MY SUGAR-GLAZED FRIENDS?
OH, NO! IT IS A NIGHTMARE!
Distributed by Universal Uclick
THERE'S NO COFFEE!
BWAH HA! HA! HA!

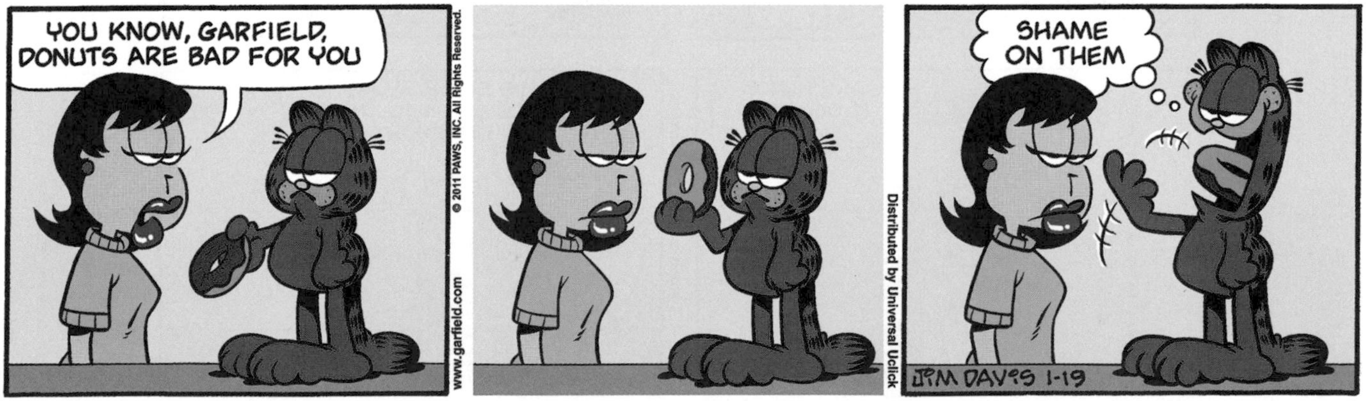
YOU KNOW, GARFIELD, DONUTS ARE BAD FOR YOU
© 2011 PAWS, INC. All Rights Reserved.
www.garfield.com
Distributed by Universal Uclick
SHAME ON THEM
JIM DAVIS 1-19

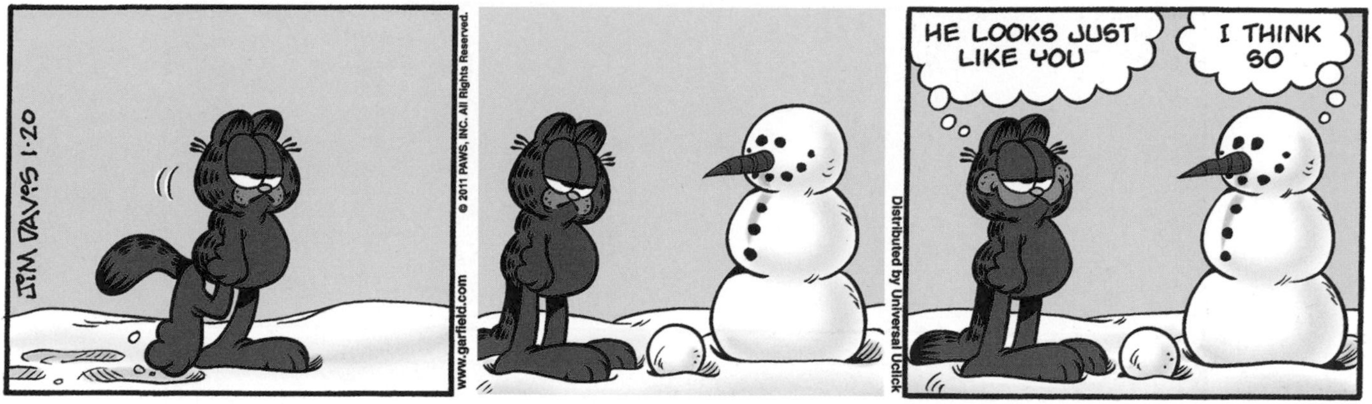
JIM DAVIS 1·20
© 2011 PAWS, INC. All Rights Reserved.
www.garfield.com
Distributed by Universal Uclick
HE LOOKS JUST LIKE YOU
I THINK SO

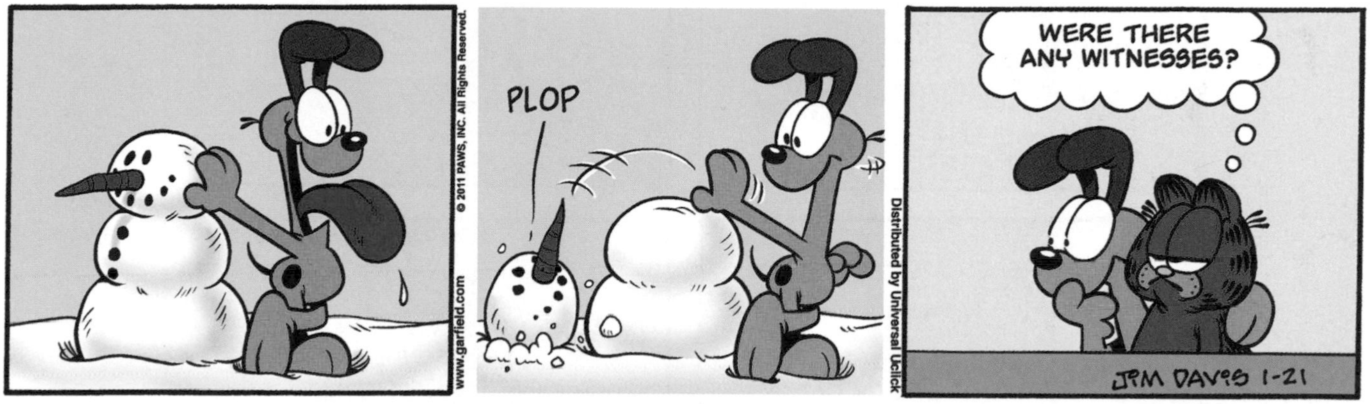
© 2011 PAWS, INC. All Rights Reserved.
www.garfield.com
PLOP
Distributed by Universal Uclick
WERE THERE ANY WITNESSES?
JIM DAVIS 1-21

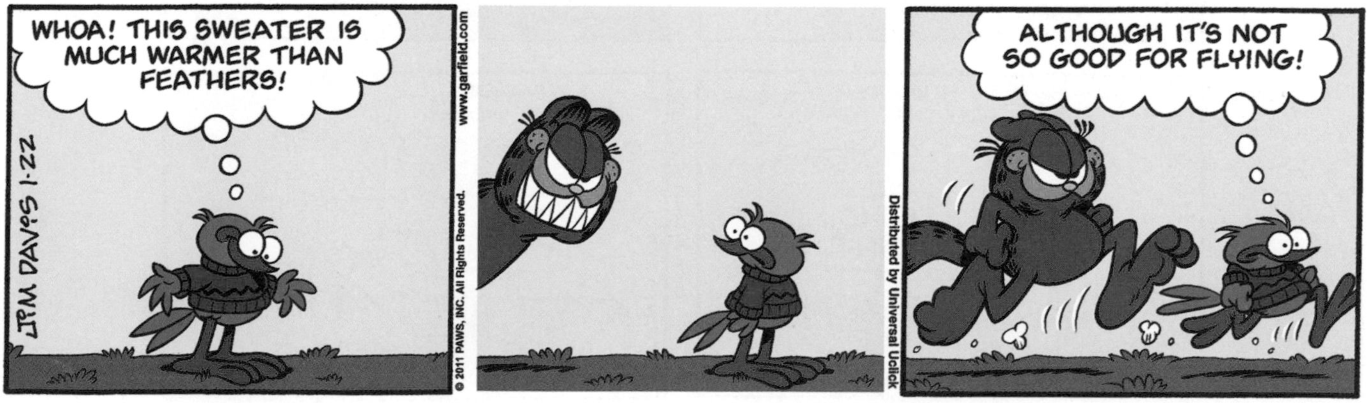
WHOA! THIS SWEATER IS MUCH WARMER THAN FEATHERS!
JIM DAVIS 1·22
www.garfield.com
© 2011 PAWS, INC. All Rights Reserved.
Distributed by Universal Uclick
ALTHOUGH IT'S NOT SO GOOD FOR FLYING!

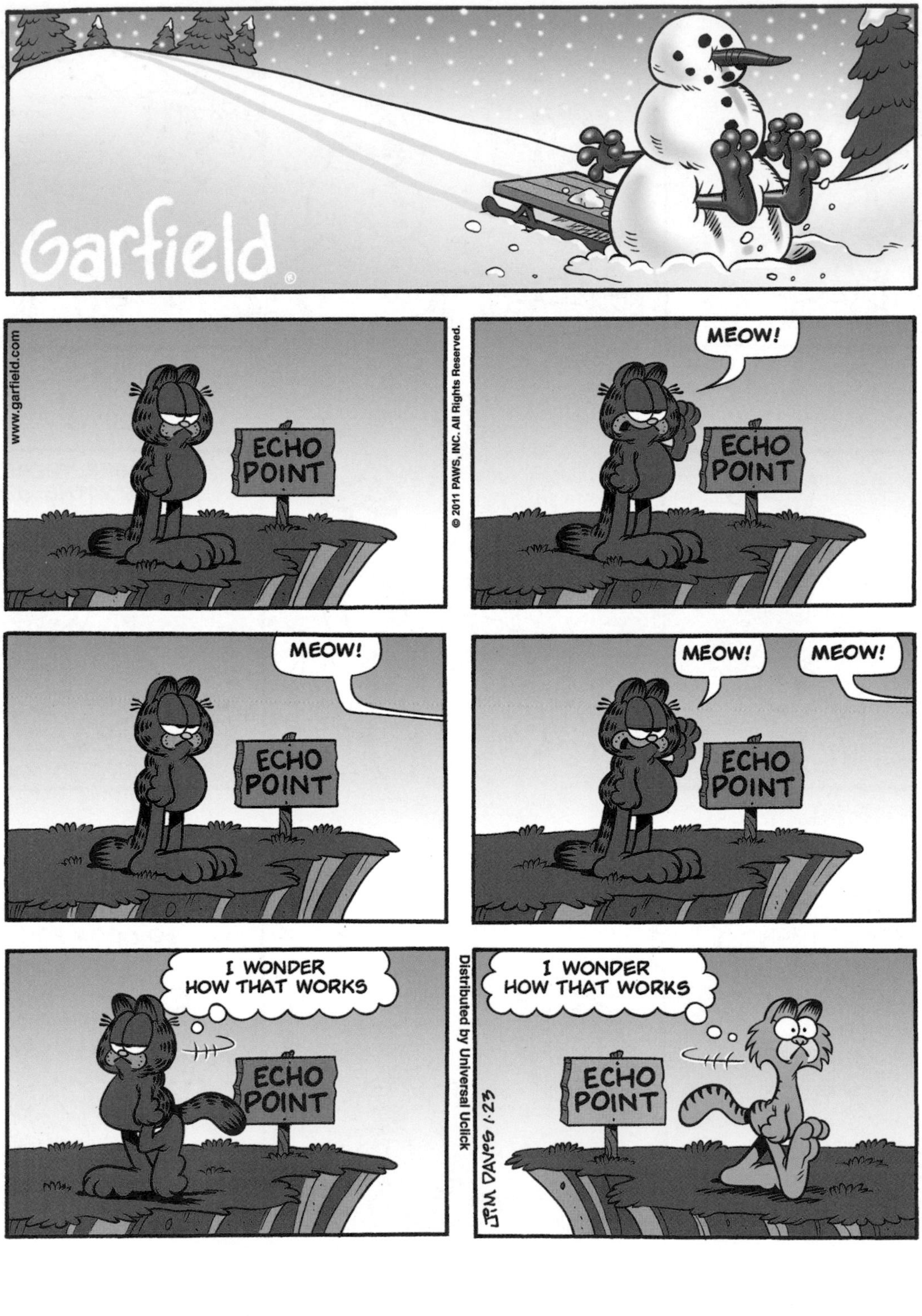
Garfield
www.garfield.com
© 2011 PAWS, INC. All Rights Reserved.
ECHO POINT
MEOW!
ECHO POINT
MEOW!
ECHO POINT
MEOW!
MEOW!
ECHO POINT
I WONDER HOW THAT WORKS
ECHO POINT
Distributed by Universal Uclick
JPM DAVPS 1-23
I WONDER HOW THAT WORKS
ECHO POINT

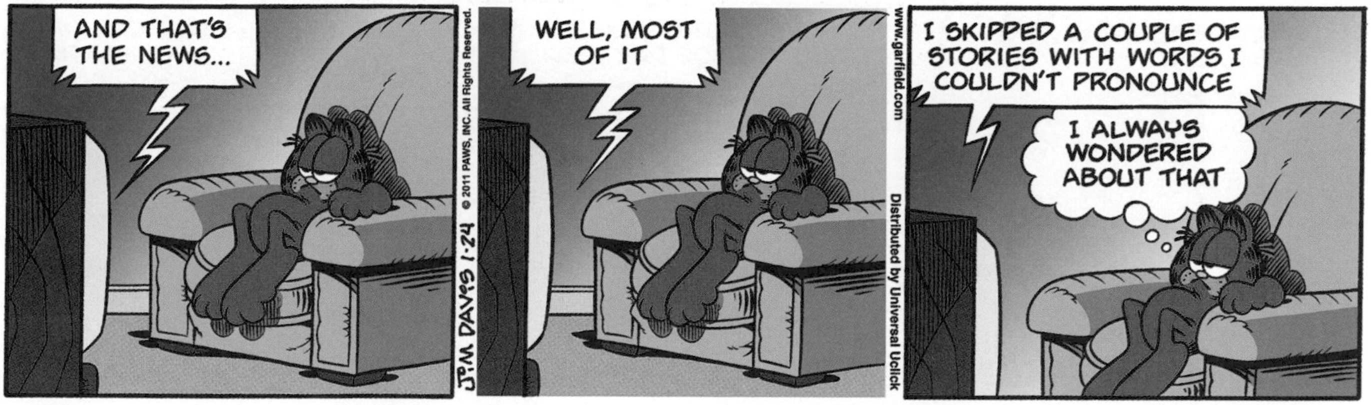
AND THAT'S THE NEWS...
WELL, MOST OF IT
I SKIPPED A COUPLE OF STORIES WITH WORDS I COULDN'T PRONOUNCE
I ALWAYS WONDERED ABOUT THAT
JIM DAVIS 1·24
© 2011 PAWS, INC. All Rights Reserved.
www.garfield.com
Distributed by Universal Uclick

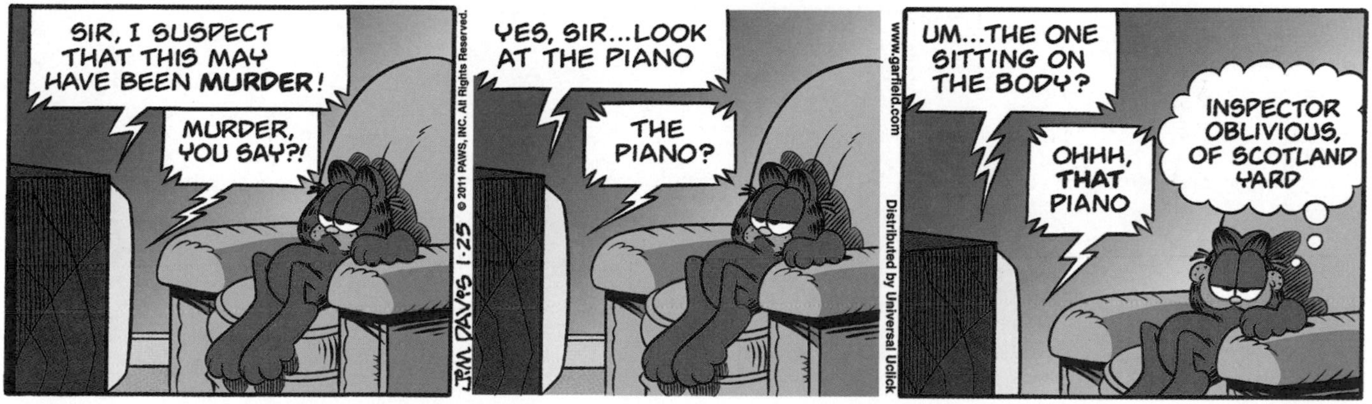
SIR, I SUSPECT THAT THIS MAY HAVE BEEN MURDER!
MURDER, YOU SAY?!
YES, SIR...LOOK AT THE PIANO
THE PIANO?
UM...THE ONE SITTING ON THE BODY?
OHHH, THAT PIANO
INSPECTOR OBLIVIOUS, OF SCOTLAND YARD
JIM DAVIS 1·25
© 2011 PAWS, INC. All Rights Reserved.
www.garfield.com
Distributed by Universal Uclick

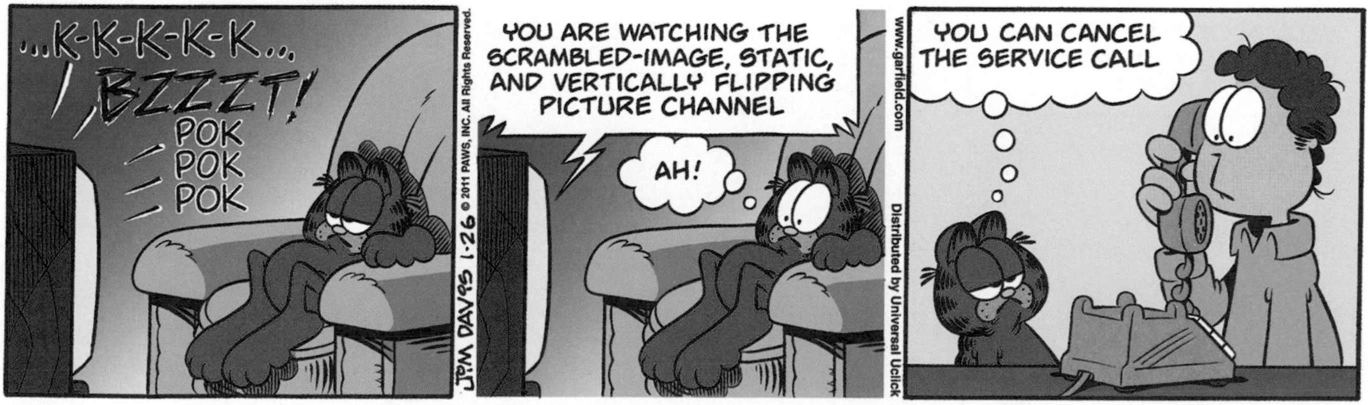
...K-K-K-K-K...
BZZZT!
POK
POK
POK
YOU ARE WATCHING THE SCRAMBLED-IMAGE, STATIC, AND VERTICALLY FLIPPING PICTURE CHANNEL
AH!
YOU CAN CANCEL THE SERVICE CALL
JIM DAVIS 1·26
© 2011 PAWS, INC. All Rights Reserved.
www.garfield.com
Distributed by Universal Uclick

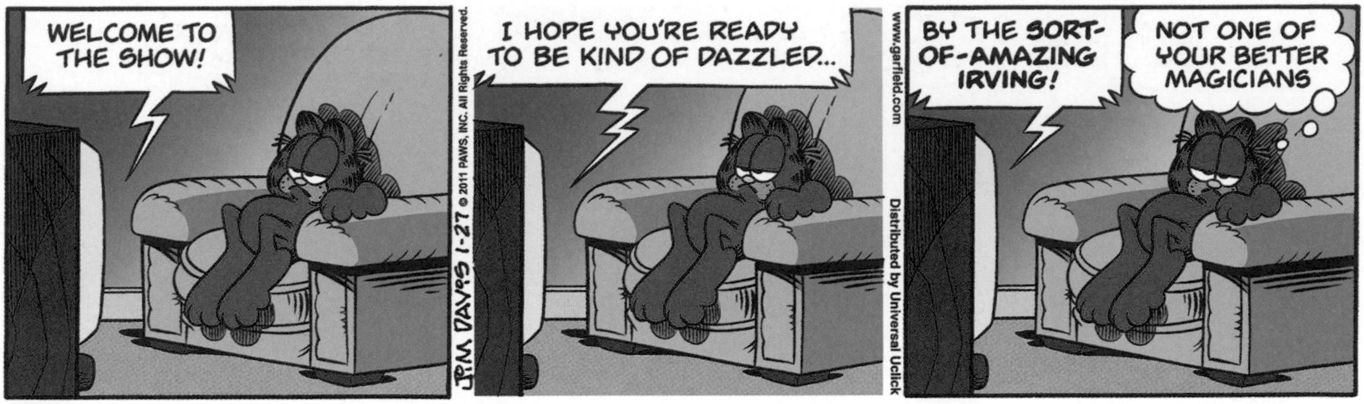
WELCOME TO THE SHOW!
JIM DAVIS 1-27 © 2011 PAWS, INC. All Rights Reserved.
I HOPE YOU'RE READY TO BE KIND OF DAZZLED...
www.garfield.com Distributed by Universal Uclick
BY THE SORT-OF-AMAZING IRVING!
NOT ONE OF YOUR BETTER MAGICIANS

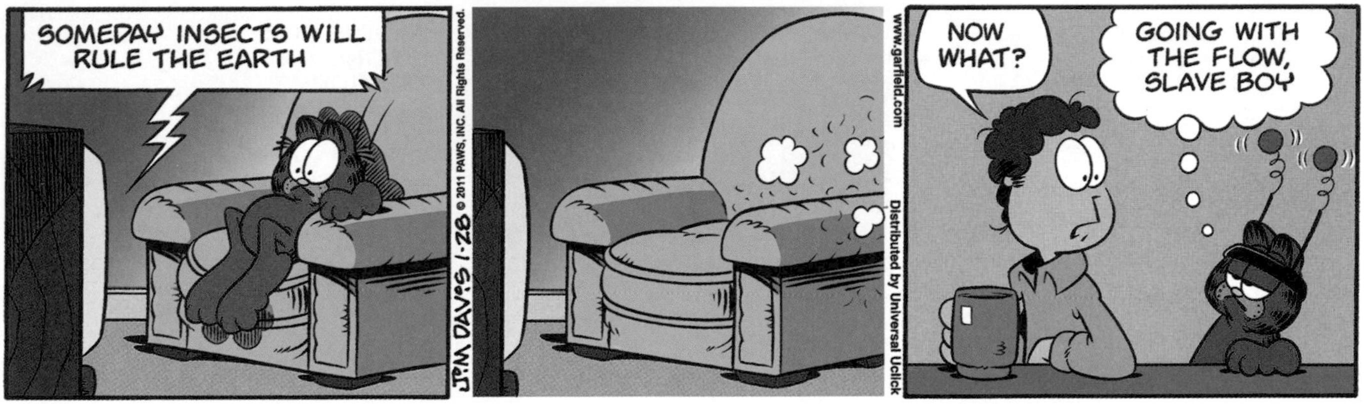
SOMEDAY INSECTS WILL RULE THE EARTH
JIM DAVIS 1-28 © 2011 PAWS, INC. All Rights Reserved.
www.garfield.com Distributed by Universal Uclick
NOW WHAT?
GOING WITH THE FLOW, SLAVE BOY

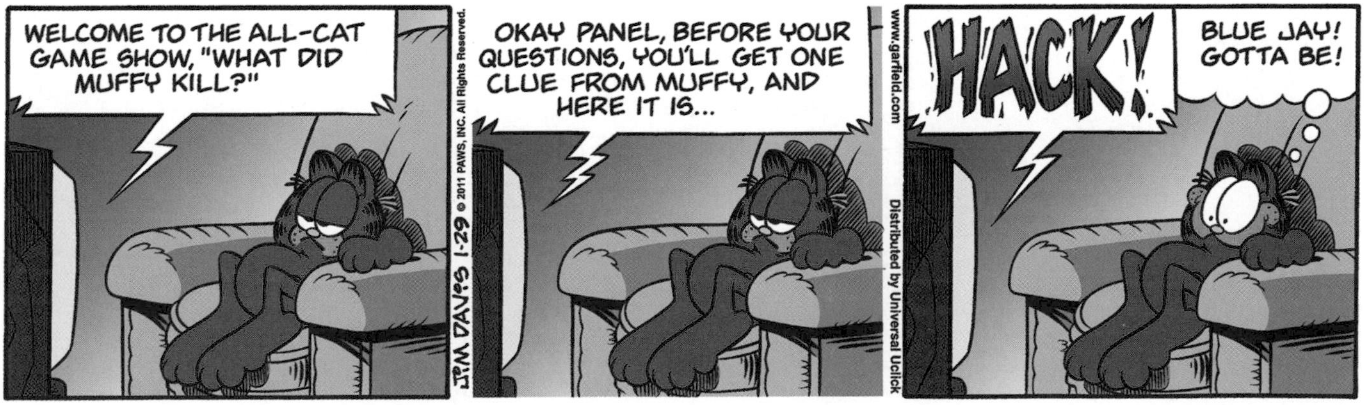
WELCOME TO THE ALL-CAT GAME SHOW, "WHAT DID MUFFY KILL?"
JIM DAVIS 1-29 © 2011 PAWS, INC. All Rights Reserved.
OKAY PANEL, BEFORE YOUR QUESTIONS, YOU'LL GET ONE CLUE FROM MUFFY, AND HERE IT IS...
www.garfield.com Distributed by Universal Uclick
HACK!
BLUE JAY! GOTTA BE!

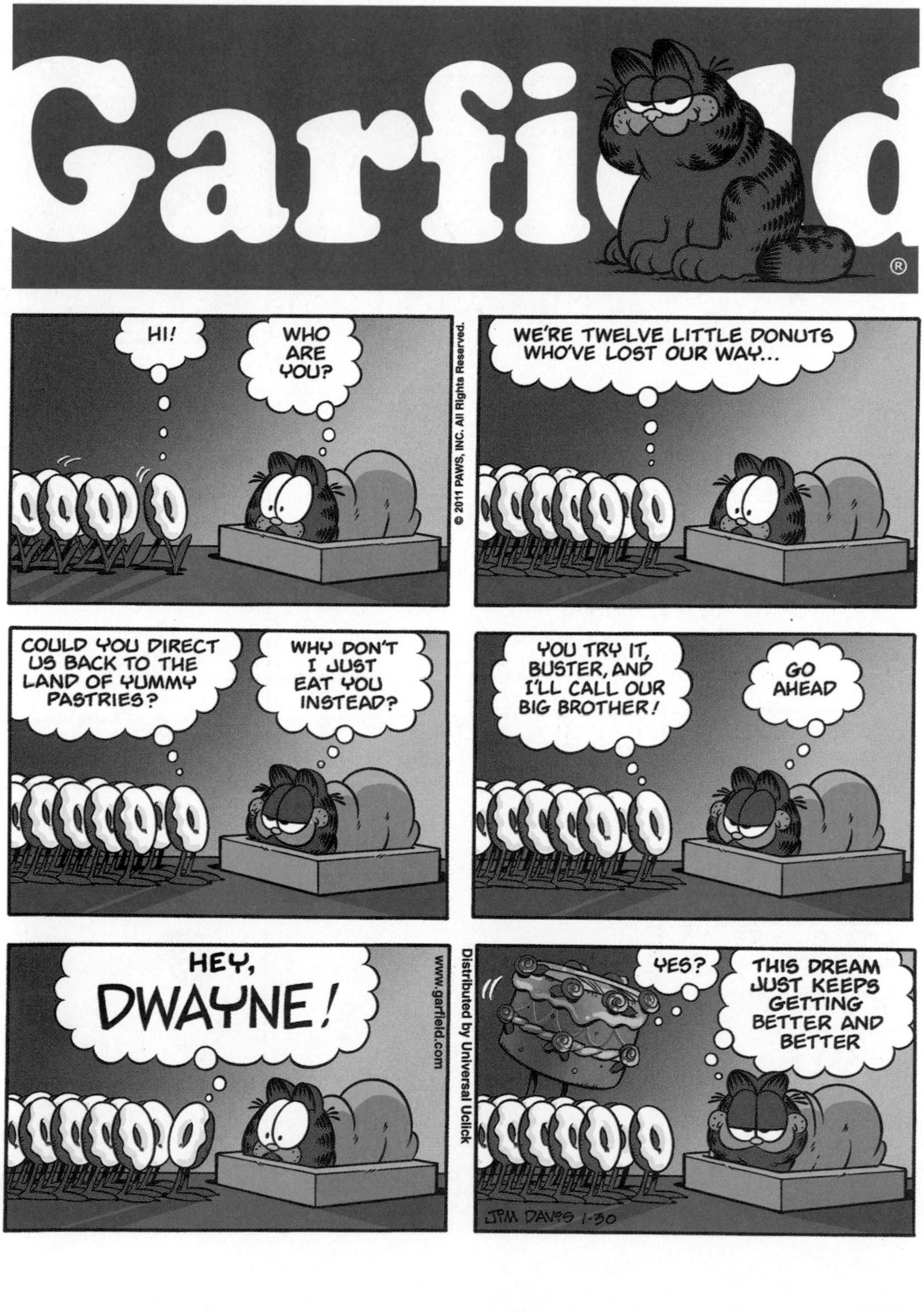
Garfield®
HI!
WHO ARE YOU?
© 2011 PAWS, INC. All Rights Reserved.
WE'RE TWELVE LITTLE DONUTS WHO'VE LOST OUR WAY...
COULD YOU DIRECT US BACK TO THE LAND OF YUMMY PASTRIES?
WHY DON'T I JUST EAT YOU INSTEAD?
YOU TRY IT, BUSTER, AND I'LL CALL OUR BIG BROTHER!
GO AHEAD
HEY, DWAYNE!
www.garfield.com
Distributed by Universal Uclick
YES?
THIS DREAM JUST KEEPS GETTING BETTER AND BETTER
JPM DAVIS 1-30

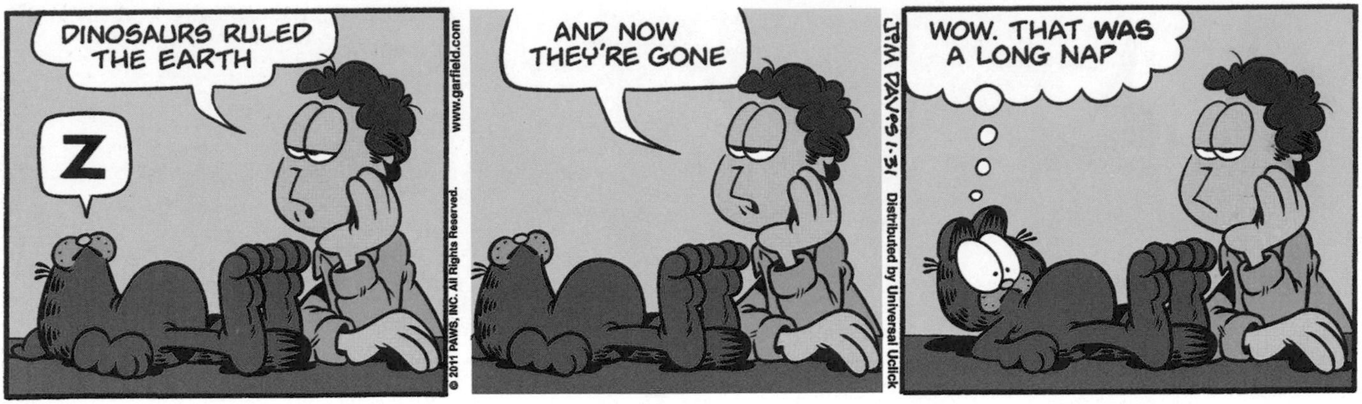
DINOSAURS RULED THE EARTH
Z
AND NOW THEY'RE GONE
WOW. THAT WAS A LONG NAP
© 2011 PAWS, INC. All Rights Reserved. www.garfield.com
JIM DAVIS 1-31 Distributed by Universal Uclick

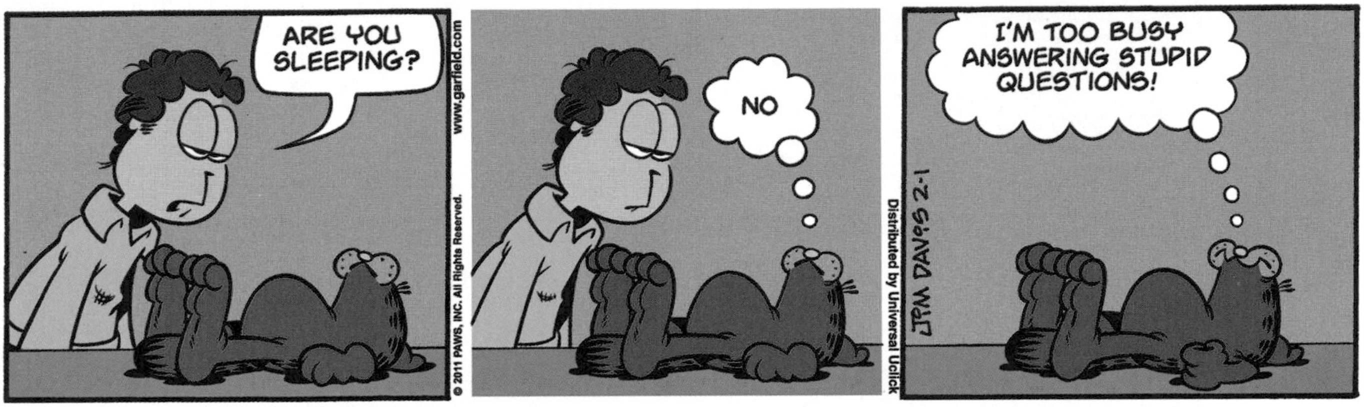
ARE YOU SLEEPING?
NO
I'M TOO BUSY ANSWERING STUPID QUESTIONS!
© 2011 PAWS, INC. All Rights Reserved. www.garfield.com
Distributed by Universal Uclick JIM DAVIS 2-1

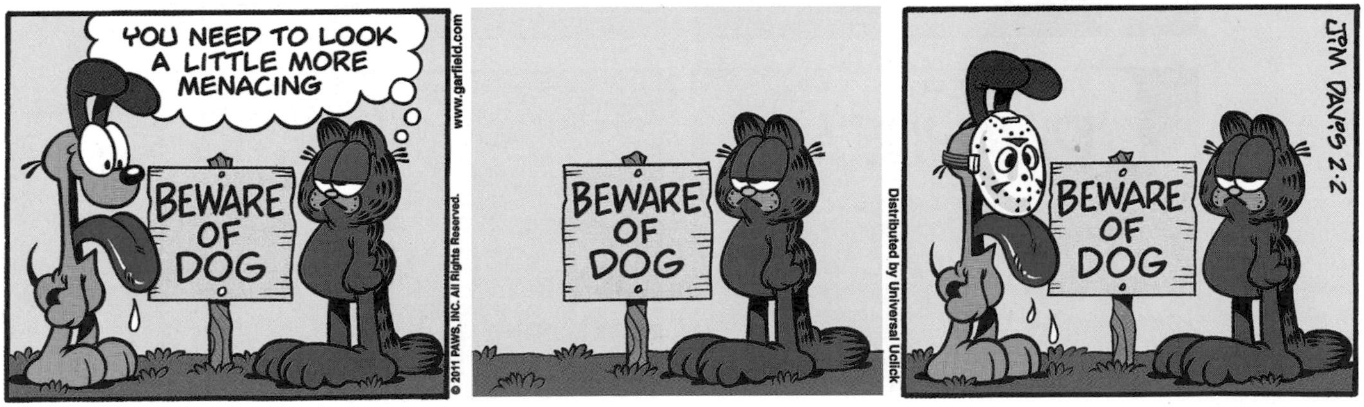
YOU NEED TO LOOK A LITTLE MORE MENACING
BEWARE OF DOG
BEWARE OF DOG
BEWARE OF DOG
© 2011 PAWS, INC. All Rights Reserved. www.garfield.com
Distributed by Universal Uclick
JIM DAVIS 2-2

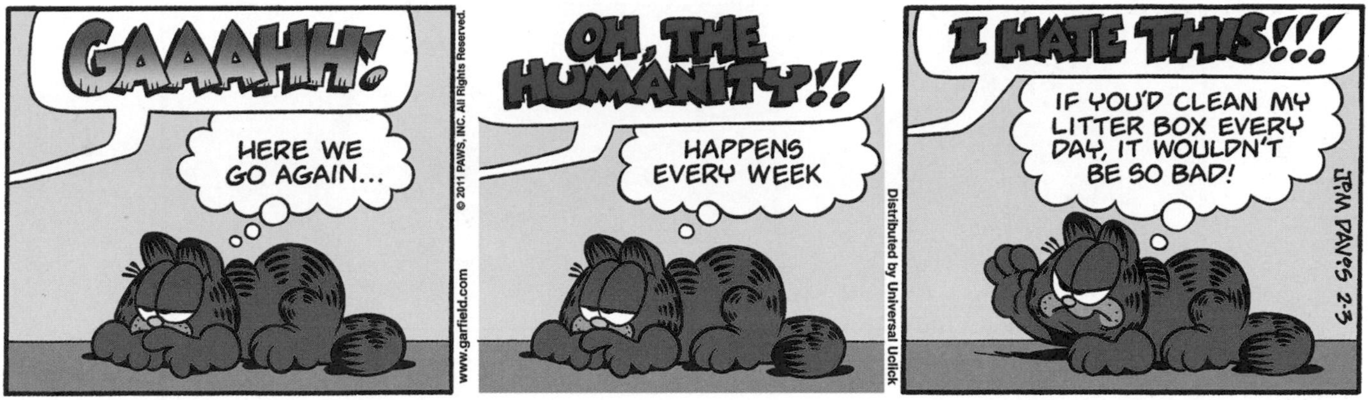
GAAAHH!
HERE WE GO AGAIN...
© 2011 PAWS, INC. All Rights Reserved.
www.garfield.com
OH, THE HUMANITY!!
HAPPENS EVERY WEEK
Distributed by Universal Uclick
I HATE THIS!!!
IF YOU'D CLEAN MY LITTER BOX EVERY DAY, IT WOULDN'T BE SO BAD!
JPM DAVIS 2-3

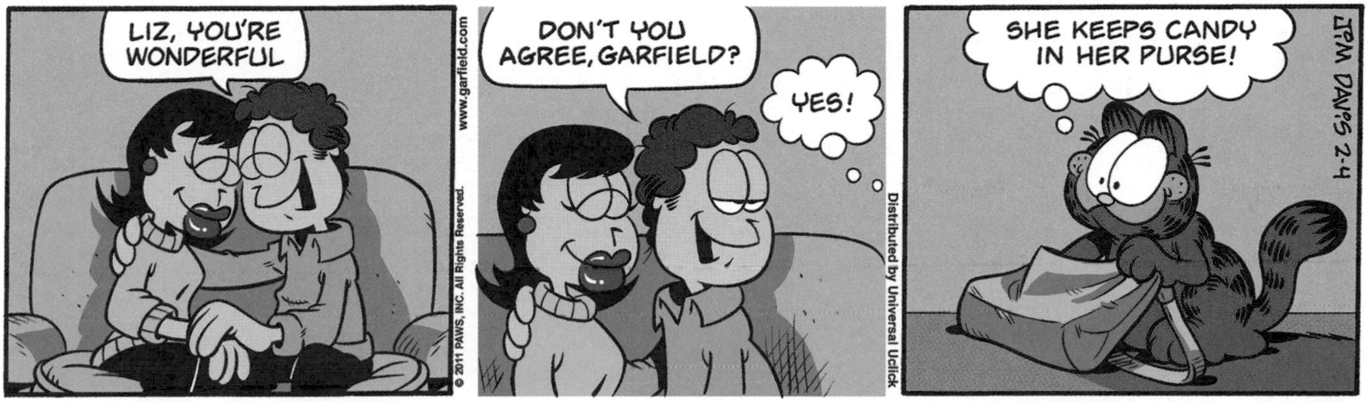
LIZ, YOU'RE WONDERFUL
www.garfield.com
© 2011 PAWS, INC. All Rights Reserved.
DON'T YOU AGREE, GARFIELD?
YES!
Distributed by Universal Uclick
SHE KEEPS CANDY IN HER PURSE!
JPM DAVIS 2-4

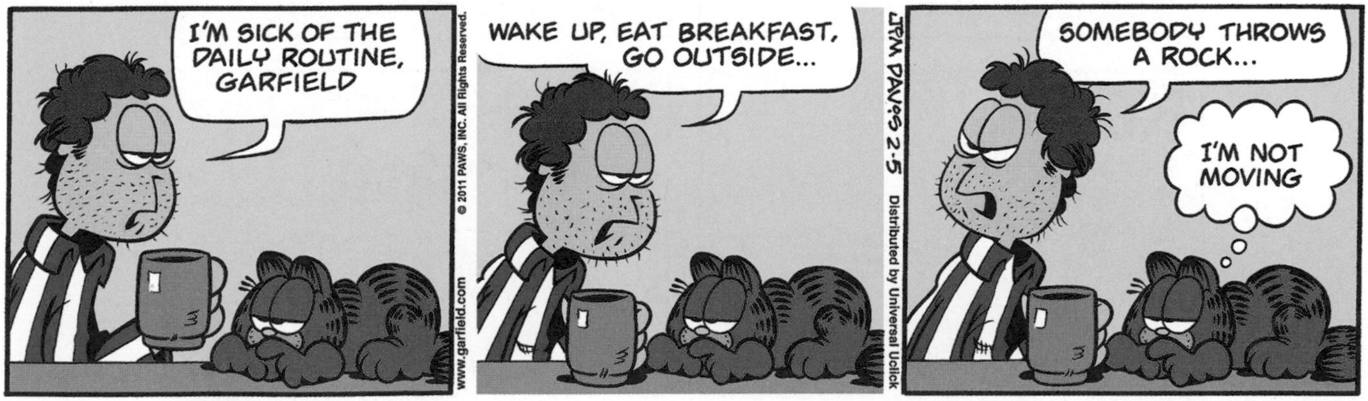
I'M SICK OF THE DAILY ROUTINE, GARFIELD
© 2011 PAWS, INC. All Rights Reserved.
www.garfield.com
WAKE UP, EAT BREAKFAST, GO OUTSIDE...
JPM DAVIS 2-5
Distributed by Universal Uclick
SOMEBODY THROWS A ROCK...
I'M NOT MOVING

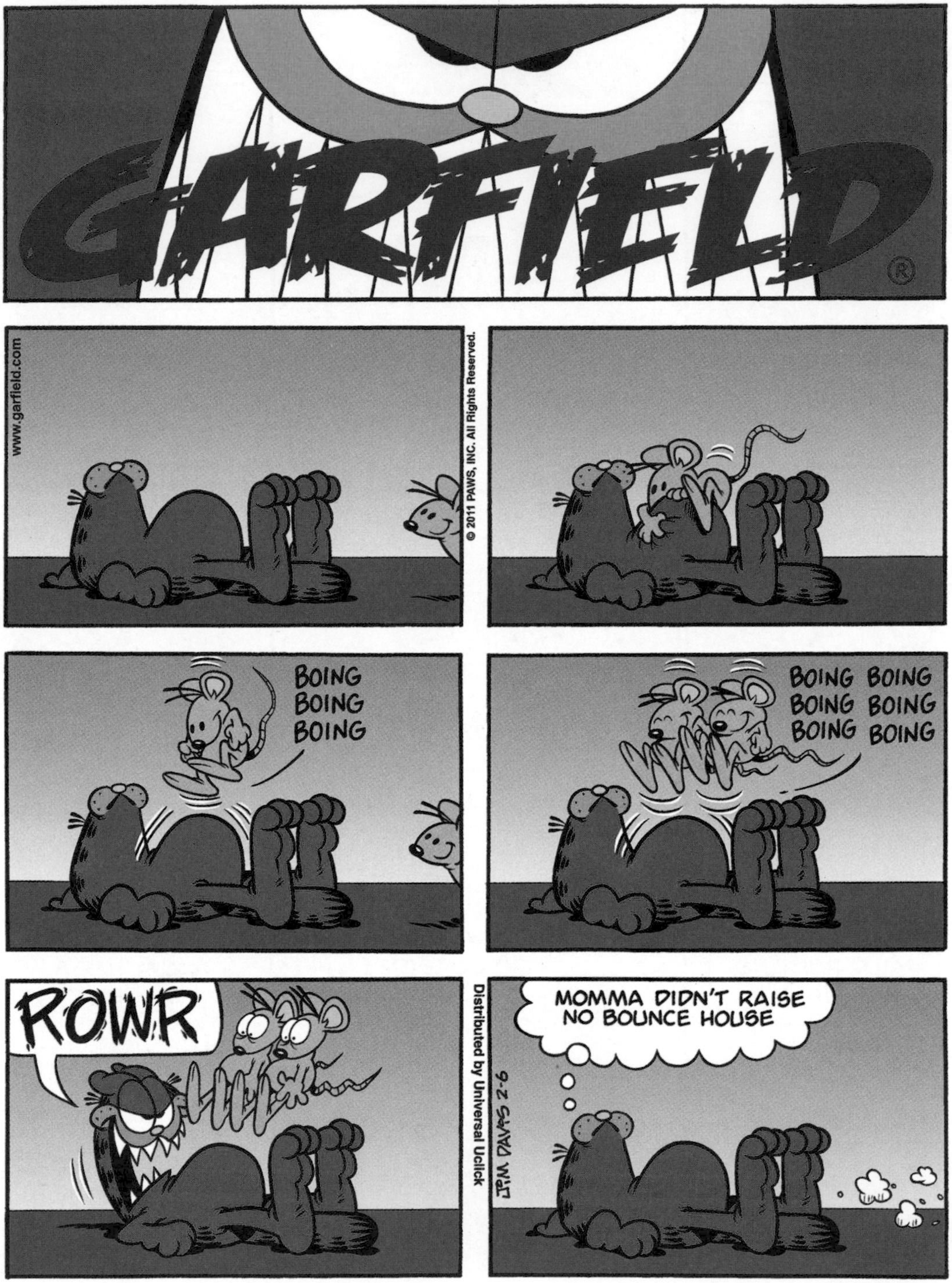
GARFIELD
www.garfield.com
© 2011 PAWS, INC. All Rights Reserved.
BOING
BOING
BOING
BOING BOING
BOING BOING
BOING BOING
ROWR
Distributed by Universal Uclick
JIM DAVIS 2-6
MOMMA DIDN'T RAISE NO BOUNCE HOUSE

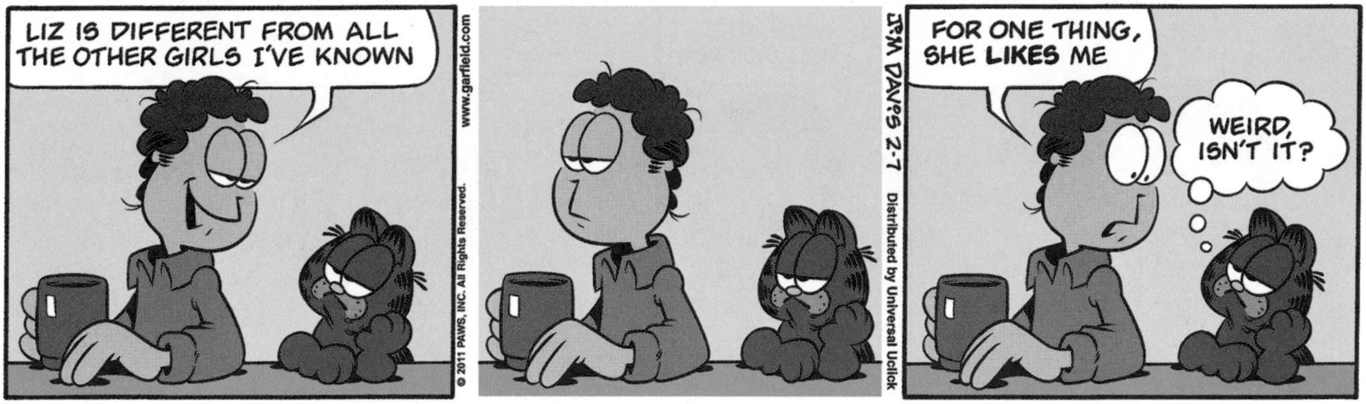
LIZ IS DIFFERENT FROM ALL THE OTHER GIRLS I'VE KNOWN
© 2011 PAWS, INC. All Rights Reserved. www.garfield.com
JIM DAVIS 2-7 Distributed by Universal Uclick
FOR ONE THING, SHE LIKES ME
WEIRD, ISN'T IT?

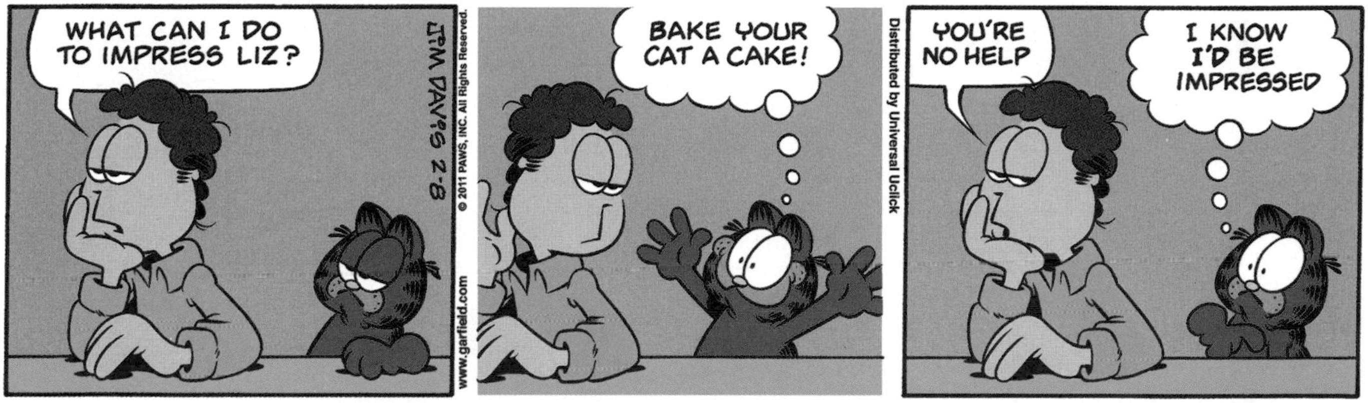
WHAT CAN I DO TO IMPRESS LIZ?
JIM DAVIS 2-8
© 2011 PAWS, INC. All Rights Reserved. www.garfield.com
BAKE YOUR CAT A CAKE!
Distributed by Universal Uclick
YOU'RE NO HELP
I KNOW I'D BE IMPRESSED

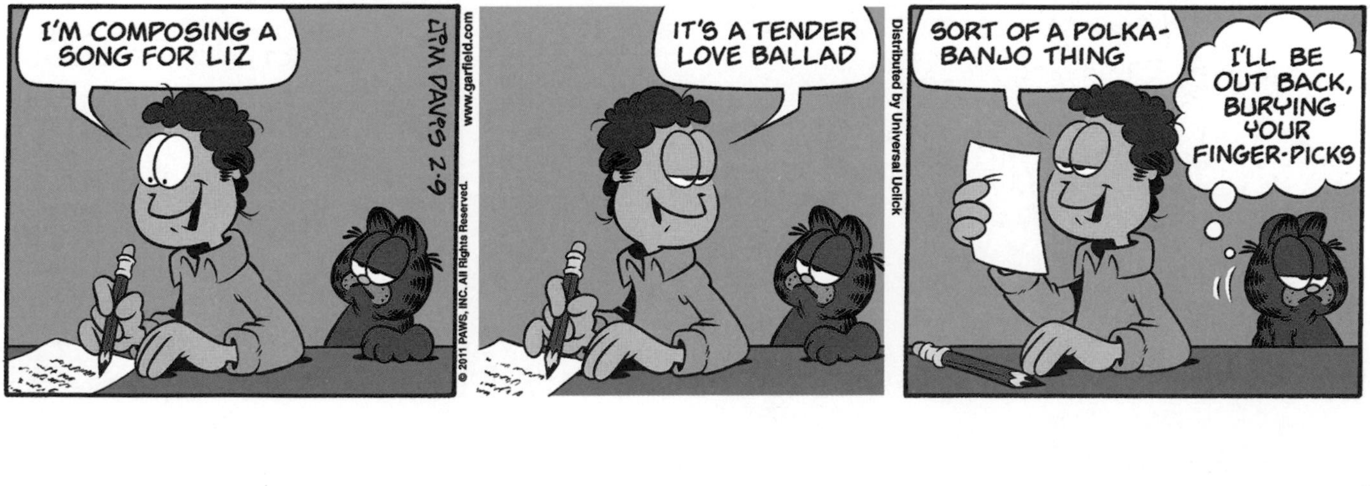
I'M COMPOSING A SONG FOR LIZ
JIM DAVIS 2-9
© 2011 PAWS, INC. All Rights Reserved. www.garfield.com
IT'S A TENDER LOVE BALLAD
Distributed by Universal Uclick
SORT OF A POLKA-BANJO THING
I'LL BE OUT BACK, BURYING YOUR FINGER-PICKS

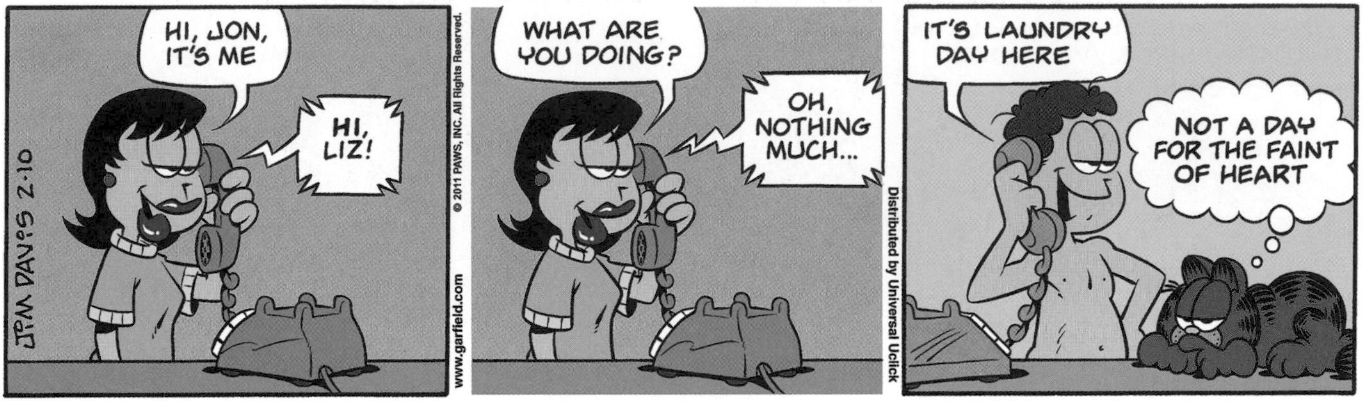
JIM DAVIS 2·10
HI, JON, IT'S ME
HI, LIZ!
© 2011 PAWS, INC. All Rights Reserved.
www.garfield.com
WHAT ARE YOU DOING?
OH, NOTHING MUCH...
Distributed by Universal Uclick
IT'S LAUNDRY DAY HERE
NOT A DAY FOR THE FAINT OF HEART

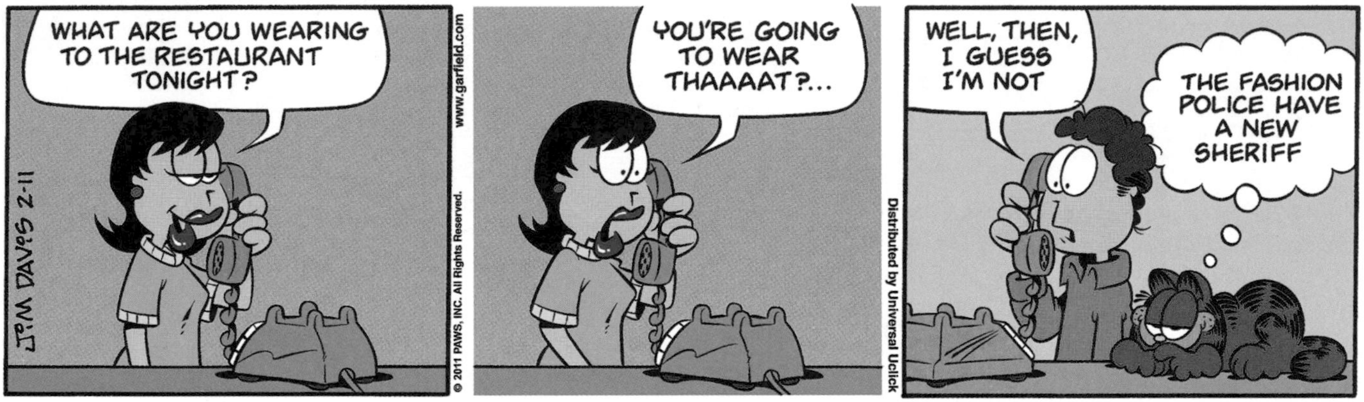
JIM DAVIS 2·11
WHAT ARE YOU WEARING TO THE RESTAURANT TONIGHT?
www.garfield.com
© 2011 PAWS, INC. All Rights Reserved.
YOU'RE GOING TO WEAR THAAAAT?...
Distributed by Universal Uclick
WELL, THEN, I GUESS I'M NOT
THE FASHION POLICE HAVE A NEW SHERIFF

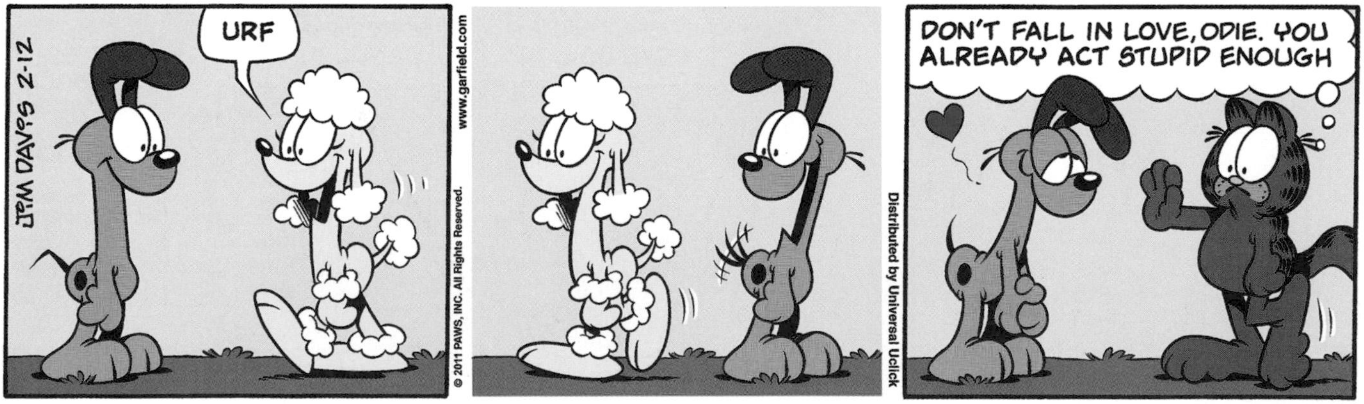
JIM DAVIS 2·12
URF
www.garfield.com
© 2011 PAWS, INC. All Rights Reserved.
Distributed by Universal Uclick
DON'T FALL IN LOVE, ODIE. YOU ALREADY ACT STUPID ENOUGH

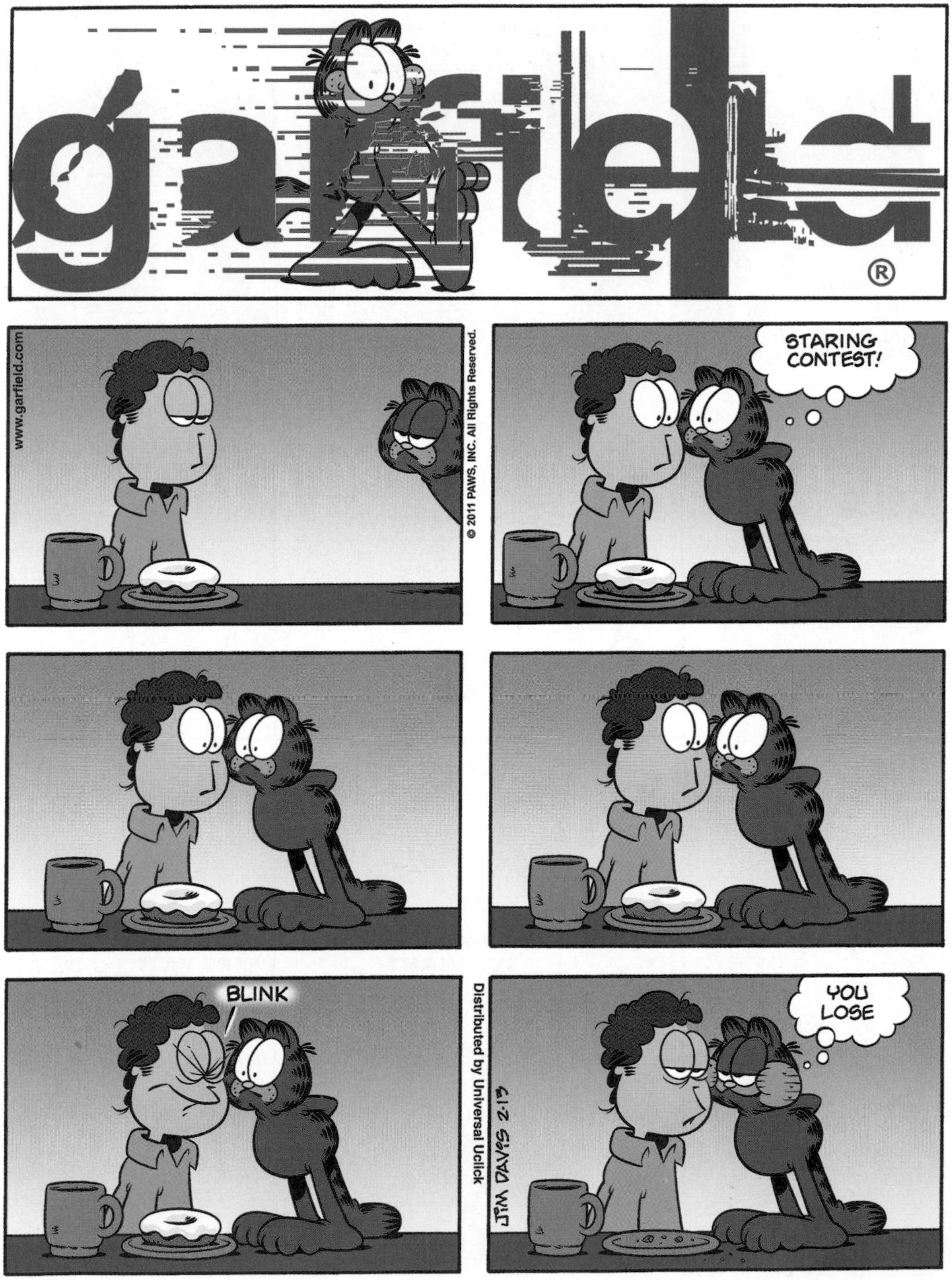
garfield
www.garfield.com
© 2011 PAWS, INC. All Rights Reserved.
STARING CONTEST!
BLINK
Distributed by Universal Uclick
JIM DAVIS 2-13
YOU LOSE

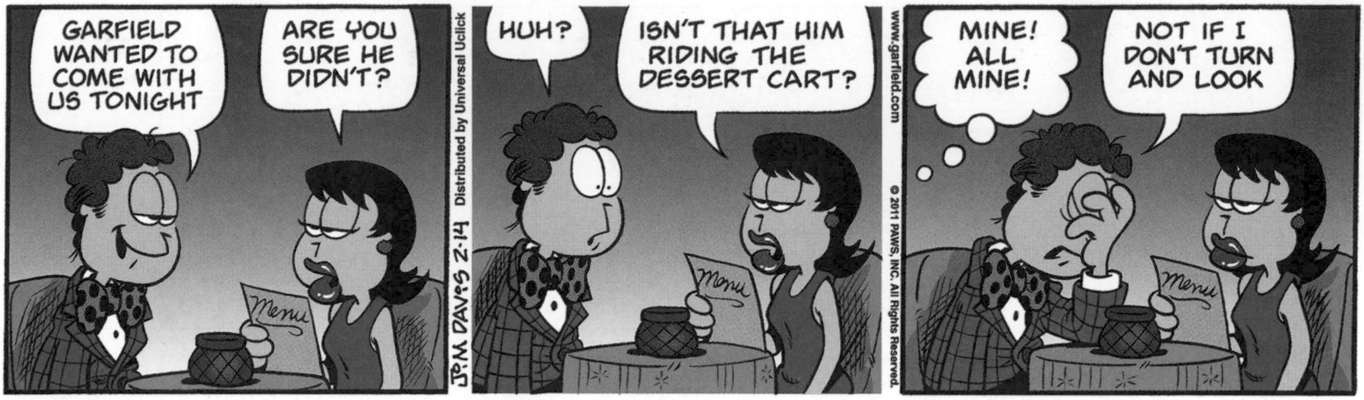
GARFIELD WANTED TO COME WITH US TONIGHT
ARE YOU SURE HE DIDN'T?
JPM DAVIS 2-14
Distributed by Universal Uclick
HUH?
ISN'T THAT HIM RIDING THE DESSERT CART?
www.garfield.com
© 2011 PAWS, INC. All Rights Reserved.
MINE! ALL MINE!
NOT IF I DON'T TURN AND LOOK

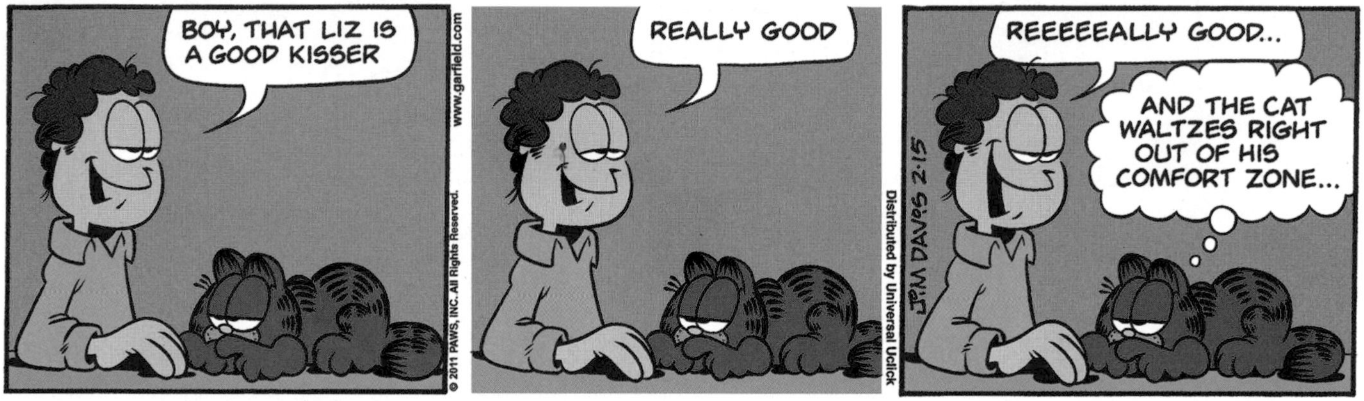
BOY, THAT LIZ IS A GOOD KISSER
www.garfield.com
© 2011 PAWS, INC. All Rights Reserved.
REALLY GOOD
Distributed by Universal Uclick
JPM DAVIS 2-15
REEEEEALLY GOOD...
AND THE CAT WALTZES RIGHT OUT OF HIS COMFORT ZONE...

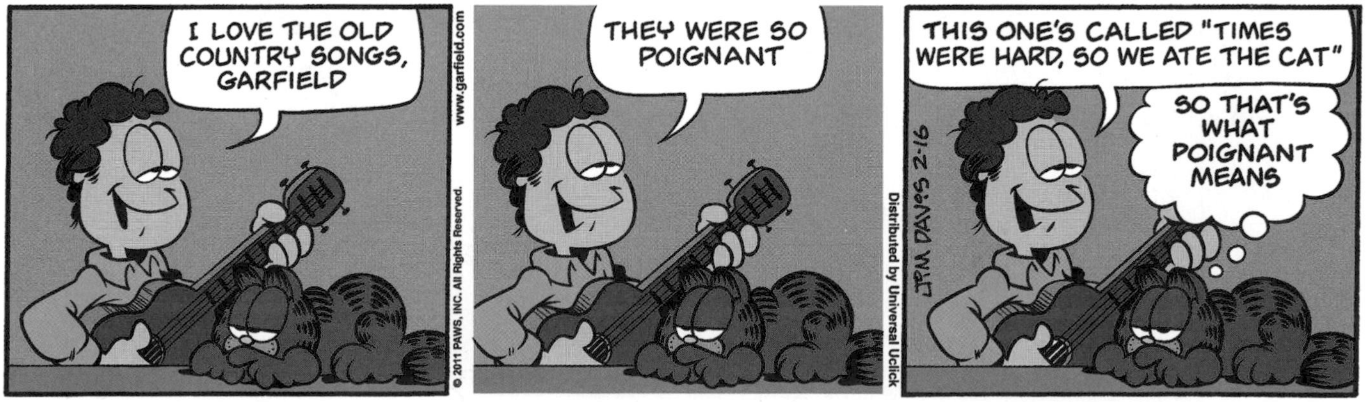
I LOVE THE OLD COUNTRY SONGS, GARFIELD
www.garfield.com
© 2011 PAWS, INC. All Rights Reserved.
THEY WERE SO POIGNANT
Distributed by Universal Uclick
JPM DAVIS 2-16
THIS ONE'S CALLED "TIMES WERE HARD, SO WE ATE THE CAT"
SO THAT'S WHAT POIGNANT MEANS

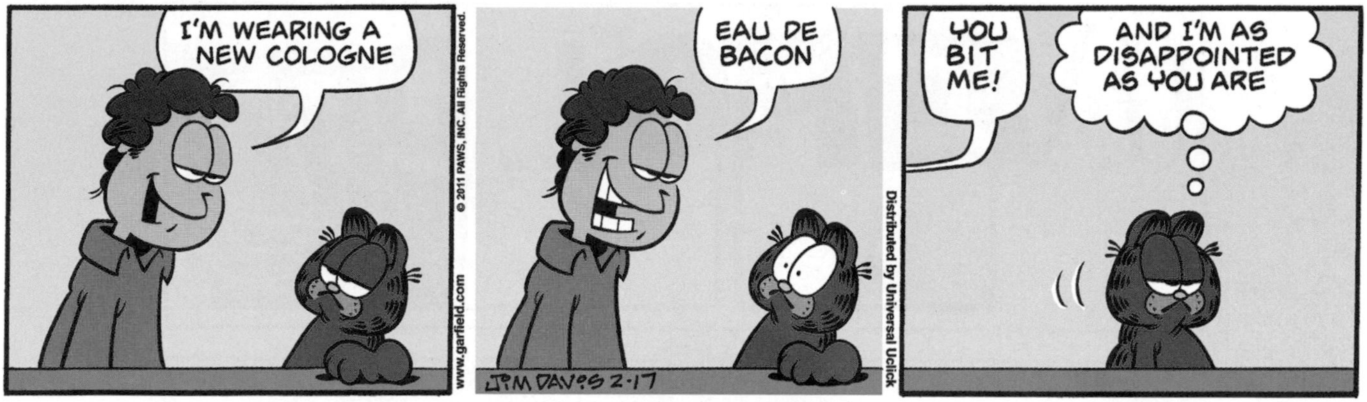
I'M WEARING A NEW COLOGNE
www.garfield.com
© 2011 PAWS, INC. All Rights Reserved.
EAU DE BACON
JIM DAVIS 2-17
Distributed by Universal Uclick
YOU BIT ME!
AND I'M AS DISAPPOINTED AS YOU ARE

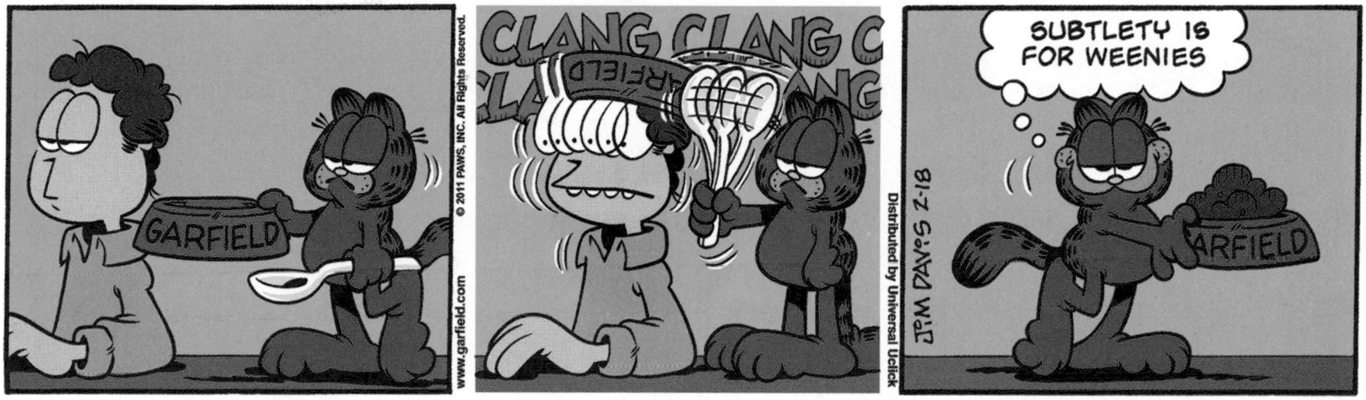
GARFIELD
www.garfield.com
© 2011 PAWS, INC. All Rights Reserved.
CLANG CLANG C
CLA ANG
JIM DAVIS 2-18
Distributed by Universal Uclick
SUBTLETY IS FOR WEENIES
ARFIELD

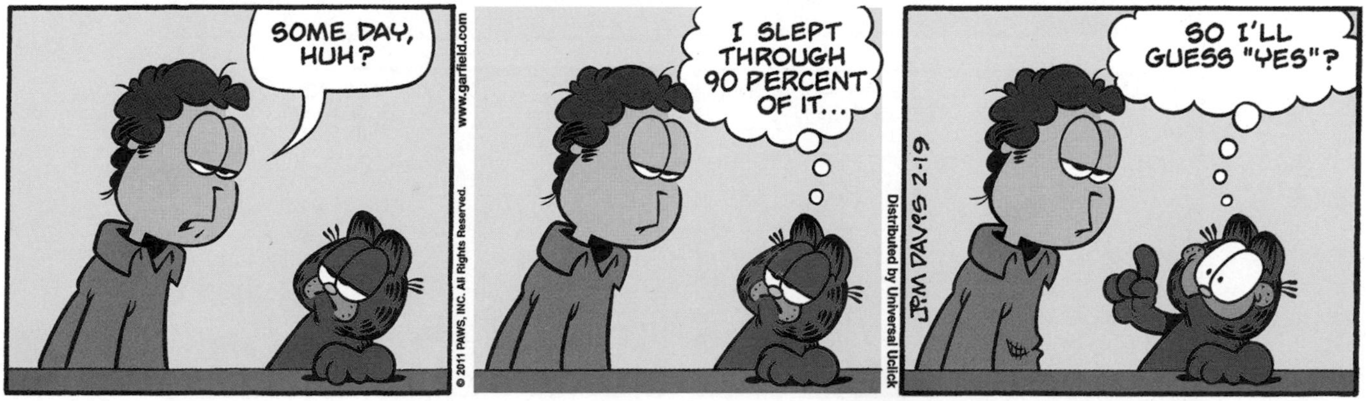
SOME DAY, HUH?
© 2011 PAWS, INC. All Rights Reserved.
www.garfield.com
I SLEPT THROUGH 90 PERCENT OF IT...
Distributed by Universal Uclick
JIM DAVIS 2-19
SO I'LL GUESS "YES"?

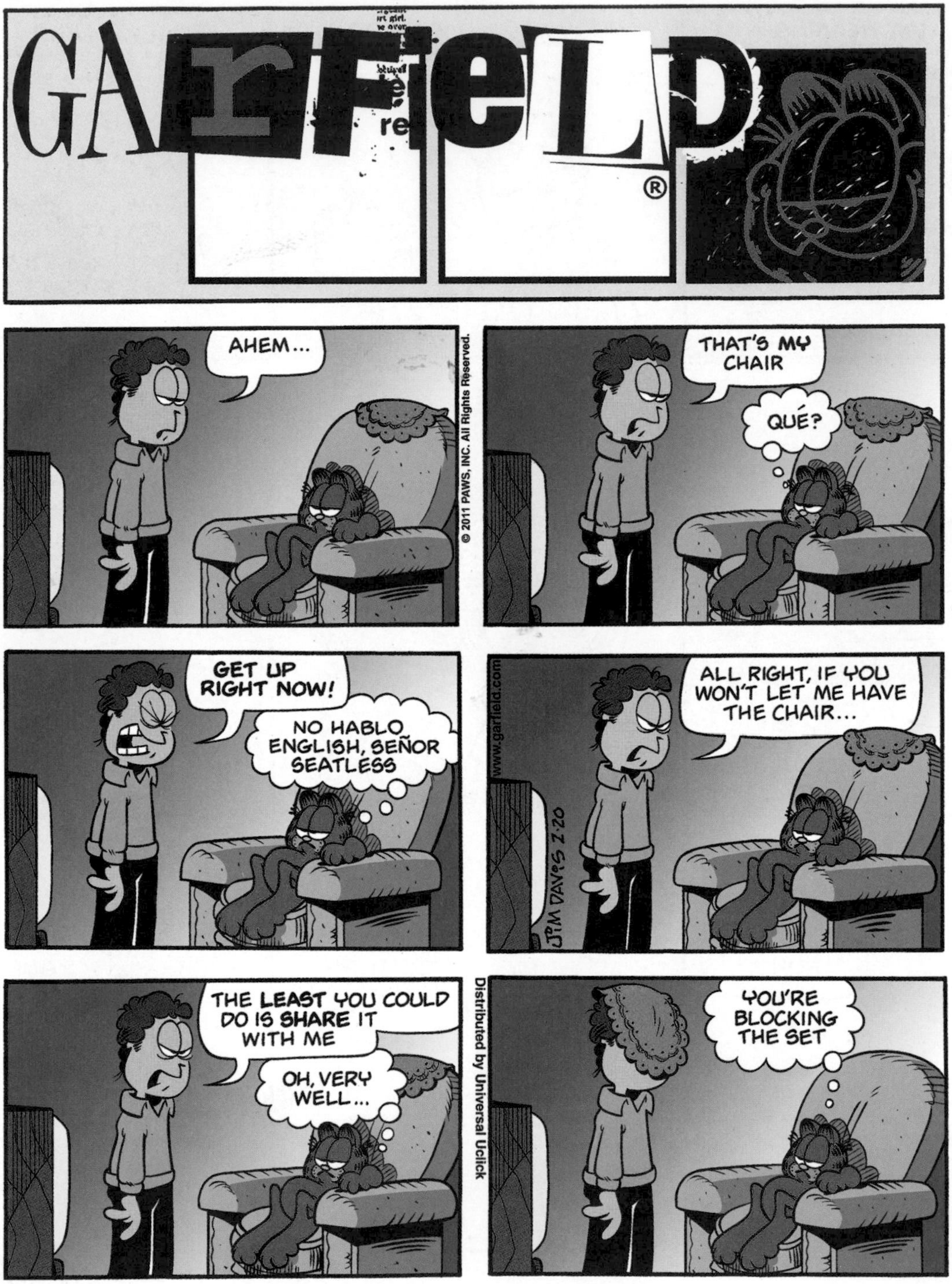
GARFIELD
AHEM...
© 2011 PAWS, INC. All Rights Reserved.
THAT'S MY CHAIR
QUÉ?
GET UP RIGHT NOW!
NO HABLO ENGLISH, SEÑOR SEATLESS
www.garfield.com
ALL RIGHT, IF YOU WON'T LET ME HAVE THE CHAIR...
JPM DAVPS 2-20
THE LEAST YOU COULD DO IS SHARE IT WITH ME
OH, VERY WELL...
Distributed by Universal Uclick
YOU'RE BLOCKING THE SET

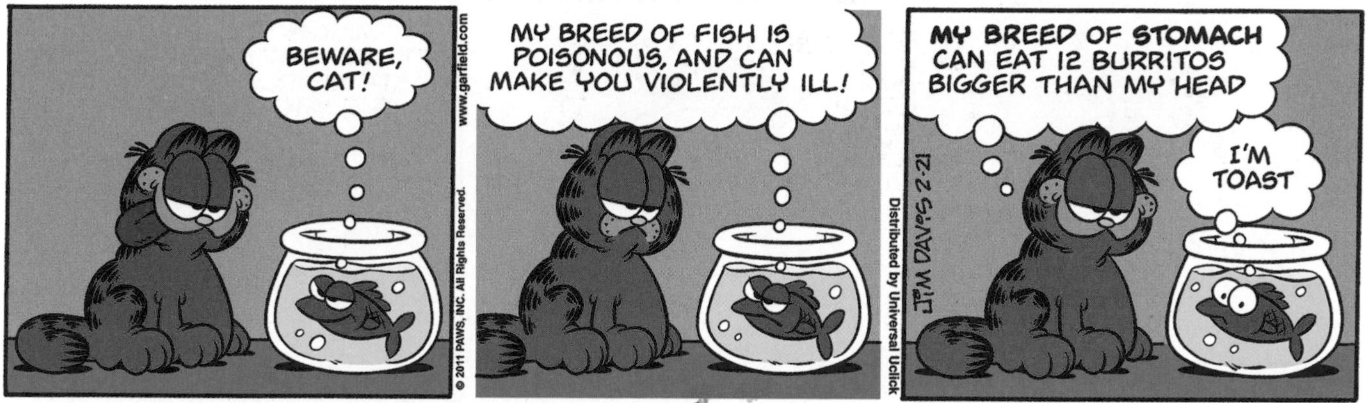
BEWARE, CAT!
© 2011 PAWS, INC. All Rights Reserved. www.garfield.com
MY BREED OF FISH IS POISONOUS, AND CAN MAKE YOU VIOLENTLY ILL!
Distributed by Universal Uclick
MY BREED OF STOMACH CAN EAT 12 BURRITOS BIGGER THAN MY HEAD
I'M TOAST
JIM DAVIS 2·21

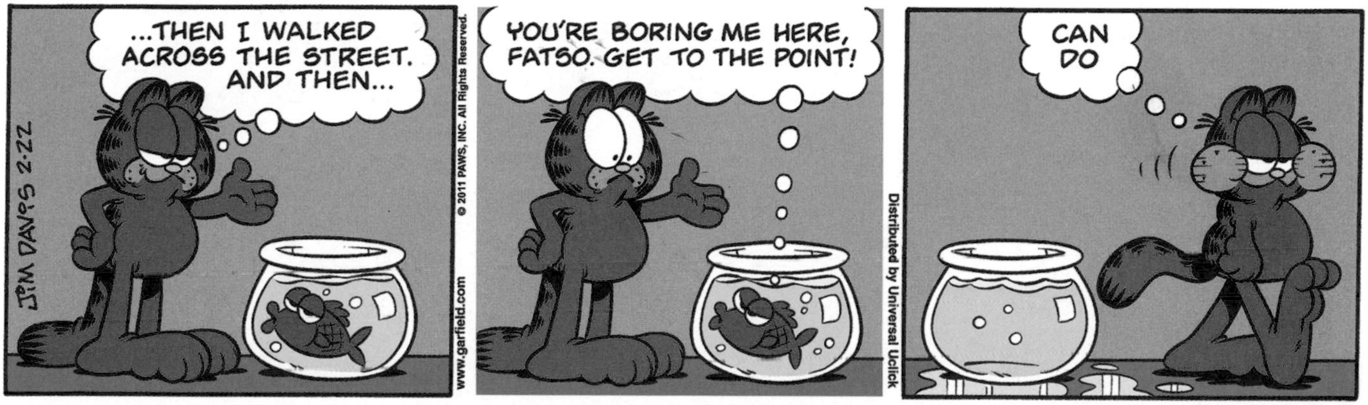
JIM DAVIS 2·22
...THEN I WALKED ACROSS THE STREET. AND THEN...
© 2011 PAWS, INC. All Rights Reserved. www.garfield.com
YOU'RE BORING ME HERE, FATSO. GET TO THE POINT!
Distributed by Universal Uclick
CAN DO

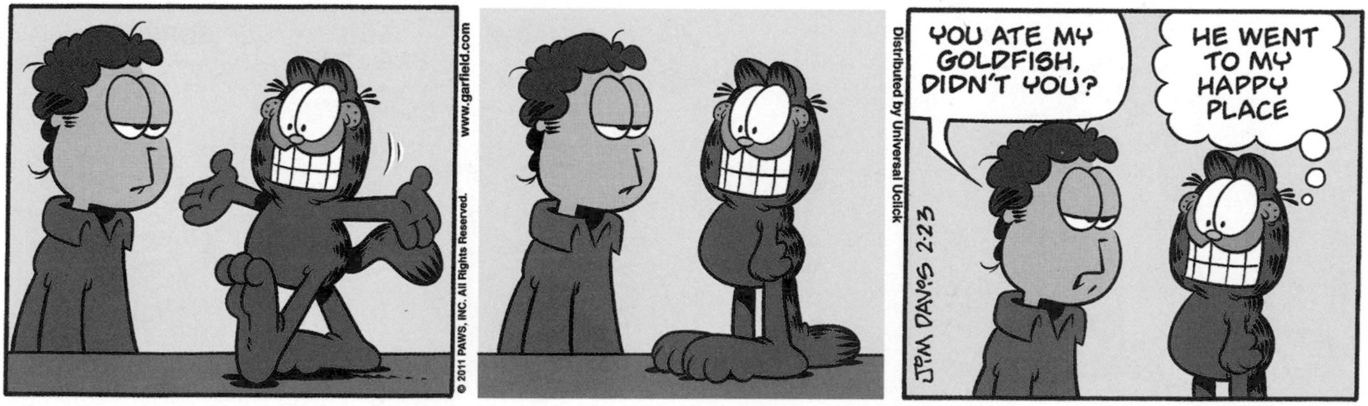
© 2011 PAWS, INC. All Rights Reserved. www.garfield.com
Distributed by Universal Uclick
JIM DAVIS 2·23
YOU ATE MY GOLDFISH, DIDN'T YOU?
HE WENT TO MY HAPPY PLACE

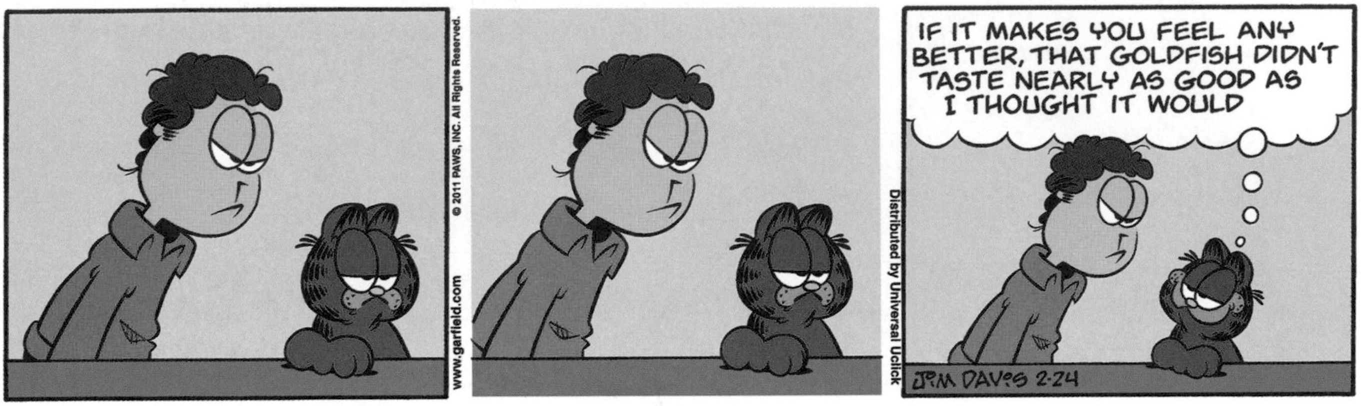
© 2011 PAWS, INC. All Rights Reserved.
www.garfield.com
IF IT MAKES YOU FEEL ANY BETTER, THAT GOLDFISH DIDN'T TASTE NEARLY AS GOOD AS I THOUGHT IT WOULD
Distributed by Universal Uclick
JIM DAVIS 2-24

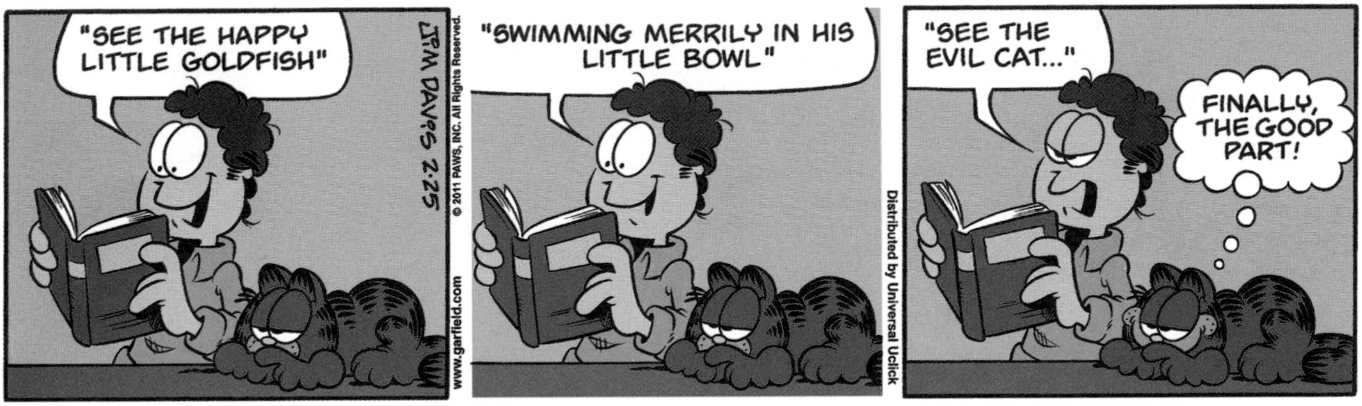
"SEE THE HAPPY LITTLE GOLDFISH"
JIM DAVIS 2-25
© 2011 PAWS, INC. All Rights Reserved.
www.garfield.com
"SWIMMING MERRILY IN HIS LITTLE BOWL"
Distributed by Universal Uclick
"SEE THE EVIL CAT..."
FINALLY, THE GOOD PART!

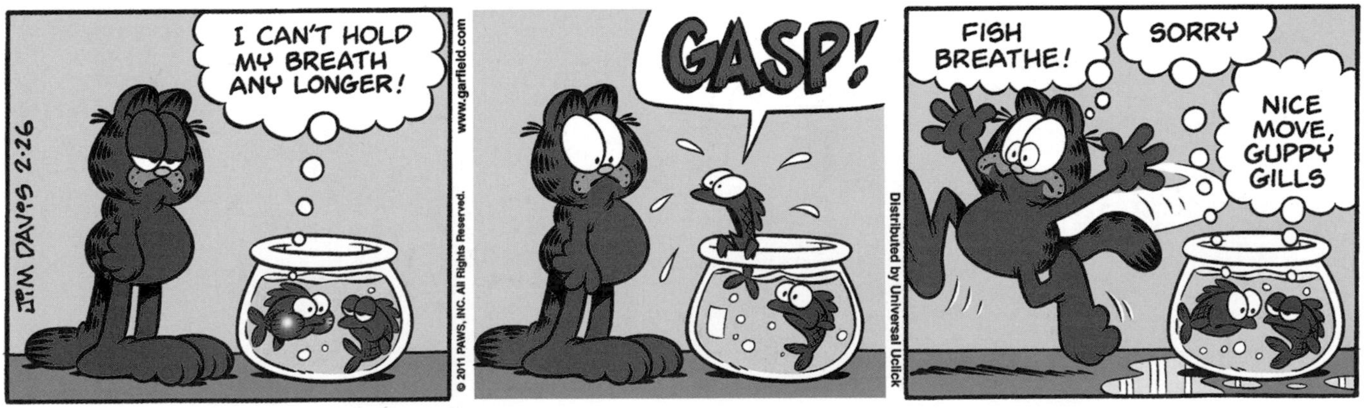
JIM DAVIS 2-26
I CAN'T HOLD MY BREATH ANY LONGER!
www.garfield.com
© 2011 PAWS, INC. All Rights Reserved.
GASP!
Distributed by Universal Uclick
FISH BREATHE!
SORRY
NICE MOVE, GUPPY GILLS

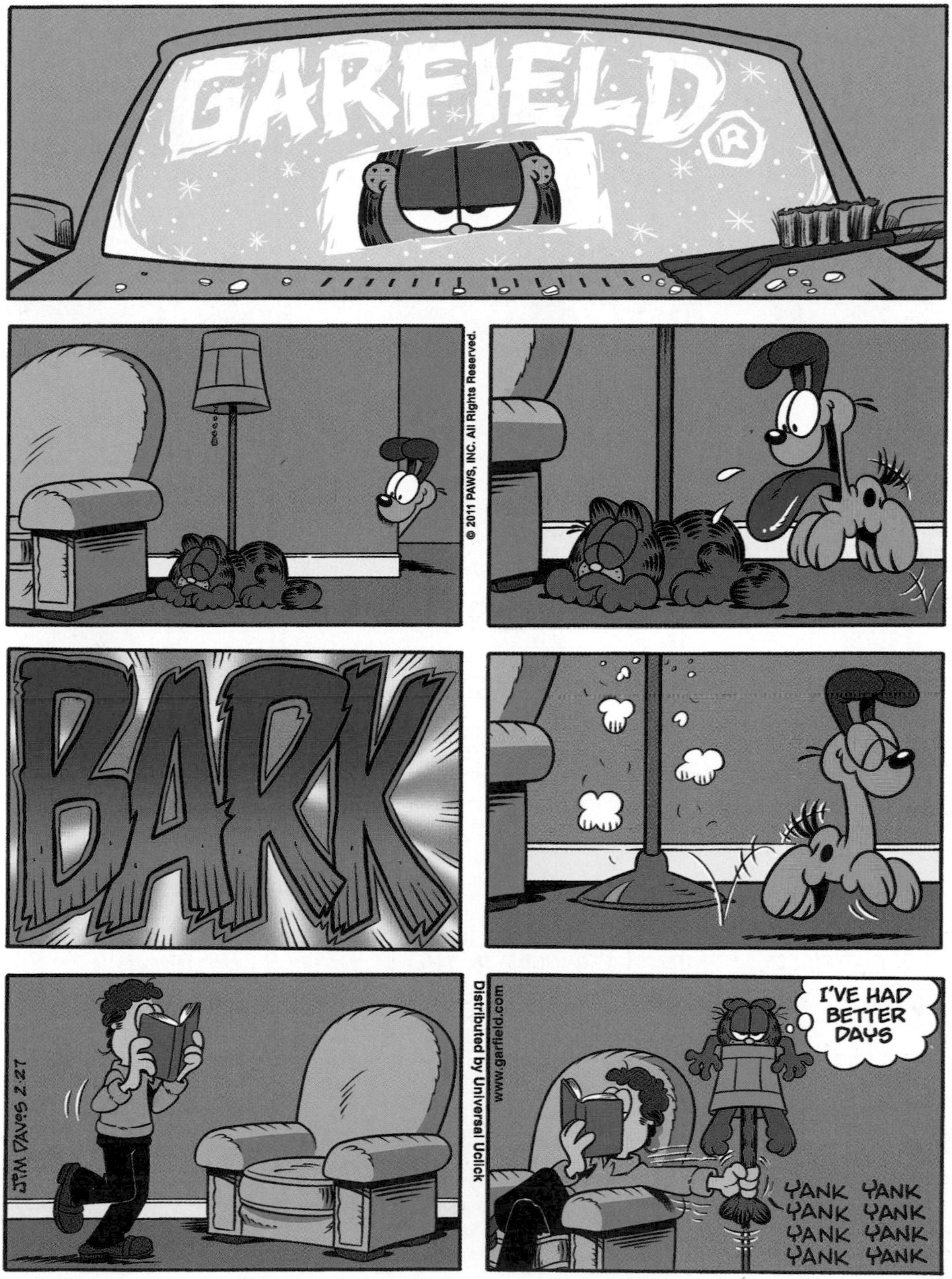
GARFIELD®
© 2011 PAWS, INC. All Rights Reserved.
BARK
JPM DAVIS 2-27
Distributed by Universal Uclick
www.garfield.com
I'VE HAD BETTER DAYS
YANK YANK YANK YANK YANK YANK YANK YANK

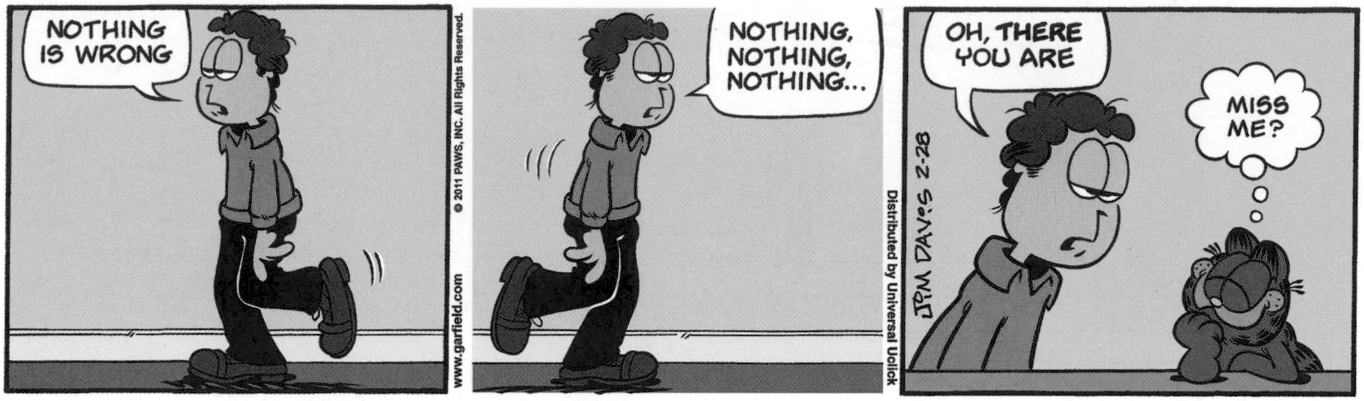
NOTHING IS WRONG
NOTHING, NOTHING, NOTHING...
OH, THERE YOU ARE
MISS ME?
JIM DAVIS 2-28
© 2011 PAWS, INC. All Rights Reserved.
www.garfield.com
Distributed by Universal Uclick

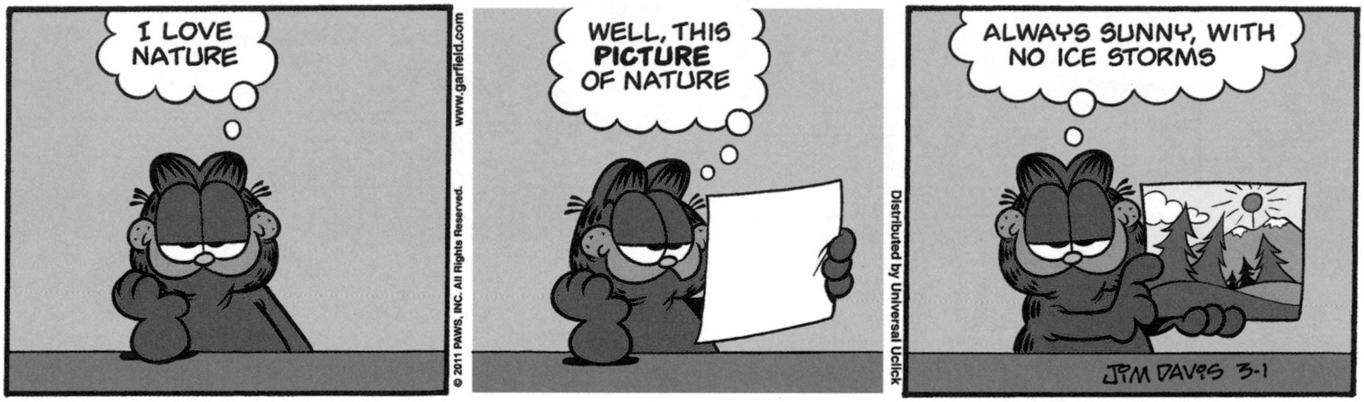
I LOVE NATURE
WELL, THIS PICTURE OF NATURE
ALWAYS SUNNY, WITH NO ICE STORMS
JIM DAVIS 3-1
© 2011 PAWS, INC. All Rights Reserved.
www.garfield.com
Distributed by Universal Uclick

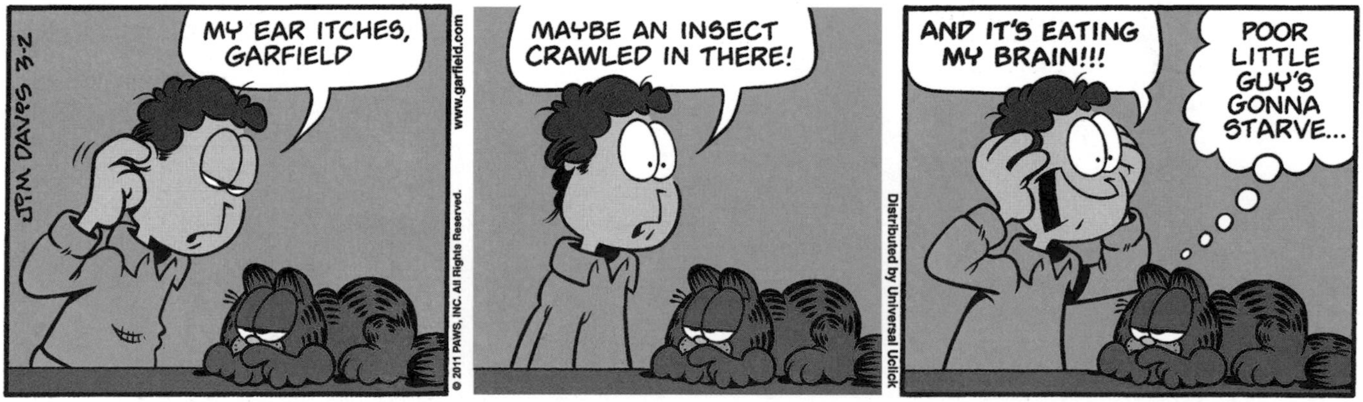
MY EAR ITCHES, GARFIELD
MAYBE AN INSECT CRAWLED IN THERE!
AND IT'S EATING MY BRAIN!!!
POOR LITTLE GUY'S GONNA STARVE...
JIM DAVIS 3-2
© 2011 PAWS, INC. All Rights Reserved.
www.garfield.com
Distributed by Universal Uclick

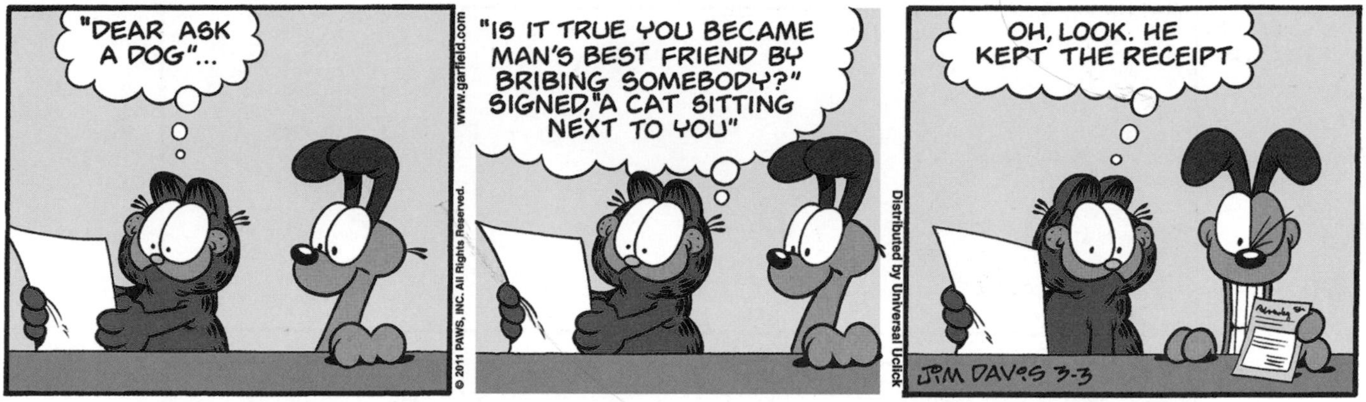
"DEAR ASK A DOG"...
"IS IT TRUE YOU BECAME MAN'S BEST FRIEND BY BRIBING SOMEBODY?" SIGNED,"A CAT SITTING NEXT TO YOU"
OH, LOOK. HE KEPT THE RECEIPT
© 2011 PAWS, INC. All Rights Reserved. www.garfield.com
Distributed by Universal Uclick
JIM DAVIS 3-3

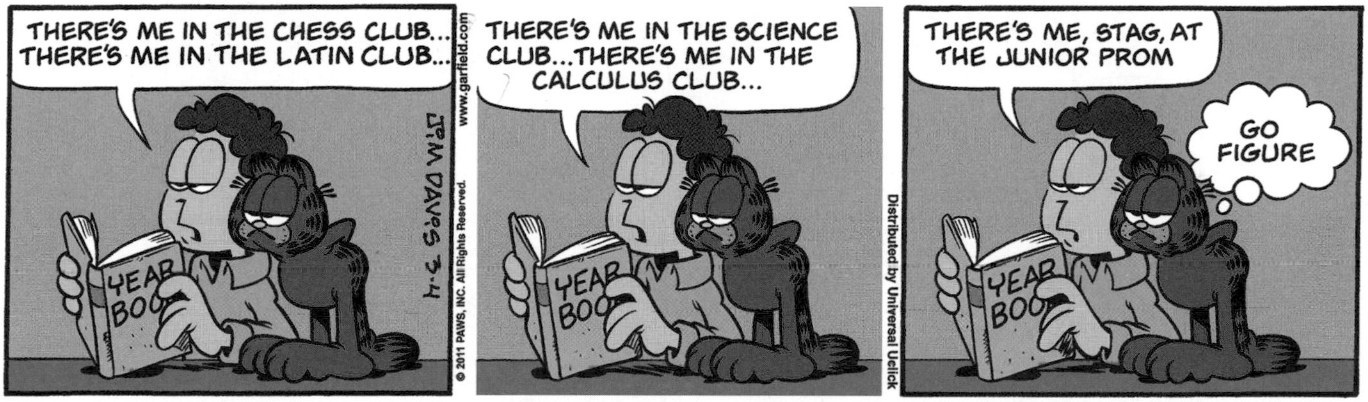
THERE'S ME IN THE CHESS CLUB... THERE'S ME IN THE LATIN CLUB...
THERE'S ME IN THE SCIENCE CLUB...THERE'S ME IN THE CALCULUS CLUB...
THERE'S ME, STAG, AT THE JUNIOR PROM
GO FIGURE
YEAR BOO
JIM DAVIS 3-4
© 2011 PAWS, INC. All Rights Reserved. www.garfield.com
Distributed by Universal Uclick

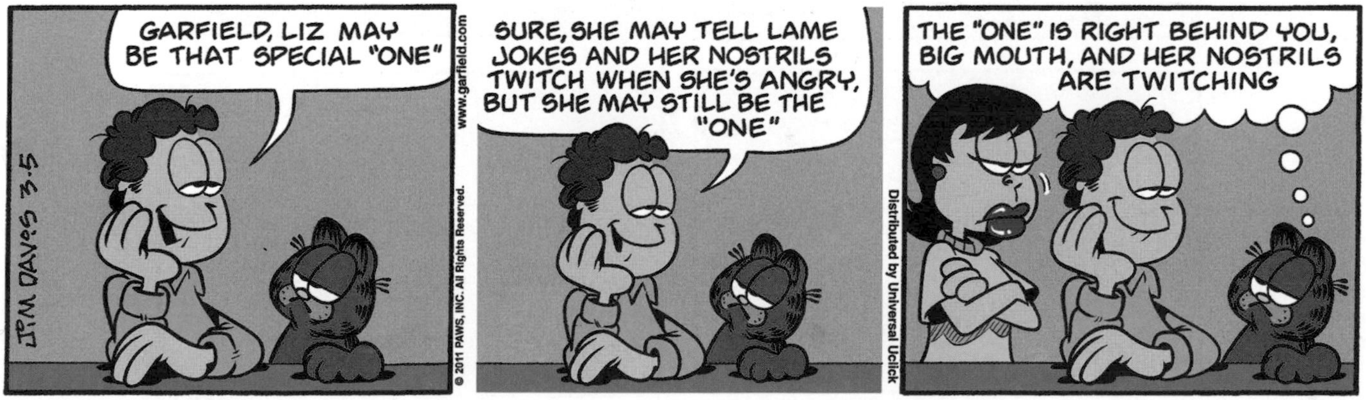
GARFIELD, LIZ MAY BE THAT SPECIAL "ONE"
SURE, SHE MAY TELL LAME JOKES AND HER NOSTRILS TWITCH WHEN SHE'S ANGRY, BUT SHE MAY STILL BE THE "ONE"
THE "ONE" IS RIGHT BEHIND YOU, BIG MOUTH, AND HER NOSTRILS ARE TWITCHING
JIM DAVIS 3-5
© 2011 PAWS, INC. All Rights Reserved. www.garfield.com
Distributed by Universal Uclick

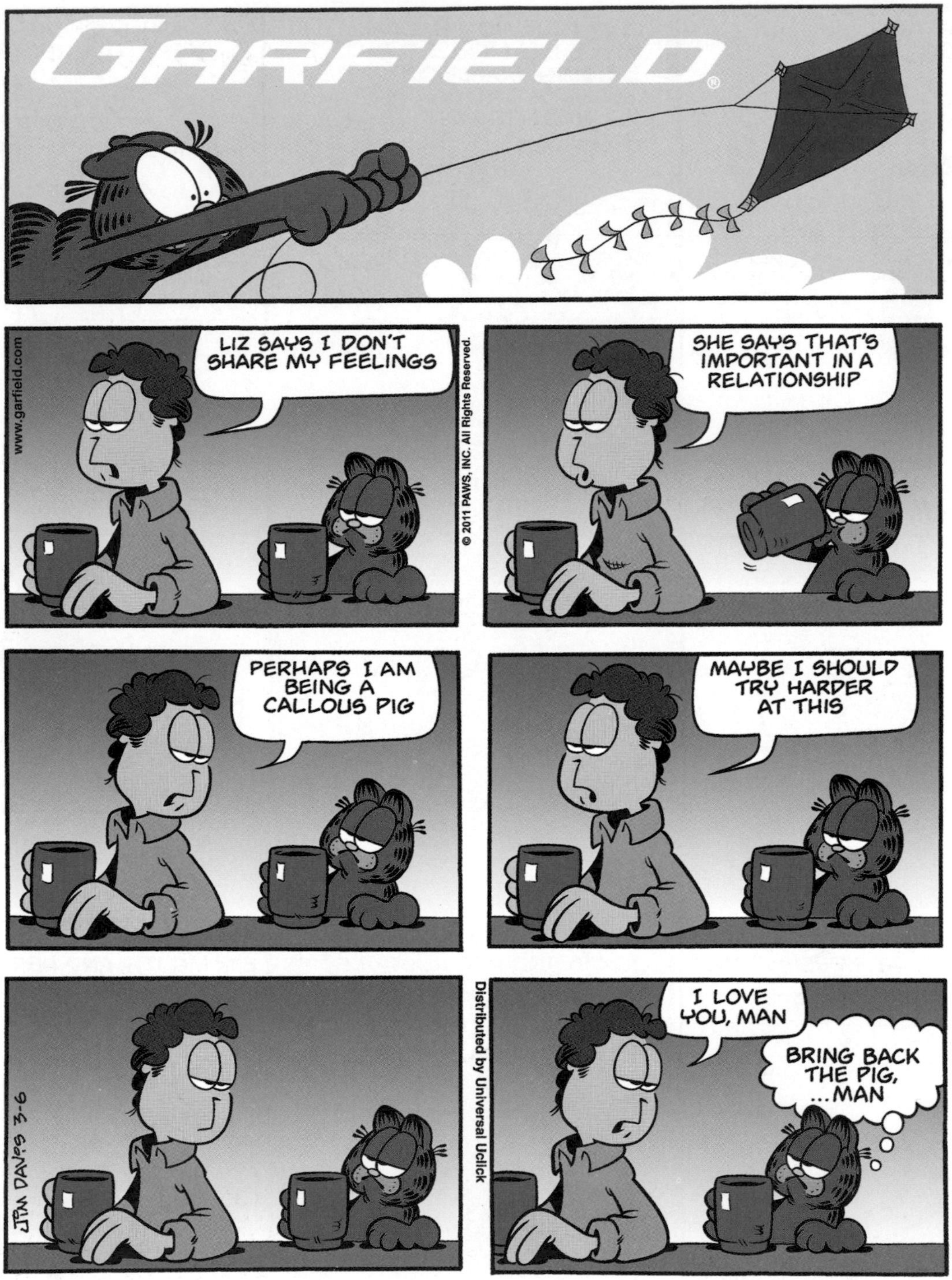
GARFIELD®
www.garfield.com
© 2011 PAWS, INC. All Rights Reserved.
LIZ SAYS I DON'T SHARE MY FEELINGS
SHE SAYS THAT'S IMPORTANT IN A RELATIONSHIP
PERHAPS I AM BEING A CALLOUS PIG
MAYBE I SHOULD TRY HARDER AT THIS
JIM DAVIS 3-6
Distributed by Universal Uclick
I LOVE YOU, MAN
BRING BACK THE PIG, ...MAN

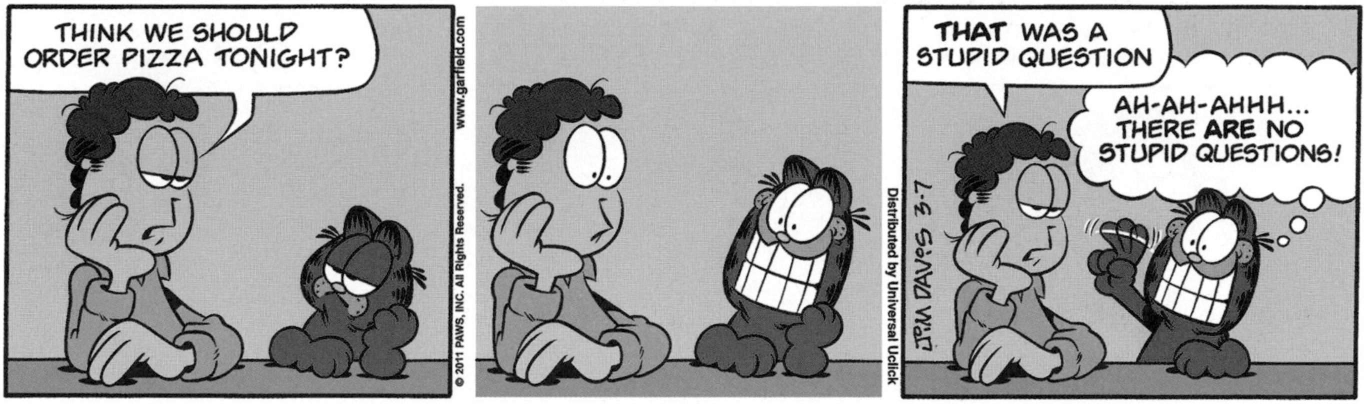
THINK WE SHOULD ORDER PIZZA TONIGHT?
THAT WAS A STUPID QUESTION
AH-AH-AHHH... THERE ARE NO STUPID QUESTIONS!
JIM DAVIS 3-7
© 2011 PAWS, INC. All Rights Reserved. www.garfield.com
Distributed by Universal Uclick

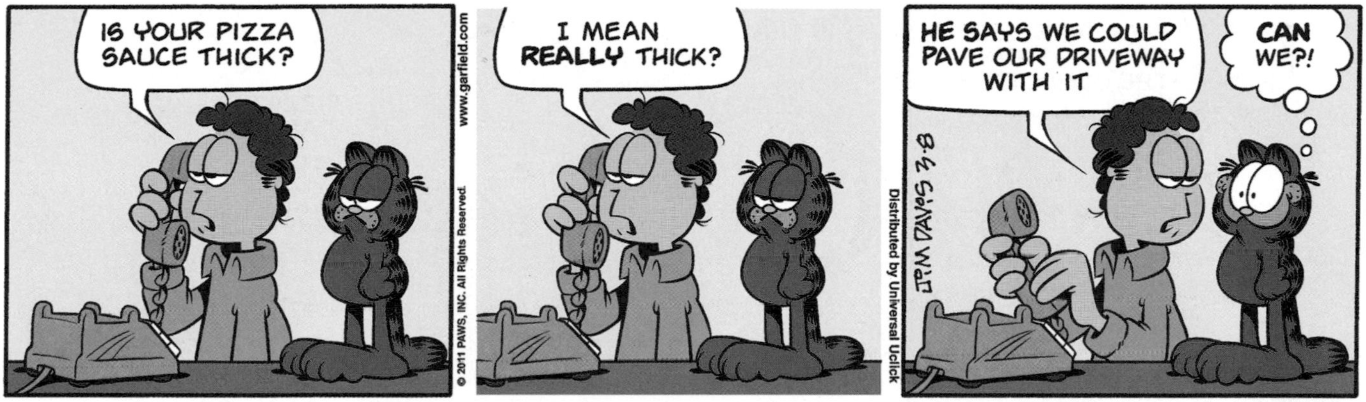
IS YOUR PIZZA SAUCE THICK?
I MEAN REALLY THICK?
HE SAYS WE COULD PAVE OUR DRIVEWAY WITH IT
CAN WE?!
JIM DAVIS 3-8
© 2011 PAWS, INC. All Rights Reserved. www.garfield.com
Distributed by Universal Uclick

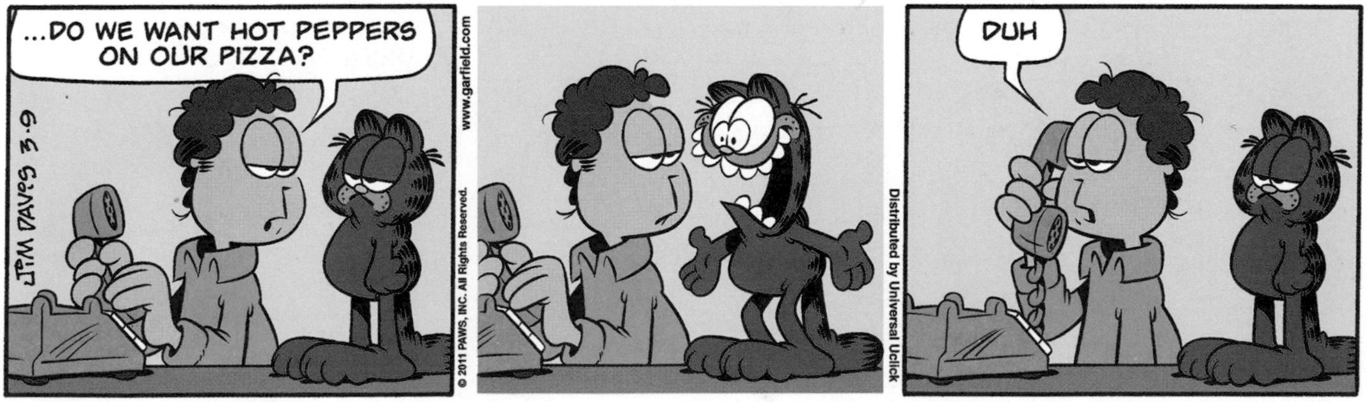
...DO WE WANT HOT PEPPERS ON OUR PIZZA?
DUH
JIM DAVIS 3-9
© 2011 PAWS, INC. All Rights Reserved. www.garfield.com
Distributed by Universal Uclick

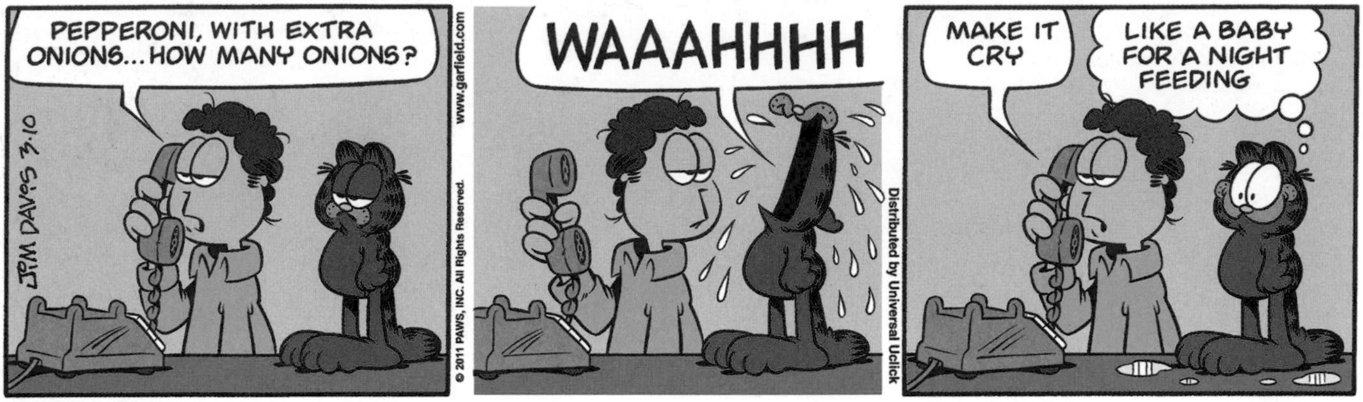
PEPPERONI, WITH EXTRA ONIONS... HOW MANY ONIONS?
JIM DAVIS 3-10
© 2011 PAWS, INC. All Rights Reserved. www.garfield.com
WAAAHHHH
Distributed by Universal Uclick
MAKE IT CRY
LIKE A BABY FOR A NIGHT FEEDING

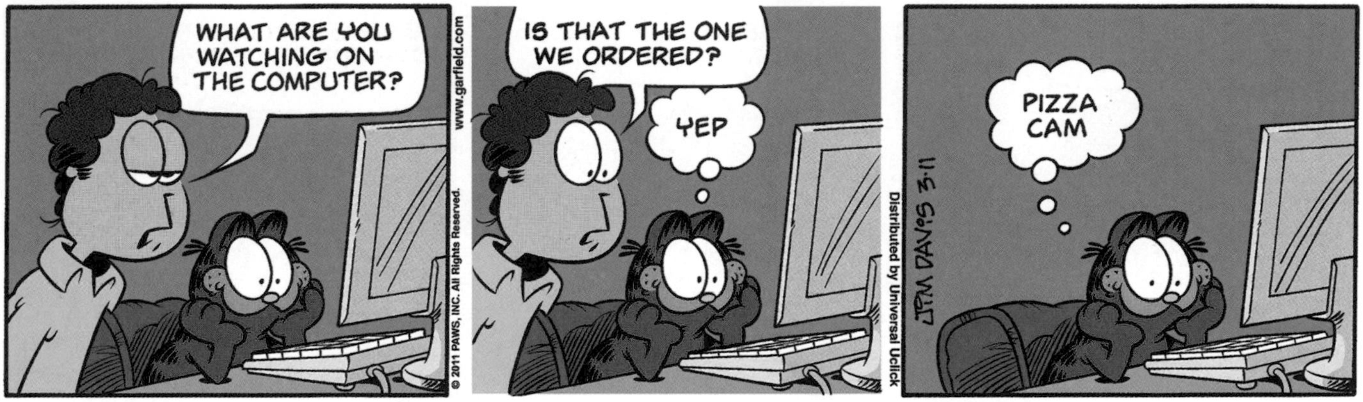
WHAT ARE YOU WATCHING ON THE COMPUTER?
© 2011 PAWS, INC. All Rights Reserved. www.garfield.com
IS THAT THE ONE WE ORDERED?
YEP
Distributed by Universal Uclick
JIM DAVIS 3-11
PIZZA CAM

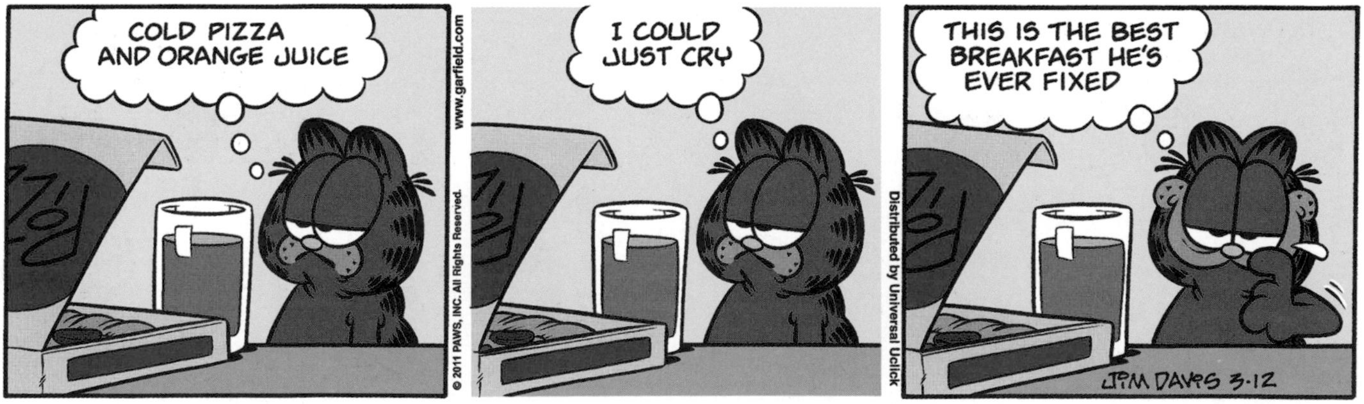
COLD PIZZA AND ORANGE JUICE
© 2011 PAWS, INC. All Rights Reserved. www.garfield.com
I COULD JUST CRY
Distributed by Universal Uclick
THIS IS THE BEST BREAKFAST HE'S EVER FIXED
JIM DAVIS 3-12

NOT-SO-MONSTROUS MONSTERS

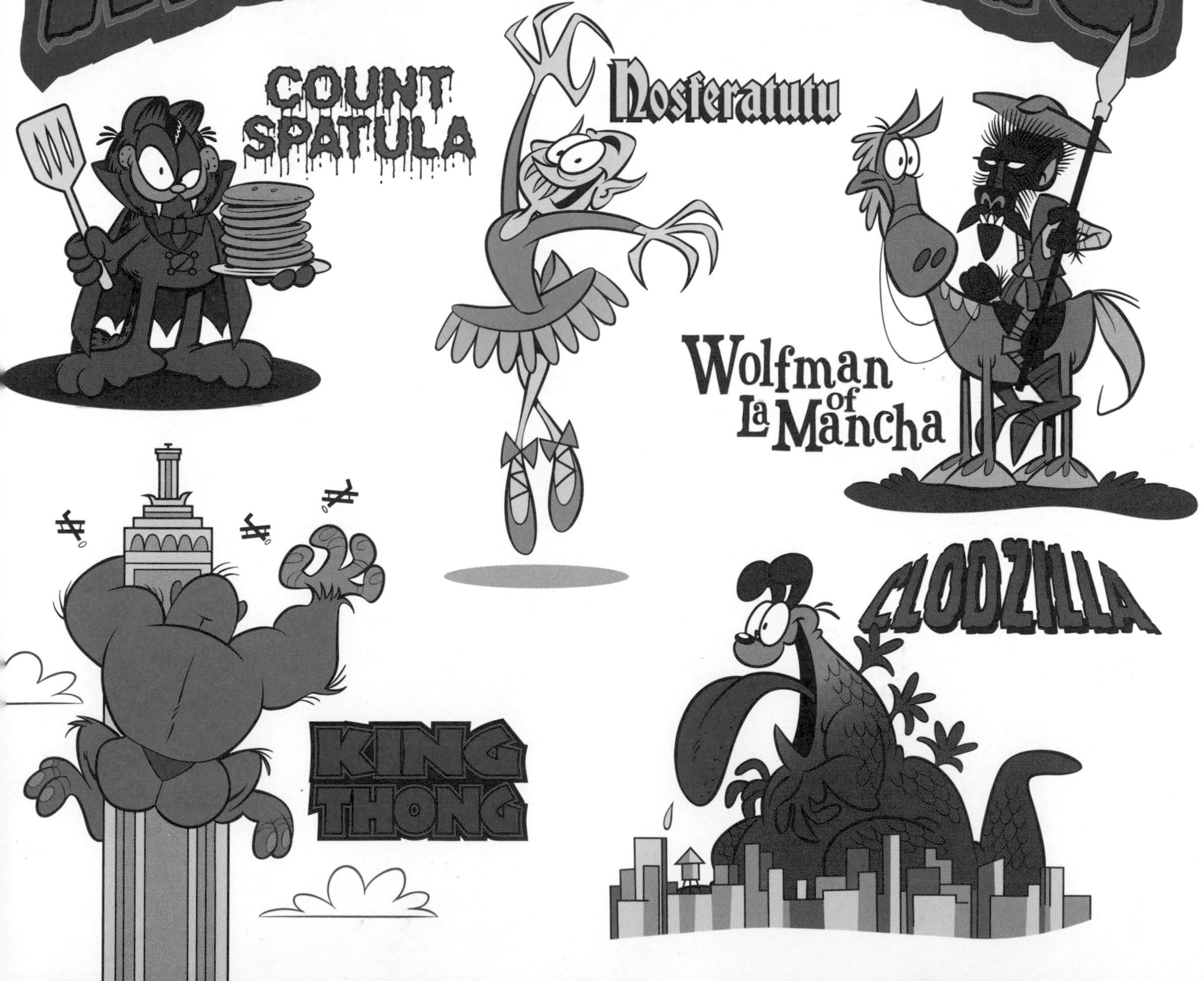
COUNT SPATULA
Nosferatutu
Wolfman of La Mancha
KING THONG
CLODZILLA

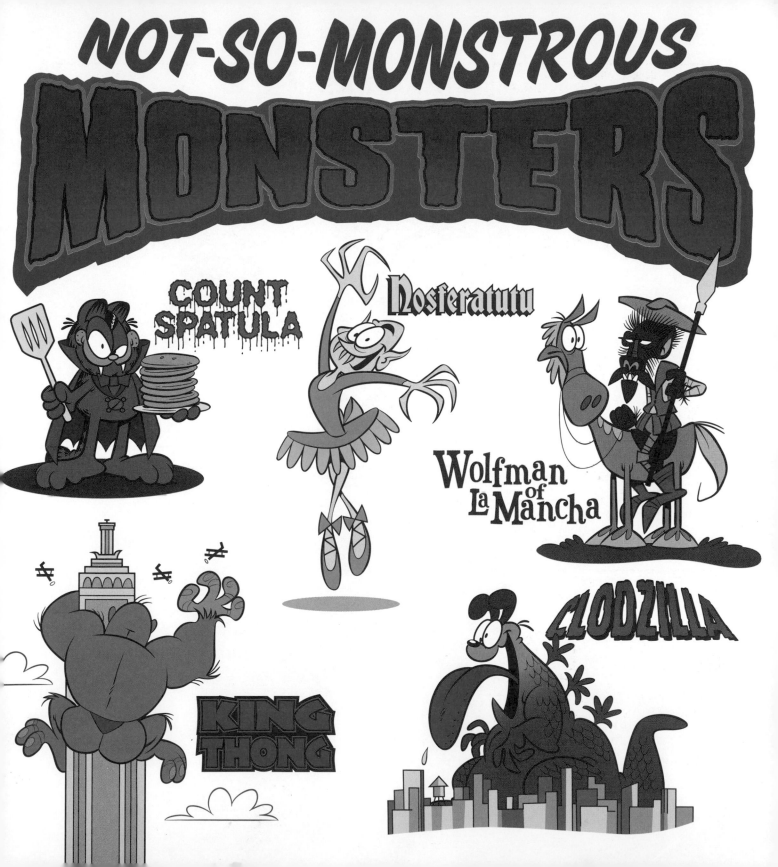

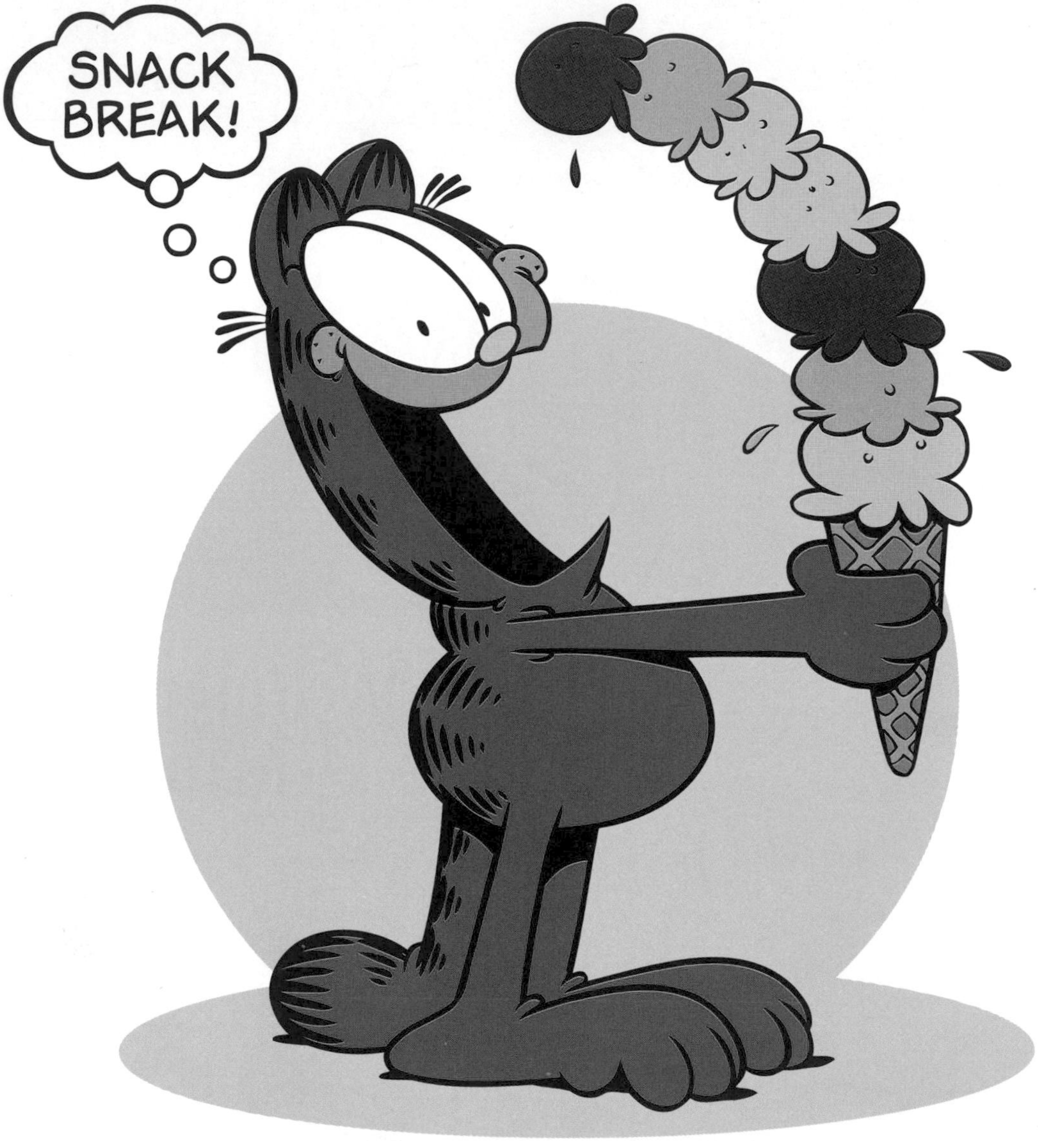
SNACK BREAK!

Garfield
SOUPED UP

BY JIM DAVIS

Ballantine Books • **New York**

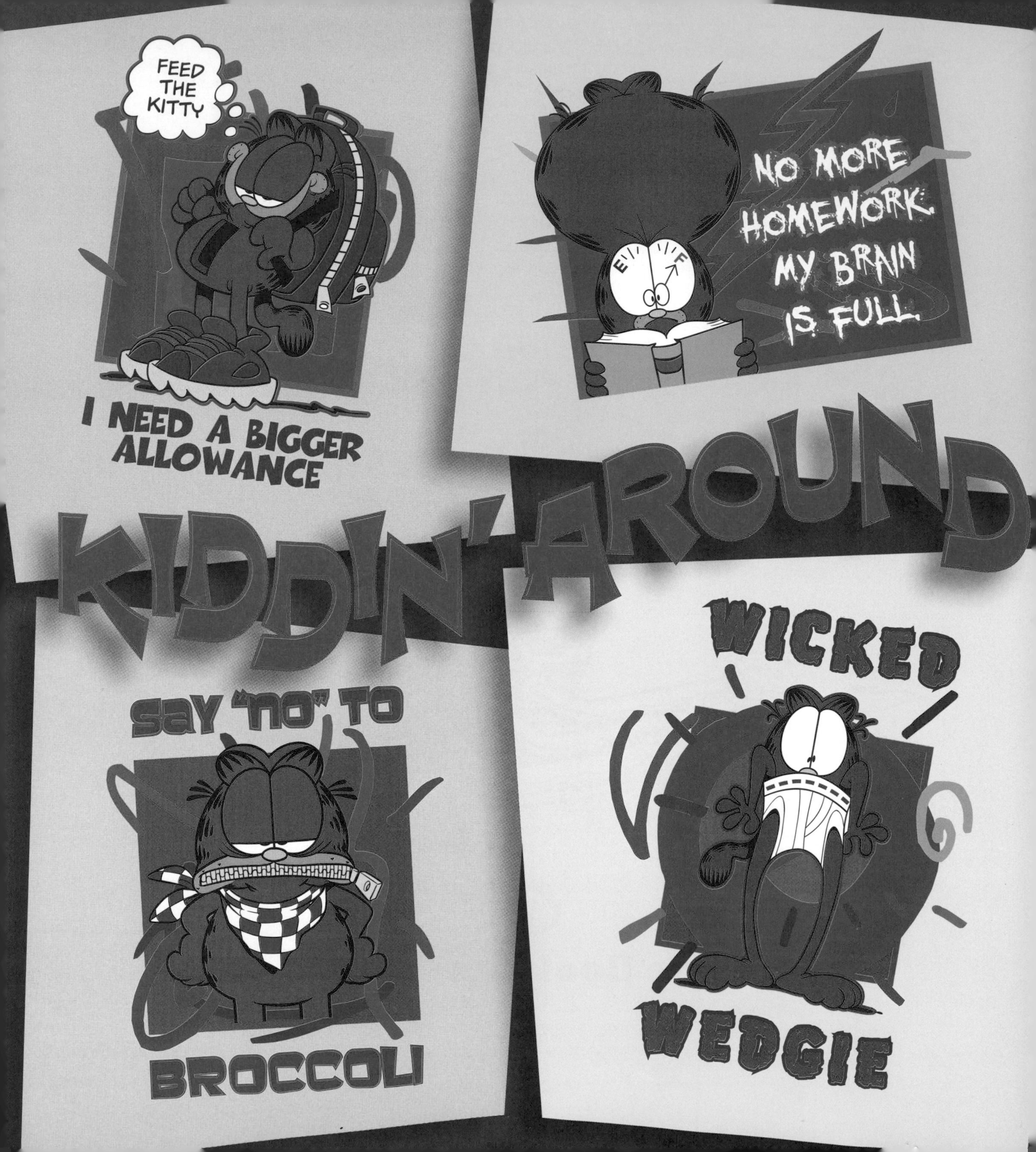
FEED THE KITTY
I NEED A BIGGER ALLOWANCE
NO MORE HOMEWORK MY BRAIN IS FULL
KIDDIN' AROUND
SAY "NO" TO BROCCOLI
WICKED WEDGIE

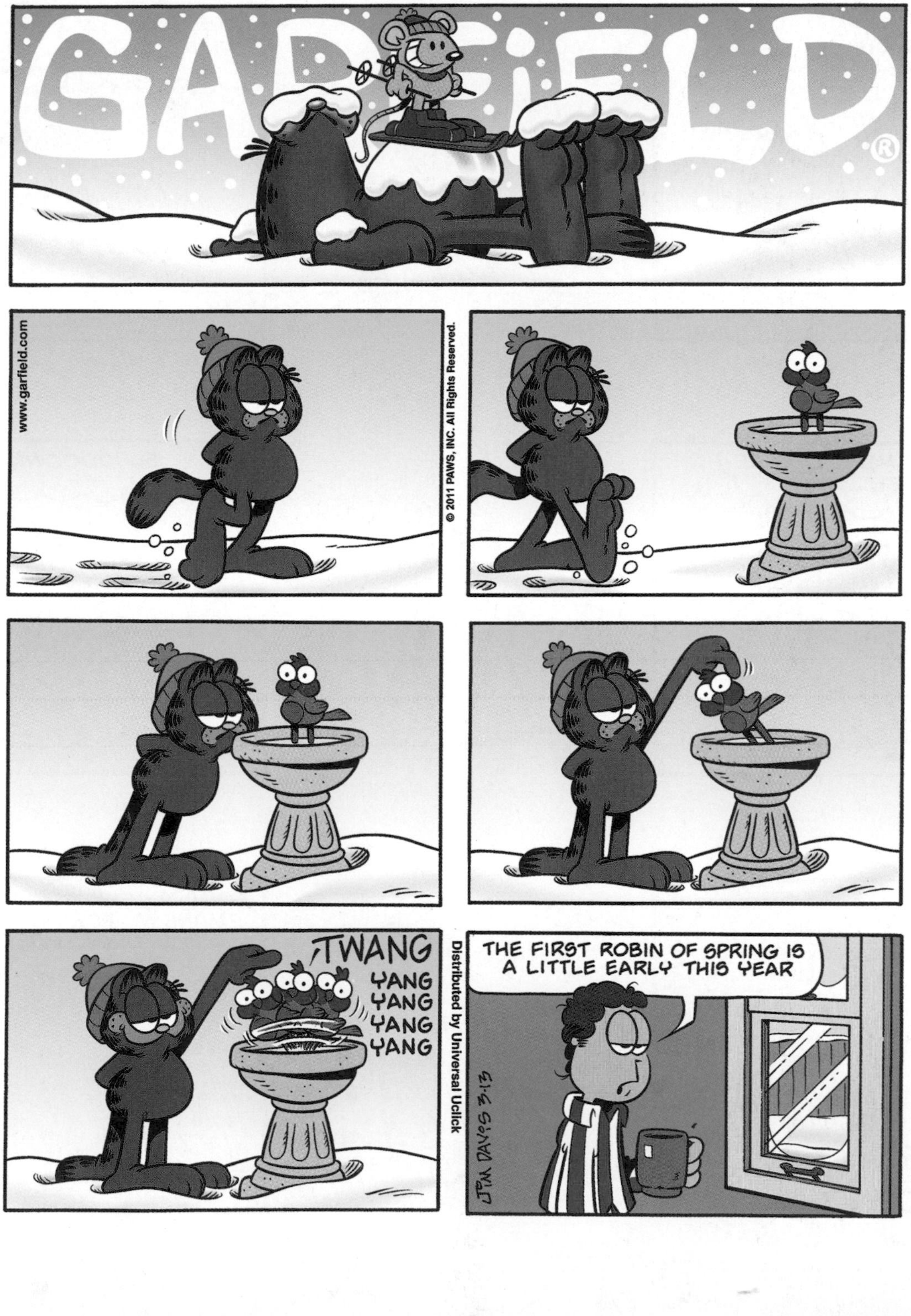
GARFIELD®
www.garfield.com
© 2011 PAWS, INC. All Rights Reserved.
TWANG
YANG
YANG
YANG
YANG
Distributed by Universal Uclick
JPM DAVPS 3-13
THE FIRST ROBIN OF SPRING IS A LITTLE EARLY THIS YEAR

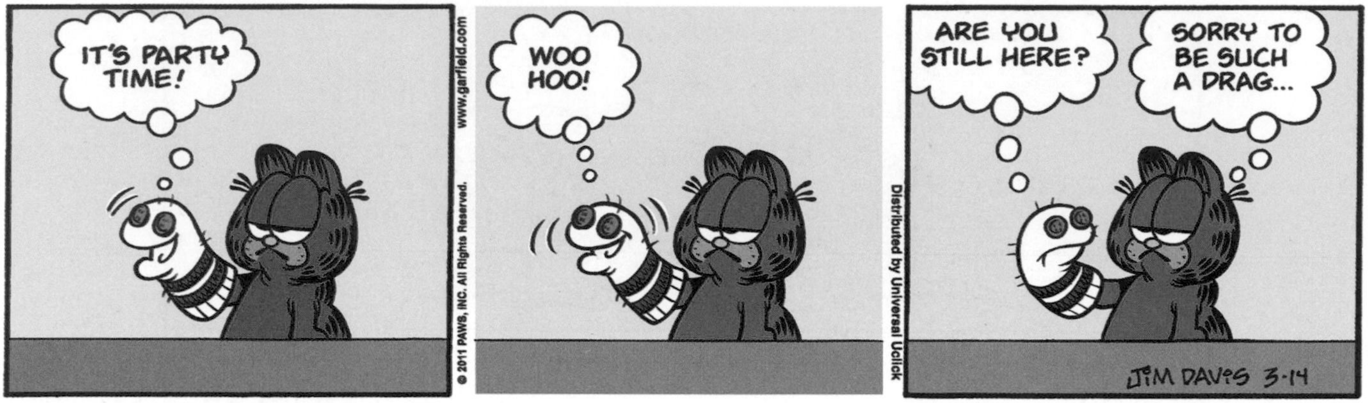
IT'S PARTY TIME!
WOO HOO!
ARE YOU STILL HERE?
SORRY TO BE SUCH A DRAG...
JIM DAVIS 3-14
© 2011 PAWS, INC. All Rights Reserved. www.garfield.com
Distributed by Universal Uclick

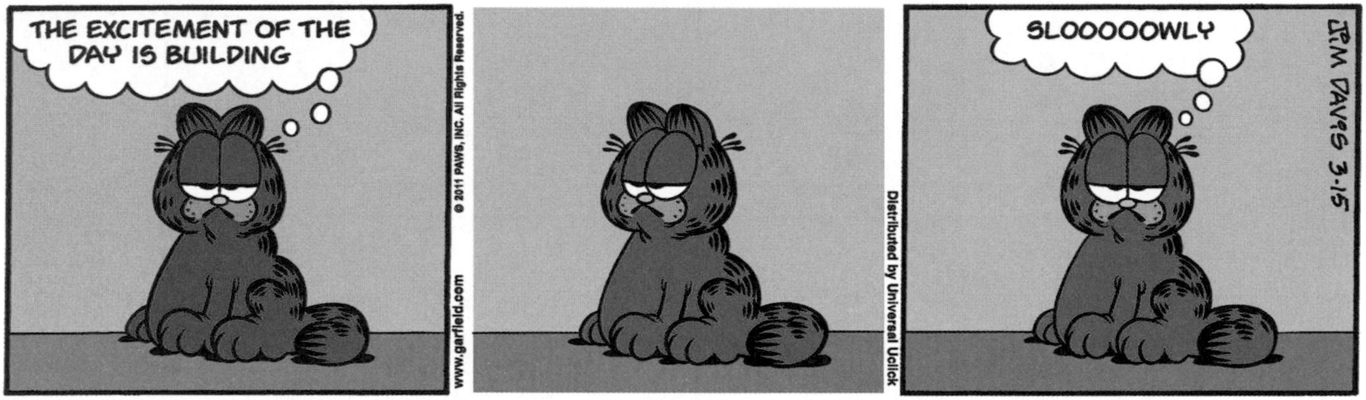
THE EXCITEMENT OF THE DAY IS BUILDING
SLOOOOOWLY
JIM DAVIS 3-15
© 2011 PAWS, INC. All Rights Reserved. www.garfield.com
Distributed by Universal Uclick

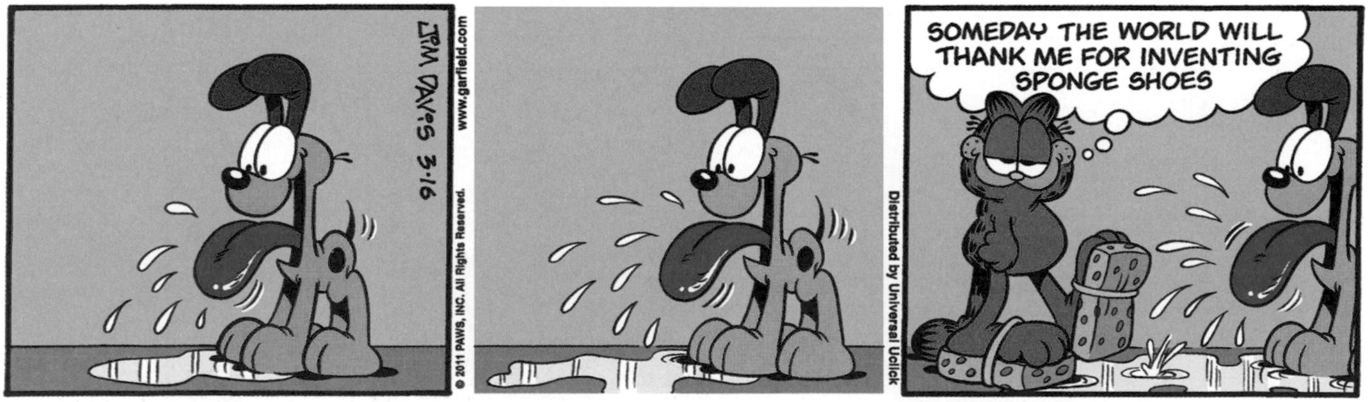
JIM DAVIS 3-16
SOMEDAY THE WORLD WILL THANK ME FOR INVENTING SPONGE SHOES
© 2011 PAWS, INC. All Rights Reserved. www.garfield.com
Distributed by Universal Uclick

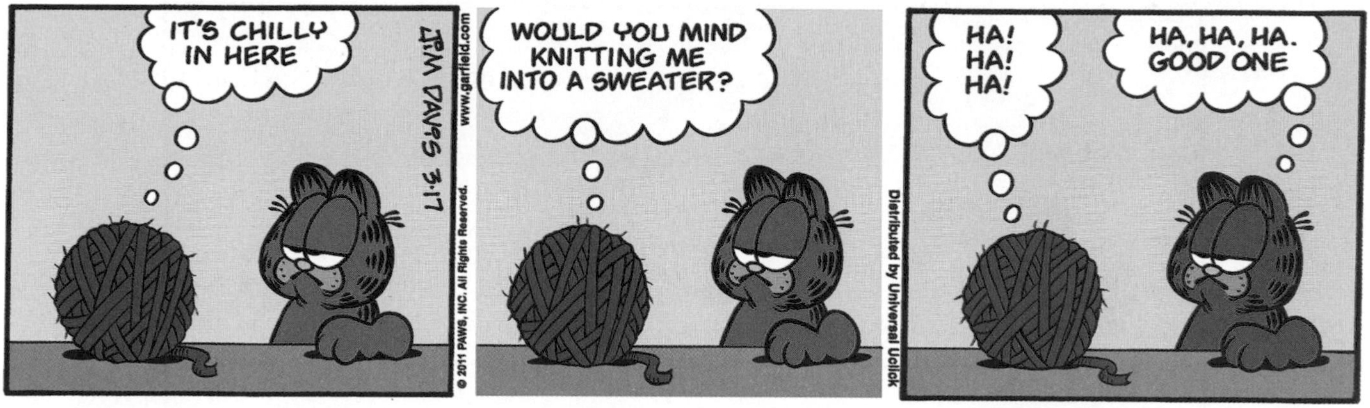
IT'S CHILLY IN HERE
JIM DAVIS 3-17
www.garfield.com
© 2011 PAWS, INC. All Rights Reserved.
WOULD YOU MIND KNITTING ME INTO A SWEATER?
Distributed by Universal Uclick
HA! HA! HA!
HA, HA, HA. GOOD ONE

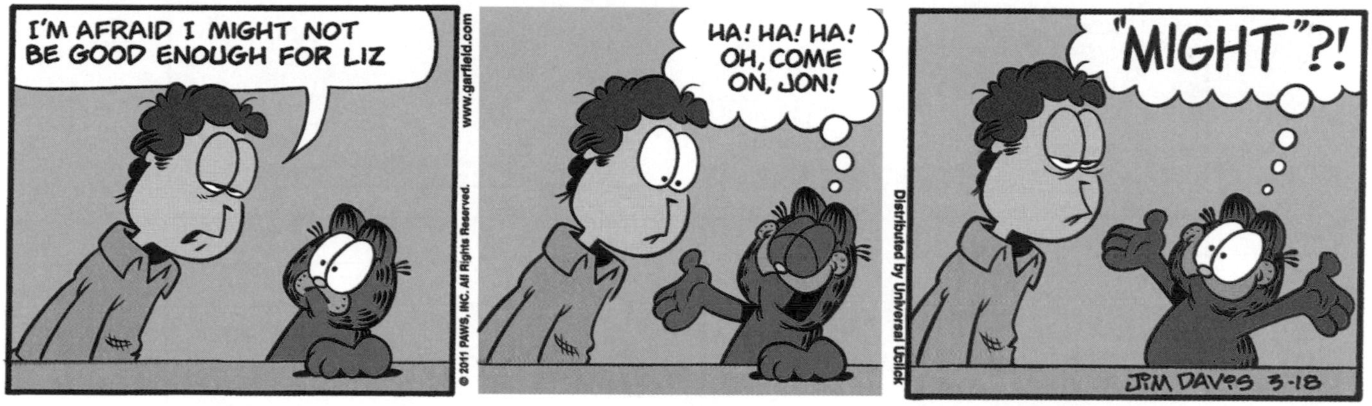
I'M AFRAID I MIGHT NOT BE GOOD ENOUGH FOR LIZ
www.garfield.com
© 2011 PAWS, INC. All Rights Reserved.
HA! HA! HA! OH, COME ON, JON!
Distributed by Universal Uclick
"MIGHT"?!
JIM DAVIS 3-18

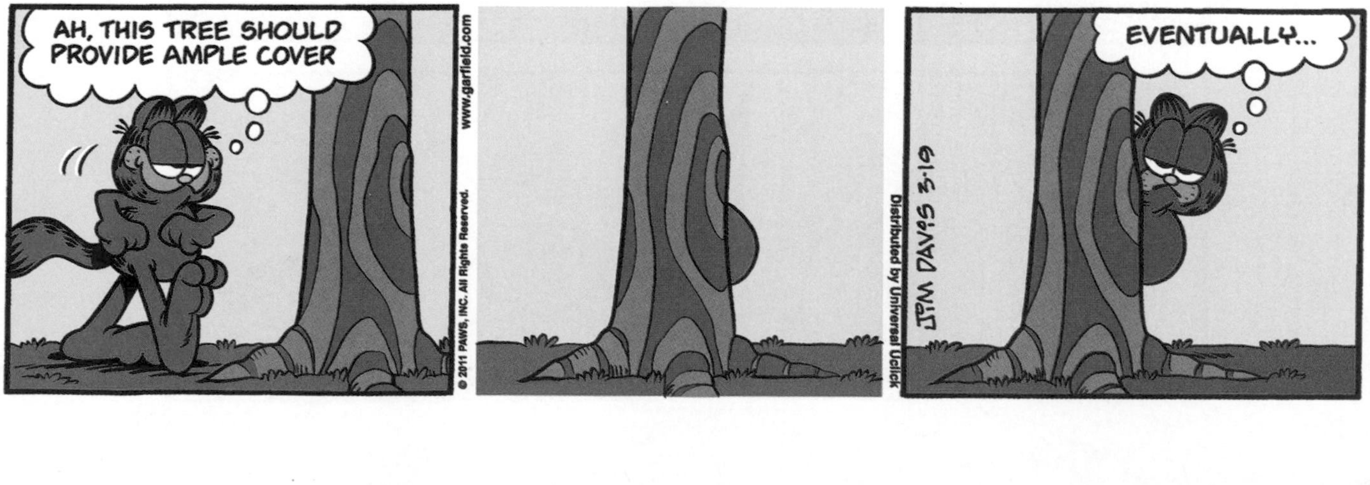
AH, THIS TREE SHOULD PROVIDE AMPLE COVER
www.garfield.com
© 2011 PAWS, INC. All Rights Reserved.
JIM DAVIS 3-19
Distributed by Universal Uclick
EVENTUALLY...

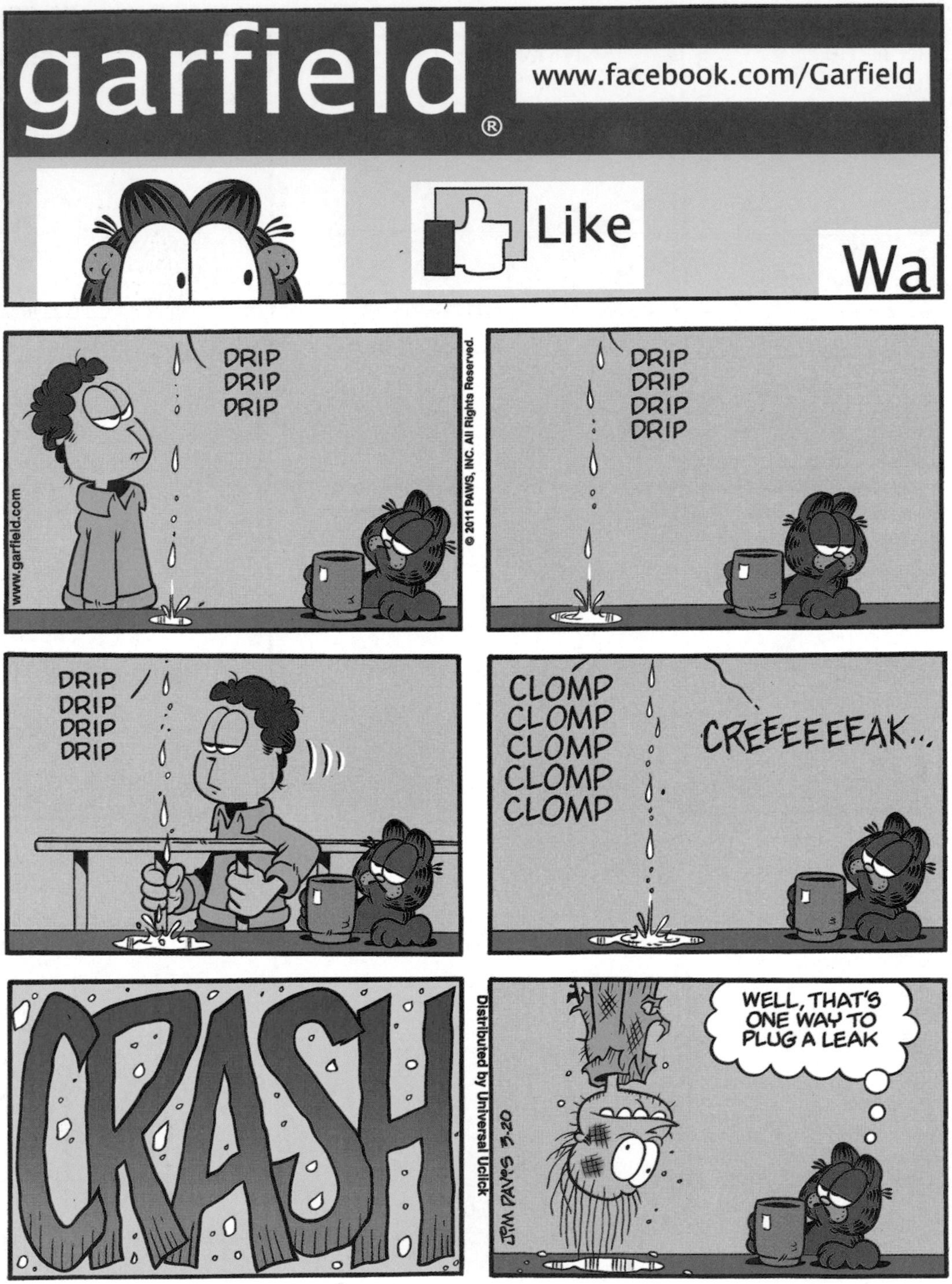
garfield®
www.facebook.com/Garfield
Like
Wal
DRIP
DRIP
DRIP
www.garfield.com
© 2011 PAWS, INC. All Rights Reserved.
DRIP
DRIP
DRIP
DRIP
DRIP
DRIP
DRIP
DRIP
CLOMP
CLOMP
CLOMP
CLOMP
CLOMP
CREEEEEEAK...
CRASH
Distributed by Universal Uclick
JIM DAVIS 3-20
WELL, THAT'S ONE WAY TO PLUG A LEAK

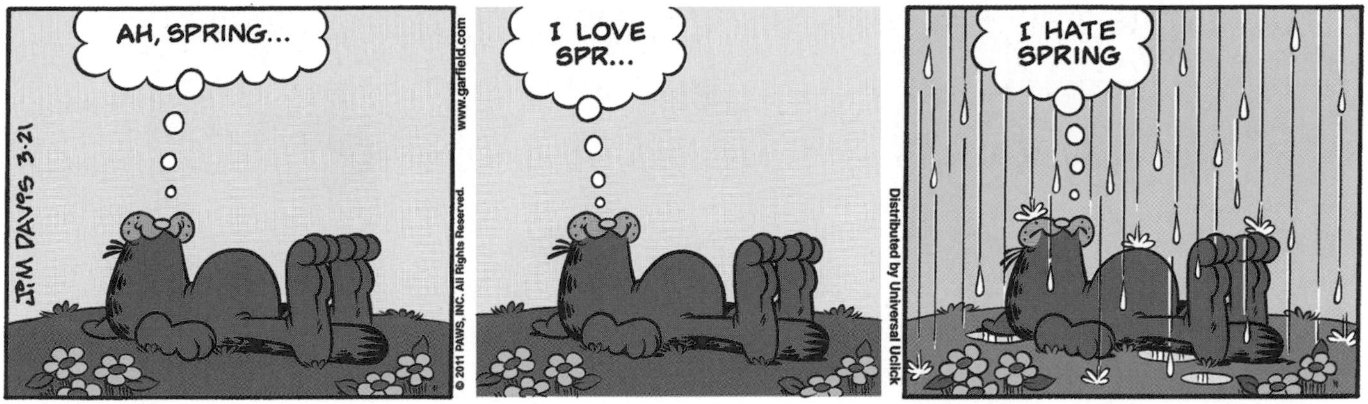
AH, SPRING...
JIM DAVIS 3-21
© 2011 PAWS, INC. All Rights Reserved.
www.garfield.com
I LOVE SPR...
Distributed by Universal Uclick
I HATE SPRING

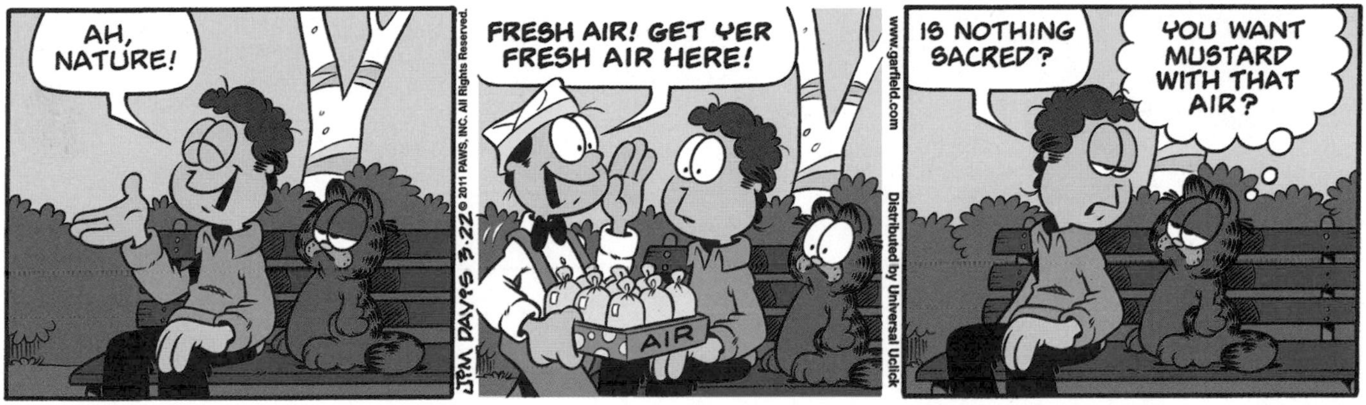
AH, NATURE!
© 2011 PAWS, INC. All Rights Reserved.
JIM DAVIS 3-22
FRESH AIR! GET YER FRESH AIR HERE!
AIR
www.garfield.com
Distributed by Universal Uclick
IS NOTHING SACRED?
YOU WANT MUSTARD WITH THAT AIR?

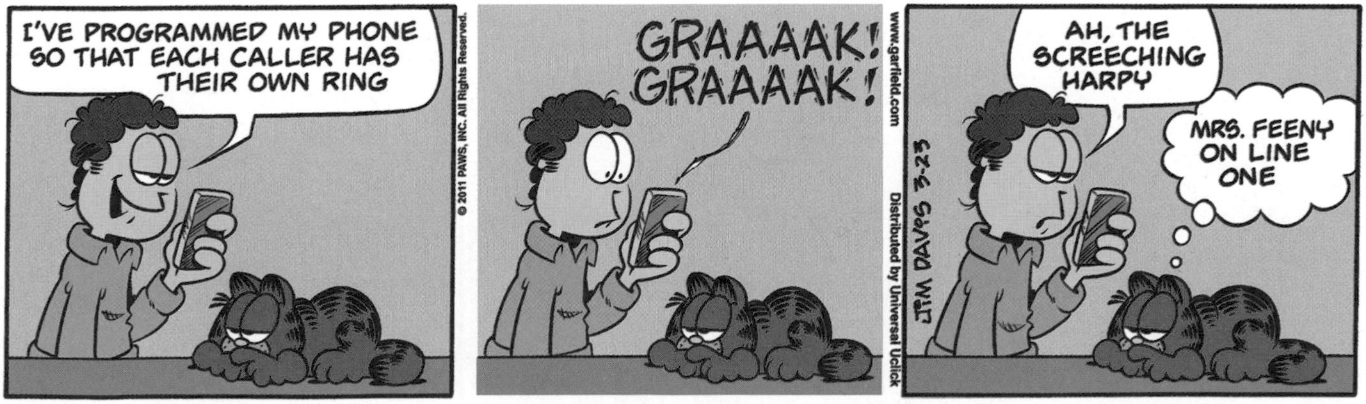
I'VE PROGRAMMED MY PHONE SO THAT EACH CALLER HAS THEIR OWN RING
© 2011 PAWS, INC. All Rights Reserved.
GRAAAAK! GRAAAAK!
www.garfield.com
Distributed by Universal Uclick
JIM DAVIS 3-23
AH, THE SCREECHING HARPY
MRS. FEENY ON LINE ONE

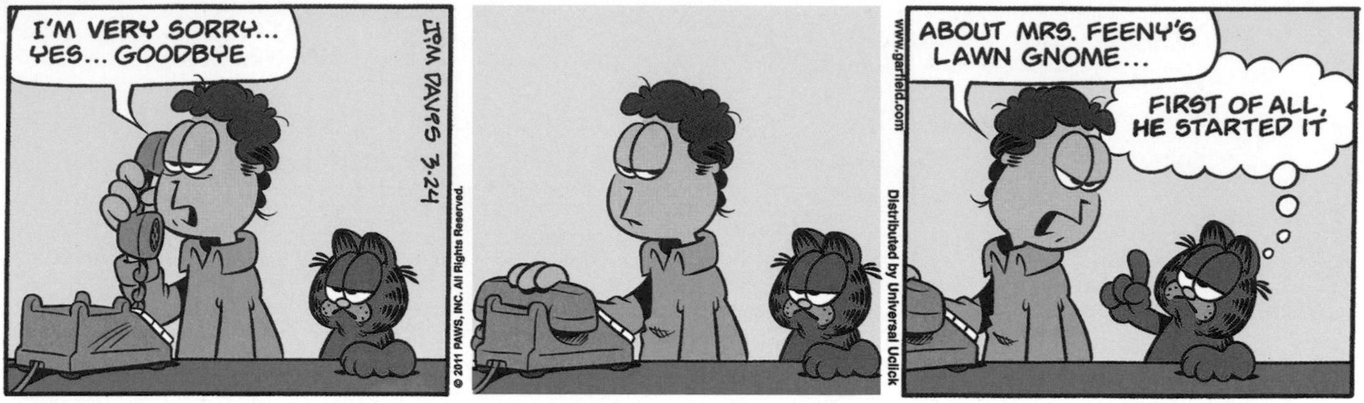
I'M VERY SORRY... YES... GOODBYE
JIM DAVIS 3-24
© 2011 PAWS, INC. All Rights Reserved.
www.garfield.com
Distributed by Universal Uclick
ABOUT MRS. FEENY'S LAWN GNOME...
FIRST OF ALL, HE STARTED IT

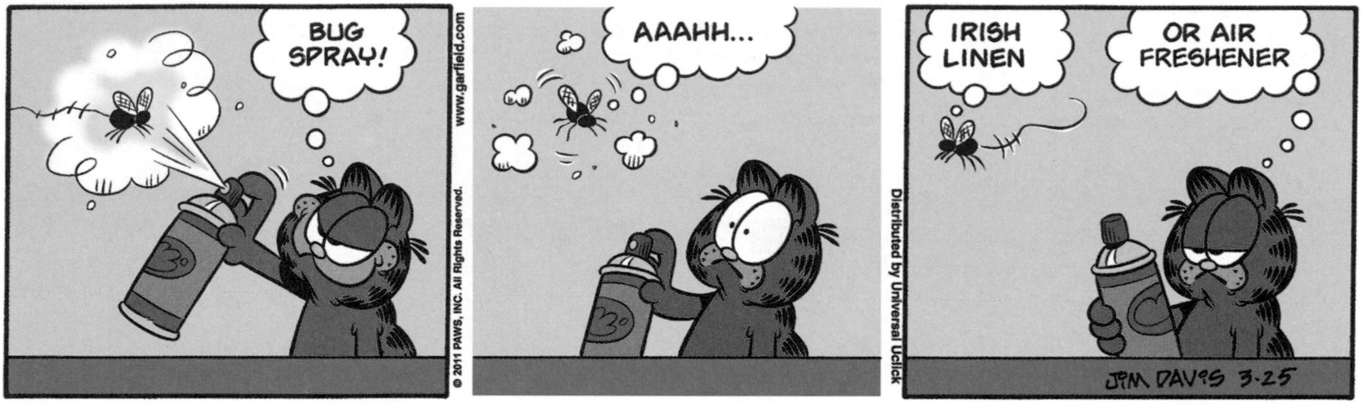
BUG SPRAY!
© 2011 PAWS, INC. All Rights Reserved.
www.garfield.com
AAAHH...
Distributed by Universal Uclick
IRISH LINEN
OR AIR FRESHENER
JIM DAVIS 3-25

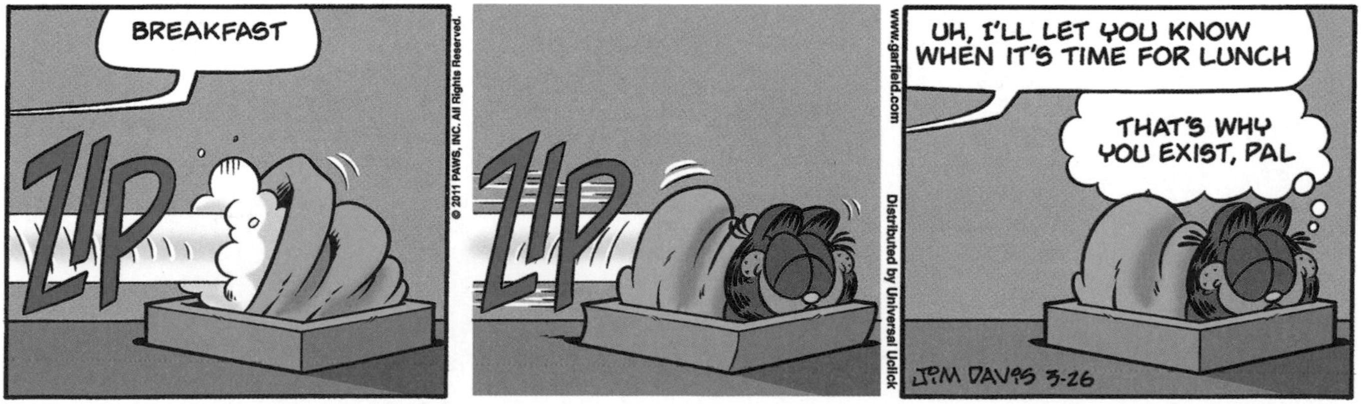
BREAKFAST
ZIP
© 2011 PAWS, INC. All Rights Reserved.
ZIP
www.garfield.com
Distributed by Universal Uclick
UH, I'LL LET YOU KNOW WHEN IT'S TIME FOR LUNCH
THAT'S WHY YOU EXIST, PAL
JIM DAVIS 3-26

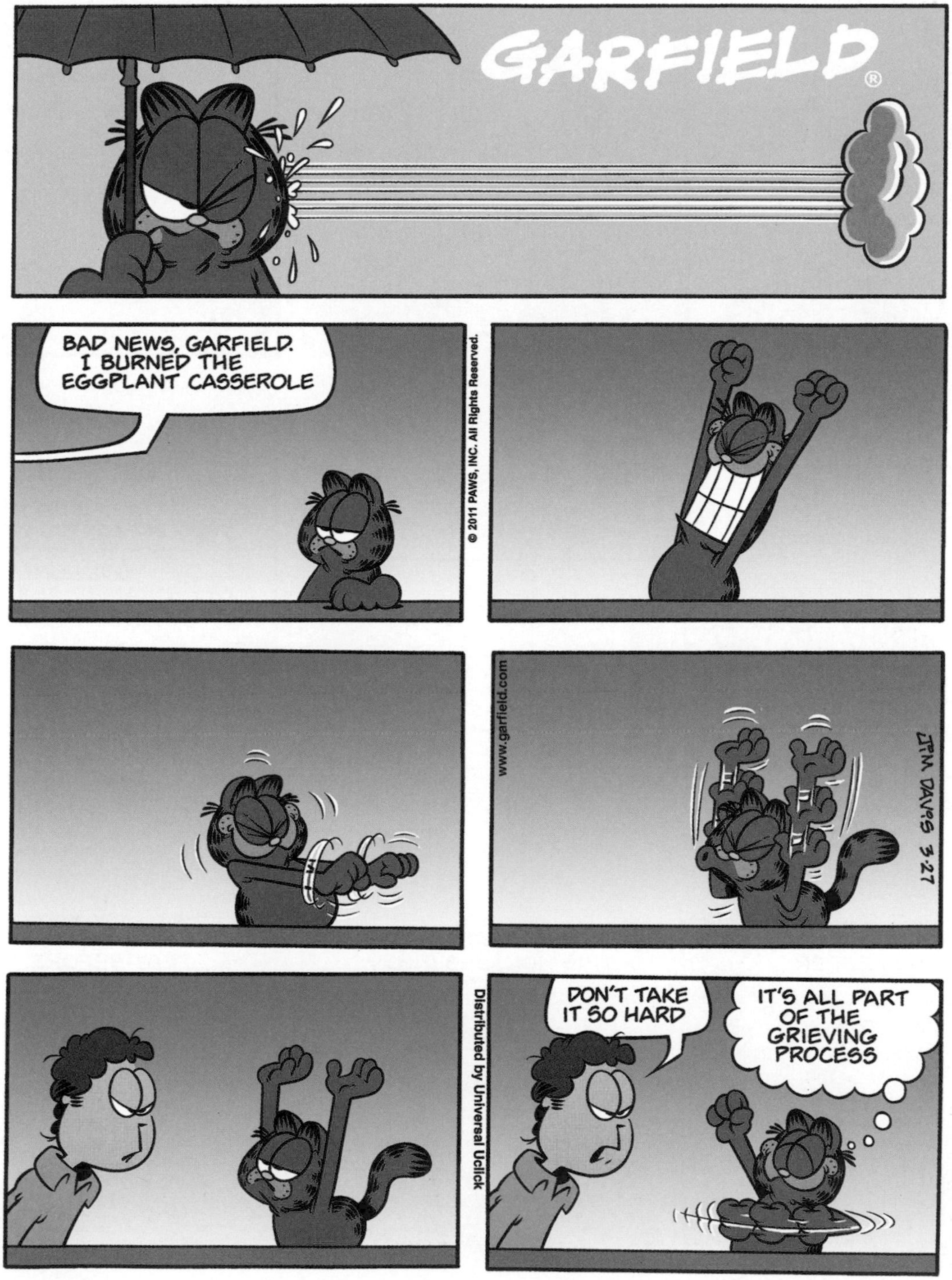
GARFIELD®
BAD NEWS, GARFIELD. I BURNED THE EGGPLANT CASSEROLE
© 2011 PAWS, INC. All Rights Reserved.
www.garfield.com
JIM DAVIS 3-27
Distributed by Universal Uclick
DON'T TAKE IT SO HARD
IT'S ALL PART OF THE GRIEVING PROCESS

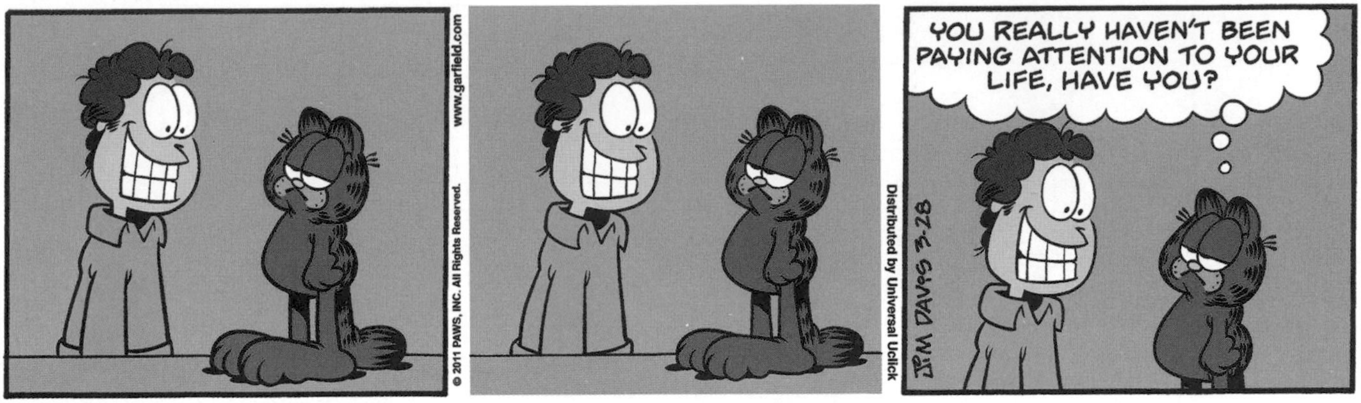
© 2011 PAWS, INC. All Rights Reserved. www.garfield.com
Distributed by Universal Uclick
YOU REALLY HAVEN'T BEEN PAYING ATTENTION TO YOUR LIFE, HAVE YOU?
JIM DAVIS 3-28

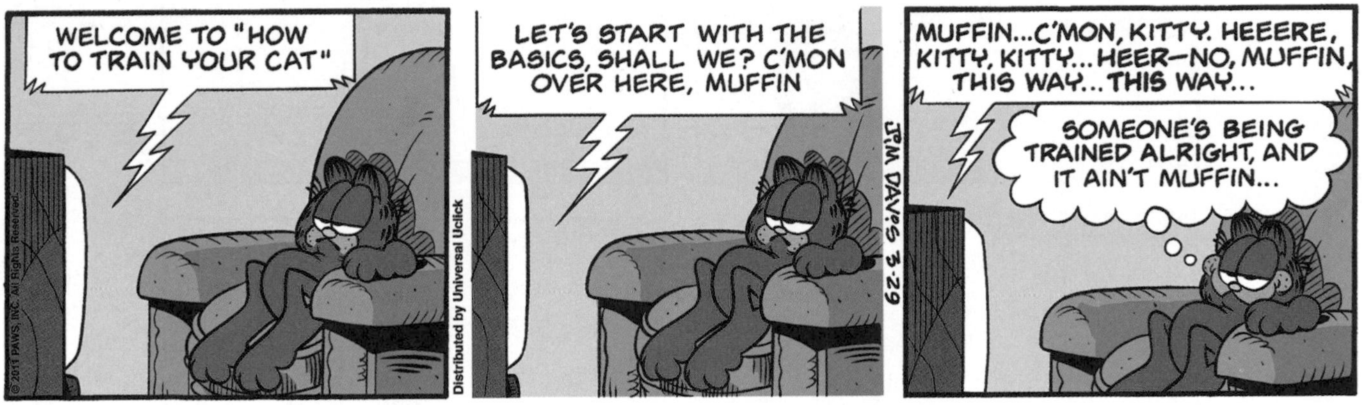
WELCOME TO "HOW TO TRAIN YOUR CAT"
© 2011 PAWS, INC. All Rights Reserved.
Distributed by Universal Uclick
LET'S START WITH THE BASICS, SHALL WE? C'MON OVER HERE, MUFFIN
JIM DAVIS 3-29
MUFFIN...C'MON, KITTY. HEEERE, KITTY, KITTY... HEER—NO, MUFFIN, THIS WAY... **THIS** WAY...
SOMEONE'S BEING TRAINED ALRIGHT, AND IT AIN'T MUFFIN...

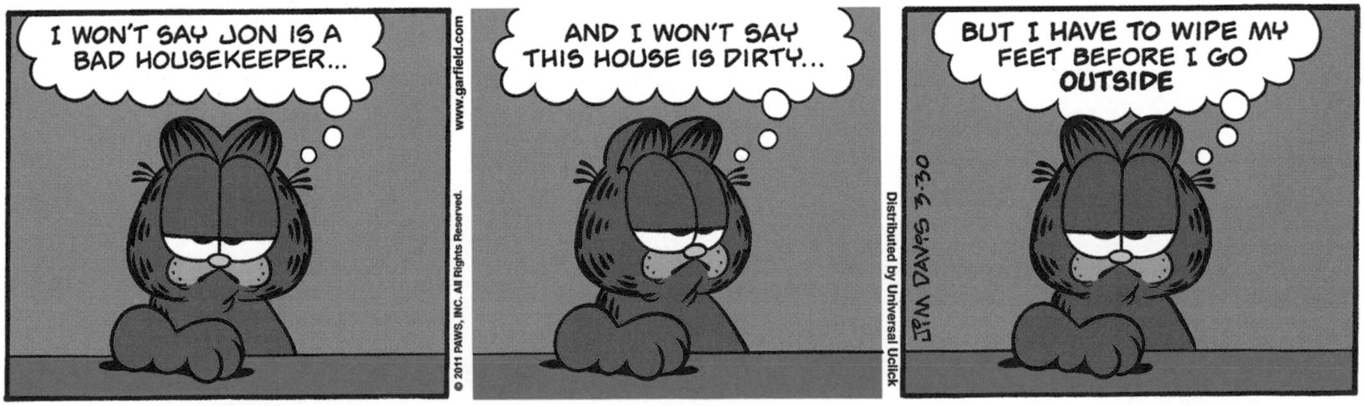
I WON'T SAY JON IS A BAD HOUSEKEEPER...
© 2011 PAWS, INC. All Rights Reserved. www.garfield.com
AND I WON'T SAY THIS HOUSE IS DIRTY...
Distributed by Universal Uclick
JIM DAVIS 3-30
BUT I HAVE TO WIPE MY FEET BEFORE I GO **OUTSIDE**

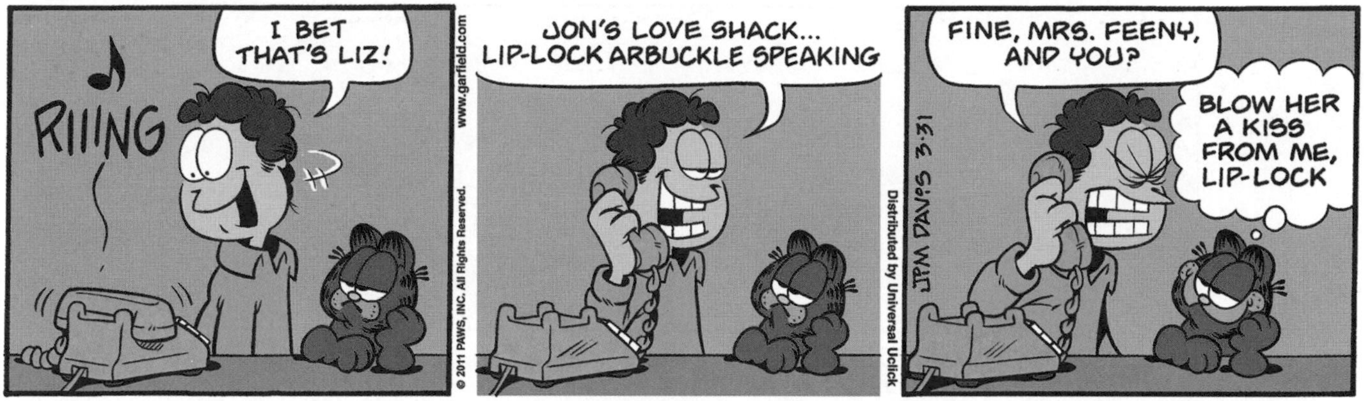
RIIING
I BET THAT'S LIZ!
© 2011 PAWS, INC. All Rights Reserved. www.garfield.com
JON'S LOVE SHACK... LIP-LOCK ARBUCKLE SPEAKING
Distributed by Universal Uclick
JIM DAVIS 3·31
FINE, MRS. FEENY, AND YOU?
BLOW HER A KISS FROM ME, LIP-LOCK

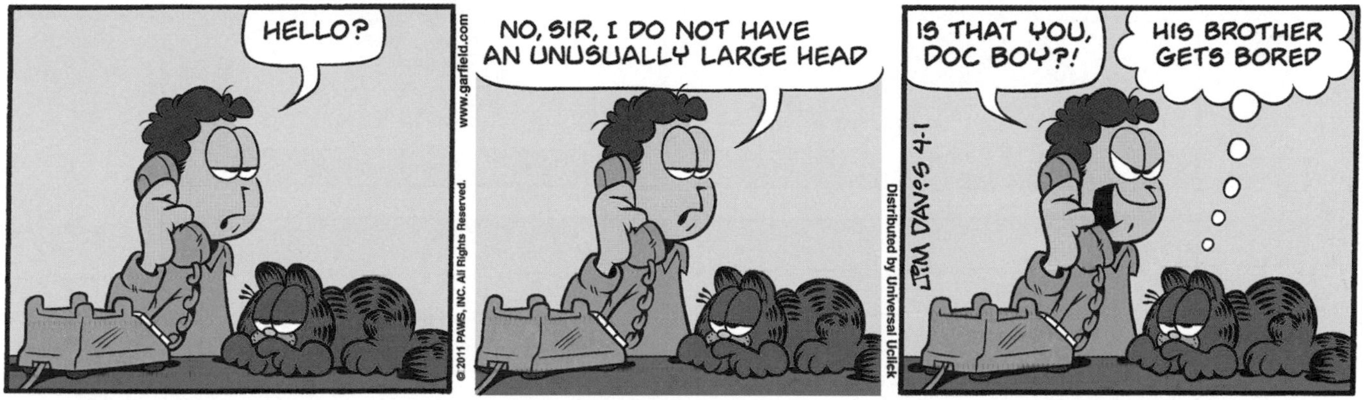
HELLO?
© 2011 PAWS, INC. All Rights Reserved. www.garfield.com
NO, SIR, I DO NOT HAVE AN UNUSUALLY LARGE HEAD
Distributed by Universal Uclick
JIM DAVIS 4-1
IS THAT YOU, DOC BOY?!
HIS BROTHER GETS BORED

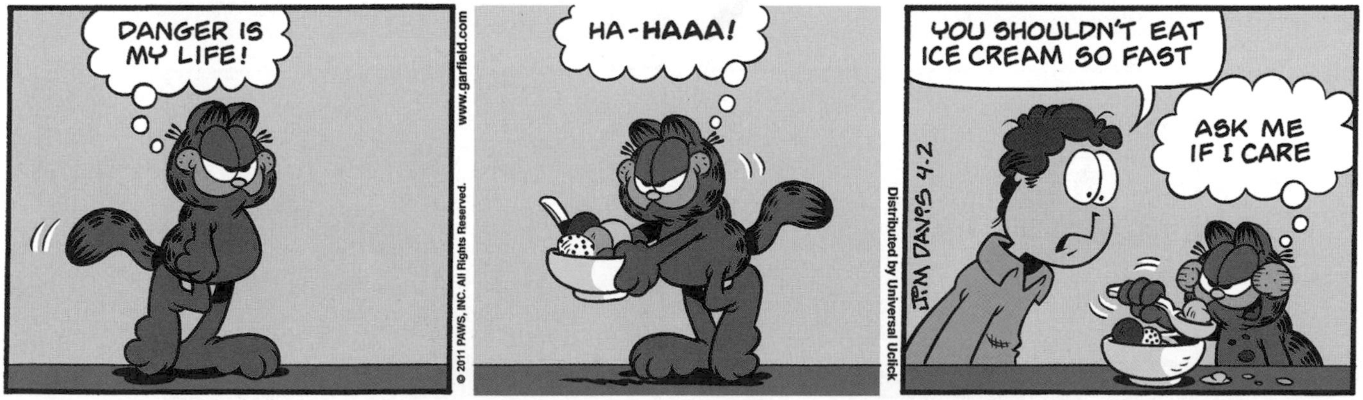
DANGER IS MY LIFE!
© 2011 PAWS, INC. All Rights Reserved. www.garfield.com
HA-HAAA!
Distributed by Universal Uclick
JIM DAVIS 4-2
YOU SHOULDN'T EAT ICE CREAM SO FAST
ASK ME IF I CARE

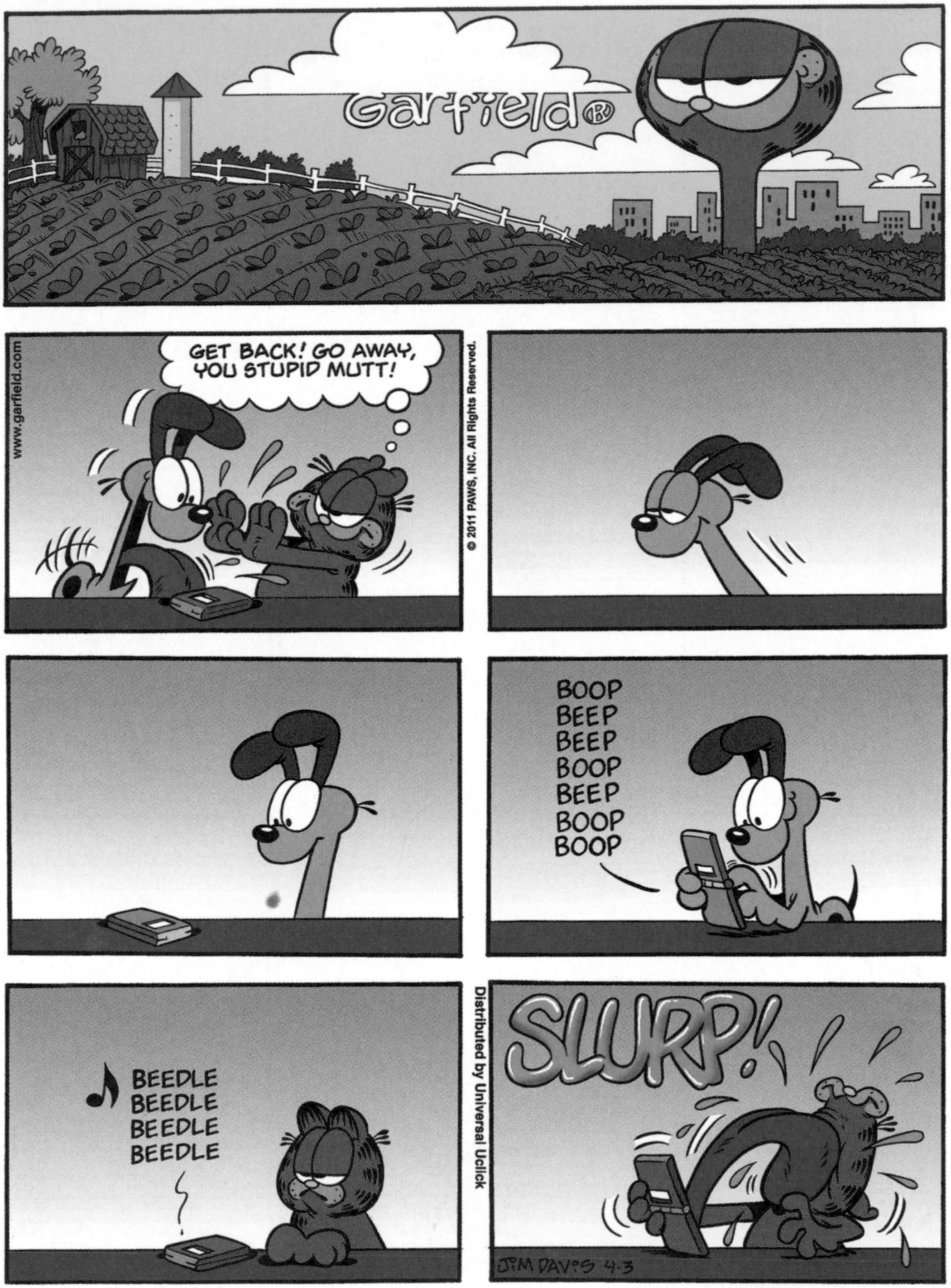
GARFIELD®
www.garfield.com
GET BACK! GO AWAY, YOU STUPID MUTT!
© 2011 PAWS, INC. All Rights Reserved.
BOOP
BEEP
BEEP
BOOP
BEEP
BOOP
BOOP
BEEDLE
BEEDLE
BEEDLE
BEEDLE
Distributed by Universal Uclick
SLURP!
JIM DAVIS 4-3

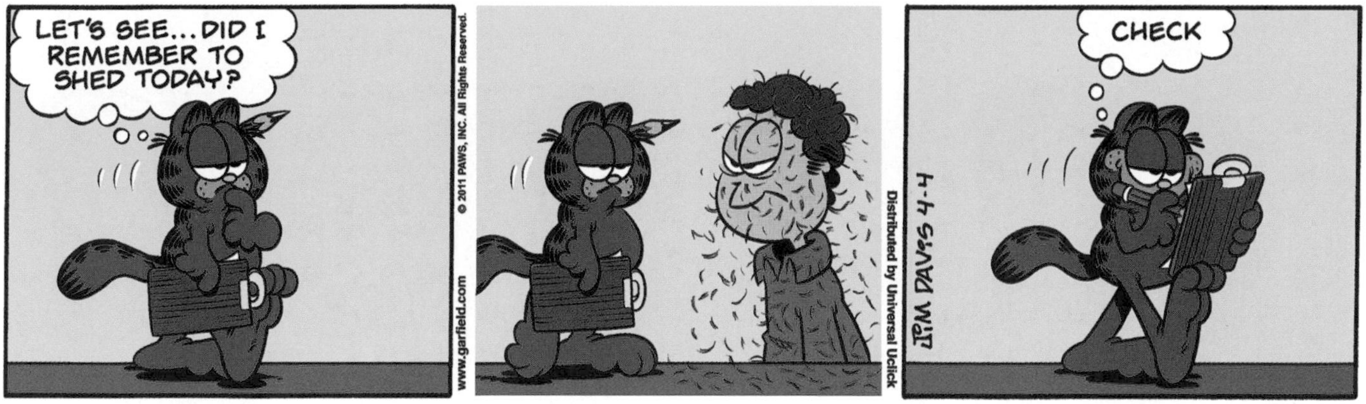
LET'S SEE...DID I REMEMBER TO SHED TODAY?
© 2011 PAWS, INC. All Rights Reserved.
www.garfield.com
Distributed by Universal Uclick
JPM DAVPS 4-4
CHECK

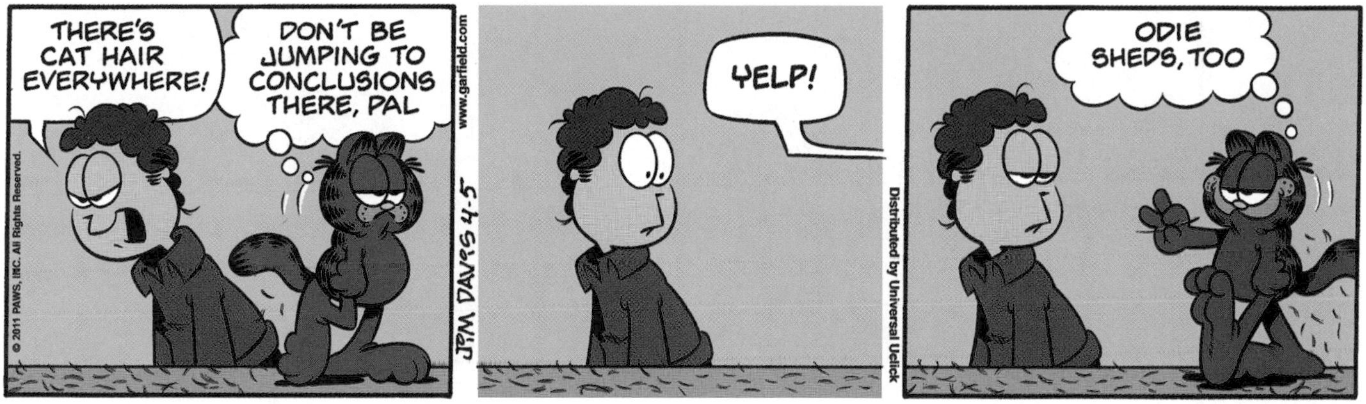
THERE'S CAT HAIR EVERYWHERE!
DON'T BE JUMPING TO CONCLUSIONS THERE, PAL
© 2011 PAWS, INC. All Rights Reserved.
JPM DAVPS 4-5
www.garfield.com
YELP!
Distributed by Universal Uclick
ODIE SHEDS, TOO

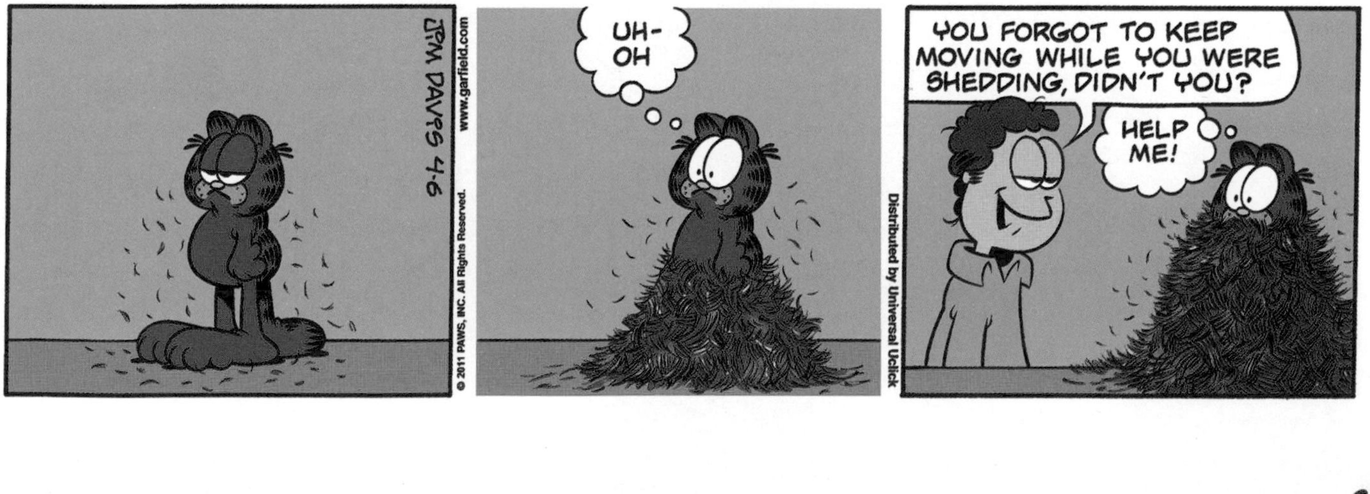
JPM DAVPS 4-6
www.garfield.com
© 2011 PAWS, INC. All Rights Reserved.
UH-OH
Distributed by Universal Uclick
YOU FORGOT TO KEEP MOVING WHILE YOU WERE SHEDDING, DIDN'T YOU?
HELP ME!

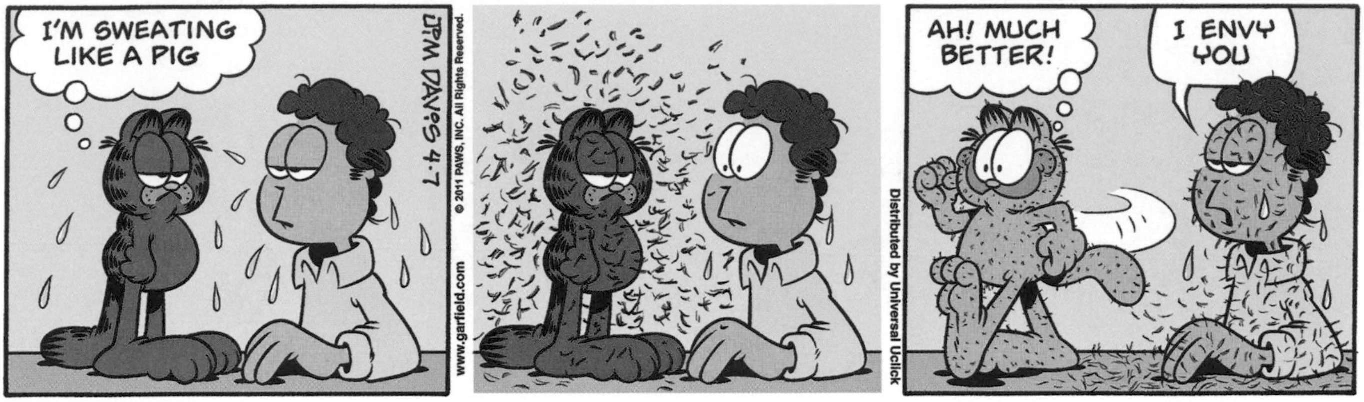
I'M SWEATING LIKE A PIG
AH! MUCH BETTER!
I ENVY YOU
JPM DAVPS 4-7
© 2011 PAWS, INC. All Rights Reserved.
www.garfield.com
Distributed by Universal Uclick

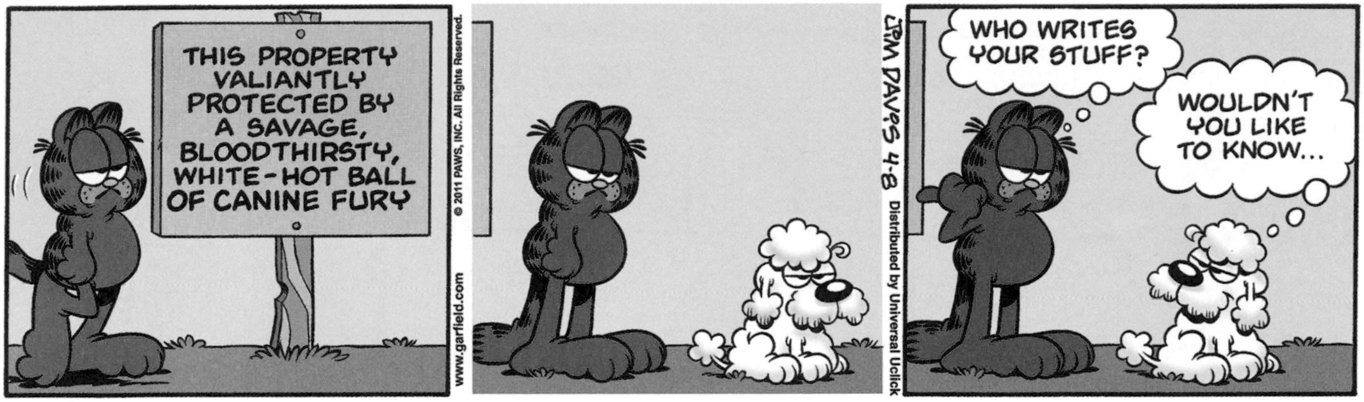
THIS PROPERTY VALIANTLY PROTECTED BY A SAVAGE, BLOODTHIRSTY, WHITE-HOT BALL OF CANINE FURY
WHO WRITES YOUR STUFF?
WOULDN'T YOU LIKE TO KNOW...
JPM DAVPS 4-8
© 2011 PAWS, INC. All Rights Reserved.
www.garfield.com
Distributed by Universal Uclick

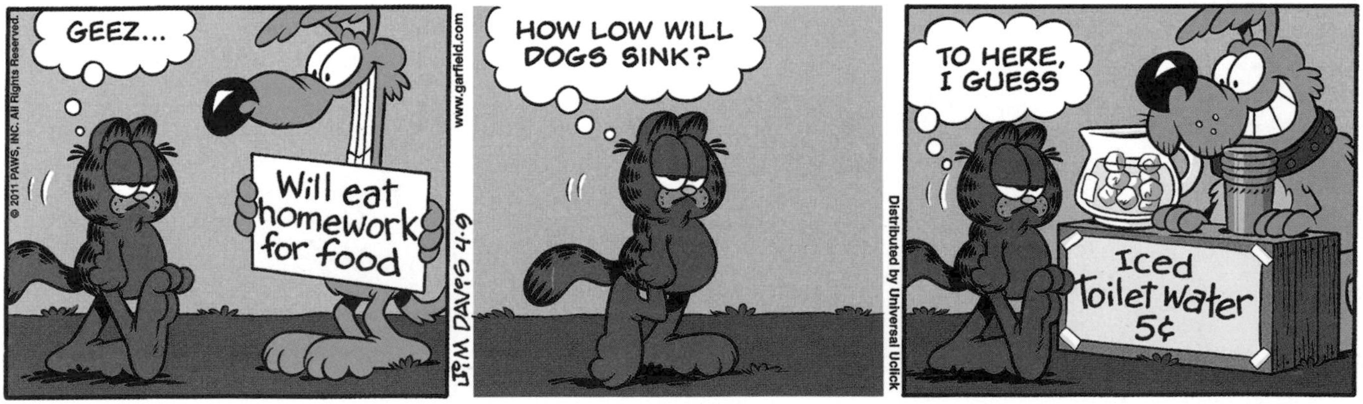
GEEZ...
Will eat homework for food
HOW LOW WILL DOGS SINK?
TO HERE, I GUESS
Iced Toilet Water 5¢
JPM DAVPS 4-9
© 2011 PAWS, INC. All Rights Reserved.
www.garfield.com
Distributed by Universal Uclick

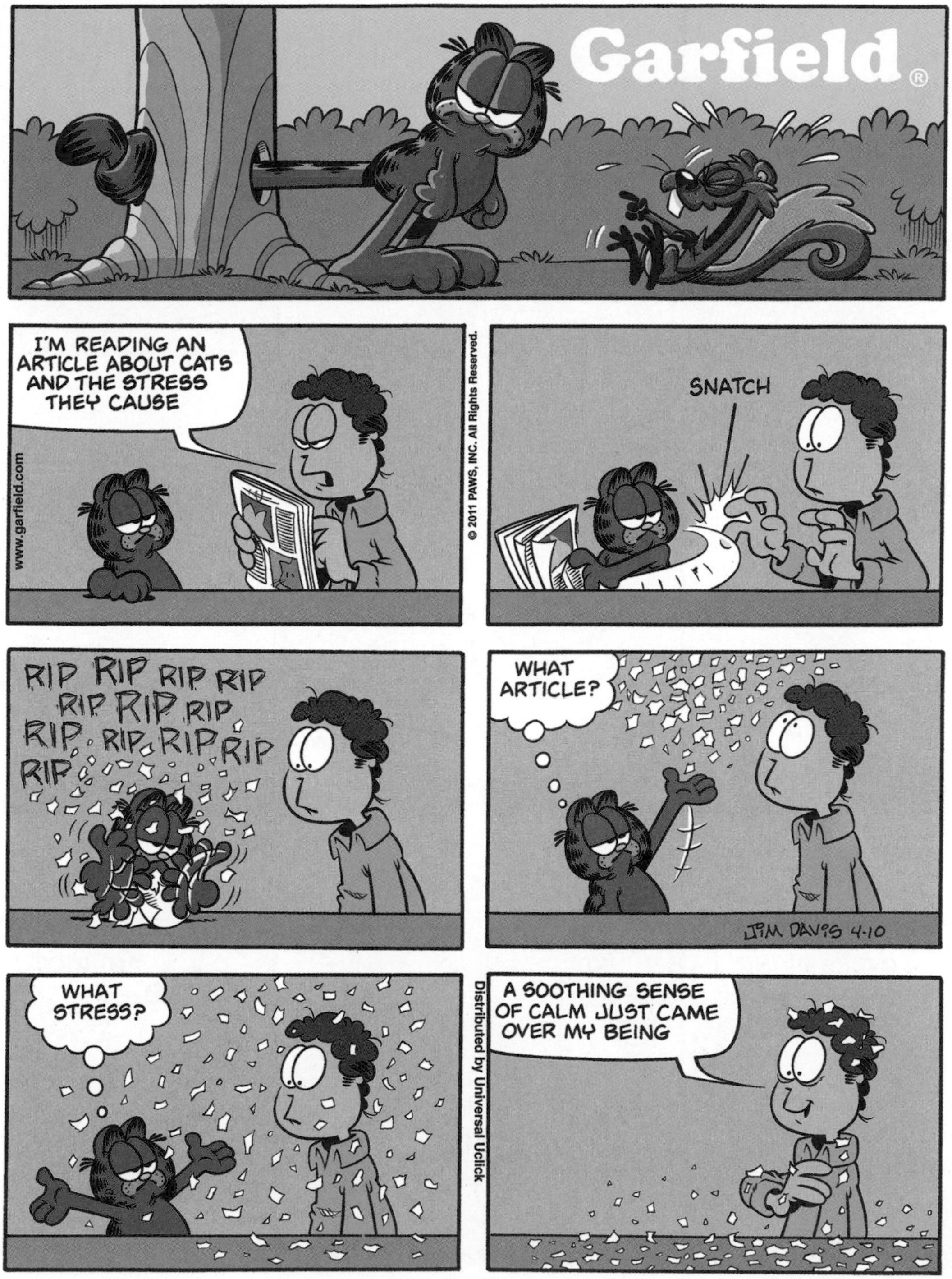
Garfield®
I'M READING AN ARTICLE ABOUT CATS AND THE STRESS THEY CAUSE
www.garfield.com
© 2011 PAWS, INC. All Rights Reserved.
SNATCH
RIP RIP RIP RIP RIP RIP RIP RIP RIP RIP RIP RIP
WHAT ARTICLE?
JIM DAVIS 4-10
WHAT STRESS?
Distributed by Universal Uclick
A SOOTHING SENSE OF CALM JUST CAME OVER MY BEING

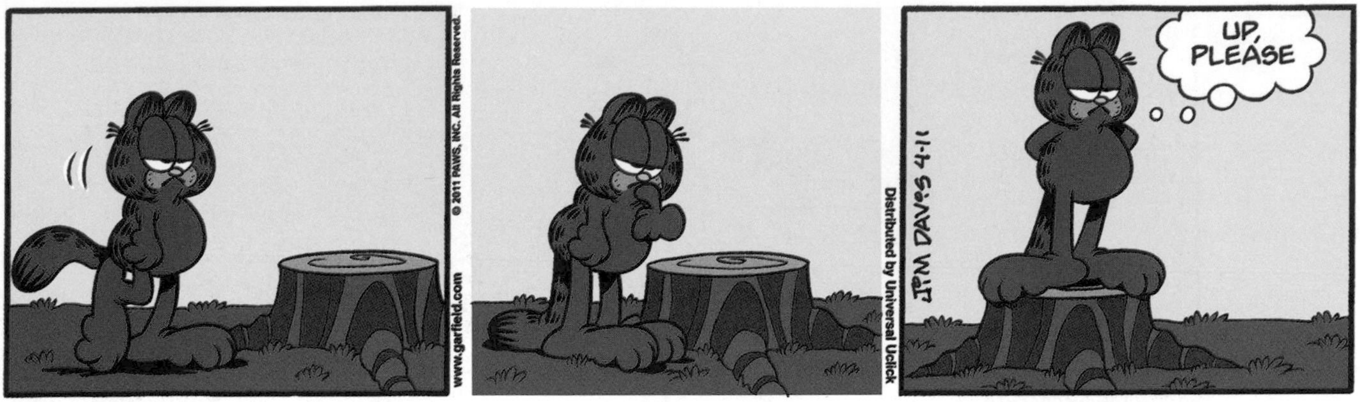
© 2011 PAWS, INC. All Rights Reserved.
www.garfield.com
Distributed by Universal Uclick
JPM DAVPS 4-11
UP, PLEASE

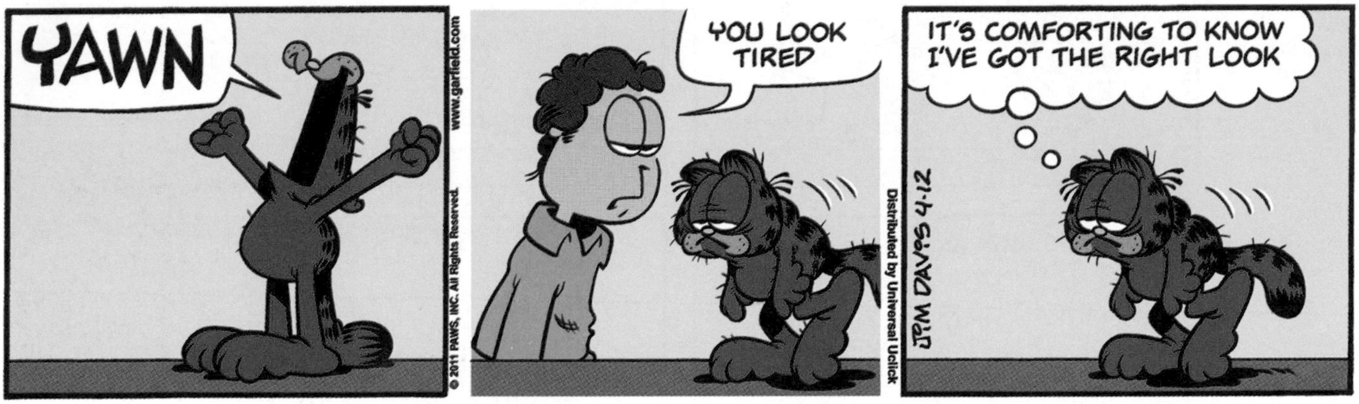
YAWN
© 2011 PAWS, INC. All Rights Reserved.
www.garfield.com
YOU LOOK TIRED
Distributed by Universal Uclick
JPM DAVPS 4-12
IT'S COMFORTING TO KNOW I'VE GOT THE RIGHT LOOK

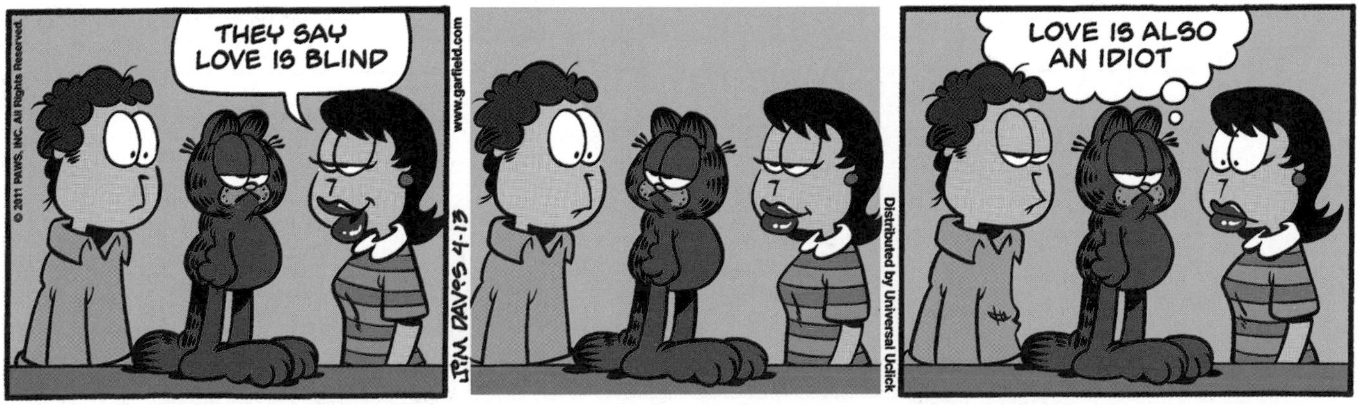
© 2011 PAWS, INC. All Rights Reserved.
THEY SAY LOVE IS BLIND
www.garfield.com
JPM DAVPS 4-13
Distributed by Universal Uclick
LOVE IS ALSO AN IDIOT

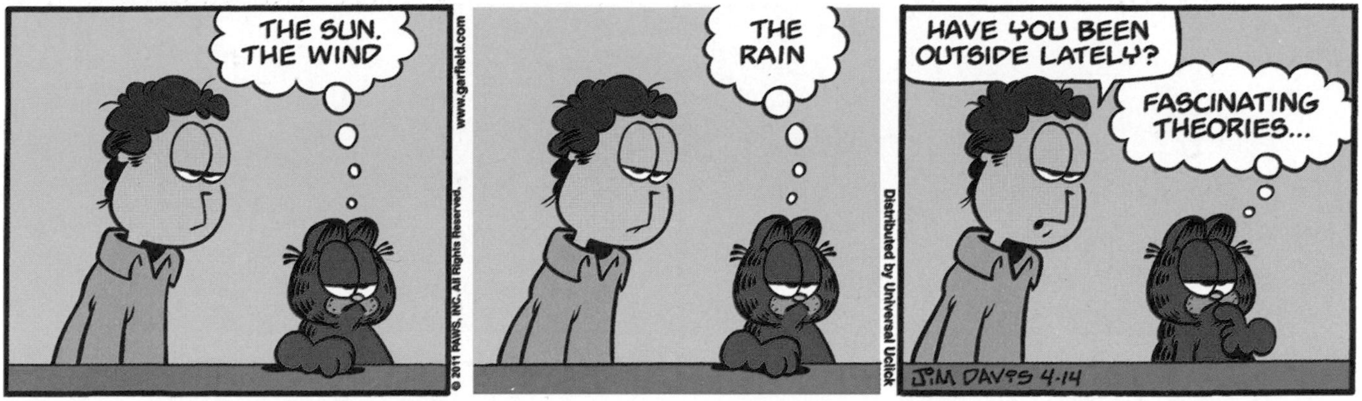
THE SUN. THE WIND
THE RAIN
HAVE YOU BEEN OUTSIDE LATELY?
FASCINATING THEORIES...
JIM DAVIS 4-14
© 2011 PAWS, INC. All Rights Reserved. www.garfield.com
Distributed by Universal Uclick

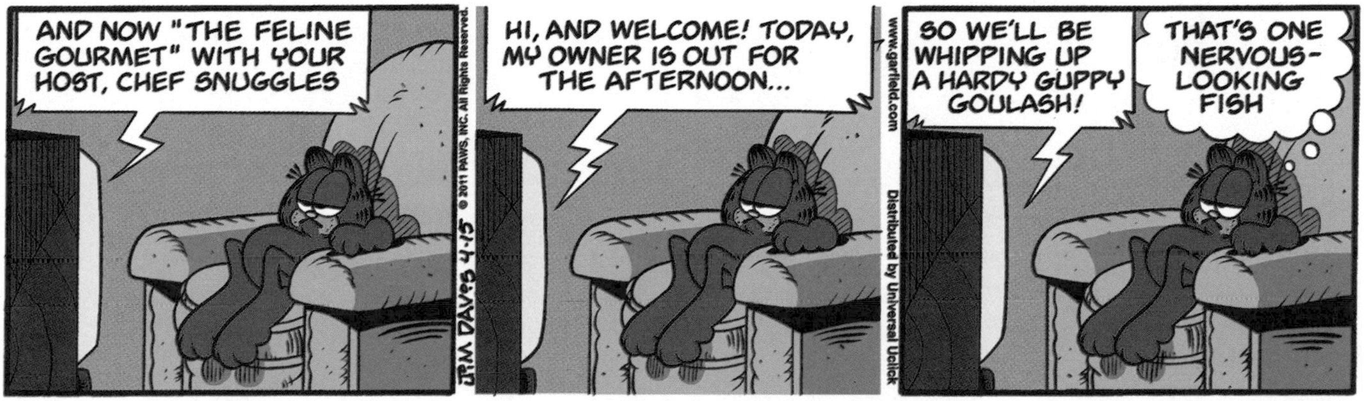
AND NOW "THE FELINE GOURMET" WITH YOUR HOST, CHEF SNUGGLES
HI, AND WELCOME! TODAY, MY OWNER IS OUT FOR THE AFTERNOON...
SO WE'LL BE WHIPPING UP A HARDY GUPPY GOULASH!
THAT'S ONE NERVOUS-LOOKING FISH
JIM DAVIS 4-15
© 2011 PAWS, INC. All Rights Reserved.
www.garfield.com
Distributed by Universal Uclick

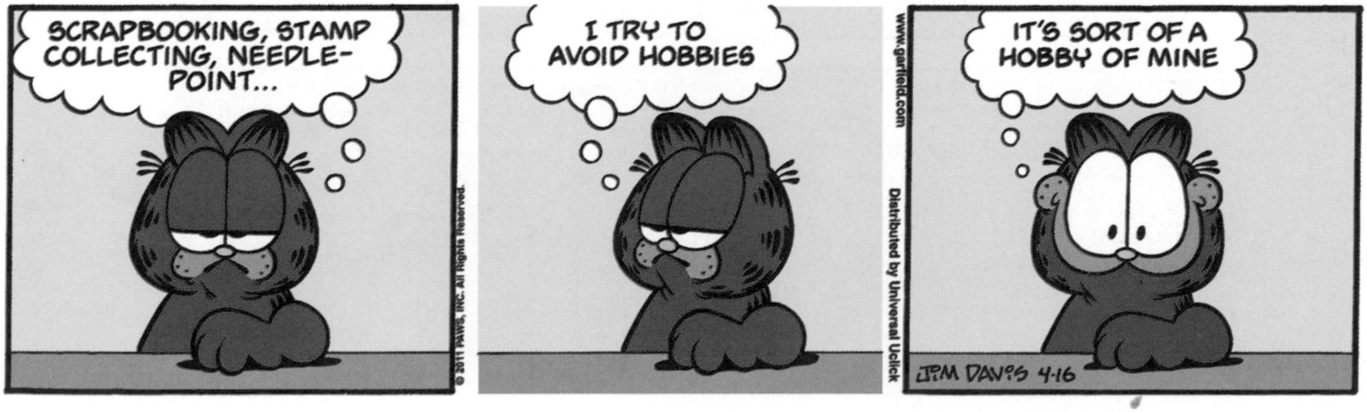
SCRAPBOOKING, STAMP COLLECTING, NEEDLE-POINT...
I TRY TO AVOID HOBBIES
IT'S SORT OF A HOBBY OF MINE
JIM DAVIS 4-16
© 2011 PAWS, INC. All Rights Reserved.
www.garfield.com
Distributed by Universal Uclick

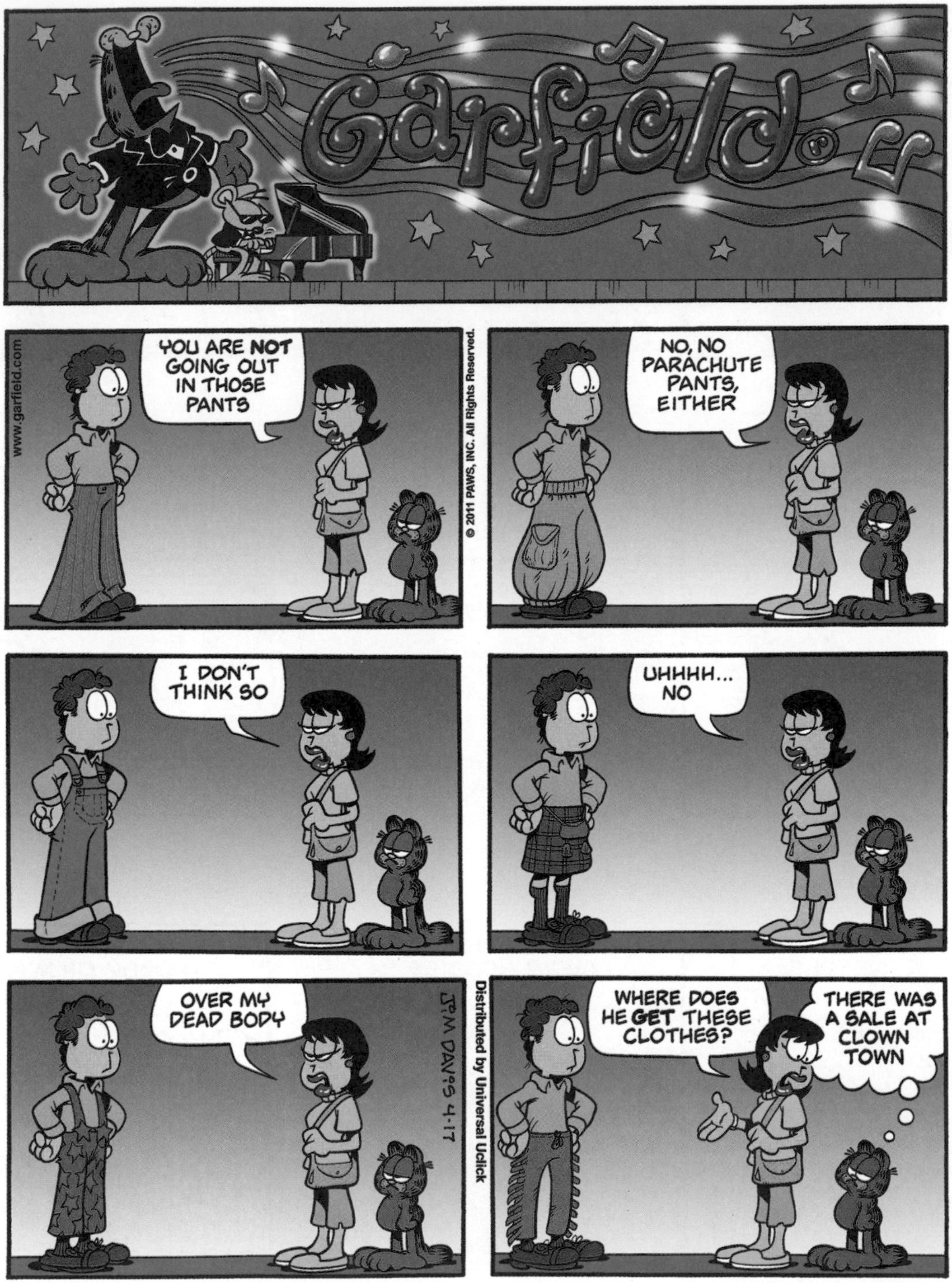
Garfield
www.garfield.com
YOU ARE NOT GOING OUT IN THOSE PANTS
© 2011 PAWS, INC. All Rights Reserved.
NO, NO PARACHUTE PANTS, EITHER
I DON'T THINK SO
UHHHH... NO
OVER MY DEAD BODY
JIM DAVIS 4-17
Distributed by Universal Uclick
WHERE DOES HE GET THESE CLOTHES?
THERE WAS A SALE AT CLOWN TOWN

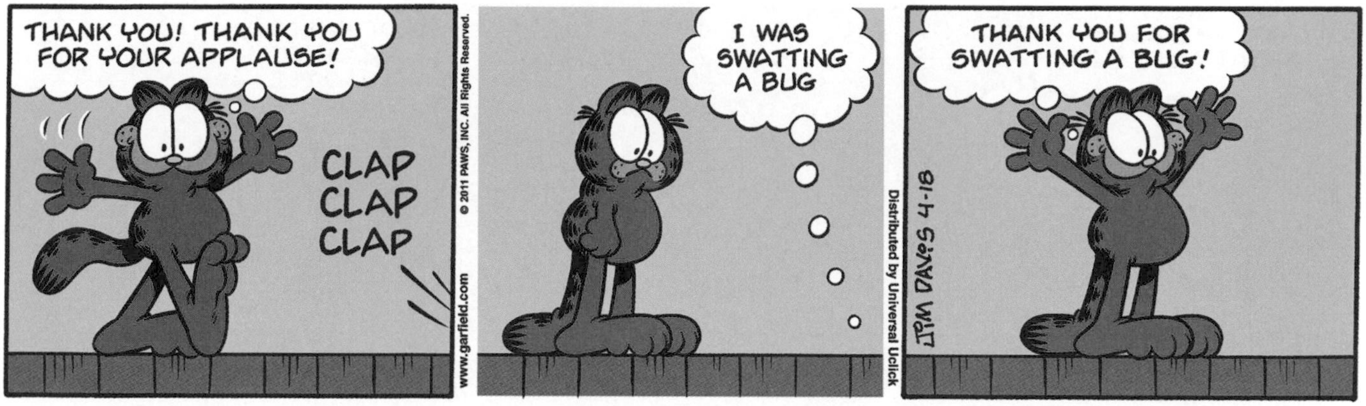
THANK YOU! THANK YOU FOR YOUR APPLAUSE!
CLAP CLAP CLAP
© 2011 PAWS, INC. All Rights Reserved.
www.garfield.com
I WAS SWATTING A BUG
JIM DAVIS 4-18
Distributed by Universal Uclick
THANK YOU FOR SWATTING A BUG!

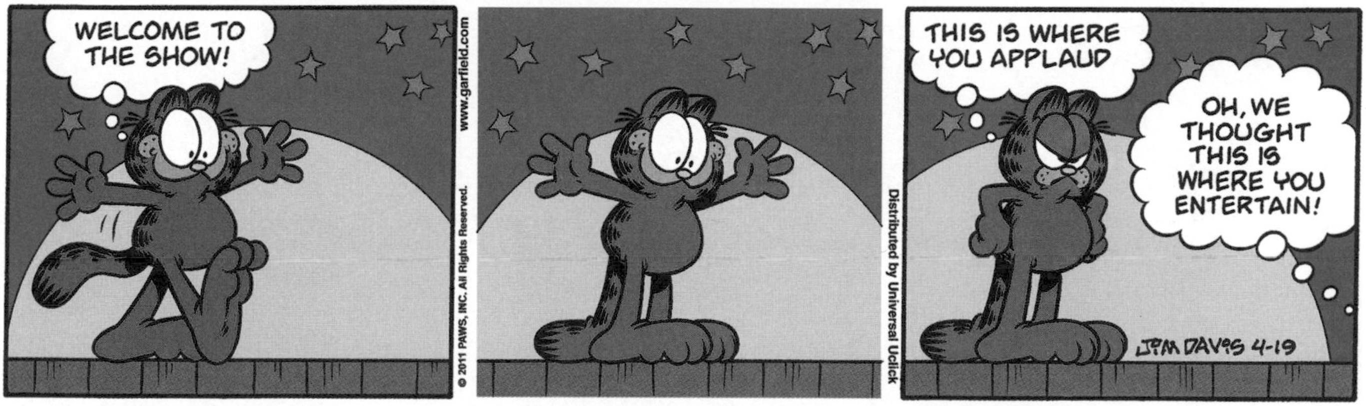
WELCOME TO THE SHOW!
© 2011 PAWS, INC. All Rights Reserved.
www.garfield.com
Distributed by Universal Uclick
THIS IS WHERE YOU APPLAUD
OH, WE THOUGHT THIS IS WHERE YOU ENTERTAIN!
JIM DAVIS 4-19

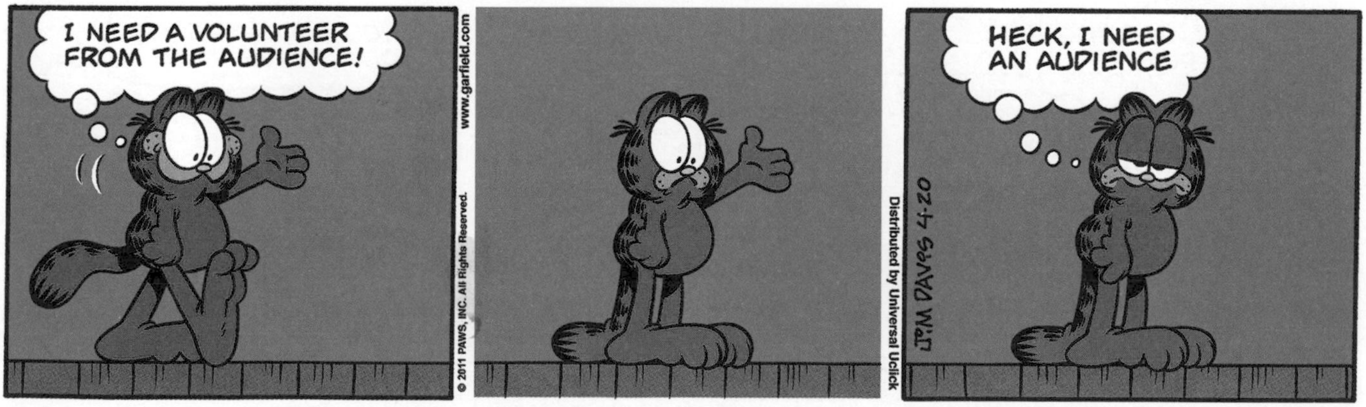
I NEED A VOLUNTEER FROM THE AUDIENCE!
© 2011 PAWS, INC. All Rights Reserved.
www.garfield.com
JIM DAVIS 4-20
Distributed by Universal Uclick
HECK, I NEED AN AUDIENCE

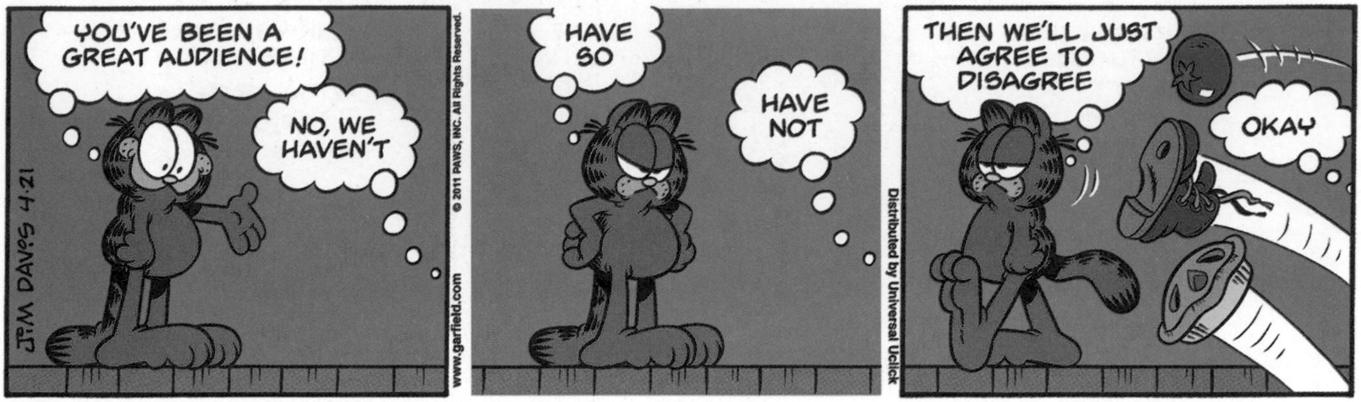
JIM DAVIS 4-21
YOU'VE BEEN A GREAT AUDIENCE!
NO, WE HAVEN'T
www.garfield.com © 2011 PAWS, INC. All Rights Reserved.
HAVE SO
HAVE NOT
Distributed by Universal Uclick
THEN WE'LL JUST AGREE TO DISAGREE
OKAY

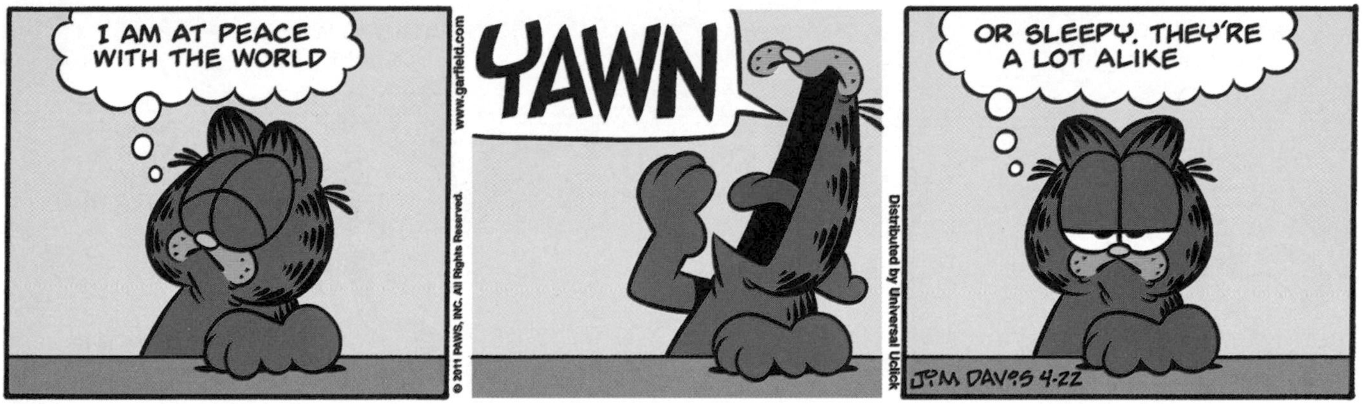
I AM AT PEACE WITH THE WORLD
© 2011 PAWS, INC. All Rights Reserved. www.garfield.com
YAWN
Distributed by Universal Uclick
OR SLEEPY. THEY'RE A LOT ALIKE
JIM DAVIS 4-22

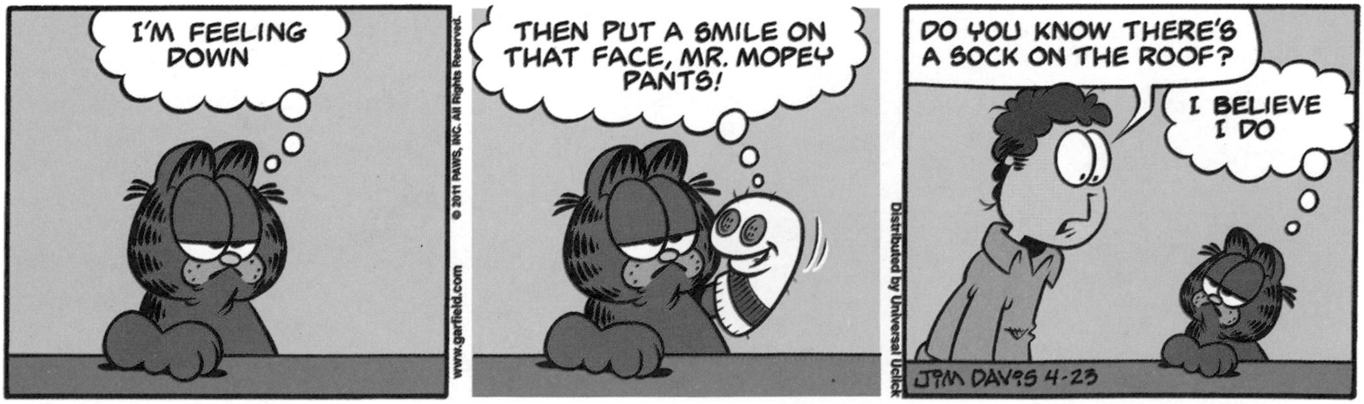
I'M FEELING DOWN
www.garfield.com © 2011 PAWS, INC. All Rights Reserved.
THEN PUT A SMILE ON THAT FACE, MR. MOPEY PANTS!
Distributed by Universal Uclick
DO YOU KNOW THERE'S A SOCK ON THE ROOF?
I BELIEVE I DO
JIM DAVIS 4-23

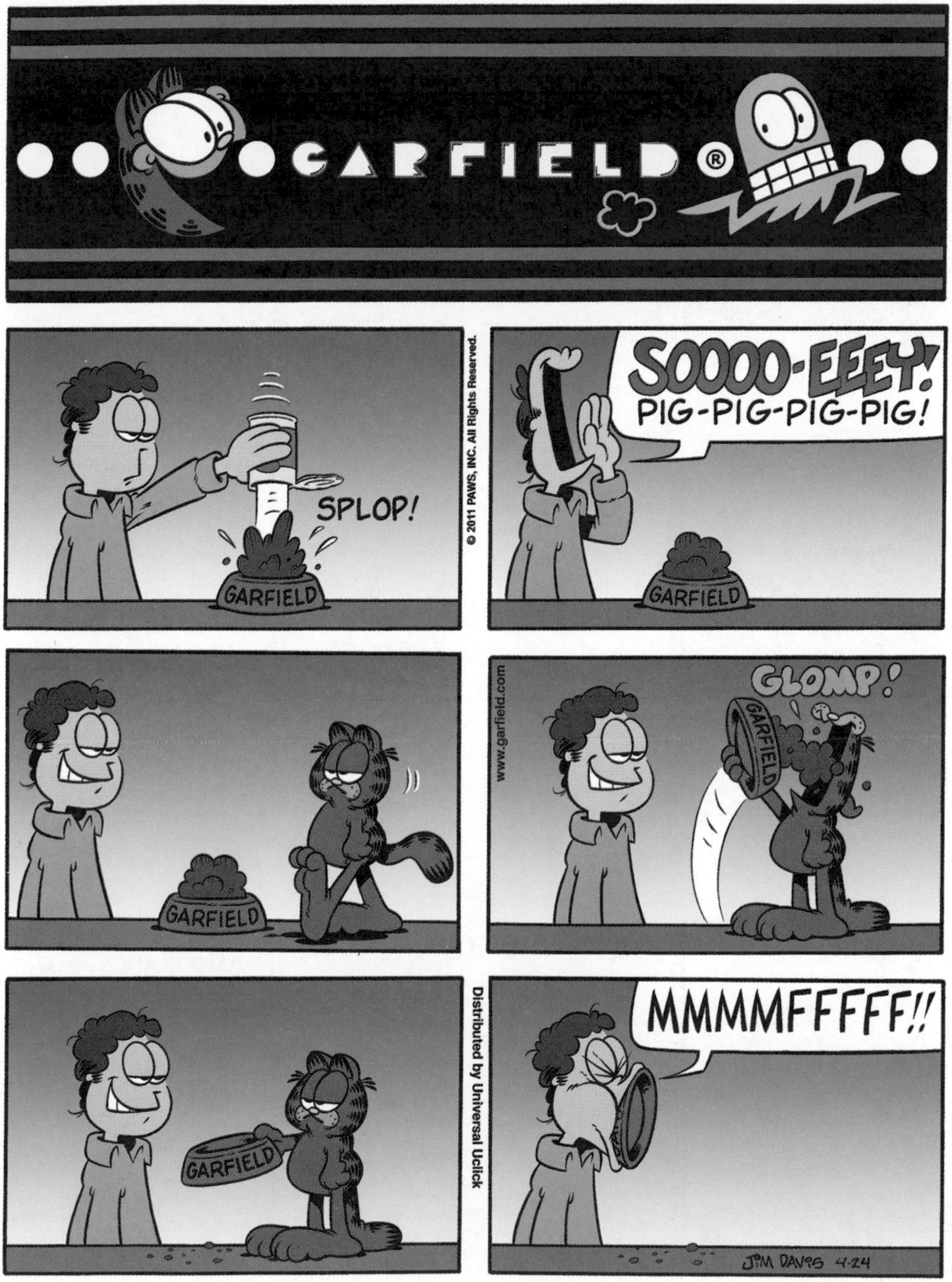
GARFIELD®
© 2011 PAWS, INC. All Rights Reserved.
SPLOP!
GARFIELD
SOOOO-EEEY! PIG-PIG-PIG-PIG!
GARFIELD
GARFIELD
www.garfield.com
GLOMP!
GARFIELD
GARFIELD
Distributed by Universal Uclick
MMMMFFFFF!!
JIM DAVIS 4-24

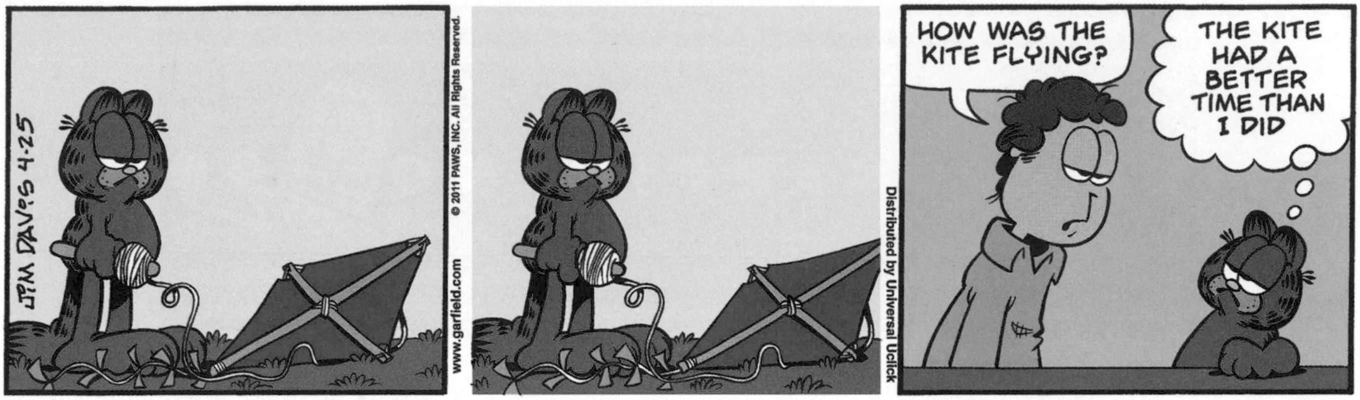
JIM DAVIS 4·25
© 2011 PAWS, INC. All Rights Reserved.
www.garfield.com
Distributed by Universal Uclick
HOW WAS THE KITE FLYING?
THE KITE HAD A BETTER TIME THAN I DID

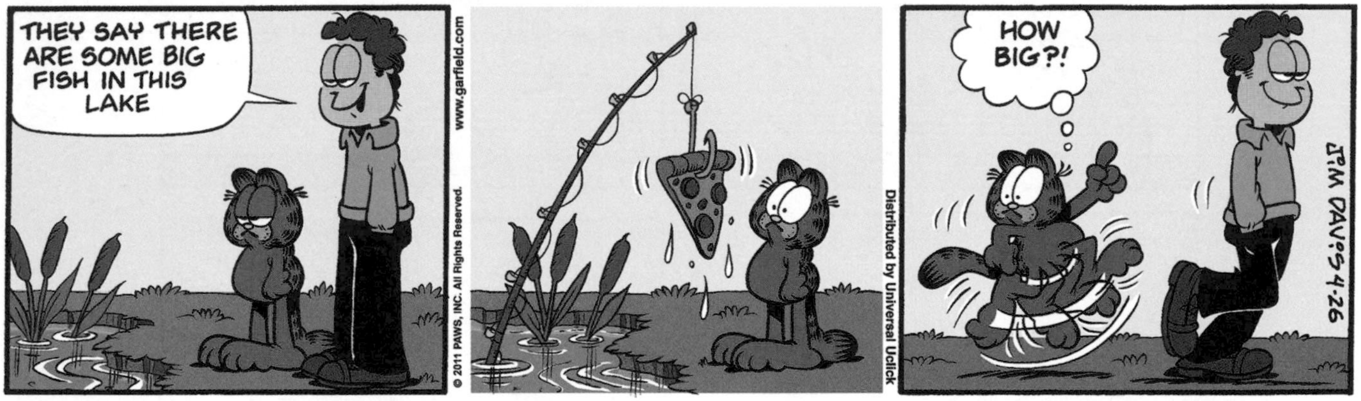
THEY SAY THERE ARE SOME BIG FISH IN THIS LAKE
www.garfield.com
© 2011 PAWS, INC. All Rights Reserved.
Distributed by Universal Uclick
HOW BIG?!
JIM DAVIS 4·26

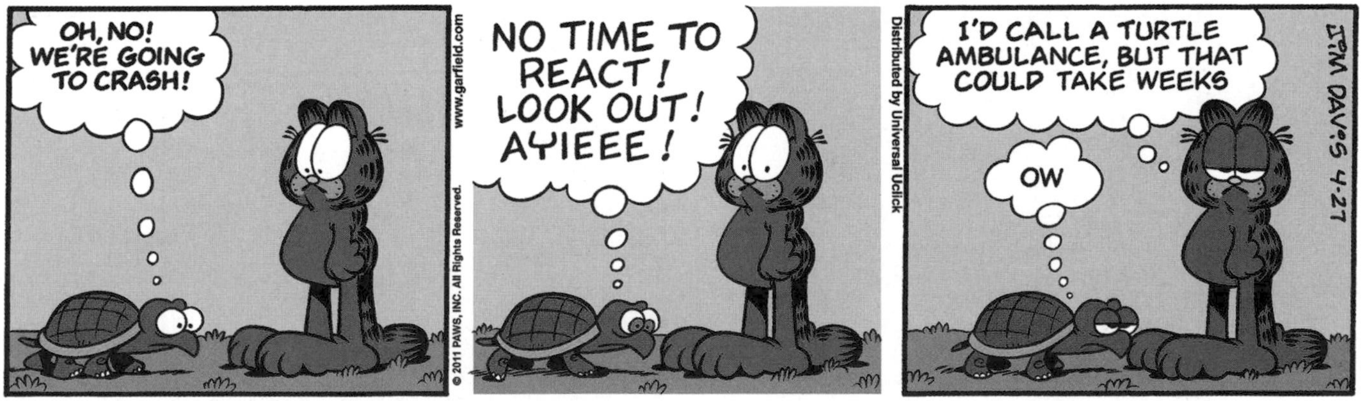
OH, NO! WE'RE GOING TO CRASH!
www.garfield.com
© 2011 PAWS, INC. All Rights Reserved.
NO TIME TO REACT! LOOK OUT! AYIEEE!
Distributed by Universal Uclick
I'D CALL A TURTLE AMBULANCE, BUT THAT COULD TAKE WEEKS
OW
JIM DAVIS 4·27

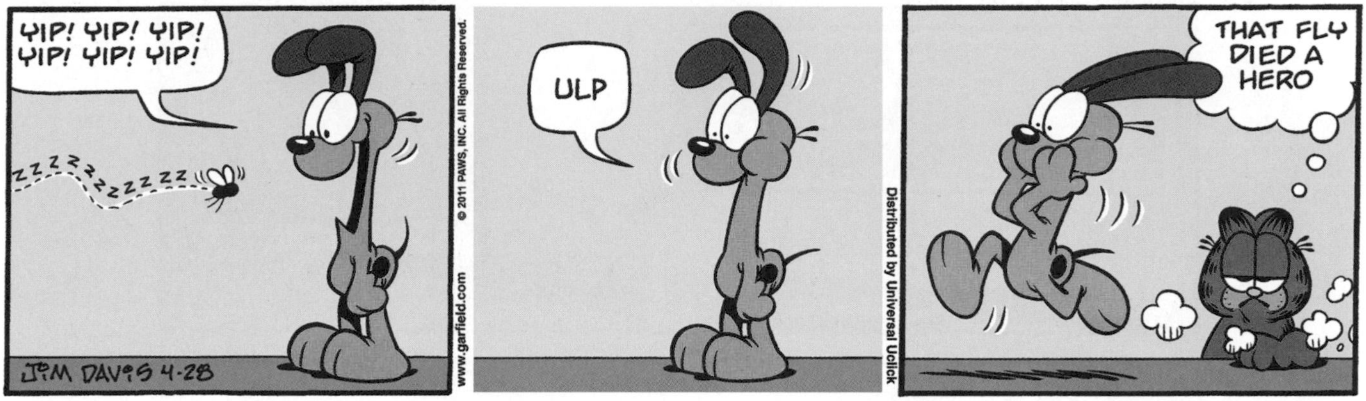
YIP! YIP! YIP! YIP! YIP! YIP!
ZZZZZZZZZZZZZ
JIM DAVIS 4-28
© 2011 PAWS, INC. All Rights Reserved.
www.garfield.com
ULP
Distributed by Universal Uclick
THAT FLY DIED A HERO

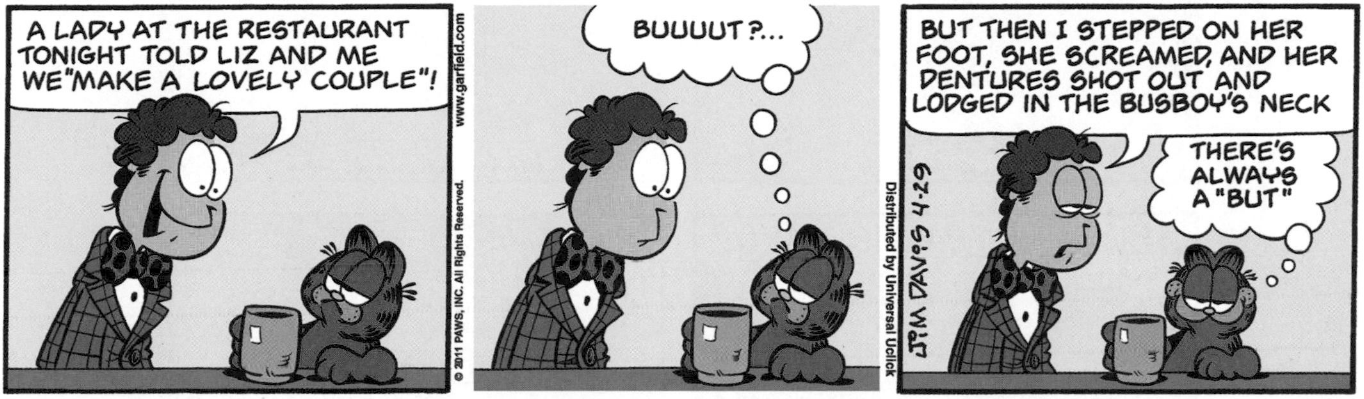
A LADY AT THE RESTAURANT TONIGHT TOLD LIZ AND ME WE"MAKE A LOVELY COUPLE"!
www.garfield.com
© 2011 PAWS, INC. All Rights Reserved.
BUUUUT?...
Distributed by Universal Uclick
BUT THEN I STEPPED ON HER FOOT, SHE SCREAMED, AND HER DENTURES SHOT OUT AND LODGED IN THE BUSBOY'S NECK
THERE'S ALWAYS A "BUT"
JIM DAVIS 4-29

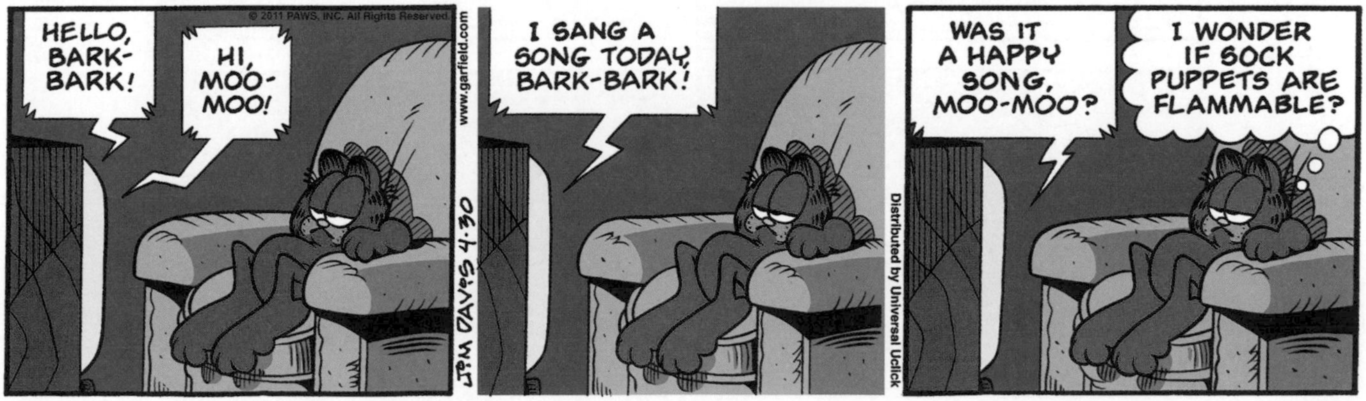
© 2011 PAWS, INC. All Rights Reserved.
HELLO, BARK-BARK!
HI, MOO-MOO!
www.garfield.com
JIM DAVIS 4-30
I SANG A SONG TODAY, BARK-BARK!
Distributed by Universal Uclick
WAS IT A HAPPY SONG, MOO-MOO?
I WONDER IF SOCK PUPPETS ARE FLAMMABLE?

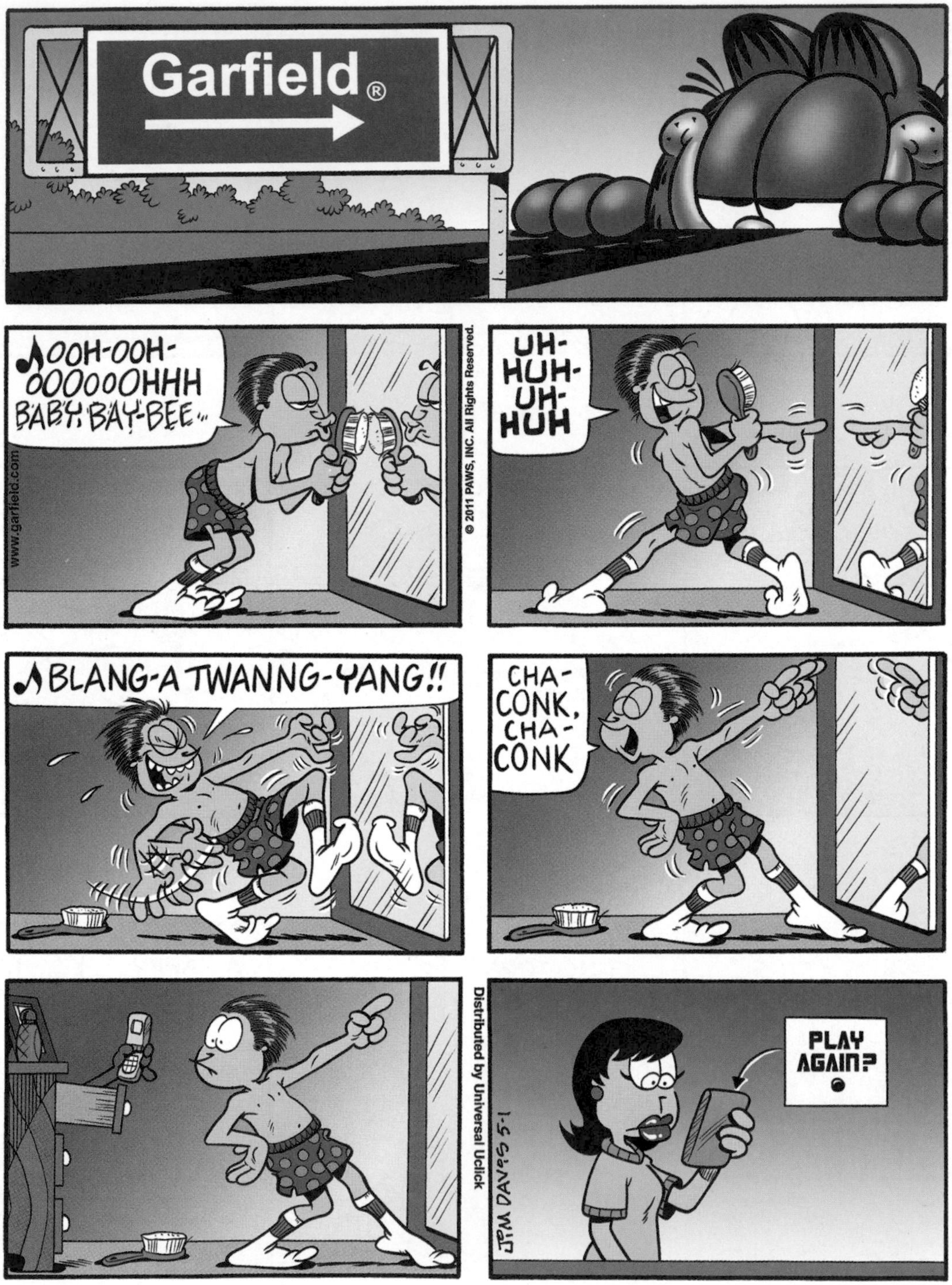
Garfield®
OOH-OOH-OOOOOOHHH BABY, BAY-BEE...
www.garfield.com
© 2011 PAWS, INC. All Rights Reserved.
UH-HUH-UH-HUH
BLANG-A TWANNG-YANG!!
CHA-CONK, CHA-CONK
Distributed by Universal Uclick
JPM DAVPS 5-1
PLAY AGAIN?

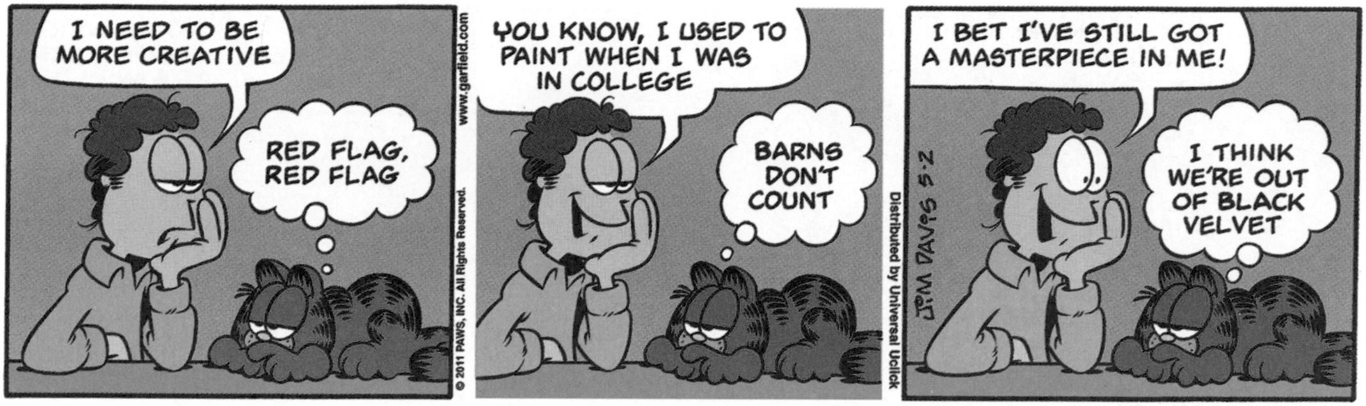
I NEED TO BE MORE CREATIVE
RED FLAG, RED FLAG
© 2011 PAWS, INC. All Rights Reserved. www.garfield.com
YOU KNOW, I USED TO PAINT WHEN I WAS IN COLLEGE
BARNS DON'T COUNT
Distributed by Universal Uclick
I BET I'VE STILL GOT A MASTERPIECE IN ME!
I THINK WE'RE OUT OF BLACK VELVET

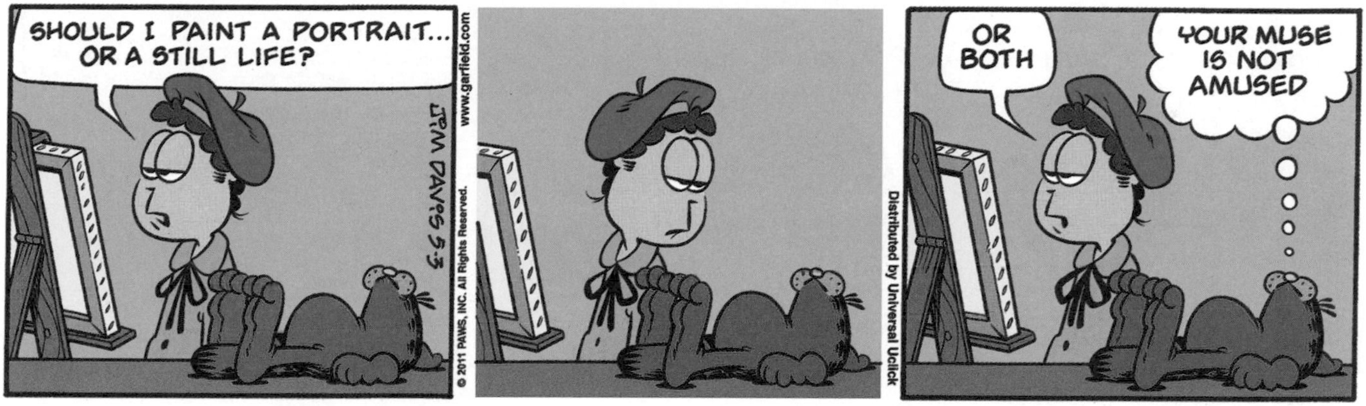
SHOULD I PAINT A PORTRAIT... OR A STILL LIFE?
© 2011 PAWS, INC. All Rights Reserved. www.garfield.com
Distributed by Universal Uclick
OR BOTH
YOUR MUSE IS NOT AMUSED

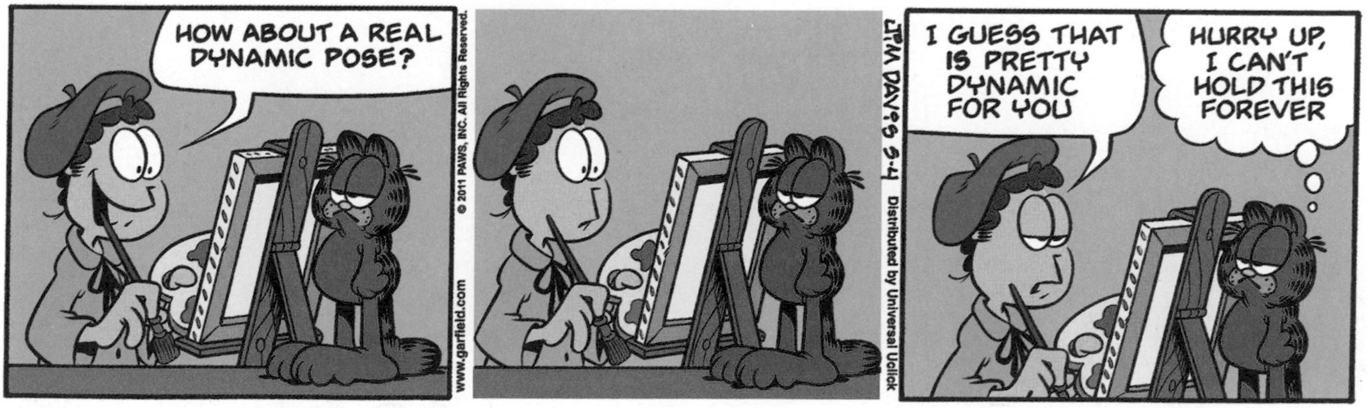
HOW ABOUT A REAL DYNAMIC POSE?
www.garfield.com © 2011 PAWS, INC. All Rights Reserved.
Distributed by Universal Uclick
I GUESS THAT IS PRETTY DYNAMIC FOR YOU
HURRY UP, I CAN'T HOLD THIS FOREVER

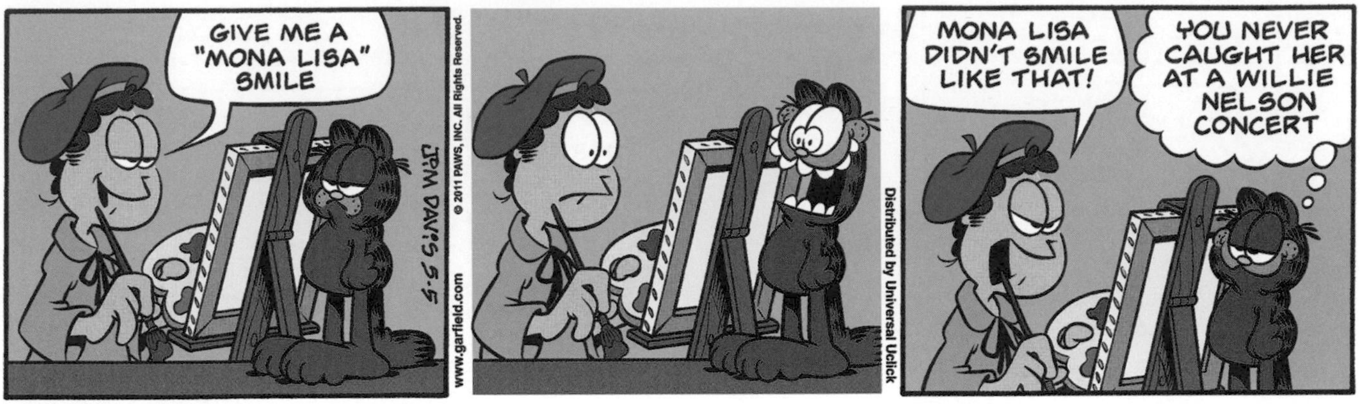
GIVE ME A "MONA LISA" SMILE
JIM DAVIS 5-5
© 2011 PAWS, INC. All Rights Reserved.
www.garfield.com
Distributed by Universal Uclick
MONA LISA DIDN'T SMILE LIKE THAT!
YOU NEVER CAUGHT HER AT A WILLIE NELSON CONCERT

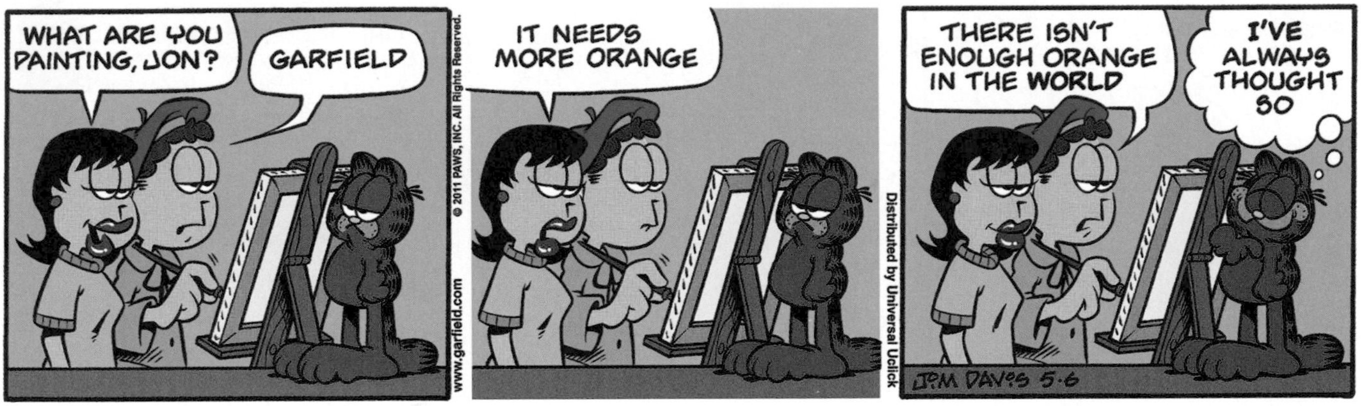
WHAT ARE YOU PAINTING, JON?
GARFIELD
© 2011 PAWS, INC. All Rights Reserved.
www.garfield.com
IT NEEDS MORE ORANGE
Distributed by Universal Uclick
THERE ISN'T ENOUGH ORANGE IN THE WORLD
I'VE ALWAYS THOUGHT SO
JIM DAVIS 5-6

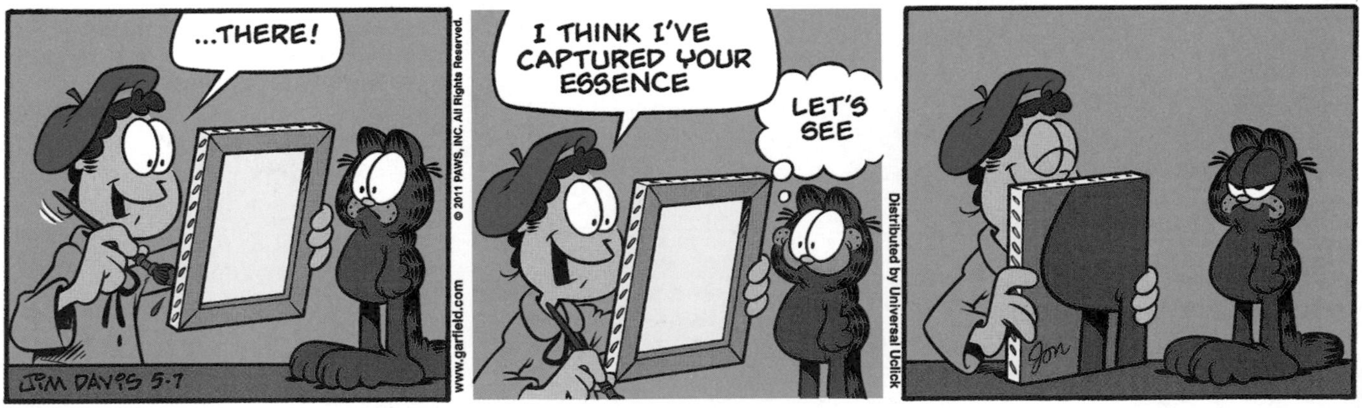
...THERE!
JIM DAVIS 5-7
© 2011 PAWS, INC. All Rights Reserved.
www.garfield.com
I THINK I'VE CAPTURED YOUR ESSENCE
LET'S SEE
Distributed by Universal Uclick
Jon

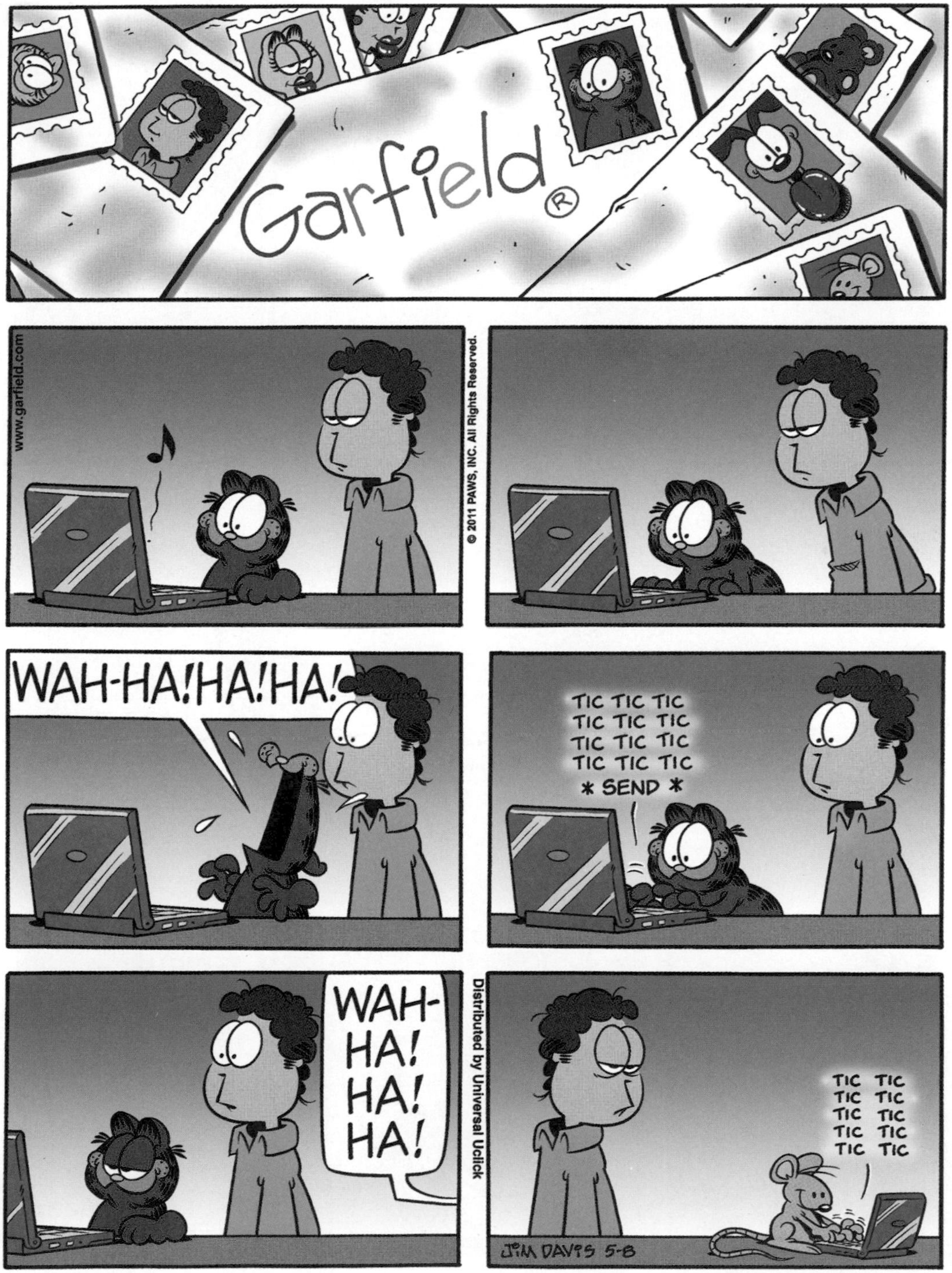
Garfield®
www.garfield.com
© 2011 PAWS, INC. All Rights Reserved.
WAH-HA!HA!HA!
TIC TIC TIC
TIC TIC TIC
TIC TIC TIC
TIC TIC TIC
* SEND *
Distributed by Universal Uclick
WAH-HA! HA! HA!
TIC TIC
TIC TIC
TIC TIC
TIC TIC
TIC TIC
JIM DAVIS 5-8

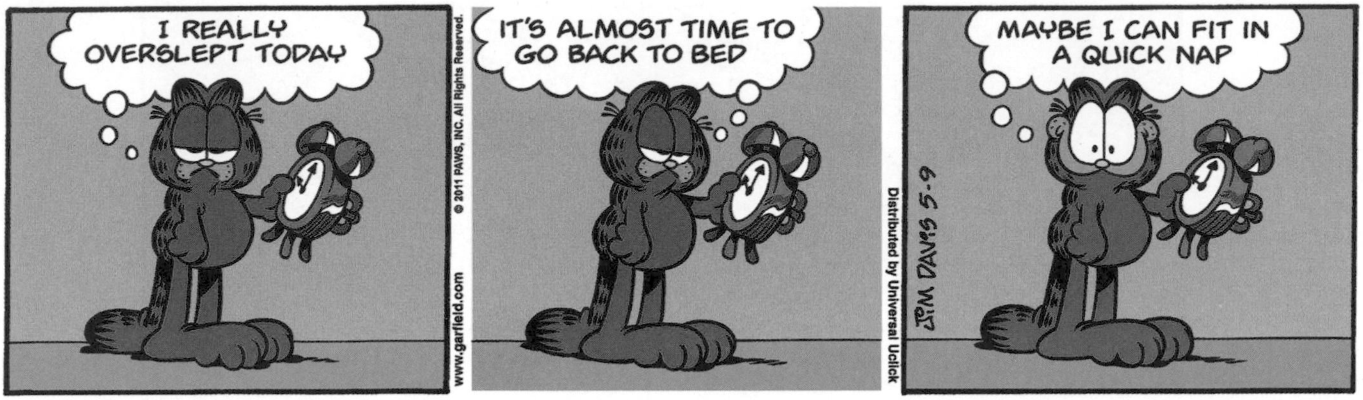
I REALLY OVERSLEPT TODAY
IT'S ALMOST TIME TO GO BACK TO BED
MAYBE I CAN FIT IN A QUICK NAP
www.garfield.com © 2011 PAWS, INC. All Rights Reserved.
Distributed by Universal Uclick
JPM DAVIS 5-9

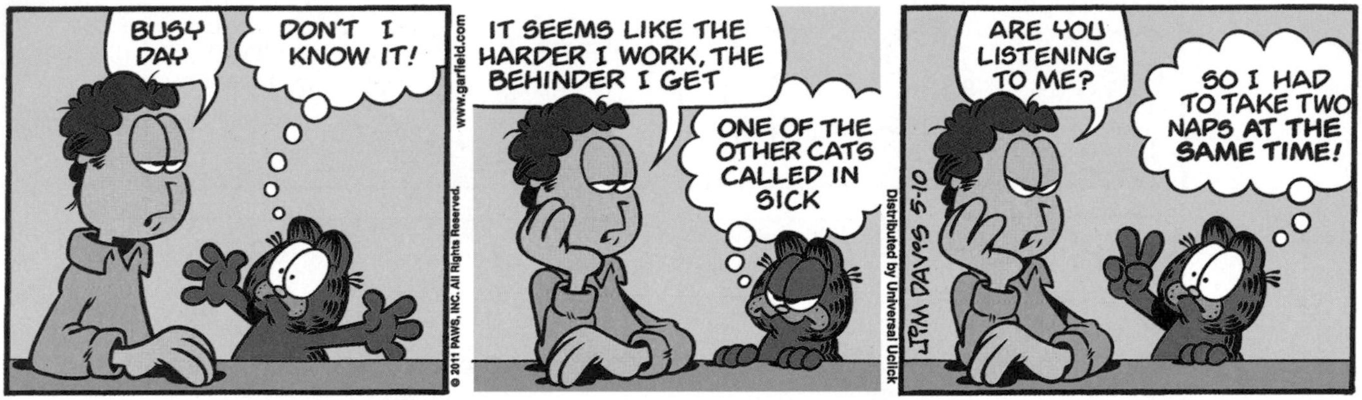
BUSY DAY
DON'T I KNOW IT!
IT SEEMS LIKE THE HARDER I WORK, THE BEHINDER I GET
ONE OF THE OTHER CATS CALLED IN SICK
ARE YOU LISTENING TO ME?
SO I HAD TO TAKE TWO NAPS AT THE SAME TIME!
© 2011 PAWS, INC. All Rights Reserved. www.garfield.com
Distributed by Universal Uclick
JPM DAVIS 5-10

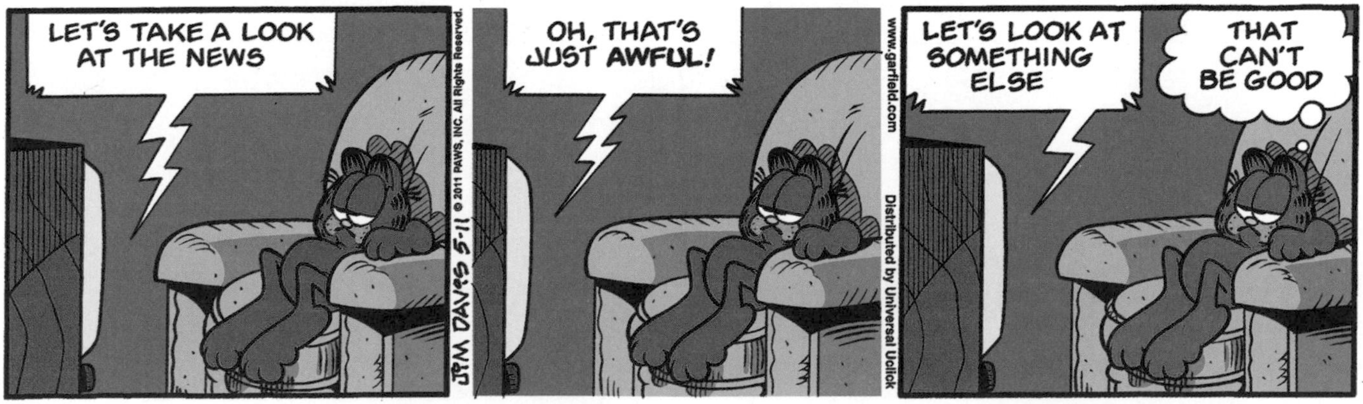
LET'S TAKE A LOOK AT THE NEWS
OH, THAT'S JUST AWFUL!
LET'S LOOK AT SOMETHING ELSE
THAT CAN'T BE GOOD
JPM DAVIS 5-11 © 2011 PAWS, INC. All Rights Reserved.
www.garfield.com Distributed by Universal Uclick

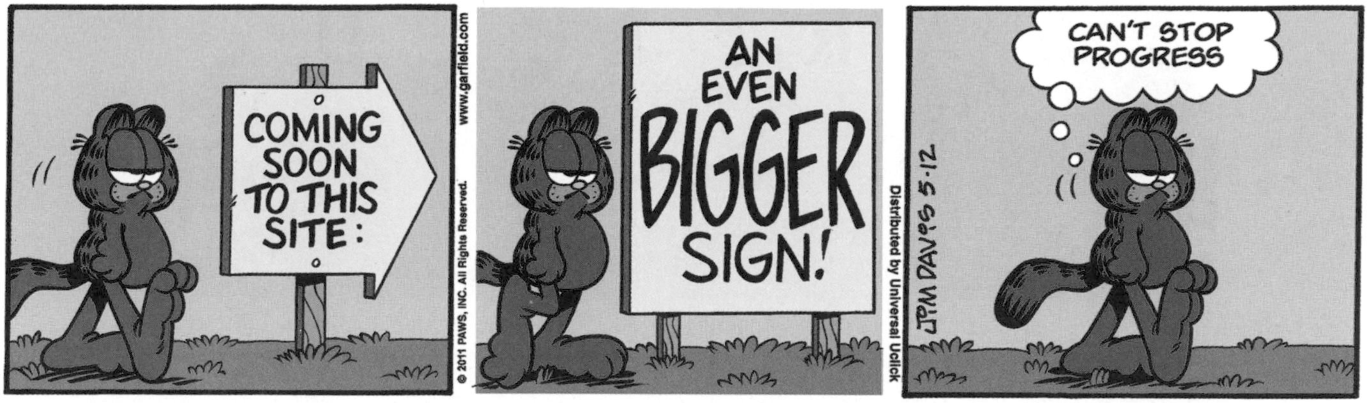
COMING SOON TO THIS SITE:
www.garfield.com
© 2011 PAWS, INC. All Rights Reserved.
AN EVEN BIGGER SIGN!
Distributed by Universal Uclick
JIM DAVIS 5-12
CAN'T STOP PROGRESS

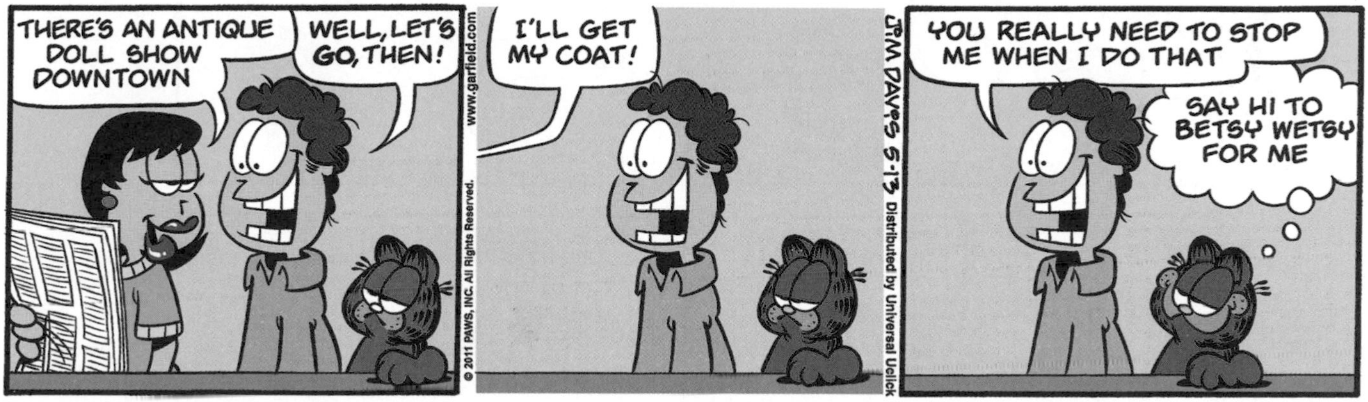
THERE'S AN ANTIQUE DOLL SHOW DOWNTOWN
WELL, LET'S GO, THEN!
www.garfield.com
© 2011 PAWS, INC. All Rights Reserved.
I'LL GET MY COAT!
JIM DAVIS 5-13
Distributed by Universal Uclick
YOU REALLY NEED TO STOP ME WHEN I DO THAT
SAY HI TO BETSY WETSY FOR ME

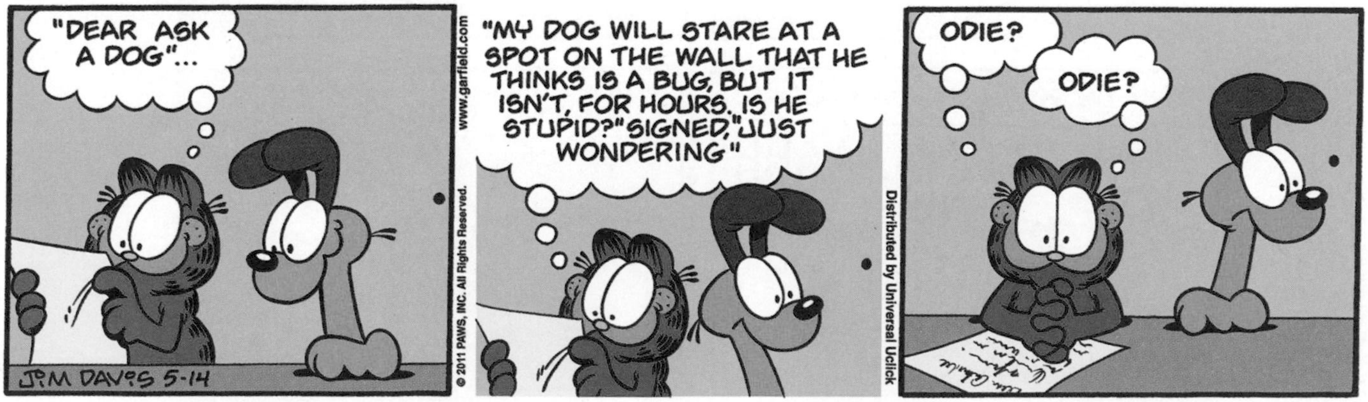
"DEAR ASK A DOG"...
JIM DAVIS 5-14
www.garfield.com
© 2011 PAWS, INC. All Rights Reserved.
"MY DOG WILL STARE AT A SPOT ON THE WALL THAT HE THINKS IS A BUG, BUT IT ISN'T, FOR HOURS. IS HE STUPID?" SIGNED, "JUST WONDERING"
Distributed by Universal Uclick
ODIE?
ODIE?

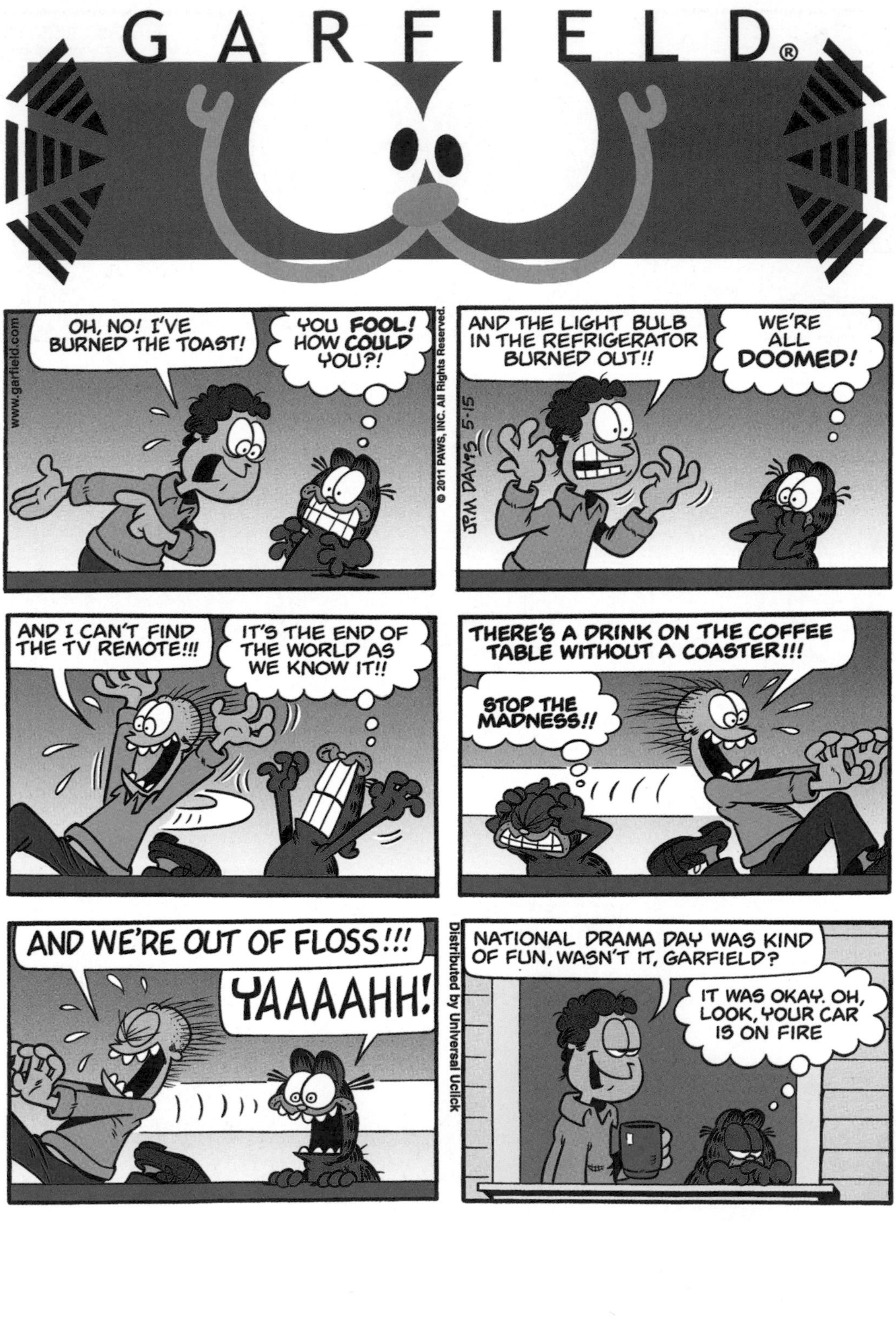

www.garfield.com
OH, NO! I'VE BURNED THE TOAST!
YOU FOOL! HOW COULD YOU?!
© 2011 PAWS, INC. All Rights Reserved.
JPM DAVIS 5-15
AND THE LIGHT BULB IN THE REFRIGERATOR BURNED OUT!!
WE'RE ALL DOOMED!
AND I CAN'T FIND THE TV REMOTE!!!
IT'S THE END OF THE WORLD AS WE KNOW IT!!
THERE'S A DRINK ON THE COFFEE TABLE WITHOUT A COASTER!!!
STOP THE MADNESS!!
AND WE'RE OUT OF FLOSS!!!
YAAAAHH!
Distributed by Universal Uclick
NATIONAL DRAMA DAY WAS KIND OF FUN, WASN'T IT, GARFIELD?
IT WAS OKAY. OH, LOOK, YOUR CAR IS ON FIRE

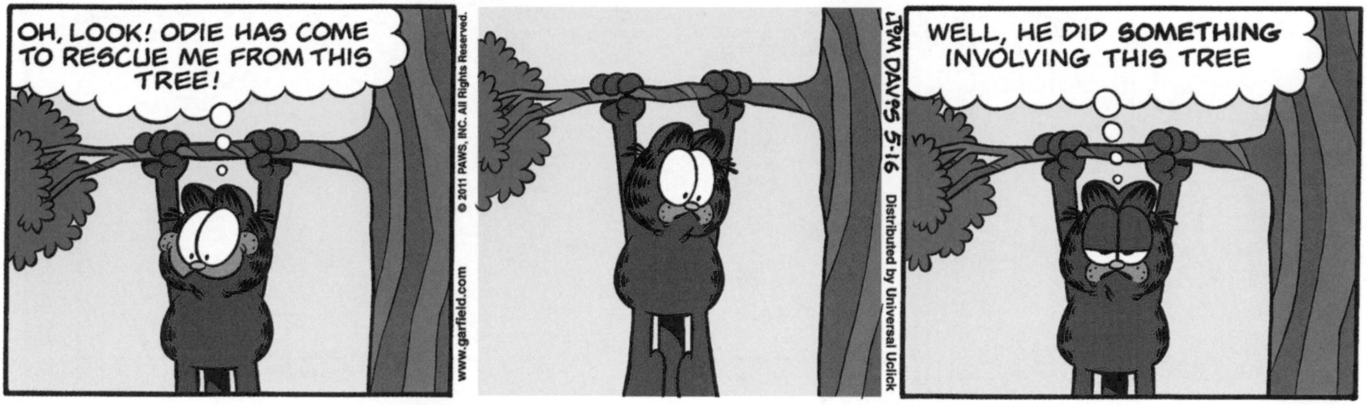
OH, LOOK! ODIE HAS COME TO RESCUE ME FROM THIS TREE!
© 2011 PAWS, INC. All Rights Reserved.
www.garfield.com
JIM DAVIS 5-16
Distributed by Universal Uclick
WELL, HE DID SOMETHING INVOLVING THIS TREE

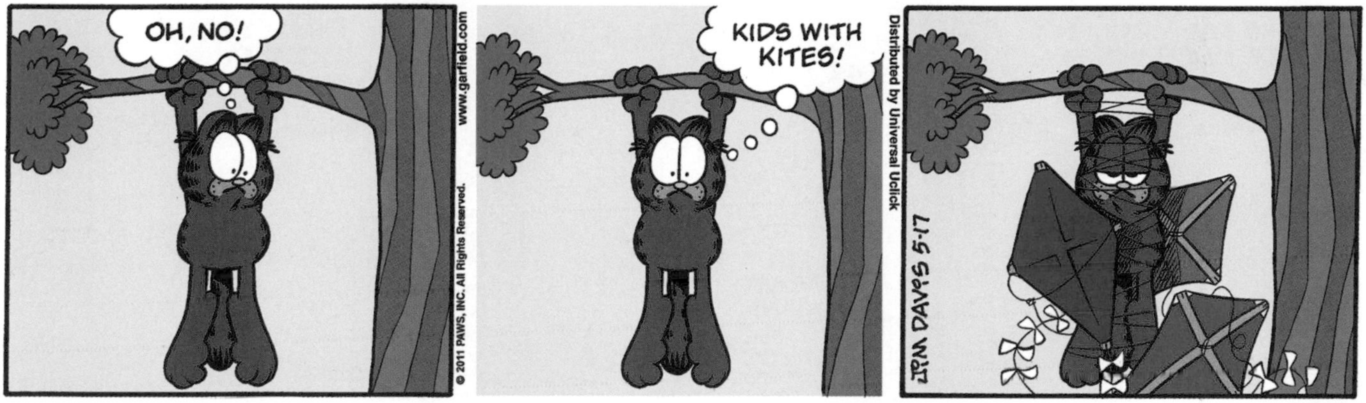
OH, NO!
© 2011 PAWS, INC. All Rights Reserved.
www.garfield.com
KIDS WITH KITES!
Distributed by Universal Uclick
JIM DAVIS 5-17

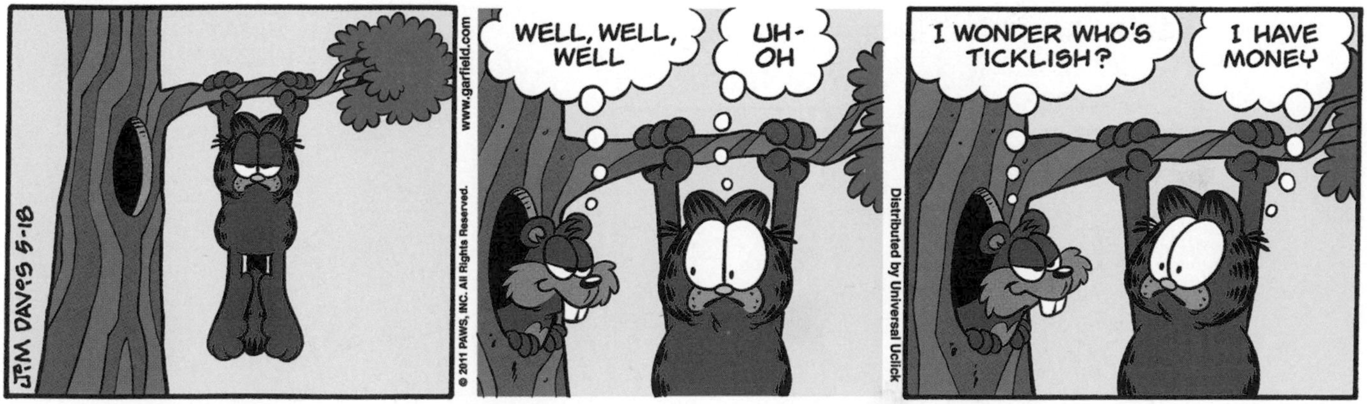
JIM DAVIS 5-18
© 2011 PAWS, INC. All Rights Reserved.
www.garfield.com
WELL, WELL, WELL
UH-OH
Distributed by Universal Uclick
I WONDER WHO'S TICKLISH?
I HAVE MONEY

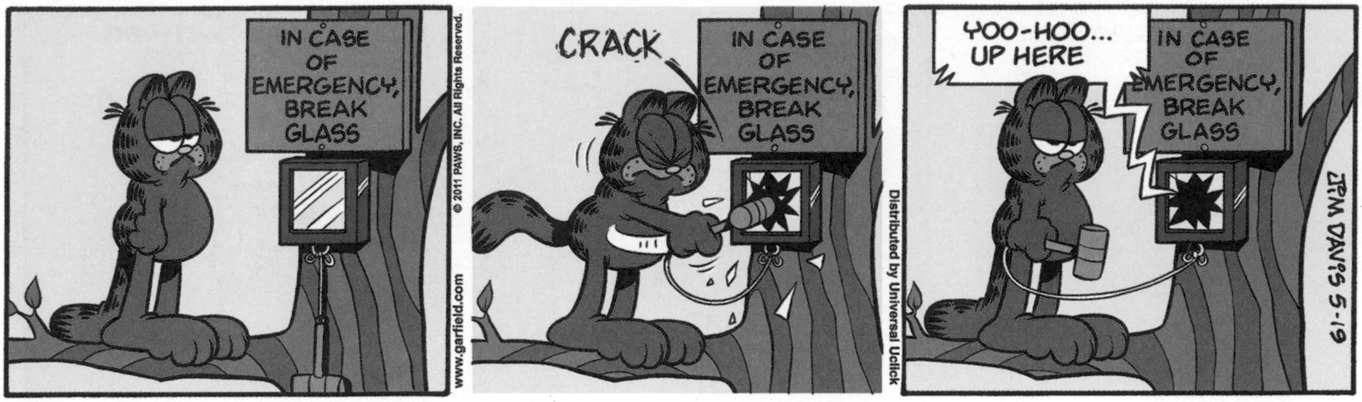
IN CASE OF EMERGENCY, BREAK GLASS
© 2011 PAWS, INC. All Rights Reserved.
www.garfield.com
CRACK
IN CASE OF EMERGENCY, BREAK GLASS
Distributed by Universal Uclick
YOO-HOO... UP HERE
IN CASE OF EMERGENCY, BREAK GLASS
JIM DAVIS 5-19

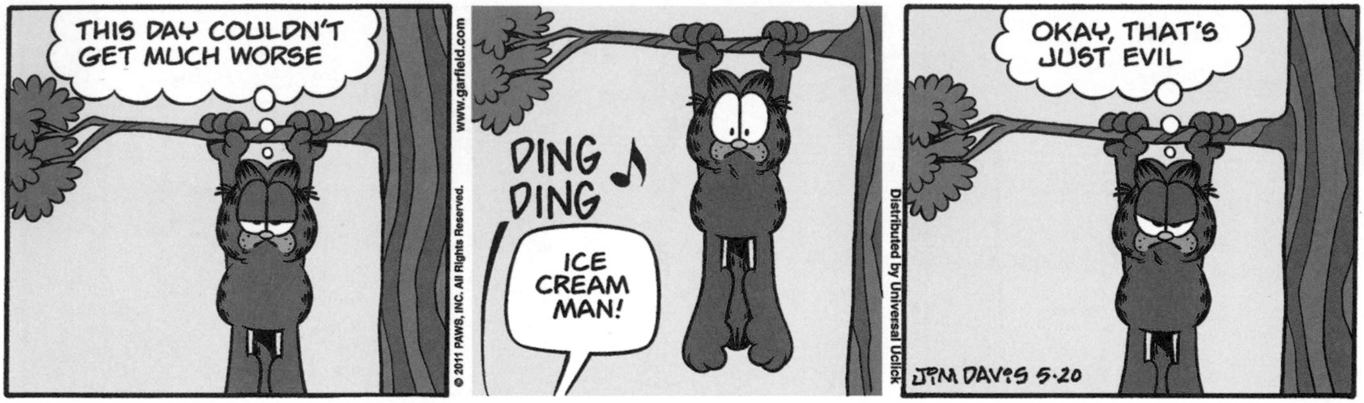
THIS DAY COULDN'T GET MUCH WORSE
© 2011 PAWS, INC. All Rights Reserved.
www.garfield.com
DING DING
ICE CREAM MAN!
Distributed by Universal Uclick
OKAY, THAT'S JUST EVIL
JIM DAVIS 5-20

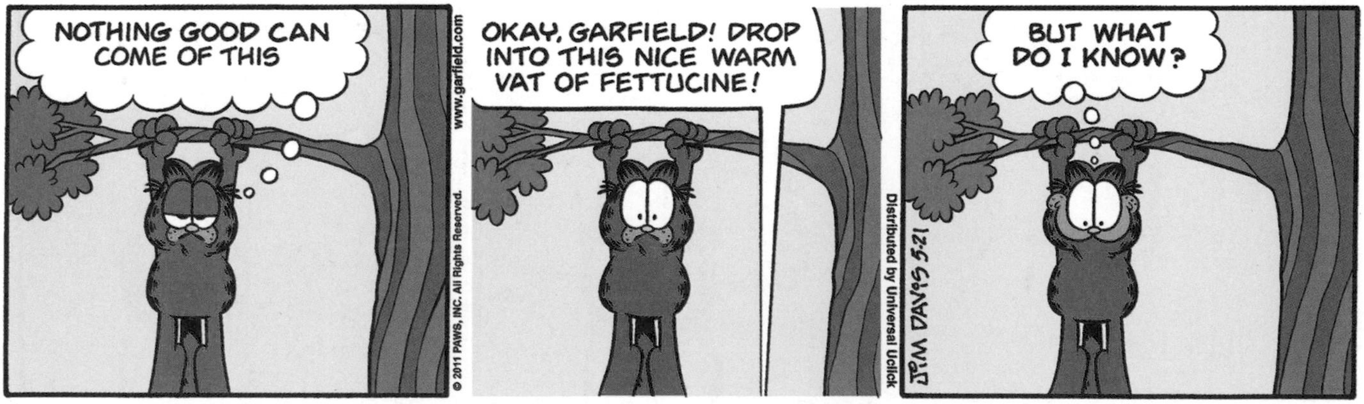
NOTHING GOOD CAN COME OF THIS
© 2011 PAWS, INC. All Rights Reserved.
www.garfield.com
OKAY, GARFIELD! DROP INTO THIS NICE WARM VAT OF FETTUCINE!
Distributed by Universal Uclick
BUT WHAT DO I KNOW?
JIM DAVIS 5-21

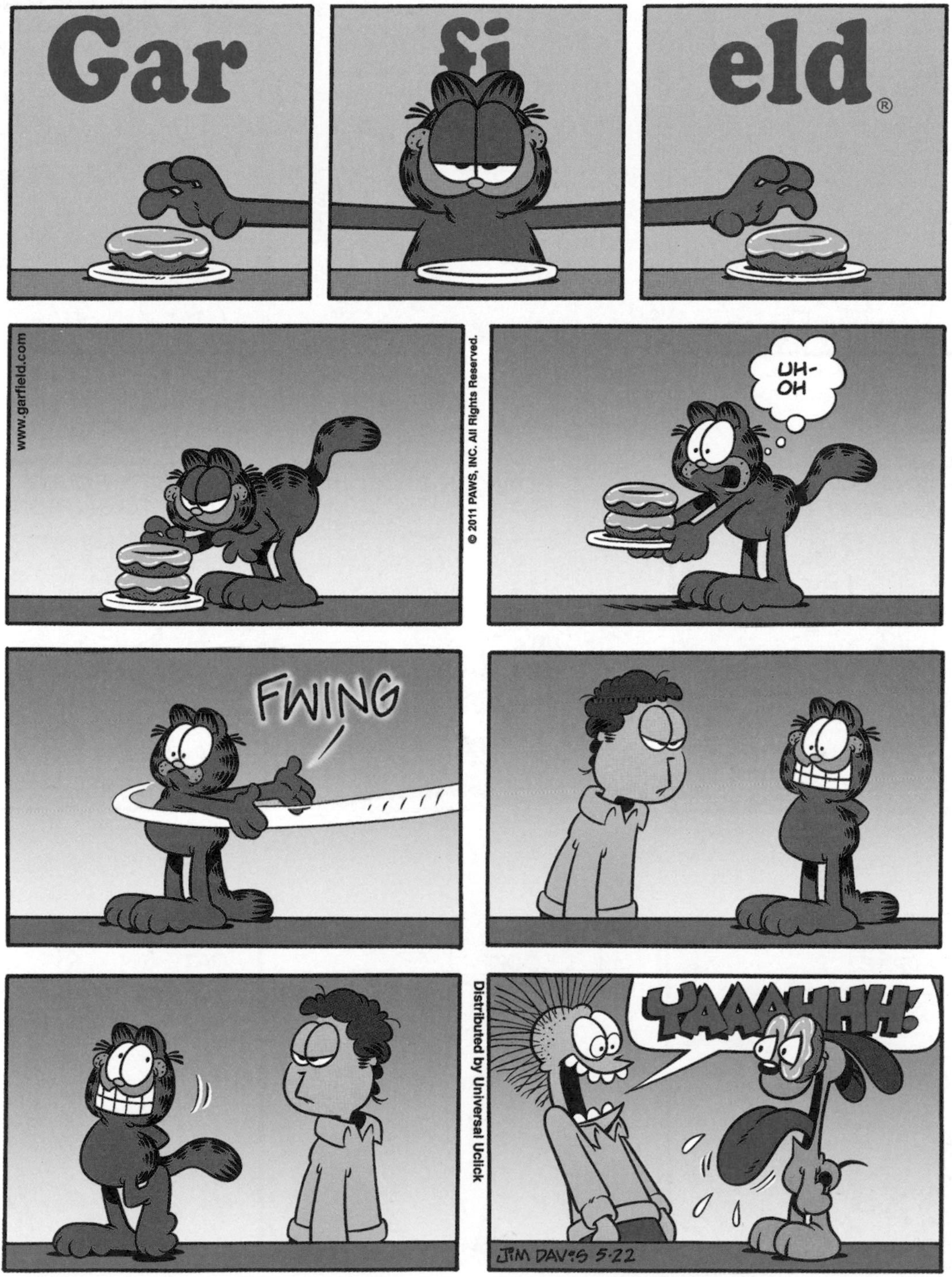
Garfield®
www.garfield.com
© 2011 PAWS, INC. All Rights Reserved.
UH-OH
FWING
Distributed by Universal Uclick
YAAAHHH!
JIM DAVIS 5-22

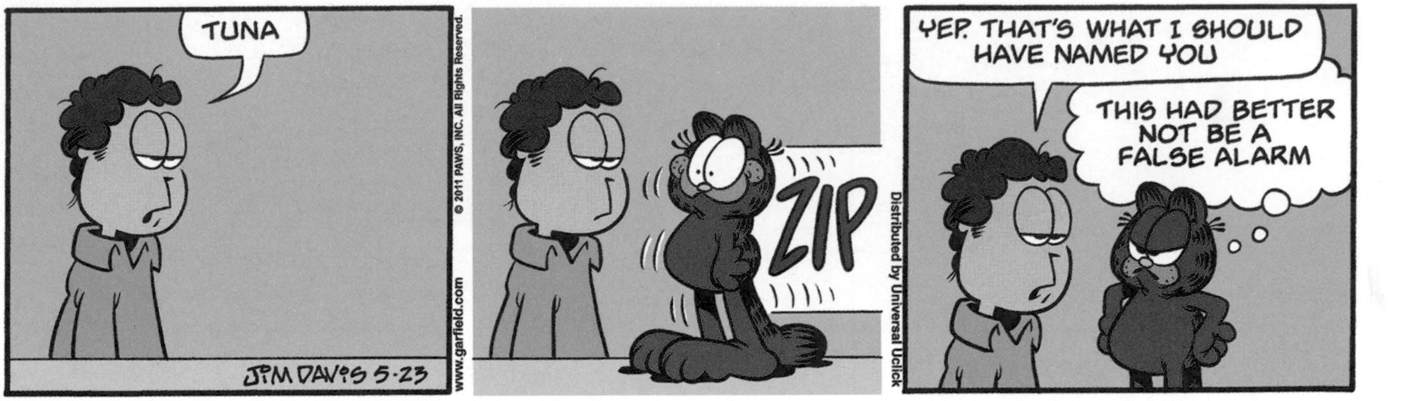
TUNA
ZIP
YEP. THAT'S WHAT I SHOULD HAVE NAMED YOU
THIS HAD BETTER NOT BE A FALSE ALARM
JIM DAVIS 5-23
© 2011 PAWS, INC. All Rights Reserved.
www.garfield.com
Distributed by Universal Uclick

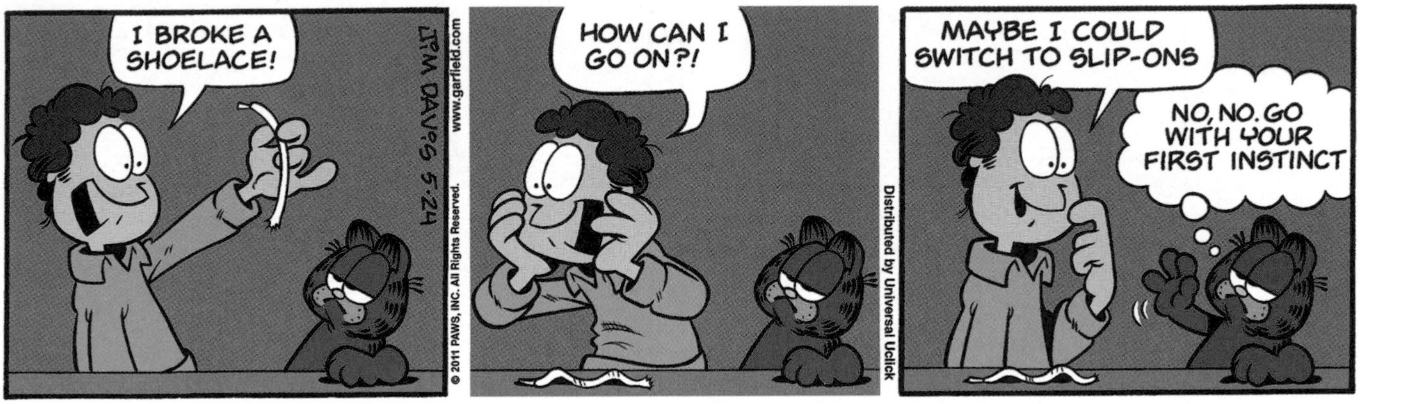
I BROKE A SHOELACE!
HOW CAN I GO ON?!
MAYBE I COULD SWITCH TO SLIP-ONS
NO, NO. GO WITH YOUR FIRST INSTINCT
JIM DAVIS 5-24
© 2011 PAWS, INC. All Rights Reserved.
www.garfield.com
Distributed by Universal Uclick

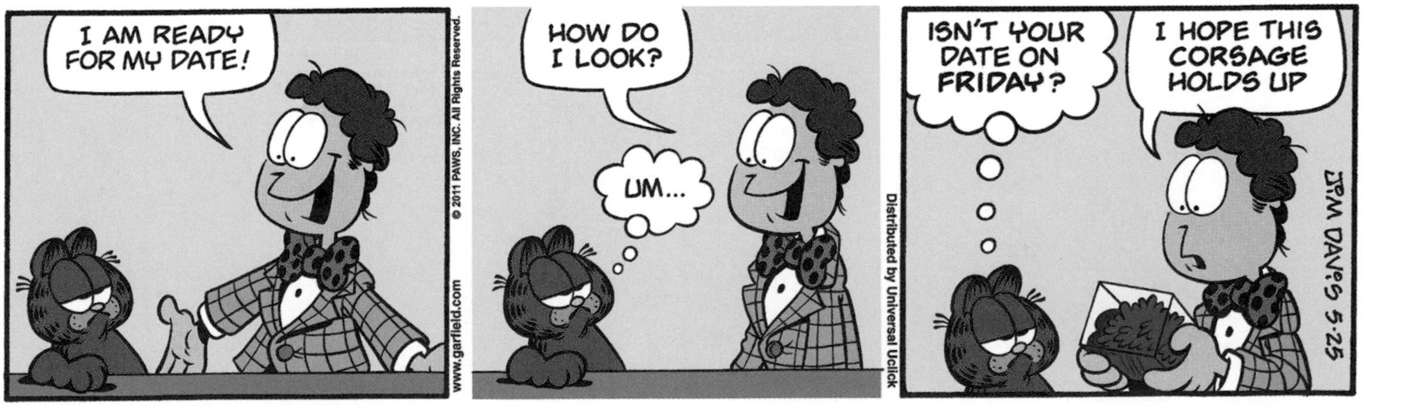
I AM READY FOR MY DATE!
HOW DO I LOOK?
UM...
ISN'T YOUR DATE ON FRIDAY?
I HOPE THIS CORSAGE HOLDS UP
JIM DAVIS 5-25
© 2011 PAWS, INC. All Rights Reserved.
www.garfield.com
Distributed by Universal Uclick

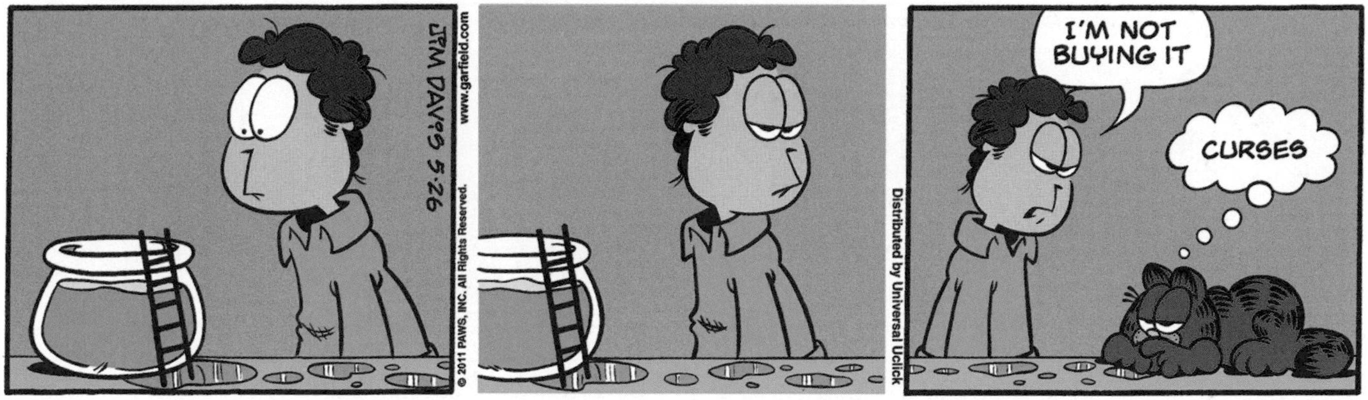
JIM DAVIS 5-26
© 2011 PAWS, INC. All Rights Reserved.
www.garfield.com
Distributed by Universal Uclick
I'M NOT BUYING IT
CURSES

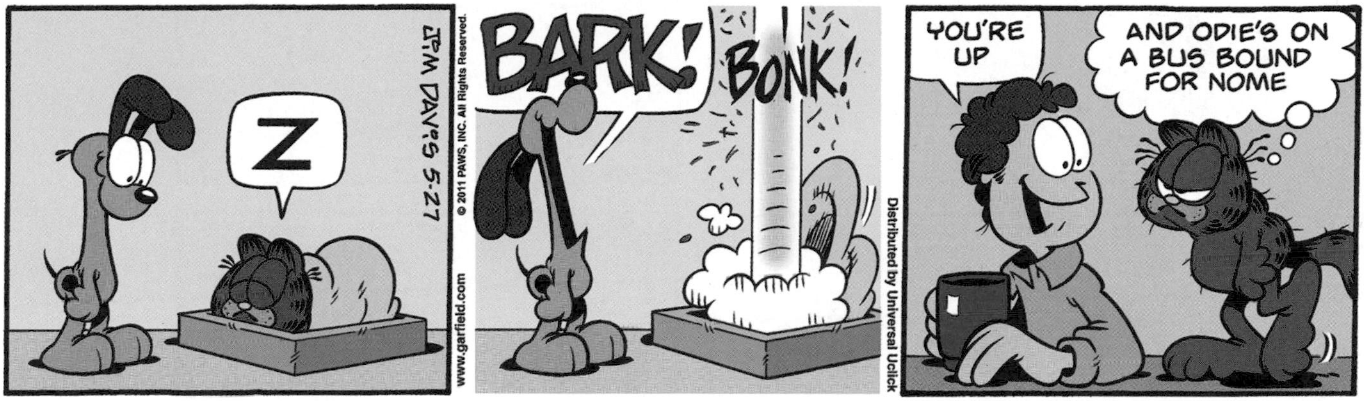
Z
JIM DAVIS 5-27
© 2011 PAWS, INC. All Rights Reserved.
www.garfield.com
BARK!
BONK!
Distributed by Universal Uclick
YOU'RE UP
AND ODIE'S ON A BUS BOUND FOR NOME

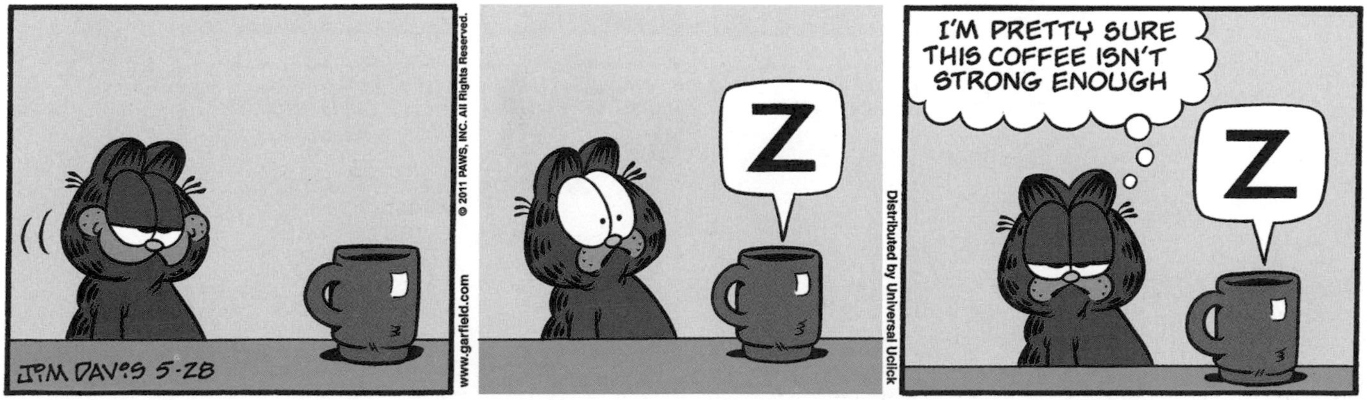
JIM DAVIS 5-28
© 2011 PAWS, INC. All Rights Reserved.
www.garfield.com
Z
Distributed by Universal Uclick
I'M PRETTY SURE THIS COFFEE ISN'T STRONG ENOUGH
Z

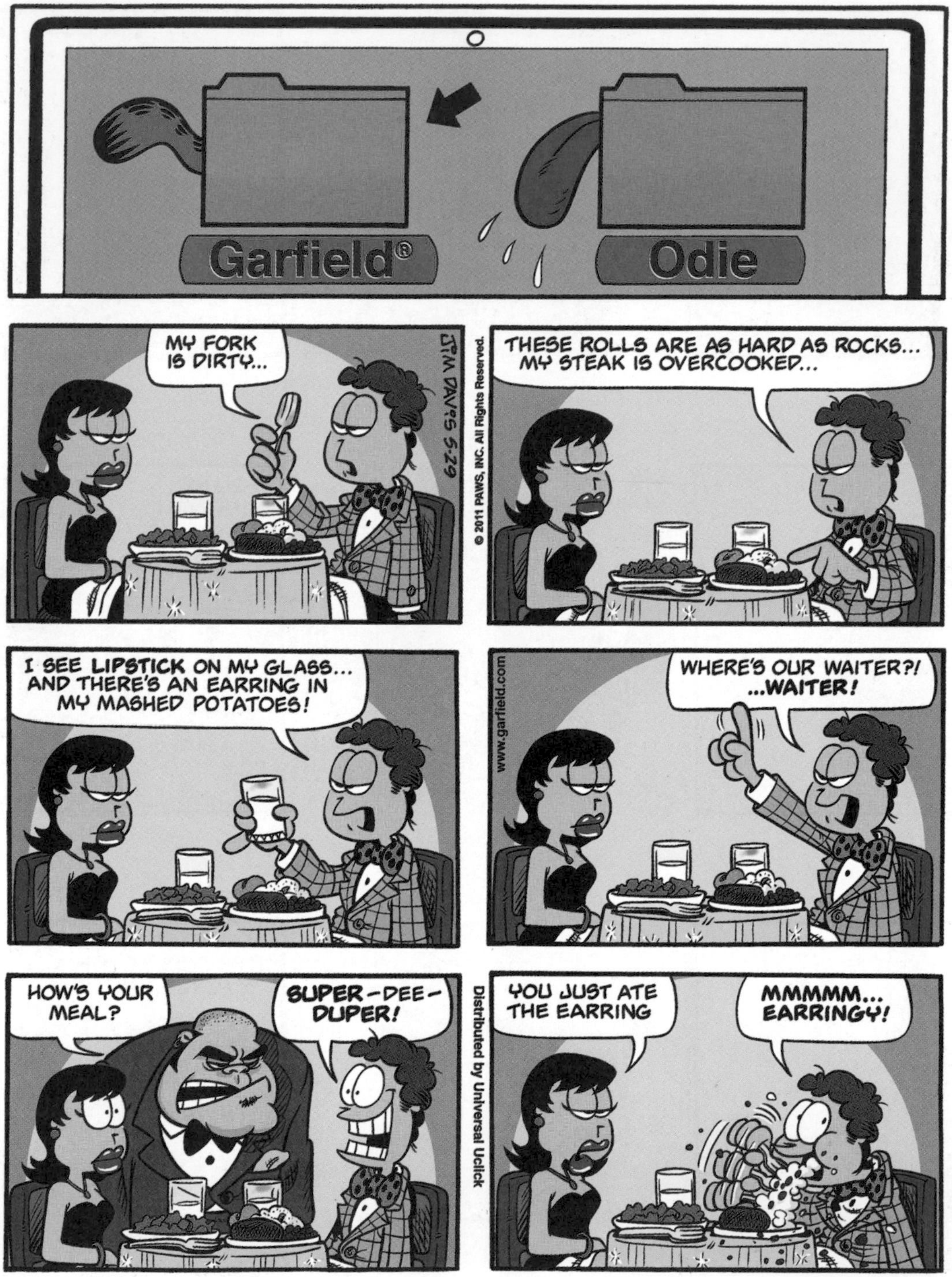
Garfield®
Odie
MY FORK IS DIRTY...
JPM DAVPS 5-29
© 2011 PAWS, INC. All Rights Reserved.
THESE ROLLS ARE AS HARD AS ROCKS... MY STEAK IS OVERCOOKED...
I SEE LIPSTICK ON MY GLASS... AND THERE'S AN EARRING IN MY MASHED POTATOES!
www.garfield.com
WHERE'S OUR WAITER?! ...WAITER!
HOW'S YOUR MEAL?
SUPER-DEE-DUPER!
Distributed by Universal Uclick
YOU JUST ATE THE EARRING
MMMMM... EARRINGY!

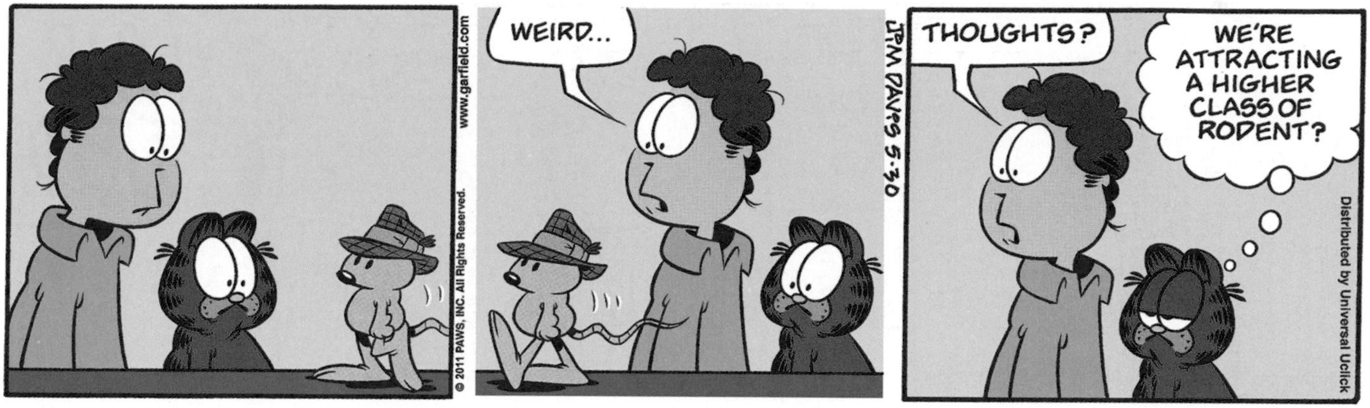
WEIRD...
THOUGHTS?
WE'RE ATTRACTING A HIGHER CLASS OF RODENT?
© 2011 PAWS, INC. All Rights Reserved. www.garfield.com
JIM DAVIS 5-30
Distributed by Universal Uclick

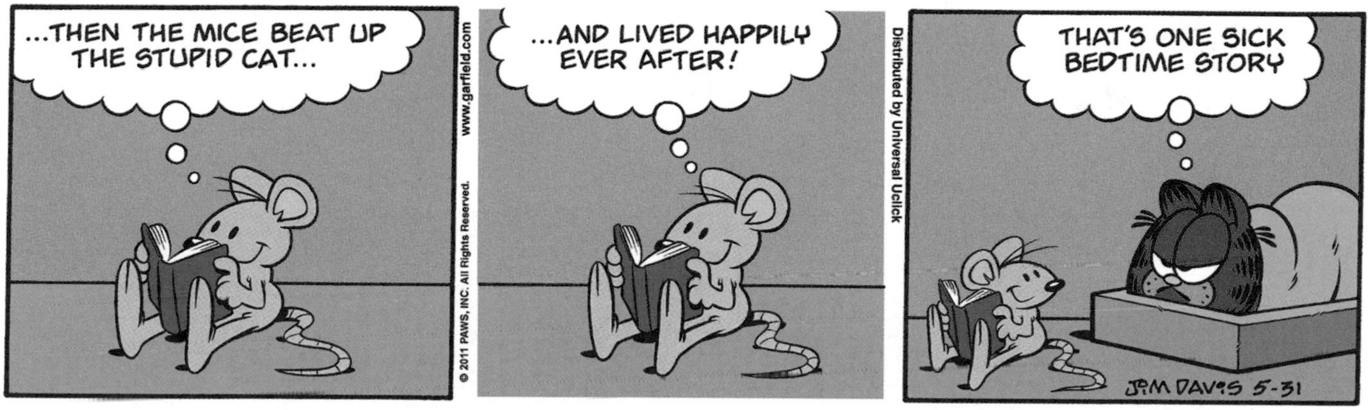
...THEN THE MICE BEAT UP THE STUPID CAT...
...AND LIVED HAPPILY EVER AFTER!
THAT'S ONE SICK BEDTIME STORY
© 2011 PAWS, INC. All Rights Reserved. www.garfield.com
Distributed by Universal Uclick
JIM DAVIS 5-31

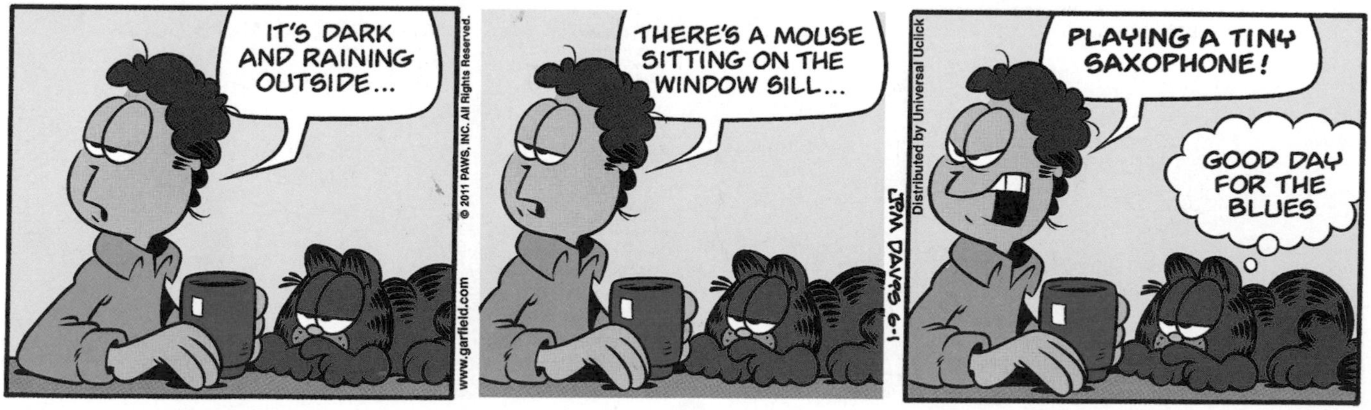
IT'S DARK AND RAINING OUTSIDE...
THERE'S A MOUSE SITTING ON THE WINDOW SILL...
PLAYING A TINY SAXOPHONE!
GOOD DAY FOR THE BLUES
© 2011 PAWS, INC. All Rights Reserved. www.garfield.com
JIM DAVIS 6-1
Distributed by Universal Uclick

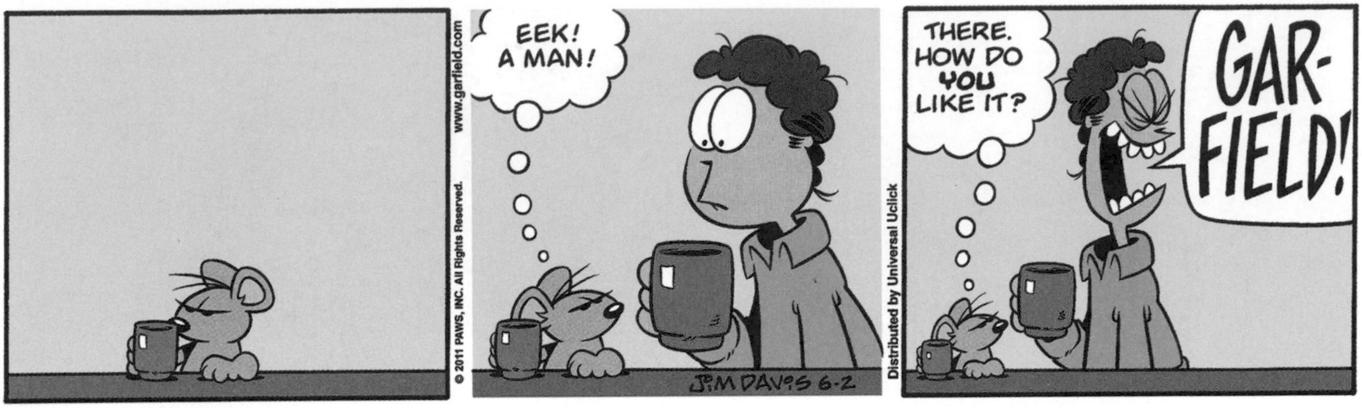
EEK! A MAN!
THERE. HOW DO YOU LIKE IT?
GAR-FIELD!
JIM DAVIS 6-2
© 2011 PAWS, INC. All Rights Reserved. www.garfield.com
Distributed by Universal Uclick

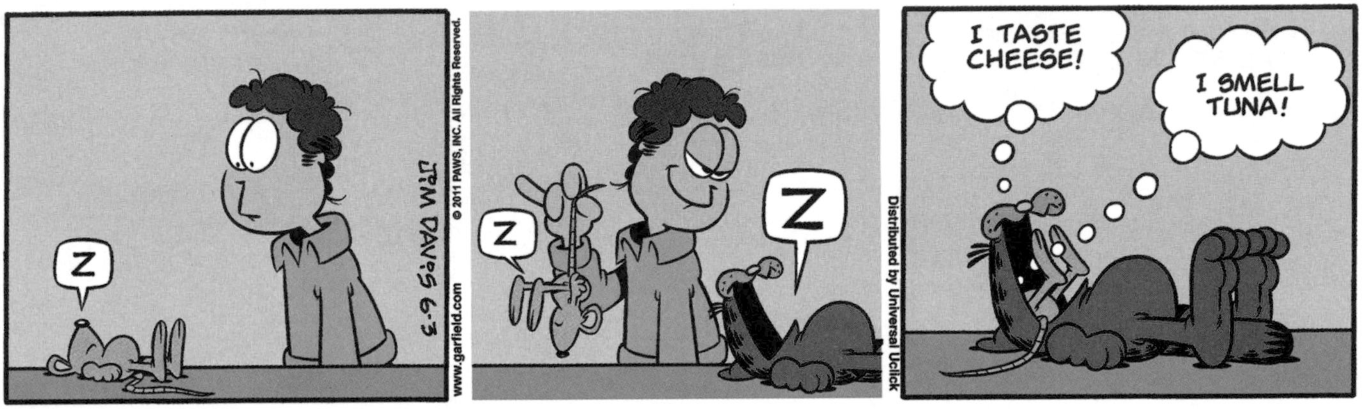
Z
JIM DAVIS 6-3
© 2011 PAWS, INC. All Rights Reserved. www.garfield.com
Z
Z
Distributed by Universal Uclick
I TASTE CHEESE!
I SMELL TUNA!

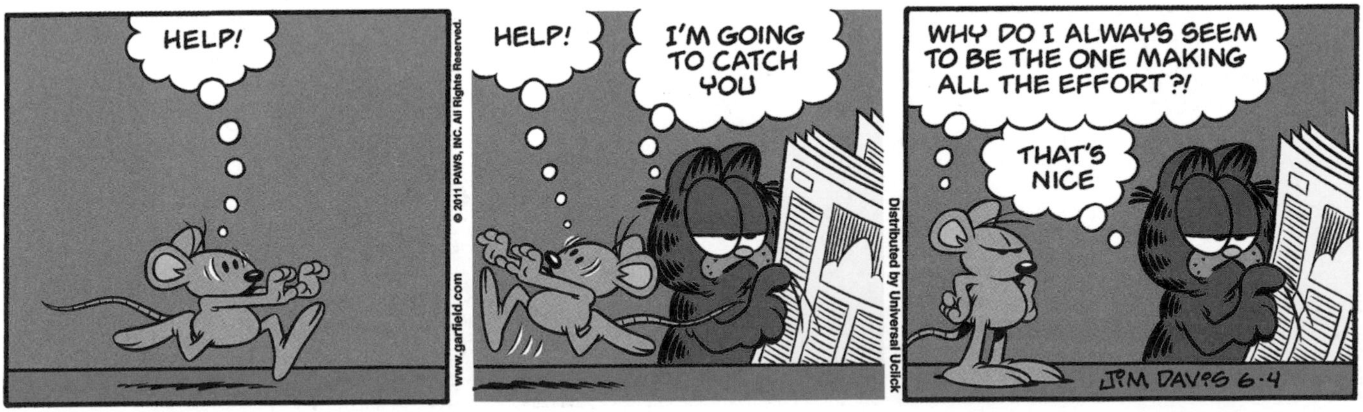
HELP!
© 2011 PAWS, INC. All Rights Reserved. www.garfield.com
HELP!
I'M GOING TO CATCH YOU
Distributed by Universal Uclick
WHY DO I ALWAYS SEEM TO BE THE ONE MAKING ALL THE EFFORT?!
THAT'S NICE
JIM DAVIS 6-4

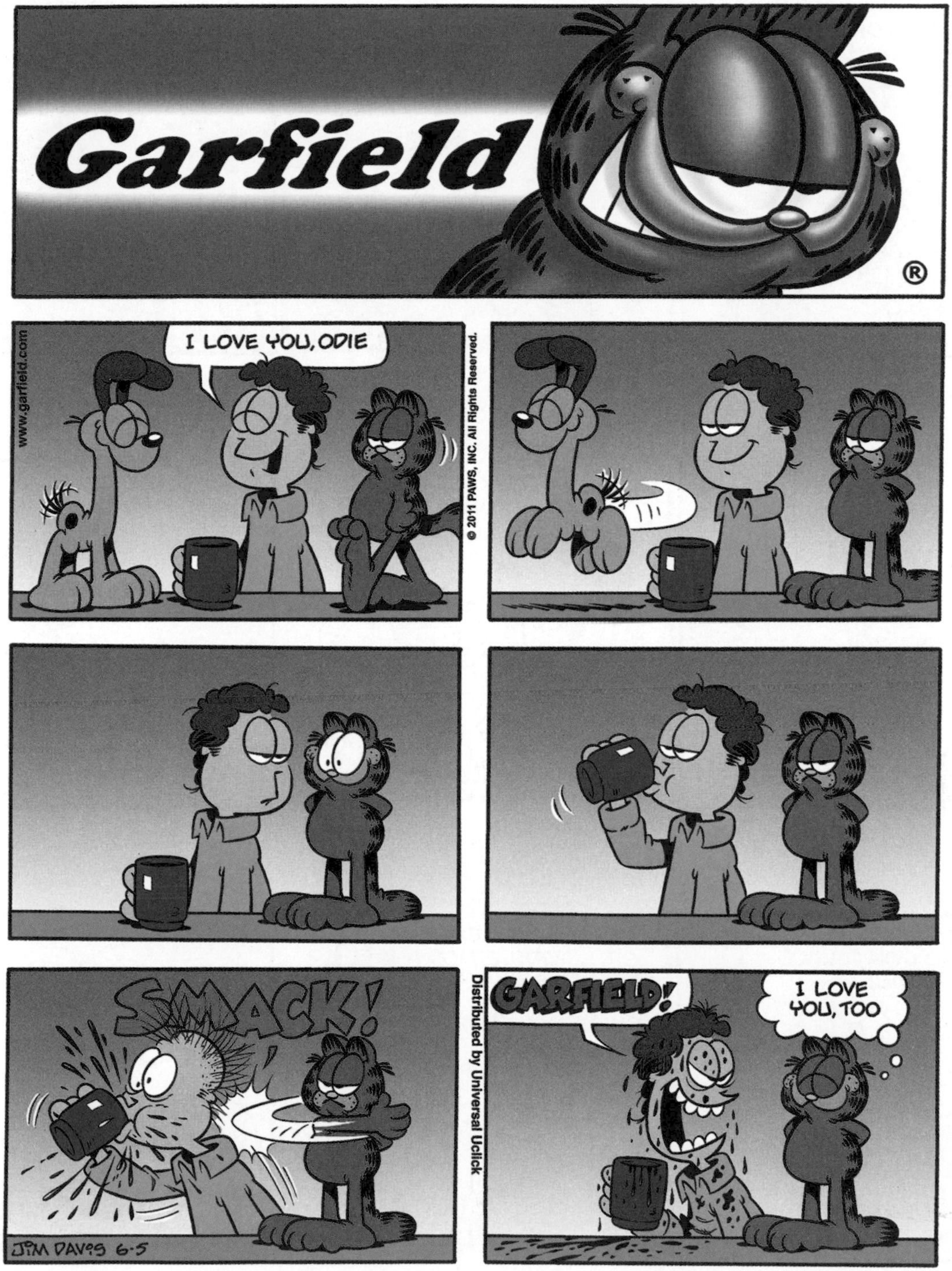
Garfield®
www.garfield.com
I LOVE YOU, ODIE
© 2011 PAWS, INC. All Rights Reserved.
SMACK!
JIM DAVIS 6-5
Distributed by Universal Uclick
GARFIELD!
I LOVE YOU, TOO

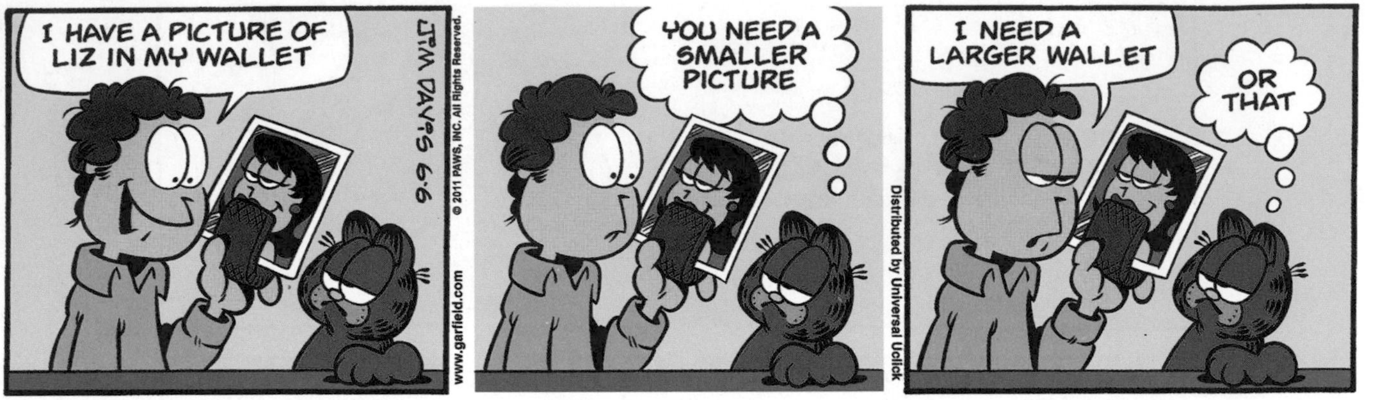
I HAVE A PICTURE OF LIZ IN MY WALLET
JIM DAVIS 6-6
© 2011 PAWS, INC. All Rights Reserved. www.garfield.com
YOU NEED A SMALLER PICTURE
Distributed by Universal Uclick
I NEED A LARGER WALLET
OR THAT

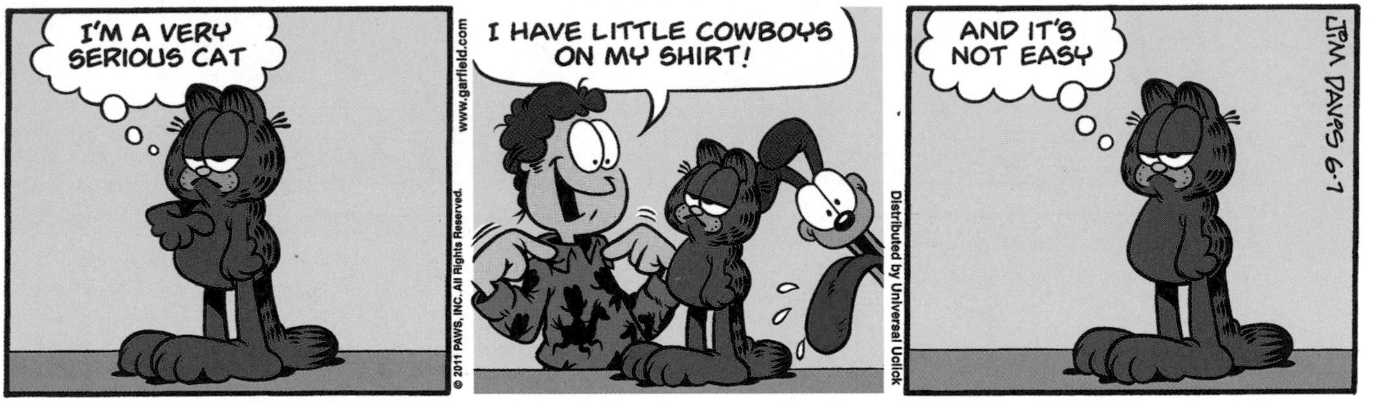
I'M A VERY SERIOUS CAT
© 2011 PAWS, INC. All Rights Reserved. www.garfield.com
I HAVE LITTLE COWBOYS ON MY SHIRT!
Distributed by Universal Uclick
AND IT'S NOT EASY
JIM DAVIS 6-7

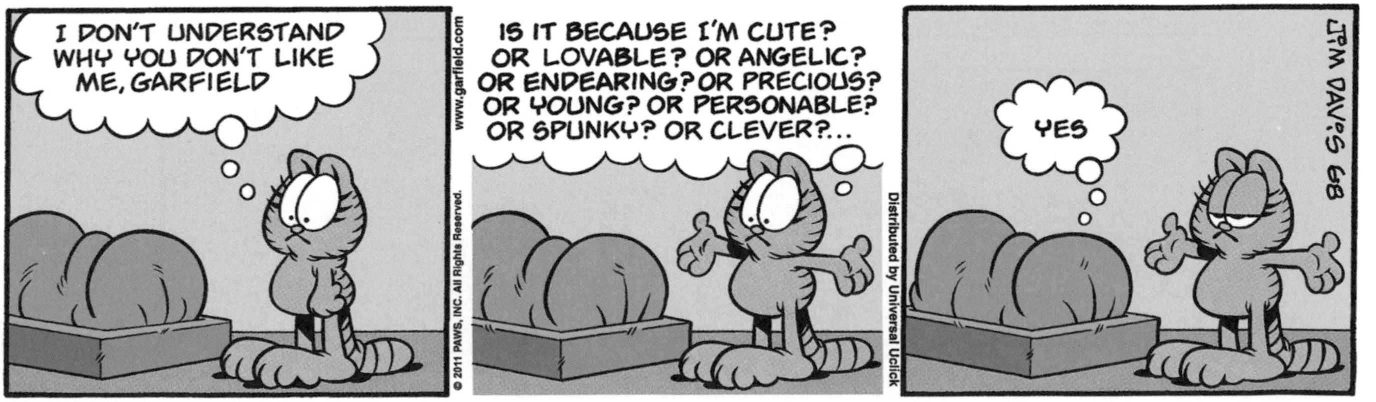
I DON'T UNDERSTAND WHY YOU DON'T LIKE ME, GARFIELD
© 2011 PAWS, INC. All Rights Reserved. www.garfield.com
IS IT BECAUSE I'M CUTE? OR LOVABLE? OR ANGELIC? OR ENDEARING? OR PRECIOUS? OR YOUNG? OR PERSONABLE? OR SPUNKY? OR CLEVER?...
Distributed by Universal Uclick
YES
JIM DAVIS 6-8

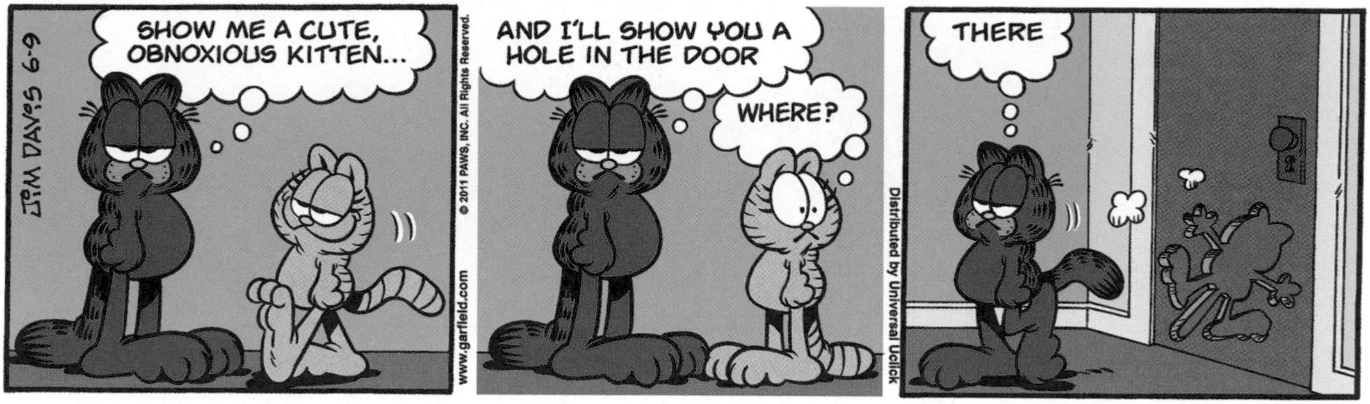
SHOW ME A CUTE, OBNOXIOUS KITTEN...
AND I'LL SHOW YOU A HOLE IN THE DOOR
WHERE?
THERE
© 2011 PAWS, INC. All Rights Reserved.
www.garfield.com
Distributed by Universal Uclick

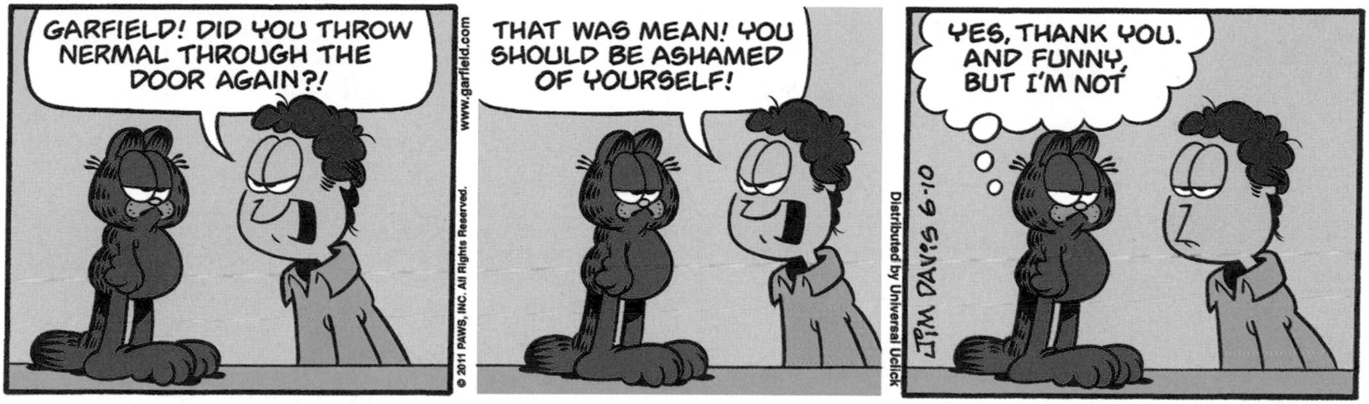
GARFIELD! DID YOU THROW NERMAL THROUGH THE DOOR AGAIN?!
THAT WAS MEAN! YOU SHOULD BE ASHAMED OF YOURSELF!
YES, THANK YOU. AND FUNNY, BUT I'M NOT
© 2011 PAWS, INC. All Rights Reserved.
www.garfield.com
Distributed by Universal Uclick

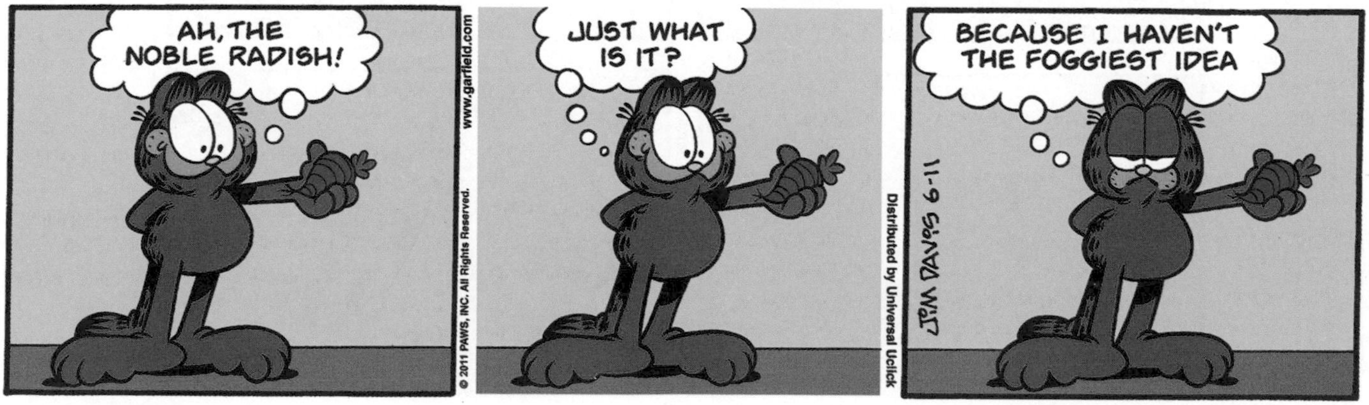
AH, THE NOBLE RADISH!
JUST WHAT IS IT?
BECAUSE I HAVEN'T THE FOGGIEST IDEA
© 2011 PAWS, INC. All Rights Reserved.
www.garfield.com
Distributed by Universal Uclick

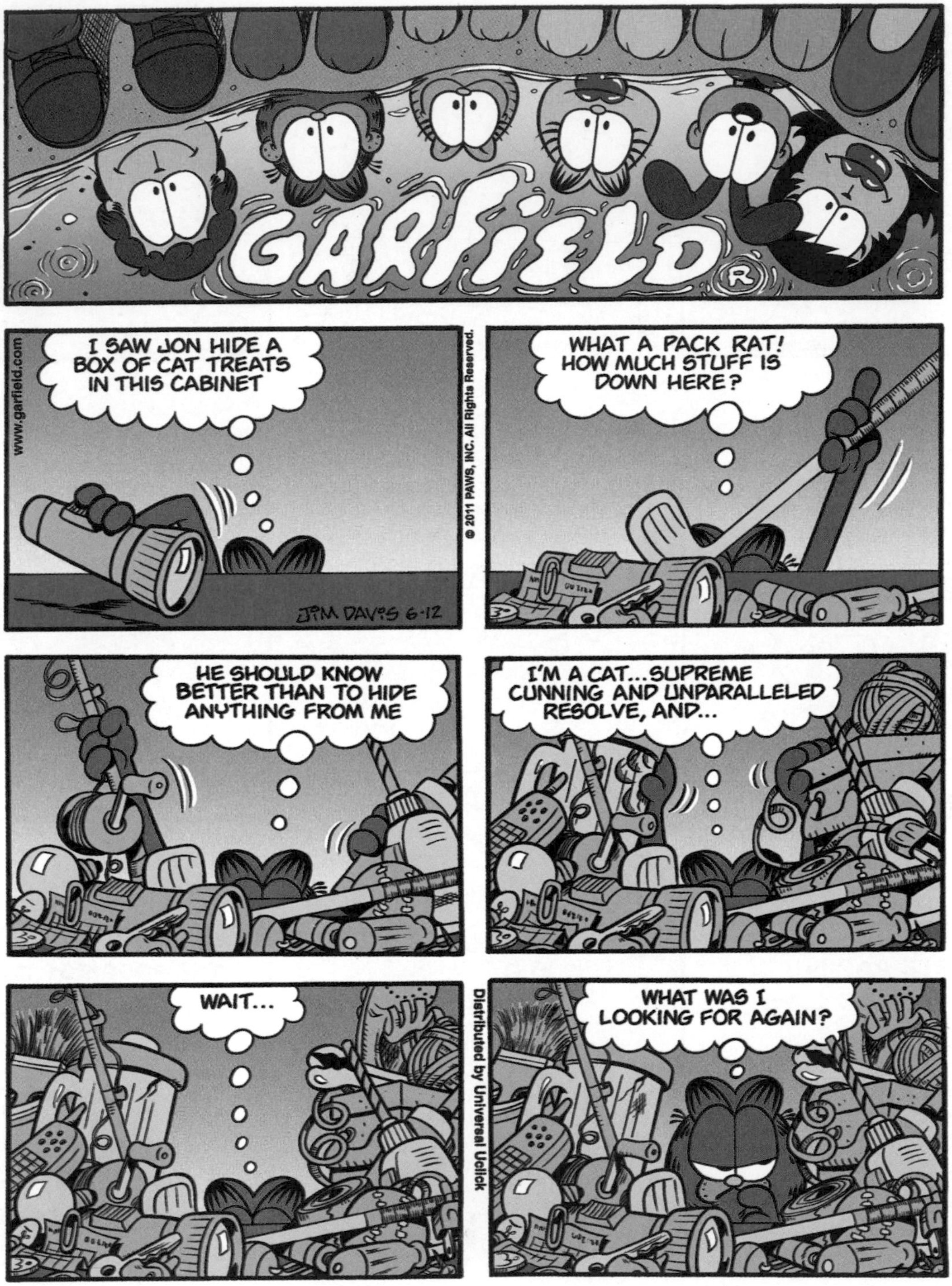
GARFIELD®
I SAW JON HIDE A BOX OF CAT TREATS IN THIS CABINET
www.garfield.com
JPM DAVPS 6-12
© 2011 PAWS, INC. All Rights Reserved.
WHAT A PACK RAT! HOW MUCH STUFF IS DOWN HERE?
HE SHOULD KNOW BETTER THAN TO HIDE ANYTHING FROM ME
I'M A CAT...SUPREME CUNNING AND UNPARALLELED RESOLVE, AND...
WAIT...
Distributed by Universal Uclick
WHAT WAS I LOOKING FOR AGAIN?

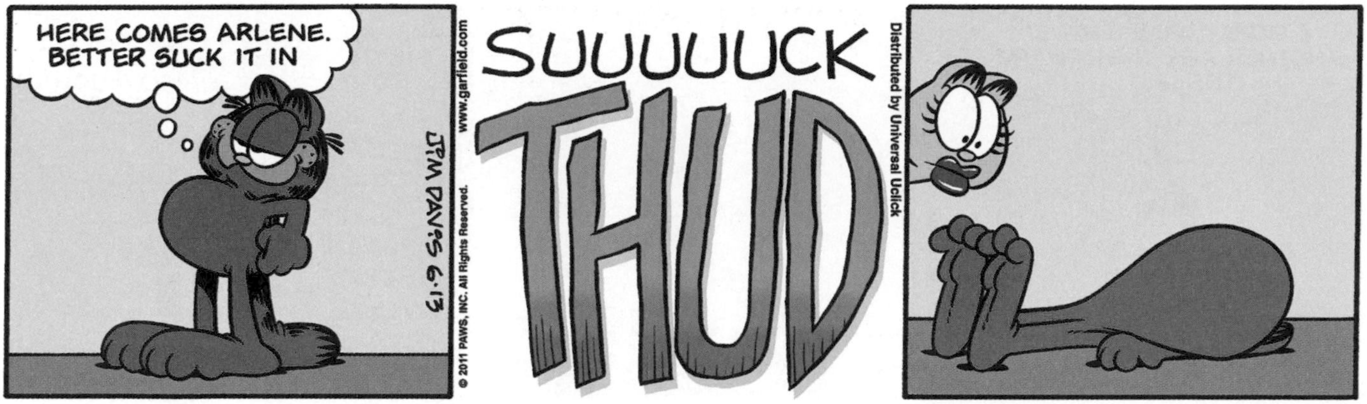
HERE COMES ARLENE. BETTER SUCK IT IN
JIM DAVIS 6-13
© 2011 PAWS, INC. All Rights Reserved.
www.garfield.com
SUUUUUCK
THUD
Distributed by Universal Uclick

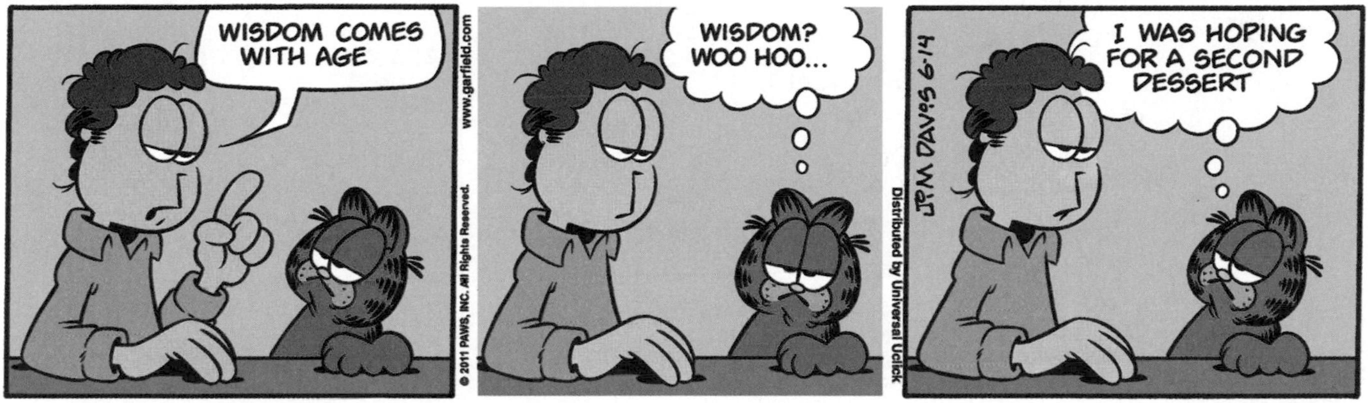
WISDOM COMES WITH AGE
© 2011 PAWS, INC. All Rights Reserved.
www.garfield.com
WISDOM? WOO HOO...
Distributed by Universal Uclick
JIM DAVIS 6-14
I WAS HOPING FOR A SECOND DESSERT

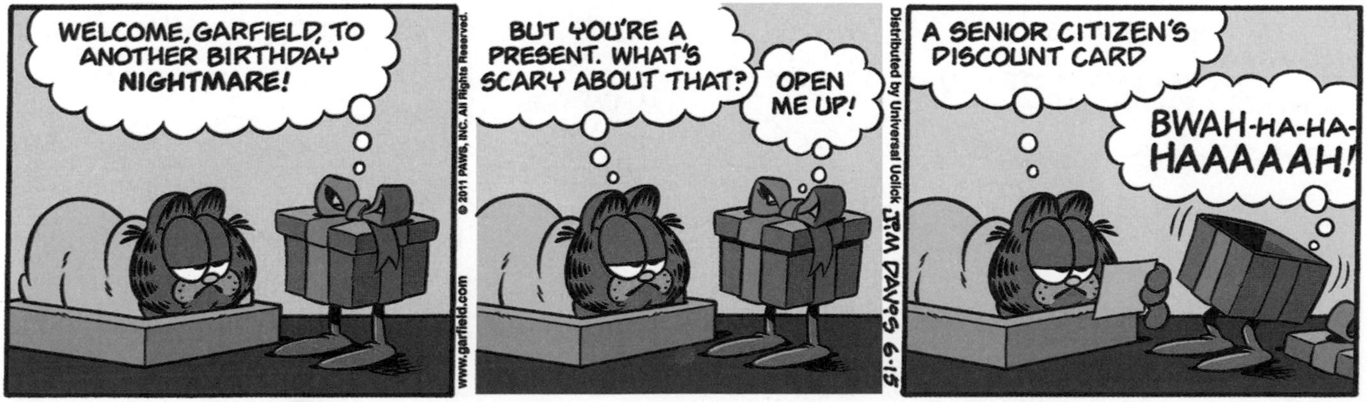
WELCOME, GARFIELD, TO ANOTHER BIRTHDAY NIGHTMARE!
www.garfield.com
© 2011 PAWS, INC. All Rights Reserved.
BUT YOU'RE A PRESENT. WHAT'S SCARY ABOUT THAT?
OPEN ME UP!
Distributed by Universal Uclick
JIM DAVIS 6-15
A SENIOR CITIZEN'S DISCOUNT CARD
BWAH-HA-HA-HAAAAAH!

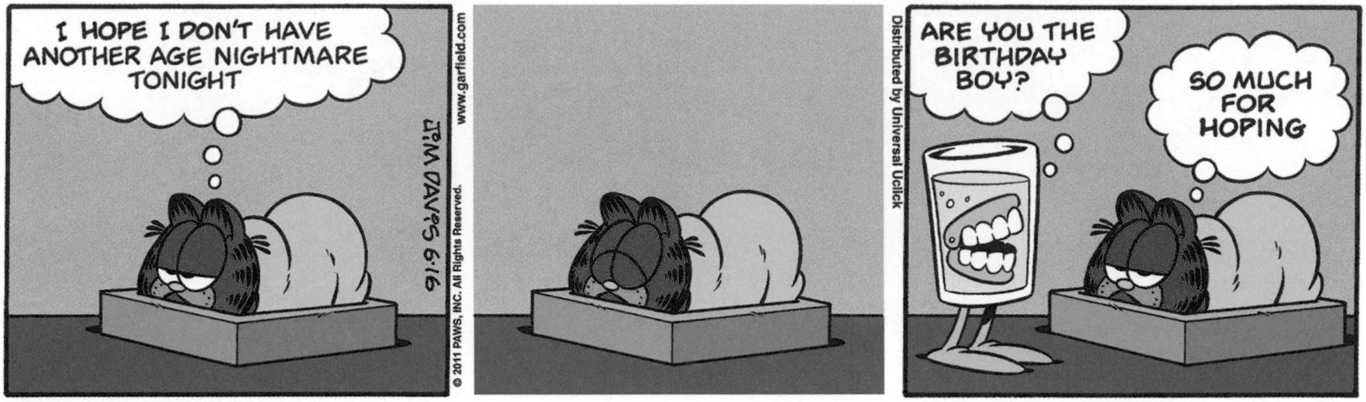
I HOPE I DON'T HAVE ANOTHER AGE NIGHTMARE TONIGHT
JIM DAVIS 6-16
© 2011 PAWS, INC. All Rights Reserved.
www.garfield.com
Distributed by Universal Uclick
ARE YOU THE BIRTHDAY BOY?
SO MUCH FOR HOPING

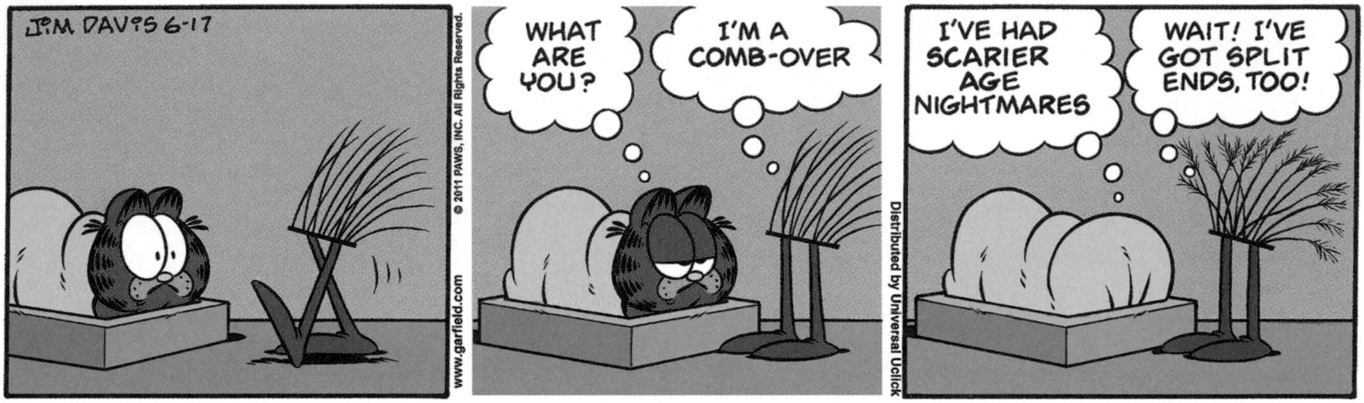
JIM DAVIS 6-17
www.garfield.com
© 2011 PAWS, INC. All Rights Reserved.
WHAT ARE YOU?
I'M A COMB-OVER
Distributed by Universal Uclick
I'VE HAD SCARIER AGE NIGHTMARES
WAIT! I'VE GOT SPLIT ENDS, TOO!

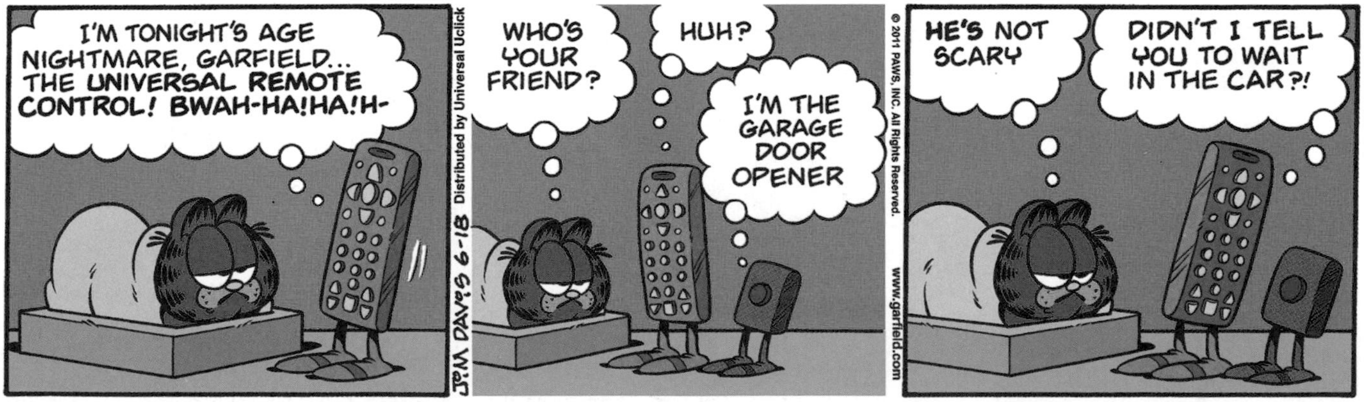
I'M TONIGHT'S AGE NIGHTMARE, GARFIELD... THE UNIVERSAL REMOTE CONTROL! BWAH-HA!HA!H-
JIM DAVIS 6-18
Distributed by Universal Uclick
WHO'S YOUR FRIEND?
HUH?
I'M THE GARAGE DOOR OPENER
© 2011 PAWS, INC. All Rights Reserved.
www.garfield.com
HE'S NOT SCARY
DIDN'T I TELL YOU TO WAIT IN THE CAR?!

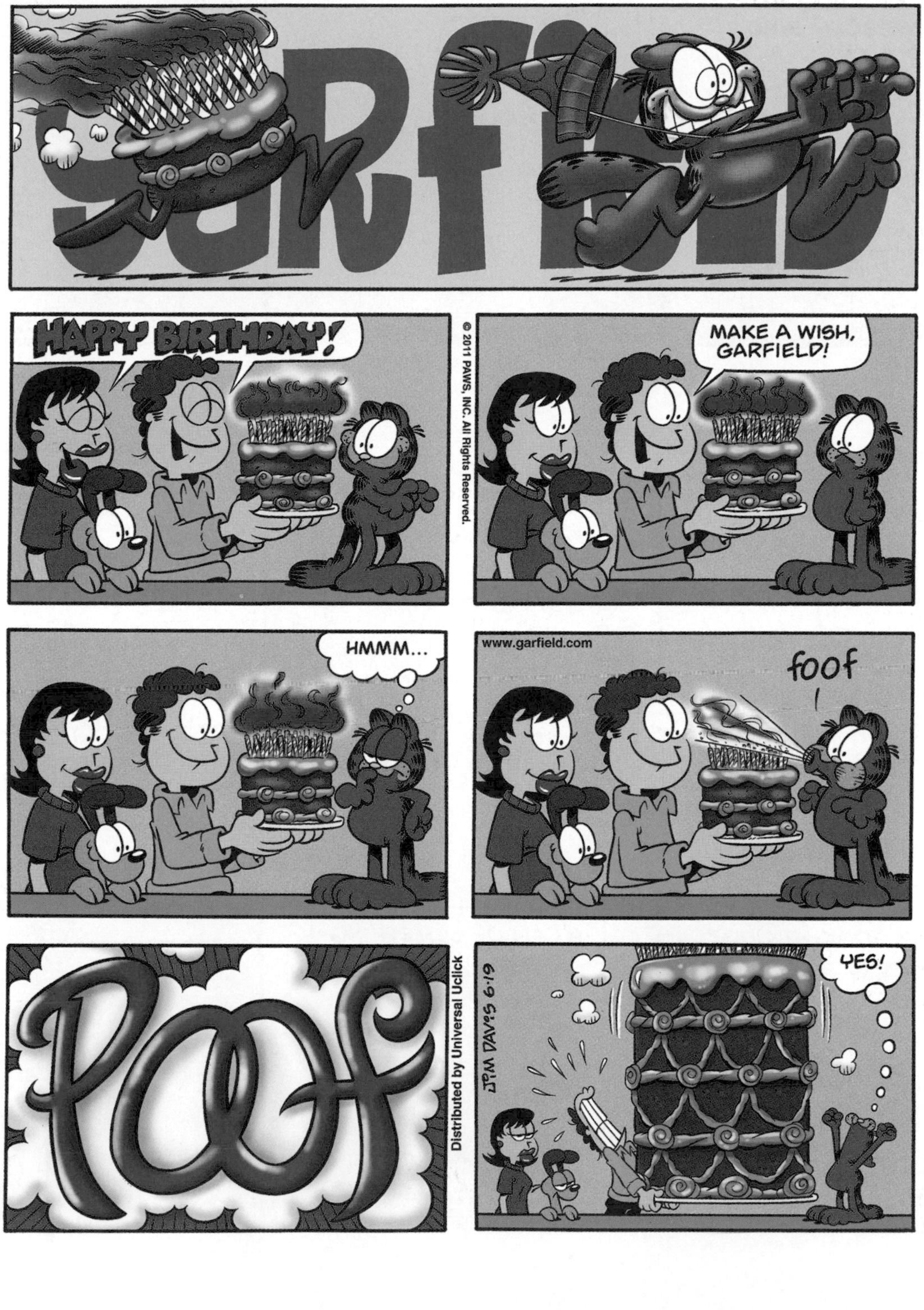
HAPPY BIRTHDAY!
MAKE A WISH, GARFIELD!
HMMM...
foof
POOF
YES!
© 2011 PAWS, INC. All Rights Reserved.
www.garfield.com
Distributed by Universal Uclick
JPM DAVIS 6·19

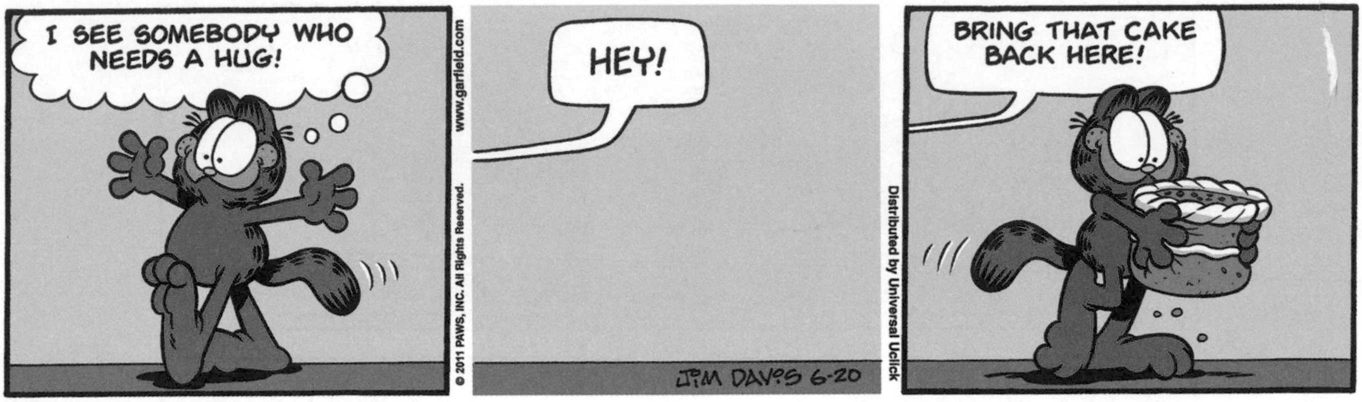
I SEE SOMEBODY WHO NEEDS A HUG!
HEY!
BRING THAT CAKE BACK HERE!
JIM DAVIS 6-20
© 2011 PAWS, INC. All Rights Reserved.
www.garfield.com
Distributed by Universal Uclick

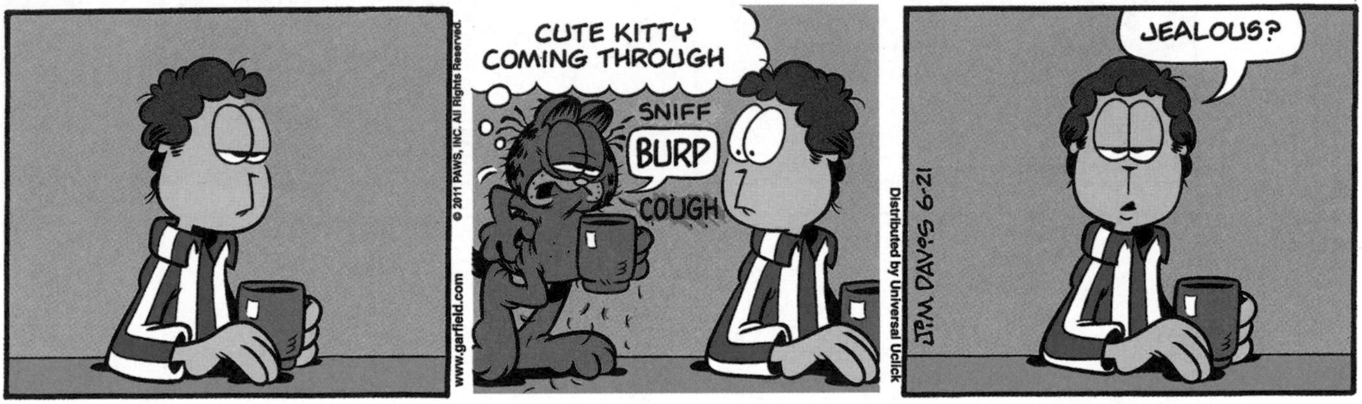
CUTE KITTY COMING THROUGH
SNIFF
BURP
COUGH
JEALOUS?
JIM DAVIS 6-21
© 2011 PAWS, INC. All Rights Reserved.
www.garfield.com
Distributed by Universal Uclick

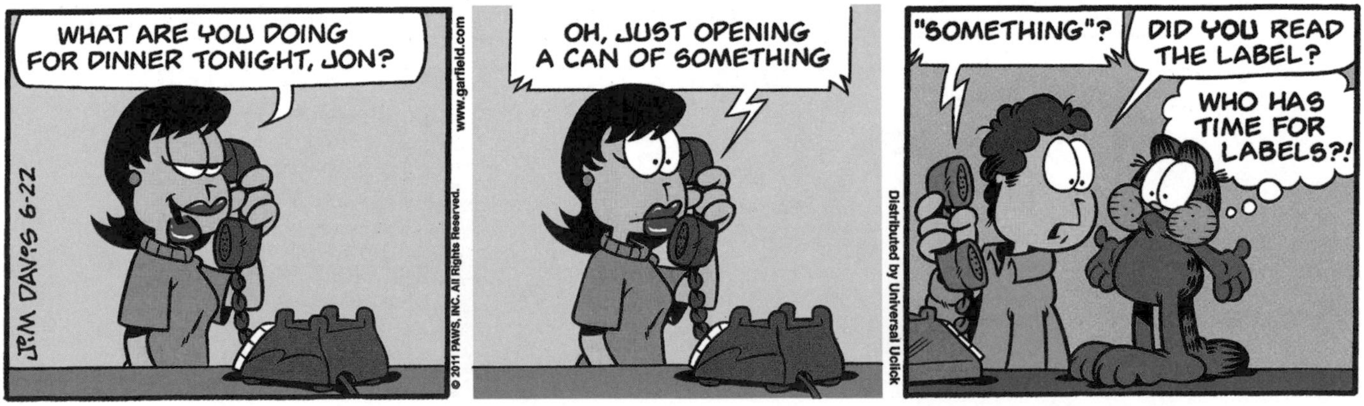
WHAT ARE YOU DOING FOR DINNER TONIGHT, JON?
OH, JUST OPENING A CAN OF SOMETHING
"SOMETHING"?
DID YOU READ THE LABEL?
WHO HAS TIME FOR LABELS?!
JIM DAVIS 6-22
© 2011 PAWS, INC. All Rights Reserved.
www.garfield.com
Distributed by Universal Uclick

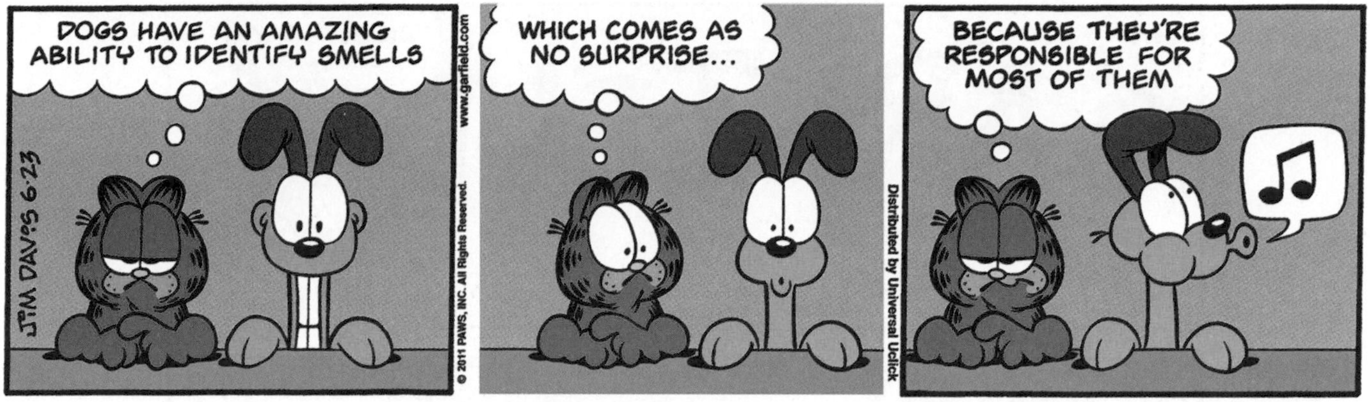
DOGS HAVE AN AMAZING ABILITY TO IDENTIFY SMELLS
JIM DAVIS 6-23
© 2011 PAWS, INC. All Rights Reserved. www.garfield.com
WHICH COMES AS NO SURPRISE...
Distributed by Universal Uclick
BECAUSE THEY'RE RESPONSIBLE FOR MOST OF THEM

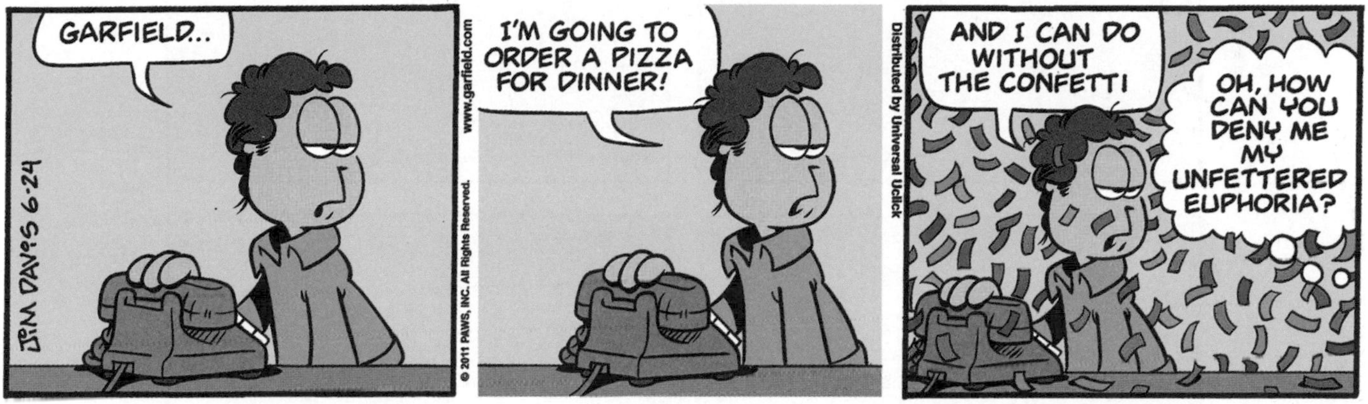
GARFIELD...
JIM DAVIS 6-24
© 2011 PAWS, INC. All Rights Reserved. www.garfield.com
I'M GOING TO ORDER A PIZZA FOR DINNER!
Distributed by Universal Uclick
AND I CAN DO WITHOUT THE CONFETTI
OH, HOW CAN YOU DENY ME MY UNFETTERED EUPHORIA?

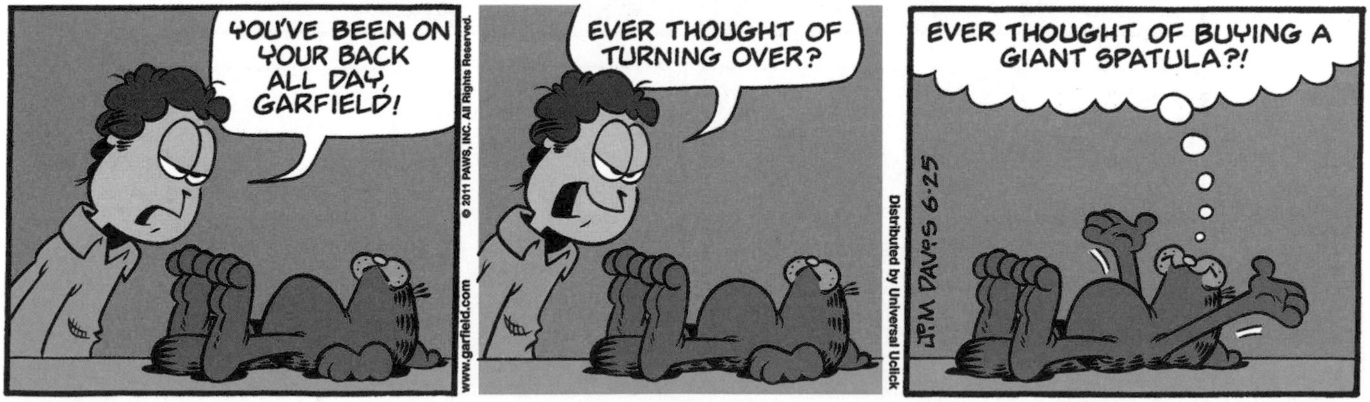
YOU'VE BEEN ON YOUR BACK ALL DAY, GARFIELD!
© 2011 PAWS, INC. All Rights Reserved. www.garfield.com
EVER THOUGHT OF TURNING OVER?
Distributed by Universal Uclick
JIM DAVIS 6-25
EVER THOUGHT OF BUYING A GIANT SPATULA?!

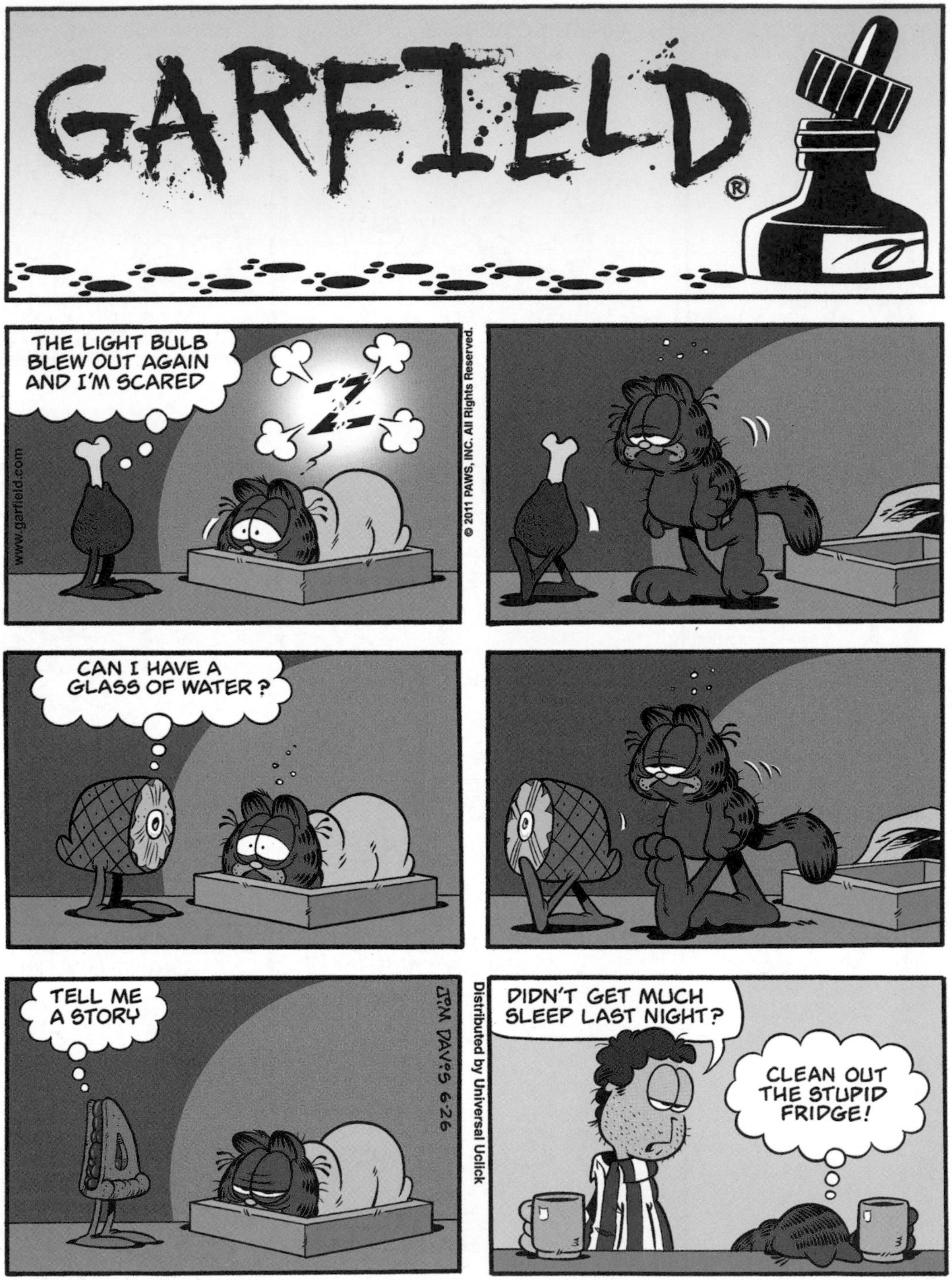
GARFIELD®
THE LIGHT BULB BLEW OUT AGAIN AND I'M SCARED
www.garfield.com
© 2011 PAWS, INC. All Rights Reserved.
CAN I HAVE A GLASS OF WATER?
TELL ME A STORY
JIM DAVIS 6-26
Distributed by Universal Uclick
DIDN'T GET MUCH SLEEP LAST NIGHT?
CLEAN OUT THE STUPID FRIDGE!

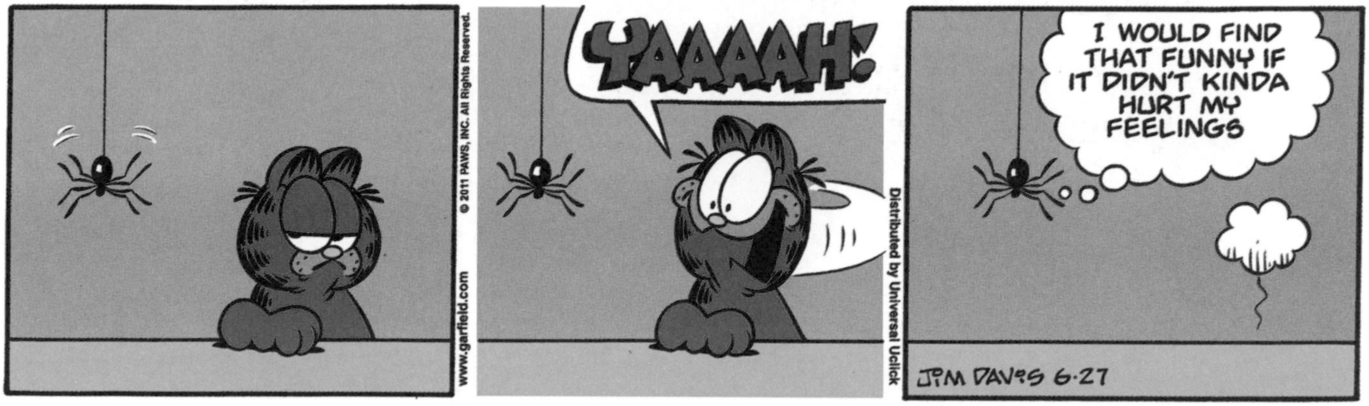

YAAAAH!
I WOULD FIND THAT FUNNY IF IT DIDN'T KINDA HURT MY FEELINGS
JIM DAVIS 6·27
© 2011 PAWS, INC. All Rights Reserved.
www.garfield.com
Distributed by Universal Uclick

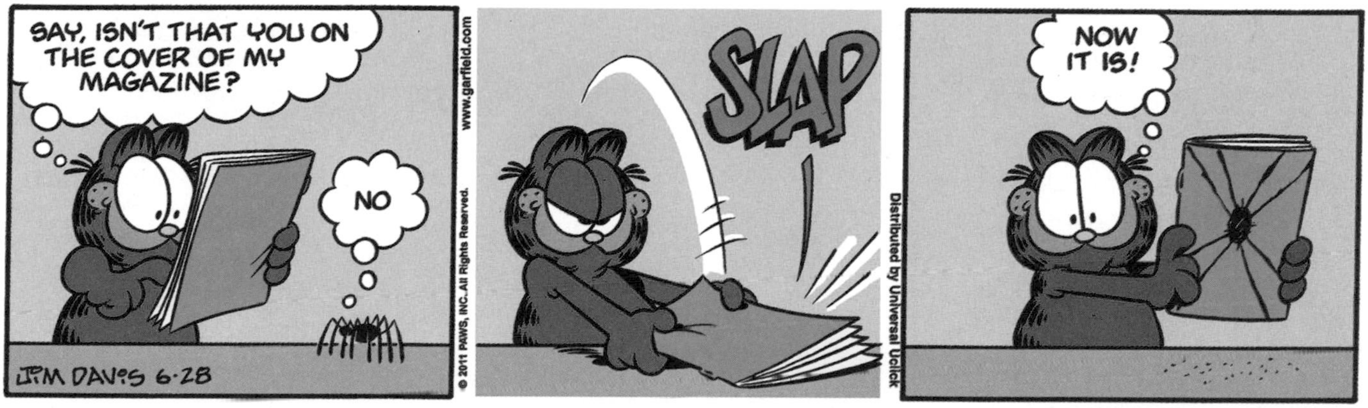

SAY, ISN'T THAT YOU ON THE COVER OF MY MAGAZINE?
NO
JIM DAVIS 6·28
SLAP
NOW IT IS!
www.garfield.com
© 2011 PAWS, INC. All Rights Reserved.
Distributed by Universal Uclick

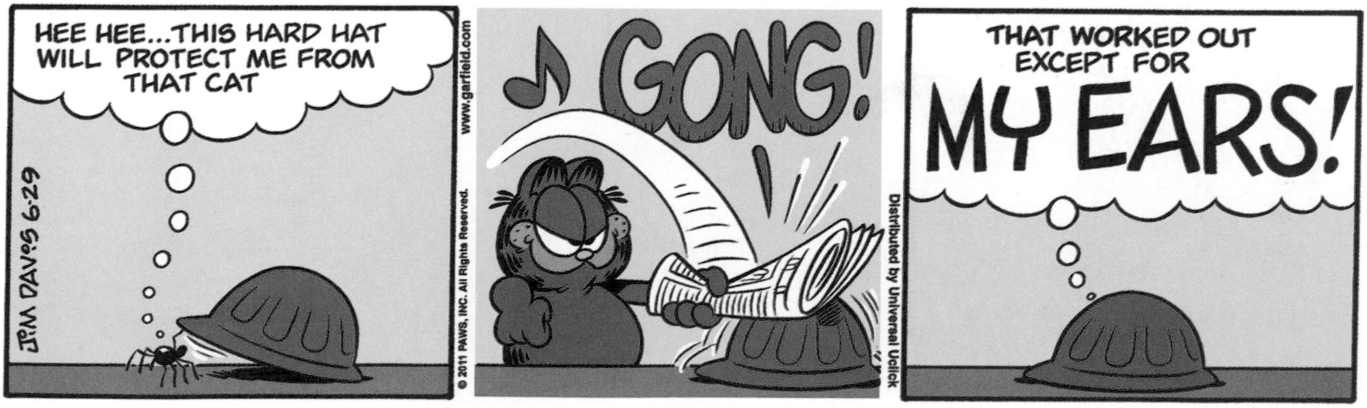

HEE HEE...THIS HARD HAT WILL PROTECT ME FROM THAT CAT
JIM DAVIS 6·29
GONG!
THAT WORKED OUT EXCEPT FOR
MY EARS!
www.garfield.com
© 2011 PAWS, INC. All Rights Reserved.
Distributed by Universal Uclick

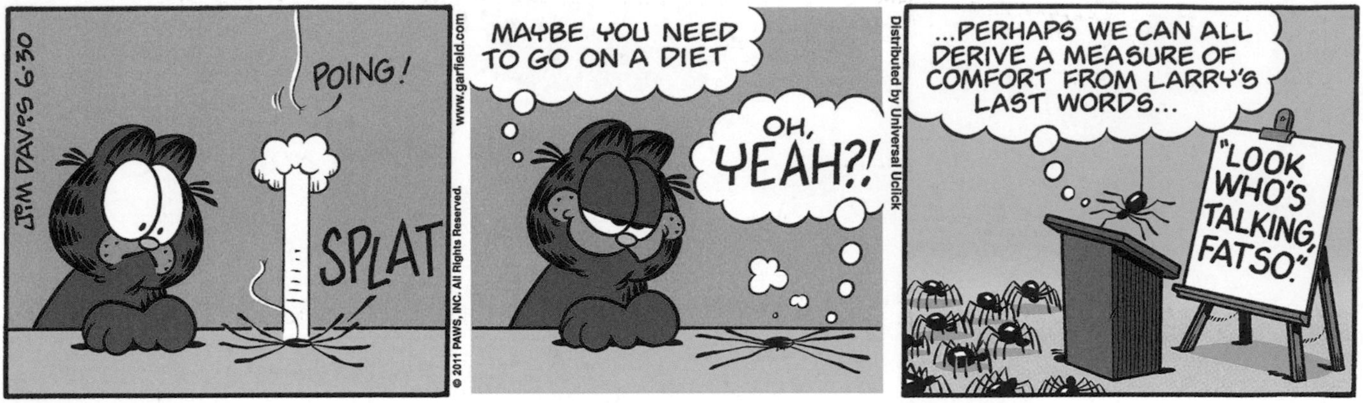
JIM DAVIS 6·30
POING!
SPLAT
www.garfield.com
© 2011 PAWS, INC. All Rights Reserved.
MAYBE YOU NEED TO GO ON A DIET
OH, YEAH?!
Distributed by Universal Uclick
...PERHAPS WE CAN ALL DERIVE A MEASURE OF COMFORT FROM LARRY'S LAST WORDS...
"LOOK WHO'S TALKING, FATSO."

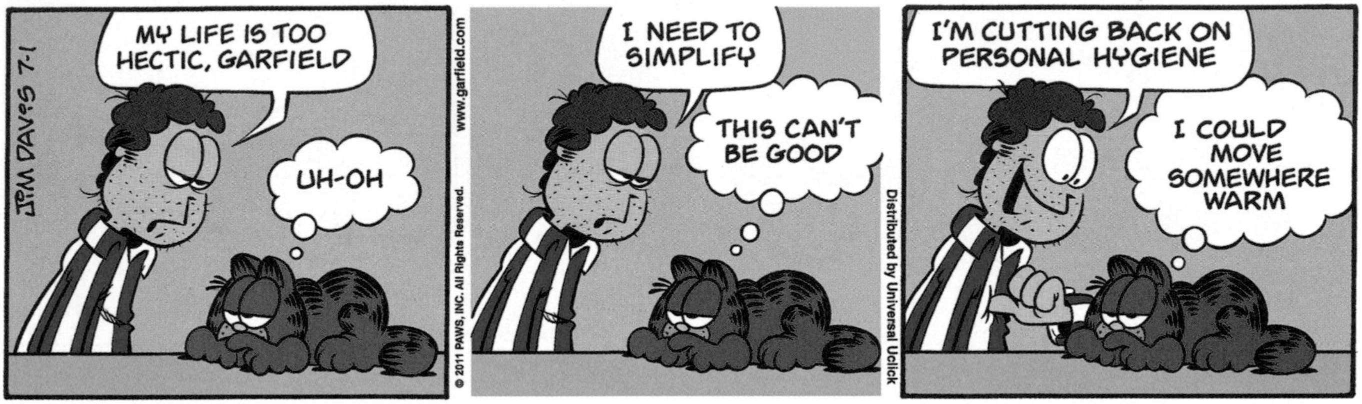
JIM DAVIS 7·1
MY LIFE IS TOO HECTIC, GARFIELD
UH-OH
www.garfield.com
© 2011 PAWS, INC. All Rights Reserved.
I NEED TO SIMPLIFY
THIS CAN'T BE GOOD
Distributed by Universal Uclick
I'M CUTTING BACK ON PERSONAL HYGIENE
I COULD MOVE SOMEWHERE WARM

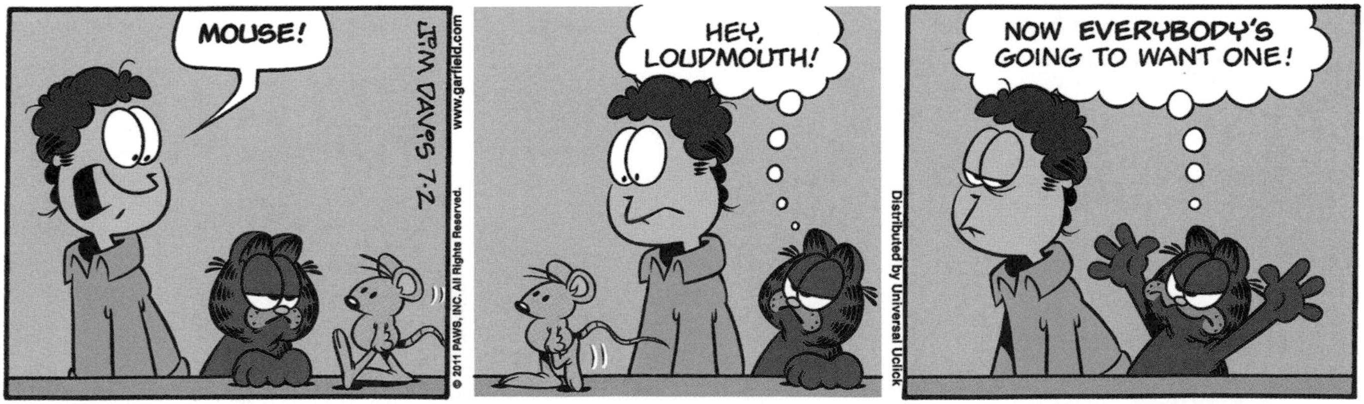
MOUSE!
JIM DAVIS 7·2
www.garfield.com
© 2011 PAWS, INC. All Rights Reserved.
HEY, LOUDMOUTH!
Distributed by Universal Uclick
NOW EVERYBODY'S GOING TO WANT ONE!

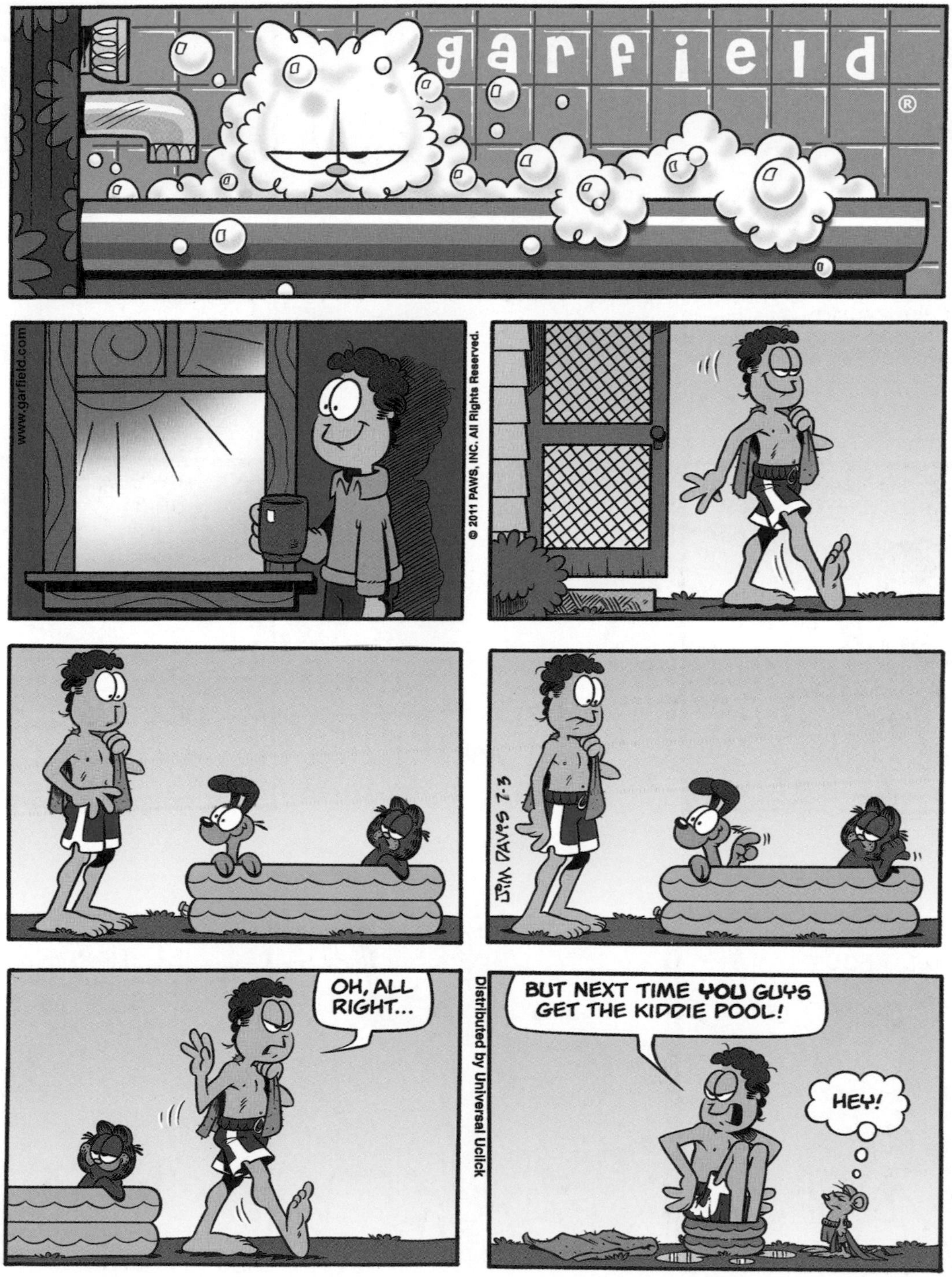
garfield®
www.garfield.com
© 2011 PAWS, INC. All Rights Reserved.
JIM DAVIS 7-3
Distributed by Universal Uclick
OH, ALL RIGHT...
BUT NEXT TIME YOU GUYS GET THE KIDDIE POOL!
HEY!

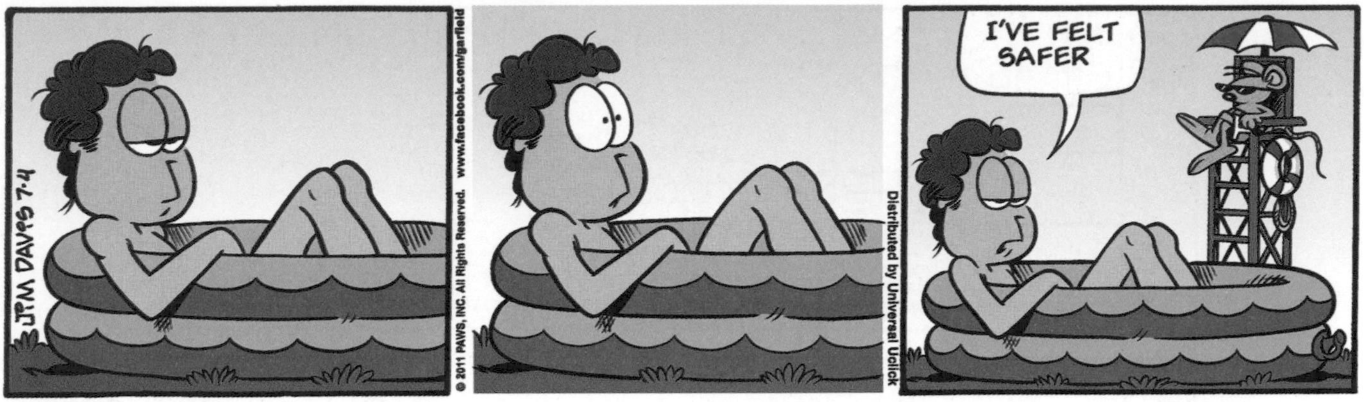
JPM DAVPS 7-4
© 2011 PAWS, INC. All Rights Reserved. www.facebook.com/garfield
Distributed by Universal Uclick
I'VE FELT SAFER

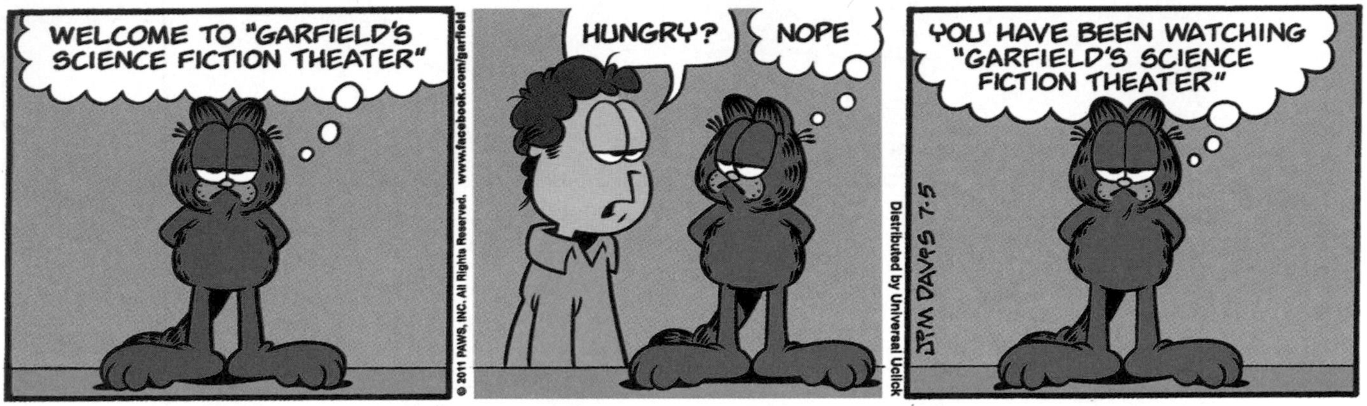
WELCOME TO "GARFIELD'S SCIENCE FICTION THEATER"
© 2011 PAWS, INC. All Rights Reserved. www.facebook.com/garfield
HUNGRY?
NOPE
Distributed by Universal Uclick
JPM DAVPS 7-5
YOU HAVE BEEN WATCHING "GARFIELD'S SCIENCE FICTION THEATER"

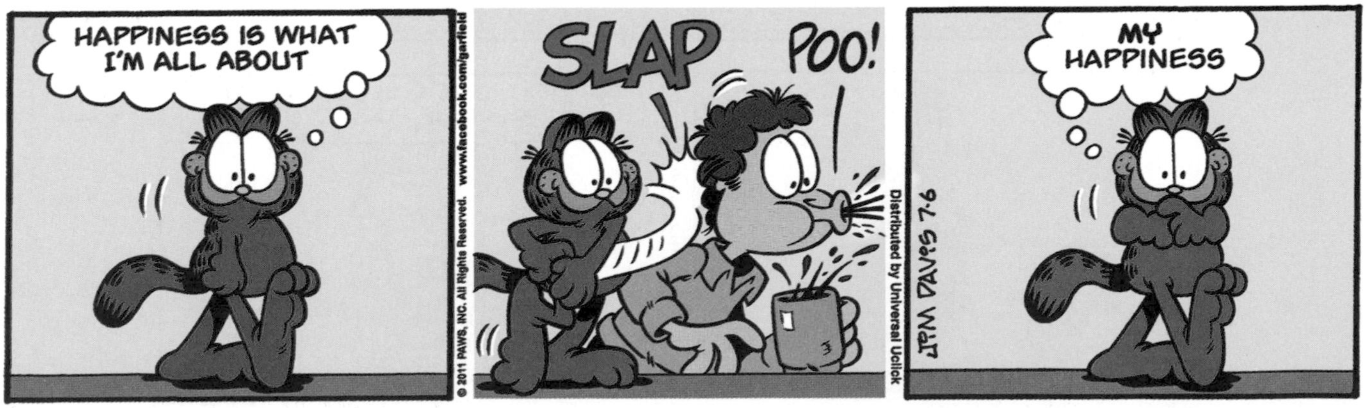
HAPPINESS IS WHAT I'M ALL ABOUT
© 2011 PAWS, INC. All Rights Reserved. www.facebook.com/garfield
SLAP
POO!
Distributed by Universal Uclick
JPM DAVPS 7-6
MY HAPPINESS

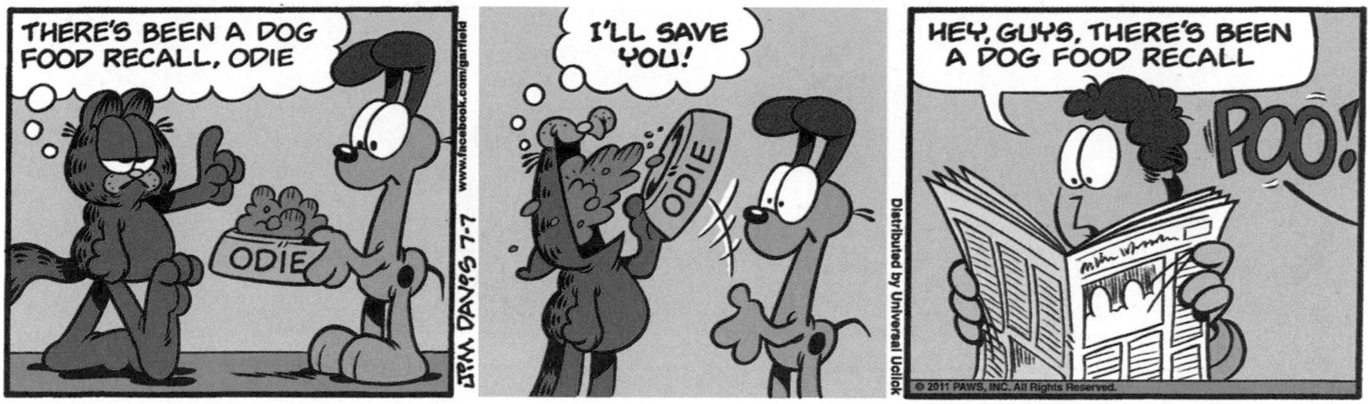
THERE'S BEEN A DOG FOOD RECALL, ODIE
ODIE
JIM DAVIS 7-7
www.facebook.com/garfield
I'LL SAVE YOU!
ODIE
Distributed by Universal Uclick
HEY, GUYS, THERE'S BEEN A DOG FOOD RECALL
POO!
© 2011 PAWS, INC. All Rights Reserved.

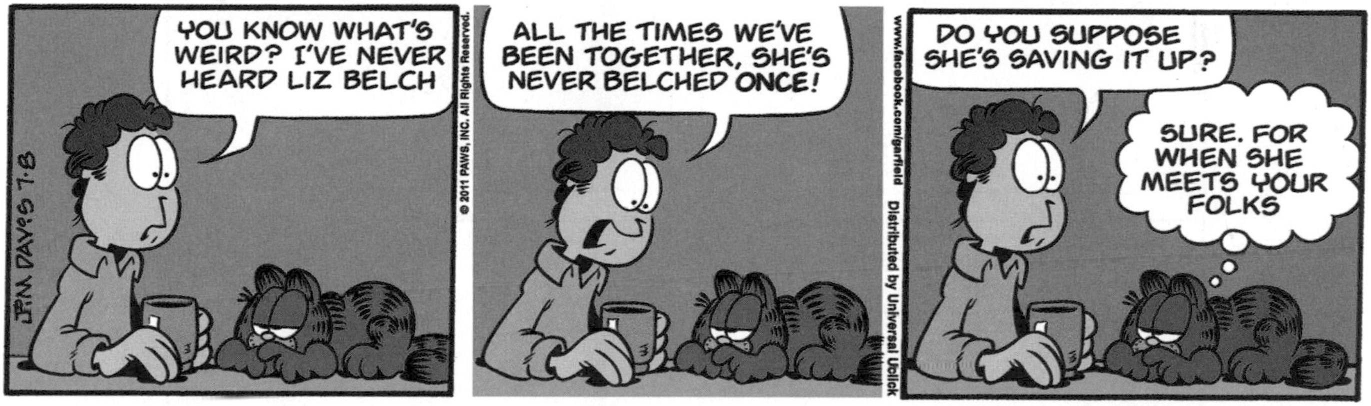
YOU KNOW WHAT'S WEIRD? I'VE NEVER HEARD LIZ BELCH
JIM DAVIS 7-8
© 2011 PAWS, INC. All Rights Reserved.
ALL THE TIMES WE'VE BEEN TOGETHER, SHE'S NEVER BELCHED ONCE!
www.facebook.com/garfield
Distributed by Universal Uclick
DO YOU SUPPOSE SHE'S SAVING IT UP?
SURE. FOR WHEN SHE MEETS YOUR FOLKS

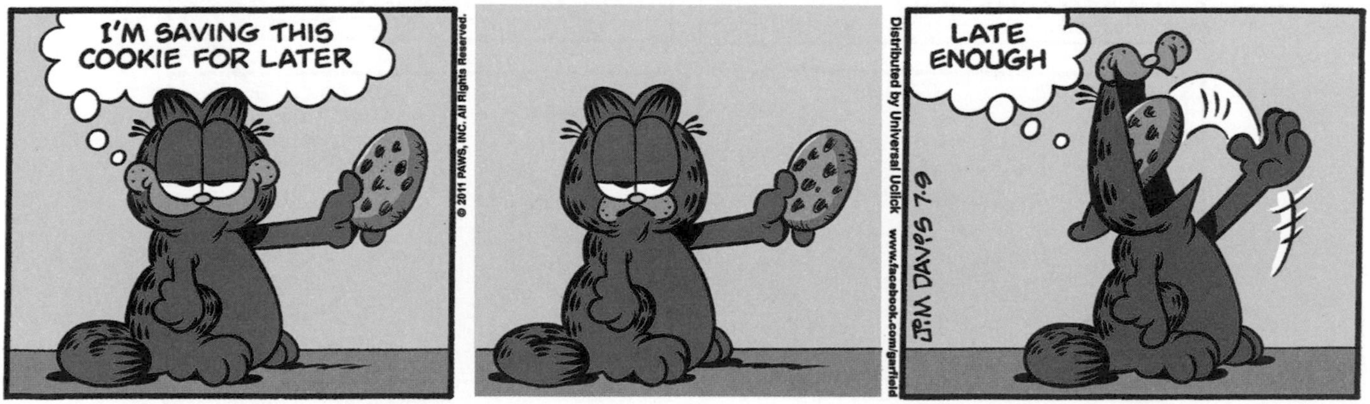
I'M SAVING THIS COOKIE FOR LATER
© 2011 PAWS, INC. All Rights Reserved.
Distributed by Universal Uclick
JIM DAVIS 7-9
www.facebook.com/garfield
LATE ENOUGH

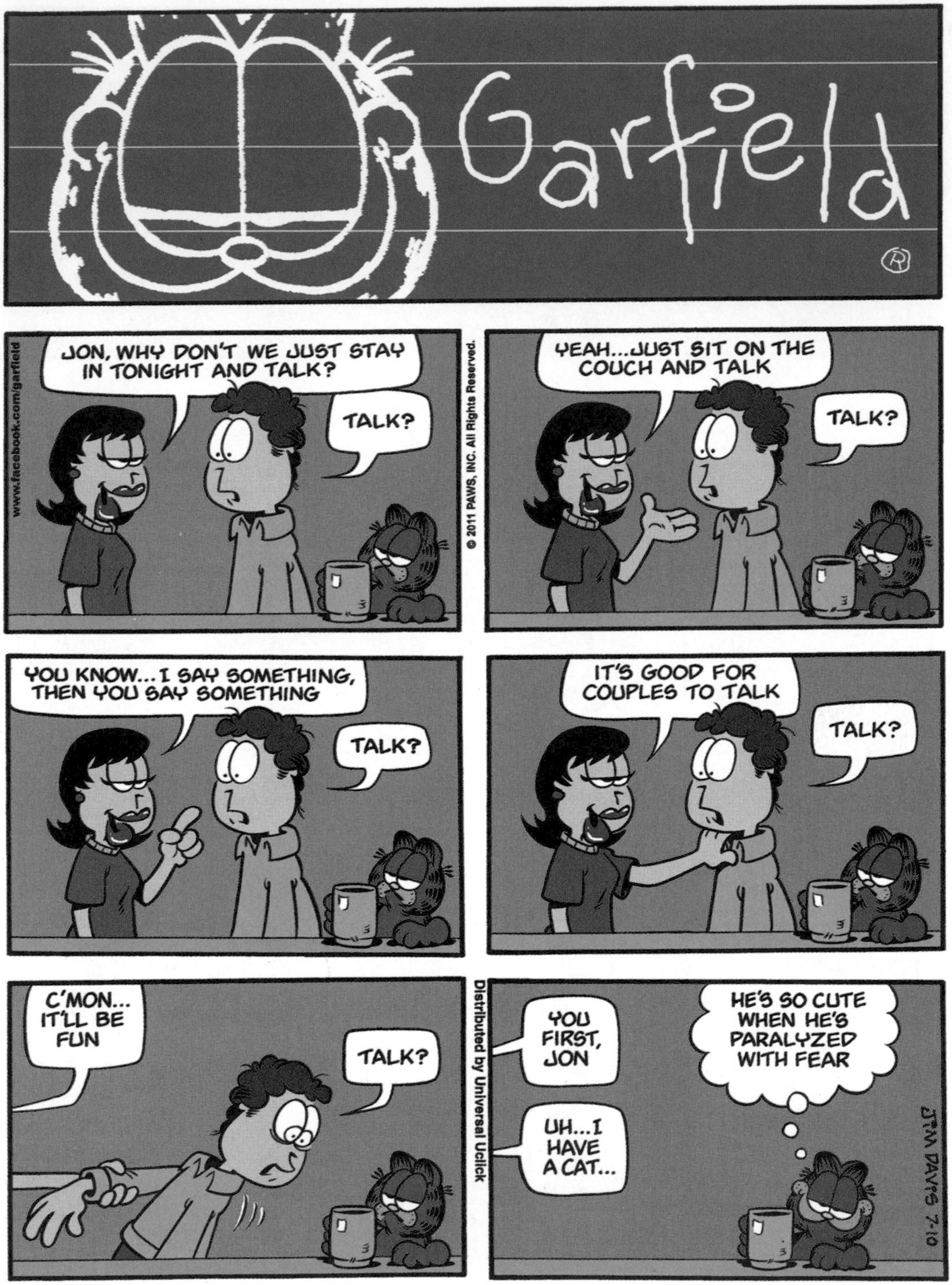
Garfield ®
www.facebook.com/garfield
JON, WHY DON'T WE JUST STAY IN TONIGHT AND TALK?
TALK?
© 2011 PAWS, INC. All Rights Reserved.
YEAH...JUST SIT ON THE COUCH AND TALK
TALK?
YOU KNOW... I SAY SOMETHING, THEN YOU SAY SOMETHING
TALK?
IT'S GOOD FOR COUPLES TO TALK
TALK?
C'MON... IT'LL BE FUN
TALK?
Distributed by Universal Uclick
YOU FIRST, JON
UH...I HAVE A CAT...
HE'S SO CUTE WHEN HE'S PARALYZED WITH FEAR
JIM DAVIS 7-10

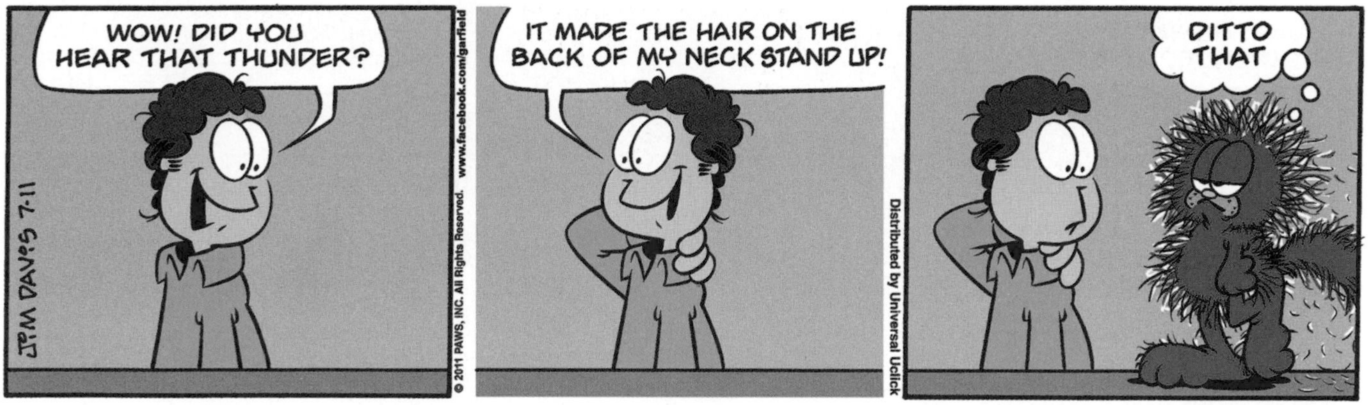
WOW! DID YOU HEAR THAT THUNDER?
IT MADE THE HAIR ON THE BACK OF MY NECK STAND UP!
DITTO THAT
© 2011 PAWS, INC. All Rights Reserved. www.facebook.com/garfield
Distributed by Universal Uclick

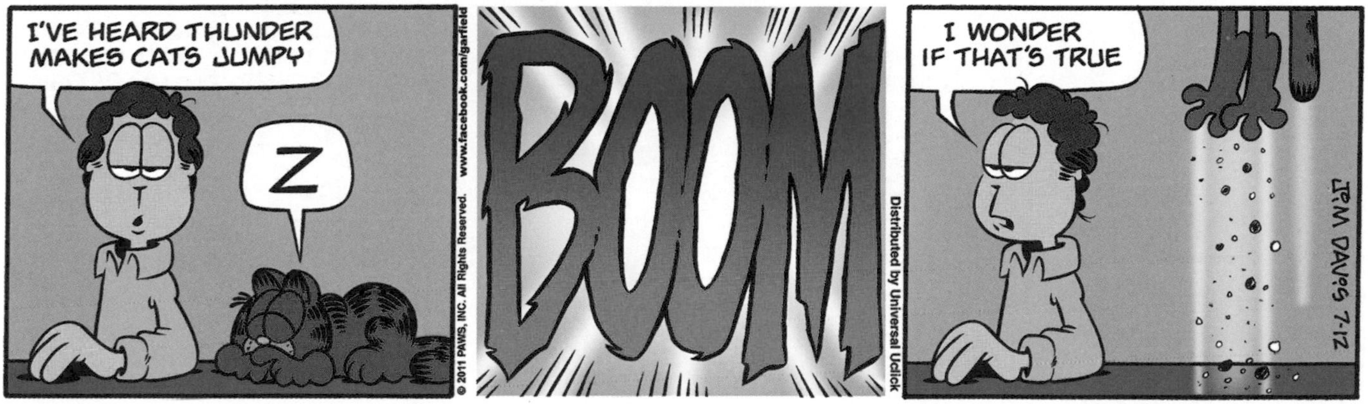
I'VE HEARD THUNDER MAKES CATS JUMPY
Z
BOOM
I WONDER IF THAT'S TRUE
© 2011 PAWS, INC. All Rights Reserved. www.facebook.com/garfield
Distributed by Universal Uclick

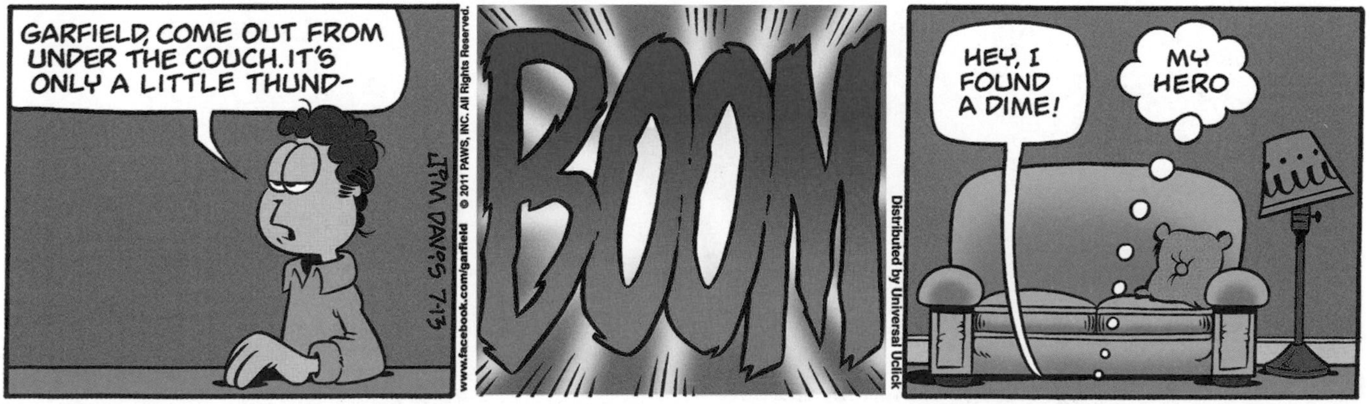
GARFIELD, COME OUT FROM UNDER THE COUCH. IT'S ONLY A LITTLE THUND-
BOOM
HEY, I FOUND A DIME!
MY HERO
www.facebook.com/garfield © 2011 PAWS, INC. All Rights Reserved.
Distributed by Universal Uclick

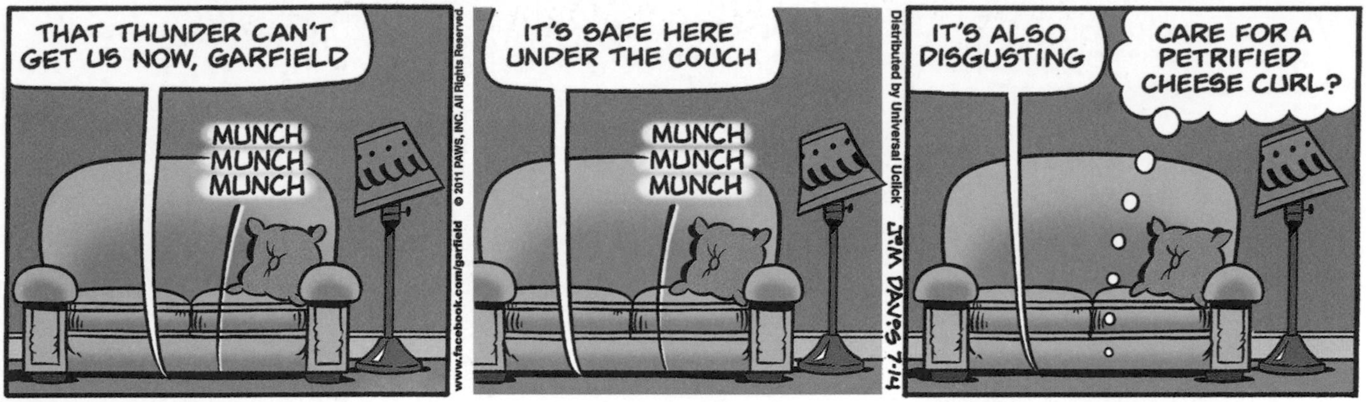
THAT THUNDER CAN'T GET US NOW, GARFIELD
MUNCH MUNCH MUNCH
IT'S SAFE HERE UNDER THE COUCH
MUNCH MUNCH MUNCH
IT'S ALSO DISGUSTING
CARE FOR A PETRIFIED CHEESE CURL?
www.facebook.com/garfield © 2011 PAWS, INC. All Rights Reserved.
Distributed by Universal Uclick
JIM DAVIS 7-14

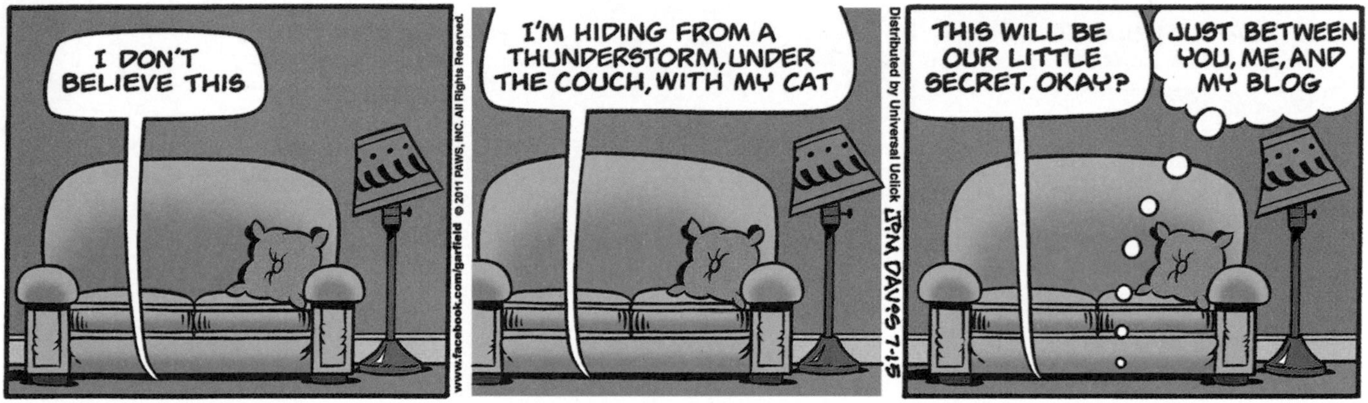
I DON'T BELIEVE THIS
I'M HIDING FROM A THUNDERSTORM, UNDER THE COUCH, WITH MY CAT
THIS WILL BE OUR LITTLE SECRET, OKAY?
JUST BETWEEN YOU, ME, AND MY BLOG
www.facebook.com/garfield © 2011 PAWS, INC. All Rights Reserved.
Distributed by Universal Uclick
JIM DAVIS 7-15

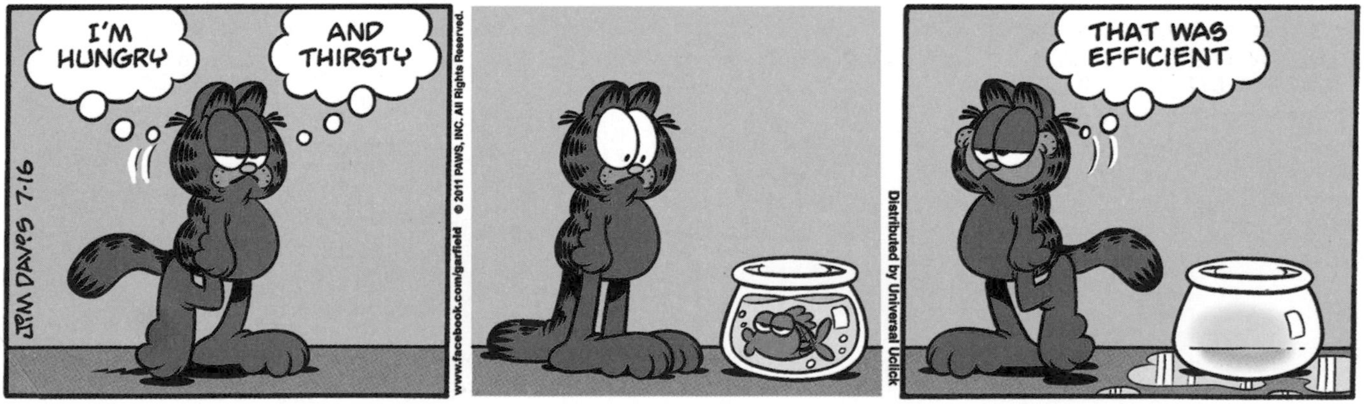
I'M HUNGRY
AND THIRSTY
THAT WAS EFFICIENT
JIM DAVIS 7-16
www.facebook.com/garfield © 2011 PAWS, INC. All Rights Reserved.
Distributed by Universal Uclick

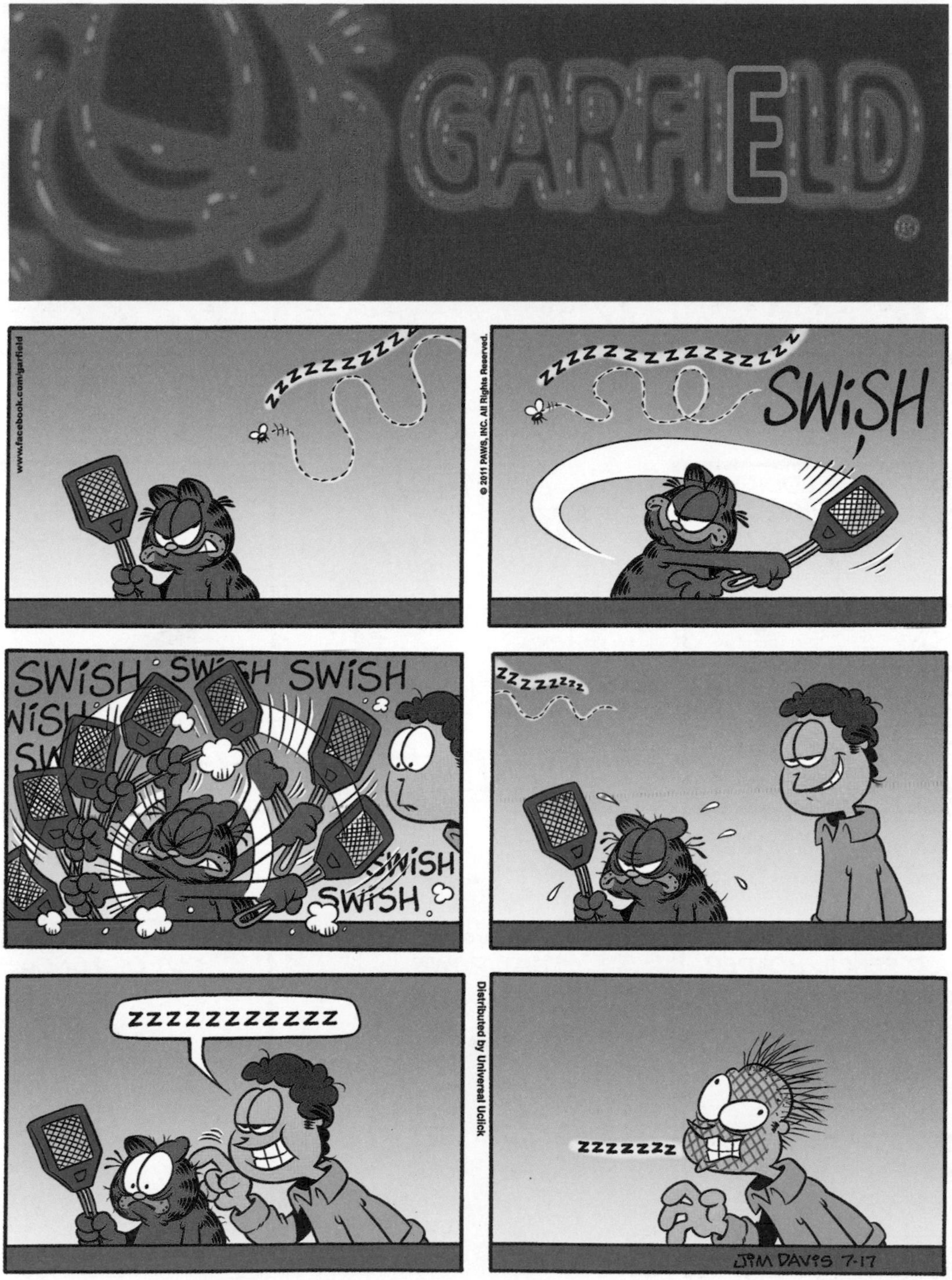
GARFIELD
www.facebook.com/garfield
© 2011 PAWS, INC. All Rights Reserved.
SWISH
SWISH SWISH SWISH
SWISH
SWISH
ZZZZZZZZZZZ
Distributed by Universal Uclick
ZZZZZZZ
JIM DAVIS 7-17

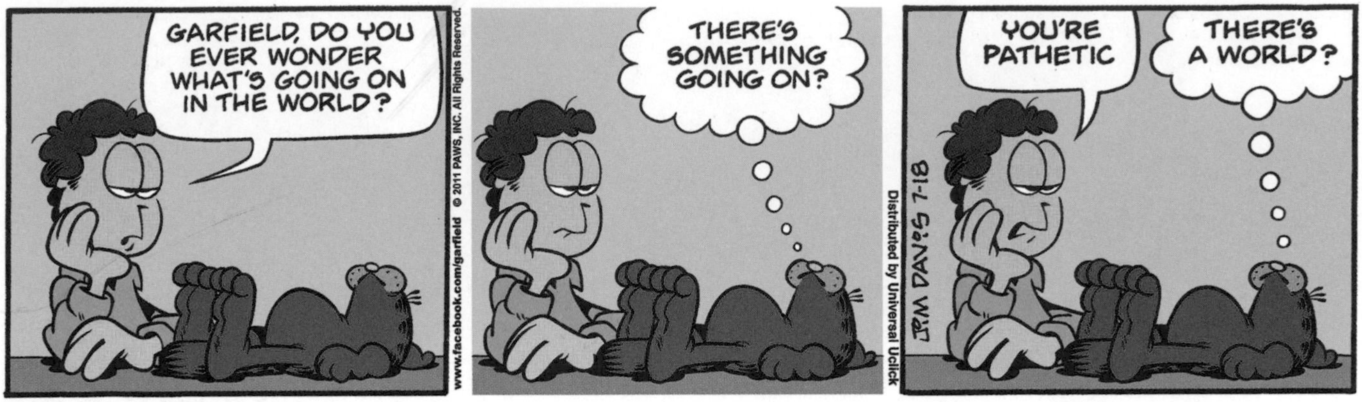
GARFIELD, DO YOU EVER WONDER WHAT'S GOING ON IN THE WORLD?
THERE'S SOMETHING GOING ON?
YOU'RE PATHETIC
THERE'S A WORLD?
JPM DAVPS 7-18

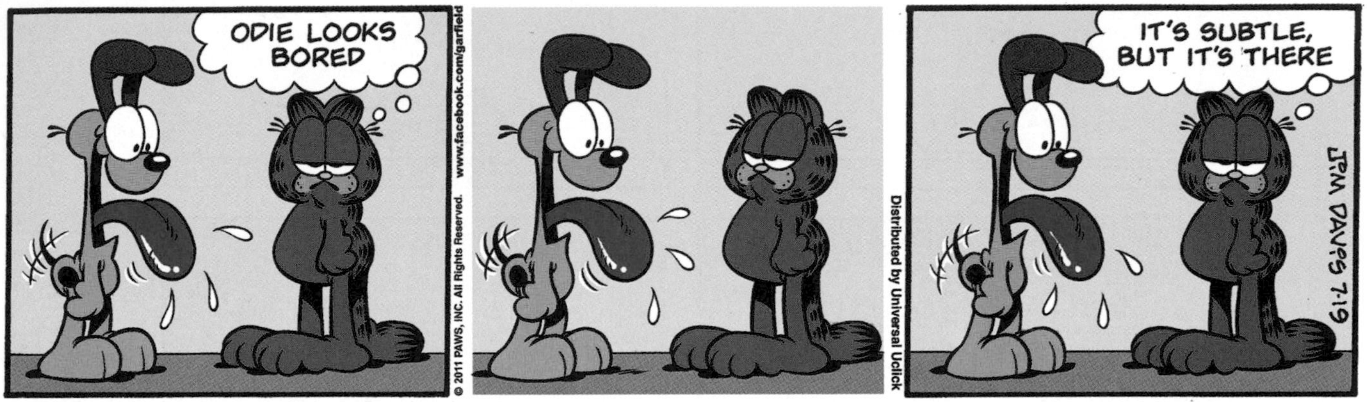
ODIE LOOKS BORED
IT'S SUBTLE, BUT IT'S THERE
JPM DAVPS 7-19

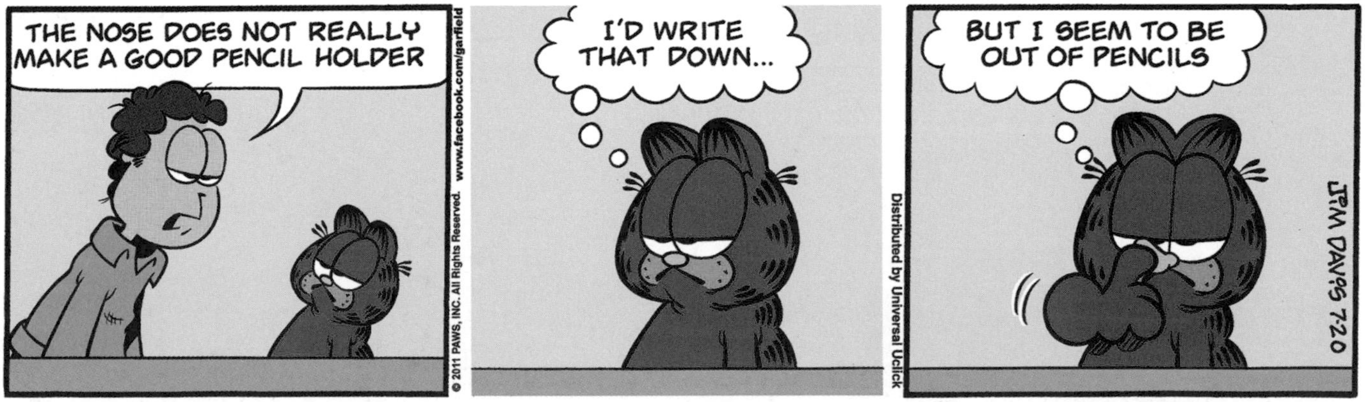
THE NOSE DOES NOT REALLY MAKE A GOOD PENCIL HOLDER
I'D WRITE THAT DOWN...
BUT I SEEM TO BE OUT OF PENCILS
JPM DAVPS 7-20

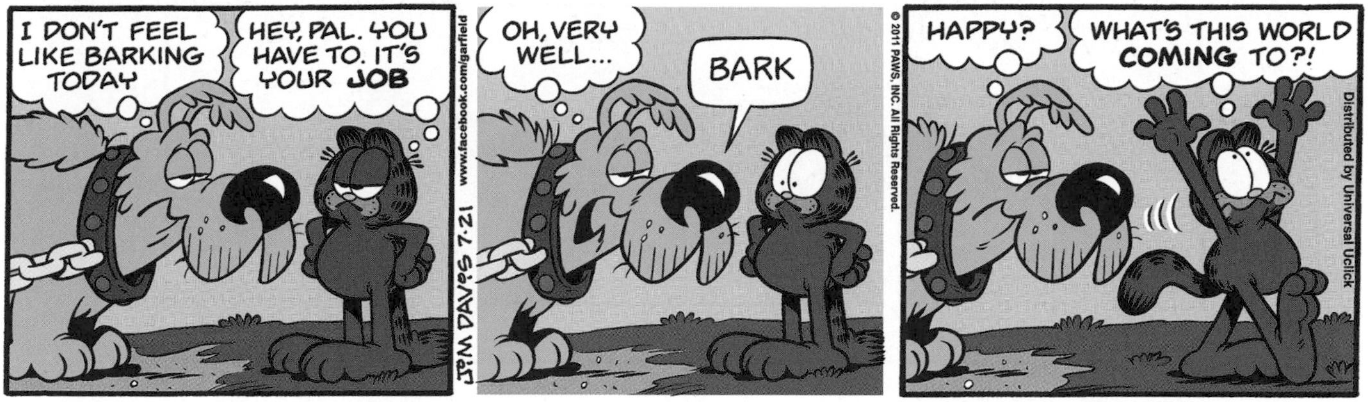
I DON'T FEEL LIKE BARKING TODAY
HEY, PAL. YOU HAVE TO. IT'S YOUR JOB
JIM DAVIS 7·21
www.facebook.com/garfield
OH, VERY WELL...
BARK
© 2011 PAWS, INC. All Rights Reserved.
HAPPY?
WHAT'S THIS WORLD COMING TO?!
Distributed by Universal Uclick

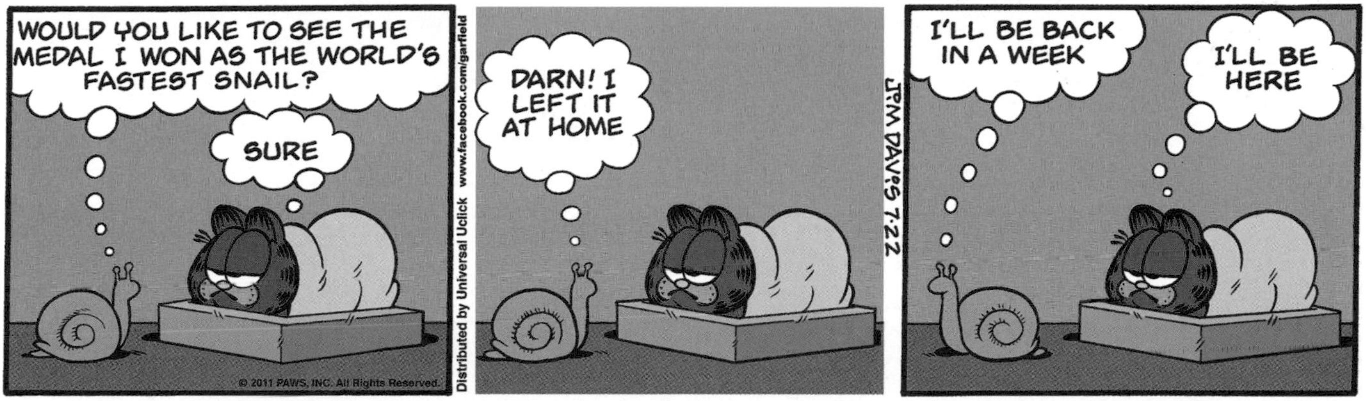
WOULD YOU LIKE TO SEE THE MEDAL I WON AS THE WORLD'S FASTEST SNAIL?
SURE
© 2011 PAWS, INC. All Rights Reserved.
Distributed by Universal Uclick www.facebook.com/garfield
DARN! I LEFT IT AT HOME
JIM DAVIS 7·22
I'LL BE BACK IN A WEEK
I'LL BE HERE

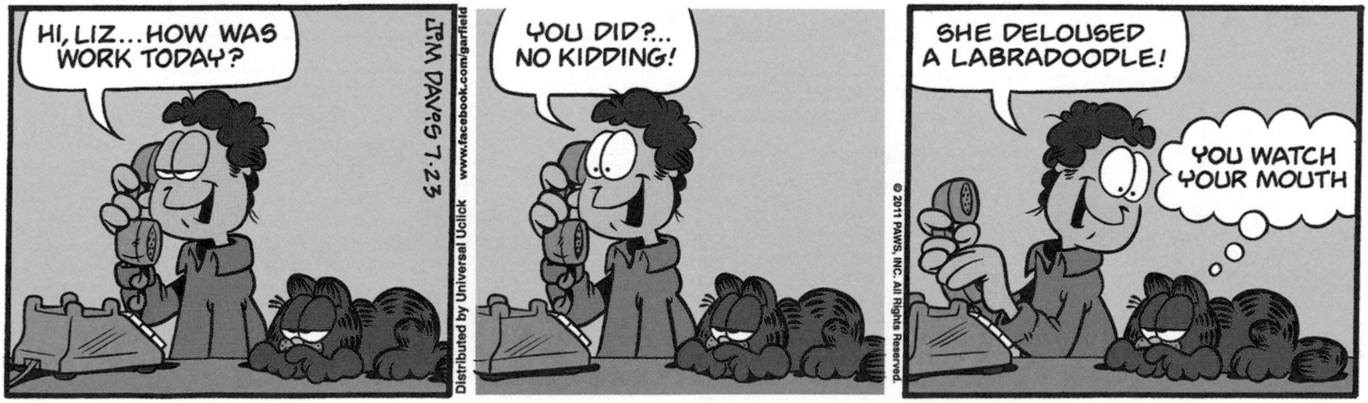
HI, LIZ...HOW WAS WORK TODAY?
JIM DAVIS 7·23
Distributed by Universal Uclick www.facebook.com/garfield
YOU DID?... NO KIDDING!
© 2011 PAWS, INC. All Rights Reserved.
SHE DELOUSED A LABRADOODLE!
YOU WATCH YOUR MOUTH

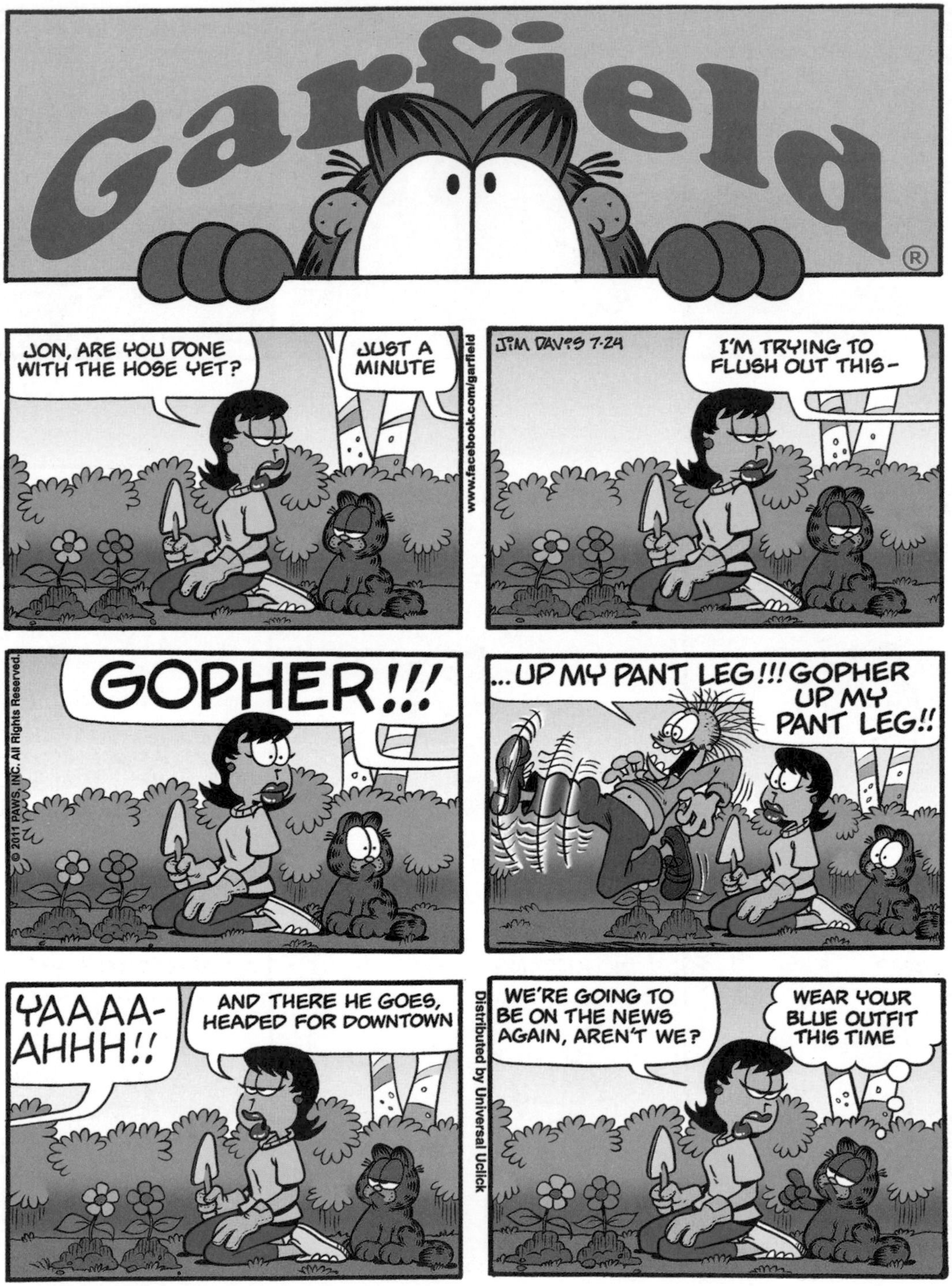
Garfield®
JON, ARE YOU DONE WITH THE HOSE YET?
JUST A MINUTE
www.facebook.com/garfield
JIM DAVIS 7-24
I'M TRYING TO FLUSH OUT THIS–
© 2011 PAWS, INC. All Rights Reserved.
GOPHER!!!
...UP MY PANT LEG!!!
GOPHER UP MY PANT LEG!!
YAAAA-AHHH!!
AND THERE HE GOES, HEADED FOR DOWNTOWN
Distributed by Universal Uclick
WE'RE GOING TO BE ON THE NEWS AGAIN, AREN'T WE?
WEAR YOUR BLUE OUTFIT THIS TIME

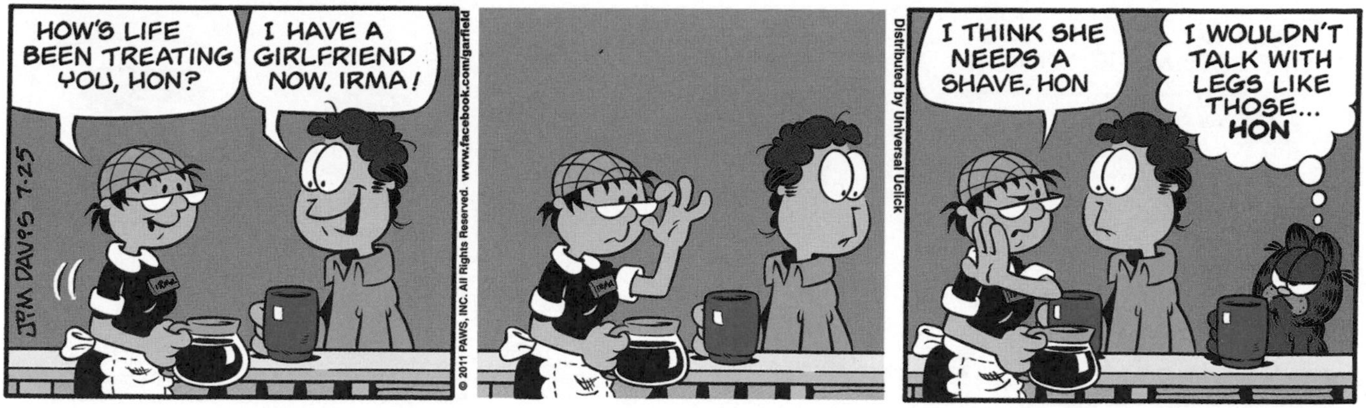
HOW'S LIFE BEEN TREATING YOU, HON?
I HAVE A GIRLFRIEND NOW, IRMA!
JPM DAVPS 7-25
I THINK SHE NEEDS A SHAVE, HON
I WOULDN'T TALK WITH LEGS LIKE THOSE... HON
© 2011 PAWS, INC. All Rights Reserved. www.facebook.com/garfield
Distributed by Universal Uclick

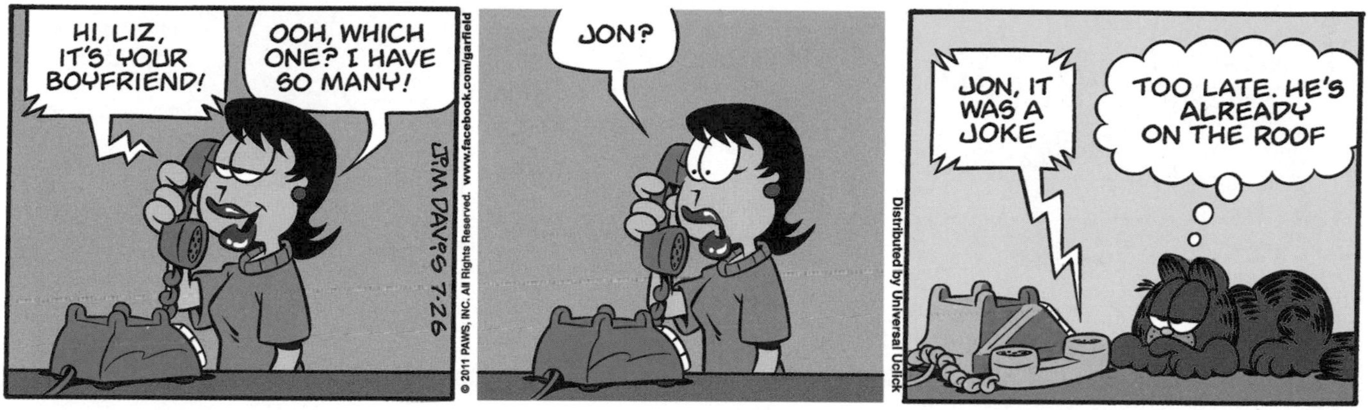
HI, LIZ, IT'S YOUR BOYFRIEND!
OOH, WHICH ONE? I HAVE SO MANY!
JPM DAVPS 7-26
JON?
JON, IT WAS A JOKE
TOO LATE. HE'S ALREADY ON THE ROOF
© 2011 PAWS, INC. All Rights Reserved. www.facebook.com/garfield
Distributed by Universal Uclick

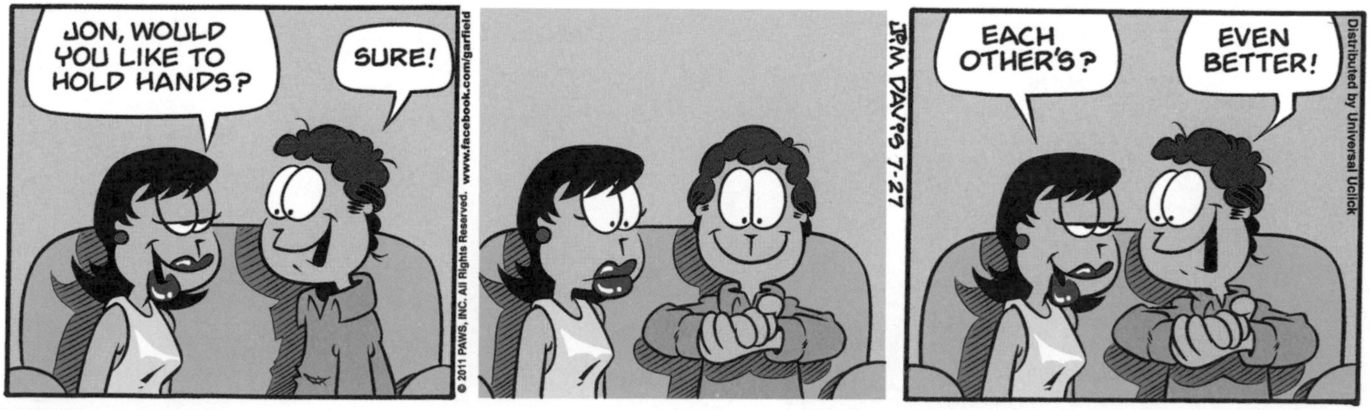
JON, WOULD YOU LIKE TO HOLD HANDS?
SURE!
JPM DAVPS 7-27
EACH OTHER'S?
EVEN BETTER!
© 2011 PAWS, INC. All Rights Reserved. www.facebook.com/garfield
Distributed by Universal Uclick

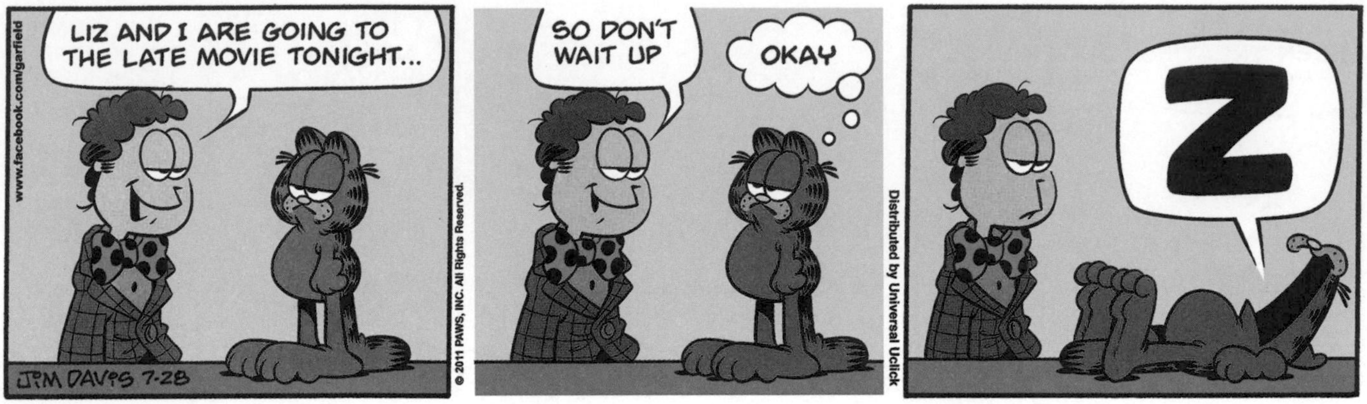
LIZ AND I ARE GOING TO THE LATE MOVIE TONIGHT...
SO DON'T WAIT UP
OKAY
Z
JIM DAVIS 7-28
www.facebook.com/garfield
© 2011 PAWS, INC. All Rights Reserved.
Distributed by Universal Uclick

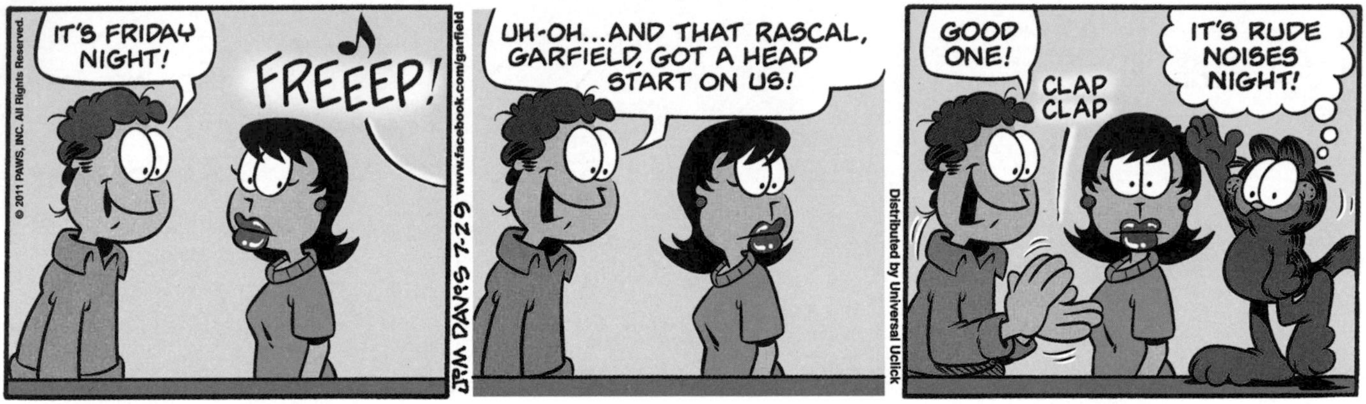
IT'S FRIDAY NIGHT!
FREEEP!
UH-OH...AND THAT RASCAL, GARFIELD, GOT A HEAD START ON US!
GOOD ONE!
CLAP CLAP
IT'S RUDE NOISES NIGHT!
JIM DAVIS 7-29
© 2011 PAWS, INC. All Rights Reserved.
www.facebook.com/garfield
Distributed by Universal Uclick

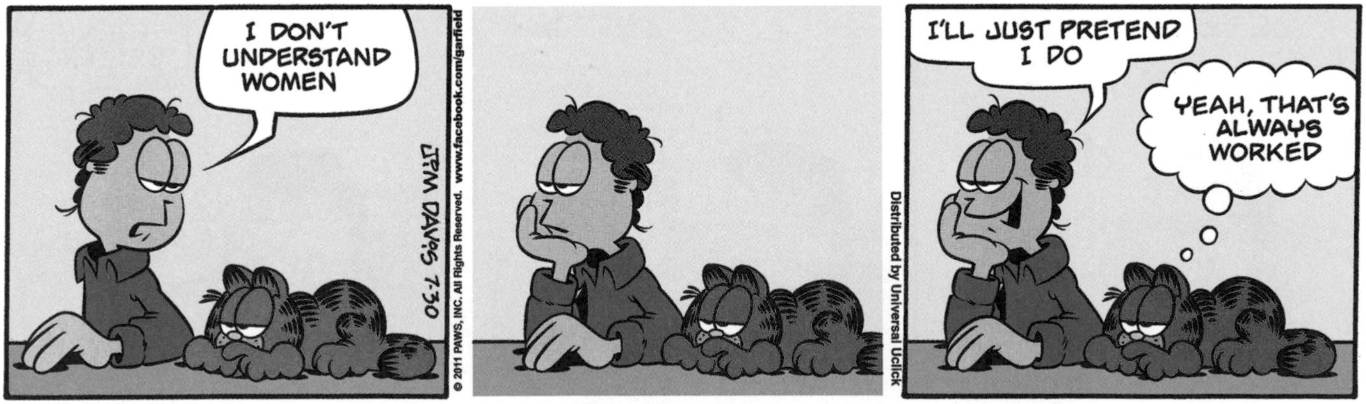
I DON'T UNDERSTAND WOMEN
I'LL JUST PRETEND I DO
YEAH, THAT'S ALWAYS WORKED
JIM DAVIS 7-30
© 2011 PAWS, INC. All Rights Reserved. www.facebook.com/garfield
Distributed by Universal Uclick

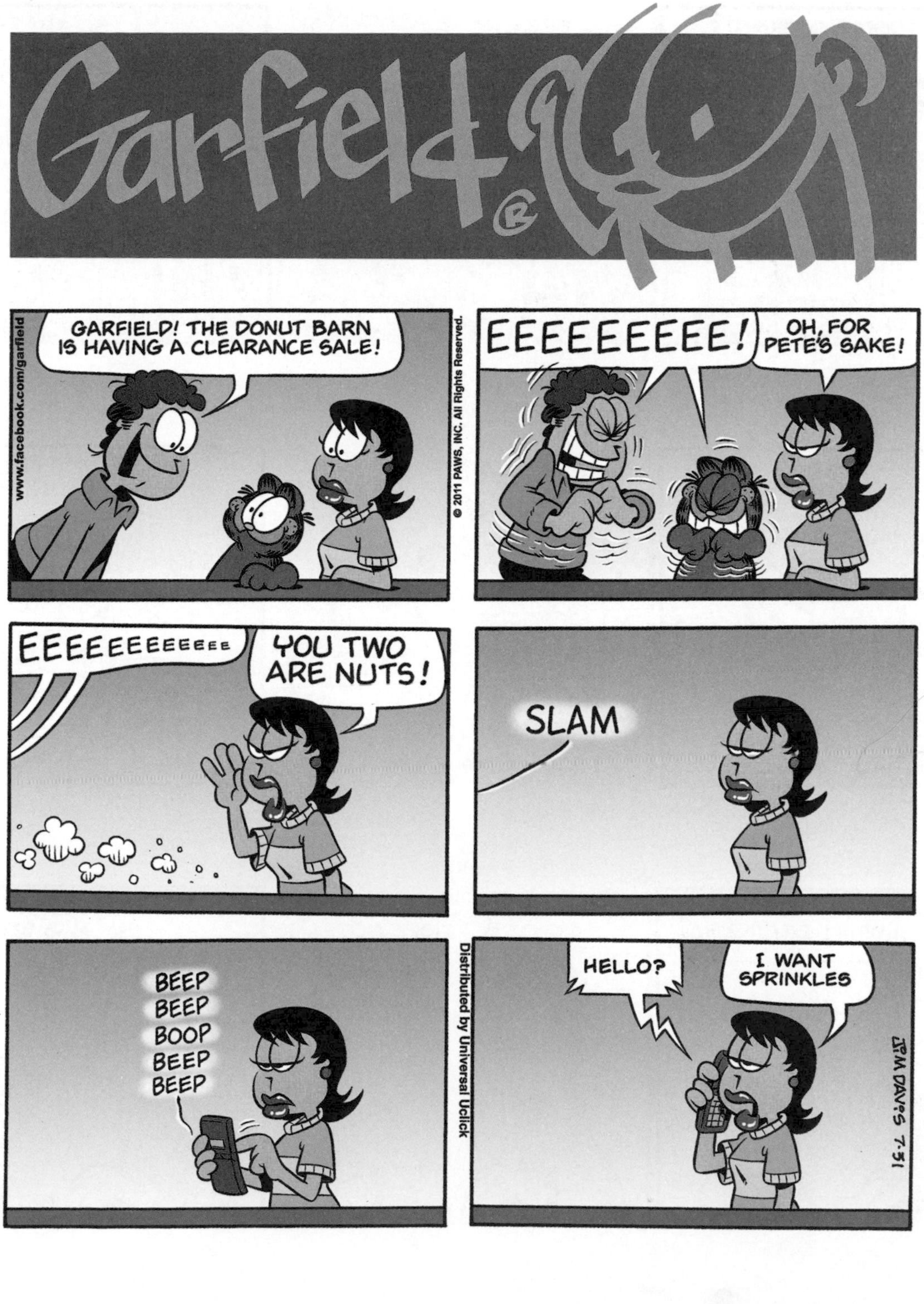
GARFIELD! THE DONUT BARN IS HAVING A CLEARANCE SALE!
www.facebook.com/garfield
© 2011 PAWS, INC. All Rights Reserved.
EEEEEEEEEE!
OH, FOR PETE'S SAKE!
EEEEEEEEEEEE
YOU TWO ARE NUTS!
SLAM
BEEP
BEEP
BOOP
BEEP
BEEP
Distributed by Universal Uclick
HELLO?
I WANT SPRINKLES
JPM DAVPS 7-31

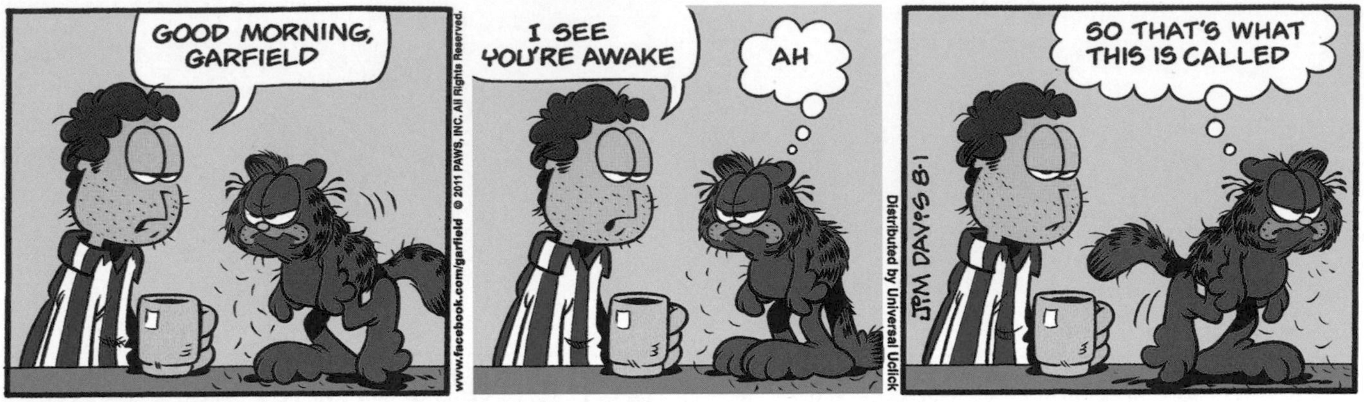
GOOD MORNING, GARFIELD
I SEE YOU'RE AWAKE
AH
SO THAT'S WHAT THIS IS CALLED
www.facebook.com/garfield © 2011 PAWS, INC. All Rights Reserved.
Distributed by Universal Uclick
JPM DAVIS 8-1

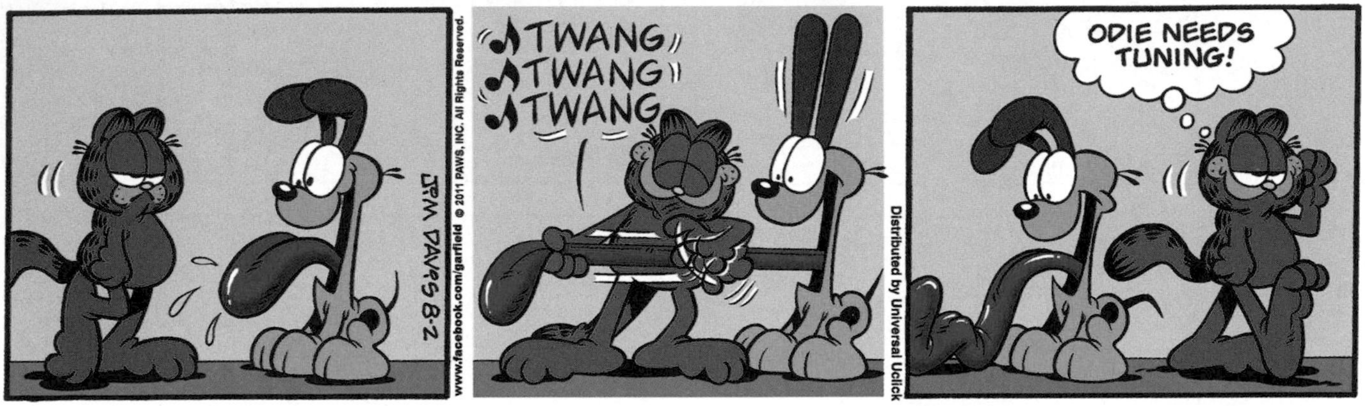
JPM DAVIS 8-2
www.facebook.com/garfield © 2011 PAWS, INC. All Rights Reserved.
TWANG
TWANG
TWANG
Distributed by Universal Uclick
ODIE NEEDS TUNING!

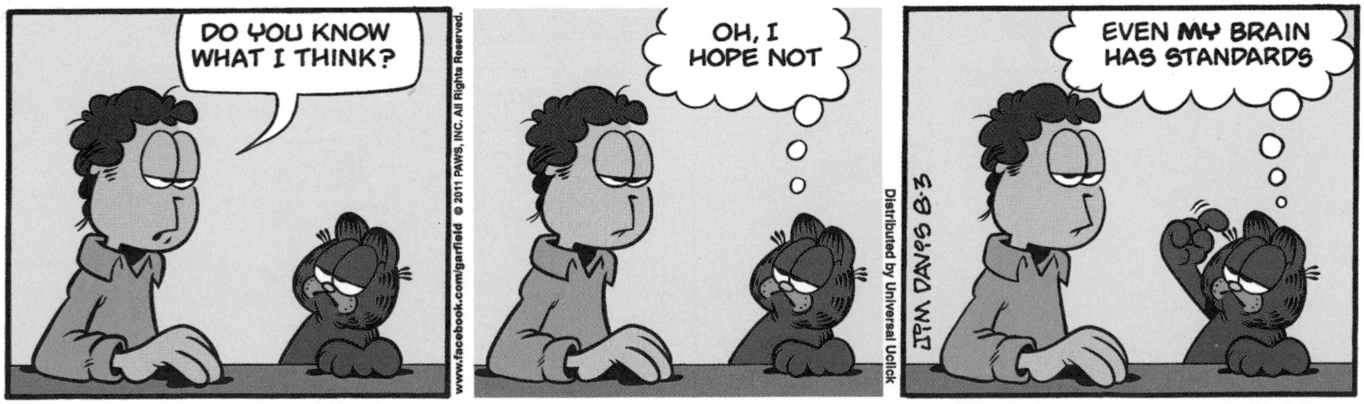
DO YOU KNOW WHAT I THINK?
www.facebook.com/garfield © 2011 PAWS, INC. All Rights Reserved.
OH, I HOPE NOT
Distributed by Universal Uclick
JPM DAVIS 8-3
EVEN MY BRAIN HAS STANDARDS

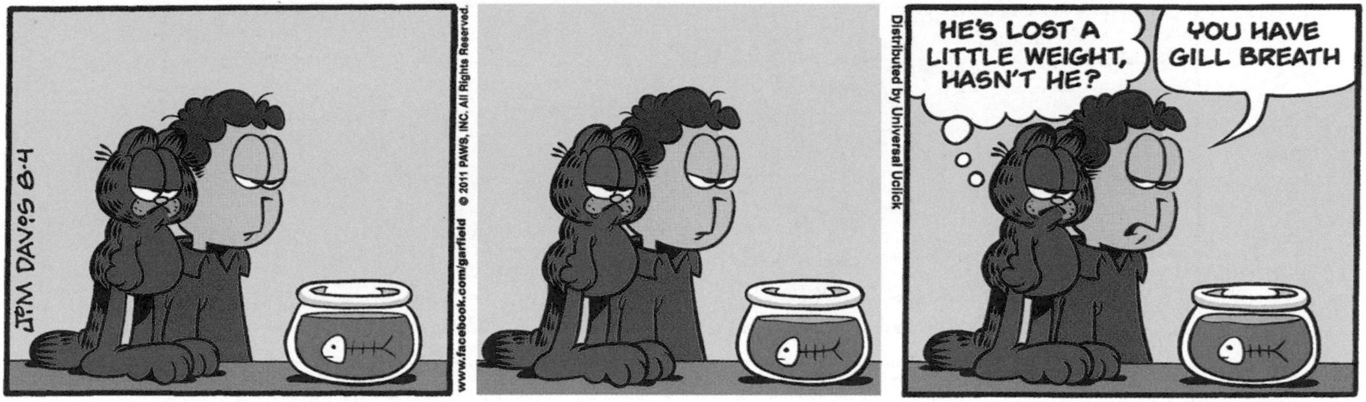
JIM DAVIS 8-4
www.facebook.com/garfield © 2011 PAWS, INC. All Rights Reserved.
Distributed by Universal Uclick
HE'S LOST A LITTLE WEIGHT, HASN'T HE?
YOU HAVE GILL BREATH

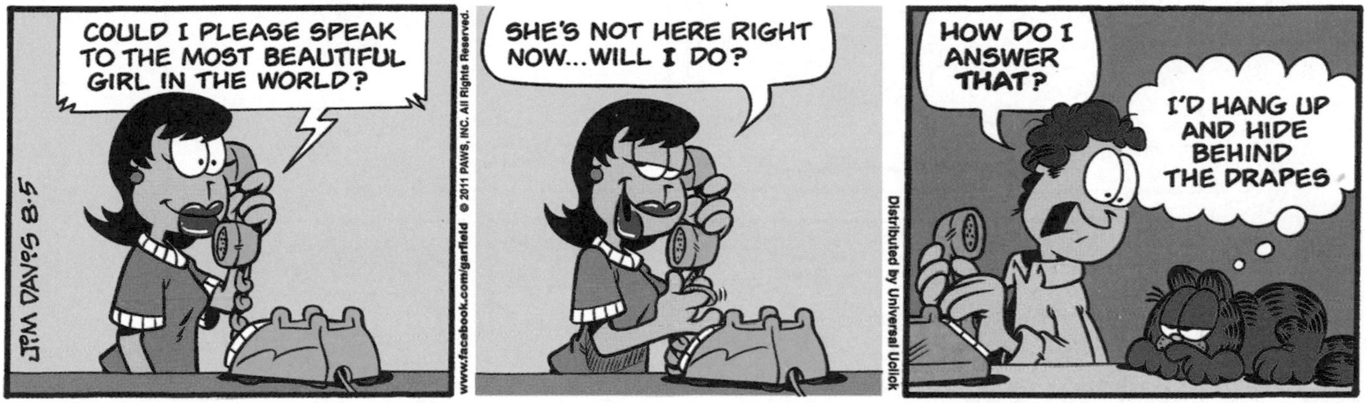
JIM DAVIS 8-5
COULD I PLEASE SPEAK TO THE MOST BEAUTIFUL GIRL IN THE WORLD?
www.facebook.com/garfield © 2011 PAWS, INC. All Rights Reserved.
SHE'S NOT HERE RIGHT NOW... WILL I DO?
Distributed by Universal Uclick
HOW DO I ANSWER THAT?
I'D HANG UP AND HIDE BEHIND THE DRAPES

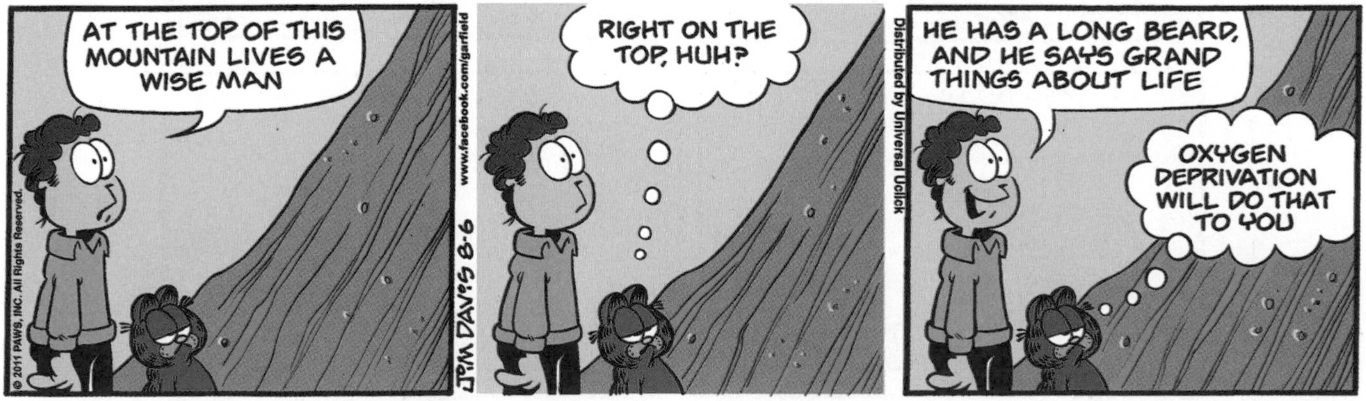
© 2011 PAWS, INC. All Rights Reserved.
AT THE TOP OF THIS MOUNTAIN LIVES A WISE MAN
www.facebook.com/garfield
JIM DAVIS 8-6
RIGHT ON THE TOP, HUH?
Distributed by Universal Uclick
HE HAS A LONG BEARD, AND HE SAYS GRAND THINGS ABOUT LIFE
OXYGEN DEPRIVATION WILL DO THAT TO YOU

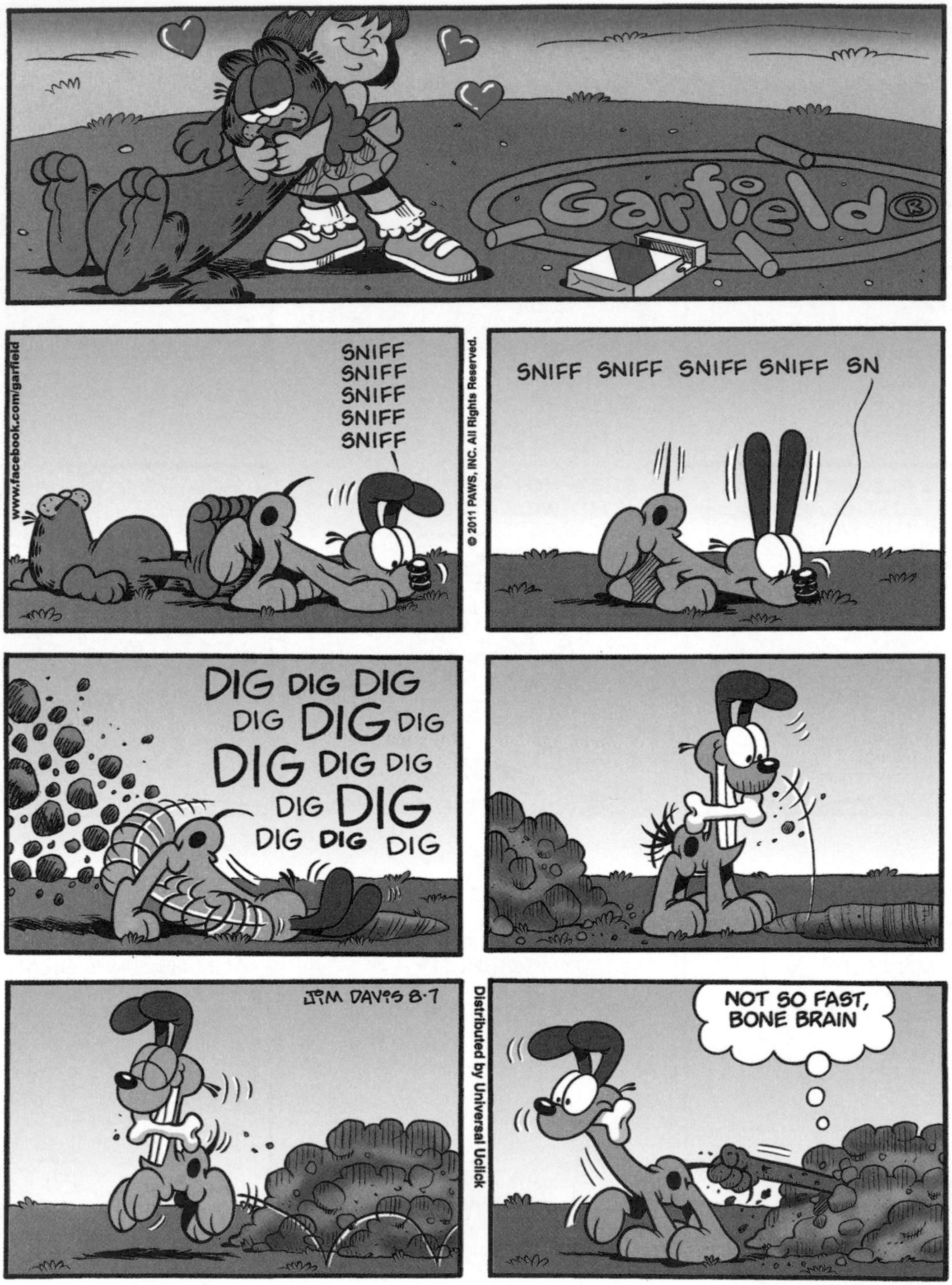

Garfield®
www.facebook.com/garfield
SNIFF SNIFF SNIFF SNIFF SNIFF
© 2011 PAWS, INC. All Rights Reserved.
SNIFF SNIFF SNIFF SNIFF SN
DIG DIG DIG DIG DIG DIG DIG DIG DIG DIG DIG DIG DIG DIG
JIM DAVIS 8-7
Distributed by Universal Uclick
NOT SO FAST, BONE BRAIN

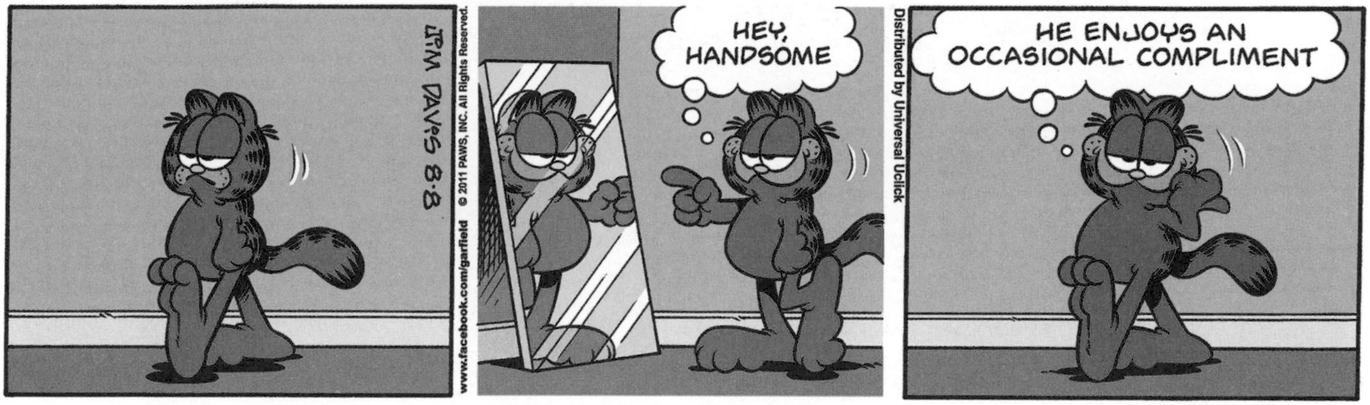
JIM DAVIS 8-8
www.facebook.com/garfield © 2011 PAWS, INC. All Rights Reserved.
HEY, HANDSOME
Distributed by Universal Uclick
HE ENJOYS AN OCCASIONAL COMPLIMENT

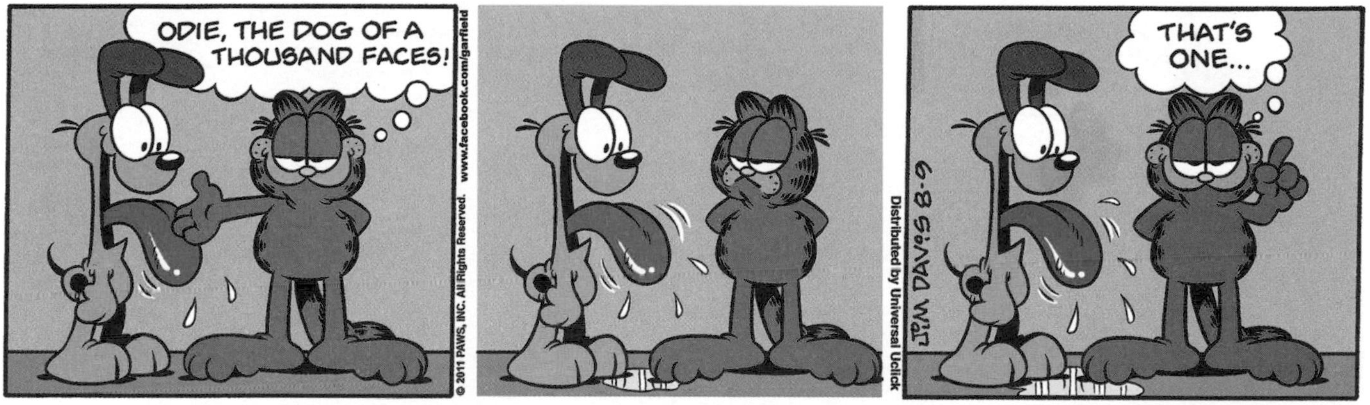
ODIE, THE DOG OF A THOUSAND FACES!
© 2011 PAWS, INC. All Rights Reserved. www.facebook.com/garfield
Distributed by Universal Uclick
JIM DAVIS 8-9
THAT'S ONE...

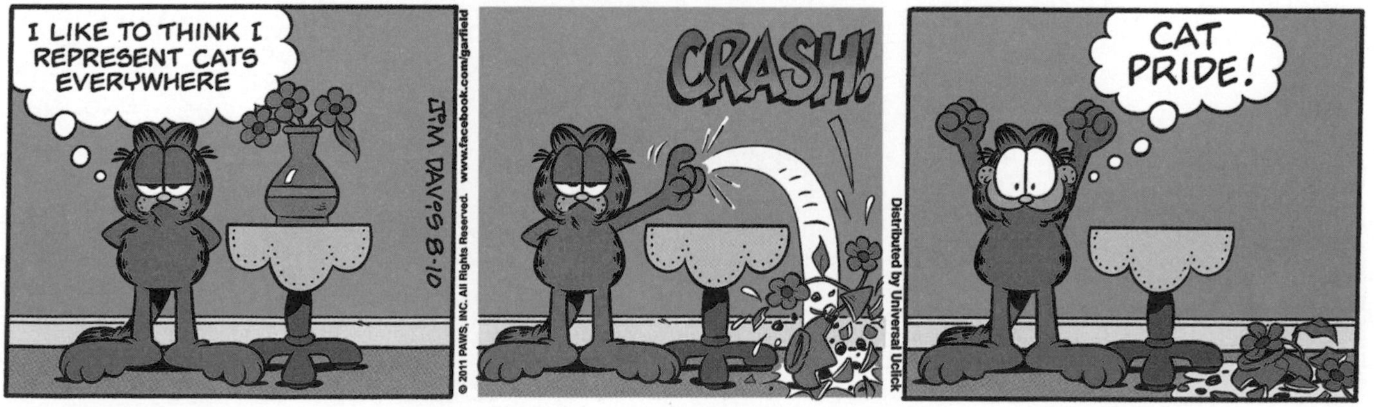
I LIKE TO THINK I REPRESENT CATS EVERYWHERE
JIM DAVIS 8-10
© 2011 PAWS, INC. All Rights Reserved. www.facebook.com/garfield
CRASH!
Distributed by Universal Uclick
CAT PRIDE!

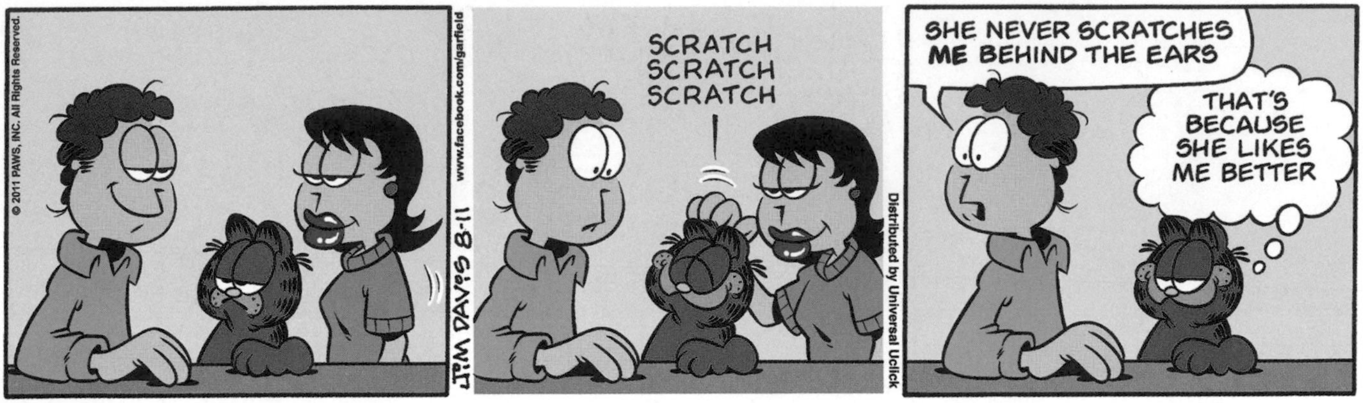
© 2011 PAWS, INC. All Rights Reserved.
www.facebook.com/garfield
JIM DAVIS 8-11
SCRATCH
SCRATCH
SCRATCH
Distributed by Universal Uclick
SHE NEVER SCRATCHES **ME** BEHIND THE EARS
THAT'S BECAUSE SHE LIKES ME BETTER

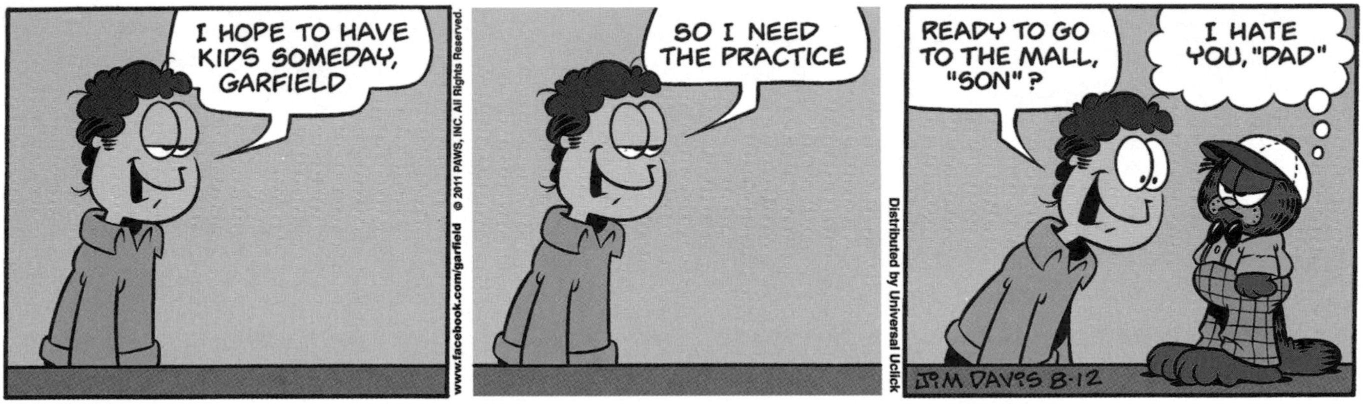
I HOPE TO HAVE KIDS SOMEDAY, GARFIELD
www.facebook.com/garfield © 2011 PAWS, INC. All Rights Reserved.
SO I NEED THE PRACTICE
Distributed by Universal Uclick
READY TO GO TO THE MALL, "SON"?
I HATE YOU, "DAD"
JIM DAVIS 8-12

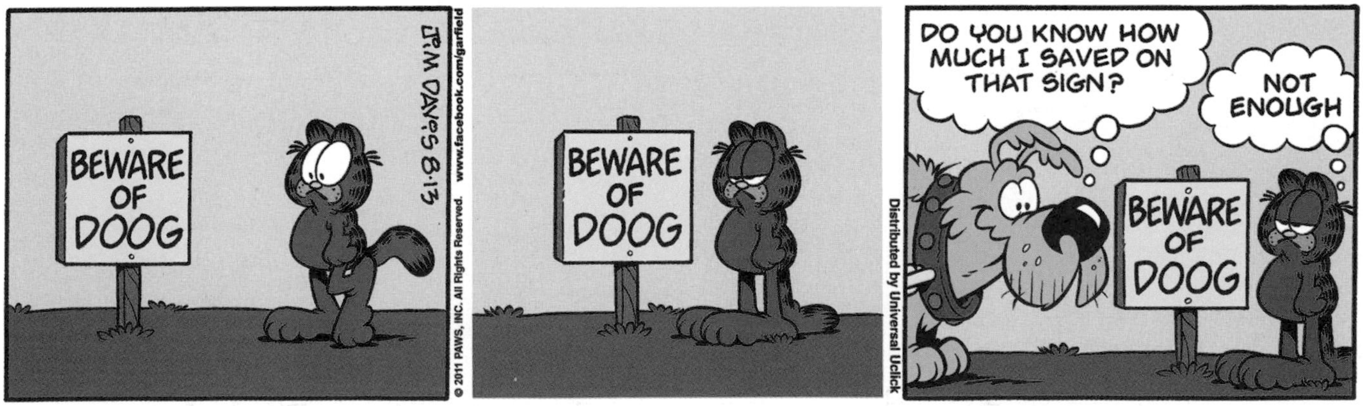
BEWARE OF DOOG
JIM DAVIS 8-13
© 2011 PAWS, INC. All Rights Reserved. www.facebook.com/garfield
BEWARE OF DOOG
Distributed by Universal Uclick
DO YOU KNOW HOW MUCH I SAVED ON THAT SIGN?
NOT ENOUGH
BEWARE OF DOOG

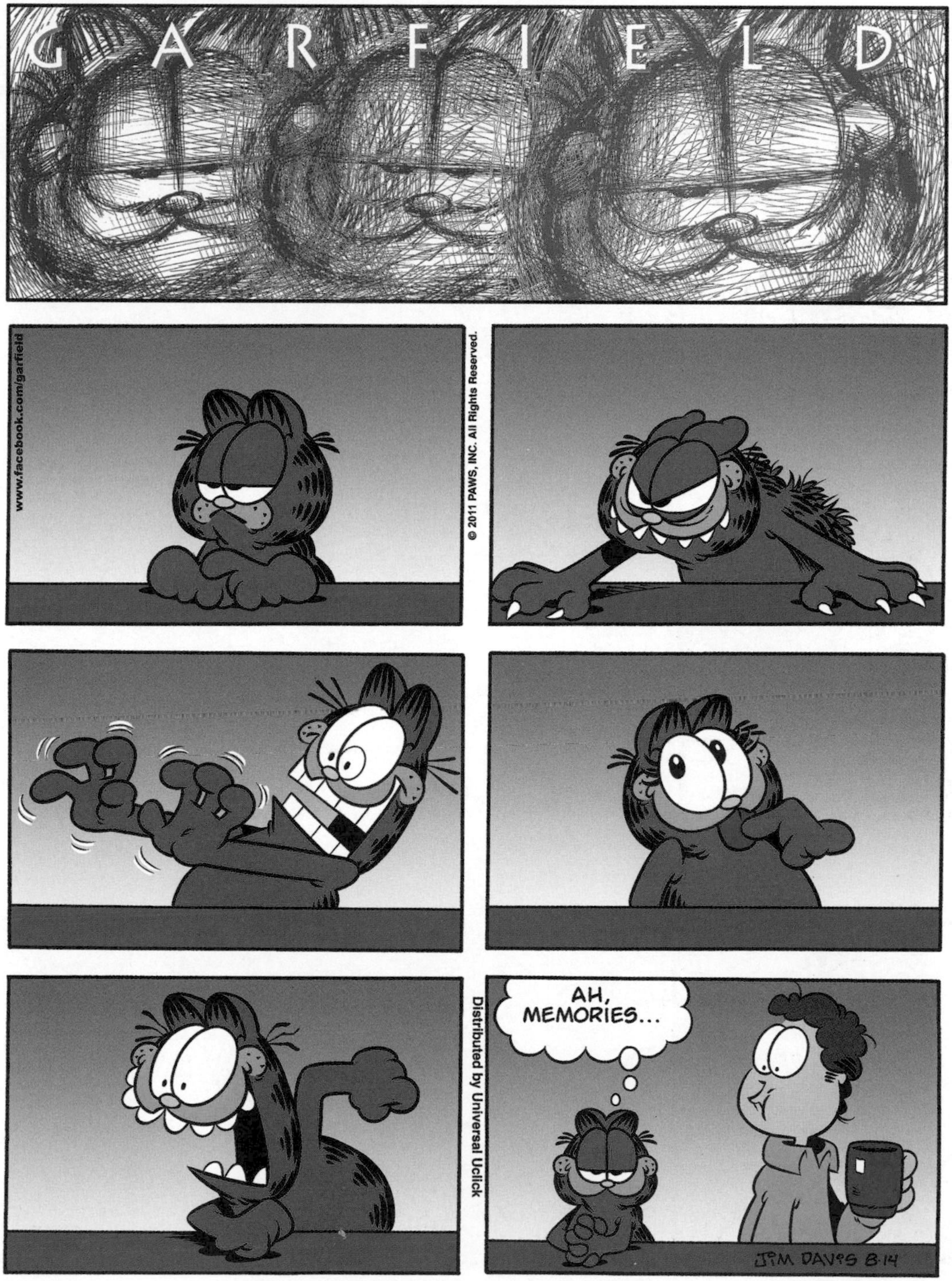
GARFIELD
www.facebook.com/garfield
AH, MEMORIES...
JIM DAVIS 8-14
Distributed by Universal Uclick

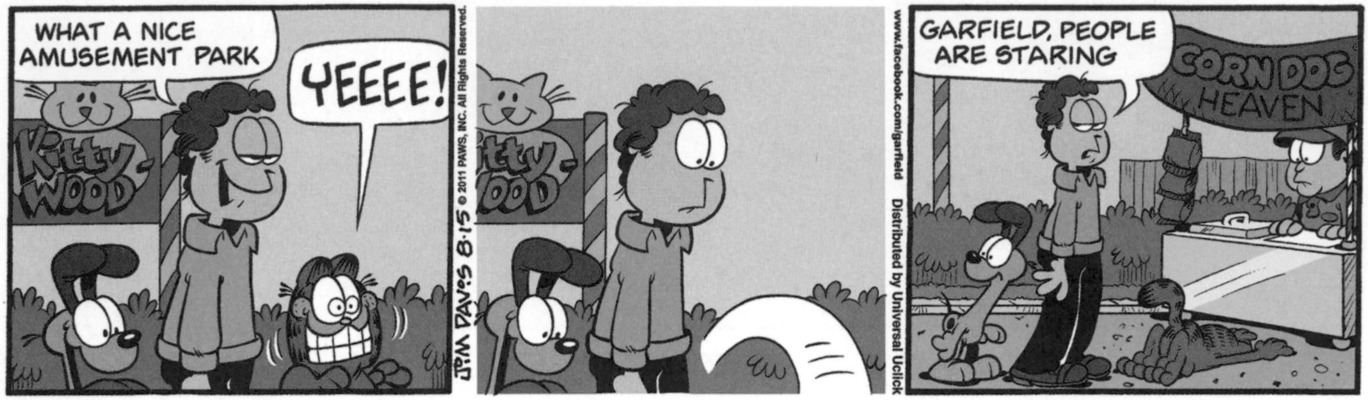
WHAT A NICE AMUSEMENT PARK
YEEEE!
KITTY-WOOD
JIM DAVIS 8·15
© 2011 PAWS, INC. All Rights Reserved.
www.facebook.com/garfield
Distributed by Universal Uclick
GARFIELD, PEOPLE ARE STARING
CORN DOG HEAVEN

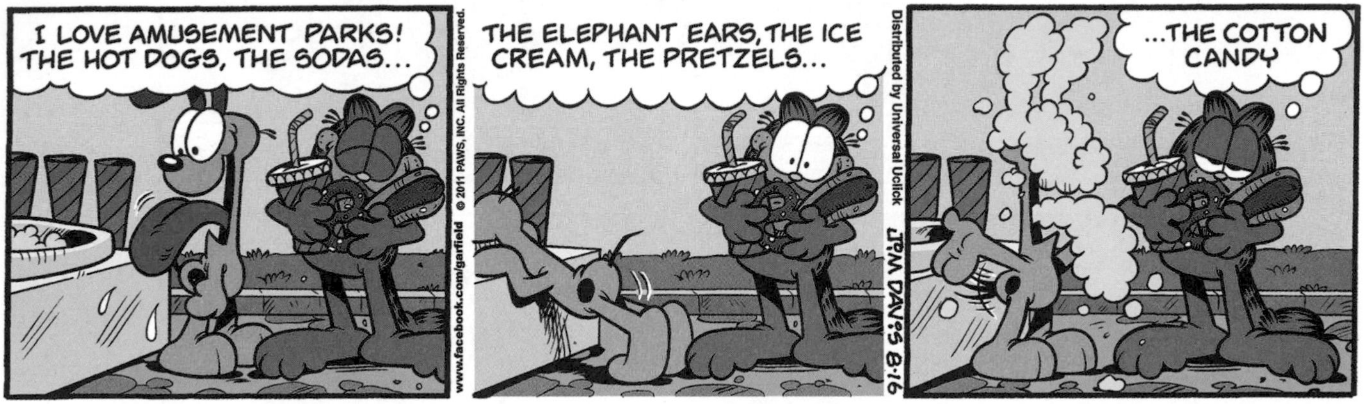
I LOVE AMUSEMENT PARKS! THE HOT DOGS, THE SODAS...
www.facebook.com/garfield © 2011 PAWS, INC. All Rights Reserved.
THE ELEPHANT EARS, THE ICE CREAM, THE PRETZELS...
Distributed by Universal Uclick
JIM DAVIS 8·16
...THE COTTON CANDY

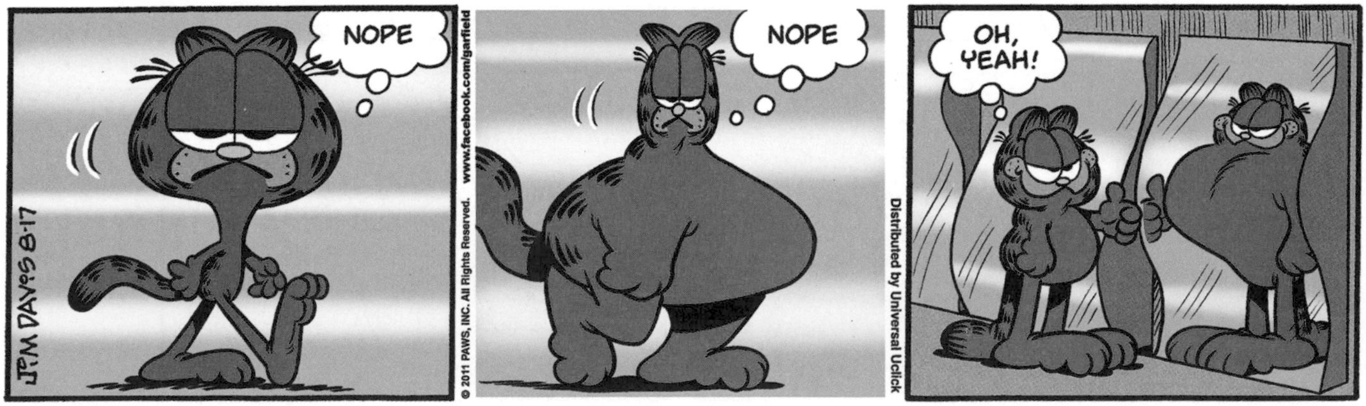
NOPE
JIM DAVIS 8·17
© 2011 PAWS, INC. All Rights Reserved. www.facebook.com/garfield
NOPE
Distributed by Universal Uclick
OH, YEAH!

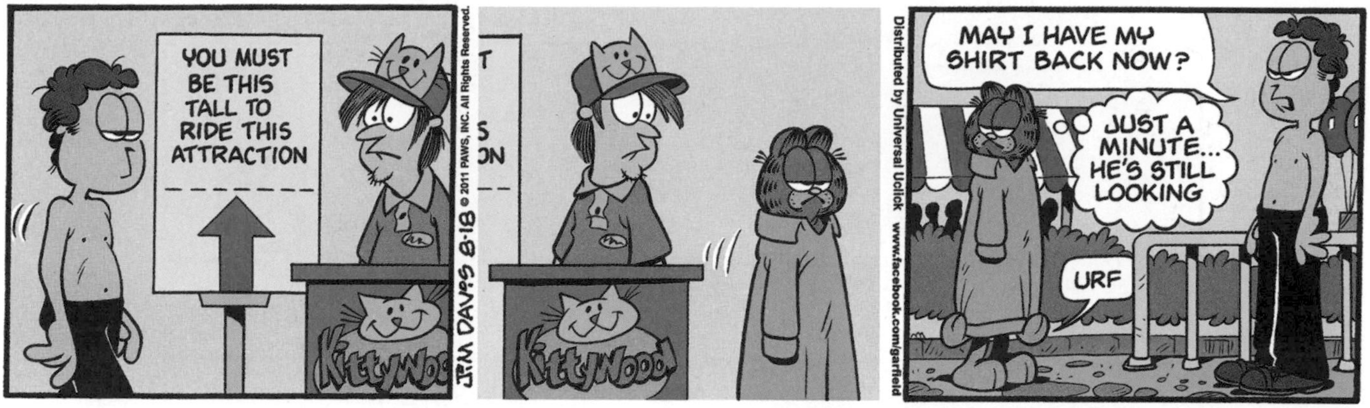
YOU MUST BE THIS TALL TO RIDE THIS ATTRACTION
KittyWood
JIM DAVIS 8-18 © 2011 PAWS, INC. All Rights Reserved.
KittyWood
Distributed by Universal Uclick www.facebook.com/garfield
MAY I HAVE MY SHIRT BACK NOW?
JUST A MINUTE... HE'S STILL LOOKING
URF

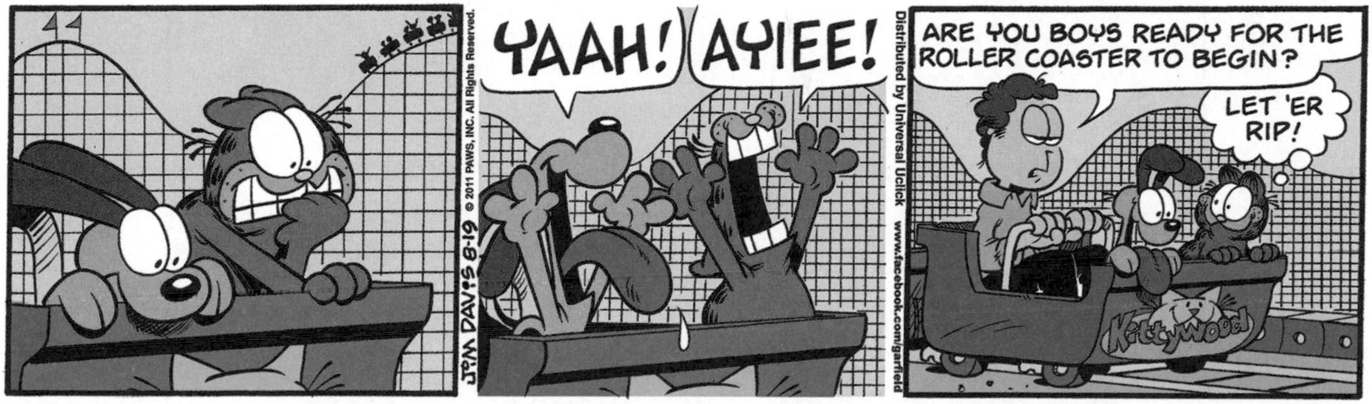
JIM DAVIS 8-19 © 2011 PAWS, INC. All Rights Reserved.
YAAH!
AYIEE!
Distributed by Universal Uclick www.facebook.com/garfield
ARE YOU BOYS READY FOR THE ROLLER COASTER TO BEGIN?
LET 'ER RIP!
KittyWood

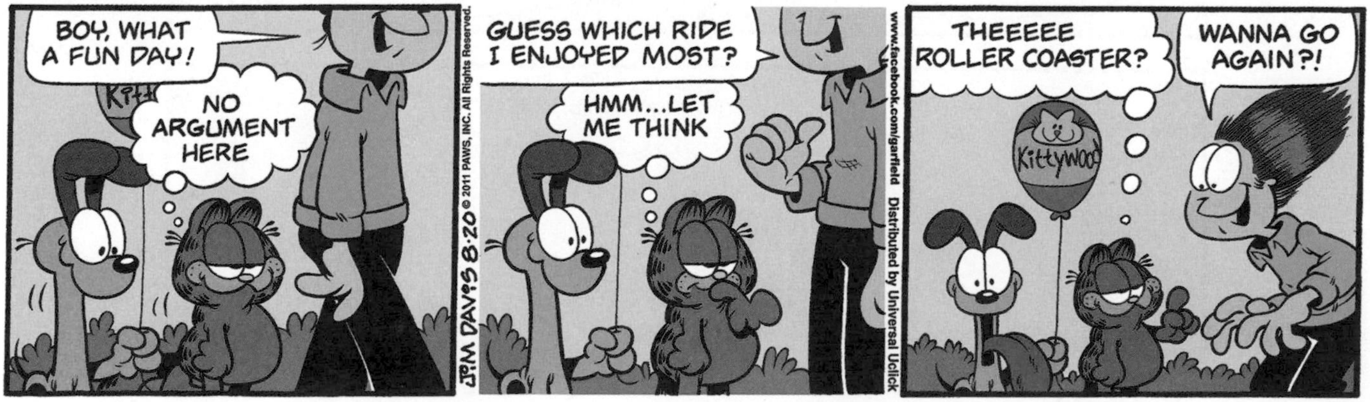
BOY, WHAT A FUN DAY!
NO ARGUMENT HERE
JIM DAVIS 8-20 © 2011 PAWS, INC. All Rights Reserved.
GUESS WHICH RIDE I ENJOYED MOST?
HMM...LET ME THINK
www.facebook.com/garfield Distributed by Universal Uclick
THEEEEE ROLLER COASTER?
WANNA GO AGAIN?!
Kittywood

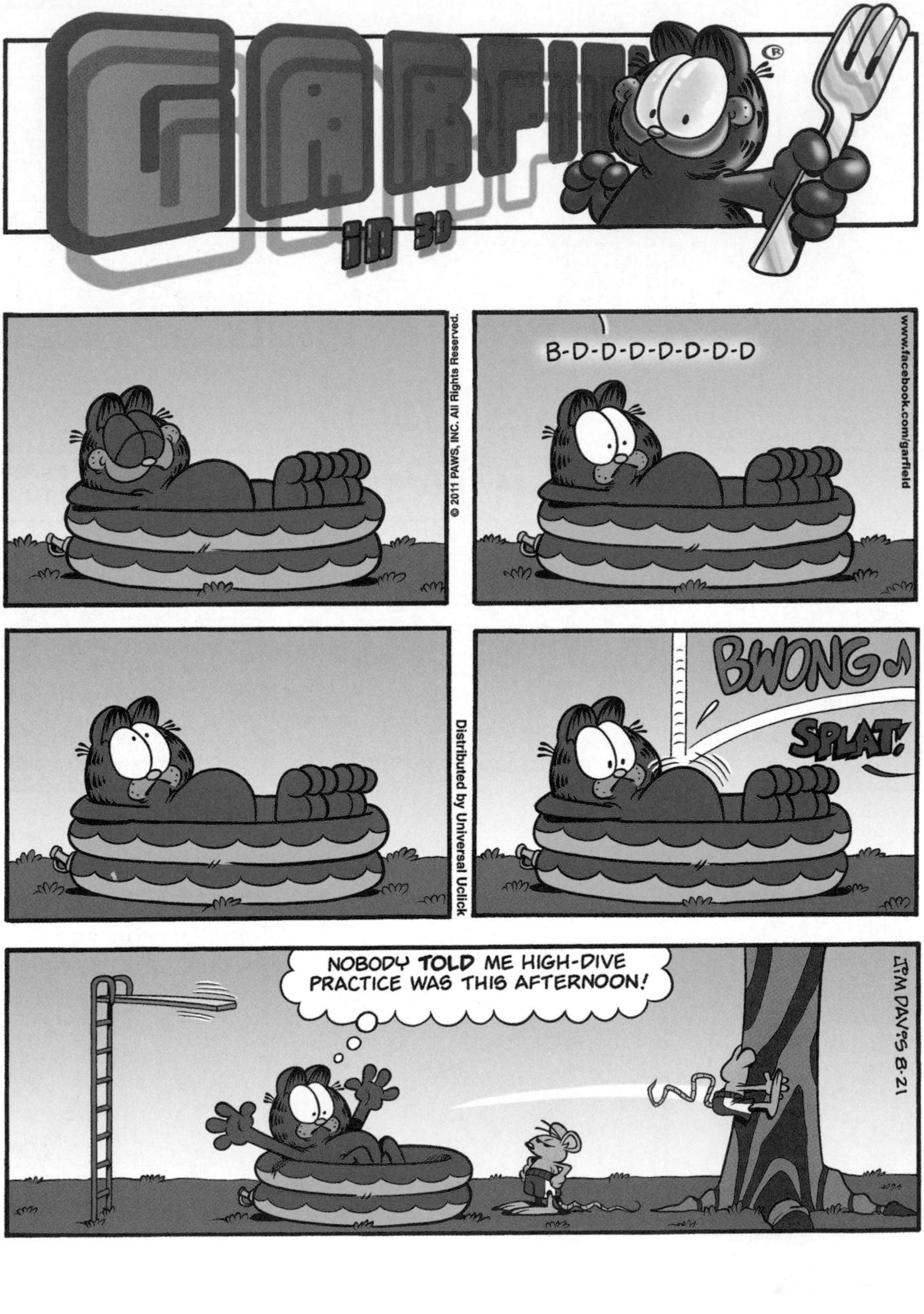

B-D-D-D-D-D-D-D
BWONG
SPLAT!
NOBODY TOLD ME HIGH-DIVE PRACTICE WAS THIS AFTERNOON!
© 2011 PAWS, INC. All Rights Reserved.
www.facebook.com/garfield
Distributed by Universal Uclick
JIM DAVIS 8-21

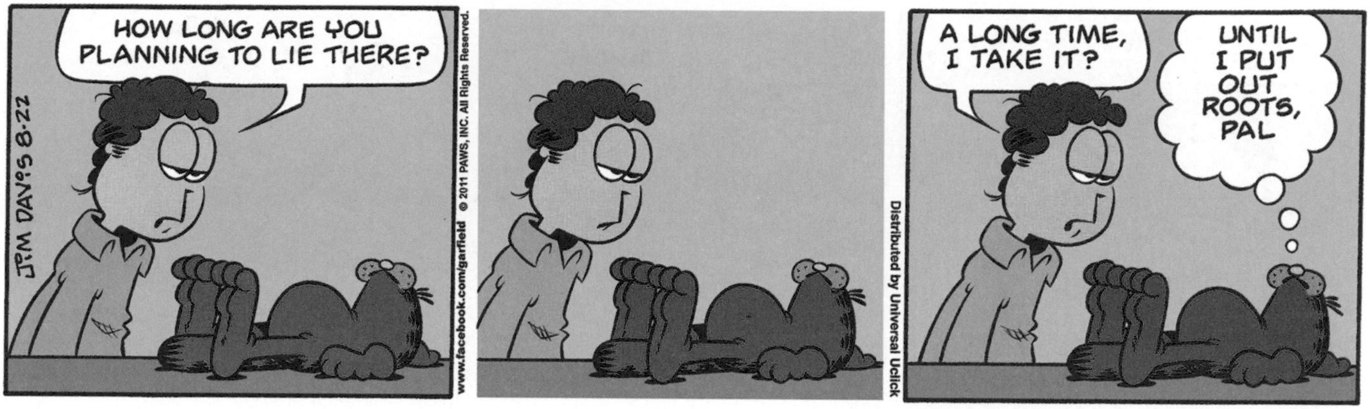
HOW LONG ARE YOU PLANNING TO LIE THERE?
JIM DAVIS 8-22
www.facebook.com/garfield © 2011 PAWS, INC. All Rights Reserved.
Distributed by Universal Uclick
A LONG TIME, I TAKE IT?
UNTIL I PUT OUT ROOTS, PAL

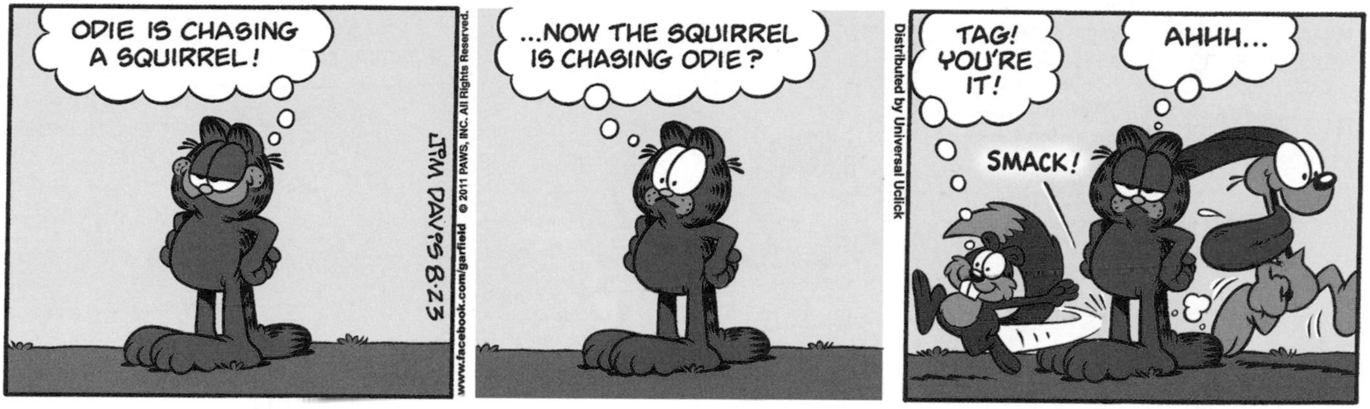
ODIE IS CHASING A SQUIRREL!
JIM DAVIS 8-23
www.facebook.com/garfield © 2011 PAWS, INC. All Rights Reserved.
...NOW THE SQUIRREL IS CHASING ODIE?
Distributed by Universal Uclick
TAG! YOU'RE IT!
AHHH...
SMACK!

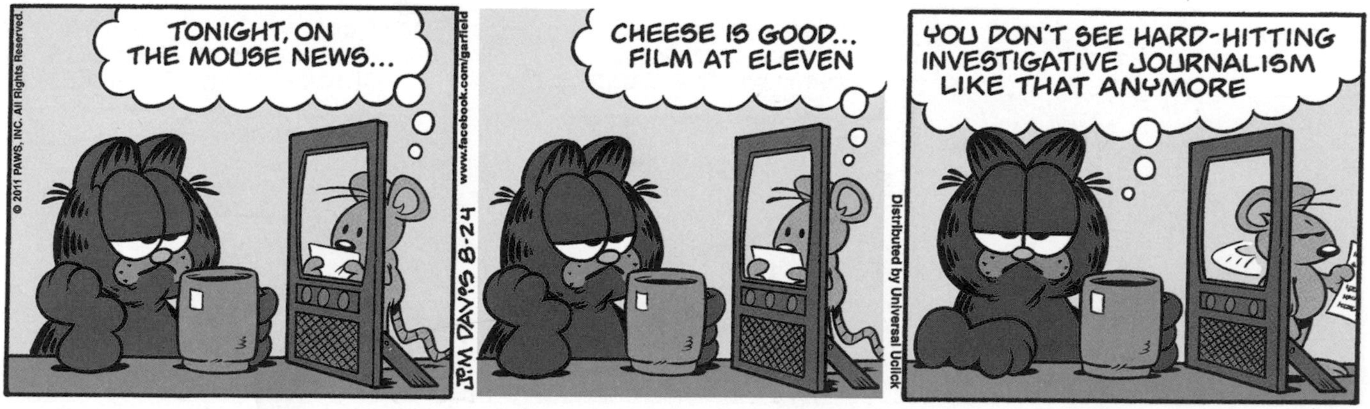
© 2011 PAWS, INC. All Rights Reserved.
TONIGHT, ON THE MOUSE NEWS...
www.facebook.com/garfield
JIM DAVIS 8-24
CHEESE IS GOOD... FILM AT ELEVEN
Distributed by Universal Uclick
YOU DON'T SEE HARD-HITTING INVESTIGATIVE JOURNALISM LIKE THAT ANYMORE

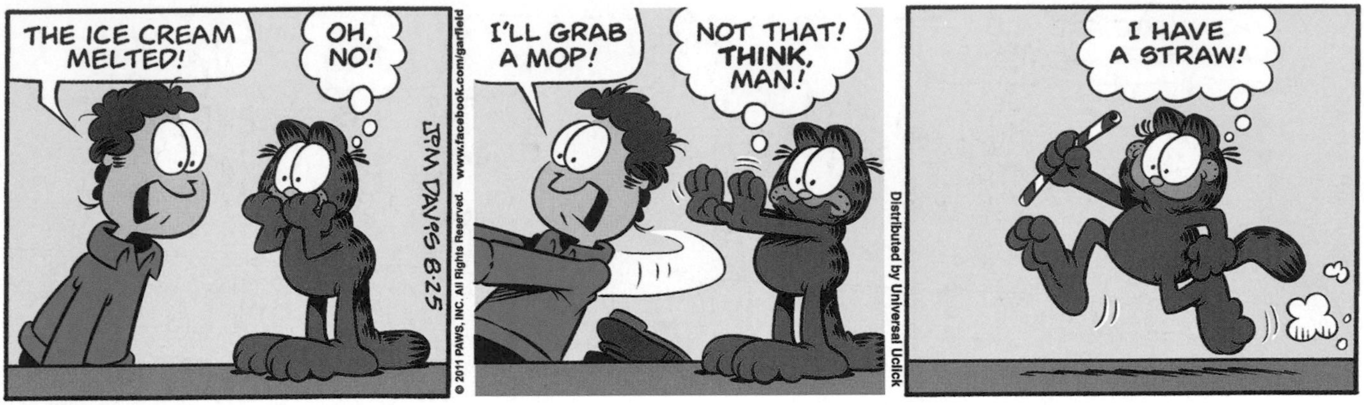
THE ICE CREAM MELTED!
OH, NO!
JIM DAVIS 8-25
© 2011 PAWS, INC. All Rights Reserved. www.facebook.com/garfield
I'LL GRAB A MOP!
NOT THAT! THINK, MAN!
Distributed by Universal Uclick
I HAVE A STRAW!

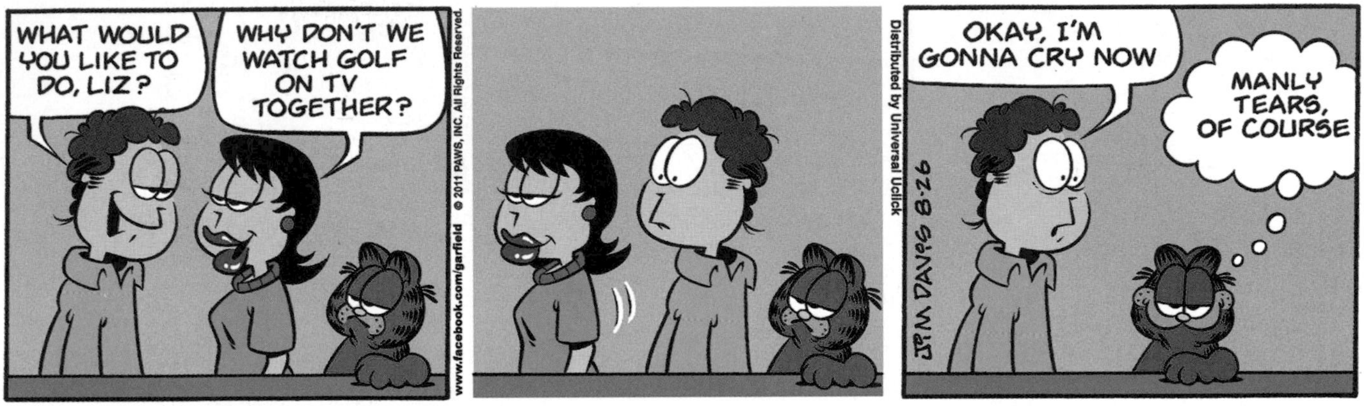
WHAT WOULD YOU LIKE TO DO, LIZ?
WHY DON'T WE WATCH GOLF ON TV TOGETHER?
www.facebook.com/garfield © 2011 PAWS, INC. All Rights Reserved.
Distributed by Universal Uclick
OKAY, I'M GONNA CRY NOW
MANLY TEARS, OF COURSE
JIM DAVIS 8-26

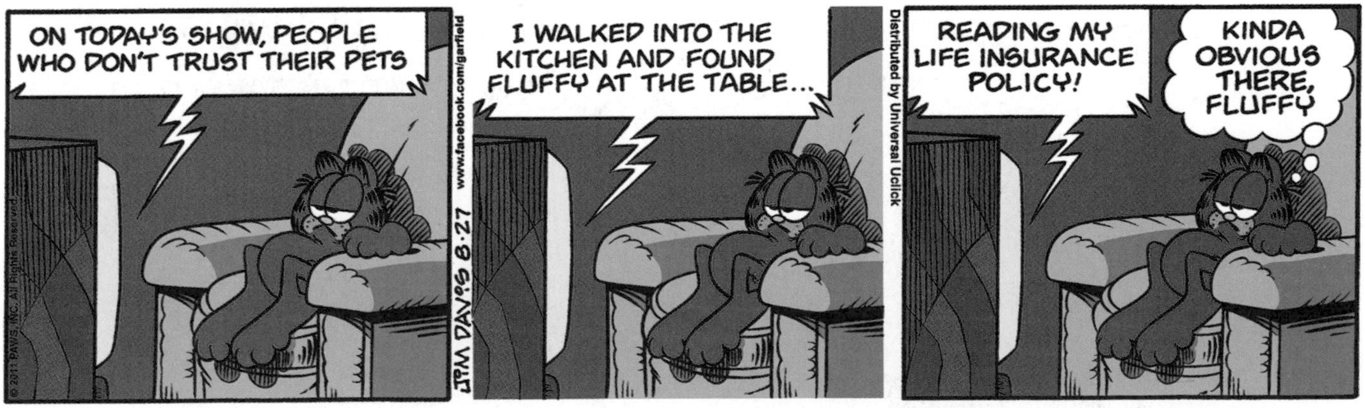
ON TODAY'S SHOW, PEOPLE WHO DON'T TRUST THEIR PETS
© 2011 PAWS, INC. All Rights Reserved.
JIM DAVIS 8-27
www.facebook.com/garfield
I WALKED INTO THE KITCHEN AND FOUND FLUFFY AT THE TABLE...
Distributed by Universal Uclick
READING MY LIFE INSURANCE POLICY!
KINDA OBVIOUS THERE, FLUFFY

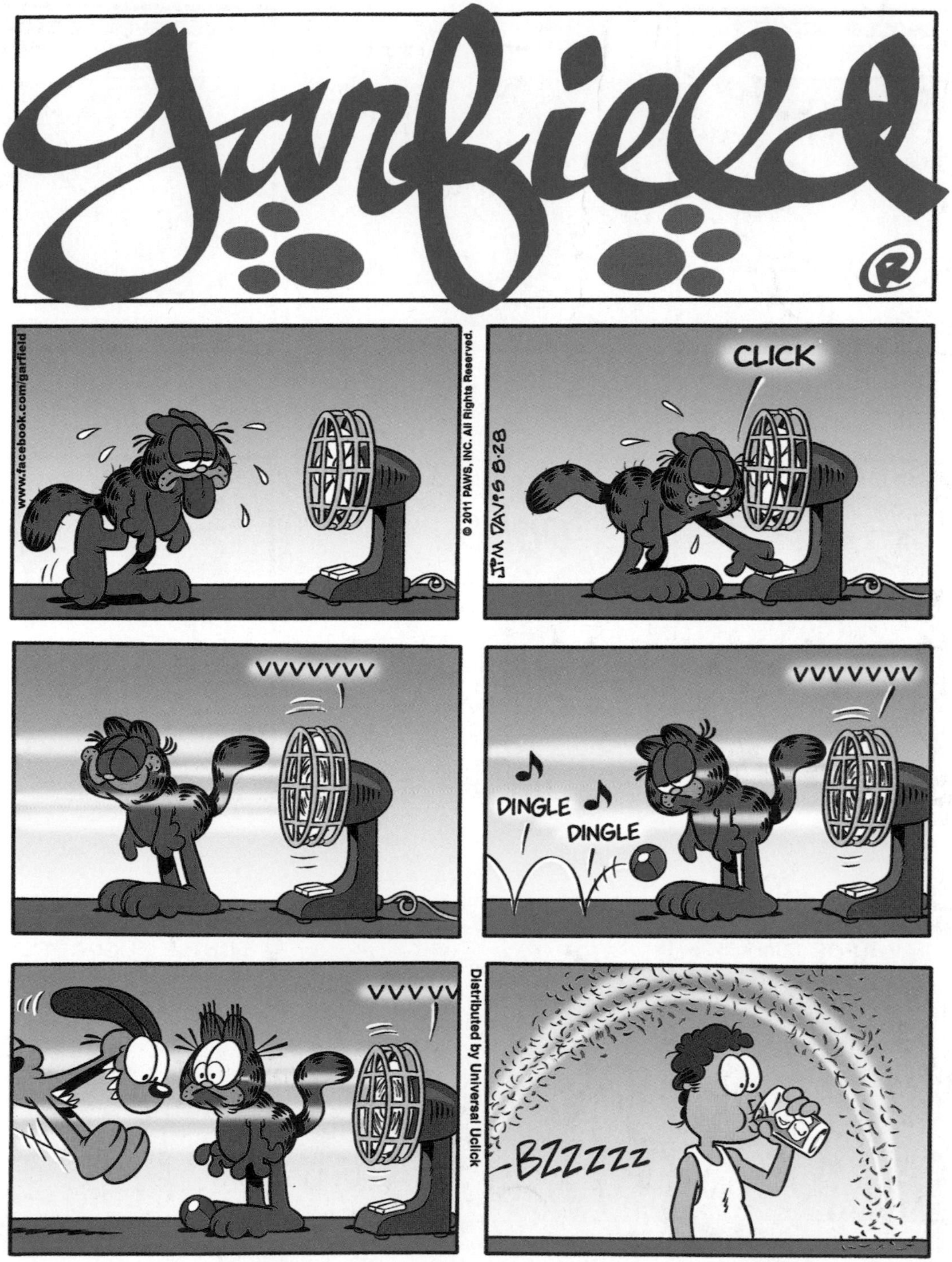
garfield
www.facebook.com/garfield
© 2011 PAWS, INC. All Rights Reserved.
JIM DAVIS 8·28
CLICK
VVVVVVV
VVVVVVV
DINGLE
DINGLE
VVVVV
Distributed by Universal Uclick
BZZZZz

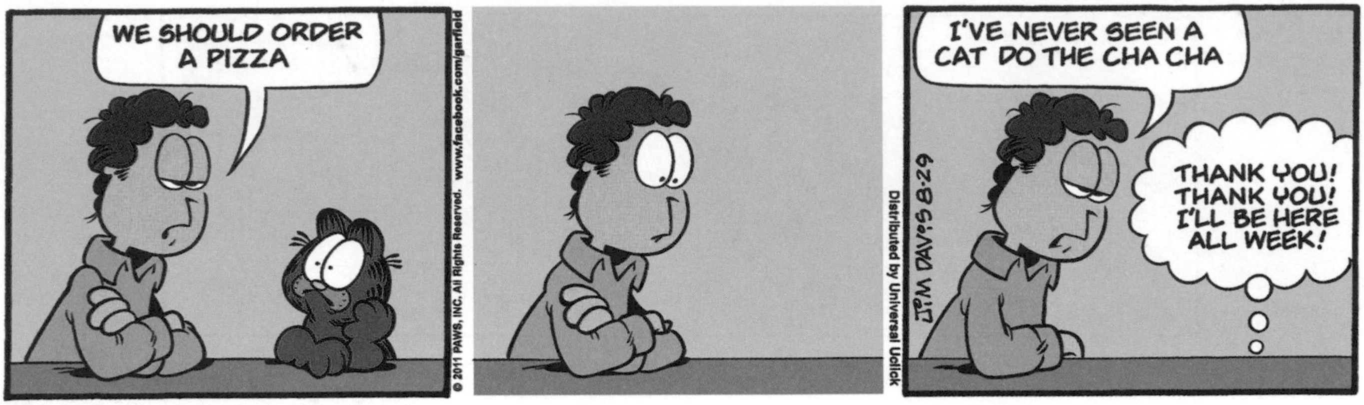
WE SHOULD ORDER A PIZZA
I'VE NEVER SEEN A CAT DO THE CHA CHA
THANK YOU! THANK YOU! I'LL BE HERE ALL WEEK!
JIM DAVIS 8-29
© 2011 PAWS, INC. All Rights Reserved. www.facebook.com/garfield
Distributed by Universal Uclick

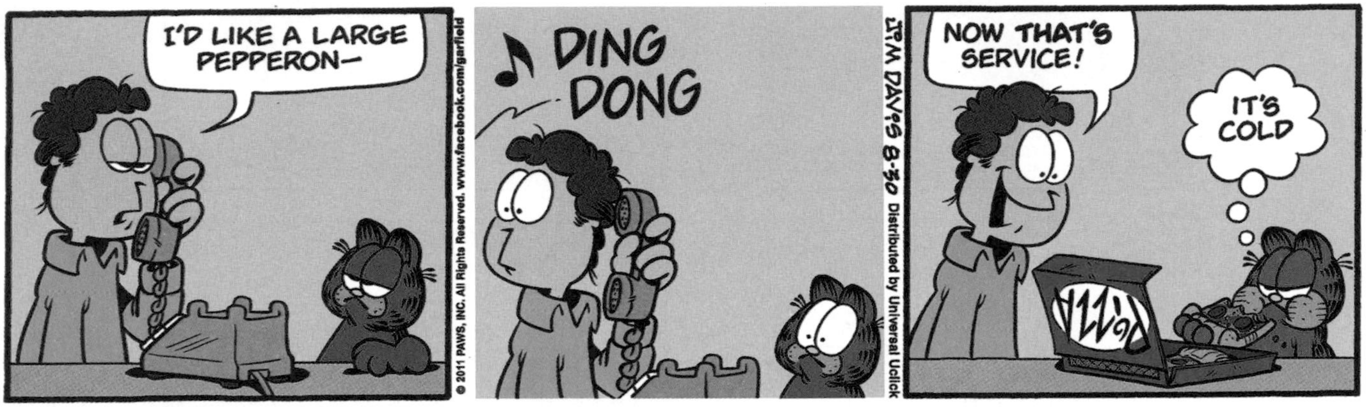
I'D LIKE A LARGE PEPPERON—
DING DONG
NOW THAT'S SERVICE!
IT'S COLD
JIM DAVIS 8-30
© 2011 PAWS, INC. All Rights Reserved. www.facebook.com/garfield
Distributed by Universal Uclick

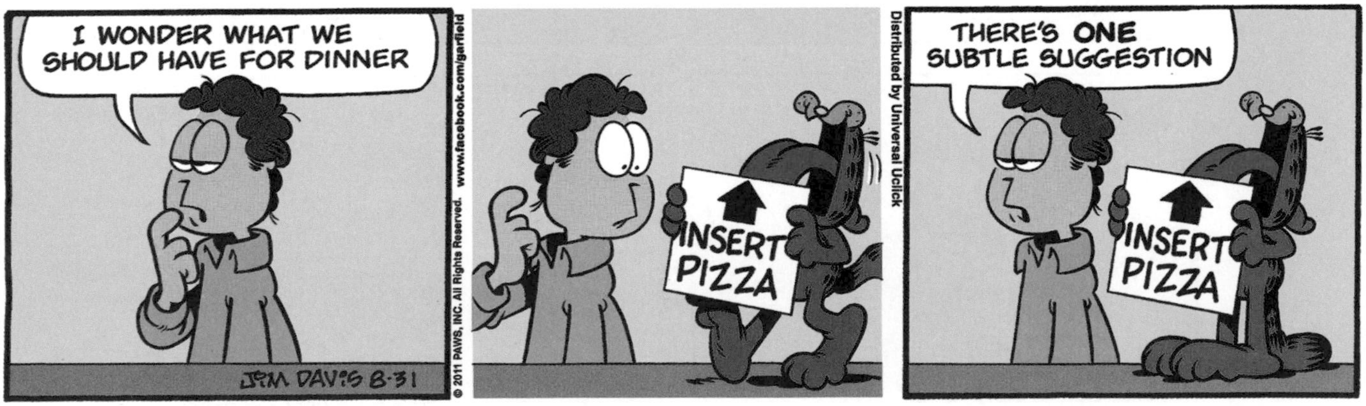
I WONDER WHAT WE SHOULD HAVE FOR DINNER
JIM DAVIS 8-31
INSERT PIZZA
THERE'S ONE SUBTLE SUGGESTION
INSERT PIZZA
© 2011 PAWS, INC. All Rights Reserved. www.facebook.com/garfield
Distributed by Universal Uclick

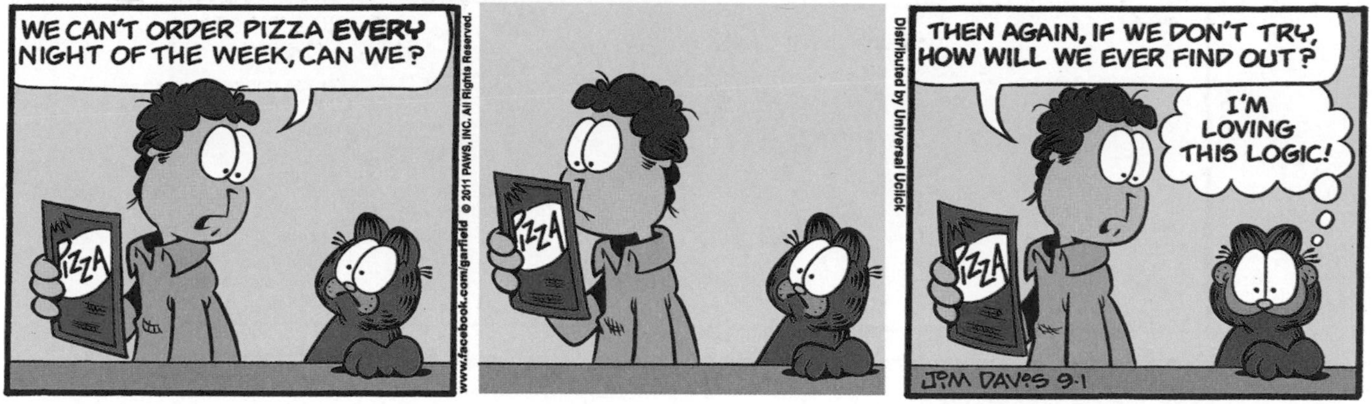
WE CAN'T ORDER PIZZA EVERY NIGHT OF THE WEEK, CAN WE?
PIZZA
© 2011 PAWS, INC. All Rights Reserved. www.facebook.com/garfield
PIZZA
Distributed by Universal Uclick
THEN AGAIN, IF WE DON'T TRY, HOW WILL WE EVER FIND OUT?
I'M LOVING THIS LOGIC!
PIZZA
JIM DAVIS 9-1

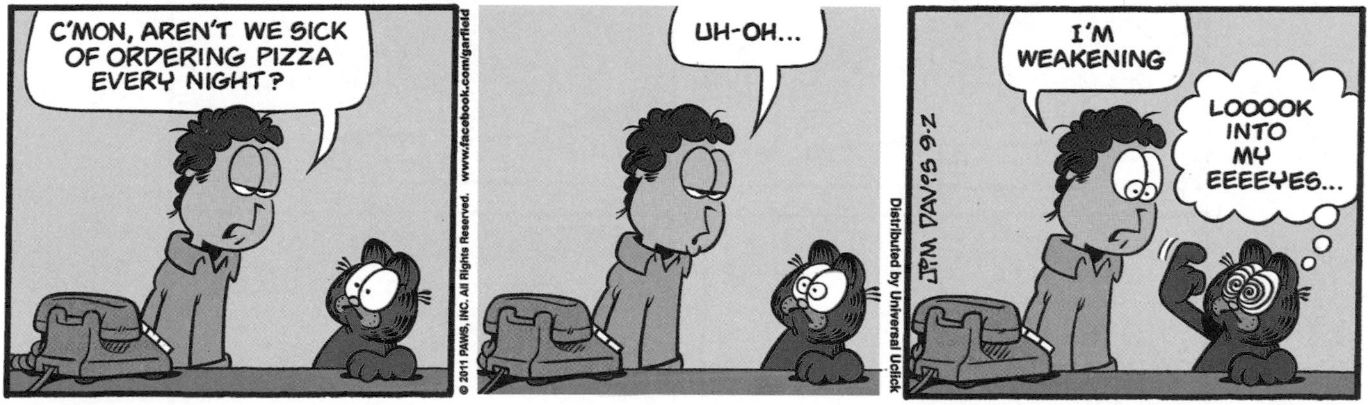
C'MON, AREN'T WE SICK OF ORDERING PIZZA EVERY NIGHT?
© 2011 PAWS, INC. All Rights Reserved. www.facebook.com/garfield
UH-OH...
Distributed by Universal Uclick
JIM DAVIS 9-2
I'M WEAKENING
LOOOOK INTO MY EEEEYES...

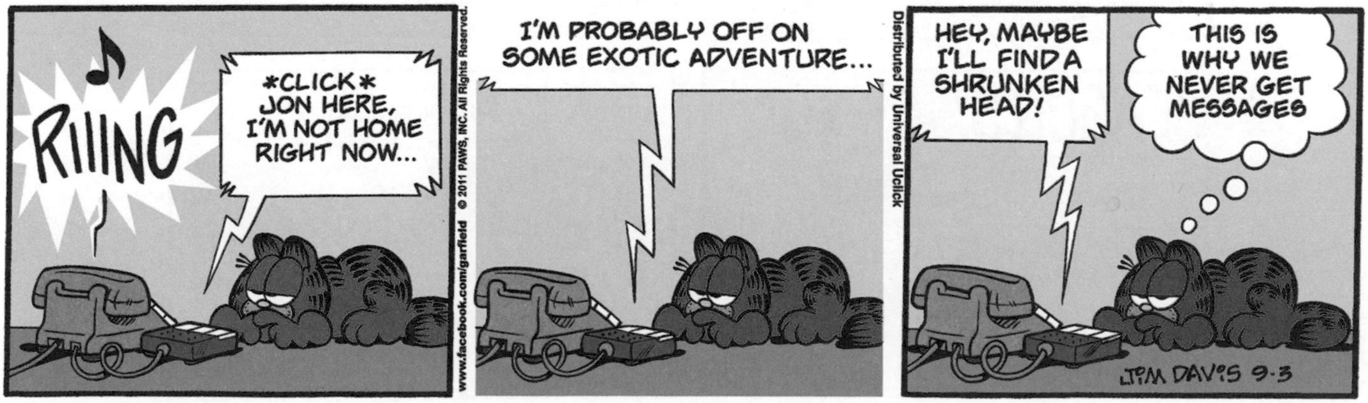
RIIING
CLICK JON HERE, I'M NOT HOME RIGHT NOW...
© 2011 PAWS, INC. All Rights Reserved. www.facebook.com/garfield
I'M PROBABLY OFF ON SOME EXOTIC ADVENTURE...
Distributed by Universal Uclick
HEY, MAYBE I'LL FIND A SHRUNKEN HEAD!
THIS IS WHY WE NEVER GET MESSAGES
JIM DAVIS 9-3

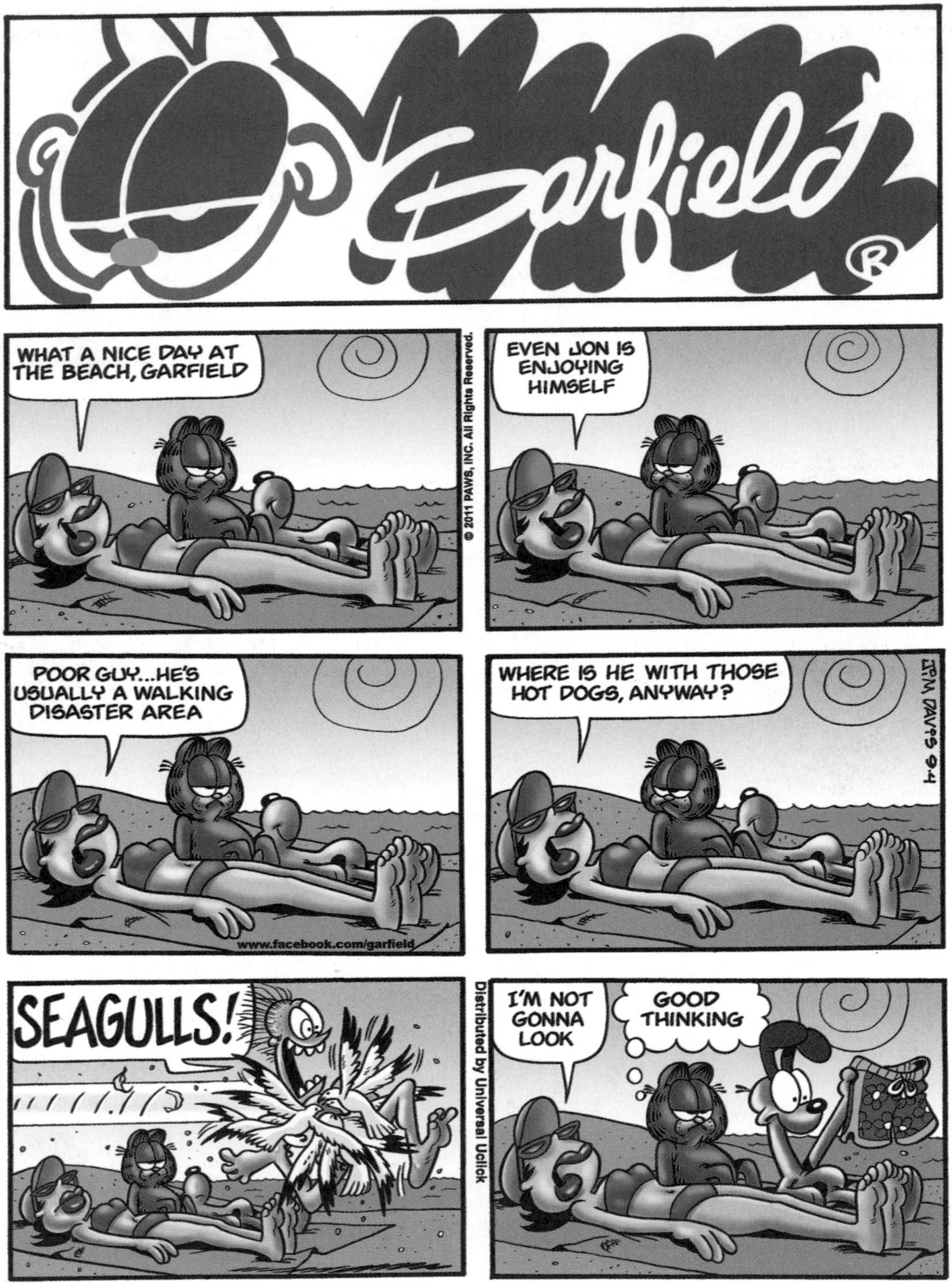
Garfield®
WHAT A NICE DAY AT THE BEACH, GARFIELD
© 2011 PAWS, INC. All Rights Reserved.
EVEN JON IS ENJOYING HIMSELF
POOR GUY...HE'S USUALLY A WALKING DISASTER AREA
www.facebook.com/garfield
WHERE IS HE WITH THOSE HOT DOGS, ANYWAY?
JIM DAVIS 9-4
SEAGULLS!
Distributed by Universal Uclick
I'M NOT GONNA LOOK
GOOD THINKING

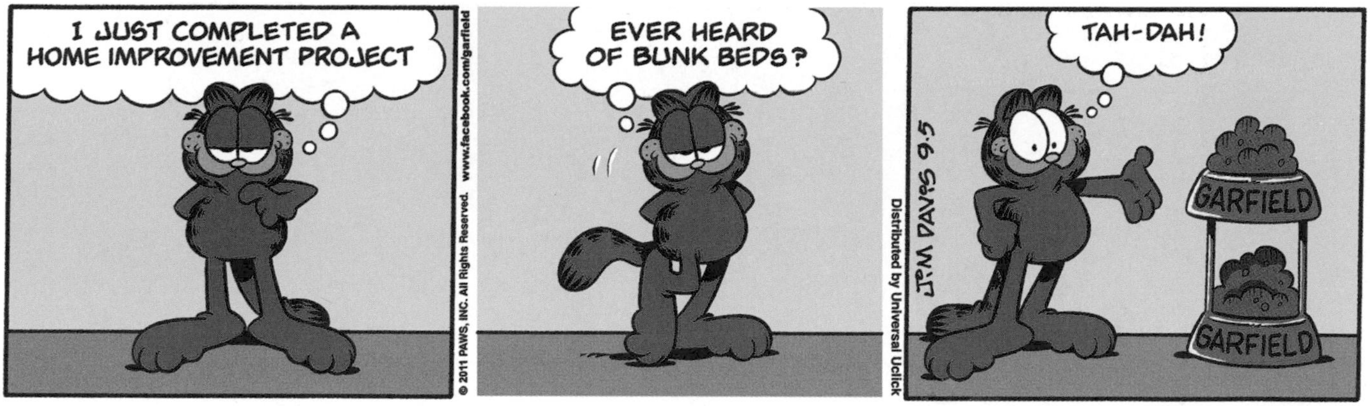
I JUST COMPLETED A HOME IMPROVEMENT PROJECT
© 2011 PAWS, INC. All Rights Reserved. www.facebook.com/garfield
EVER HEARD OF BUNK BEDS?
Distributed by Universal Uclick
JIM DAVIS 9-5
TAH-DAH!
GARFIELD
GARFIELD

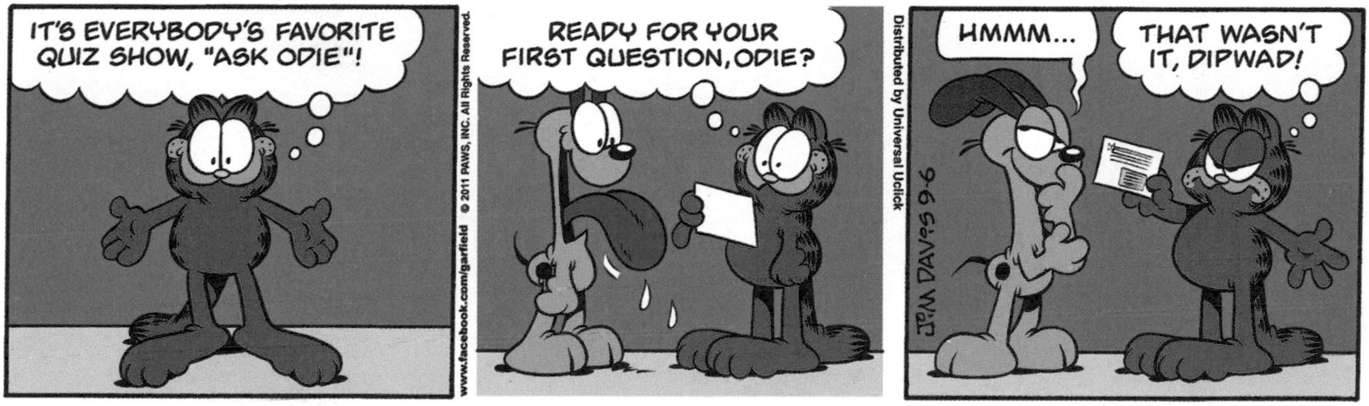
IT'S EVERYBODY'S FAVORITE QUIZ SHOW, "ASK ODIE"!
www.facebook.com/garfield © 2011 PAWS, INC. All Rights Reserved.
READY FOR YOUR FIRST QUESTION, ODIE?
Distributed by Universal Uclick
JIM DAVIS 9-6
HMMM...
THAT WASN'T IT, DIPWAD!

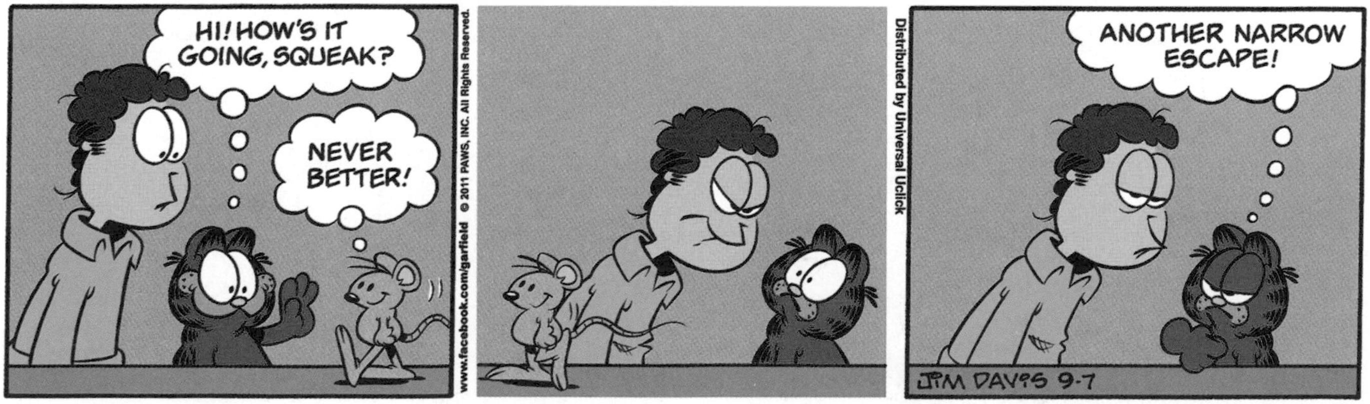
HI! HOW'S IT GOING, SQUEAK?
NEVER BETTER!
www.facebook.com/garfield © 2011 PAWS, INC. All Rights Reserved.
Distributed by Universal Uclick
ANOTHER NARROW ESCAPE!
JIM DAVIS 9-7

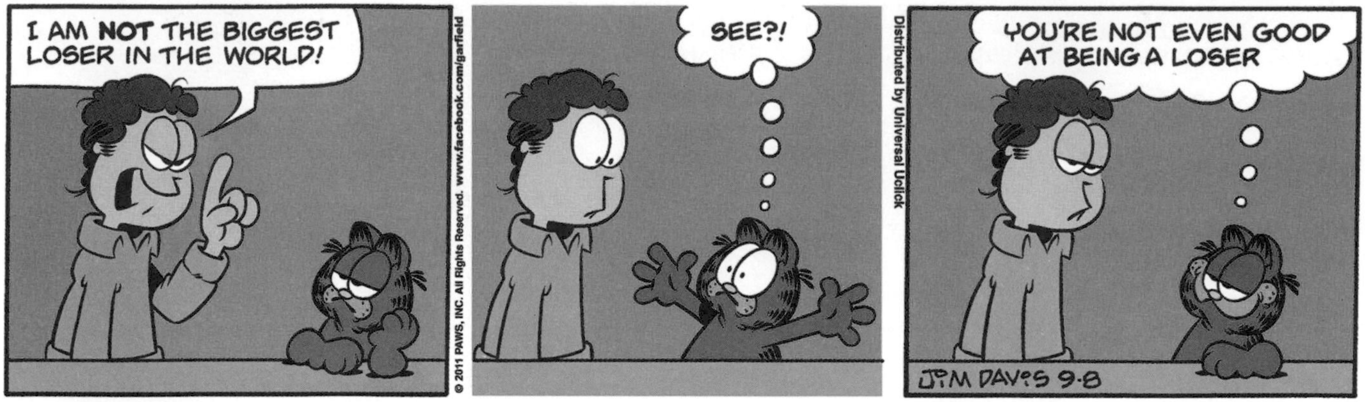
I AM **NOT** THE BIGGEST LOSER IN THE WORLD!
SEE?!
YOU'RE NOT EVEN GOOD AT BEING A LOSER
© 2011 PAWS, INC. All Rights Reserved. www.facebook.com/garfield
Distributed by Universal Uclick
JIM DAVIS 9-8

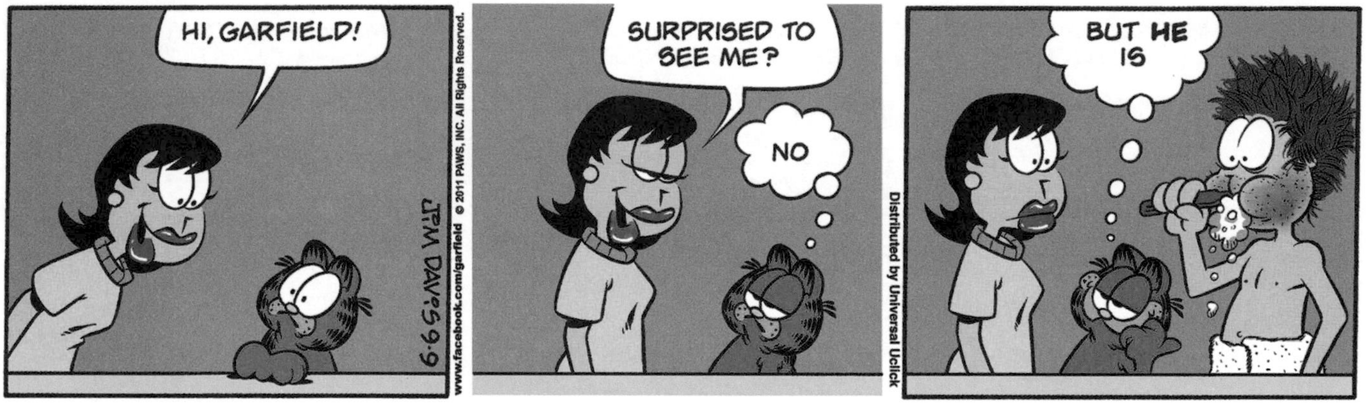
HI, GARFIELD!
SURPRISED TO SEE ME?
NO
BUT **HE** IS
JIM DAVIS 9-9
www.facebook.com/garfield © 2011 PAWS, INC. All Rights Reserved.
Distributed by Universal Uclick

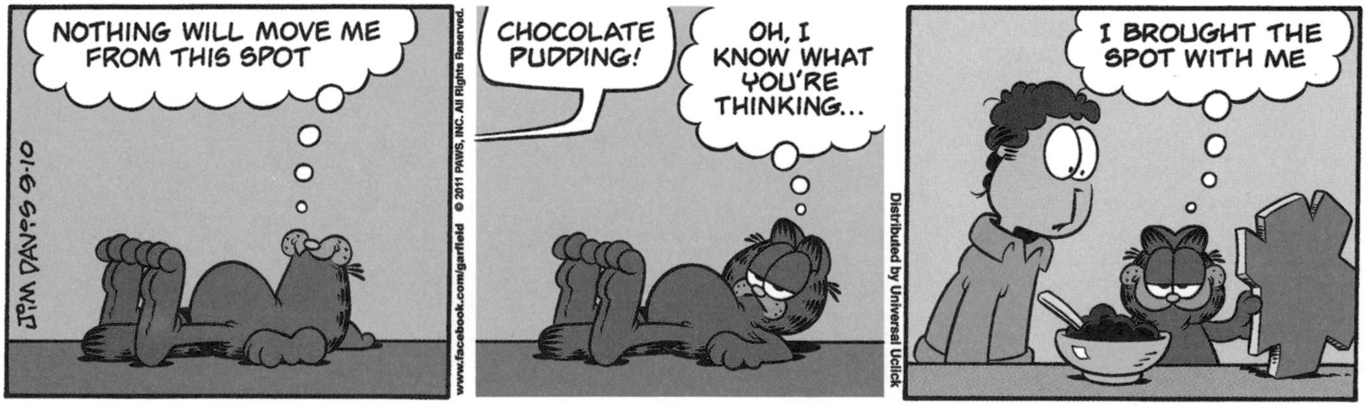
NOTHING WILL MOVE ME FROM THIS SPOT
CHOCOLATE PUDDING!
OH, I KNOW WHAT YOU'RE THINKING...
I BROUGHT THE SPOT WITH ME
JIM DAVIS 9-10
www.facebook.com/garfield © 2011 PAWS, INC. All Rights Reserved.
Distributed by Universal Uclick

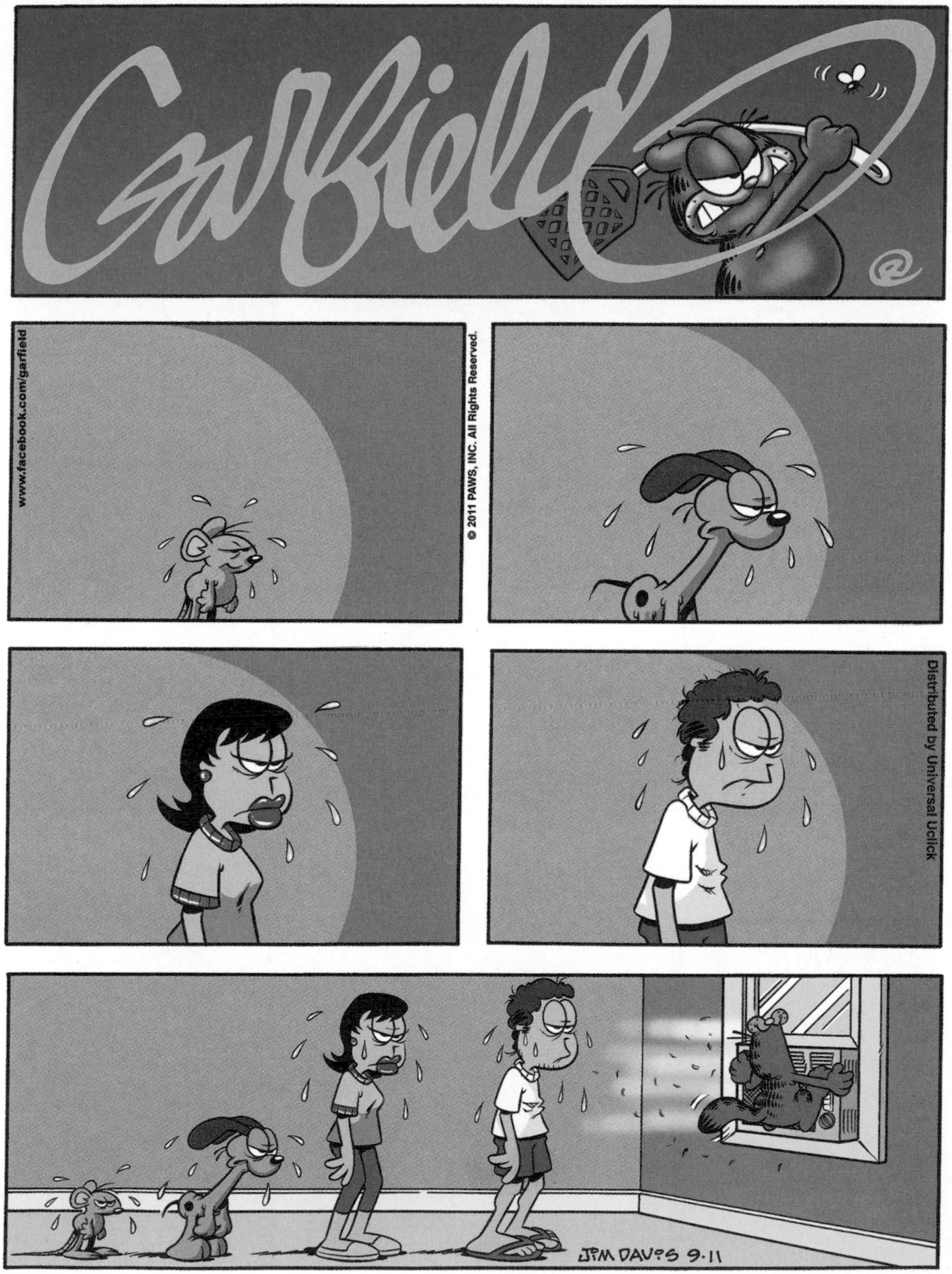

Garfield
www.facebook.com/garfield
© 2011 PAWS, INC. All Rights Reserved.
Distributed by Universal Uclick
JIM DAVIS 9-11

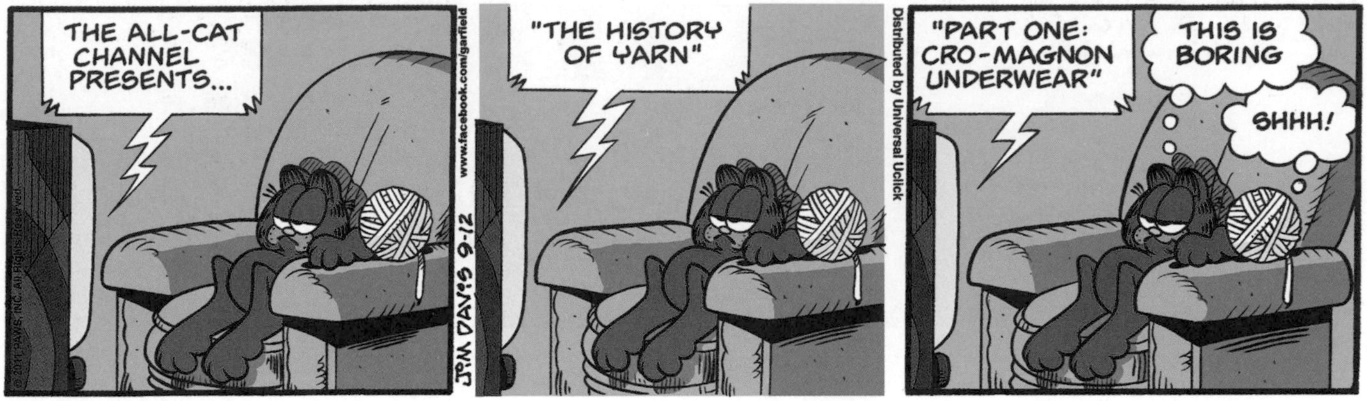
THE ALL-CAT CHANNEL PRESENTS...
"THE HISTORY OF YARN"
"PART ONE: CRO-MAGNON UNDERWEAR"
THIS IS BORING
SHHH!
© 2011 PAWS, INC. All Rights Reserved.
JIM DAVIS 9-12
www.facebook.com/garfield
Distributed by Universal Uclick

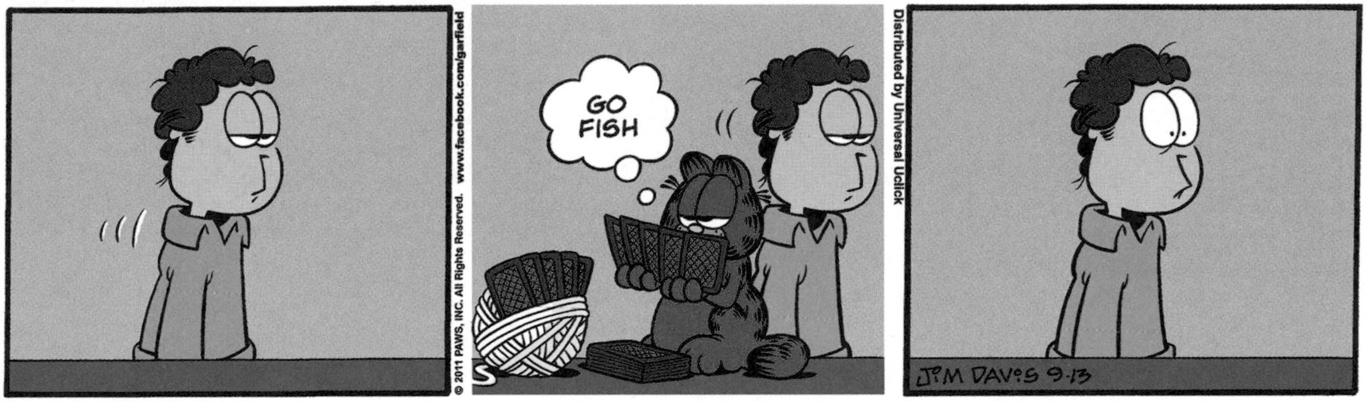
GO FISH
© 2011 PAWS, INC. All Rights Reserved. www.facebook.com/garfield
Distributed by Universal Uclick
JIM DAVIS 9-13

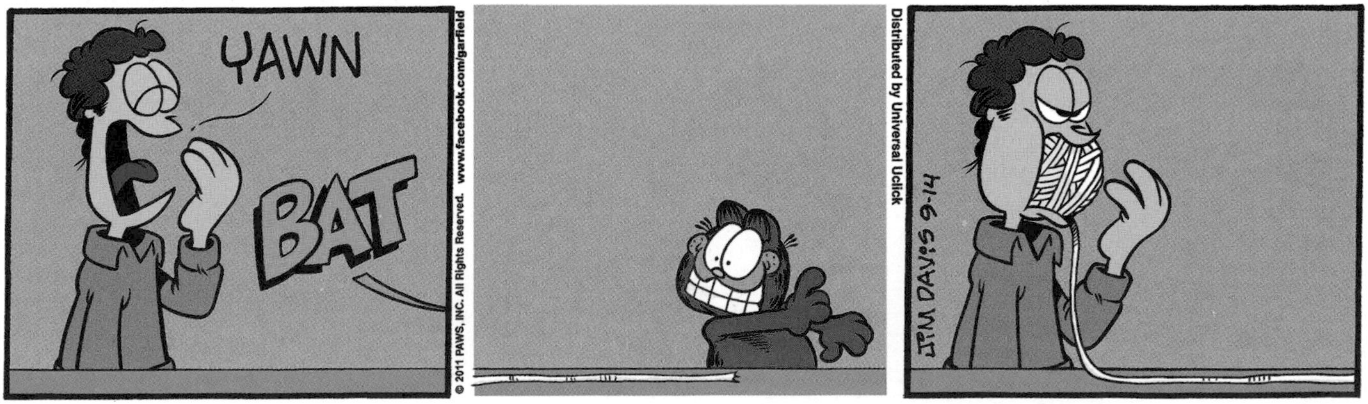
YAWN
BAT
© 2011 PAWS, INC. All Rights Reserved. www.facebook.com/garfield
Distributed by Universal Uclick
JIM DAVIS 9-14

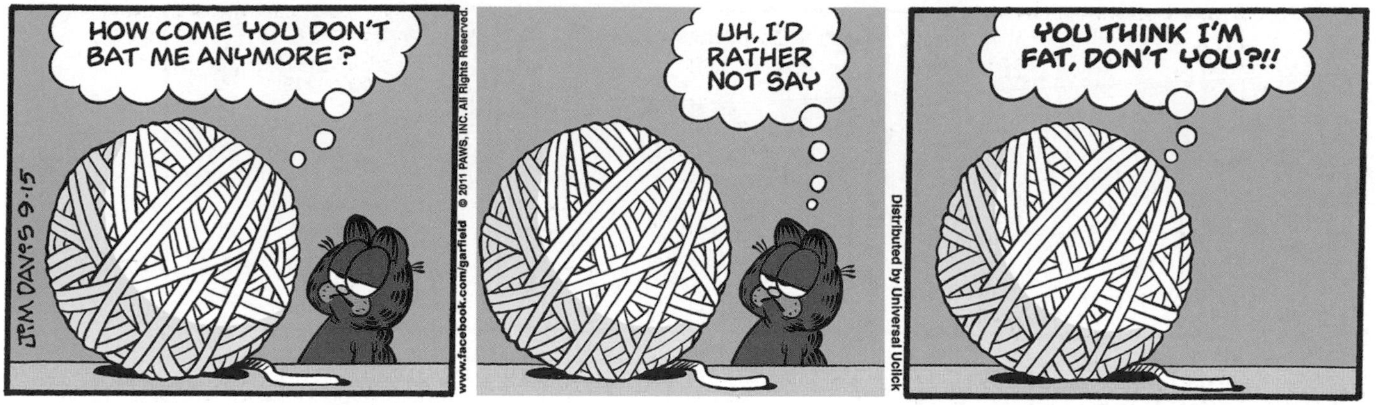
HOW COME YOU DON'T BAT ME ANYMORE?
JPM DAVPS 9·15
© 2011 PAWS, INC. All Rights Reserved. www.facebook.com/garfield
UH, I'D RATHER NOT SAY
Distributed by Universal Uclick
YOU THINK I'M FAT, DON'T YOU?!!

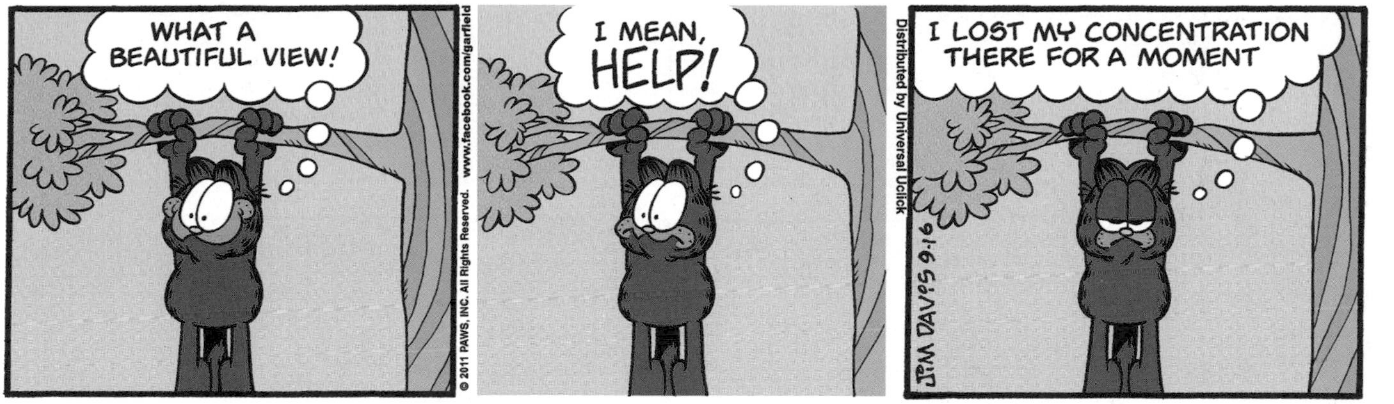
WHAT A BEAUTIFUL VIEW!
© 2011 PAWS, INC. All Rights Reserved. www.facebook.com/garfield
I MEAN, HELP!
Distributed by Universal Uclick
I LOST MY CONCENTRATION THERE FOR A MOMENT
JPM DAVPS 9·16

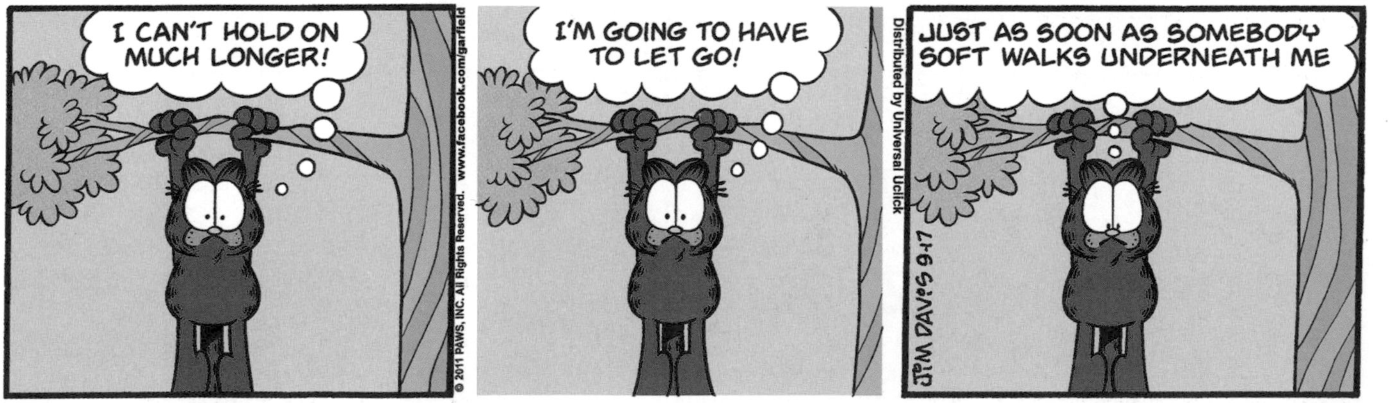
I CAN'T HOLD ON MUCH LONGER!
© 2011 PAWS, INC. All Rights Reserved. www.facebook.com/garfield
I'M GOING TO HAVE TO LET GO!
Distributed by Universal Uclick
JUST AS SOON AS SOMEBODY SOFT WALKS UNDERNEATH ME
JPM DAVPS 9·17

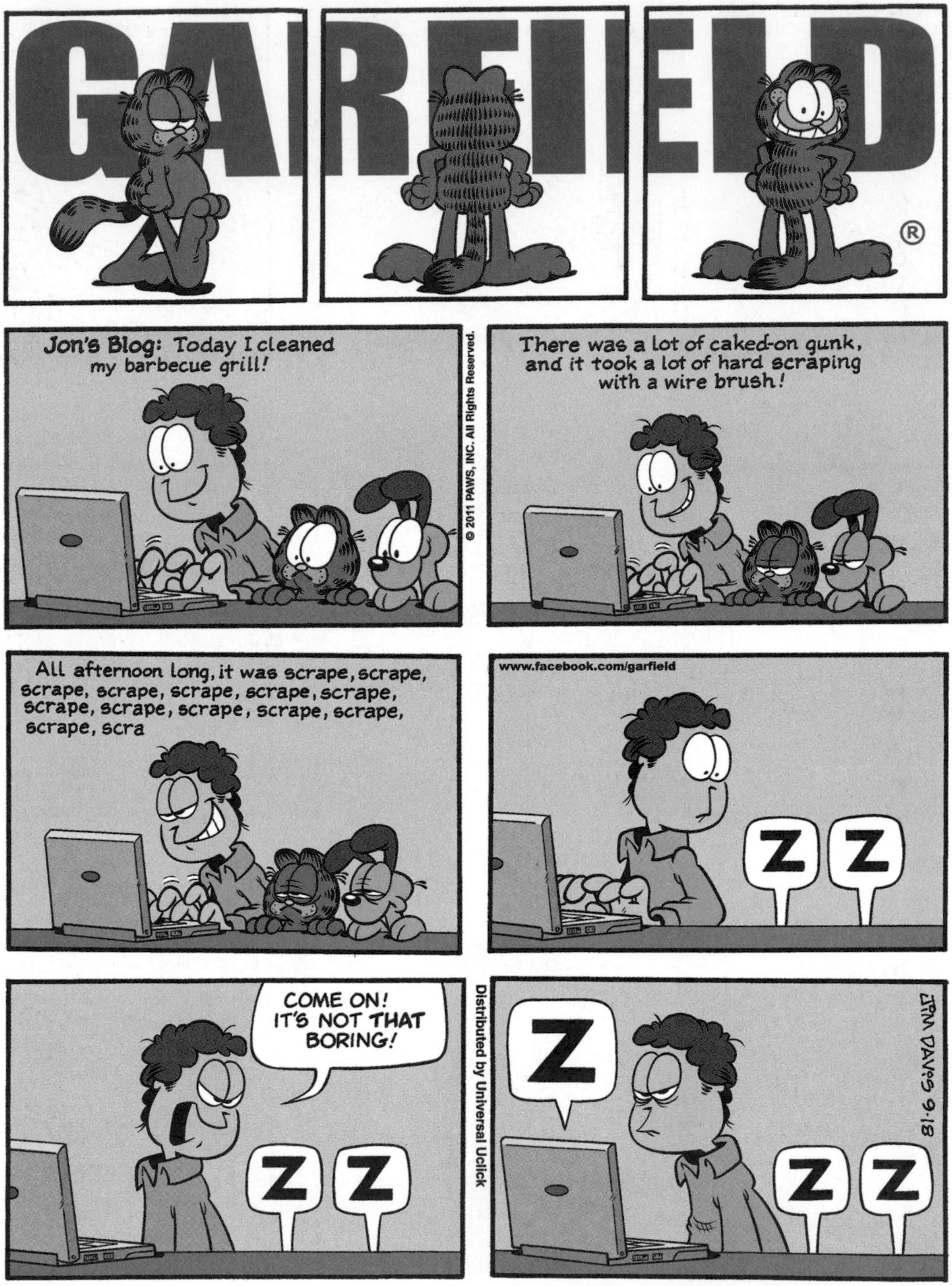
GARFIELD®
Jon's Blog: Today I cleaned my barbecue grill!
© 2011 PAWS, INC. All Rights Reserved.
There was a lot of caked-on gunk, and it took a lot of hard scraping with a wire brush!
All afternoon long, it was scrape, scrape, scrape, scrape, scrape, scrape, scrape, scrape, scrape, scrape, scrape, scrape, scrape, scra
www.facebook.com/garfield
Z Z
COME ON! IT'S NOT THAT BORING!
Z Z
Distributed by Universal Uclick
JPM DAVPS 9-18
Z
Z Z

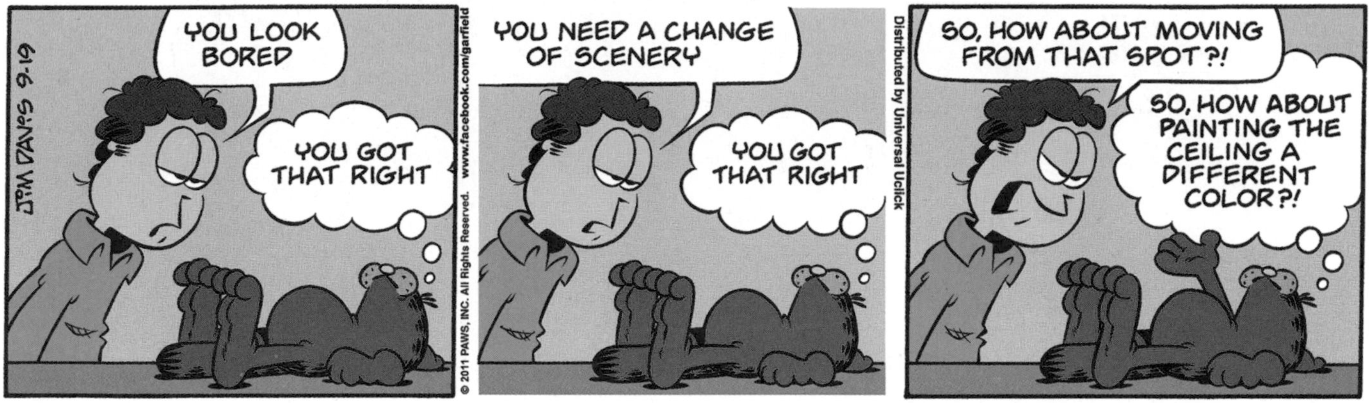
JIM DAVIS 9-19
YOU LOOK BORED
YOU GOT THAT RIGHT
YOU NEED A CHANGE OF SCENERY
YOU GOT THAT RIGHT
SO, HOW ABOUT MOVING FROM THAT SPOT?!
SO, HOW ABOUT PAINTING THE CEILING A DIFFERENT COLOR?!
© 2011 PAWS, INC. All Rights Reserved. www.facebook.com/garfield
Distributed by Universal Uclick

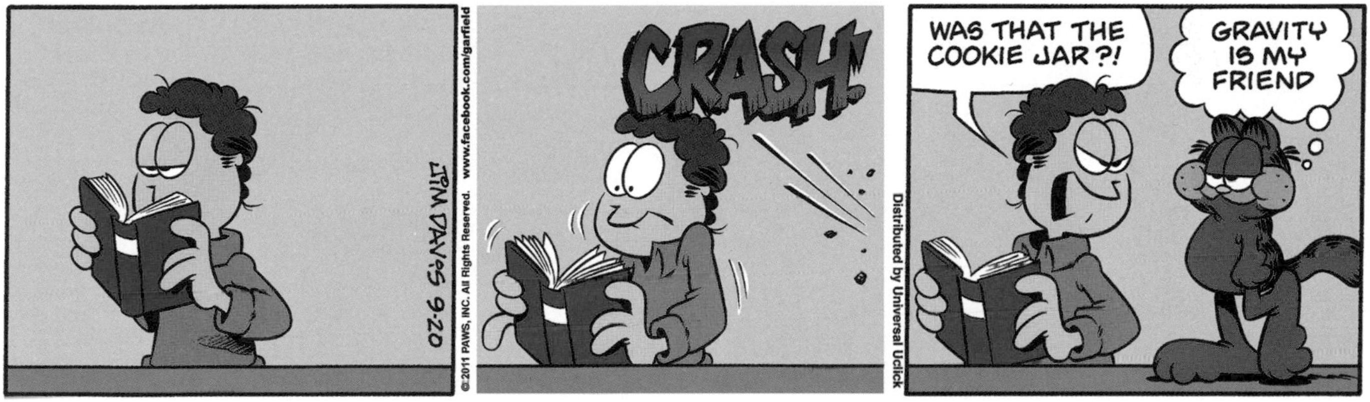
JIM DAVIS 9-20
CRASH!
WAS THAT THE COOKIE JAR?!
GRAVITY IS MY FRIEND
© 2011 PAWS, INC. All Rights Reserved. www.facebook.com/garfield
Distributed by Universal Uclick

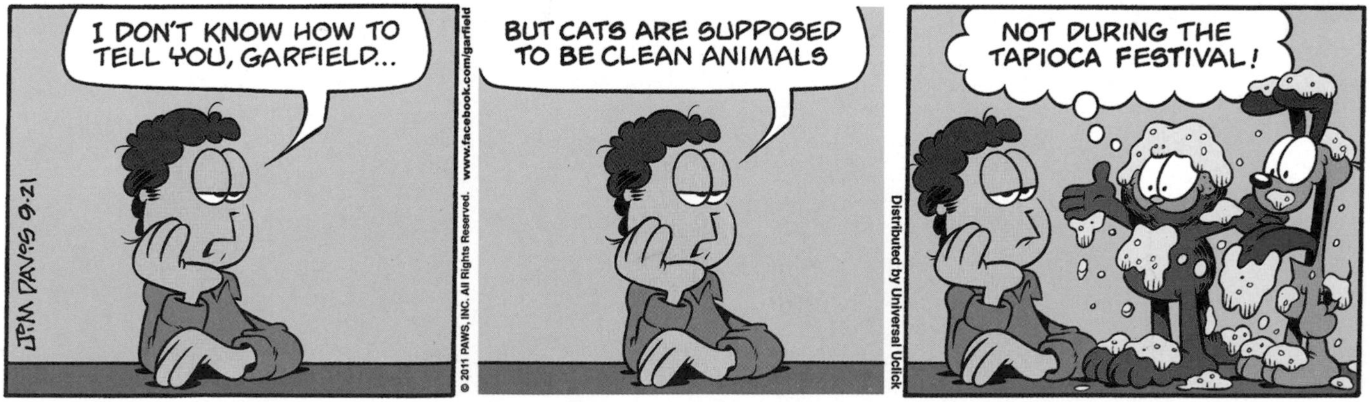
JIM DAVIS 9-21
I DON'T KNOW HOW TO TELL YOU, GARFIELD...
BUT CATS ARE SUPPOSED TO BE CLEAN ANIMALS
NOT DURING THE TAPIOCA FESTIVAL!
© 2011 PAWS, INC. All Rights Reserved. www.facebook.com/garfield
Distributed by Universal Uclick

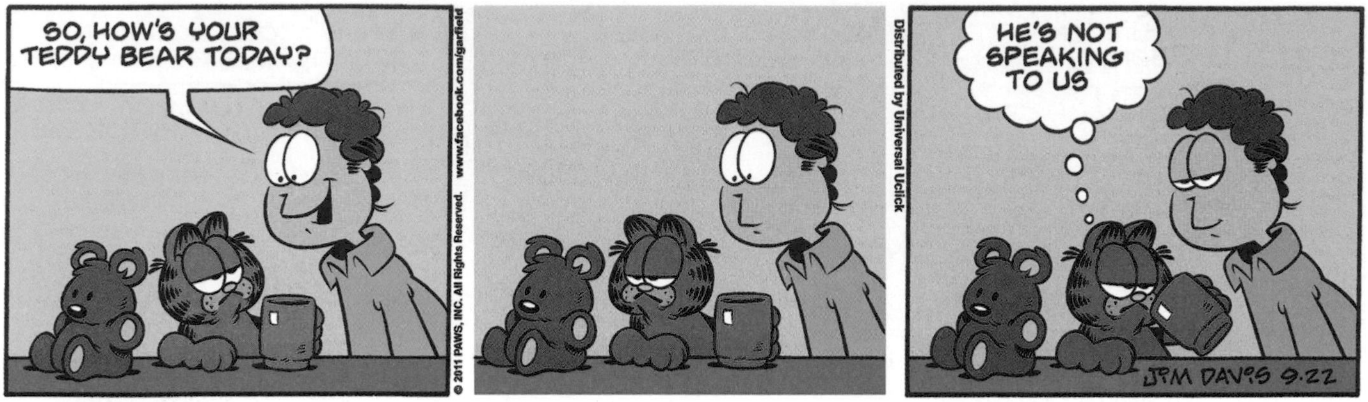
SO, HOW'S YOUR TEDDY BEAR TODAY?
HE'S NOT SPEAKING TO US
JIM DAVIS 9·22

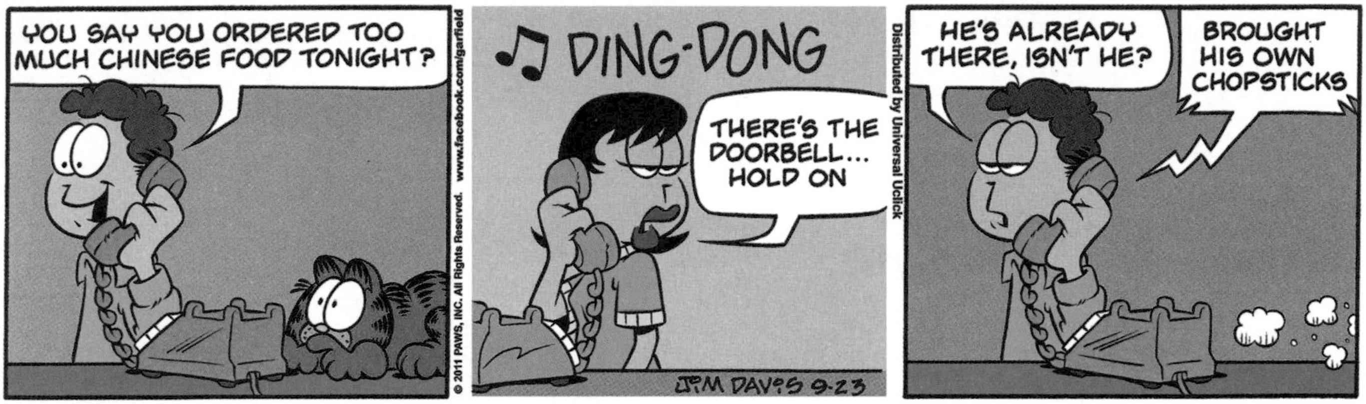
YOU SAY YOU ORDERED TOO MUCH CHINESE FOOD TONIGHT?
♫ DING-DONG
THERE'S THE DOORBELL... HOLD ON
JIM DAVIS 9·23
HE'S ALREADY THERE, ISN'T HE?
BROUGHT HIS OWN CHOPSTICKS

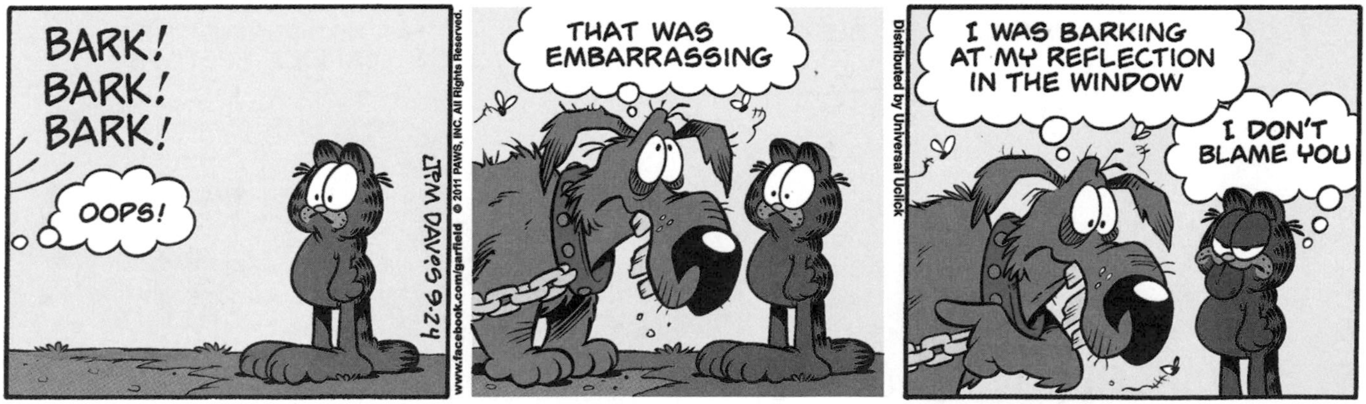
BARK! BARK! BARK!
OOPS!
JIM DAVIS 9·24
THAT WAS EMBARRASSING
I WAS BARKING AT MY REFLECTION IN THE WINDOW
I DON'T BLAME YOU

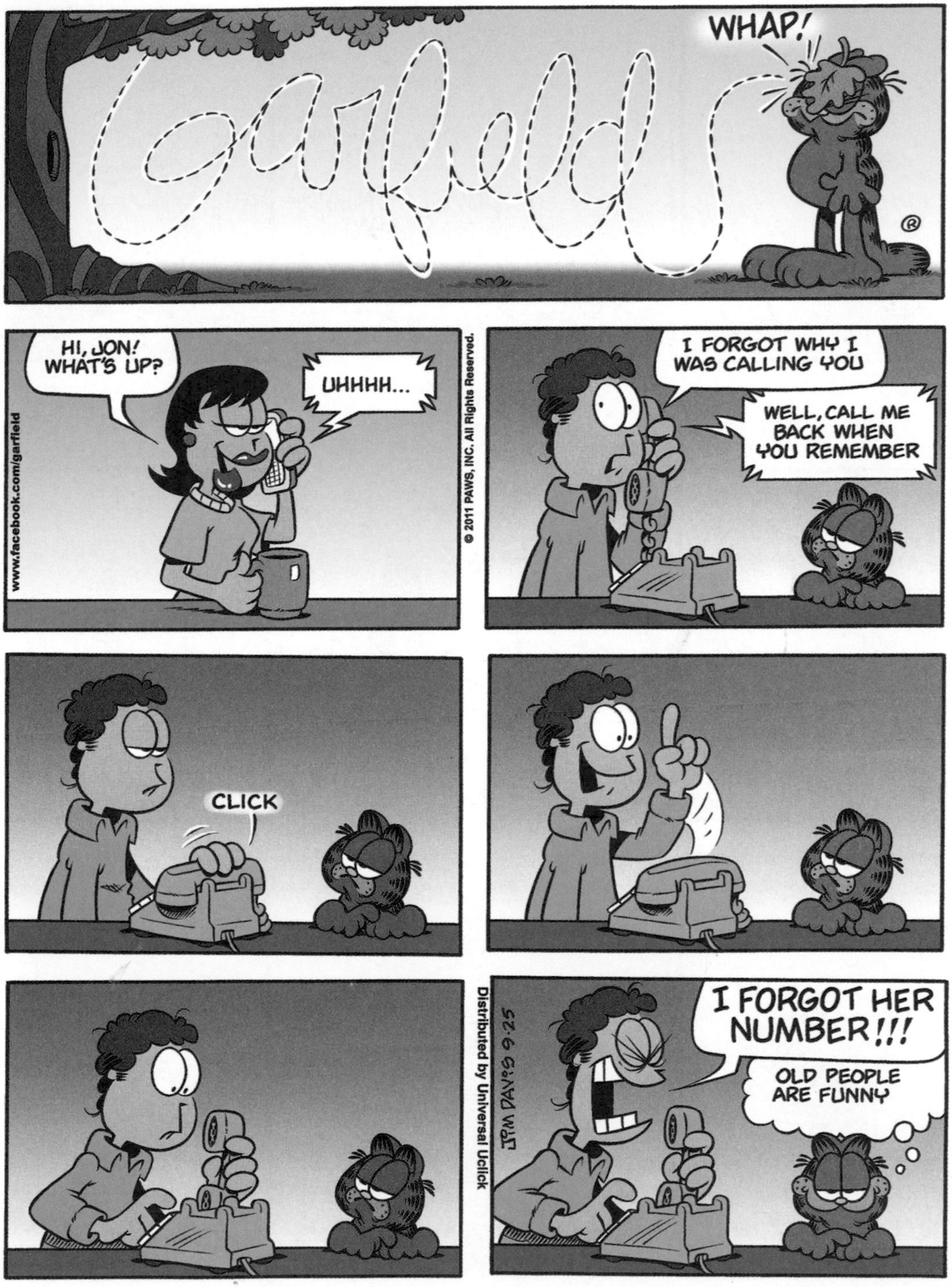
WHAP!
garfield
www.facebook.com/garfield
HI, JON! WHAT'S UP?
UHHHH...
© 2011 PAWS, INC. All Rights Reserved.
I FORGOT WHY I WAS CALLING YOU
WELL, CALL ME BACK WHEN YOU REMEMBER
CLICK
Distributed by Universal Uclick
JIM DAVIS 9-25
I FORGOT HER NUMBER!!!
OLD PEOPLE ARE FUNNY

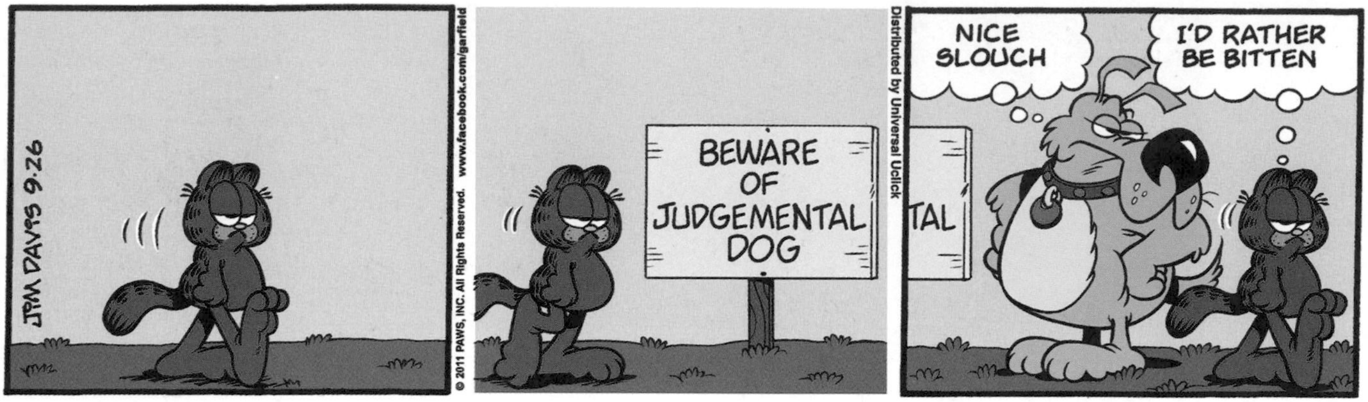
JIM DAVIS 9-26
© 2011 PAWS, INC. All Rights Reserved. www.facebook.com/garfield
BEWARE OF JUDGEMENTAL DOG
Distributed by Universal Uclick
TAL
NICE SLOUCH
I'D RATHER BE BITTEN

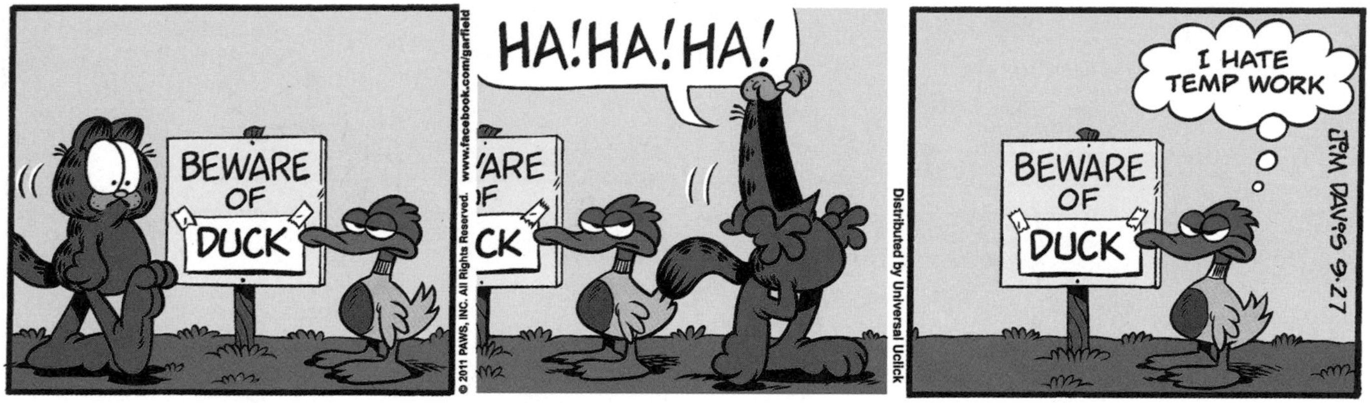
BEWARE OF DUCK
© 2011 PAWS, INC. All Rights Reserved. www.facebook.com/garfield
HA! HA! HA!
ARE OF CK
Distributed by Universal Uclick
I HATE TEMP WORK
BEWARE OF DUCK
JIM DAVIS 9-27

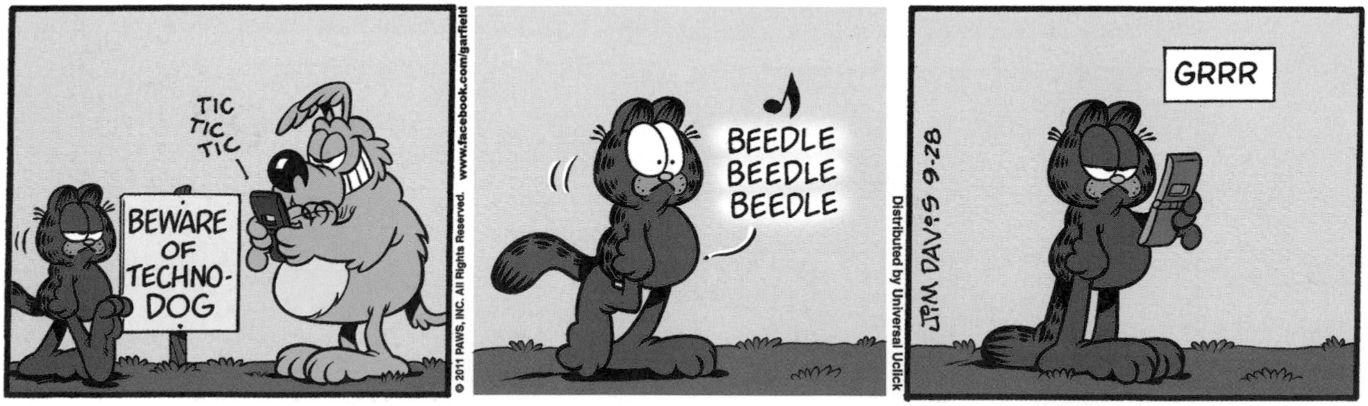
TIC TIC TIC
BEWARE OF TECHNO-DOG
© 2011 PAWS, INC. All Rights Reserved. www.facebook.com/garfield
BEEDLE BEEDLE BEEDLE
Distributed by Universal Uclick
JIM DAVIS 9-28
GRRR

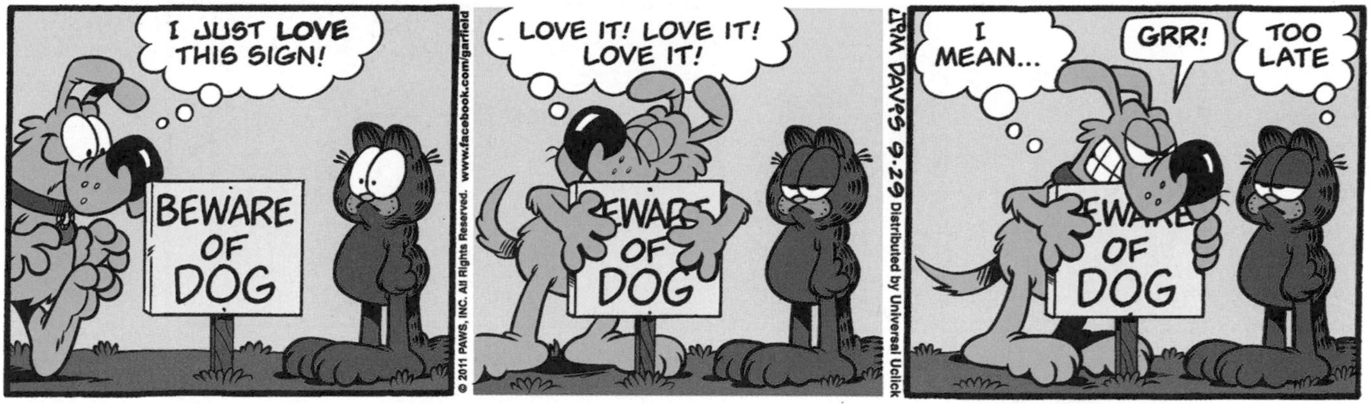
I JUST LOVE THIS SIGN!
BEWARE OF DOG
© 2011 PAWS, INC. All Rights Reserved. www.facebook.com/garfield
LOVE IT! LOVE IT! LOVE IT!
JIM DAVIS 9-29 Distributed by Universal Uclick
I MEAN...
GRR!
TOO LATE

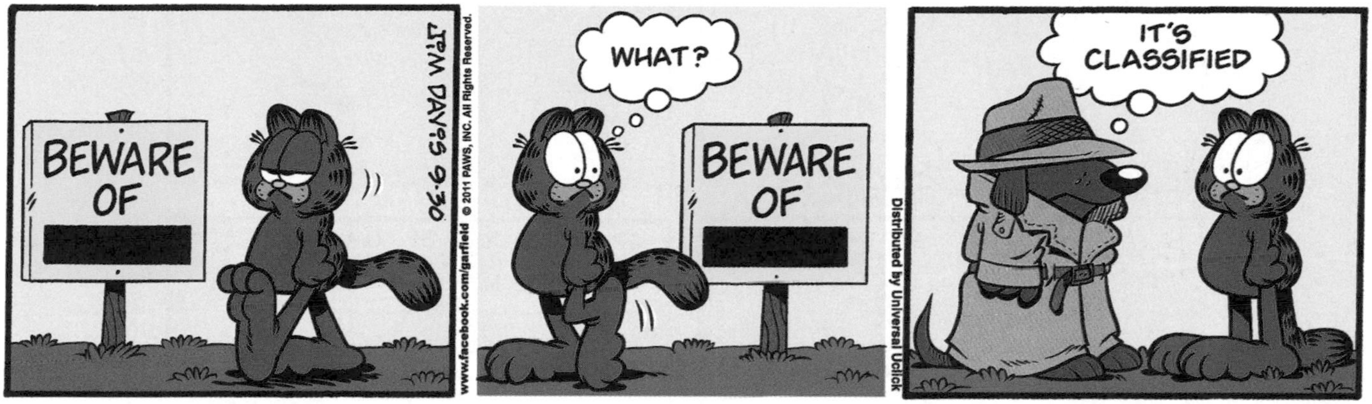
BEWARE OF
JIM DAVIS 9-30
www.facebook.com/garfield © 2011 PAWS, INC. All Rights Reserved.
WHAT?
BEWARE OF
Distributed by Universal Uclick
IT'S CLASSIFIED

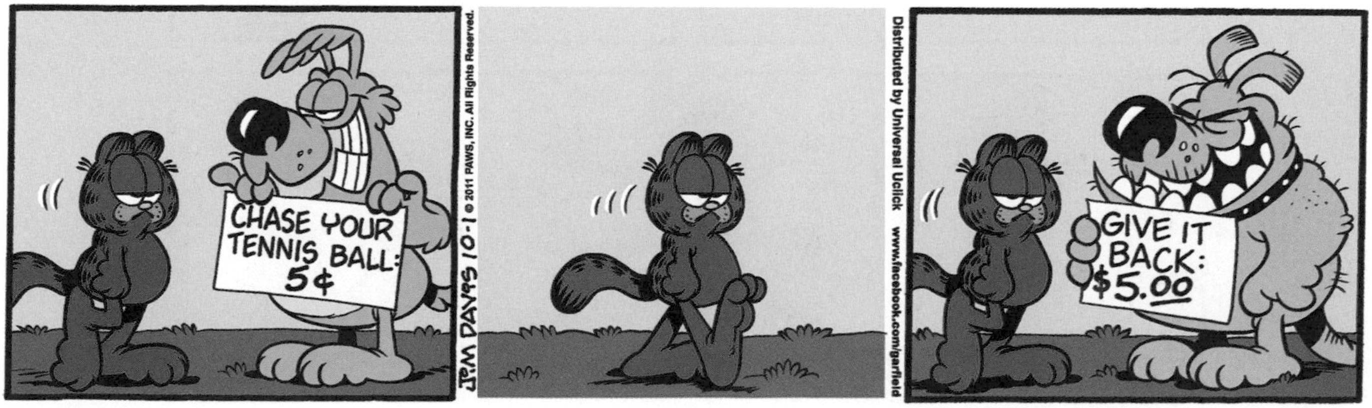
CHASE YOUR TENNIS BALL: 5¢
JIM DAVIS 10-1 © 2011 PAWS, INC. All Rights Reserved.
Distributed by Universal Uclick www.facebook.com/garfield
GIVE IT BACK: $5.00

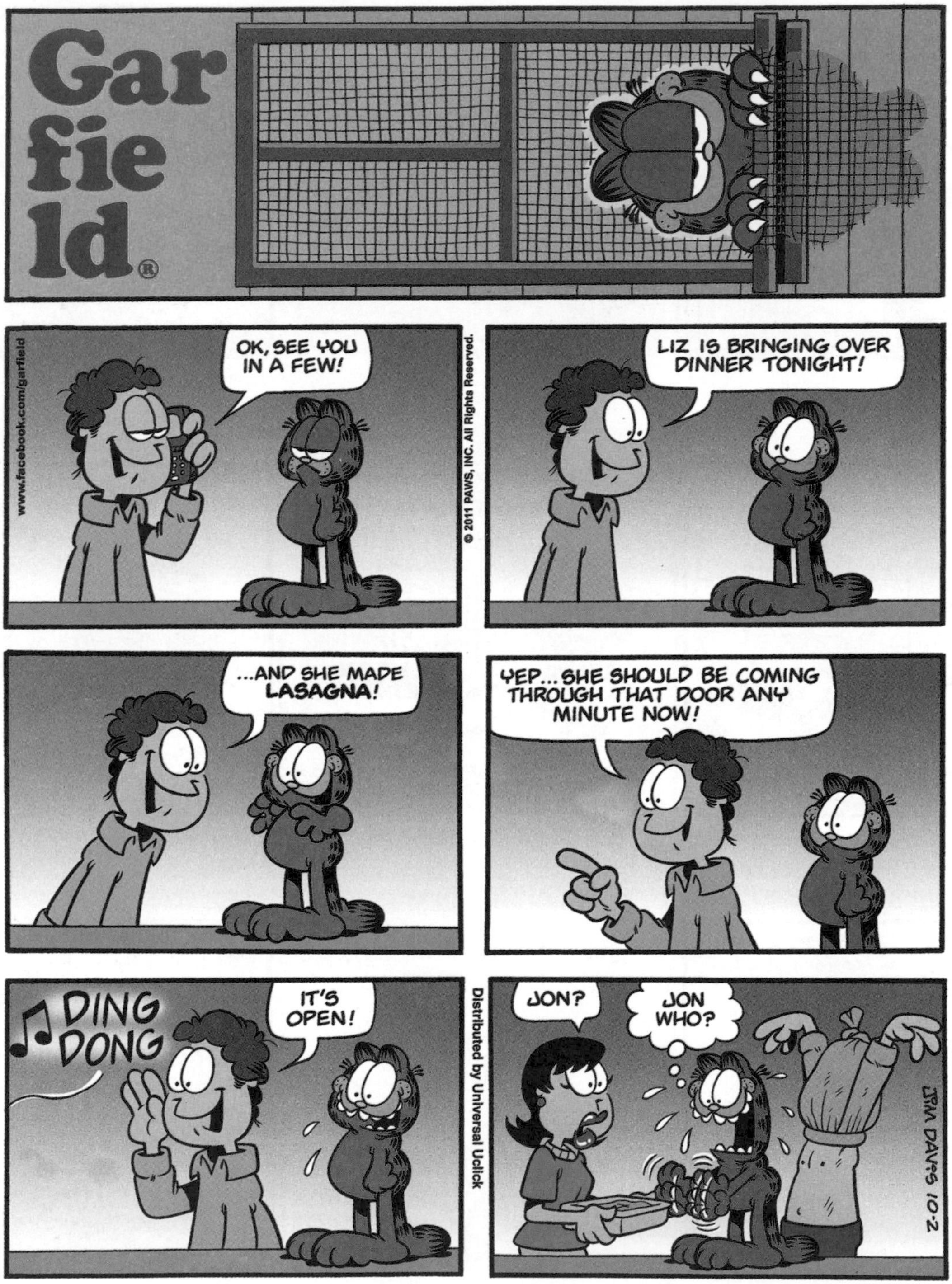
Garfield®
www.facebook.com/garfield
OK, SEE YOU IN A FEW!
© 2011 PAWS, INC. All Rights Reserved.
LIZ IS BRINGING OVER DINNER TONIGHT!
...AND SHE MADE LASAGNA!
YEP... SHE SHOULD BE COMING THROUGH THAT DOOR ANY MINUTE NOW!
DING DONG
IT'S OPEN!
Distributed by Universal Uclick
JON?
JON WHO?
JIM DAVIS 10-2

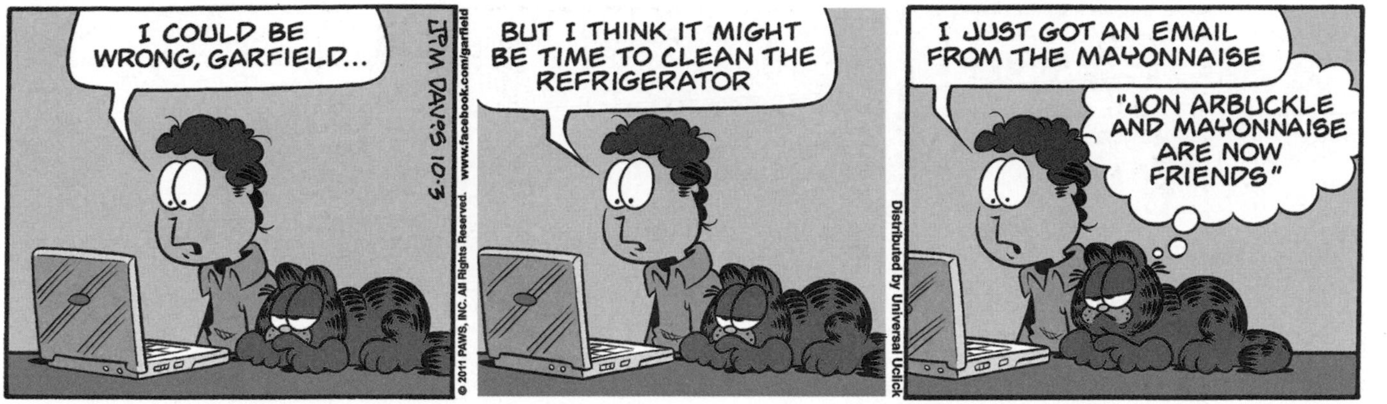
I COULD BE WRONG, GARFIELD...
JIM DAVIS 10-3
© 2011 PAWS, INC. All Rights Reserved. www.facebook.com/garfield
BUT I THINK IT MIGHT BE TIME TO CLEAN THE REFRIGERATOR
Distributed by Universal Uclick
I JUST GOT AN EMAIL FROM THE MAYONNAISE
"JON ARBUCKLE AND MAYONNAISE ARE NOW FRIENDS"

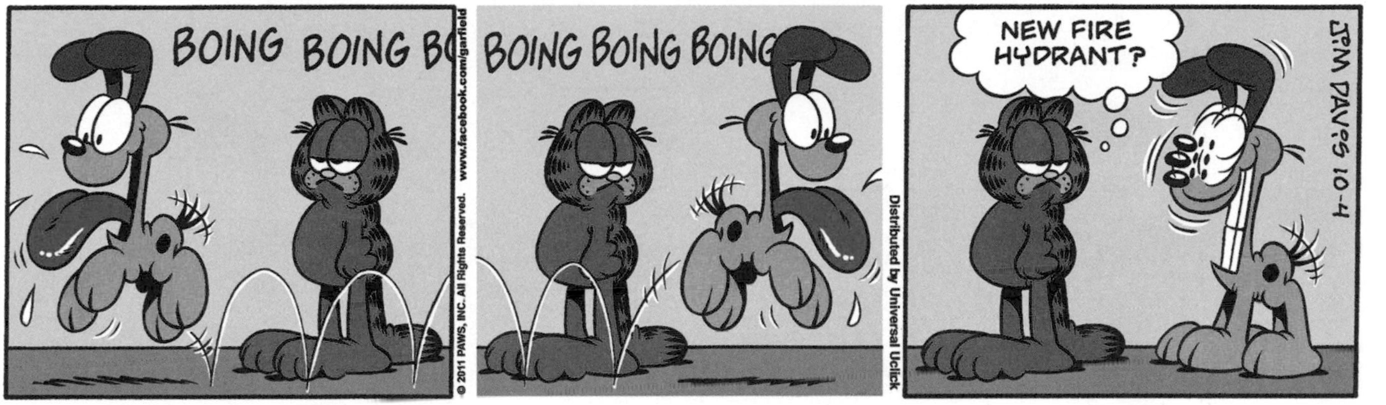
BOING BOING BO
© 2011 PAWS, INC. All Rights Reserved. www.facebook.com/garfield
BOING BOING BOING
Distributed by Universal Uclick
NEW FIRE HYDRANT?
JIM DAVIS 10-4

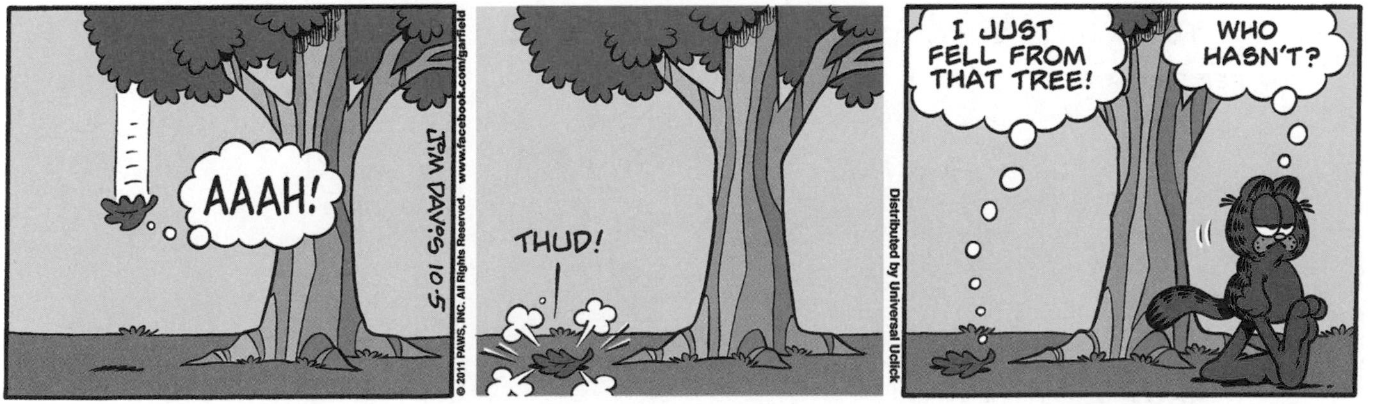
AAAH!
JIM DAVIS 10-5
© 2011 PAWS, INC. All Rights Reserved. www.facebook.com/garfield
THUD!
Distributed by Universal Uclick
I JUST FELL FROM THAT TREE!
WHO HASN'T?

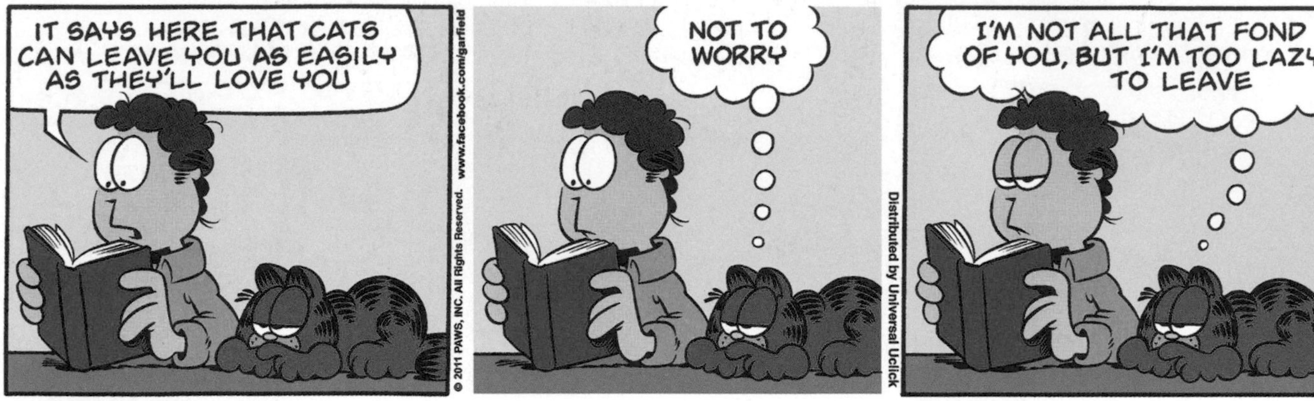
IT SAYS HERE THAT CATS CAN LEAVE YOU AS EASILY AS THEY'LL LOVE YOU
© 2011 PAWS, INC. All Rights Reserved. www.facebook.com/garfield
NOT TO WORRY
Distributed by Universal Uclick
I'M NOT ALL THAT FOND OF YOU, BUT I'M TOO LAZY TO LEAVE
JIM DAVIS 10-6

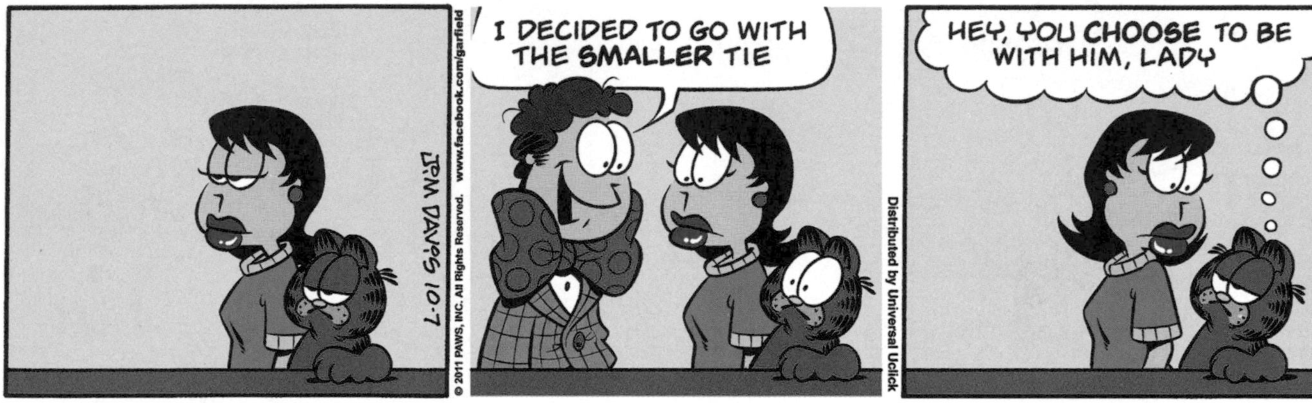
JIM DAVIS 10-7
© 2011 PAWS, INC. All Rights Reserved. www.facebook.com/garfield
I DECIDED TO GO WITH THE **SMALLER** TIE
Distributed by Universal Uclick
HEY, YOU **CHOOSE** TO BE WITH HIM, LADY

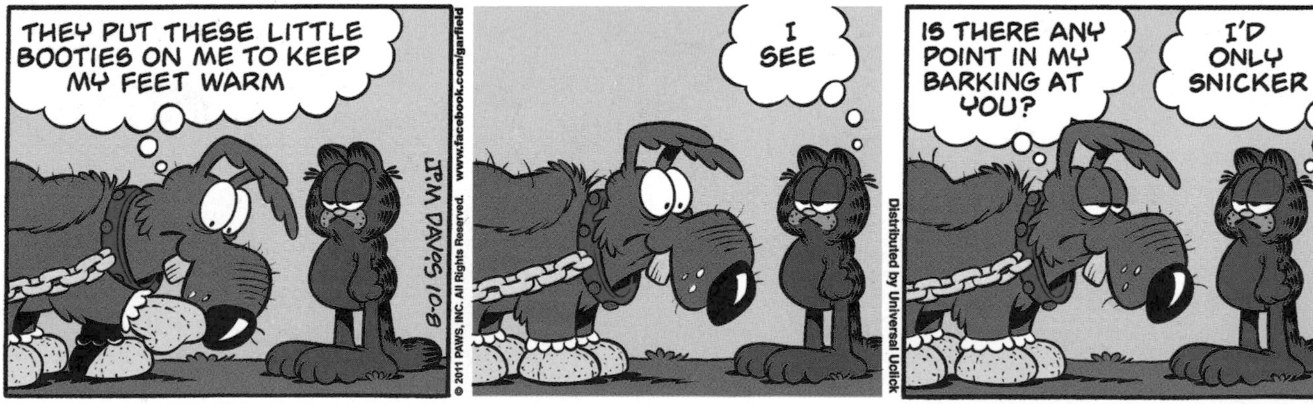
THEY PUT THESE LITTLE BOOTIES ON ME TO KEEP MY FEET WARM
JIM DAVIS 10-8
© 2011 PAWS, INC. All Rights Reserved. www.facebook.com/garfield
I SEE
Distributed by Universal Uclick
IS THERE ANY POINT IN MY BARKING AT YOU?
I'D ONLY SNICKER

VINTAGE GARFIELD

...from, like, the totally awesome '80s!

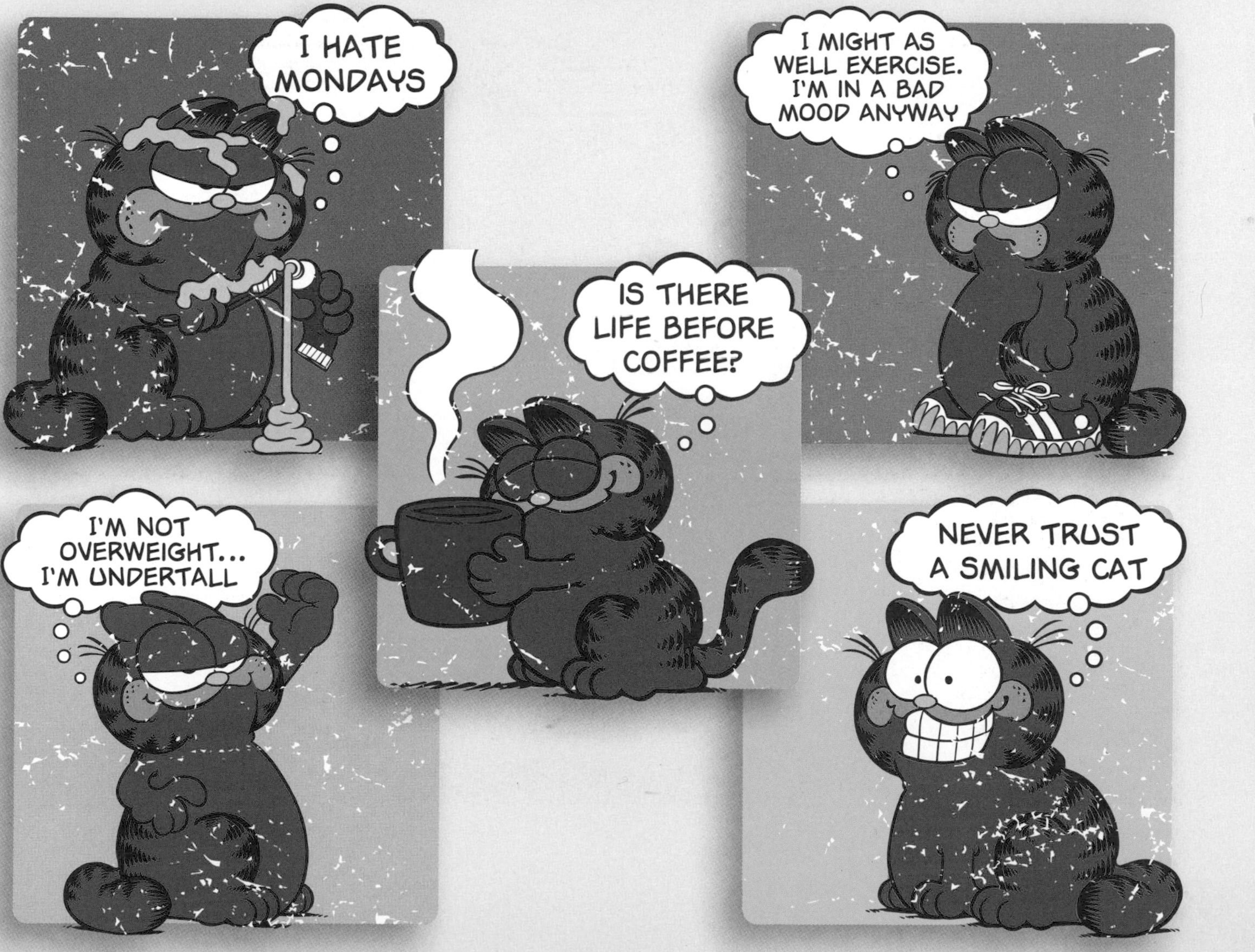
I HATE MONDAYS
I MIGHT AS WELL EXERCISE. I'M IN A BAD MOOD ANYWAY
IS THERE LIFE BEFORE COFFEE?
I'M NOT OVERWEIGHT... I'M UNDERTALL
NEVER TRUST A SMILING CAT

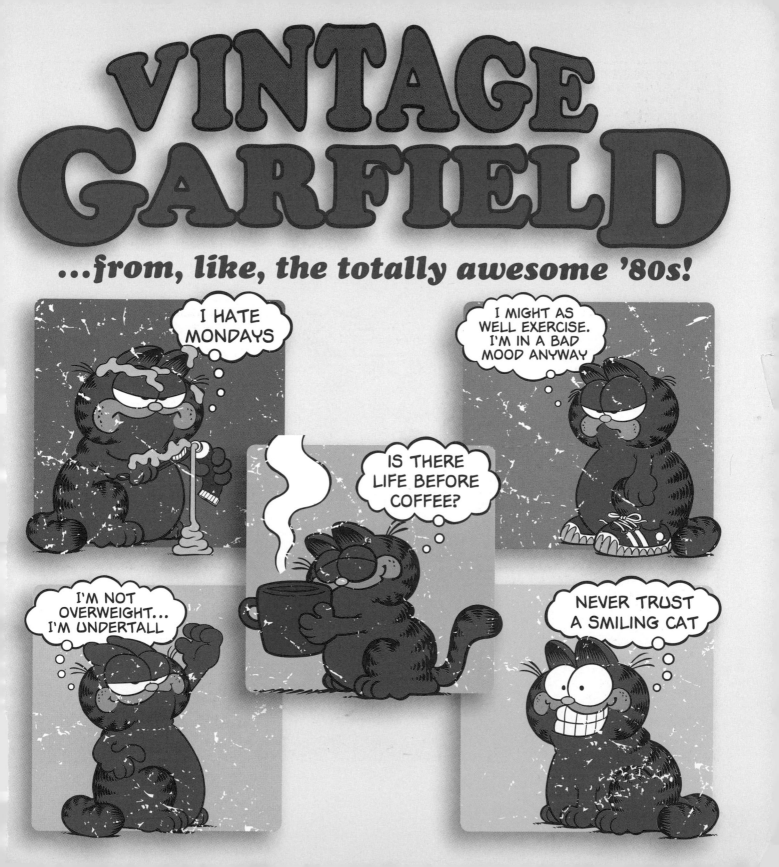

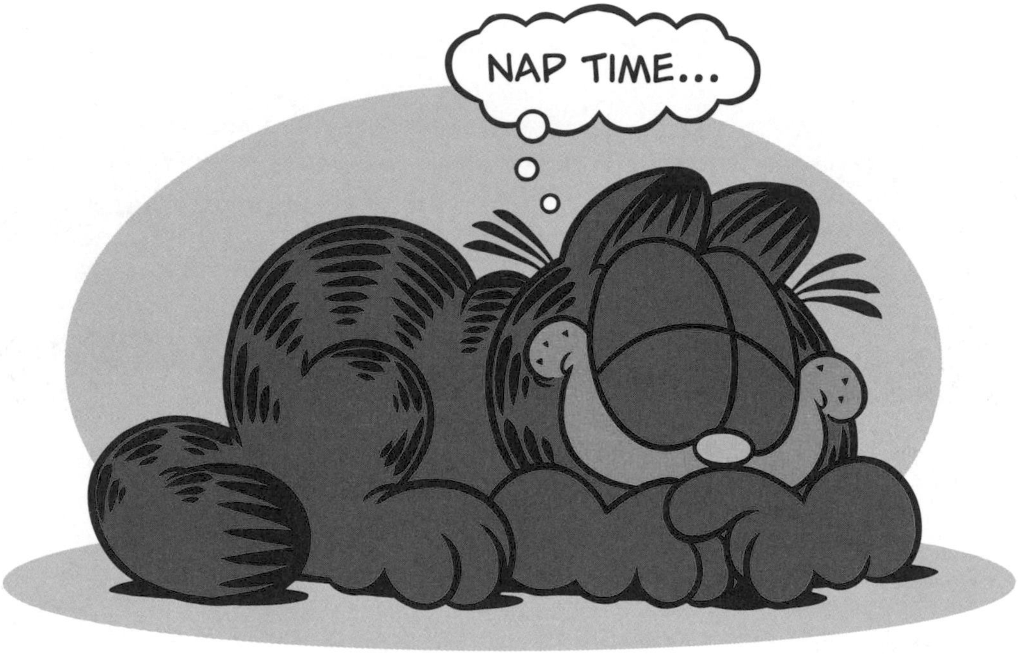
NAP TIME...

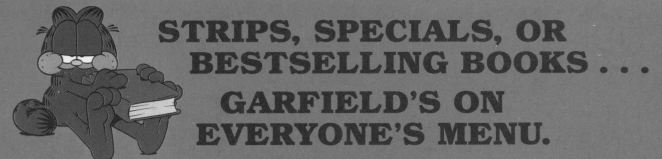

STRIPS, SPECIALS, OR BESTSELLING BOOKS . . . GARFIELD'S ON EVERYONE'S MENU.

Don't miss even one episode in the Tubby Tabby's hilarious series!

GARFIELD AT LARGE	(#1)	978-0-345-44382-3
GARFIELD GAINS WEIGHT	(#2)	978-0-345-44975-7
GARFIELD BIGGER THAN LIFE	(#3)	978-0-345-45027-2
GARFIELD WEIGHS IN	(#4)	978-0-345-45205-4
GARFIELD TAKES THE CAKE	(#5)	978-0-345-44978-8
GARFIELD EATS HIS HEART OUT	(#6)	978-0-345-46459-0
GARFIELD SITS AROUND THE HOUSE	(#7)	978-0-345-46463-7
GARFIELD TIPS THE SCALES	(#8)	978-0-345-46909-0
GARFIELD LOSES HIS FEET	(#9)	978-0-345-46467-5
GARFIELD MAKES IT BIG	(#10)	978-0-345-46468-2
GARFIELD ROLLS ON	(#11)	978-0-345-47561-9
GARFIELD OUT TO LUNCH	(#12)	978-0-345-47562-6
GARFIELD FOOD FOR THOUGHT	(#13)	978-0-345-47563-3
GARFIELD SWALLOWS HIS PRIDE	(#14)	978-0-345-91386-9
GARFIELD WORLDWIDE	(#15)	978-0-345-91754-6
GARFIELD ROUNDS OUT	(#16)	978-0-345-49169-5
GARFIELD CHEWS THE FAT	(#17)	978-0-345-49170-1
GARFIELD GOES TO WAIST	(#18)	978-0-345-49173-2
GARFIELD HANGS OUT	(#19)	978-0-345-49174-9
GARFIELD TAKES UP SPACE	(#20)	978-0-345-49178-7
GARFIELD SAYS A MOUTHFUL	(#21)	978-0-345-49179-4
GARFIELD BY THE POUND	(#22)	978-0-345-52558-1
GARFIELD KEEPS HIS CHINS UP	(#23)	978-0-345-52559-8
GARFIELD TAKES HIS LICKS	(#24)	978-0-345-52587-1
GARFIELD HITS THE BIG TIME	(#25)	978-0-345-52589-5
GARFIELD PULLS HIS WEIGHT	(#26)	978-0-345-52594-9
GARFIELD DISHES IT OUT	(#27)	978-0-345-52595-6
GARFIELD LIFE IN THE FAT LANE	(#28)	978-0-345-52600-7
GARFIELD TONS OF FUN	(#29)	978-0-345-52601-4
GARFIELD BIGGER AND BETTER	(#30)	978-0-345-52605-2
GARFIELD HAMS IT UP	(#31)	978-0-345-52606-9
GARFIELD THINKS BIG	(#32)	978-0-425-28516-9
GARFIELD THROWS HIS WEIGHT AROUND	(#33)	978-0-425-28559-6
GARFIELD LIFE TO THE FULLEST	(#34)	978-0-345-43239-1
GARFIELD FEEDS THE KITTY	(#35)	978-0-345-43673-3
GARFIELD HOGS THE SPOTLIGHT	(#36)	978-0-345-43922-2
GARFIELD BEEFS UP	(#37)	978-0-345-44109-6
GARFIELD GETS COOKIN'	(#38)	978-0-345-44582-7
GARFIELD EATS CROW	(#39)	978-0-345-45201-6
GARFIELD SURVIVAL OF THE FATTEST	(#40)	978-0-345-46458-3
GARFIELD OLDER AND WIDER	(#41)	978-0-345-46462-0
GARFIELD PIGS OUT	(#42)	978-0-345-46466-8
GARFIELD BLOTS OUT THE SUN	(#43)	978-0-345-46615-0
GARFIELD GOES BANANAS	(#44)	978-0-345-91346-3
GARFIELD LARGE & IN CHARGE	(#45)	978-0-345-49172-5
GARFIELD SPILLS THE BEANS	(#46)	978-0-345-49177-0
GARFIELD GETS HIS JUST DESSERTS	(#47)	978-0-345-91387-6
GARFIELD WILL EAT FOR FOOD	(#48)	978-0-345-49176-3
GARFIELD WEIGHS HIS OPTIONS	(#49)	978-0-345-49181-7
GARFIELD POTBELLY OF GOLD	(#50)	978-0-345-52244-3
GARFIELD SHOVELS IT IN	(#51)	978-0-345-52419-5
GARFIELD LARD OF THE JUNGLE	(#52)	978-0-345-52584-0
GARFIELD BRINGS HOME THE BACON	(#53)	978-0-345-52586-4
GARFIELD GETS IN A PICKLE	(#54)	978-0-345-52590-1
GARFIELD SINGS FOR HIS SUPPER	(#55)	978-0-345-52593-2
GARFIELD CAUTION: WIDE LOAD	(#56)	978-0-345-52596-3
GARFIELD SOUPED UP	(#57)	978-0-345-52598-7
GARFIELD GOES TO HIS HAPPY PLACE	(#58)	978-0-345-52602-1
GARFIELD THE BIG CHEESE	(#59)	978-0-345-52604-5
GARFIELD CLEANS HIS PLATE	(#60)	978-0-345-52608-3
GARFIELD CHICKENS OUT	(#61)	978-0-425-28515-2
GARFIELD LISTENS TO HIS GUT	(#62)	978-0-425-28557-2

DVD TIE-INS

GARFIELD AS HIMSELF	978-0-345-47805-4
GARFIELD HOLIDAY CELEBRATIONS	978-0-345-47930-3
GARFIELD TRAVEL ADVENTURES	978-0-345-48087-3

AND DON'T MISS . . .

GARFIELD AT 25: IN DOG YEARS I'D BE DEAD	978-0-345-45204-7
GARFIELD'S JOKE ZONE/INSULTS	978-0-345-46263-3
GARFIELD FAT CAT 3-PACK/ VOL. 1	978-0-345-46455-2
GARFIELD FAT CAT 3-PACK/ VOL. 2	978-0-345-46465-1
GARFIELD FAT CAT 3-PACK/ VOL. 3	978-0-345-48088-0
GARFIELD FAT CAT 3-PACK/ VOL. 4	978-0-345-49171-8
GARFIELD FAT CAT 3-PACK/ VOL. 5	978-0-345-49180-8
GARFIELD FAT CAT 3-PACK/ VOL. 6	978-0-345-52420-1
GARFIELD FAT CAT 3-PACK/ VOL. 7	978-0-345-52588-8
GARFIELD FAT CAT 3-PACK/ VOL. 8	978-0-345-52599-4
GARFIELD FAT CAT 3-PACK/ VOL. 9	978-0-345-52607-6
GARFIELD FAT CAT 3-PACK/ VOL. 10	978-0-425-28558-9
GARFIELD FAT CAT 3-PACK/ VOL. 13	978-0-345-46460-6
GARFIELD FAT CAT 3-PACK/ VOL. 14	978-0-345-49175-6
GARFIELD FAT CAT 3-PACK/ VOL. 15	978-0-345-52585-7
GARFIELD FAT CAT 3-PACK/ VOL. 16	978-0-345-52592-5
GARFIELD FAT CAT 3-PACK/ VOL. 17	978-0-345-52603-8
GARFIELD FAT CAT 3-PACK/ VOL. 18	978-0-399-59440-3
SEASON'S EATINGS: A VERY MERRY GARFIELD CHRISTMAS	978-0-345-47560-2
GARFIELD'S GUIDE TO EVERYTHING	978-0-345-46461-3
ODIE UNLEASHED!	978-0-345-46464-4
GARFIELD'S BOOK OF CAT NAMES	978-0-345-48516-8
THE GARFIELD JOURNAL	978-0-345-46469-9
LIGHTS, CAMERA, HAIRBALLS!: GARFIELD AT THE MOVIES	978-0-345-49134-3
30 YEARS OF LAUGHS AND LASAGNA	978-0-345-50379-4
GARFIELD MINUS GARFIELD	978-0-345-51387-8
GARFIELD FROM THE TRASH BIN	978-0-345-51881-1
GARFIELD LEFT SPEECHLESS	978-0-345-53058-5
MY LAUGHABLE LIFE WITH GARFIELD	978-0-345-52591-8
GARFIELD'S SUNDAY FINEST	978-0-345-52597-0

New larger, full-color format!